SACRED LANGUAGE, VERNACULAR DIFFERENCE

Sacred Language, Vernacular Difference

GLOBAL ARABIC AND COUNTERIMPERIAL LITERATURES

ANNETTE DAMAYANTI LIENAU

PRINCETON UNIVERSITY PRESS
PRINCETON & OXFORD

Published by Princeton University Press
41 William Street, Princeton, New Jersey 08540
99 Banbury Road, Oxford OX2 6JX

press.princeton.edu

Library of Congress Cataloging-in-Publication Data

Names: Lienau, Annette Damayanti, author.
Title: Sacred language, vernacular difference : global Arabic and counter-imperial literatures / Annette Damayanti Lienau.
Description: Princeton : Princeton University Press, 2023. | Includes bibliographical references and index.
Identifiers: LCCN 2023036664 (print) | LCCN 2023036665 (ebook) | ISBN 9780691249834 (paperback) | ISBN 9780691249803 (hardback) | ISBN 9780691249889 (ebook)
Subjects: LCSH: Arabic language— Political aspects— History. | Languages in contact. | Egyptian literature, Modern— Arab influences. | Indonesian literature— Arab influences. | Senegalese literature— Arab influences. | Postcolonialism in literature. | Nationalism and literature. | Egypt— Intellectual life. | Indonesia— Intellectual life. | Senegal— Intellectual life. | BISAC: LITERARY CRITICISM / Comparative Literature | POLITICAL SCIENCE / Colonialism & Post-Colonialism
Classification: LCC PJ6074 .L54 2023 (print) | LCC PJ6074 (ebook) | DDC 306.442 /927— dc23/eng/20230824
LC record available at https://lccn.loc.gov/2023036664
LC ebook record available at https://lccn.loc.gov/2023036665

British Library Cataloging-in-Publication Data is available

Editorial: Anne Savarese & James Collier
Production Editorial: Jaden Young
Jacket/Cover Design: Katie Osborne
Production: Lauren Reese
Publicity: William Pagdatoon
Copyeditor: Elisabeth A. Graves

Jacket image: Robert Kawka / Alamy Stock Photo

This book has been composed in Arno

10 9 8 7 6 5 4 3 2 1

To the generous stranger
whose outstretched arms sheltered
two frail and elderly pilgrims as they circled the Kaʿaba

In memory of my grandparents

And for my parents,
who crossed great distances
and made of strangers
a family

The Arabic language is, without question, the language that has invaded the greatest expanse of countries. Only two other languages, Greek and Latin, share with her the honor of becoming universal languages, that is, instruments of religious thought or politics superior to a diversity of races. But the breadth of the conquests of Latin and of Greek do not approach that of Arabic. [. . .] What is this, compared with the immense empire of the Arabic language, embracing Spain, Africa to the equator, Southern Asia to Java, Russia to Kazan?

—ERNEST RENAN, *HISTOIRE GÉNÉRALE ET SYSTÈME COMPARÉ DES LANGUES SÉMITIQUES*, 1863

The Arab writer, then, writes for a public in disarray, one without a single or coherent cultural frame of reference. If he satisfies the Egyptian, he may not satisfy the Syrian, and if he pleases both of them, he may anger the Persian or Indian. If the Muslims are content, the Christians may be annoyed [. . .] . This is a huge obstacle.

—JURJĪ ZAYDĀN, "KUTTĀB AL-ʿARABIYYA WA-QURRĀʾUHĀ," 1899

Europe's great Africanists will tell you that black Africa [. . .] possesses a certain number of written languages. Nonetheless, I prefer, to her written literature, influenced most of the time by Arabic, and leaving the imprint of rhetoric, the oral literature of the *griots* [. . .] .

—LÉOPOLD SÉDAR SENGHOR, "VUES SUR L'AFRIQUE NOIRE OU ASSIMILER, NON ÊTRE ASSIMILÉS," 1945

CONTENTS

PREFACE

IN MAY 1998, mass uprisings in Indonesia overthrew an authoritarian government led by General Suharto. Amid the ensuing power vacuum and nationwide existential crisis that followed, I noticed an unusual social practice taking hold in my Indonesian extended family. Many of my Muslim relatives were expressing a renewed sense of religious attachment by more often engaging in Arabic "code-switching"—using Arabic terms instead of Indonesian ones in casual conversation. This annoyed others of my Indonesian relatives who were either non-Muslim or less (overtly) devout. The argument I heard among the disgruntled was that Arabic code-switching was a religious affectation and an exclusionary practice with no place in religiously mixed families or in secular public life. Some even claimed that it was a betrayal of Indonesia's national beginnings and of its pluralist and multireligious character—an affront to what my grandfather had fought for as an officer in Indonesia's anticolonial wars. The public defense of such practices I later noticed was that Islam was simply resuming its rightful place in national life after 1998, given the Muslim majority long present in Indonesia.

A few years later, as I was on the cusp of beginning my graduate studies in the United States, 9/11 altered the course of U.S. national and global history. It changed the tenor of American political discourse and the pitch of nationalist rhetoric: A drive to contain and moderate Islam globally became increasingly conflated with American security interests, bearing controversial and often tragic results. A surge of Islamophobia and of anti-Arab violence followed in the United States, as devout Muslims feared becoming random targets and reckoned with their public visibility. American university campuses responded to rising public interest in the Arabic language—at times reflecting student interest in greater understanding, at times as an instrument of war among military personnel preparing for deployment. The specter of an intractable overseas conflict and military occupation altered the climate of the Arabic programs in which I was trained in the United States.

The dust on these dynamics remains unsettled. My impression of these rifts, however, left me deeply aggrieved. Some twenty years ago, I was in no position to pursue a research project that conjoined these contexts directly—and I likely never will, given my own training as a non-Americanist. But I was compelled by these circumstances to probe the historical dynamics in which Arabic seemed central: implicated in debates over Islamic self-expression, "containment," and "moderation," a spectral presence across postcolonial forms of national distinction, controversies over cultural pluralism, and histories of empire.

As a scholar of Indonesian and (German) American descent, I have often found my research subtly informed by the controversies I witnessed across this double inheritance. My sense of Arabic's importance as a language with multiple meanings informed my approach to this book. Its controversial position across vast distances made me wonder how well we account for its global presence in the stories we usually tell about anticolonial resistance movements, counterimperial nationalisms, and postcolonial writing. It also raised questions for me about how Arabic could be viewed as an external intrusion into indigenous forms of national belonging in Indonesia, given Indonesia's own position as a multiethnic nation-state (as well as a multireligious one despite its Muslim-majority citizenry).

Arabic's global role is, of course, often understood through its qualities as a language of Islamic ritual and precolonial merchant commerce within Asia and Africa. But my own findings suggest that Arabic's transregional importance exceeds these common associations, demanding fundamentally new ways of thinking about Arabic as a medium with growing anticolonial associations in nineteenth- and twentieth-century contexts. This is true not only in the Middle East, as is well known, but in regions in West Africa and Southeast Asia. In this book, I show that it is precisely because of its cosmopolitan (transregional, interethnic) position that Arabic was viewed as a risk to be moderated by colonial agents from French West Africa to the Dutch East Indies—a trend that then conditioned Arabic's growing counterimperial associations within both regions by the early twentieth century. It is, however, also due to its cosmopolitan and ritual position that Arabic complicated debates among writers and intellectuals about questions of indigeneity, pluralism, and national belonging with the formation of new nation-states in the twentieth century as European empires declined. Where Arabic is viewed as a cultural force of narrow regional or ideological relevance, limited to Middle East studies or to Islamic studies, this story is impossible to fully appreciate. These dynamics in their transregional dimensions also remain overlooked within the fields of colonial and postcolonial studies—an oversight that my book tries to redress.

My book's title was inspired by Niloofar Haeri's *Sacred Language, Ordinary People: Dilemmas of Culture and Politics in Egypt.* Haeri's observation that Egyptian colloquial Arabic remained controversial relative to classical Arabic (*fuṣḥā*) as a "sacred language" raised questions for me about the existence of parallel controversies beyond Egypt. First trained as an Africanist, I began to read Haeri's scholarship after encountering Ngũgĩ wa Thiong'o's defense of African literary vernaculars, a coincidence that inspired me to consider whether the problem of language choice was broadly shared among formerly colonized spaces across Asia and Africa. I began my research as a comparative project in the "spirit of Bandung," gesturing to the iconic first gathering of Asian and African independent states held in Bandung, Indonesia, in 1955. The traces of these beginnings continue to surface across this book.

Niloofar Haeri's findings also led me to question the Arabic language's imbrication in enduring power dynamics and global inequalities. As she explains:

> Linguistically, Muslim countries can be divided into two kinds: those whose national and official languages are not genealogically related to Arabic, such as Iran, Turkey, Pakistan, Indonesia, Senegal and Nigeria (among others), and those that speak various Arabic "dialects" or vernaculars related to, but quite different from, the Classical Arabic of the Qur'an. In both kinds of countries, regardless of native language, a believing Muslim must know some Classical Arabic [*fuṣḥā*] in order to read the holy text, to perform the daily prayers and to carry out other religious rituals and obligations. It has come to pass [...] that the language and Islam are mutually constitutive.

Given "that so many of the instituted practices of Islam must be carried out by believers exclusively in Classical Arabic," she questioned whether such practices reconstitute "an old power struggle" subordinating more recently converted communities to their predecessors.

Due to my firsthand observations, I was compelled by Haeri's suggestion that the "battle lines" drawn around a language "are deserving of close attention because they are not merely about language and narrowly linguistic issues." As Haeri explains of regions where Arabic is ritually employed, the power of classical Arabic or *fuṣḥā* "is such that, in the nexus of state, religion and nation, it continues to stand at the center—used both to pull that triangle together and to push its constituents apart." Readers of my own book will observe the recurrence of this tension across other cases—this "push" and "pull" between state-sanctioned print practices, contested ideas about religious identity, and claims to interreligious forms of national unity. This is a matter of special importance where ideological struggles between languages "sacred" and "mundane," "spoken" and "written," emerged as proxy battles over issues of counterimperial autonomy. As Haeri observes, French and British colonial rule reinforced Egyptians' allegiance to classical Arabic, as it became "the central trope through which opposition to that rule was articulated." I notice a comparable (if qualified) dynamic of reinforced allegiance to classical Arabic as a counterimperial tactic in cases in West Africa and Southeast Asia.

The colonial and postcolonial rise of European languages as forms of cosmopolitan currency has, however, changed the nature of this defensive allegiance to Arabic. In Egypt, for example, former President Mohamed Morsi was mocked for his clumsy public code-switching between Arabic and his deeply accented English, raising questions about Arabic's status relative to European alternatives. Is Arabic mastery insufficient to mark someone as a cosmopolitan political elite in the twenty-first century? Does Arabic still read as a worldly acrolect (a prestige language), or is it more often perceived as a provincial basilect (a subordinate medium) relative to former colonial tongues? As Haeri discerned, lived practices often differ from—and temper—professed beliefs or language attitudes, even where classical Arabic is widely considered to be singular, even sacred, and a prime basis of national value. Egyptian intellectuals and elites, she observed, may profess allegiance to Arabic for religious or patriotic reasons but diminish its use in their own mouths, as they seek upward social mobility and integration into Europeanized global and labor markets.

This Eurocentric class dynamic is a postcolonial condition whose signs are seen across my own findings beyond Egypt. And not only class but gender plays a role in discrepant language practices, at times overdetermining expectations of female speakers presumed to have less intimacy with high literary or ritual Arabic than with colloquial standards. Although less central to the archive I consult within this book, the intersection of class, gender, and Arabic literacies remains controversial transregionally—an issue whose comparative dimensions and literary consequences have yet to be systematically explored.

Note:

Unless otherwise noted, all translations are my own. My transliterations from Arabic generally follow the standards used by the *International Journal of Middle Eastern Studies*. Exceptions include simplified transliterations for names commonly cited in English and the use of regional conventions for Arabic names and terms in West Africa and Southeast Asia.

ACKNOWLEDGMENTS

MY GRATITUDE extends to many colleagues and mentors whose insights and critical assessments have impacted my approach to this book. Christopher L. Miller first oversaw my work on African and francophone materials at Yale and offered me guidance and encouragement across the project's many transformations and across my own shifting institutional affiliations. Tony Day generously took me on as an advisee in Indonesian literature at Yale, offering invaluable advice as the project first took form. Nergis Ertürk, Hendrik J. Maier, Fallou Ngom, and Shaden Tageldin gave me incisive feedback on the first four chapters of this book through a manuscript workshop. Their generous advice and encouraging review of the book in progress had a vital impact on the project as it evolved. A faculty grant from Harvard's Asia Center made this interdisciplinary exchange and manuscript workshop possible, and I thank Jorge Espada and my colleagues at the Asia Center for their support.

My deepest gratitude goes to Karen Thornber for her guidance and mentorship as I transitioned to Harvard. I am extremely thankful for her enthusiastic review of several early chapters of the book and her encouragement and support as I crossed the finish line during the pandemic. I am also sincerely grateful to Bill Granara for his encouragement and for his incisive and helpful feedback on the full manuscript. David Damrosch also read the entire manuscript with care and followed its many revisions at different stages of the project. His generous editorial suggestions and insights as the book took its final form were invaluable.

Sincere thanks also go to David Atherton, Saul Zaritt, Naomi Weiss, Annabel Kim, Sarah Dimick, and Nicole Sütterlin for their extraordinary kindness and camaraderie and for their helpful suggestions as I revised several chapters—especially amid the disruptions and challenges of the pandemic. My gratitude extends to Nina Zipser, dean for Faculty Affairs at Harvard, and to her staff for first putting us in touch as a faculty writing group and for her office's support of working parents during the pandemic. Allison DiBianca's perceptive suggestions were invaluable as I regained my bearings on this project, as were my many encouraging writing exchanges with David Atherton during our pandemic lockdowns. For their generous advice, moral support, and personal encouragement throughout this process, I am also extremely grateful to Katharina Piechocki, Justine Landau, and Durba Mitra. I was very fortunate to have met Usha Reena Rungoo as I neared the final stages of this project at Harvard. I have greatly treasured her friendship and generous encouragement as the book was completed.

Many communities offered the intellectual grounds for developing my ideas before my arrival at Harvard, including at the University of Massachusetts Amherst. I am deeply grateful to Laura Doyle for her extraordinary mentorship, kindness, and intellectual generosity and for her faith in this project amid challenges that often seemed insurmountable given my ambitions for the book. My thanks also extend to Mwangi wa Gĩthĩnji, Johan Mathew, and Joselyn Almeida-Beveridge, my co-recipients of a Mellon Sawyer grant, and to Yaari Felber-Seligman, who collaborated with us throughout our workshops. The scholarly community and exchanges that they fostered through the World Studies Interdisciplinary Project were deeply impactful for my research. Sincere thanks go to Simon Gikandi, Isabel Hofmeyr, and Sahar Amer for their early enthusiasm for my work in progress. I am also grateful to Sheldon Pollock for his encouragement of the project in its earliest inception during his visit with us through the Mellon Sawyer program and to Michael Laffan for his illuminating insights as I explored my ideas for this book. Exchanges with Ngũgĩ wa Thiong'o, Mary Louise Pratt, and Anne Stoler through our Mellon Sawyer workshops were also key to guiding my ideas and methods.

I am deeply grateful to the late David Lenson and to my many departmental colleagues for their support and camaraderie during my time at the University of Massachusetts Amherst. David Lenson's personal kindness and unwavering optimism were very dear to me as the manuscript was under preparation. Special thanks also go to Kathryn Lachman for her kind support and to my dear friend Ela Gezen, whose sense of humor, sage advice, and incredible generosity and warmth were a balm through many trying times as I navigated this project. Tremendous thanks to you and to your wonderful family, Dio and Cem, who through your kindness brightened my time so much in Amherst.

It was my great fortune to have had Rebecca Johnson, Anne Marie McManus, Meg Weisberg, Bilal Orfali, Rossen Djagalov, Alice Lovejoy, and Jeanne-Marie Jackson among my extraordinary peers at Yale. Their own work and conversation impacted the way I approached materials in this book, and their companionship often brought much needed levity to my own work. I am also thankful to have benefited from early conversations with and advice from Beatrice Gruendler, Jing Tsu, Katerina Clark, Haun Saussy, Dudley Andrew, Katie Trumpener, Ala Alryyes, and Margaret Litvin as I was planning my research.

My thanks also extend to Indriyo Sukmono and to the Indonesianist student community he supported during my time at Yale—a community that made New Haven feel like a home away from home. Special thanks go especially to Richard Payne and to Andrew Conroe (my dissertation writing buddies), whose great company and generous laughter made a joy of my final year in New Haven. I am also grateful to Kevin Fogg, whose helpful insights on field research yielded important leads for me in Indonesia.

Exchanges with colleagues and peers under the direction of Shu-mei Shih and Françoise Lionnet during my fellowship through the Mellon Postdoctoral Program in Minor Transnationalism at the University of California, Los Angeles (UCLA), were formative for this project, and I am grateful to them both for their early support of my work. I would also like to extend my appreciation to the editorial collective of *boundary 2*, who facilitated several exchanges that were formative for this project on the politics of language at Dartmouth and on philology and translation at the University of Pittsburgh. Their sense of the ethical stakes of scholarly work very much informed my own. I am extremely grateful for the kindness, encouragement, and enthusiasm of Paul Bové and Jonathan Arac for this project, as well as for the supportive exchanges they facilitated through the collective with David Golumbia, Aamir Mufti, Hortense Spillers, Bruce Robbins, Christian Thorne, Colin Dayan, Anita Starosta, Leah Feldman, Ronald A. Judy, Don Pease, and Charles Bernstein.

I am also grateful to Claire Gallien, Sarah bin Tyeer, and Muhsin al-Musawi for facilitating a generative exchange through a Columbia University workshop on Arabic literature in Paris, 2019, where I enjoyed illuminating conversations with Michael Cooperson, Rana Issa, Hoda El Shakry, Marwa Elshakry, Anna Ziajka Stanton, and Jeffrey Sacks as I completed the manuscript. Thanks also go to Miya Xie for making possible an informative workshop through the Mellon Inter-Asia Workshop at Dartmouth, where counterpoints between Arabic literary studies and Sinophone studies were discussed.

I am also grateful to the Wellesley Newhouse Humanities Center Fellowship program for its support as the book was completed. Special thanks go to Eve Zimmerman, Lauren Cote, and my cohort of Newhouse faculty fellows for their encouragement and feedback on the project, including Antonio Arraiza-Rivera, Weihong Bao, Genevieve Clutario, Rebeca Héy-Colon, Susan Ellison, Nikhil Rao, Thomas Sarmiento, and Yoon Sun Yang.

The research published in this book was made possible through funding from the National Endowment for the Humanities, the American Council of Learned Societies (Faculty Fellowship and Mellon Early Career Dissertation Completion Fellowship), the Wellesley College Newhouse Center for the Humanities Faculty Fellowship, the Asia Center at Harvard University, the Mellon Postdoctoral Humanities Fellowship Program at UCLA, the Social Science Research Council's Mellon International Dissertation Research Fellowship Program, a Healey Faculty Research Grant from the University of Massachusetts Amherst, and travel grants from Yale's Macmillan Center. This project was also refined through constructive exchanges made possible by the African Literature Association, the American Comparative Literature Association, the Middle East Studies Association, the Modern Language Association, Princeton's African Humanities Colloquium, the Social Science Research Foundation, and the Yale Indonesia Forum and through other invitations to speak at Columbia, Cornell, Dartmouth, the University of Pittsburgh, Pennsylvania State University, and Stanford University, where I had the good fortune to receive helpful suggestions, generative insights, and feedback from many colleagues, including Michael Allan, Magalí Armillas-Tiseyras, Wendy Belcher, Fahad Bishara, Stephanie Bosch-Santana, Emily Drumsta, Yasser Elhariry, Ziad Fahmy, Nouri Gana, Cullen Goldblatt, Bilal Hashmi, Samuel Hodgkin, Tsitsi Ella Jaji, Alexander Key, Shuang Shen, Eric Tagliacozzo, and Rebecca Walkowitz. I am grateful to Ousmane Kane for the opportunity to have shared my work in progress through the Islam in Africa series at Harvard. I would also like to extend my thanks to my many students and advisees at Harvard, the University of Massachusetts, and UCLA, whose conversation, intellectual curiosity, and excitement about our common interests I greatly appreciated as I completed this project.

Many other mentors and colleagues facilitated my early research and travels overseas. In Senegal, I had the great fortune of Souleymane Faye's mentorship and training in Wolof at the Centre de Linguistique Appliquée de Dakar at the Université Cheikh Anta Diop in Senegal; Professor Faye, instructor extraordinaire of Wolof and lecturer on Senegalese sociolinguistics, was an absolute delight to learn from, offering me vital research contacts and leads—and regaling me with the most entertaining personal memories of Senghor. His erudition and warmth made my visits to Dakar a joy on many occasions. I am extremely grateful as well to Seydou Nourou Ndiaye, Pathé Diagne, and Cheikh Aliou Ndao for sharing their personal memories of Ousmane Sembene and for their reflections on the founding of *Kaddu* as a pioneering publication in Dakar. I am also pleased to have made the acquaintance of Alain Sembene, Arame Fal, and Abdallah Fahmi Aidara, who also offered me research leads. Melani Budianta, who served as a research sponsor in Indonesia, drew my attention to key sources and cultural debates of relevance to my work in Jakarta and facilitated my meeting with Hilmar Farid Setiadi, whose work on Pramoedya's personal biography offered me key insights for this book. Dr. Mona Lohanda, the renowned Indonesian historian and archivist (whom I'd known since childhood as "Tante Mona"), also offered me valuable guidance during my early research, pointing me to the right collections as I began my work. I am grateful to Seynabou Mbaye and her family, who embodied for me the meanings of *teranga* during my repeated stays in Dakar. I am also thankful to my Indonesian extended family for their hospitality and support during my return visits to Indonesia.

I am grateful to the many staff and librarians who assisted me when visiting and navigating materials in several collections and libraries in the United States and overseas, including at the Bibliothèque nationale de France in Paris; the Archives nationales d'outre-mer in Aix-en-Provence; the Egyptian National Library and Archives (Dār al-Kutub wa-l-Wathā'iq al-Qawmiyya), and the library of the American University in Cairo; the Indonesian National Library (Perpustakaan Nasional), Pusat Perfilman Usmar Ismael, and Pusat Dokumentasi H. B. Jassin in Jakarta; the Perpustakaan Negara Malaysia in Kuala Lumpur; collections at Leiden University and Amsterdam's International Institute for Social History; and the Archives Nationales du Sénégal, the collections of the Institut Fondamental d'Afrique Noir in Dakar, and the Mouride library collection in Touba, Senegal. Librarians and staff at Yale, Harvard, Cornell, UCLA, and the University of Massachusetts Amherst were also extremely helpful throughout the many years I completed my research.

Although the late Helen Tartar never saw this project to its final form, my memory of her early enthusiasm and gentle encouragement after workshopping an early book proposal through a Mellon Mentoring Grant was a tremendous gift given the magnitude of this ambitious undertaking. I also had the exceptional good fortune to work with Ellen Tilton-Cantrell as the manuscript was revised. Her generous insights and deft editorial guidance helped to transform a complex and initially ponderous manuscript into its current form.

I would also like to express my sincere appreciation for my editors at Princeton University Press for their assistance and professional expertise throughout the publication process. I am extremely grateful to Emily Apter for her continued support of this project, and to Anne Savarese for her tremendous generosity, patience, and guidance as Princeton University Press ushered this book into its final form amidst the disruptions and delays of the pandemic. I greatly appreciate the feedback I received from two anonymous reviewers, whose insights and suggestions were central to the revision process. I am also grateful to James Collier, Jaden Young, and Bob Bettendorf for their editorial support. Tremendous thanks also to Elisabeth A. Graves for her careful copyediting, to Lori Holland for her typesetting assistance, and to Steven Moore and Sheila Hill for their assistance with the index. I am also very grateful for support from the Schofield Publication Fund of the Department of Comparative Literature at Harvard. My thanks extend to Liam Klein for his aid with translations from Dutch and to Korka Sall for her generous help with Wolof translations from the journal *Kaddu*. Muhammad Habib also graciously checked and corrected my translations of Egyptian colloquial Arabic poetry. Portions of my research in this book previously appeared in the journal *PMLA*.

I am also grateful for the generous support, patience, and encouragement of many other friends and family as I completed my research for this project. Meg, Catherine, Laura, Emily, Sarah, Mihaela and Saul, Alice, Yoni, Christine, and Yu: Reconnecting with you over the years has been a tremendous gift, and I will be forever grateful for your warmth, laughter, and moral support through life's many turns. For my dear parents: I hope seeing this book in print offers you a less pixelated view of the work that engrossed me over the past many years—and gives you a glimpse into how your personal influences yielded an unorthodox research project in my hands. Consider this, with love, an homage to your shared story, impressed on me through childhood accounts of the Indonesian independence struggle, the Bandung Conference, the U.S. civil rights movement, and the tragedy of lost friends and imprisoned relatives in Indonesia after 1965. Meg and Denette, who often heard a play-by-play account through tired phone calls of my worries and frustrations as I finished this book: Thank you for kindness and moral support (and even for early touches of copyediting here and there). Odette: I will also be forever grateful for your unwavering faith in me over the many long years it took to finish this book and for your invaluable advice as I reframed the stakes of this project across its many incarnations. And Aziz: My greatest thanks to you for reading the final manuscript in full and for offering incisive suggestions and warm encouragement as the book crossed the finish line. To Meg, Odette, Aziz, and Dadu—words cannot express my thanks to you for your incredible love and care for our family as I finally sent off my manuscript.

I am so grateful for the children in my life, who have brought me tremendous joy and laughter amid work that often felt solemn. Sophie and Gwynnie, Navaz and Liam, Taleb and Noah, and little Ava (and your delightful friends)—your presence has been my greatest blessing. Hesham: This book would have been difficult to finish without your support and encouragement. I am so grateful for the countless occasions when you lovingly provided me the time and space that I needed to complete this manuscript. Thank you for bringing your beautiful and loving family into my life.

My daughter was two years old when she learned that her mother was writing a book. Having wandered onto my lap as I was typing at my desk, she offered to help me finish my book by coloring its pages. In the subtlest of ways, but with the brightest of colors, I am sure she already has.

—Cambridge, Massachusetts, June 1, 2023

SACRED LANGUAGE,
VERNACULAR DIFFERENCE

INTRODUCTION

Arabic as a Contact Language

> Since the Renaissance, since the grand discoveries that marked the beginnings of Europe's hold upon the world, extraordinary in its hegemony over peoples of color, no event bears an equal historical importance [. . .]. The [Asia-Africa] Conference of Bandung was more than a military triumph, which established a new, initially provisional equilibrium of political forces [. . .] : it was a moral victory for peoples of color.
>
> —LÉOPOLD SÉDAR SENGHOR, "LES NATIONALISMES D'OUTREMER ET L'AVENIR DES PEUPLES DE COULEUR"

WITH THE MASTERY OF a single language—Arabic—seventeenth-century merchants could voyage without the help of a translator from the Strait of Gibraltar in the eastern Mediterranean to the Strait of Malacca, which marks the passage from the Indian Ocean to the Pacific.[1] By the mid-twentieth century, this same transregional expanse would be described at the Bandung Conference as the "main artery" of European imperialism, against which newly independent states were rising in opposition.[2] Across this transcontinental African and Asian space, the Arabic language connected many regions—and also coexisted with other languages, which were envisioned at times as complements and at times as rivals. How have communities across this expanse interpreted those points of contact and coexistence—and through what ideological grounds? A broad comparison underscores the stakes of these questions. Vernacular-language literatures in Western Europe are often interpreted through their development against a Latin imperial or ecumenical tradition. How, then, might we compare the study of national and vernacular literatures developing within an Arabic context? What implications might this comparison have for how we assess decolonizing national cultures—cultures shaped both by European imperial pressures and by the cultural impact of ritual (or Qur'anic) Arabic?

Beyond its status as a ritual language among Muslims worldwide, Arabic had served as an unrivaled medium of commercial access between Asia and Africa since the thirteenth century, after the secrets of monsoon seafaring were discovered, opening trade routes between the Arabian Peninsula and coastal regions from East Africa to Southeast Asia. In the fifteenth century, Arabic's unrivaled status as a commercial lingua franca from the Strait of Gibraltar to the "spice islands" of the East Indies meant that Portuguese voyagers to the Indian Ocean relied heavily on Arabic interpreters, and seventeenth-century Dutch merchant travelers considered Arabic mastery an asset worthy of scholarly investment. By the nineteenth and early twentieth centuries, however, as European rivalries intensified and coalesced across continental Asia and Africa, Arabic became progressively overshadowed by European literacies within its former channels of transregional exchange.

New biases against Arabic also gained traction among European Orientalists and colonial agents, many of whom associated Arabic and Arabicized literacies with globally "second-class" status. As the influential French scholar and colonial officer Alfred Le Chatelier expressed this prejudice in 1899, "Muslim society is divided into two neatly distinct classes wherever the Muslim literate in European languages progresses beside the Muslim literate in Arabic," between "a class whose thinking remains exclusively Qur'anic, through use of the religious language, Arabic, Persian, or Turkish, and a class whose minds awaken to civilization" through exposure to European languages.[3] Arabicized literacies, in other words, were becoming viewed by colonial commentators as the mark of a new global underclass.

The effects of this shifting status for Arabic varied across Europe's colonies. The process gave rise to the uneven displacement of Arabic as an administrative language and script across arabophone regions and print markets. While generalities are difficult to draw, emerging ideas within circles of Orientalist scholarship naturalized the progressively marginal status of Arabic relative to European literacies—as though Arabic had always been destined to a position of global subordination and "civilizational" irrelevance, inimical to "progress" in European-dominated terms.

These attitudes elicited responses across Europe's colonial frontiers. Under the growing influence of metropolitan European scholarship and the pressures of colony-based policy makers and colonial publishing houses, writers across Arabic-Islamic "contact zones" in Asia and Africa were increasingly compelled to respond to colonial biases against Arabic as a cultural artifice, an orthographic constraint, and a regressive local presence. Across emerging print platforms, colonial ideologies of language converged with defensive claims about Arabic's enduring relevance and its long-standing coexistence with a diversity of languages and dialects.

This book argues that, against these shifting asymmetries of imperial power, writing across Arabic-Islamic contact zones gave the Arabic language and script new political meaning. No longer merely a commercial lingua franca or a ritual language for Muslim communities globally, Arabic became an anticolonial medium for many writers. Writers from West and North Africa to Southeast Asia defended Arabic as a counterimperial medium for challenging cultural asymmetries imposed by imperial Europe, though others questioned the prestigious status that both ritual Arabic and European languages held relative to local vernaculars and languages across Asia and Africa. I take these intersecting hierarchies as my point of departure, to illustrate how Arabic's contact with colonial rivals and vernacular alternatives had generative results, both culturally and aesthetically. Debates comparing the status of Arabic with other languages were central to new modes of imagining a more equitable world with the formation of counterimperial ideologies and the emergence of newly independent states in the twentieth century.

Against seismic shifts in the exchange value of Arabic and European languages during the nineteenth and twentieth centuries, the writers I examine promoted different visions of cultural parity in the wake of European imperialism. In three comparative cases, I examine how the status of Arabic as a charismatic medium, script, and symbol factored into evolving ideas about egalitarian futures across several regions. Moving in focus from French West Africa and the Dutch East Indies to Egypt under Ottoman and British control, I emphasize a thread of commonality across a multilingual corpus of counterimperial writing in the shadow of Arabic as an acrolect or prestige language. Within these regions, assertions of cultural equality were at times expressly aligned with traditional Arabic-Islamic teachings on parity between Arabs and non-Arabs. Such assertions were also at times expressed through positionally subordinate "vernacular" sensibilities in the wake of colonial language hierarchies. To make legible both forms of expression and alignment, I begin with Arabic literacy as a common ground for many writers, before moving across a broader dispersion across languages and dialects that were elevated alongside

Arabic as emancipatory media by the mid- to late twentieth century—from Wolof to colloquial Egyptian and Indonesian Malay. The book ends with observations on how writers both within and beyond the regions labeled by Europeans as the "Middle East" advanced vernacular, subaltern sensibilities against both Arabocentric and Eurocentric forms of ethnic and linguistic prejudice.

By examining the formation of national cultures at the convergence of scriptural, colonial, and local languages, I offer a lens for reassessing the rise of anticolonial nationalisms as reflected through debates on language politics across a historically arabophone space. In consequence, I draw attention to the following dynamics. Arabic literacies and Islamic cultural assimilation were contending with two centrifugal forces that gained momentum during the nineteenth century and into the twentieth century. The first was the genesis of new forms of (proto-)national self-consciousness emerging against an imperial European or Ottoman presence, which lent urgency to the reappraisal of ethnic and linguistic differences within a transregional Muslim community. The second was the growing politicization of Arabic as an interconfessional mark of identity. Tensions surrounding new regionalisms or nationalisms, linguistic difference, and Islamic orthodoxy were interpreted across a broad political spectrum in late colonial and postcolonial contexts. This spectrum ranged from defenders of ritual orthodoxies (who equated Arabic literacy with Islamic cultural belonging) to writers espousing a more qualified acceptance (if not outright rejection) of scriptural standards of Arabic as a cultural force and local literary medium.

Within colonial and postcolonial studies, much of the discussion of contact zones and center-periphery relations has focused on the impact of imperial European languages on local vernaculars, with scholars often framing these dynamics as oppositional.[4] Pursuing an alternative approach, I argue that the relationship between ritual Arabic and its linguistic others was often not one of binary opposition. Their coexistence gave rise to creative tensions and literary innovations irreducible to European imperial influences or to Eurocentric paradigms of progressive vernacularization in the model of post-Reformation Europe. Examining the uneven transition to independence across sites drawn from Southeast Asia, sub-Saharan Africa, and the Middle East, this book works against tendencies to interpret the history of postcolonial literature and postindependence writing through singularly European influences and paradigms. The polycentric status of Arabic as a foundationally interethnic medium, from its complex history of codification through its geographically expanding vocation as a ritual presence, importantly factored into this dynamic.

By highlighting what has been gained rather than lost through Arabic's history as a language in contact with a diversity of alternatives, I hope to counter two common misconceptions about Arabic's status relative to other languages or vernaculars. Despite periodic claims of the "untranslatability" of Arabic, Arabic was not rigidly immutable or untranslatable in its historical contact with other languages and unstandardized dialects.[5] Nor was it a cultural obsolescence lagging behind (but destined to follow) a more "modern," post-Latinate European precedent of vernacularization. These misconceptions gained traction with the rise of European Orientalist writing during the nineteenth and early twentieth centuries as European literacies gained prominence over Arabic alternatives, a shift discussed in the opening chapter. As ritual Arabic remained a force of continued importance across arabophone regions, it coexisted with a diversity of translational practices that at times positioned Arabic and non-Arabic languages on an equal footing and tempered notions of Arabic linguistic mastery as a sign of cultural distinction and unrivaled Muslim piety. I demonstrate this common pattern across a series of cases from West Africa, the Middle East, and Southeast Asia, within the long shadow of Arabic's historical influence as a language of high ritual culture. Across many literary variations, a conciliation between ritual Arabic and local vernaculars appears, giving rise to innovations in literary form. Such innovations play on the meanings of cultural parity between the sacred and the vernacular, between the worldly and the otherworldly, and between ethnolinguistic Arabness and non-Arabness.

Key Concepts and Their Limits

Several concepts central to the book—the concept of the vernacular, the notion of Arabic as a sacralized "truth language" in Islamic contexts, and the notion of Arabic-Islamic contact zones—require further definition. In general, I use the term "vernacular" to designate a language in structural opposition to a more prestigious lingua franca—whether the latter is a European language serving as an elite and hegemonic medium within a colonial territory (English, French, or Dutch) or a ritual variety of Arabic (*fuṣḥā*) connecting Muslim communities transregionally. Notwithstanding this general usage, at times I qualify my reliance on the term "vernacular" to reveal the translational risks involved in the application of the concept beyond European contexts.

Deriving from the Latin term *vernaculus,* meaning the language of the "homeborn slave" (*verna*) in imperial Roman domains, the term carries connotations of the *domestic, native,* and *indigenous.* Arising through these associations, the concept in English tends "to describe the structurally inferior position of many European languages with regard to Latin" until the sixteenth century.[6] The term "vernacular" has acquired an additional association within colonial and postcolonial studies, however, where it is often associated with counterhegemonic projects that challenged the global dominance of imperial Europe itself. In the context of African literary history in particular, designations of "vernacular-language" literature—from Gĩkũyũ to Wolof—often align with anti-elitist literary projects advanced in the twentieth century by writers such as Ngũgĩ wa Thiong'o who employed indigenous-language writing to unsettle the prestige of colonial alternatives.

Certain caveats, however, are vital to bear in mind. As Tobias Warner has aptly noted of West African language debates, "[T]here are no 'value neutral' terms for discussing languages" in the wake of imperial European contact.[7] Joseph Errington explains this non-neutrality in the following pithy formulation: "[C]olonial agents made alien ways of speaking into objects of knowledge, so that their speakers could be made subjects of colonial power."[8] The disciplinary dominance of European linguistic concepts can be viewed as a by-product of this process. Despite its counterhegemonic associations within postcolonial studies, then, the term "vernacular" is complicated by the history of vernacular-language literacies as objects of colonial distortion and policy manipulation, as colonial agents and linguists mobilized European linguistic categories to legitimize their authority over languages beyond Europe's colonial frontiers. Across vast distances, colonial agents taxonomized "unfamiliar tongues" as "vernacular" or "nonvernacular" forms of speech and used these categories to engineer state-sanctioned literacies for rising generations of colonial subjects within the so-called Muslim world. Such concepts accrued a disciplinary currency that remains difficult to dislodge after centuries of European global dominance.[9]

As a result, it may be difficult to disentangle any discussion of vernacular language debates from Eurocentric concepts and modes of framing. Yet, by comparing subaltern, "vernacular" literatures relative to both European and Arabic prestige languages, we can develop a more accurate sense of how histories of language contact remain ideologically fraught at the global intersection of Eurocentric and Arabocentric hierarchies. At times I will therefore use "vernacular" to designate positionally subordinate languages and dialects relative to high literary Arabic (*fuṣḥā*) and to colonial European languages, and at others I bracket the term as a borrowed and relatively Eurocentric concept within Arabic-Islamic contact zones, in the search for alternatives to nuance this conceptual common ground.

In this book, I frequently employ the term "contact zone" to designate "social spaces where disparate cultures meet, clash, grapple with each other," through "highly asymmetrical relations of domination and subordination"—as Mary Louise Pratt explained the phrase in *Imperial Eyes*.[10] Against the term "colonial frontier," which she suggests "is grounded within a European expansionist perspective (the frontier is a frontier only with respect to Europe),"[11] Pratt employed "contact zone" to privilege more polycentric copresences and perspectives beyond an expansionary colonial center. I borrow from Pratt's notion but add the qualifier "Arabic-Islamic" to designate the imbrication of two forms of stratification and hierarchy within the regions I examine. These include hierarchies imposed not only through colonial contact with Europe but through spaces of encounter in which formerly remote peoples became connected by the twinned processes of Islamization and Arabicization.

Throughout the book, I use "contact language" not to describe Arabic as a "pidgin," as sociolinguists frequently use the term, but more simply to describe its position as a language of transregional connection. Arabic's status as a medium used between non-native speakers necessarily implicates a transregional "zone of translation."[12] In the following chapters, I focus on what is gained rather than lost through Arabic's history as a contact language, in its movement across the regional frontiers of an expanding arabophone realm. Rather than framing its histories of contact through anxieties about linguistic corruption and attenuation in its movement away from an "originary" center, I recover the innovations of intercultural texts developed by communities in contact with Arabic, including in regions where non-native speakers were preponderant. From West Africa to Southeast Asia, writers who were self-consciously marginal—relative to Arabic-Islamic cultural centers and sites of early conversion—engaged in selective forms of cultural borrowing, innovation, and autoethnographic writing, contending with local histories of stratification and cultural minoritization in the shadow of Arabic as a language of high ritual and cultural prestige.

The term "arabophone" (a calque on the term "francophone") is frequently used in French-language scholarship to designate writers and speakers of Arabic. Building on Jurjī Zaydān's expansive notion of a transregional arabophone readership (as discussed later in chapter 2), I broaden the term's application to designate a cultural community beyond a "core" of native Arabic-language writers in North Africa and the Middle East, to encompass non-native West African and Southeast Asian writers and speakers of Arabic. By beginning with arabophone writing as a comparative common ground, I draw attention to horizons of literary comparison that move beyond Eurocentric paradigms and disciplinary configurations. To engage with Asian and African cultural histories impacted by both Arabic and European languages, I sometimes use the term "Europhone" as a shorthand to designate modern European languages as a group. This term admittedly occludes the heterogeneity of European languages themselves, but it is useful to provisionally frame how certain authors "write back" to both European metropolitan and Arabic cultural centers.

Global Arabic: "Cosmopolitan" and "Sacred"

The prestige accorded to Arabic was in part indebted to its status as a sacralized language of revelation and as what some scholars have called a "truth language." Benedict Anderson coined the term to designate "the idea that a particular script-language offered privileged access to ontological truth." Anderson illustrates the concept through the examples of both Church Latin and Qur'anic Arabic, languages that "called into being the great transcontinental sodalities of Christendom" and an Islamic *umma* or global community.[13] Despite their illustrative value, such broad classifications of "truth languages" bracket the singular importance of the multilingual interpreters and translators who employ these languages—figures whose translingual work tempers the monolingual force of any language as a supposedly unrivaled means to access a higher ontological reality.

This terminological shorthand on Anderson's part also raises questions of commensurability—not least between Church Latin and ritual Arabic. Broadly unaddressed in Anderson's coinage are the risks of employing largely European terms of analysis within Islamized arabophone regions and beyond the Latinate boundaries of early European Christendom. What analytical nuances are gained when European terms are displaced by alternatives drawn from Arabic lineages and source materials, as the histories of Arabic as a contact language are retraced across Asian and African territories? These observations bear not only on the application of the terms "vernacular" and "truth language" to Arabic-Islamic contexts but also on using Eurocentric notions of "racial" and "national" difference to frame histories of contact between Arabic and other languages.

Following Ronit Ricci's example in *Islam Translated,* I see Arabic as a "cosmopolitan language," viewing it as a prestigious medium used by literary elites to communicate across regional and linguistic differences. Arabic, however, also inaugurated a new "vernacular age" wherever it was regionally introduced, as Ricci explains.[14] Dynamics of Islamic conversion and translation contributed to the formation of a new repository of shared stories, religious motifs, and narrative traditions in Arabicized vernaculars across South and Southeast Asia, or what she calls an Arabic "cosmopolis."[15] Like Ricci, I approach Arabic's cosmopolitan presence as a basis for exploring literary innovations across a diversity of vernacular contexts, though I consider regions of a different dispersion than the South and Southeast Asian sites that Ricci examines.

Arabic's cosmopolitan function often intersects with its sacred one. Though scholars frequently differentiate between the roles functionally occupied by a "sacred language" and a "cosmopolitan language," I use both terms to frame Arabic's transregional vocation, switching between the two according to my own shifting emphasis. What is consistent, however, is that I approach Arabic as a charismatic language, understood to be both "sacred" (ritually important) and "cosmopolitan" (conferring prestige to writers). Arabic, in this regard, often appears as a sign of distinction among writers who used it to express their sense of Muslim belonging and their cultivation (or *adab*).

One of my core aims is to emphasize Arabic's status as a dynamic language of print, literary experimentation, and transcultural influence, rather than one of stasis and cultural stagnation. Literary Arabic (*fuṣḥā*) underwent an uneven process of reform during the nineteenth and twentieth centuries in the Middle East, becoming a grammatically simplified and lexically enriched print standard that evolved over the period treated within the book. In connection to this, Arabic's taxonomic designation as a "living" (rather than "moribund") language by European Orientalists and native speakers became a matter of public controversy, especially as attached to the designation of *fuṣḥā* after the nineteenth century (often equated with "classical" or "Qurʾanic" Arabic, though not universally accepted as such). Underlying these controversies over terminology were questions and anxieties about Arabic's capacity to modernize as a print medium, given its formidable history—its association with a "classical" poetic canon and with ideals of eloquence (or *faṣāḥa*) associated with the Qurʾan. Several authors featured in this book theorized Arabic's capacity to balance between its ritual vocation for Muslims worldwide and its role as a cosmopolitan language of print that would interact with and borrow from other languages.

Arabic speakers historically described the Arabic of the Qurʾan, of classical literature, and of erudite literary texts with a single term: *al-lugha al-ʿarabiyya al-fuṣḥā*, or "eloquent Arabic." European commentators beginning in the nineteenth century in contrast tended to variegate their designations for Arabic according to context and function, variously translating *fuṣḥā* as "classical," "Qurʾanic," "premodern," or "written" Arabic. The unique anglophone term "Modern Standard Arabic," now used to describe literary Arabic after its linguistic reforms as a print standard in the late nineteenth and early twentieth centuries, was a later contribution by U.S.-based linguists in the wake of these debates. Though we can think of "modern" literary Arabic (*fuṣḥā*) as historically connected to "Qurʾanic Arabic," the two are not identical, in part due to the impact of these debates and associated reforms dating from the nineteenth century. The histories of contact between Western European commentators and native Arabic literary elites contributed to this complex history of taxonomic differentiation, a differentiation that remains controversial.[16] Contact with European linguists resulted in innovations among native Arabic speech communities to describe *fuṣḥā* before and after its nineteenth- and early twentieth-century print reforms—for example, differentiating *fuṣḥā al-turāth* (classical Arabic) from *fuṣḥā al-ʿāṣr* or *al-ʿarabiyya al-muʿāṣira* (modern Arabic).[17]

In framing Arabic as a "sacred language" for the purposes of this book, I found Webb Keane's working definition of religious language to be particularly useful. He sees religious languages as linguistic practices that are perceived by speakers or users themselves to be marked or unusual, "distinct from ordinary experience, or situated across some sort of ontological divide from something understood as a more everyday 'here and now.'" Keane suggests that religious language "commonly helps make present what would otherwise, in the course of ordinary experience, be absent or imperceptible."[18] I interpret this definition to encompass the perceptions not only of users or speakers but also of listeners of a language deemed sacred.

Across the contexts and cases examined in this book, two exemplars recur of this marked experience of sacred or religious language. One is the perceived experience of Arabic as an unrivaled form of divine or divinely inspired speech. The second is connected but not reducible to Arabic, through verse 30:22 in the Qurʾan, which sanctifies linguistic differences. This second case can be described as an intense religious experience of linguistic otherness that is grounded in a listener's perception of differences in human speech as a sign from beyond the "here and now." Where difference ordinarily threatens to alienate speakers of distinct languages, its discernment in sacred or religious terms ascribes a divine origin to that difference. At times I describe this second experience as the perception of a sanctified heteroglossia—where the variegation of languages is itself viewed as a sign of the wonders of a divinely created universe, an experience in which human hearers imagine themselves bridging (if not quite overcoming) an ontological divide between different speech communities. The experience thus connects ordinary speakers to what they understand as the universe's otherworldly origins. Any languages "foreign" to a hearer—including non-Arabic languages to the Arabic speaker—are by this logic divine imprints, extensions of a divine message if not exactly divine or divinely inspired speech itself. These two experiences of religious or sacred language at times correspond to xenophilic and xenophobic attitudes that wend their way throughout this book, demonstrating the push and pull between purist ideologies of language that are attached to Arabic as a sacred medium and more heteroglossic values that reflect a history of linguistic intermingling among arabophone communities.

Thresholds of Arabness and Non-Arabness

The term *ʿajam* is generally undertheorized and underscrutinized, but it is crucial to understanding dynamics within Arabic-Islamic contact zones. The terms *ʿajam* for non-Arab peoples and *ʿajamiyya* for non-Arabic languages offer a vital conceptual trace for Arabic's itinerant movement across ethnolinguistic and racial boundaries. As Yasir Suleiman observes, *ʿajami* (pl. *ʿajam*) is used in the Qurʾan "to designate a binary group classification between Arabs and non-Arabs on the basis of language," and it appears as a marked category to signify "what is—in terms of the Qurʾan as revelation—a deviation from the standard or norm."[19]

These terms apparently circulated in pre-Islamic Arabian communities to designate speakers of inscrutable forms of garbled or accented speech (not unlike *barbaros* in ancient Greek and Latin contexts). Qurʾanic scripture enshrined these relational terms, as the Qurʾan self-referentially characterizes its own status as a clear, Arabic revelation against an *ʿajamiyya* alternative or counterfactual across several verses.[20] With the spread of ritual Arabic, the terms *ʿajam* and *ʿajamiyya* were increasingly applied across ethnic lines to groups near the Arabian Peninsula, most notably to a Persian populace (a designation that they continue to retain), notwithstanding their more generalizable usage for non-Arab peoples and their languages.[21] Etymologically associated with the Arabic term *ʿujma*, meaning "deficiencies in pronunciation or speech," *ʿajam(iyya)* is often opposed in classical Arabic texts to a purist ideal of eloquence (or *faṣāḥa*) and to "eloquent speech" (*fuṣḥā*). These terms vitally frame how Arabic is characterized within the Qurʾan as an unrivaled language of ritual prestige, and they are crucial for framing subaltern sensibilities and interpretive practices relative to Arabic *fuṣḥā*, the language register associated with both Qurʾanic scripture and the most elevated forms of classical poetry.

Across Arabic regions of contact, the notion of *ʿajam(iyya)* difference has taken on various accretions. As Islam expanded after the seventh century, the concept traveled along with Arabic as an evolving ethnonymic designation and came to describe a broader diversity of non-Arabic languages (*ʿajamiyyāt*) and non-Arab peoples (*ʿajam*, sing. *ʿajami*) across North Africa and West Asia. At times the term still refers to the garbled, accented, inscrutable, linguistically uncanny or xenophone. And at others, as an "ethnonym," it refers to the non-Arab.[22] Within sub-Saharan African contexts, the term *ʿajami* now refers to non-Arabic languages written in Arabic orthography, as the Arabic script came to transcribe at least eighty languages across continental Africa, yielding literary traditions in at least twenty-nine continental African vernaculars and attenuating the term's originally pejorative meaning.[23] In nineteenth-century Arabic canonical texts, the terms *ʿajam* and *ʿajamiyya* continued to mark the boundaries of Arabic speech communities after colonial French and British incursions in North Africa but extended to new horizons of contact with non-Arab European foreigners. This included the terms' employment as pejorative designations for European Orientalists, whose interference in questions of Arabic philology and poetics was increasingly felt by native speakers—some of whom disdained European Orientalists and missionaries as accented (*ʿajami*) speakers of Arabic.

In Arabocentric terms, then, *ʿajam* (with its derivatives) largely remained a pejorative term of scorn; it names a boundary of inclusion and exclusion for the "Arabophone" and ethnolinguistically marks those who fail to pass. In Islamic intellectual traditions, however, the term is more ambiguous. On the one hand, it frames the uniqueness of the Qurʾan as a clear, Arabic revelation. Yet it is equally invoked to advance heteroglossic or pluralist ideologies of language that attach to Muslim communities, pointing to an internal tension between Arabic's historically centripetal and centrifugal movements, between a linguistic or scriptural orthodoxy in Arabic and the translational needs of a growing, linguistically diverse *umma* (or "community of believers") among the *ʿajam*.[24] Although a pejorative term and a marked category among a core of native Arabic speakers, *ʿajam* has also been used to assert parity across

Arabic-Islamic contact zones among non-Arab Muslims—and to affirm the right to ethnolinguistic difference within an *umma* conjoined by a shared ritual language. The term appears, for example, in hadith, or "sayings," attributed to the Prophet Muhammad's last sermon (*khuṭbah al-widāʿ*), in which he is believed to have proclaimed: "[T]he Arab has no superiority over the non-Arab [*ʿajam*], nor the non-Arab over the Arab, except in piety to God."[25] Variations on this hadith tradition extend ideals of parity between *sudān* and *bayḍān*—black and white—in addition to *ʿajam* and *ʿarab*.[26] On these grounds, as we will see, challenges to linguism and colorism were intertwined across diversifying Muslim communities.

In the early classical period (the first three centuries A.H.), exegetical elaborations on such notions of equality were at times idiomatically expressed (with claims that peoples were level as the surface of water or equal like the teeth of a comb), though Qur'anic verses and hadith on unity and equality were often conceptually referenced through the Arabic term *taswiyya* ("leveling" or "equality") among the pious.[27] Such sanctified notions of equality between *ʿarab* and *ʿajam* are reinforced by Qur'anic verses that either proclaim the equality of peoples and tribes (*shuʿūb wa-qabāʾil*) or uphold linguistic diversity as a benediction:

> Oh, Mankind! We have created you from a male and a female, and We have made you into groups and tribes [*shuʿūb wa qabāʾil*], so that you may know one another. Truly the noblest [*akrām*] among you before God is the most righteous [or pious]. (49:13)[28]

> And among His wonders is the creation of the heavens and the earth, and the diversity [or differences: *ikhtilāf*] of your languages and your colors. In these are signs for mankind. (30:22)[29]

Alongside notions of the Qur'an as a self-referentially unrivaled *Arabic* revelation, then, the Qur'an itself presents linguistic diversity (heteroglossia) as a divine sign.[30]

Although these egalitarian precepts and interpretive traditions reinforce a right to *ʿajami* (non-Arab) difference from Arab counterparts within global Muslim communities, they are difficult to translate in ways that are culturally relevant to the Eurocentric terms and histories that dominate our current disciplines. The notion of *ʿajam(iyya)* difference as a protean, shifting concept remains underexamined and translationally eclipsed, despite the term's centrality for framing subaltern sensibilities within Arabic-Islamic contact zones.

In European Orientalist texts, as Arabic literacies became increasingly politicized by colonial agents in the nineteenth and early twentieth centuries, the term *ʿajam* is variously translated as *barbaros* against a Greco-Roman template and as "non-Arabs" in phil-Aryan and pan-Latinate terms. After the mid- nineteenth century, *ʿajami* came to be polemically translated as the non-Arab Indo-Aryan, applying especially to Greeks and Persians (relative to Arab "Semites"). Certain Orientalist commentators translated the term to frame competitive "Arab" and "non-Arab" forms of what they considered national pride or protonational consciousness. Each of these translational decisions has freighted the autochthonous Arabic opposition of *ʿajam* to *ʿarab* with new meanings and, arguably, with new distortions. But the most durable way the stakes of this opposition were translated in colonial-era Orientalist circles was through histories of what was described as Arab and non-Arab racial difference, racial competition, and racial equality or egalitarianism. Evidence of these colonial-era dependencies on racial and political-national terminology continue to resurface across the book, as *ʿajam-ʿarab* conceptual dynamics are explored with various overlays.

Notwithstanding these translational difficulties, the recuperation—or rendering visible—of the concept of *ʿajami* otherness advances the important labor of making legible a shared Arabic-Islamic idealist tradition of ethnolinguistic parity. This idealism connects writers within regions considered both "centers" and "peripheries" of Arabic language use—from the Middle East to Southeast Asia and West Africa. In the nineteenth and twentieth centuries, its pluralist implications gained meaning among Wolof poets, novelists writing in Malay, Egyptian colloquial poets, and even writers using high literary Arabic or *fuṣḥā*.

This book begins with the comparative reframing of the Arabophone, unsettling notions of centrality and peripherality among speakers of Arabic. The final arc of the book considers the obverse or inverse side of the *ʿajam(iyya)* as a relational concept. Where *ʿajam(iyya)* has crossed boundaries, it has gained in meaning; it offers a prism through which Arabic has traveled and—orthographically, scripturally, exegetically, and literarily—has mingled with the languages of non-Arab communities from continental West Africa to South Africa, from Persia, the Maghreb, and Iberia to insular Southeast Asia.

It has to be said, however, that the egalitarian claims central to this book—between *ʿajam* and *ʿarab*, black and white—are largely *idealist* claims. Forms of color prejudice and linguistic bias were complex and changeable among early Arab and Muslim communities and were reflected by diverse exegetical practices. For example, the Qur'anic verse 49:13 on the parity between peoples and tribes, which was used to defend egalitarian ideals by many of the writers featured in this book, has also been used to assert forms of ethnonationalism and tribalism in very different contexts.[31] Although such divergent uses of verse 49:13 may appear to undercut the claims of the authors I discuss, these nonuniform practices make their invocation of the verse in the name of parity all the more poignant.

It would be a mistake to assume that dynamics of linguistic and racial prejudice were uniform—or were understood in conceptual terms equivalent to those of European commentators. I underscore this point on conceptual incommensurability to avoid "flattening out" a complex historical dynamic. As Bruce Hall, Ghenwa Hayek, and others have noted, however, this quandary does not mean that we should refrain from engaging with evidence of colorism and racial prejudice—or, I should add, language bias—for fear of misnaming these dynamics but, rather, that we should treat conceptual incommensurabilities with nuance across varied contexts.[32]

Beyond the Margins of an Arabophone "Muslim World"

In examining egalitarian forms of literary expression, I focus on three sites with distinct imperial legacies that collectively represent both the custodial Middle Eastern "centers" and the Southeast Asian and West African "peripheries" of a realm politicized by European Orientalist scholars in the late nineteenth century as the "Muslim world."[33] I focus on Senegal, formerly controlled by the French; Indonesia, a former Dutch colony; and semiautonomous Egypt, which emerged as a regional print center within the Ottoman Empire before it was occupied by the British in the late nineteenth century. Beginning with an interimperial approach to the questions that opened this introduction, my discussion builds toward a comparative focus on the discrete national contexts of Senegal, Indonesia, and Egypt in the mid- to late twentieth century. This comparison, however, ultimately yields claims among writers within the "peripheral" regions of West Africa and Southeast Asia that challenge the very grounds of that marginality, at times with reference to Qur'anically enshrined traditions of parity within a global Muslim religious community. Equally important are literary contributions from Egypt that unsettle or bracket notions of Arabic distinction and Arab Egyptian cultural centrality, despite Egypt's position as a center of Islamic learning and Arabic print culture during the nineteenth and twentieth centuries.

The book moves through a centrifugal structure. Beginning with a focus on Arabic as a transregional and interethnic contact language, the discussion progresses through a linguistic and literary dispersion, encompassing literary languages native to Southeast Asia and sub-Saharan West Africa in the spirit of lateral comparisons. Moving through a diversity of languages in contact with ritual Arabic, I also connect controversies on subaltern vernacular writing in Southeast Asia and sub-Saharan West Africa to parallel debates about the literary representation of nonstandard, colloquial varieties of Arabic in the Middle East. These comparisons bypass connections to colonial Europe as a primary common ground and present an alternative approach to the often binary colonial/postcolonial constructions used in more isolated studies of national literatures emerging within Europe's former colonies. Even though I draw evidence from three regional or "area studies" sites, I aim to unsettle the common disciplinary lines that divide scholarship on these regions. I hope to bring greater visibility to global dynamics that cannot be explained through regional scales of analysis, highlighting the history of egalitarian ideals that gain meaning when understood beyond a regional or provincial frame.

The first section, "Reframing the Arabophone," focuses on influential authors from roughly the 1820s through the 1940s. I begin by introducing Orientalist polemics and colonial language policies that contributed to the marginalization of Arabic and the segregation of Arabic and European literacies across several of Europe's colonial territories. I also consider how writing in the late colonial period gave the Arabic language and script new meaning across imperial lines: No longer merely a religious, sacralized language, it became a counterimperial medium, portrayed as a language of symbolic opposition to a colonial or imperial presence.

The second section, "Vernacular Difference and Emerging Nationalisms," considers how the politicization of colonial languages and scriptural Arabic influenced the work of poets in Egypt, Senegal, and Indonesia in the decades surrounding independence (1930s–60s). This section considers how the interchange and competition between Arabic and vernacular traditions helped shape the emergent poetry of three national poetic canons. I also show how the relationship between Arabic and its surrounding vernaculars changed through the controversial search for an egalitarian and liberationist aesthetic in the mid-twentieth century. In addition, this section explores connections between poetic language and the rhetoric of emerging heads of state (Sukarno, Nasser, and Senghor) during an era of transformative political change, along with reference to the Bandung Conference as a leitmotif. The section draws attention to the political catalysts and afterlives of poetic form and plays on the transnational visibility of the Bandung Conference as both a historical event and a near-mythic symbol within a decolonizing Asia-Africa.[34]

Focusing on postcolonial writing toward the latter half of the twentieth century, the third section, "Connected Histories and Competing Literacies," examines authors associated with an emerging "Third World" literary canon in Asia-Africa who challenged the status of Arabic as a language of religious prestige. Of leftist political sympathies, these authors either depicted the religious rise of Arabic as a matter of historical accident or sought to reconcile its sacralized status with a more secular, populist vision for local culture. By considering how the coexistence of sacred and vernacular languages is depicted in historical fiction, I also develop in this section a method of reading that considers how the traces of historically marginalized languages or dialects are nonetheless sustained in individual texts and in the apparent fissures of national literary histories. Drawing attention to questions of language and class, this final arc of the book emphasizes how novelists, from Senegal and Indonesia to Egypt, expressed commitments to linguistic egalitarianism, within the shared penumbra of ritual Arabic.

The enduring coexistence of sacralized Arabic with a diversity of vernacular languages has implications for the comparative study of emerging twentieth-century nationalisms, bearing on the secularity or religious pluralism of new nation-states and the nature of their linguistically bounded forms of communal imagining. In my concluding chapters, I invite readers to reconsider how vernacular literatures in the sites I examine scaffold an emerging national consciousness according to egalitarian contours. While Benedict Anderson influentially argued that national communities were foundationally mediated through the rise of print vernaculars against the decline of religious "truth languages" such as Latin or Arabic, this book demonstrates how that claim is complicated by the legacies of late colonial language policies and the enduring influence of Qur'anic Arabic on postcolonial writing and contemporary culture.

"Sacred Language" as a World Literary "Thread"

Retracing the politicization of Arabic in the wake of European empires also yields insights into polycentric cultural formations relevant to "world literature" as a frame of perennial resurgence. As Tobias Warner has observed in *The Tongue-Tied Imagination*, the iterative nature of the counterimperial "language question" draws us toward a renewed attention to the global dynamics of literary commensurability and incommensurability, of cultural integration and autonomy across various scales of world literary analysis. Warner further suggests that if language itself can be read as a kind of connective cross-thread, aligning readers and speakers across vast distances, language debates amount to the worked-over knots of these cross-threads. Attitudes in favor of linguistic purism and cultural distinction, he argues, are tantamount to perennial attempts to rend apart the entwined cross-threads of literary languages and the seams that connect literary texts.[35] A study of literary innovations at the interstices of language debates and translational dynamics, by this logic, can illuminate the constitutive tensions of globally interconnected forms.

Interest in world literature as both subject and literary frame has tended to surface during periods of major global transformation and crisis, as Djelal Kadir has observed of critical approaches to literature beyond narrowly national confines.[36] In European and American contexts, interest in world literature first emerged with the heights of European imperialism through intellectuals such as Goethe, resurged in the wake of World War II with critics such as Auerbach, and more recently arose as the end of the Cold War has redrawn the world's national and ideological boundaries. Scholars debating this most recent critical resurgence have noted that "world literature" as a frame at its best carries the promise of inclusive literary horizons, while also questioning whether this inclusive purview exists mostly on an aspirational or idealized plane, given the persistence of global inequalities that condition forms of literary circulation. Has translation as a globalized practice in the wake of European imperialism overdetermined what rises to the surface of "worldly" circulation in European languages such as English? Have the colonial beginnings of disciplines such as comparative linguistics constrained the taxonomies through which "literature" has come to be defined, translated, and globally consumed? Some critics have suggested that the interpretive frame of world literature privileges texts that circulate among cosmopolitan literary elites, to the detriment of more localized literary forms that travel less well—including those in provincial "vernaculars."[37]

In different ways, my project aligns with both sides of the argument. On the one hand, David Damrosch's observations about the generative quality of literary circulation—rendering literature itself a "worldly" object—offer a useful frame for certain dimensions of this book. I trace the generative circulation of Qur'anic interpretive practices and Islamic narrative inheritances as they surface in literary texts. Such practices moved through Arabic as a historically connective language, far beyond a core of native Arabic speech communities in West Asia and North Africa (or beyond a "point of origin," to use Damrosch's turn of phrase).[38] My book, however, is also attuned to Arabic's distinctive position in the "push and pull" of world literary space. Although Arabic's position in this space can be viewed as centrifugal (holding to itself, resisting translation), it can also be viewed as generative and centripetal. "Worldliness," in this context, might refer to the transcultural effects of literary borrowing and adaptation, enabled in this case by Arabic's enduring porousness and proximity to other languages.

I approach Arabic's untranslatability not as a "given" or foreclosed fact associated with religious orthodoxies but, rather, as a claim posited and challenged by countervailing practices of translation, at times defended by ideas about Arabic's coequal position to other languages, as already suggested in verse 30:22 of the Qur'an. It is through this push and pull between the monoglossic and heteroglossic—between the untranslatable and translatable—that world literary tensions appear. It is also through this push and pull between language attitudes that literature's "normative force," in Pheng Cheah's terms, might be discerned.[39] By exploring the politics of language across historically colonized Asian and African regions, I trace the circulation of pluralist and egalitarian ideas within Muslim communities as a more equitable "world" was being envisioned after European empires.

Although this book ends with observations on heteroglossia as a pluralist value—drawing evidence from late twentieth-century Arabic literature—it begins with an account of how linguistic diversities were also once colonially usable, viewed by European Orientalists as a way to divide and disarm subjects across a colonized "Muslim world." In the wake of an Orientalist past, "'diversity' itself is [or was] a colonial and Orientalist problematic" that "emerges precisely on the plane of equivalence that is literature," as Aamir Mufti reminds us.[40] Aligning with this observation, the book begins with a chapter on controversial Orientalist and interimperial approaches to arabophone and Muslim diversity during the nineteenth century.

While it may seem counterintuitive to begin with a treatment of European Orientalist and colonial texts, my opening chapter foregrounds how European colonial engagements with Arabic—including efforts to moderate, contain, or displace the language—vested Arabic with new counterimperial associations (as explored in later chapters). Arabic's characterization by many colonial European authorities as a globally underclass language also conditioned how subaltern authors would rally to Arabic's defense as a language of enduring prestige. Moving from British-occupied Egypt as a rising center of Arabic print to French West Africa and Southeast Asia, where Arabic was colonially marginalized, I uncover defensive attachments to Arabic as a common development within and beyond the "Middle East."

1

Reframing the Arabophone

1

Orientalism and Muslim Diversity

"Islam and the Race Problem"

> It is undeniable that the human groups that, on the basis of whichever somatic and psychological kinship factors, feel united and are called races, presently bring humanity into troubles hitherto unknown. In making their proposal to overcome the impending crisis, the American writers [Lothrop Stoddard and Madison Grant] assume the total superiority of the white race, especially a particular part of that race, and aim at the preservation, for that human group, of all living conditions, under which it can stay what it is, regardless of what happens to yellow, red, brown, and black. They urge haste in erecting the necessary dams; they fail to see, however, that these would not turn the flood, but rather would bring about a struggle for life and death, compared to which the most recent war was mere child's play.
>
> —CHRISTIAAN SNOUCK HURGRONJE, "DE ISLAM EN HET RASSENPROBLEEM," FEBRUARY 8, 1922

The redrawing of the global map in the wake of World War I coincided with the re-equilibrium of imperial rivalries, the formation of new protectorates and mandates, and the assertion of national boundaries across former Asian and African colonies of a war-torn Europe. Ruminating on this postwar cartography in a speech at Leiden University in 1922, the influential Dutch Orientalist (and former advisor to the Dutch East Indies colonial government) Christiaan Snouck Hurgronje observed with foreboding that this was a redrawing of the global map that would simply hold "until the next war."[1] His premonition was that this demarcation of state-centered boundaries was opposed by the force of "inextricable" human networks that transcended them on the basis of a multitude of factors, including race and religion. These factors, and in particular racial egotism and racial supremacy, he claimed, offered the prospect of an endless global struggle that would make the latest war appear like "child's play."

Citing incendiary pseudo-academic tracts such as the American Lothrop Stoddard's *The Rising Tide of Color: The Threat against White World-Supremacy* (1920), Snouck Hurgronje presented an overview of "racial" antagonisms and their envisioned resolution within Islam's own history as a point of contrast. Yet Snouck Hurgronje—like Orientalists who came before him—was still projecting European-language concepts upon his subject. The term "race," ambiguous and polysemous itself in European contexts, had no clear equivalent in Arabic upon the term's earliest translations into the Arabic language.[2] By translating into European terms what he called "racial" dynamics internal to Islamic history, Snouck Hurgronje was making a series of selective choices about what in Arabic and arabophone Muslim contexts might represent these European-derived notions: "racial difference" (*rasverschil*), "racial conflict" (*rasconflicten*), and "racial equality" (*gelijkwaardigheid*).

As previously noted, with Islam's expansion after the seventh century, the terms *ʿajami*/*ʿajam* and *ʿajamiyyāt* traveled along with Arabic, to respectively designate a growing diversity of non-Arab demographics and non-Arabic languages. At times referring to the garbled, accented, or inscrutable, and at times, to the non-Arab as a pejorative or marked category, the terms were also invoked to assert ideals of equality between *ʿajam* and *ʿarab* and to affirm the right to ethnic and linguistic difference within an expanding *umma* otherwise unified by Arabic as a ritual language. The present chapter focuses not on these Arabic concepts for ethnolinguistic difference per se (a topic explored in later chapters) but, rather, on their distortive translation and interpretation in Western European Orientalist circles—distortions that paved the way for Snouck Hurgronje's remarks in Leiden. I also explore how racialized characterizations of internal Muslim diversity—across *ʿarabi* and *ʿajami* difference—resonated across scholarly and policy platforms, informing colonial theories of "divide and rule" and of Islam's ideological "containment."

In the late nineteenth century, the Arabic language was perceived to be expanding in influence—and Islam to be gaining in converts—in Africa and Southeast Asia, across regions where European empires had growing commercial ambitions and intensifying strategic interests. In the course of the mid- to late nineteenth century, Orientalist scholarship itself was correlatively gaining in comparative dimensions—transregionally and transhistorically—in keeping with the exigencies of expansionary colonial ambitions within these territories.[3] As the future of a progressively colonized "Muslim world" was being assessed by the turn of the twentieth century, racialized European interpretations of *ʿajam* and *ʿarab* difference gained meaning within circles of Orientalist interpreters and colonial stakeholders. Against this broader context, this chapter foregrounds how certain ideas on Islamic racial difference, strife, and accommodation were projected, circulated, and reinterpreted among influential Orientalist scholars and colonial agents. The fraught deployment of classically oriented scholarship to racially assess Islam's contemporary diversity gained ground through the materials explored in the present chapter, with significant repercussions.

This chapter focuses on a spectrum of influential Orientalist voices in conversation about the future of Islam as a racialized global force. It arcs from the 1840s, with the rise of comparative Semitic philology and (proto-)Islamic studies in Europe, to the 1920s, after Orientalist exchanges were beset by the antagonisms of World War I. It moves in roughly chronological order. Among the most controversial figures featured is the French philosopher and philologist Ernest Renan (1823–92), whose early scholarship on "Semitic" and "Aryan" linguistic "races" set the tone for later scholarly debates. Ignaz Goldziher (1850–1921), a Hungarian scholar whose work transformed European Islamic studies, appears among Renan's most ardent critics; the lifelong clerk of a Hungarian synagogue, Goldziher published his groundbreaking work avocationally, in part on the persistent encouragement of his close friend Snouck Hurgronje.

The Dutch Islamicist Snouck Hurgronje (1857–1936)—whose 1922 speech on racial dynamics was dedicated to Goldziher—emerges as one of the most fascinating and contradictory figures I examine here. Deployed by the Dutch government for the covert surveillance of Indonesian pilgrims on the Hajj (a mission during which he nominally converted to Islam), Snouck Hurgronje later became an architect of Islamist suppression in northern Sumatra (Aceh) as a Dutch colonial advisor. He also gained renown in European academic circles as an eminent scholar of Islamic law. His vacillation between colonial pragmatist and liberal academic offers a through line across this chapter. Other figures mentioned in the chapter include Alfred Le Chatelier (1855–1929), an African-based French colonial official and scholar of Islamic sociology, who was responsible for translating and publishing Snouck Hurgronje's ideas in French.

This chapter looks principally at how Orientalist scholars and colonial stakeholders considered themselves to be interpreting transhistorical racial or ethnolinguistic dynamics in a set of texts from colonial European metropoles. The Orientalist texts and colonial commentaries examined here generally conflated Arabic literacies and Islamization, de-emphasizing the position of Arabic as a historically interreligious medium (an issue considered in the following chapter). Polemical attention was instead placed on the role of Arabic as a culturally isolationist medium for racialized Arabs, a medium often conflated with the origins of Islam, or else as an inter-"racial" ritual language for historically expanding Muslim communities. Yet European "master concepts"—such as "race"—prove problematic in their remarks, as signs of cross-cultural distortion, incommensurability, and anachronism surface within their commentaries on the stakes of *ʿarab* and *ʿajam* difference and acculturation.

We will begin with influential publications by Ernest Renan and Ignaz Goldziher, to trace how European racial and national taxonomies in foundational Orientalist scholarship displaced and politicized the autochthonous boundary terms of *ʿarab* and *ʿajam* (Arab and non-Arab ethnolinguistic differences). The conceptual translation of *ʿarab* and *ʿajam* difference through Eurocentric terms of racial and national diversity assumed real-world repercussions beyond scholarly exchanges, as European colonial agents became invested in the causes of Islam's ongoing expansion and its containment in sub-Saharan West Africa and Southeast Asia. I then consider how the progressive dominance of European frameworks for understanding *ʿarab* and *ʿajam* distinctions resonated within colonial policy circles. After examining how racialized Orientalist characterizations of Muslim diversity informed policy justifications for "divide and rule" in a colonial query on the "future of Islam" (in 1900–1901), the chapter concludes by comparing strategies for Islam's ideological containment as envisioned by Snouck Hurgronje and his French counterpart and publisher, Le Chatelier. These figures theorized in parallel ways the dissociation of a non-Arab West African and Southeast Asian populace from Arabic-Islamic influences at the colonized margins of what they called the "Muslim world"—a problematic blanket designation that remains in current use. As with "the Middle East," we should always refer to "the Muslim world" in awareness of its colonial derivation, noting the diversities too often hidden within these terms.

Mistranslation and Racial Becoming: When *ʿAjam* Became "Aryan"

A leading European interpreter of the diversity of the "Muslim world" was the French Orientalist Ernest Renan, from the 1840s until his death in 1892. Renan was the first European scholar to position Arabic language studies within the emerging field of comparative Semitic philology. Renan has been largely discredited for his contributions to an anti-Semitic and phil-Aryan racial imaginary through his scholarly pursuits,[4] but Renan's polemical writing overdetermined the parameters through which nineteenth-century debates on Muslim diversity would proceed in both scholarly domains and circles of colonial policy makers.

Renan's scholarship notably eclipsed the variety of Arabic terms for Arabic and non-Arabic languages and communities. These include the vital concept that frames the Qur'an as an "Arabic" revelation against an *ʿajami* alternative—the latter Arabic term appearing nowhere in Renan's foundational *Histoire Générale et Systèmes Comparés des Langues Sémitiques* (1855). Equally eclipsed are terms for designating non-Arabic languages that had adopted the Arabic script. Instead, he translated (or approximated) the taxonomic meaning of *ʿajamiyya* otherness (without citing the original Arabic term) as solecisms or *patois grossiers*, using this translation to racially characterize Arab communities as culturally closed, predisposed to dismiss all other languages as disorderly and ungrammatical, "incapables de règle."[5] This was no small fault, for, by translating *ʿajami* into the French term *patois* and overlooking the original term's philological traces in Arabic scholarship, he disregarded the way that this boundary term had framed historically shifting notions of Arabness itself, discounting forms of dynamism internal to the history of the Arabic language and its changing communities of speakers. This oversight was central to his reductive assertion that Arab (and ancient Bedouin) communities were exemplary "Semites" characterized by linguistic purism, closure, and self-regard. He notoriously contrasted this Semitic cultural and racial rigidity with an allegedly superior "Indo-Aryan" cultural and linguistic dynamism.[6]

Such arguments broadly served his claims that forms of grammatical rigidity and stasis reflected the communal mentality of Semitic speech communities, in contrast to the progressive dynamism of Indo-Aryan alternatives. Semitic dogmatisms and unities, he claimed, had given rise to the origins of monotheism—Judaism and Islam—in their Hebrew and Arabic conveyances; against these tendencies were the cultural leaven of allegedly more "dynamic" and variegated Indo-Aryan civilizations and their changeable languages (such as those of Greek and Persian communities), which countervailed Semitic forms of cultural conservativism and stasis across the history of world civilizations.[7]

What Renan misses is that the French term *patois* fails to convey other vital meanings of *ʿajamiyya* as a boundary term—one that conveys not only monoglossic attachments to Arabic but also Arabic-Islamic defenses of heteroglossia and ethnolinguistic parity. Renan thereby dismisses a constitutive tension evident within arabophone communities as Arabic expanded across an unrivaled diversity of regions and ritual users. Across Arabic-Islamic contact zones, monoglossic ideologies of language (defending the unrivaled preserve of Arabic as a sacralized, ritual language) were perennially in tension with heteroglossic ideologies of language (advancing the expansion of Arabic as an interethnic, "universal" medium in dynamic coexistence with *non-Arabic* tongues, or *ʿajamiyyāt*). He thereby de-emphasized the historical dynamism and fluidity of Arabic as a complex language of transregional contact and as an embodied medium: of mixed genealogies, social affect, shifting accent, and linguistic "passing," at the intersection of spoken and written media, across a complex matrix of mixed ethnic affiliations.

Across Renan's corpus of scholarship, Arabic terms of relational difference understood as *ʿajami* otherness come to be increasingly translated as a taxonomically non-Semitic, *Indo-Aryan* otherness. Beyond his translation of *ʿajami* difference to Arabic as a patois, as the "foreign influences" and "solecisms of new converts,"[8] Renan engaged in other forms of distortive translation—and eclipsing—of the notion of *ʿajami* difference through phil-Aryan and anti-Semitic interpretive gestures. It would take a later generation of Orientalist scholars to partially redress this oversight, bringing greater visibility to these conceptual terms within the emerging field of Islamic studies in the late nineteenth century. But Renan's early conceptual oversights and reliance on Eurocentric racial terminology to frame differences between *ʿarab* and *ʿajam* remained entrenched in his wake and were carried forward even among later generations of more nuanced and scrupulous European scholars.

Regarding Arabic's widespread and growing orthographic usage across continental Asia and Africa—what Renan called Arabic's "promiscuity" with the languages of Muslim Asia and its active "conquering" of the African continent—he characterized the Arabic script as an ossified and even "destructive" writing system, a script that he claimed was a liability for "non-Arab" communities from Iberia to Java.[9] Renan's unfavorable judgment of Arabic as a written medium pertained as much to contemporary Muslim communities of "non-Arabs" as to arabographic or arabophone communities of medieval or classical antiquity. Indeed, within his own scholarly corpus, much ink was spilled to dissociate Arabic as a mere writing system from the supposedly original racial identity of non-Arab figures who employed Arabic to speak or write. This was a trend anticipated in his work on comparative philology and extended in his later work, where Renan claimed that Arab philosophy was not authentically "Arab" and referred instead to Greek innovations merely "*written in Arabic*."[10]

Renan further developed this view in his later work *Averroès et l'Averroïsme* (1882) and then most directly and controversially developed these claims in an 1883 essay entitled "Islam and Science." There he asserted that what had come to be called "Arab science" in European scholarly circles was due principally to the work not of Arabs but of Persian and Andalusian innovators: ethnic or racially non-Arab figures who merely spoke the Arabic language or used it as a written medium. What is often overlooked in overviews of Renan's commentary is that he proceeded by racially distinguishing Arabs from Arabophones, arguing that use of the Arabic language was insufficient grounds for the assimilation of "non-Arabs" into "Arabness." He ultimately differentiated between the native Arab and Arabophone—or the racially *Arab* and the racially *non-Arab* speaker or writer of Arabic—through an obverse, Eurocentric framing of the relational difference between (in Arabocentric terms) *ʿarab* and *ʿajam*.

Renan's perspective strongly affected his use of his Arabic sources. His discussion seems to be borrowing from Ibn Khaldun, but without referencing Ibn Khaldun's view of Arabic as an acquired and embodied habit rather than an intrinsic quality of a particular community.[11] What conventionally passes, Renan claims, as scientific and civilizational progress in early Islamic histories were instead racially Indo-Aryan, Sassanian Persian, Andalusian, or classical Greek cultural borrowings—with Semitic Arabs merely and passively proffering their language as a medium for these advancements. Renan's positions on non-native speakers of Arabic characterized the language not as a reflection but as a constraint, an ill-fitting garb and superficial overlay. In this connection, he characterized the misfit between Arabic and its early non-Arab Muslim users, again racially disparaging the very notion of "Arab philosophy" and "Arab science":

> But what is Arab in this allegedly Arab science? The language, nothing but the language. The Muslim conquest had brought the language of the Hejaz to the ends of the world. The same fate befell Arabic as did Latin, which, in the West, came to express feelings and thoughts that had nothing in common with the old Latium. [. . .] What is quite remarkable, in fact, is that of all the allegedly Arab philosophers and scholars [of the earliest Muslim dynasties], there was in practice only one, Al-Kindi, who had Arab origins; all the others are Persians, inhabitants of Transoxiana, Spaniards, people of Bukhara, Samarkand, Córdoba, Seville. Not only are they not Arabs by

> blood; their character has nothing Arab about it. They employ Arabic; but they are hampered by it, the way the thinkers of the Middle Ages are hampered by Latin and break its rules for their purposes.[12]

To challenge the practice of attaching an Arab identity to non-Arab communities who used Arabic, Renan resorted to the following comparative analogy: "It is as great a mistake to attribute Arab science and philosophy to Arabia as it would be to attribute the entirety of Christian Latin literature, all the Scholastics, all the Renaissance, all the science of the sixteenth and part of the seventeenth centuries to the city of Rome simply because it is written in Latin."[13]

This Eurocentric analogy designates as paradigmatic the fate of Latin Christendom and of European history in the wake of the Roman Empire. It also, however, builds on an anti-Semitic and phil-Aryan eclipse of autochthonous Arabic concepts that were at times deployed to level apparent differences between Arabs and Arabophones, or *ʿarab* and *ʿajam*—a difference that Renan implicitly reads as a racialized contrast between allegedly static, Semitic Arabs and dynamic, Aryan non-Arabs. In this way, Renan imposes a framework for naming "racial" divisions internal to an arabophone Muslim community, to offer an ethnolinguistically stratified genealogy of "progress" within early or foundational Islamic histories.

Renan's inaugural work in comparative Semitic philology bequeathed to later European scholars an authoritative precedent for judging Arabic a static or moribund language and for dismissing its orthography as a regressive constraint.[14] In the 1820s the Egyptian scholar Rifāʿah al-Ṭahṭāwī (who studied with one of Renan's forebears, Silvestre de Sacy) could take for granted that Arabic was classed as a "living language" (*langue vivante*) within French taxonomies,[15] but this would no longer be uncontestable after Renan's scholarship of the mid-century. By then, Renan had contributed to the polemical characterization of Arabic as a moribund language and an ossified orthographic practice—a bias against the writing system with a long-standing, transregional impact that we will explore in subsequent chapters.

Framing Parity: *ʿAjami* Difference as "Race" or "Nation"

Among a generation of scholars and Orientalists who assessed Renan's ideas in the late nineteenth century, one of the most impactful rejoinders was by Ignaz Goldziher, the Hungarian Orientalist and pioneer of modern Islamic studies in Europe.[16] Although he discredited several of Renan's claims, his work nonetheless bore the stamp of Renan's foundational framing of *ʿajami* difference as a "racial" question. A figure more philologically scrupulous than Renan—and a Jewish scholar troubled by Renan's anti-Semitism—Goldziher challenged Renan for his reductive and ahistorical conclusions on the linguistic stasis of Semitic communities and highlighted Islamic traditions of parity between *ʿarab* and *ʿajam* that Renan overlooked.

Goldziher's response to Renan was to emphasize the importance of ethnolinguistic competition and synthesis at the evolving foundations of Islam, challenging the conflation of "Arabness" and "Islam" in ways that insisted on the historicization of these terms and suggested their potential disaggregation. In a letter to fellow Orientalist Martin Hartmann, for example, he raised his objections to Renan by asking rhetorically, "Was not Mohammad the exact opposite of all, what the racial drives of his people demanded?"[17] Goldziher's question reveals a slippage back into the racially reductive, however, as his criticism of Renan also assumes the reductive existence of "racial drives" among pre-Islamic Arabian communities. In such rejoinders, one might discern how Renan's foundational arguments on what Goldziher called "racial character," "abstracted from the flow of history,"[18] had overdetermined the framing of Arab(ic) histories of ethnolinguistic contact as resumed by Renan's later challengers, who would still translate the meaning and value of *ʿarab* and *ʿajam* coexistence as a "racial" question.

Goldziher's own pioneering scholarship nonetheless illuminated for a European audience the history of early Arab resistance to the Prophet Muhammad's teachings, rendering Renan's attribution of Islam's origins to a monolithic Semitic Arab community untenable. In his own feat of conceptual translation, Goldziher argued that the Prophet's egalitarian doctrine (*Gleichheitslehre*) and tribally unifying teachings posed a direct challenge to the "racial presumptions" of his own Arab contemporaries.[19] The latter, Goldziher argued, was encompassed by the tribally competitive, factionalizing values (*muruwwa*) embodied in "pagan" Arabian poetry, a sensibility that Goldziher would associate with a provincial Arab "racial arrogance" in early Muslim communities.[20] He equally argued that the Arabic language was not, as Renan assumed, extant in static form when Islam historically emerged, as though reflecting a primordial source of racially Arab "Semitic genius." Its development instead reflected the ethnolinguistic diversity and intermingling of early Muslim communities—a fact underacknowledged by Renan, though evident across extensive philological sources.

In a two-volume monograph that transformed the field of Islamic studies in Europe, *Muhammedanische Studien* (1889–90), Goldziher countered Renan by illuminating the dynamic beginnings of what passed for both "Arabic" linguistically and "Arabness" genealogically. Genealogical and linguistic assertions of Arabness, he concluded, were in fact the result of an agonistic process of commingling among racially diverse, early Muslim communities. Notwithstanding his dependency on reductive terminologies of "racial" and "tribal" differences, Goldziher was the first European scholar after Renan to more systematically examine (and cite) the autochthonous, relational Arabic terms of *ʿarab* and *ʿajam* to historicize this ethnolinguistic diversity. (Goldziher generally translated *ʿarab* and *ʿajam* as *Araber* and *Nichtaraber*.) In contrast to Renan's claims on the irreducible difference between racialized Arab "Semites" and "Aryan" non-Arabs, Goldziher examined the fluid boundaries between "Arab" and "non-Arab" communities on both linguistic and genealogical grounds, highlighting practices of ethnolinguistic "passing" between *ʿarab* and *ʿajam* as chronicled in early poetic and philological sources. To this end, Goldziher's work also illuminated Islamic traditions (hadith) through which "Arabness" effectively encompassed an *ʿajami* otherness, collapsing the differences between the two.

As Goldziher claimed, "around an authentic kernel" of precepts from the Qurʾan, didactic narrative traditions sanctifying ideals of parity in early Muslim communities arose to commemorate the life and deeds of the Prophet Muhammad.[21] Admonitions of genealogical pride through these traditions extended across the shifting boundaries between Arabs and *ʿajam*, challenging the endurance of "tribal" and "racial" prejudice within the earliest Muslim communities.[22] Goldziher also emphasized the attachment of "pious" Muslims to such ideals of parity and to the notion that "all who speak Arabic are Arabs":

> No pious co-religionist would ever have reproached [. . .] Muslim scholars of foreign extraction with being of lower standing than the true Arab because of his foreign origin. The fact that these foreign authorities [*ʿajam*] could find such a firm foothold in the ecclesiastical language of Islam [. . .] so that they even contributed to the scientific study of this language more than the members of the race of which it was the native tongue, gave them legitimate opportunity to bridge the racial difference even more easily. This also has, of course, to be expressed by no less a person than Mohammad himself: "Oh men," he is made to say [in an attributed hadith], "verily God is one God and the ancestor of all men is the same ancestor, religion is the

same religion and the Arabic language is neither the father nor the mother of any one of you but is nothing but a language. Therefore all who speak Arabic are Arabs."[23]

Through such traditions, the linguistic assimilation of the non-Arab *ʿajam* into Arabness, or the "opening up" of Arabness to *ʿajam* otherness, appears possible, though such traditions were still in tension with assertions of genealogical pride and the mockery of "mixed-bred" converts (*mawlā* clients), as Goldziher noted.[24]

After Goldziher's scholarship, Islam and Arabic as its privileged ritual medium would no longer be so easily reduced to racially monolithic "Semitic" origins (at least among informed commentators). But European Orientalist understandings of the diversity of Muslim communities would remain entrenched within the translational parameters of nineteenth-century European scholarship, made legible through ambiguous terminologies of "racial rivalry," "racial coexistence," "racial equality," and "racial egalitarianism." This conceptual entrenchment persisted across disagreements on the topic of Islamic acculturation and Muslim diversity. The ambiguous, conceptual language of race to translate and frame *ʿajam* and *ʿarab* dynamics would persist in Goldziher's scholarship, even when devoid of the phil-Aryan and anti-Semitic overtones to which Renan would attach these distinctions.

Goldziher's important addition or overlay, however, to these translational choices deserves emphasis: Beyond these racial terms, Goldziher also employed the terms "nation" and "national consciousness" or "national pride" to describe historically competitive *ʿajam*-*ʿarab* polemics and their evolving conciliation.[25] These terminologies were central to his explanation of these polemics as they arose among early Muslim elites. Concepts such as "nation" and "race" may have offered Goldziher the clearest contours through which dynamics of *ʿarab* and *ʿajam* became relevant and legible within European scholarship. To this end, he framed these early Muslim polemics through the translational language of an anachronistic nationalist sensibility, explaining that these were "competitive polemics" proceeding from the "positions of various nationalities of Islam," including those of Persians, Nabateans, and Copts, who sought to "restore their national and literary traditions" through reference to Islamic teachings of "racial equality."[26] This translational issue arguably still holds true and has yet to be fully assessed, though scholars have more recently opposed the anachronistic application of "nationalist" terms to the early classical period.[27]

Egalitarianism as Propaganda or Liberality

Following Goldziher's death in 1921, Christiaan Snouck Hurgronje presented his lecture entitled "Islam and the Race Problem" as "homage" to his "fallen colleague" in February 1922, as national and territorial boundaries were being redrawn across global maps after World War I. He summarized several of Goldziher's foundational conclusions in ways that attest to the continuing entrenchment of "racial" and "national" terms to translate the stakes of *ʿarab-ʿajam* historical dynamics. He emphasized on this occasion how Islam as a "system" had conceptually managed what he called its perennial "racial question," that is, the recurrent problem of "racial" coexistence as Islam shifted from a provincial belief system to a religion of universal relevance and interracial community.

Snouck Hurgronje traced how an ethnolinguistic exceptionalism among early Arab communities gave way to practices of broader interethnic assimilation within an expanding Muslim community. He further emphasized how a foundationally monolingual, Arabic revelation became the basis for a universal, interethnic community grounded on a principle of "racial and national equality" ("gelijkwaardigheid aller rassen of natiën").[28] He observed that the Prophet Muhammad's initial revelation, characterized as an Arabic revelation against "barbarous tongues," signaled its intended confinement to a "racially" Arab rather than non-Arab community.[29] As Snouck Hurgronje argued on multiple occasions, it was, beyond economic or geographic factors, the historical "sharpening" of Islamic principles of equality that contributed to Islam's expansion and to "the mind-boggling power of Islam."[30] He concluded: "It is the principle of racial equality" and "the near-miraculous spread" of the Arabic language that "accomplished miracles as great as the Arab armies" in Islam's expansion.[31]

These conclusions were written with a certain sobriety in 1922, after the internecine violence of World War I.[32] On this occasion, Snouck Hurgronje considered such Arabic-Islamic teachings in relatively humanistic terms, presenting, he claimed, a reason for hope in light of perennial problems of "racial" coexistence and postwar racial tensions that threatened to resurface during what he predicted would be the world's "next war."[33] He here advanced relatively liberal, sympathetic positions toward the subject of intra-Muslim "racial equality," concluding with an optimistic gesture to new horizons of cultural progress and transregional association that might level the disparities between Dutch metropoles and colonial subjects of the Dutch East Indies.[34]

Snouck Hurgronje's emphases when interpreting questions of "racial difference" in Arabic-Islamic terms, however, shifted depending on context and political contingency. As a colonial administrator and policy advisor writing some ten years earlier, he had considered these same egalitarian traditions to be a form of "Muslim propaganda," levied from "superior" Muslims to "inferior" pagans in the outlying islands of the Dutch East Indies, and he had suggested that such doctrines of parity and inclusivity needed to be recognized within colonial policy circles, to contain Islam's expansion among pagan communities under Europe's colonial watch.[35] Within Snouck Hurgronje's own writing, then, one can see two emerging tendencies through which Islamic teachings of "racial parity" were viewed by European scholars (and colonial agents) after the turn of the twentieth century. One tendency was to view such teachings with liberal admiration and recognition; another was to view them with colonial hostility as a form of religious "propaganda" that facilitated the spread of Islam as a restive force within European-governed territories.

The remainder of this chapter considers how such patterns of scholarly interpretation would resonate across policy documents and publishing platforms, as European Orientalist scholars were increasingly drawn into interimperial circuits of policy exchange.[36] To throw these interpretive patterns into relief, I present Snouck Hurgronje's more hostile comments on Muslim teachings of racial parity as a counterpoint to the British Persianist Edward Browne's writing in 1901 on the same Islamic traditions as a sign of Islam's "openness." Both commentaries offer a glimpse into the discursive resonances between Orientalist scholarship and colonial policy publications where questions of Muslim diversity and equality were concerned. Snouck Hurgronje and Browne—Dutch and British Orientalists—were notably publishing within semiofficial colonial French journals (*Revue du Monde Musulman* and *Questions Diplomatiques et Coloniales*).

Browne was responding to an editorial inquiry in the latter journal by the journalist Edmond Fazy asking for insight into "l'avenir de l'Islam," "the future of Islam," as France was (re)styling itself as a "Muslim power" (*puissance musulmane*) in continental Africa at the turn of the twentieth century. What Snouck Hurgronje reads as Muslim propaganda, Browne understands as the sign of a remarkable inclusivity, as the traces of a relatively unprecedented, historical embodiment of cultural tolerance and equality among Muslim communities. Browne also suggests that it is difficult to find or reduce "Islam" to an originary cultural source—challenging the notion of an original center or a true periphery within "Islam" as a global presence. He professes a difficulty in privileging an origin of Islamic civilization, culture, or "science," citing the ease of conversion into the faith and the accretive influences long at work in "what we have taken the habit of naming 'Arab sciences.'"[37] Here we can hear echoes of Renan on the questionable "Arabness" of the "Arab sciences"; but where Renan's observations culminate in a derisive, racialized point, suggesting that "science" among Arabs was a borrowed object, Browne instead proceeds to characterize Islam as a movement of foundational absorption and expansive assimilation central to the faith, an openness that calls into question the very notion of its racially determined origins.

In his sequence of lectures published as *Politique Musulmane de la Hollande*, Snouck Hurgronje in contrast emphasized the role of violence in the process of Islam's historical expansion, but he also drew attention to "the use of less violent means" in Islam's appeal to "culturally inferior" prospective converts at its regional peripheries.[38] He argued that Islam benefited from a process of "easily facilitated conversion" and from teachings that emphasize internal states of piety over external signs of difference among the faithful, a doctrinal teaching that eased the assimilation of new entrants into the faith and was responsible for Islam's gains relative to Christian missionary alternatives in European-controlled territories.[39] To characterize the ease with which the Islamic community expands across lines of difference and among allegedly "inferior peoples," Snouck Hurgronje indirectly referenced an Islamic hadith on the Prophet Muhammad's last sermon and a Qur'anic verse (49:13) to frame Islam's accommodation of its own diversity. He later referred to this as Islam's "race verse" in "De Islam en het rassenprobleem," where he more liberally states: "The racial doctrine of the Islamic system has greatly contributed to its initial, not insignificant, success, and it serves as an everlasting ornament to this international community."[40]

In *Politique Musulmane de la Hollande*, Snouck Hurgronje proceeded to characterize Islam's inclusive accommodation of a diverse populace as part of "a system of Muslim propaganda," a doctrine of inbuilt permissiveness allowing for a spectrum of de facto heterodox behaviors and irreligious practices among Muslims and newly converted communities:

> If we have understood well this system of Muslim propaganda, we possess at the same time the key to the secret of the missionary force, so much admired, from which Islam benefits; we would understand also why Islam is such a dangerous competitor for the Christian mission, above all when both are at work among peoples of an inferior culture.[41]

Against charges of nominal belief, "superficial conversion," or "believers in appearance only" across lines of difference, Islamic doctrine carries a refutation, Snouck Hurgronje claimed, as Islamic doctrine asserted that "God alone can judge the authenticity of our faith, whereas human beings judge themselves merely by external signs."[42] Developing ideas he had previously advanced in his essay "L'Avenir de l'Islam," he proceeded to offer policy recommendations on how Islam's missionary force might be curtailed in European-controlled territories, by limiting the use of Muslim intermediaries at the frontiers between Muslim and "pagan" communities.[43]

It is worth returning to the original verse and narrative tradition (hadith) that Snouck Hurgronje indirectly cites here as "Muslim propaganda" to underscore their diverse interpretation within Orientalist circles. What he considers a pretext and defense of "superficial" conversions, others upheld as a sign of Islam's more equitable accommodation of its internal and foundational diversity. Here, Snouck Hurgronje exposes his own sense of racialized cultural hierarchies, to explain why Islam is a faith to which "inferior peoples" are susceptible.[44] Ten years earlier, Edward Browne had commented more liberally on the same traditions and verse (49:13) in his response to Edmond Fazy's inquiry on the future of Islam. Browne professed that the more we seek an "origin" to Islamic practices, the more confounded we are by the venture of determining their fixed provenance. It is in this light that Browne underscores "two or three facts about 'Islam' too frequently ignored in Europe," illuminating in the process egalitarian Islamic teachings through European notions of "patriotism" and "racial" difference.[45] Muhammad, he says, "not only effectively unified Arab tribes, awakening in [their] people a patriotic spirit, but impressed upon all believers ideas of solidarity, equality, and fraternity." In illustration, he translates verse 49:13 from the Qur'an ("The most noble among you according to God is the one who fears God the most") and introduces to his European readership hadith, or "traditions," on the Prophet Muhammad's final sermon in the following terms:

> [E]xplicit in its condemnation of racial pride and chauvinism is the following tradition [hadith] on the Prophet's final sermon: "O, people! God has forbidden you the arrogance of pagan times, and the ancient pride of lineage; the Arab has no superiority over the barbarian [*'ajam*] but for their piety; you are all children of Adam, and Adam was himself created from dust!"[46]

The notion that Browne cites—that there is no superiority of Arab over "barbarian" (but for the piety of each)—is what Snouck Hurgronje indirectly references on the primacy of internal piety over "external signs" in his lecture on the "propagation of Islam" and Islam's "missionary force."[47]

Here Browne translates into French (and through the Greco-Roman term *barbaros*, or "barbarian") Islamic traditions on the equitable accommodation of "Islam's" own diversity—a diversity and equality understood in the original Arabic as existing between *ʿarab* and *ʿajam*. His rejection of racially purist attachments is further underscored by his commentary's opening, in which he suggests that colonial Europe would do best by learning from the negative historical example of antecedent Muslim empires, especially the decline in the eighth century of the ʿUmayyad dynasty, which he suggests was weakened by Arab racial presumptions and contraventions over their foreign subjects among the (*ʿajam*) Persians.[48] Notwithstanding the anti-imperial and antiracist point of Browne's comment, his conclusions, drawn from the German Orientalist Van Vloten (whom he directly cites), are informed by a phil-Aryan, nationalist German reading of the ʿUmayyad decline. According to Van Vloten, the rise of a "national" "Persian" sense of self-determination against an "Arab" ʿUmayyad dynasty caused the dynasty's decline.[49]

Browne's comments seem to admonish the racial arrogance of a jingoistic, colonial Europe; but a second rebuke might also be understood in his remarks. European colonial interests aligned with the rehabilitation of a racially Arab caliphal seat in the Maghreb (a French aspiration) or in the Arabian Peninsula (a British ambition) to challenge non-Arab, Ottoman Turkey's caliphal claims and pan-Islamic overtures, but Browne implies the political folly and failed precedents of such racialized projects and their European imperial supports (projects that were a subject of discussion within the pages of the journal where Browne published his comments).[50] As this broader political context suggests, Orientalist readings of internal Muslim diversity—as racial difference or (proto-)national distinction—were implicated in colonial-era attempts to redraw the internal boundaries of the "Muslim world" by the turn of the twentieth century.

From Diversity to "Divide and Rule": The 1901 "Future of Islam"

The 1901 French inquiry on the "future of Islam" where Browne published these remarks sought to present a crucible of informed opinion on a topic of growing interest to the French Empire in its African expansion. Eliciting contributions from leading Orientalists and *arabisants* across an interimperial dispersion, the inquiry illustrates how contributing colonial functionaries and Orientalist scholars connected questions of "racial" difference and parity to matters of imperial calculus—to policies of Islamic containment and tactics of "divide and rule."[51]

For many contributors to the inquiry, Islam's expansion across continental Africa and Asia was a central concern. At times their sense of foreboding was connected to Ottoman Turkey's growing overtures to pan-Islamic unity in ways that implicated Muslim territories beyond direct Ottoman control after the 1870s.[52] Colonial ambitions to disarm Ottoman Turkish claims to solidarity among Muslims worldwide were broadly considered through the inquiry, as contributors probed how "racial" differences within Islam could be exploited as a moderating force. The long shadow of Renan's controversial ideas on foundational Muslim "races" resurfaced within the inquiry. But alongside references to Renan among the contributors (a cross section of leading Orientalists in 1900–1901), reference to Goldziher's scholarship on egalitarian Islamic teachings and on Islam's accommodation of "racial" and "national" differences also appeared.[53]

The inquiry begins with a striking opening response from the prominent French Orientalist Baron Carra de Vaux. Carra de Vaux's status as a specialist of medieval and classical subjects (Avicenna in particular) placed him in the self-conscious position of deploying his historical expertise for "prophetic" purposes. He expressed his reluctance with an opening (if somewhat disingenuous) demurral, claiming that "affirmative positive documents for this period of history"—the future twentieth century—"do not yet exist." He nonetheless proceeded to examine "forces in play" and "movements initiated" to make certain "predictions" about the "Muslim world."[54] According to Carra de Vaux, these movements and forces depended on a racially differentiated reading of the Muslim world's internal constituents. He characterized the "black" Muslim occupants of central Africa and the Malays and Javanese of the "extreme Orient" as peripheral, regressive, and racially subordinate.[55] He singled out an Aryan Persian imprint on Islamic civilization as Islam's only source of dynamism and cultural redemption—without which Islam's constituents would allegedly remain prone to stasis and conservatism. This conservatism, he asserted, would be in keeping with Islam's Arab Semitic racial origins, its Turkish and Berber influences, and its black African and Oriental Malay embodiments of lassitude and stagnation.[56] Carra de Vaux concludes, however, that progress within the Muslim world was stymied by the marginal position of Aryan Persia (beset by its heterodox status as a majority-Shiʿite region)—a marginalization therefore condemning Islam to continued stasis if not for the intervention of "external [read: colonial, European] forces."[57]

Carra de Vaux's contribution illustrates how differences within the "Muslim world" were still translationally understood by the turn of the twentieth century through earlier nineteenth-century Indo-Aryan and Semitic racial divisions and cultural hierarchies. In this regard, Carra de Vaux claimed that Aryan racial elements within the contemporary Muslim world should be protected from inferior incursions: "[O]nce glorious races, kindred to ours," including the "Greek, Armenian, Persian," "deserve deliverance from Turkish threats and domination."[58] Here, elements of French philhellenism and solidarities with (Eastern) Christian communities under Ottoman subjection were apparent, at the expense of racially subordinated Arab Semitic, Turkish, African, and East Asian others.

Against this diverse racial spectrum, Carra de Vaux characterized pan-Islamism as "the greatest threat" to Europe's "Christian powers" in their rapports with the "world of Islam." He identified a simultaneous "resumption of arms" ("prise d'armes") from North Africa to the extreme Orient as a possibility, to be reduced by avoiding "imprudences" and "overt injuries" through certain policies ("une certaine politique").[59] In Carra de Vaux's estimation, "racial" differences offered the logic of a colonial solution to potential pan-Islamic hostilities. The prescription, he suggested, lay in making use of preexisting divisions in the "néo-Mahométan monde." Noting that "the Islam of the Sudanese, of the Chinese, of the Persians, of the Malays" were each "distinct," he proposed that colonial powers foster nationalist sentiments at the expense of religious solidarities. Carra de Vaux argued that the position of Egypt and its ascendant attachments to territorial nationalism could assume an exemplary dividing role between an "Asian Islam" and an "African Islam": "Let us make of Egypt a barrier between the domains of African Islam and Asian Islam. In a word, let us *section* Islam."[60]

By this logic, racial differences could be reinforced to foster divisions within Islam itself. Carra de Vaux suggested that colonial policy must cultivate such divisions by reinforcing discrete national polities. In his vision, a broad global emulation of a (model) nationalist Egypt would ideally lead the more peripheral regions of "Muslim Asia" and "Muslim Africa" into nationalist isolation—with interests more conciliatory to those of colonial Europe. Here again, Muslim diversity appears legible through Eurocentric terms of "racial" and "national" difference. Carra de Vaux deploys through racialized Eurocentric notions of "progress" an interpretive analysis of the "classical" histories of Islam for prescriptive colonial interests. As Marwan Buheiry has observed, Carra de Vaux's opening contribution thus brings into focus the regional peripheries and centers of the "world of Islamism" (*le monde de l'islamisme*).[61]

The inquiry attests to the increasingly politicized stakes of assessing the dynamics of racial diversity and assimilation across colonized Arabic-Islamic "contact zones," here understood through the interimperial calculus of a French foreign policy platform, the colonial French journal *Questions Diplomatiques et Coloniales*. Responses to the journal's inquiry on the "future of Islam" also suggest that Orientalism as a field was gaining unprecedented comparative dimensions at the turn of the twentieth century, in keeping with the logic of Western Europe's colonial expansion and new commercial interests. Early Orientalist scholarship had centered on a "classical" past (as many historians of the field have observed); but the 1901 inquiry attests to the increasingly predictive and prescriptive demands made of Orientalists. In addition, the logic of expansionary colonial interests was bringing within a panoptic scholarly lens the "margins" of the "Muslim world," giving the field its increasingly comparative dimensions.[62]

If Carra de Vaux initially demurred in his submission on "Islamism in the twentieth century" due to his "medieval" (rather than "current") expertise, Snouck Hurgronje expressed his reluctance to "prophesy" on different grounds. Writing his submission from Sumatra as an active colonial agent in 1901, he professed his distance from European centers of scholarly authority. He nonetheless also traced Islam's inherent lines of fracture to explain—and predict—the political fragmentation of the "Muslim world" and to counter claims of pan-Islamic unity arising from an Ottoman Turkish caliphal center.[63] Snouck Hurgronje challenged the legitimacy of diplomatic overtures to pan-Islamic unity advanced by Ottoman Turkey, by comparing Islam's political present with its foundational history. Islam's foundational communities became politically decentralized "very early" in history, he claimed, and the "theory" or doctrine of an Islamic caliphate was a belated emergence—a sign of political decadence—just as theories and codified rules of Arabic grammar emerged after the high marks of a classical Arabic language had passed and the language was experiencing a state of decline.[64] He further claimed that Ottoman pretensions to this caliphal inheritance profited from European diplomatic misunderstandings and presumed equivalences between an Islamic caliphate and a Catholic papacy.[65] He concluded with the following remark to fellow European readers: that it was possible to "tolerate the Ottomans" as a "fellow political dynasty," while being disabused of their claims to caliphal unity over Muslims worldwide, because "religious unity is vested not in a [centralized] caliphate but in the [decentralized] *ulema*"—that is, in a decentralized class of elite religious scholars and arbiters.[66]

Here Snouck Hurgronje challenges as idealized fictions two interrelated foundations of pan-Islamic solidarity. The first, he claimed, was the notion of a unified polity vested in a caliphal model of government; the second was the unifying force of ritual Arabic, whose integrity depended on a grammatical idealization of the classical language distinct from contemporary human speech. Any vestiges of unity, he claimed, inhered in a decentralized interpretive class of elite religious scholars (*ulema*) who arbitrated between the ideal and the lived. In his view, both the de facto decentralization of these religious elites and the disjuncture between their historical ideals and the contemporary communities over which they claimed authority meant that real Muslim political unity and cultural uniformity were unachievable. The logic of this conclusion derives from his analogy between the codification of caliphal doctrines and the fixing of grammatical rules for the Arabic language, both processes occurring at a historical inflection point, marking a period of political decadence and cultural nostalgia. Arabic grammar was itself only scrutinized when the purest forms of the language were in the process of dissolution, just as theories of caliphal sovereignty were asserted after the de facto political unity of Islam's foundational dynasties had disappeared.[67]

That Snouck Hurgronje draws an analogy between the idealization of an Arabic linguistic community through the historical fixing of grammatical norms and the idealization of an Islamic community of shared governance is telling. The analogy suggests the disjuncture between the real and the ideal in both linguistic and juridical-political terms. The laws of both the Arabic language (its grammar) and Islamic political unity (doctrines of caliphal sovereignty) are indexed to an irretrievable past; the irretrievable conditions on which they are based and their status as nostalgic abstractions condemn them to a position of tenuous relevance for contemporary and future subjects of a (pan-)Islamic community. Although Snouck Hurgronje did not extend this analogy on Arabic to its logical conclusion, this much is implied: The religiously sanctified terms of both Arabic literacy and pan-Islamic unity had from their foundations a quality of historical inauthenticity. They were the products of an effort to arrest what had already been lost to the passage of time.[68]

Although the question of Arabic and Islamic cultural literacies is a subordinate issue within this policy-oriented memorandum, important implications can be drawn from Snouck Hurgronje's observations on language. The most significant of these implications is that ritual Arabic amounts to an unrepresentative abstraction for contemporary and future Muslim communities. His conclusions suggest that, to the extent that contemporary Muslim communities depended on Arabic literacy as a form of self-representation (a literacy embodied in the language's allegedly ossified grammar), they also depended on an artificial displacement of contemporary forms of speech.

On the grounds of these observations, I explore the following implications of Snouck Hurgronje's claims. His contribution attests to the historical position of ritual Arabic as an idealized prestige language sustained by an interpretive class of clerical elites—elites who traditionally occupied positions of political influence and mediation across Arabic-Islamic "contact zones." His broader policy aims, however, were to limit Arabic's reach as a medium of political mediation and prestige within the territories under his advisory jurisdiction, in keeping with colonial Dutch objectives for Islam's containment and moderation in the Dutch East Indies.[69] Snouck Hurgronje's policy recommendations corresponded with Arabic's displacement by Europeanized literacies for rising generations of local elites in the Dutch East Indies.

Snouck Hurgronje's tactics and justifications for moderating Islam's influence and Arabic's presence in the Dutch East Indies also had striking repercussions and parallels interimperially. This is attested by the interested audience of French colonial officials and Orientalists who read and translated his work and who shared parallel concerns about Islam's expansion in sub-Saharan African regions where Islam was actively gaining converts. In line with Snouck Hurgronje's ideas on parity and inclusivity as "Muslim propaganda," for example, another commentator to the survey on *l'avenir de l'Islam*, the Algeria-based Arabist and colonial official Henry de Castries, implied that forms of racial inclusion and an "absence of color prejudice" among Muslim communities were responsible for Islam's expansion in continental Africa. This, according to de Castries, was why Islam appeared to outdo Christian missionaries by extending to new converts a superior practice of racial parity and inclusivity. Prejudice, he claimed, "was an enduring feature of the Christian missionary even when he gave the black his most tender compassion and even when he proclaimed him to be his brother."[70]

I focus in the next section on the parallels and connections between the Dutch East Indies and French West Africa—connections in part corroborated by the translation and publication of Snouck Hurgronje's policy recommendations in French colonial journals. I also draw attention to one of the figures who facilitated these translations within French colonial circles: Alfred Le Chatelier, a veteran colonial officer in Algeria and the Congo, first chair of

Islamic sociology at the Collège de France, and founder of the groundbreaking journal *Revue du Monde Musulman,* through which Snouck Hurgronje's ideas were published in French. Le Chatelier penned an enthusiastic introduction to the French translation of Snouck Hurgronje's lectures on Dutch Muslim policy, lauding developments in the Dutch East Indies as progressive policy models worthy of emulation.[71] Transperipheral comparisons between sub-Saharan African and East Indies Muslim communities were implicated in his efforts, facilitated by the pioneering journal he founded to survey developments across the "Muslim world."[72]

Theories of Containment

The semiofficial French publication *Revue du Monde Musulman* (founded in 1906) through which Snouck Hurgronje published his remarks on "the propagation of Islam" provided an important space for transperipheral comparisons of the colonized "Muslim world" and discussions of possible measures for moderating Islam's influence in Europe's colonies. As with the inquiry on the "future of Islam" published by *Questions Diplomatiques et Coloniales,* the journal was responding to the perceived need for greater collaboration between circles of European Orientalists, imperial policy makers, and colonial agents tasked with print surveillance across the Muslim world. This was a need partially met by the *Revue* itself, which dedicated up to a quarter of its pages to a summary of new publications within Muslim regions globally.[73] An early appeal by Le Chatelier for interimperial surveillance on the Muslim world articulated these motivations with an eye to the following challenge to colonial policy makers, in an open letter published in the British press, later republished in French as a political pamphlet, *Politique Musulmane.*[74] Although ritual Arabic conferred on Europe's Muslim subjects a certain measure of "social homogeneity," Le Chatelier wrote, the breadth, diversity, and dynamism of contemporary Muslim territories meant that the Muslim world could no longer be understood purely through the prism of classical Arabic texts. He argued that the Muslim world can no longer be monitored and governed through recourse to "fourth-century Hijri" manuscripts; it must "now" be understood through the careful review of a growing proliferation of new print publications within its boundaries.[75]

Le Chatelier proceeded to argue that new forms of Orientalist scholarship were required to meet imminent threats wrought by modern print networks—new networks conjoining (what we might call) Arabic-Islamic "contact zones" globally. He seemed particularly concerned about publications circulating from Egypt to French-controlled African territories.[76] He prophesied that without greater interimperial cooperation on surveillance of the Muslim world, the consequence would be the declining influence and economic obsolescence of Europe's (former) "Muslim empires," among which he counted France, Britain, the Netherlands, and Russia.[77]

Concerns about moderating and containing Islam led French colonial officials such as Le Chatelier to admire and study Holland's stable reign over the predominantly Muslim Dutch East Indies—particularly as France was considering its African expansion into Morocco and seeking to avoid its own previously failed tactics in Algeria and Egypt. On these grounds, Le Chatelier published an enthusiastic introduction to Snouck Hurgronje's translated lectures on "Holland's Muslim policy."[78] As Le Chatelier's writing attests, the logic of a transperipheral, racialized science of the "Muslim world," bringing into comparative focus "marginal" Muslim regions such as French West Africa and the Dutch East Indies, was tied to the logic of containment; racialized arguments about the status of their inhabitants as superficially assimilated and acculturated Muslims served this purpose, with conclusions drawn regarding their qualities as an ideologically malleable populace. The sites of recent (and ongoing) Muslim conversion were portrayed as both a colonial risk and an opportunity: Such regions remained susceptible to foreign influences (i.e., the "soft power" of the Ottomans and, later, their German allies) but also to countervailing influences in a reoriented colonial politics of (pro-European) "Association" (thus named in the colonies of both French West Africa and the Dutch East Indies). Both Le Chatelier in the continental African case and Snouck Hurgronje in the Dutch East Indies were central figures in theorizing these policy reorientations, and their publications leave behind a legacy of scholarly exchange and policy sharing with repercussions we will examine in subsequent chapters.[79]

Snouck Hurgronje's *Politique Musulmane de la Hollande* offers a broad and wide-ranging set of observations and policy advisements; of relevance to questions of Muslim diversity and assimilation are his remarks on the causes of Islam's expansion in the twentieth century and the possibilities of its containment among an ethnically and culturally diverse populace. The general characterization of Indies (Javanese and Malay) Muslims as superficially assimilated converts persists in the pages of Snouck Hurgronje's translated "four lectures" and complements his broader discussion of its policy implications for matters of ideological containment. Expanding on his earlier contribution to the French inquiry on the "future of Islam," he emphasized again the status of "pan-Islam" and the ideal of caliphal unity as a fiction of minimal relevance to the ordinary Indonesian practicing a syncretic form of Islam. Pan-Islamic aspirations—despite their reliance on historically inauthentic ideals—were nonetheless a source of potential agitation among a minority of more dogmatic, scripturalist *ulema* hostile to Dutch rule.[80] It is on this basis that Snouck Hurgronje offered one of the recommendations for which he is best known: a policy that would allow colonial functionaries the appearance of outward religious neutrality, by engaging in forms of ideological containment "without [explicitly] violating religious liberty."[81] To this end, he advocated for a respect for religious liberties within "private" affairs—allowing for broad freedom of passage on the Hajj pilgrimage, freedom of worship, and the free exercise of religion in private legal matters (such as family law)—while curbing religious influences and literacies elsewhere in the public, political realm—for example, by privileging over Islamic juridical practices alternative forms of customary law.[82] As Harry Benda has said, Snouck Hurgronje's conclusions proceeded from the assumption that the Dutch colonialists' enemy "was not Islam as a religion, but Islam as a political doctrine."[83] Snouck Hurgronje also identified secular Western education as a containment tactic, as "the surest means of reducing and ultimately defeating the influence of Islam in Indonesia," noting with a sense of triumph that colonial schools were making gains over their traditional Muslim counterparts.[84] In this vein, he promoted a long-term policy of European cultural "Association" for a rising generation of Indies subjects, advocating for the secular Dutch education of local elites, the assimilation of Western-educated Indonesians into the colonial civil administration, and the longer-term expansion of secular pedagogy to the Indonesian masses.[85] He had personally recommended (and overseen) the romanization of local languages historically written in Arabic script (such as Malay and Acehnese), considering the spread of Europeanized literacies a salutary moderating force.[86]

Resuming a point made in his previous publications, Snouck Hurgronje lamented the Dutch state's long-standing reliance on traditionally trained Muslim clerical functionaries as intermediaries among "pagan subjects," considering this an indirect catalyst and support for Islam's expansion within pagan communities of the Dutch East Indies.[87] He argued that "the government favors Muslim propaganda by installing Muhammadan functionaries in pagan regions. [. . .] The government must nonetheless pay attention not to place in pagan territories too many subalterns of the Muslim religion, so as to protect itself against an involuntary expansion of Islam."[88] This deserves some emphasis. In May 1911, at a time nearly coincident with the translation of Snouck Hurgronje's recommendations within French colonial publishing circuits, the governor-general of French West Africa, William Ponty, circulated a comparable memo among colonial officials to limit the use of Arabic through Muslim intermediaries, arguing that not to do so was tantamount to spreading or encouraging the "propaganda of Islam."[89]

It is clear that Dutch ideas fell on fertile ground among French Orientalists and functionaries with ties to France's West African colonies. In this connection, Le Chatelier, like his Dutch counterpart Snouck Hurgronje, had envisioned in parallel ways the distancing of Arabic as a ritual language from public circuits of commercial literacy and political mediation for a rising generation of colonial subjects. In his 1910 *Politique Musulmane*, as in *L'Islam dans l'Afrique occidentale* (1899), Le Chatelier promoted French education to compete with "Arabic-Islamic" alternatives in West Africa, and he proposed that the francophone African Muslim would act as a moderating force to the Arabophone. Racialized characterizations of sub-Saharan Africans offer a pretext for Le Chatelier's arguments on the containment of Arabic literacies and the spread of the French language.

Aligning with a claim Snouck Hurgronje had also made, Le Chatelier claimed that the "superiority of the Muslim over the [non-Muslim] fetishist" was due to the former's "possession of a written language," but this allowed Muslims to ascend to positions of importance as political intermediaries over their non-Muslim counterparts in potentially risky ways.[90] Arabographic and arabophone literacies in West Africa, he argued, should therefore be contained, limited to the "mosque" or the *zawiya*—to the nominally private realm of ritual obligations. Ranking forms of literacy within the Muslim world, he also offered a global view of the superiority of *Europhone* Muslims against their exclusively *arabophone* (or Persian- and Turkish-speaking) inferiors:

> We have only to look at what passes in the Indies, in Persia, in Egypt, in Syria, in Turkey, in Tunisia, in Algeria, wherever the Muslim literate in European languages progresses beside the Muslim literate in Arabic. In all of these countries Muslim society is divided into two neatly distinct classes: a class whose thinking remains exclusively Qur'anic, through use of the religious language, Arabic, Persian, or Turkish, and a class whose minds awaken to civilization, Westernized by their perceptions, through the language that they employ [. . .] . The same is true in West Africa. [. . .] Our

> African sub-Saharan [*soudanienne*] task is therefore entirely clear [. . .]. Let us leave Arabic in its *Zaouias* and mosques [. . .]. Beside the *Taleb* to whom Arabic is taught, the *Khodja* who employs Arabic to write, and the *Dioula* who uses Arabic [numerals] for his records, let us place the [French colonial] schoolmaster.[91]

Statements like this illustrate that the spread of the French language was considered a tactic to curb Arabic and Arabicized literacies among Muslim subjects. The promotion of French through policies of pro-European "Association" between the 1890s and 1910s can therefore be understood as an extension of colonial concerns about Muslim containment and moderation.

Le Chatelier also characterized French as a moderating commercial force, countervailing Arabic as a language of "the propaganda of Holy wars."[92] Writing on the subject in 1910, he argued that West Africa had "much evolved" since 1887; after the political decline or capture of figures such as Samory and Ahmadou Cheikhou, Islam was in a more defensive position, he claimed, making way for "our African work of expanding French civilization."[93] In line with Snouck Hurgronje's own advocacy of European literacies over Arabic or Arabicized alternatives for rising generations of local subjects, Le Chatelier concluded: "It is the propagation of the French language that will be the tactical key to our victory." He added that "we can take recourse from a variety of methods to expand it: the choice of functionaries and indigenous agents, obligatory instruction among indigenous troops, by an appropriate educational formation [*scolarité*], with fixed schools and ambulant supervisors."[94]

The following points deserve emphasis on the status of Arabic in connection to political elites and subalterns as envisioned by these influential colonial figures. Both commentators, the Dutch Snouck Hurgronje and the French Le Chatelier, observed that Arabic literacies had bestowed a significant degree of social prominence and political access on Muslim intermediaries in West Africa and the Dutch East Indies at the turn of the twentieth century. They hoped that soon Arabic literacies would no longer serve this vital mediating function; administrative access to political centers of power would become increasingly vested in the Europeanized or romanized literacies of a consolidating French or Dutch colonial state.

In parallel ways, Snouck Hurgronje and Le Chatelier theorized this eventuality: Both advocated for a division between a Europeanized public domain and the relatively "private" circumscription of Arabic-Islamic literacies—confined to the realms of religious ritual and education, "personal" affairs, and family law (in Snouck Hurgronje's case) and to "mosques and *zawiyas*" (as Le Chatelier proposed). Although such changes were envisioned with reference to divisions between public and private spheres, they would also have longer-term implications for local class stratifications (as Le Chatelier's comments on progressive Europhone and regressive arabophone Muslim "classes" imply). Whereas Arabic had once been an unrivaled medium of transregional access, it was being theorized by the late nineteenth and early twentieth centuries as a public *basilect* in a global order dominated by Europe.[95] In this new linguistic world order, arabophone literacies would mark the emergence of *a new global underclass.*

2

Thresholds of "Arabness"

"Honestly, my lord," said the servant, "though he is kind, I believe he is an *ʿajami*, for I can barely understand him when he speaks in our language."

—AḤMAD FĀRIS AL-SHIDYĀQ,
AL-SĀQ ʿALĀ AL-SĀQ FĪ MĀ HUWA AL-FIRYĀQ

THE PIONEERING nineteenth-century Lebanese Arab author Aḥmad Fāris al-Shidyāq, after venturing to Egypt as a scribe for a local patron, recounted in his semi-autobiographical travelogue the shock of being surreptitiously accused by an Egyptian manservant of being an inscrutable *ʿajami*—a non-Arab. The servant, whose suspicion supplies the epigraph above, had intended to expose an imposter: an *ʿajami* trying to pass as an Arab and to profit from this deception by posing as an erudite scholar of Arabic despite being incomprehensible to the ordinary Egyptian. The accusation derives its humor by playing on linguistic hierarchies (presumed by the servant) that subordinate non-Arabs to Arabs. It also depends on the parodic depiction of dialectal differences across regional and class lines, recast by the servant as being so vast as to render the Lebanese scribe and the underclass Egyptian mutually unintelligible. The vignette capitalizes on the humor of competing claims regarding who possesses Arabic as a native speaker and who determines its boundaries of inclusion. Whose lexical tics and habits of grammar are too extreme for him to be considered an Arabophone—the commoner or the erudite scholar? In its hyperbole, al-Shidyāq's account also prods his readers with the implied question: Is it possible to take Arabic erudition—or pedantic posturing—to such an extreme that, so alienated from the common masses (the *ʿāmma*), one can no longer be considered a speaker of Arabic?

I begin with this anecdote because it offers a vital insight on intersecting ways of framing arabophone boundaries. Axes of inclusion are not only ones of presumed nativeness, differentiating between the Arab and non-Arab (*ʿarabi* and *ʿajami*); they are also marked—and unsettled—by boundaries of class and regional difference. Such differences are associated with the term *ʿāmmiyya*, a term derived from *ʿāmma*, which can mean "common" (as opposed to elite) and which generally refers to dialects or colloquial forms of speech.[1] The value of al-Shidyāq's anecdote—parodying the difference between foreign and native speaker, between high- and lowbrow speech—lies in its inference that these differences are perhaps more spectral than oppositional.[2] The vignette provokes the question, disputed in the nineteenth century among native and non-native speakers of Arabic alike, of whether foreign influences were contaminating the integrity of Arabic speech. Wherein lie the center of "nativeness" and the frontiers of *ʿajami* foreignness?

Moved by such questions, this chapter explores how influential nineteenth- and early twentieth-century Arab Egyptian and Syrian authors interpreted the relational terms of *ʿarab* and *ʿajam* and asks what this tells us about how they envisioned the boundaries of the Arabophone. The previous chapter considered the polemical thresholds of ethnolinguistic "Arabness" and "non-Arabness" through the prism of European colonial and Orientalist texts, as Islam expanded across colonial Southeast Asia and West Africa and colonists debated issues of Muslim acculturation within these subject regions, displacing and politicizing the autochthonous Arabic notions of *ʿarab* and *ʿajam* difference. The present chapter delves into these boundary terms and the relational dynamics they describe, as portrayed within Arabic-language writing from roughly the same period (the early to mid-nineteenth century through the first decade of the twentieth century).

Throughout this chapter, I aim to bracket Eurocentric nineteenth-century taxonomies of "race" and "nation." I instead offer a different prism for framing questions of ethnolinguistic difference between *ʿarab* and *ʿajam*. Here I focus on several influential authors within an Arabic cultural and literary revival emerging across print centers of North Africa and West Asia (Ottoman Egypt and Syria), known in Arabic as the *nahḍa*. The *nahḍa* presents a vital period for considering these dynamics, as it coincided with the regional flourishing of new print technologies in North Africa and West Asia, with a vibrant translation movement, and with intensified language debates among literary figures on the reform of Arabic as a literary and print medium.[3]

Drawing from texts of the *nahḍa*, I observe how several major writers approached concepts of Arabness and non-Arabness, *ʿarab* and *ʿajam*, as native speakers and, in the process, disaggregated "Arab" identities from purely "Islamic" ones. They did so by assessing the history and future of Arabic as a both interreligious and interethnic language. In this way, Arabic mediated two centrifugal tendencies among these authors. First, Arabic mediated the tendency of many authors to assert collective forms of Arab distinction across religious lines. Second, Arabic mediated their tendency to make claims to interethnic parity between Arabs and non-Arabs and their languages, at times by referencing Islamic precepts or idealist traditions. In this connection, the authors examined in this chapter generally considered Arabic to be a medium more dynamic than did many Orientalists of the previous chapter—several of whom associated Arabic with cultural regression and ossified literacies.

Included in this chapter are print pioneers, public intellectuals, and literary writers who grappled with a common problem: the colonial-era preservation, defense, and evolution of Arabic as a print language, a language that one author, Rifāʿah al-Ṭahṭāwī, compares with pure "gold" in the global exchange of languages.[4] To extend his analogy further, a collective concern of authors featured in this chapter involves the elevation of Arabic as a form of cultural currency. Language debates between them are almost legible as exchanges over assays and currency values: How, they seem to ask, might Arabic be refashioned in journalistic and literary hands to sustain its value in globalizing print markets? Is Arabic lexically enriched or contaminated when transformed into an *alloy* through non-Arabic borrowings and influences? Was the Arabic language ever *not* an alloy in its historical contact with non-Arabic languages (or *ʿajamiyyāt*)? And who are the true arbiters in this collective "assay" over linguistic integrity and contamination—native or non-native scholars, dialect speakers or erudite writers of *fuṣḥā*?

This chapter focuses on influential Egyptian and Levantine *nahḍawi* figures, marking the historically custodial "centers" of native Arabic speech communities in the Mashriq (North Africa and West Asia). I include writing by key figures of the *nahḍa* who assessed the status of Arabic as a medium of interethnic contact and dialectal diversity and who addressed the boundaries between Arabic and foreign languages (or *ʿajamiyyāt*). These include the Egyptian translator and pedagogue Rifāʿah Rāfiʿ al-Ṭahṭāwī (1801–73), who was appointed the Muslim chaplain of a viceregal educational mission to Paris in the 1820s, and the itinerant Lebanese translator, linguist, and journalistic pioneer Aḥmad Fāris al-Shidyāq (1804–87), author of the previously cited travelogue *al-Sāq ʿalā al-sāq* (published in 1855). I also consider authors of a slightly later generation, including the Syrian Muslim scholar, linguistic reformer, and founder of the Arab Academy of Damascus ʿAbd al-Qādir al-Maghribī (1867–1956) and the prominent Lebanese Christian novelist, editor, and print entrepreneur Jurjī Zaydān (1861–1914). Both were active in Egypt by the first decade of the twentieth century but became influential figures within an Arabic print sphere that encompassed readers across Ottoman Egypt and Greater Syria. I illustrate how these authors approached ethnolinguistic dynamics in ways irreducible to racialized and Eurocentric paradigms of philological comparison, vernacularization, and linguistic descent.

I will begin with a brief introduction to the *nahḍa* as a movement of rising Arabic print and will offer an exploration of the terms *ʿajam* (sing. *ʿajami*) and *ʿajamiyya* as relational, ethnonymic concepts. I next consider how the stakes of these concepts are dramatized within several major literary texts of the *nahḍa*, moving in roughly chronological order. The chapter then shifts in focus from literary passages to more polemical language debates that occurred during the late nineteenth and early twentieth centuries, intensifying after the British occupation of Egypt in the 1880s. On the strength of these debates, the chapter concludes with remarks on the insufficiency of European terms such as "vernacular" for framing histories of Arabic language contact, given the Eurocentric pull of such concepts in colonially dominated arabophone regions.

Before moving forward, then, it is necessary to briefly revisit the relational concepts and boundary terms derived from Arabic-Islamic narrative traditions that serve as an alternative point of entry to the "vernacular." Their use enabled *nahḍawi* writers from al-Ṭahṭāwī to Zaydān to frame Arabic as a dynamic print literacy that could reconcile its diverse interethnic readership with emerging forms of solidarity through transregional print networks. These solidarities were expressed and framed through the boundary terms *ʿajam* and *ʿajamiyya*, terms that often surfaced within language debates of the *nahḍa* alongside assessments of colloquial variances among native Arabic speakers. Different writers of the *nahḍa* sought to reconcile their own sense of arabophone diversities—across colonial territories, dialectal and religious differences—with defensive attachments to Arabic as a print medium.

As we have seen, *ʿajam* (sing. *ʿajami*) is often defined as an Arabic term for "non-Arab" demographics, and *ʿajamiyyāt*, for "non-Arabic" languages, frequently associated with the linguistically debased, garbled, or inscrutable. Yet to only define *ʿajam* or *ʿajamiyya* as Arabic-language terms for ethnolinguistic non-Arabness forecloses their shifting meaning as boundary markers in both intra-Arab and interethnic contexts (as parodied in this chapter's opening).[5] Bearing this in mind, then, the following pages examine portrayals of *ʿajami* difference that refer not only to non-Arabs; the term *ʿajam(i)* (and its derivative term *ʿajamiyya*) is also understood as constitutive of historically changing notions of the Arabic language and of Arabness—constitutive of their changing relational boundaries across a broadening and ethnically diversifying expanse of Arabic speakers and writers.

Although the focus of this chapter is principally on the relational difference between *ʿajam(iyya)* and *ʿarab(iyya)*, a second concept, the notion of *ʿāmmiyya* speech, or the "common" tongue, appears entwined in these dynamics. It surfaces along with the term *ʿajamiyyāt* (foreign languages) in the language debates examined in this chapter as a second boundary term relative to "eloquent" Arabic (*al-ʿarabiyya al-fuṣḥā*)—the latter associated with the high points of classical Arabic poetry and with Qurʾanic or ritual Arabic.[6] While *ʿajamiyya* and *ʿāmmiyya* appear as solecistic, boundary concepts relative to scriptural Arabic, neither of these terms amounts to the vernacular as a European or Eurocentric notion. Across literary vignettes and language debates of the *nahḍa*, both concepts were invoked to reconcile Arabic's integrity as a print medium with its dynamism as a transregional "contact language" amid European imperial encroachments.

Arabs and Their Relational Others: Al-Ṭahṭāwī's Travelogue (1826–1831)

The travel writing of the al-Azhar-trained Egyptian scholar and translator Rifāʿah al-Ṭahṭāwī marks an important beginning when considering the tension in *nahḍawi* texts between two dynamics: forms of Arab (ethno)linguistic distinction and forms of egalitarian solidarity that extend sympathetically from Arab communities to *ʿajam* (non-Arab) others. Al-Ṭahṭāwī's travelogue, *Takhlīṣ al-Ibrīz fī Talkhīṣ Bārīz* (*Extracting Pure Gold to Render Paris, Briefly Told*), is often upheld as a foundational text reflecting an early Arabic survey of French scholarly disciplines during his sojourn as an Egyptian viceregal emissary to Paris from 1826 to 1831. Al-Ṭahṭāwī's work is instructive for the cartographic imagination it encompasses—a projection of a global order that compares an Islamocentric and culturally Arabocentric vision of the world and of Ottoman Egypt's place in the world with European (Gallocentric) practices of cartographic and taxonomic division. As such, al-Ṭahṭāwī's writing is impossible to extricate from, on the one hand, a normative cartography in which a region's relative value depends on its custodial role or centrality within Arabic-Islamic culture and, on the other, a Eurocentric sense of the world's scientific advancements as measured against the (post-Napoleonic) dominance of imperial Europe.[7]

Several opening passages of al-Ṭahṭāwī's travelogue are, in this respect, instructive. After ranking regions and continents according to technocentric measures of civilizational progress, he offers an Islamocentric vision of the world in which regions are stratified according to their religious importance; in this regard, after the irreligious Americas, it is not only the "pagan," non-Muslim regions of sub-Saharan (black) Africa that appear peripheral but also certain regions of insular Asia (among the islands of the "encircling sea"), which he implies has more recently "opened" to Islam.[8] In a trope that would gain traction in Egyptian Arabic writing of the nineteenth and early twentieth centuries, al-Ṭahṭāwī situates Egypt as a conduit for the African continent in its progress toward both scientific advancements and Islamic religious enlightenment—here in indirect praise of his viceregal patron, Muhammad ʿAli, given ʿAli's own imperial ambitions in Sudan.[9] This cartographic convergence of a European technocentrism and Islamic-Arabocentrism foregrounds al-Ṭahṭāwī's double vision as a disciplinary comparatist, a vision in which Egypt (as both a regional custodian of Arabic-Islamic learning and a vanguard in its exposure to European science) occupies a globally central position, at the nexus of both.

In homage to inherited Arabic conventions for "dividing" humankind, al-Ṭahṭāwī at times employs a stock turn of phrase that opposes Arabness to non-Arabness, invoking all of "God's creatures" or the entire "Muslim community" among both Arab and *ʿajam*; in this way, he references a division of the divinely created world enshrined in Qurʾanic verse that frames Islamic traditions of difference and parity between Arab and non-Arab (*ʿarab* and *ʿajam*).[10] Across such ethnonymic divisions between *ʿarab* and *ʿajam*, al-Ṭahṭāwī often unselfconsciously classes himself with the former; and yet, a close reading of certain passages within his text reveals that his self-identification extends across these boundaries in unexpected ways.

Notions of "Arabness" bear an ambiguous affiliation in al-Ṭahṭāwī's text. At times Arabness appears self-referential—for example, al-Ṭahṭāwī characterizes himself as a figure of Arab(ic) cultural custodianship. At other points, however, "Arabs" refers instead to provincial communities allegedly more homogeneous and linguistically pure in speech—Bedouin "Arabs." "Arab" as an ethnonym, in this sense, ambiguously refers to two distinctive groups lauded at different points in the text for either their urbane cultivation or their linguistic purity. (Al-Ṭahṭāwī likely borrowed this distinction from the fourteenth-century philosopher Ibn Khaldun, who first theorized divisions between "cultivated" urban groups and "nomadic" Arabs.)[11] Although al-Ṭahṭāwī refers to "Arab" Bedouin tribes and their long-standing reputation for retaining the purest forms of the Arabic language, it is urban centers of Islamic cultural custodianship—such as the venerable university and mosque of al-Azhar in Cairo or the Sublime Porte in Istanbul—that symbolize for al-Ṭahṭāwī the vanguards of Arabic-Islamic culture. Ottoman Egypt's cultural hybridity lends a certain authority to al-Ṭahṭāwī's position as a translational figure: He presents himself as a relatively cosmopolitan, Ottoman subject relative to his more provincial counterparts in "Arab" domains.[12] Citing a Paris-based Egyptian scholar to describe the history of Egypt as an "amalgamation of heterogeneous elements," al-Ṭahṭāwī seems to reconcile his own assessments of Arab diversity—and cosmopolitan exposure to *ʿajami(yya)* influences—with a sense of Arab distinction and arabophone pride.[13]

Al-Ṭahṭāwī's sense of cosmopolitan distance from "Arabs" in purist terms sways his appraisal of languages. As he compares French linguistic taxonomies of the 1820s with those current within the Arabic-Islamic sciences, he reconciles a belief in the superiority of Arabic and a pride in ethnolinguistic Arabness with a cosmopolitan interest in non-Arab demographics and non-Arabic languages.[14] Although Arabic for al-Ṭahṭāwī remains a medium of unrivaled eloquence "for the Arabs," he acknowledges that eloquence may at times translate poorly between languages: What appears in Arabic a marvel of rhetorical embellishment, he claims, may appear for the French a stylistic weakness.[15] His sense of Arabic exceptionality is tempered by an intuition of epistemic currencies eclipsed by an *ʿajami(yya)* otherness, complicated by nonequivalent standards of eloquence between languages.

Certain passages of al-Ṭahṭāwī's work uphold a sense of Arab distinction, but in ways detached from (what we might call) a purely "racial" or ethnic sense of identity. Al-Ṭahṭāwī regales his readers with digressive passages comparing the relative virtues and demerits of Arabs and non-Arabs, engaging a literary practice with a long classical tradition in which scribes and poets would boast of their erudition while agonistically probing the nature of cultivation (*adab*) across lines of difference.[16] Al-Ṭahṭāwī, in a presumed feat of cosmopolitan discernment, compares and contrasts "characteristically" Arab virtues (such as generosity) against the attributes of his French hosts—incomparable to Arabs in the latters' generosity, he claims, but comparable in their shared "love of freedom."[17]

Al-Ṭahṭāwī's travelogue notably concludes with a discursive exploration of this shared "love of freedom," in a passage that ends with a summary anecdote on the Prophet Muhammad's early companions (drawn from a hadith tradition). Al-Ṭahṭāwī through this reference accords a characteristically Arab respect for equality and liberty to Egypt's Arab Muslim conquerors, in their treatment of new converts and Egyptian subjects in the seventh century. According to the anecdote set amid the Arab conquests of Egypt, a native Egyptian was assaulted by the son of the seventh-century Arab commander and conqueror of Egypt, ʿAmr ibn al-ʿĀṣ, after the Egyptian surpassed the commander's son in a competitive race. The unwarranted assault was met with a punishment mandated by the caliph ʿUmar ibn al-Khaṭṭāb, who extended to the wronged Egyptian an invitation not only to strike the commander's son but to strike the commander himself for not keeping in check the filial presumptions and misplaced entitlements of his child. ʿAmr ibn al-ʿĀṣ, the Arab commander of Egypt, in other words, was threatened with a kind of poetic justice for not upholding a characteristically Arab principal of equality.

Perhaps paradoxically, in the name of Arab cultural or moral superiority, the anecdote folds within itself a kind of indifference to Arab filial or ethnic superiority. Al-Ṭahṭāwī uses this anecdote to compare what he calls the Arab "love of freedom" with an equivalent postrevolutionary French value (if not an imperial French one), appealing perhaps to new post-Napoleonic forms of cultural hierarchy and circuits of recognition.[18] On these circuits of recognition, one might mention the position of French Orientalists (such as Silvestre de Sacy) as redactors and reviewers of the travelogue, offering a poignant horizon of reception for these envisioned French and Arab resemblances on principles of "liberty."[19]

In his framing of this anecdote, al-Ṭahṭāwī's identification with Arabness appears to vacillate between a relatively Arab or Arabized Egyptian present and a pre-Islamic Egyptian past. The anecdote tellingly reflects his own double consciousness, as though mediating his assimilation and acculturation within a historic community of faith. On the one hand, al-Ṭahṭāwī speaks through the narrative past of a subordinate (ethnically non-Arab or not-yet-Arabized) Egypt amid Arab Muslim conquerors. But in the present of his own travelogue, his self-identification appears relatively (or relationally) Arab, as the Arab or Arabized subject of the ethnically Albanian, Ottoman Turkish viceroy to whom he dedicated his travelogue. In other words, al-Ṭahṭāwī's Arabness seems to reflect a self-consciously ethnic difference that marks him as a social inferior to his Ottoman patron; this difference nonetheless offers him a kind of moral authority in his custodianship of Arab cultural values. His ambiguous or liminal position as the (re)narrator of this tradition identifies him with the position of a subordinate and supplicant for equal treatment across ethnically stratified empires—whether they be dated to the seventh-century Arab conquest of Egypt or to the nineteenth-century Ottoman Turkish subjection of Egypt. In the seventh-century case, this egalitarian tradition frames the subordination of the "non-Arab" (*ʿajami*) Egyptian to the Arab; in the nineteenth-century case, it frames the subordination of the Arab to the (*ʿajami*) Turk.

Linguistic Solidarity and *ʿAjami* Incursions

Egyptian Arab and Ottoman Turkish dynamics characterized within another canonical text of the *nahḍa* by the polymath Aḥmad Fāris al-Shidyāq also dramatize relational differences between *ʿajam* and *ʿarab*. Al-Shidyāq's writing equally attests to how major writers of the *nahḍa* reconciled a sense of Arab distinction and arabophone solidarities with diversities of Arabic speech and dialect forms. He gives expression to forms of Arab(ic) distinction relative to *ʿajam(iyya)* others but parodies the fluid boundaries between Arab and *ʿajam* in ways that probe the integrity of "Arabness" on linguistic grounds.

In a semifictional account of his travels to Egypt published in 1855, *al-Sāq ʿalā al-sāq* (*Leg over Leg*), al-Shidyāq (or the narrator frequently read as his semifictional double, al-Fariyāq) remarks on an unsettling scene of elitism in Alexandria, prompting the author to challenge the subordination of Egyptian Arabs to Ottoman Turks and to defend both *Arabic* and *Arabness* on religious grounds against *ʿajami* incursions. The vignette begins with the narrator observing the submissive comportment of an Egyptian Arab toward a presumed Ottoman Turkish superior, an observation that concludes with the narrator's questioning of social hierarchies that subordinate the Egyptian to the Turk and that subordinate the Arabic language to Ottoman Turkish—an irony that gains force given the linguistic nature of the Qurʾan's revelation in Arabic, the author proclaims. In an argument invoking Qurʾanic verses that characterize the Qurʾan as an Arabic revelation, rather than an *ʿajami* alternative, al-Shidyāq writes the following:

> I have never been able to work out the reason for the sense of superiority felt by these Turks here with regard to the Arabs, when the Prophet (peace

> be upon him) was an Arab, the Qurʾān was revealed in Arabic, and the imams, rightly-guided Caliphs, and scholars of Islam were all Arabs. I think, though, that most Turks are unaware of these facts [. . .].[20]

This defense of Arabic and of Arabness is all the more striking given its provenance from an author whose religious affiliations shifted across multiple conversions—from Maronite and Protestant Christianity to Islam—though at the point of this publication he was believed to have been a recent Protestant convert.[21] In the wake of this observation, al-Shidyāq's text parodies Turkish pretenses of cultural superiority, digressing into a gibberish doggerel in what reads as vaguely Turkish sounds or accents—as though presenting to his Arabic readers a litany of inscrutable *ʿajami* injuries to the Arab ear.[22] One can conclude that this parodied performance of Turkish inscrutability was a sheer artifice, given that al-Shidyāq appeared to have been himself fluent in Ottoman Turkish (if Rana Issa's reading of al-Shidyāq's scribal archives in Beirut is correct).[23]

While this first passage addresses social and religious hierarchies between Muslim Turkish and Egyptian Arab coreligionists, al-Shidyāq elsewhere objects to *ʿajami* incursions in Christian Arab domains, suggesting the author's assertion of interreligious Arab solidarities on *linguistic* grounds. When contextualized by other passages in which this relational difference (*ʿajam* and *ʿarab*) is mentioned in al-Shidyāq's text, its usage appears to leverage a historically ascendant sense of Arab or native arabophone interreligious solidarities against *ʿajami* others. Al-Shidyāq's objections against *ʿajami* linguistic incursions are equally directed against European pastors who fail to pass in their poor use of Arabic among native Arab congregants. In one passage parodying such offenses, al-Shidyāq mocks an *ʿajami* anglophone pastor who comically (if unwittingly) preaches scatological "truths" and injunctions to a captive audience in Arabic, garbling his sermon for lack of social intimacy with the language. The accented sermon, laden with errors, becomes a social outrage, causing one righteous listener to curse the day that "these *ʿajams*" "showed their faces among us!" [[الالا بارك الله في يوم الذي راينا فيه وجوه هولآ العجم]].[24]

If al-Shidyāq's anecdote disparaging Ottoman Turks in Alexandria defends Arabic and ethnic Arabness on Islamic religious grounds, its reading against this second passage suggests that he leverages interreligious Arab solidarities on shared linguistic grounds through an attention to *ʿajami* difference. In the first passage, he challenges Turkish failures to accord the Arabic language its rightful status as a culturally and ritually superior medium, a superiority that raises its native speakers from a position of subordination in Ottoman Turkish domains. If, in the first case, the author objects to the marginality of the Arabic language within Ottoman Turkish provinces, then, in the second case, his rebuke of *ʿajami* characters has other aims: to challenge the social presumptions (and authority) of a growing number of non-native European (*ʿajami*) speakers of Arabic—figures at times explicitly cursed as *ʿajami* others.

This pejorative characterization of *ʿajami* otherness attests to the hazards of cultural interference within Arabic contact zones—an interference that both preceded and coincided with the extension of Western European colonial influences across Ottoman Arab regions in the nineteenth century. As such passages suggest, *ʿajam(i)* as a term in nineteenth-century literary currency not only encompassed long-standing cultural contacts between Arabic and its more linguistically proximate others (including Persian and Ottoman Turkish); it also referred to a new diversification and intensification of cultural contacts—marking Western Europe's and anglophone America's growing scholarly and missionary interests in Arabic and in arabophone Muslim regions.[25]

Further attesting to the characterization of European Orientalists as *ʿajami* others, I return briefly to al-Ṭahṭāwī's narrative in evidence: In a telling passage of his Parisian travelogue, he describes the accented, *ʿajami* strangeness of the Arabic spoken by the French scholar Silvestre de Sacy, a foundational philologist who trained a rising generation of major Orientalists in the early nineteenth century. Al-Ṭahṭāwī observes of de Sacy—notwithstanding the latter's zeal as a student of Arabic—that his *ʿajami* tongue fails him in the articulation of Arabic words: "[W]hen he reads, he has a foreign accent [or "pronounces as the *ʿajam* do," ينتق كالعجم] and he cannot speak Arabic unless he has a book in his hands. If he wants to explain an expression, he uses strange words, which he is unable to pronounce properly."[26] Despite this othering of the accented *ʿajami* Orientalist, al-Ṭahṭāwī's characterization of de Sacy is not devoid of a certain pathos; indeed, the passage seems to function for al-Ṭahṭāwī as one of qualified recognition and conciliation across ethnolinguistic differences. For al-Ṭahṭāwī acknowledges through de Sacy's inscrutable or uncanny efforts at Arabic expression a redeemable, inverse side to *ʿajami* subjectivity and interiority, beyond the inarticulacy of "his kind." He concludes that "[i]n spite of appearances, the idea that foreigners [*al-aʿjām*] do not understand Arabic when they do not speak it as well as the Arabs is without any foundation."[27]

Al-Ṭahṭāwī's acknowledgment of *ʿajami* interiority within this vignette has broader implications. Along with this conclusion, he accords to non-Arabic languages (*ʿajamiyyāt*) a value closer to Arabic than might be conventionally admitted by his more Arabocentric counterparts or presumed readers—an aspect of his text previously mentioned. For the passage in which de Sacy surfaces as an *ʿajami* figure also occasions al-Ṭahṭāwī's conclusion that non-Arabic languages, rather than being sole mimicry of Arabic as a gold standard, may retain their value as independent repositories of knowledge. In terms resonant with the title of his travelogue, he poses the rhetorical question: "There is no doubt that the language of the Arabs is the greatest and most splendid of languages. But is it because it is pure gold that whatever imitates it is mere tinsel?"[28] Al-Ṭahṭāwī often admits the supremacy of Arabic as an incomparable form of currency—a sacralized language and an unrivaled medium of eloquence and lexical richness—but his declaration of its linguistic superiority is tempered by his inference of valuable epistemic horizons submerged within an inarticulate *ʿajami* otherness. To these points, the Orientalist de Sacy's scholarly accomplishments as a commentator and translator of classical Arabic texts attest for al-Ṭahṭāwī that a reserve of non-Arabic and non-Arabocentric modes of knowledge exists in translation—and beyond what might be discerned by the monolingual arabophone counterpart for whom the *ʿajam* and their languages remain opaque.[29]

Such designations of European Orientalists as struggling *ʿajami* figures nonetheless coincided with a growing sense of subalternity among many *nahḍawi* writers relative to European scholars, as Eurocentric scholarly shifts occurred in global terms during the nineteenth century.[30] In al-Shidyāq's writing, an *ʿajami* designation for Orientalists appears defensive and irredeemably pejorative as a result: a matter worthy of their embarrassment, betraying their own personal histories of tutelage at the mercy of native speakers and exposing their incapacity to fully appraise the value of Arabic cultural forms (notwithstanding their professional presumptions). In this connection, al-Shidyāq levels a pejorative *ʿajami* designation against European Arabists and Orientalist figures who have earned his wrath for their indifference to the value of Arabic poetics (embodied in verse written by his own hand). Of their indifference—and stinginess—he penned the following complaint, contrasting non-Arab miserliness to what he implies is a characteristically Arab value of generosity: "in the market of the non-Arabs [الاعاجم] my words and my praises / found no buyers and were without profit [. . .] were I the Racine of my age among them and its Milton, I would get out of them barely / enough sustaining water to quench my thirst" [و قد كان في سوق الاعاجم كاسدا/مقالي واطرآي (عليهم بلا ربح [. . .] ولو انني راسين عصري فيهم/ ومِلتن ما استسقيت منهم سوى النشح)].[31]

Orientalists are elsewhere rebuked as philological amateurs who masquerade as experts. In evidence, al-Shidyāq ends his travelogue (itself a transgeneric work) with a long appendix of linguistic errors in Arabic attributed to prominent European scholars.[32] Within this plaintive conclusion, al-Shidyāq chides European Orientalists not only for their unmerited presumptions of authority as non-native speakers (or what we might call *ʿajami* imposters) but for their linguistic hypocrisies in what they privilege *as Arabic*: Why, he asks, do European and French Orientalists dignify as a scholarly object vulgar dialects of Arabic— *ʿāmmiyyāt*—when they would hardly do the same for their own (French) patois?[33] Other languages of Asia, he claims, like the languages of Persia and India, are increasingly subject to such injury among non-native, European "authorities," implying that these European pretenders are a rising and interlingually fraudulent group.[34] In al-Shidyāq's text, in other words, a new sense of subaltern solidarities—against Orientalist European intruders—transcends older boundaries of non-Arab otherness.[35] Implicated in this broader complaint is al-Shidyāq's sense of grievance regarding the diminished status of Arabic as a language of scholarly authority: declining against European alternatives and adding injury to its already marginalized position as a political and social basilect in Ottoman Turkish domains relative to Turkish. In other words, to read al-Shidyāq on these dynamics, the relational concepts of *ʿajam* and *ʿarab* frame epistemic asymmetries that inhere across nineteenth-century Arabic contact zones; they frame an Arabocentric grievance of surrendered authority on Arabness itself. A relational boundary of *ʿajam* and *ʿarab* difference animates al-Shidyāq's defense of a language under siege, with its speakers losing authority over the very language they speak.[36]

An important qualification, however, deserves to be made to this conclusion. As a boundary concept for inscrutability, the term *ʿajami* in al-Shidyāq's text marks the vanishing horizons of the Arabic language in relational terms—audially, textually, or lexically marking where the Arabic language threatens to lose its integrity. Notwithstanding its frequent legibility in translation as "foreign" and "non-Arab," the meaning of *ʿajami* otherness is not entirely reducible to the foreign—or even to the "non-Arab" in al-Shidyāq's text.[37] In al-Shidyāq's narrative, the term *ʿajam* (and its derivations) delimits a strangeness that it is often heard rather than seen and therefore speaks to the failures of linguistic passing in ways that resonate with al-Ṭahṭāwī's account of the accented Orientalist Silvestre de Sacy.[38] It becomes a linguistically and ethnically inflected boundary concept for both an unassimilated foreignness and a native strangeness, a strangeness that within al-Shidyāq's own writing also plays with the possibility of a nominally *intra-Arab* inscrutability across regional dialects, drawing attention to the language's own variability.

When the specter of *ʿajami* otherness frames an intra-Arab inscrutability, it leaves open the question of who can claim Arabness on the basis of native Arabic speech. In this respect, al-Shidyāq uses the term *ʿajami* to ironize forms of linguistic self-estrangement between speakers of Arabic across regional differences and across lines of class. Here, I return to the anecdote from *al-Sāq ʿalā al-sāq* that began this chapter, in which his protagonist is employed as a literary scribe at the court of an Egyptian patron but finds himself identified by one of his own Egyptian servants as an imposter: "Honestly, my lord," the servant declares to the Egyptian patron, "he's a good man, but I think he may not be an Arab [literally, "he may be an *ʿajami*"] because I can hardly understand him when he speaks to me in our language" [فقال له الخادم والله يا سيدي انه رجل طيب غير اني اظن انه اعجمي فاني لا اكاد افهمه حين يتكلم بلغتنا].[39] The humor in this passage is clear, but the object of the intended comedy is ambiguous: Are we to laugh at the literary master for his pedantic affectations, his presumptions of eloquence being anything but clear to the common ear? Or are we to laugh at the presumptions of an illiterate (or semiliterate) manservant, claiming to arbitrate between proper and improper forms of the language—a judgment made with such confidence that he would expose his master as an inscrutable *ʿajami* fraud (given that his master traffics in Arabic as a scribal copyist and court eulogist)? The passage comically destabilizes the interpretive grounds of Arab identity and Arab(ic) authority: Who is to say who is an Arab and who natively speaks Arabic in its proper form? Is it the Syrian literary master or his unlettered Egyptian manservant—presumably a native speaker of Egyptian colloquial Arabic (or *ʿāmmiyya*)?[40] The passage leaves the issue unsettled, and it is the mutual alienation of two figures proclaiming native Arabic mastery and ethnic Arabness that generates this comedy at the internal thresholds of the Arabophone. For all of its self-referential mockery, this passing anecdote is a testament to a language itself in flux.

Al-Shidyāq's parodic anecdote on *ʿajami* imposture is all the more poignant given that al-Shidyāq himself later faced accusations that he was unfit to publish Arabic print because his magnum opus, *al-Sāq ʿalā al-sāq*, was virtually an *ʿajami* text. His literary archrival, Ibrahim al-Yaziji, denounced al-Shidyāq's writing for being overrun with the double corruptions of *ʿajamiyyāt* and *ʿāmmiyyāt*—of inscrutable non-Arabic and colloquial interferences. The book therefore, al-Yaziji claimed, could not be admitted as a faithfully Arabic text.[41] Notwithstanding the hyperbolic nature of this accusation, advanced by the claim that al-Shidyāq's writing relied to excess on foreign-language terms, this agonistic deployment of the concept *ʿajamiyya* among major literary figures of the nineteenth century is illuminating. Among the objects of controversy within this quarrel were the parameters of Arabic as an emerging standard of print in the latter part of the nineteenth century, in its modernization and accommodation of foreign terms and concepts.

The Expanding Boundaries of the *Umma*

In the debates on the assimilation of "foreign words" and "foreign languages" (*ʿajamiyyāt*) into Arabic, at stake was the renovation and reform of Arabic as a medium receptive to nominally "non-Arab" concepts. Implicated were questions of the language's semantic, epistemic, and relational center of gravity. At stake were its coherence and authenticity as a medium with an identitarian inflection that depended on questions no less vital (and perennially unresolved) than what the licit parameters of the Arabic language were and how both the language and its literature would retain their integrity as Arabic media against the alleged double threats of both *ʿajamiyya* and *ʿāmmiyya* incursions (foreign and colloquial corruptions). These issues were negotiated through the twinned dynamics of what came to be termed in literary and scholarly circles the Arabicization (*taʿrīb*) and naturalization (*tajannus*) of foreign concepts; as late nineteenth-century language debates (carrying into the early twentieth century) demonstrated, arguments often assumed transhistorical dimensions in the redeployment of the term *ʿajami(yya)* as a concept, as certain contributors drew parallels to historically antecedent standardizations of the language. Commentators within these debates, for example, observed that terms previously marked as non-Arab (e.g., in Persian or Greek) had become lexically naturalized, in effect becoming Arabic speech.[42]

These exchanges across Ottoman Arab print centers were broadly interconfessional. The integrity of Arabic as an emerging print standard was, however, also assessed within orthodox Muslim circles in ways that implicated its ritual status. The question of Arabic's position as a sacralized medium (against an *ʿajamiyya* alternative) was at stake in this reckoning among religious scholars and intellectuals. One contributor to these debates, Sheikh ʿAbd al-Qādir al-Maghribī, is notable as a conservative religious scholar who defended the assimilation of "foreign" (*ʿajamiyya*) terms into Arabic through relatively orthodox, religious claims. In so doing, al-Maghribī characterized the Arabic language as a dynamic, inherently interethnic medium whose evolution complemented rather than challenged its Islamic ritual vocation.[43]

Al-Maghribī offered what might be considered a relatively orthodox Muslim sociological account of Arabic language development that endorses the assimilation of non-Arab cultural (and lexical) influences into Arabic in ways that map onto the expanding boundaries of a global Muslim community (or *umma*). In al-Maghribī's account, published under the title *Kitāb al-Ishtiqāq wa-l-Taʿrīb* (*The Book of Derivation and Arabization*) in 1908, a progressive, historical expansion of new Muslim converts coincided with the extension and increasing diversification of contacts between Arabic and *ʿajamiyya* languages. Perceiving this not as a cultural liability, al-Maghribī instead suggested that the Arabic language gained in dynamism through this process of expanded conversion while maintaining its integrity as a shared religious medium. In this respect, he correlated the perennial linguistic "naturalization" of *ʿajami* (foreign, non-Arab) influences to the shifting boundaries of the *umma*. Al-Maghribī claimed that the *umma*

> formed itself out of two elements and along two paths: by natural increase of the autochthonous population inside the Arab ethnic group (*al-tawālud*), and by assimilation of non-Arabic elements (*al-tajannus*). In a similar way, [the] Arabic language emerged, grew, and should continue to grow both by derivation from Arabic roots (*al-ishtiqāq*), which is analogous to *al-tawālud*, and by assimilation of foreign vocabulary (*al-taʿrīb*, which could correspond to *al-tajannus* [the naturalization of *ʿajam*, or foreign peoples]).[44]

The linguistic incorporation or domestication of *ʿajamiyyāt* (foreign terms) into Arabic, in other words, corresponded to the shifting boundaries of the *umma* and to the growing incorporation of the world's diversity into an expanding community of belief; rather than a menace to the global Muslim community, the Arabic domestication of *ʿajamiyyāt* could be understood as a progressive sign of its ritual fulfillment. These relational dynamics across Arabic contact zones suggest, in other words, that "Muslim networks did at least as much to spread diversity as enforce uniformity."[45] Al-Maghribī, in effect, offers a vision of reciprocal acculturation between Arab and *ʿajam* in linguistic and demographic terms, as the thresholds of assimilation between Arabic and foreign tongues (*ʿajamiyyāt*) mark the tension between an Arabocentric religious uniformity and a growing linguistic diversity within a globalizing *umma*. Al-Maghribī's account might be considered teleological and evolutionary in its approach, but there was a significant degree of disjuncture between his framing of Arabic as a "contact language" and racialized accounts of linguistic hierarchy and philological descent among nineteenth-century European Orientalists such as Renan.[46] This observation gains further traction given the controversial transposition into Arabic of European notions of "vernacularization" and "vernacular" variances from Qurʾanic Arabic, as we shall soon see.[47]

Finally, given that the object of al-Maghribī's remarks is the shifting boundaries of an *umma* ambiguously defined, his claims point to the ambiguities associated with nascent forms of political or civic belonging, raising questions about how a growing, interethnic *umma* would politically or cartographically transform in its allegiance to linguistic diversity and ritual uniformity. Into what final form might an expanding, interethnic *umma*—suspended between ritual Arabic and *ʿajamiyyāt*—evolve or translate in a world increasingly dominated by European concepts, epistemes, and historical paradigms? The irresolution of this question seems implied by the enduring problem that, as Cemil Aydin has suggested, *umma* as an Arabic concept—here used by al-Maghribī—has no direct, European-language translation or equivalent, notwithstanding its frequent mistranslation after the late nineteenth century as the "Muslim world" (and its racialized politicization as a "world" remote from Western Europe).[48] In al-Maghribī's theorization, the Arabic language remains territorially ambiguous: culturally changeable through its expanding boundaries but ritually stable in its globally expanding vocation. In other words, this cartographic projection of a global *umma* envisions neither the gradual displacement of a shared ritual language by its "baser" alternatives nor its dissolution or attenuation in their presence; it presupposes the perennial coexistence of a sacred medium with a sanctified plurilingualism. Here we are far from a Eurocentric "vernacularization" thesis and from its derivative arguments for associated secular nationalisms.[49]

Opposing Paradigms of Vernacularization

Models of vernacularization associated with (post-Reformation) European Christendom were opposed by Arabic language intellectuals of vastly different backgrounds. Among the most influential was the popular Lebanese Christian novelist, journalist, and publisher Jurjī Zaydān, who made some of the most holistic defenses of literary Arabic against arguments for its textual displacement by spoken "vernaculars" or regional dialects (*ʿāmmiyyāt*). As outlined in a series of articles published in the 1880s and 1890s, Zaydān argued that Arabic's evolution would not result in the progressive displacement of Qur'anic Arabic by a vernacular diversity (in the model of European vernaculars rising from the cradle of Latin Christendom); an attachment to Qur'anic Arabic as a cultural inheritance among interethnic Muslims and interreligious Arabs would instead ensure that Arabic could honor its historically Islamic cultural vocation while continuing to "evolve" by lexically borrowing from other languages as needed.[50] Zaydān's status as a non-Muslim contributor to these debates, and one promoting a shared Arabic language patrimony across religious differences, deserves emphasis given the nature of his claims as they extended across religious lines.

Zaydān argued that Arabic had always evolved. Arabic's transformations as it absorbed and accommodated an array of foreign influences illustrated the dynamism and cosmopolitan vocation of Arabic across Islamic history: with the formation of early Islamic sciences (of law, jurisprudence, and linguistic sciences), with its development of new bureaucratic and political concepts during the first Arab Muslim empires, with philosophical translations from Greek, and through its employment across non-Arab, Muslim dynasties. Notions of Arabic's linguistic immutability, Zaydān argued, were not authentic reflections of Islamic history itself but, rather, the result of a mistaken overattachment to pre-Islamic standards of the language: "Now is the time for us to free our pens from the chains of the pre-Islamic Age of Ignorance [*jāhiliyya*] and bring them out of the prison of nomadic Life. [. . .] We should not despise every word the Bedouin did not pronounce some ten centuries ago."[51] Zaydān in this way presented a transhistorical account of Arabic's development that sought to reconcile its historically Islamic ritual association with its modernization as a "supra-religious" language, characterizing the language as an entity "subject to laws of evolution," "continually renewing vocabulary and construction," and as such "living" and "growing."[52]

The Egyptian pedagogue al-Ṭahṭāwī, likely the first Egyptian scholar to translate into Arabic the European disciplinary concept of the vernacular in the 1820s (as *dārija*, meaning "popular speech"), also remarked on the emergence of French taxonomies distinguishing between "living" and "dead" languages.[53] Al-Ṭahṭāwī, in the decades that marked the transformative beginnings of European comparative philology, could unselfconsciously assume that his own written medium, Arabic, would count among "living" languages (against, he claimed, older Egyptian languages such as Coptic).[54] The status of Arabic as a living medium, however, was no longer uncontested by the end of the nineteenth century when Zaydān was publishing. By then, arguments associating literary or Qur'anic Arabic with cultural obsolescence became matters of public controversy among a growing number of Orientalists, colonial bureaucrats, and policy makers—as foregrounded in the previous chapter—with polemical repercussions in British-occupied Egypt.[55]

The 1883 Dufferin Report penned by one of the earliest architects of the British occupation of Egypt, Lord Dufferin, exemplifies this characterization of Qur'anic Arabic as a historical obsolescence, distinct from actual language use in Egypt and irrelevant for the needs of "modern" Egyptian governance: "Modern Egyptian Arabic," Lord Dufferin wrote, "bears the same relation to Koranic Arabic as Italian and modern Greek do to Latin and classic Greek." He went on to prophesy, "There is little chance of much progress being made in educating the masses in Egypt until the children are taught the vulgar Arabic instead of, as at present, Koranic Arabic."[56] While Dufferin's opinions were intended for internal government circulation, local perceptions of European colonial hostility to literary and Qur'anic Arabic intensified with the public comments and essays of Sir William Willcocks, an Anglo-Egyptian engineer and colonial functionary who advocated in the late 1880s for changes to public literacy in Egypt due to the disparity between common Egyptian speech and written standards of Arabic. Colloquial Egyptian speech, he claimed to great controversy, was entirely unrelated to written Arabic.

In a series of public lectures and essays published in both Arabic and English, Willcocks characterized Arabic as a foreign, moribund, and archaic impediment to progress in Egypt.[57] He asserted that written Arabic was artificially sustained as a false symbol of cultural unity across regions effectively divided by a spoken diversity of unconnected languages, often mistaken for Arabic dialects.[58] The situation imposed upon ordinary Egyptians an impossible bicephalism or double vision: the constant labor of translation between their native speech and an allegedly archaic and foreign written norm (*fuṣḥā*). This unnecessary mental burden, Willcocks claimed, could be lifted were spoken vernaculars transcribed as a literary and written standard.[59] In one of his entreaties summarizing his ideas, he wrote: "If Europe tried, for its own selfish ends, to keep these Mediterranean countries backward, could it find any better way than to encourage them to despise their own living spoken languages and to laud to the skies their artificial literary language?"[60] Willcocks contended that the situation "put back the hand of the Near East clock to where European linguists were 400 years ago when they thought that it was sufficient to learn Latin to be fully equipped to work in Italy, France, Spain and Portugal."[61]

Zaydān's rebuttal to Willcocks involved a variety of claims, including that written Arabic in places like Egypt was neither moribund nor foreign, as Latin had been or had become to the English. The disparities between regionally spoken and written varieties of the Arabic language were due to differences in class rather than ethnolinguistic differences, he countered. To reason by analogy, he claimed, one would not conclude by virtue of the English commoner and British elite's mutual inscrutability that elevated standards of written English should disappear or be displaced by baser standards of colloquial English.[62] The same was true for Arabic. Written Arabic merely required reform and simplification to accommodate the class diversity of an Arabic-reading public. Zaydān also disputed that arabophone regions would undergo the linguistic fragmentation that had beset a post-Latinate, post-Reformation European Christendom.[63] Transregional and interconfessional attachments to high literary and Qurʾanic Arabic ensured that Arabic would be sustained as a "living" language rather than deteriorate as a moribund archaicism. To dispense with written Arabic would disinherit future generations of Arabic speakers from centuries of local scholarship, he argued, and disunify regions that had historically shared Arabic as a written standard.[64]

According to Zaydān, written Arabic simply needed to be streamlined to assume its rightful place as a "modern" written and literary standard, balancing its exposure to foreign (*ʿajamiyya*) influences with its address of the common reader (the *ʿāmma*, or "common public," speakers of *ʿāmmiyyāt*, "common or colloquial speech"). Colloquial speech was not "foreign" to Arabic, by Zaydān's estimation; nor, he argued, would Arabic lose its integrity if it borrowed foreign terms in a measured way.[65] As he proposed, writers should "not corrupt the language with words and expressions of the common people [*ʿāmmiyyāt*], or introduce an excessive amount of foreign words [*ʿajamiyyāt*] so that our language becomes like Ottoman Turkish" or like "Urdu or Maltese."[66] As noted by Shaden Tageldin and Anne-Laure Dupont, though Zaydān enjoined writers of Arabic to compose from the position of a generalist and to effectively "hew to a middle register" for the sake of a common public, such efforts did not require adopting as a literary standard the "common tongue" (*lughat al-ʿāmma*).[67]

Framing Ethnolinguistic Difference in Arabic Print

In 1899, Jurjī Zaydān, as publisher and print entrepreneur, was witnessing the signs of a striking solidarity in the making. The Arabic language, he claimed in an editorial published that year, was enjoying an unprecedented revival, connecting the regional margins of the "Islamic world" to Arabic's rising print centers in places such as Cairo, where his own publication, *al-Hilāl, The Crescent,* had been based since the early 1890s. Colonial incursions, he claimed, had provoked a defensive attachment to Arabic among Muslims worldwide, eliciting a global revitalization of Arabic language studies. Such defenses had prompted South Asian Muslim readers of his journal to contact him for advice on the latest advancements in Arabic language pedagogy, notwithstanding his own status as an Arab Christian.[68] As Zaydān's publications attest, a global Arabic reading public was continuing to expand and diversify toward the turn of the twentieth century, conjoining the non-Arab "margins" of the "Islamic world" to locally minoritized, Christian Arab editors and print entrepreneurs like himself. Against the equation of Arabic with a single ethnicity or religious patrimony, Zaydān historically records the existence of solidarities across a kind of chiasmus, a solidarity struck between Arab religious minorities and non-Arab (*ʿajam*) Muslims, communities conjoined in their shared commitment to the Arabic language as a cultural inheritance.

While lauding this transregional resurgence, Zaydān describes the challenges that this diverse readership presented to Arabic language writers as they faced a troubling horizon of expectations, or what Zaydān called a readership "in disarray."[69] As Arabic extended its reach as an interethnic and interconfessional print language in the late nineteenth century, carrying across an imperially divided and politically fragmented public, writers, he lamented, were beset by exceptional dilemmas:

> The Arab writer, then, writes for a public in disarray [*li-qurrāʾ fawḍā*], one without a single or coherent cultural frame of reference. If he satisfies the Egyptian, he may not satisfy the Syrian, and if he pleases both of them, he may anger the Persian or Indian. If the Muslims are content, the Christians may be annoyed [. . .] . This is a huge obstacle [. . .] whereas the European writer may satisfy his readers with only a few needs.[70]

Arabic print publics, Zaydān claimed, were further divided by the heterogeneous influence of colonial pedagogies, fostering differences in taste and orientation among an already divided readership. The Arabic readership in Ottoman Egypt, which was invaded by the French in the late eighteenth century and occupied by the British after the 1880s, was to his mind exemplarily riven between Francophile and Anglophile tastes. This was, however, not irredeemable, as Zaydān considered pedagogical standardization the best possible antidote to "the heterogeneous and chaotic character" of an Arabic print public.[71] His conclusions were optimistic: "The Arabic reading public is increasing day by day and will continue to do so and time will come when tastes will become less diverse and clearly differentiated, since education will improve, becoming universalized and more standardized."[72]

Notwithstanding the pedagogical revival of Arabic across what Zaydān called the "Islamic world" (*al-ʿālam al-Islamī*) in 1899, political vicissitudes and colonial policies would in the twentieth century further variegate the conditions of historically arabophone publics. Zaydān could not have foreseen, for example, Turkish divestment from the Arabic script, the rise across the Muslim world of colonial literacies and colonially modified orthographies, the growth of romanized print markets, and the progressive eclipse of Arabic language pedagogies by Europeanized alternatives across regional lines. Zaydān's vision of a global arabophone public in 1899, however, vitally attests to the following: Unilateral conflations of ethnolinguistic Arabness with Islam deserve scrutiny (if not skepticism), given the ethnolinguistic diversity of a global Muslim community (or *umma*) and the interreligious attachment of self-identifying Arabs to Arabic.

This deserves emphasis given the conflation of Arabic literacies and Islam by many influential colonial agents, noted in the previous chapter. This discursive conflation intensified at the height of the Arabic *nahḍa* (coinciding with a proliferation of Arabic print periodicals after the 1870s).[73] The perspective of the major French Orientalist Alfred Le Chatelier, founder of the transformative Orientalist publication *Revue du Monde Musulman*, offers a vital counterpoint to Zaydān's impressions of a transregional Arabic readership during this time. Le Chatelier explained that the use of Arabic assured Muslims worldwide a certain measure of social uniformity—as the English language did for a diverse British Commonwealth. But Muslims globally, he qualified, could no longer be understood through classical manuscripts of the fourth century A.H. Instead, they could be understood through a growing number of print publications, which were gradually adapting to occidental influences. These, he argued, threatened to transform colonized Muslim territories into autonomous regions commercially indifferent to Europe. Writing in 1907 in an open plea for greater interimperial surveillance across Western Europe of print networks emerging across the "Muslim world," Le Chatelier lamented and prophesied:

> At the end of the nineteenth century, the Muslim world barely counted a hundred journals. There are now close to a thousand, and there will easily

> be 2,500 or 3,000 in 1915. [. . .] If the proportion of "evolved" Muslims (that is, possessing occidental culture) is now no more than 2–3 percent, it will be not many years before that figure attains 10 percent. [. . .] When Egypt attains 10 percent of "*evolués*" she will pass without a fight, by the simple force of things, from the rank of [colonial] *Realm in Trust* to that of [independent] *Nation in the Making*. The same will be true for Algeria and Tunisia, as for Russian Asia. It would have been otherwise, if Muslim nations were isolated within narrow borders; but the global expansion of Islam necessarily provokes a reaction from country to country through the development of the press.[74]

When "Islam," he warned, assimilated and mastered what were then considered "European technologies" such as modern print, Europe would again become commercially inferior—or irrelevant—across an African and Asian space.[75]

By juxtaposing these views from the turn of the twentieth century on an arabophone print renaissance as prospect or risk, I underscore the different emphases of the present chapter and the previous one. Within the Orientalist and colonial texts examined in chapter 1, Arabic literacies were often unilaterally conflated with the risk of Islamic resurgence as a potential ideological threat. Public exchanges between Western European colonists often conflated arabophone communities with a progressively othered "Muslim world"—as exemplified by Le Chatelier's own assessment of the late nineteenth-century Arabic print revival, a matter of years after Zaydān's own.[76] But a more complex chiasmus of solidarities appears within Arabic writing of the *nahḍa*, conjoining interethnic Muslim communities globally with interreligious ones in Ottoman Arab territories.

Nineteenth-century colonial incursions across predominantly Muslim regions of Africa and Asia contributed to Western Europe's differentiation of the Ottoman Empire and its subjects as an allegedly non-Christian, non-European polity, giving rise to the characterization of the "Muslim world" as Europe's "racialized" other, according to historian Cemil Aydin. Aydin also notes that toward the latter half of the nineteenth century and early twentieth century, the assertion that the "Muslim world" was racially distinct and culturally subordinate in turn fostered responses and counterclaims from within this notional realm about "its own" nature.[77] Aydin's vital observation, however, raises the question of how Europe's progressively "racialized" Muslim and Ottoman others expressed their own self-understanding across their linguistic and religious diversity. When Western Europe's Muslim subjects and religiously diverse Ottoman others reconciled their emerging solidarities to their ethnolinguistic diversity, what shared conceptual language did they use beyond the European-language terms of "race" and "racialization"?

Evidence within this chapter (and the subsequent two) presents an answer to this question. The arabophone authors examined here referred to alternative terms and concepts to give expression to emerging forms of interethnic arabophone solidarity across (as Zaydān would call it) *al-ʿālam al-Islamī*—the "Islamic world"—despite the heterogeneous influences and growing cultural dominance of colonial Western Europe within Asia and Africa.[78] Canonical authors of the nineteenth and early twentieth centuries invoked relational differences between Arab and "non-Arab" (*ʿajam*) communities to frame interreligious modes of solidarity between Arabs, just as these differences were referenced to frame interethnic assertions of equality across a global *umma*. Arabic was believed to mediate two diverging forces among arabophone authors within Ottoman Arab print centers: a collective sense of Arab distinction, on the one hand, and Muslim assertions of interethnic affiliation and parity between Arabs and non-Arabs, on the other. The conceptual terms—*ʿajam* and *ʿajamiyya*—referenced to frame these emerging solidarities were precisely those that had been politicized by European colonial agents and Orientalists as "racial differences" between Arabs and non-Arabs, across colonial exchanges on inter-"racial" acculturation and containment within the "Muslim world" (as shown in the previous chapter).

Although nineteenth-century European Orientalists often described *ʿarab* and *ʿajam* differences as "racial" or "national," Arabic language readers of the same period were unlikely to have recognized such translational overlays. The English term *race* had no universally accepted equivalents in Arabic upon its reception as a pseudo-scientific idea either with Darwin's translations into Arabic (after the 1860s) or with the translation of European social and ethnographic texts in the late nineteenth century.[79] The transposition was rife with ambiguity given the difficulties of finding direct Arabic cognates for the European term "race." It may be tempting to analytically return to the European-language concepts privileged in the previous chapter to frame these autochthonous (*ʿarab* and *ʿajam*) dynamics or to claim that linguistic dynamics represent a proxy for racial dynamics. Writers discussed in this chapter, however, offer reasons to challenge the dominance and explanatory value of borrowed European terms—such as "race," "nation," and "vernacular"—and to consider the historical (Arabic/non-Arabic) dynamics that they describe, but also the Arabic concepts that such terms displace.

Vernacular Nonequivalence (*ʿAjamiyya* Otherness)

As exemplified by Zaydān's defensive statements on Arabic as a living language, the concepts of *ʿāmmiyyāt* (translationally glossed as "colloquialisms") and *ʿajamiyyāt* (non-Arabic, foreign-language terms) polemically resurfaced as double thresholds for Arabic during the *nahḍa*.[80] They collectively offer, in other words, a double boundary to Arabic in its integrity, *ʿāmmiyya* registering as an ethnically internal boundary (often across class and regional differences) and *ʿajamiyya* registering as a nominally external boundary (across ethnic differences). As implied by the anecdote drawn from al-Shidyāq that opened this chapter, however, the distinction between those internal and external boundaries is not always clear, suggesting a relationship more spectral than oppositional between the two. Where, in other words, does *ʿajamiyya* otherness end and *ʿāmmiyya* inscrutability begin? This is particularly enigmatic when both terms seem to describe an *intra-Arab* otherness or linguistic margin (as evident, for example, in al-Shidyāq's parodic vignette, in which regional and class differences mutually estrange two native speakers of Arabic).

The twinned historical surfacing of these boundary terms, *ʿajamiyya* and *ʿāmmiyyāt*, also invites questions about their value for non-Eurocentric literary comparisons. A case for their comparison appears possible—and is in effect pursued across this book's later chapters; for both *ʿajamiyya* and *ʿāmmiyya* texts may be understood as culturally creolized formations and literary media relative to a ritual Arabic legacy. To engage in *ʿāmmiyya* and *ʿajamiyya* comparisons would therefore entail comparisons of minoritized literatures from within a ritually inflected Arabic tradition, with one margin "speaking to" another in contrapuntal ways and through high ritual Arabic as a common contact language. Such a comparison necessarily engages the challenging task of comparing and historicizing cultural forms without overrelying on a distortive, evolutionary arc that excessively veers toward either Eurocentric or Arabocentric measures of cultural value.

It may be tempting to frame *ʿajamiyya* and *ʿāmmiyya* comparisons by equating the two terms (in different ways) to the European-language concept of the vernacular; but each is clearly irreducible to this borrowed Eurocentric concept, freighted with unique genealogies and historical valences. Both *ʿajamiyya* and *ʿāmmiyya* appear as solecistic, boundary concepts for ritual Arabic; but neither easily aligns with "vernacular" as a European or Eurocentric term, as attested by the diversity of figures featured within this chapter. To put this otherwise (and as implied by Zaydān and al-Maghribī on the evolution of Arabic), unlike the relationship of scriptural or ecumenical Church Latin to its successive national vernaculars in Europe, the historical relationship of ritual Arabic to *ʿāmmiyya* and *ʿajamiyya* otherness is not one of successive displacement but, rather, of perennial, if controversial, coexistence. The anxieties that attend the transmission and preservation of charismatic texts and their interpretive traditions in Arabic are at stake in such controversies. Rendering this untranslatability or inequivalence more clearly might move European language observers of these dynamics to (re)privilege organizing concepts from historically subaltern places and to move against asymmetries of knowledge colonially inherited or imposed. This effort should not eclipse asymmetries of knowledge precolonially inherited, however, on the opacity of *ʿajami(yya)* as a conceptual term.

I end with a note on how this chapter serves as an important counterpoint to the previous one. Western Europe's discursive racialization of Ottoman and Muslim subjects (as described by Aydin) corresponded, I argue, to defensive tactics understood in very different terms by Ottoman Arab and Muslim arabophone writers—terms incommensurate with Western European notions of race and racialization. In this connection, this chapter has traced Arabic concepts vital for exploring how emerging solidarities among Europe's racialized Muslim and Ottoman Arab others were expressed across the fact of their own linguistic diversity through the shared conceptual terms *ʿajam(i)* and *ʿajamiyya*. And non-Muslim Arabs across Ottoman territories of the nineteenth century invoked these same terms to express a sense of Arab cultural distinction and interreligious solidarity.

ʿAjam(iyya) as a conceptual term is nonetheless troubling for its lingering opacity. To engage in a form of cultural translation, and to gesture to what Plato implied of a potentially (if not perfectly) analogous designation, as a binary term in opposition to the *Greek*, the term *barbaros* tells us little about the *barbaroi*.[81] The same might be said of *ʿajam* otherness, which beckons us beyond its inscrutability as an oppositional term for the xenophone, beyond its ambiguous definition as *indistinction*. *ʿAjam(iyya)* might be considered a Janus-faced term. Linguistically, geographically, and historically, it turns both toward the *ʿarab*—itself an ethnolinguistic infixity—and radially outward. At the interface of a pre-Islamic past and an Islamic present, it belies in its singularity the many tongues that distinguish an *ʿajam(iyya)* diversity (or "babel"). The historical traces of *ʿajam(iyya)* cultural forms therefore bear within themselves this heteroglossic or translational interface. *ʿAjam(iyya)*, as the conceptual threshold between the familiar and the strange, if not the sacred and profane, is also the site through which cultural conflict and coexistence, diversity and solidarity, are mediated at the boundaries of the Arabophone.

3

Arabic Mastery and Racial Parity

All that is in this [poem] is right and steady
So hone yourself with it readily [. . .]
And turn not away from its acceptance
For the blackness of my skin
As the greatest of God's devotees [*ʿibād*]
Are the greatest in piety, worshipping with detachment.

—AHMADU BAMBA MBAKKE, "MASĀLIK AL-JINĀN"

AHMADU BAMBA MBAKKE, founder of the most widespread Sufi movement in sub-Saharan West Africa in the late nineteenth and early twentieth centuries, the Murid movement (or Muridiyya), versified in one of his most renowned poems an assertion of parity between black and white, *sudān* and *bayḍān*. His emphasis on piety over differences in skin color invoked longstanding Islamic teachings on the equal status of black and white, Arab and non-Arab (*ʿarab* and *ʿajam*)—on people being differentiated only by their righteousness. The poem, "Masālik al-Jinān," written in Arabic, contributed to the Wolof poet's exceptional literary corpus between the 1890s and early 1900s, distinguishing him as one of the most prolific composers of Arabic verse in West Africa.[1] Writing as colonial French influence was expanding across the region, Ahmadu Bamba used Arabic to counter this growing influence while also enhancing his status as a non-native speaker of Arabic. By his own account, his Arabic mastery elevated him across an interethnic arabophone community, as a non-native speaker of Arabic and a black poet among "white" (*bayḍān*) Muslims. His attachment to Arabic, however, was also defensive relative to the colonial promotion of French across his native region of Senegal; by the late nineteenth century, France was working to curb and displace Arabic literacies in its West African colonies. Bamba's pride in Arabic mastery can therefore be seen as responding to two intersecting hierarchies taking root in sub-Saharan West Africa during his lifetime. These include an Arabocentric stratification within many regional Muslim communities, which accorded a higher value to Arabic competency as a sacralized language over *ʿajamiyya* (non-Arabic) alternatives, and Eurocentric hierarchies associated with the consolidation of French colonial control in West Africa after the 1890s.[2]

In light of these intersecting hierarchies, the present chapter and the one that follows draw attention to parallel dynamics shared across arabophone Muslim communities in sub-Saharan West Africa and Southeast Asia. Writers across both regions, including Bamba, reconciled a sense of pride in Arabic linguistic passing as non-native speakers with a self-conscious awareness of their non-Arab difference—a difference defended through reference to Islamic teachings on parity between black and white, Arab and non-Arab communities. Even as Arabic literacies were being curtailed within both regions (in Dutch-controlled Southeast Asia as in French West Africa), parallel claims of Arabic-Islamic assimilation survived imperial attempts to distance local Muslim communities from the widespread use of Arabic. As we will see, colonial efforts to weaken local attachments to Arabic were resisted by influential writers who asserted that ritual Arabic bore a complementary rather than antagonistic relationship to local languages and cultural forms.

This chapter and the next underscore how Bamba and one of his later counterparts in Muslim Southeast Asia, Hamka, upheld Arabic as a symbol of transregional Islamic solidarity. Both authors grappled, however, with the endurance of cultural and linguistic hierarchies that privileged Arabic within a shared community of faith. Their writing in this connection illustrates the traces of what could be called an *ʿajami* literary self-consciousness. Each writer's legacy attests to an enduring tension between efforts to sustain Arabic as a ritual language of universal vocation and efforts to accommodate ethnic and linguistic differences within a transregional Muslim community. Bamba's legacy—as an arabophone Wolof writer who dignified a tradition of cultural egalitarianism—in turn gave rise to an ascendant generation of twentieth-century Wolof and Pulaar poets who defended the use of non-Arabic (*ʿajamiyya*) languages for devotional ends in the Murid movement. This younger generation of poets, while literate in Arabic and trained in the Arabic script, defended the use of local vernaculars in devotional and literary contexts, often by invoking Bamba's teachings on ethnolinguistic parity as a pretext.[3]

Bamba himself, however, chose to write primarily in Arabic. I will probe the historical implications of that choice and offer contextual details that clarify the stakes of Bamba's relationship to the Arabic language as a self-consciously black, non-Arab poet in West Africa. Navigating a period when French colonial agents were working to displace Arabic as an official medium, Bamba depicted his use of the language as a sign of autonomy and of devotion to a higher authority, and he reconsecrated Arabic as an esoteric language of divine access in his poetry. We will also consider his emancipatory claims to Arabic mastery as a figure exiled from his homeland by French colonial authorities (in the late nineteenth and early twentieth centuries).[4] The first half of this chapter presents an overview of how Arabic moved from public prominence in much of the region as a de facto official, transactional language and script to its status as a more circumscribed devotional language during Senegal's subjection to colonial control. The second half of the chapter explores how French efforts to weaken a politically autonomous or allegedly hostile Muslim leadership in the region, and to displace the Arabic language as a potential conduit of their influence, coincided with the Sufi poet's reinterpretation of his exile as a divinely sanctioned and voluntary removal from the public realm.

Despite early French efforts to diminish his influence, Ahmadu Bamba is a figure whose legacy is now evident across the soundscapes, mediascapes, and public art of contemporary Senegal: The sole colonial-era photograph taken of him—a reclusive figure garbed in white, with a shawl covering his head and obscuring his face—has inspired a local iconography that pervades the region and remains prominent within the capital of Dakar.[5] Itinerant strains of his sung poetry are heard all over Senegal, and informal markets hawking prints of his venerated poetry are widespread. His Murid devotees speak reverently of his personal biography, highlighting his objection to the enslavement of fellow Muslims at the court of the regent Lat Joor, his religious devotion amid long periods of incarceration and exile at the hands of colonial officials, and his superiority to or parity with Mauritanian sheikhs as an erudite religious scholar. While he is a figure of anticolonial resistance and black racial pride to many of his followers, scholarship more critical of the Murid order also highlights the eventual accommodation by Murid leaders of French colonial authorities toward the end of Bamba's life. This accommodation, as many scholars have observed, would imprint itself on postindependence patterns of political and electoral brokering between Murid leaders and more secular francophone political elites.

The first portion of this chapter will be devoted to the perception of French and Arabic as ideologically antagonistic forces by French colonial agents toward the turn of the century (a perception intensifying between 1895 and 1914). I will then proceed with a selective reading of Bamba's poetry, focusing on the poet's self-referential presentation of his writing in Arabic. This paired reading of Arabic's symbolic value within the French colonial archives and Bamba's poetry exemplifies how Arabic was not merely institutionally marginalized by French colonial agents but also upheld by one of its most influential writers in Senegal as a language of high ritual prestige. The poet in this way characterized his use of Arabic as a sign of counterimperial autonomy in the midst of colonial coercion, with long-standing implications for local culture.

The chapter concludes by exploring how early French colonial perceptions of an ideological contest between the French and Arabic languages in Senegal ended with a certain equilibrium. A symbiosis emerged between the colonial state and Bamba as one of Senegal's most influential and popular Muslim leaders. While the French controlled public office in Senegal, Bamba believed that his ambitions and influence involved a higher realm of devotion—a realm in which the esoteric mastery of the Arabic language assumed a paramount form of symbolic capital, transcending French efforts to limit the language to "private," devotional contexts.[6] This double perspective enabled the French and Arabic languages to eventually assume a symbiotic coexistence as discrete acrolects in Senegal.[7]

These conditions, however, left unresolved how local vernaculars would be transcribed at the crossroads of Arabic and Europeanized literacies. The inheritance of this predicament by mid- to late twentieth-century Senegalese writers—who sought to elevate local languages relative to both acrolects—is a subject explored by the chapter's conclusion and resumed in later chapters on liberationist writing in the shadow of both Arabic and colonial French influences.

Imperial Front Lines: Advancing French, Displacing Arabic

Following the Portuguese and the Dutch, the French maintained a mercantile presence on the West African coast from the early seventeenth century; incursions into the interior of present-day Senegal began in the 1830s and proceeded over the course of a century. A period of intensified military expansion was followed by the establishment of a military government at the mouth of the Senegal River and by the appointment in 1854 of the naval engineer Louis Faidherbe as colonial governor. From its incipiency, the French colonial administration considered Islam the most formidable ideological threat to the expansion of French authority in sub-Saharan West Africa, a perception informed by earlier campaigns and encounters with Muslim clerics in northwest Africa.[8] A speech by Governor Faidherbe to native Senegalese interpreters in 1860 suggests the extent to which France's West African expansion was viewed as a countervailing force to Islam, conceived as a rival extraterritorial influence in the region:

> Residents of Senegal, for the most part you have received from your fathers the religion of the Arabs; but, questions of belief aside, you are by no means obliged to imitate the Arabs in their morals, in their ignorance [. . .] . It is not to them that you must go to seek your examples [. . .] .[9]

This envisioned dissociation of Islam from its pejoratively characterized, regional origins in Arab North Africa and West Asia indicates the eventual direction of French cultural policy with regard to Senegal's overwhelmingly (and increasingly) Muslim demographic, favoring colonial French models of institutional authority and culminating in the local projection of a "Muslim civilization which expresses itself in French."[10]

Early French colonial policy toward Islam in West Africa was marked by ambivalence and inconsistency, due not only to poor initial intelligence gathering from Arabic-language sources but also to the paradoxical task of converting what seemed an "insuperable" source of opposition into an invaluable "instrument of conquest."[11] A general trend can nonetheless be discerned with regard to colonial language policy, whereby the Arabic language in sub-Saharan West Africa came to be considered a potentially radicalizing force and was increasingly conflated with politicized Islam (and later with religiously inflected nationalist ideas imported from the Middle East).[12] Despite these colonial anxieties, Arabic nonetheless remained an important medium of diplomatic and written exchange between local rulers and French colonial agents until the early twentieth century—as late as 1906, the administration of Governor Roume considered the training of local interpreters in Arabic a paramount colonial asset. The French administration nonetheless increasingly sought to displace the public use of Arabic, citing the necessity to maintain linguistic barriers to "separate" "our West African Islam" from alternative centers of religious power in West Asia.[13]

Although French military expansion in sub-Saharan West Africa and Mauritania continued into the 1930s—with Senegal "pacified" by the 1890s—in the late nineteenth century the increasing cost to France of military conquests in the region resulted in a shift away from overt military campaigns toward alternative modes of coercion and control.[14] In 1895, the seat of French colonial power was transferred from a military to a civilian administration, and a regional Federation of French West Africa (L'Afrique Occidentale Française, the AOF) was established to consolidate the economic potential of the colonies under a program of "rational economic development" (*mise en valeur*).[15] The push toward economic consolidation under a regional, federal system corresponded with a greater policy emphasis on the region's linguistic integration, with the French language promoted as both a unifying force and a cultural front for a French *mission civilisatrice* in France's West African colonies.[16] According to historian Alice Conklin, debates within the colonial French West African administration about a regionally unifying language concluded with French as the sole contender by the early 1900s: "West Africa needed a common language as badly as it needed a common railroad system, and, by default, French was the only one available," for "there were simply too many dialects to master."[17]

The colonial promotion of French within the public domain reached its height under the administration of Governor William Ponty (1908–14), when French was established as the official language of the AOF. The decision to exclusively employ French in official correspondence, however, involved the active displacement of an Arabic language and script whose de facto status as a transactional medium until 1911 (between colonial agents and local leaders) implies the disingenuousness of claims that French was the only contender for a unifying, regional language. In May 1911, Governor Ponty issued a circular banning the use of Arabic in judicial and administrative matters, arguing that

> Arabic only enters into African countries with Muslim proselytism. For the Black it is a sacred language. Even indirectly to oblige those under our jurisdiction to learn it in order to maintain official relations with us comes to the same as encouraging the propaganda of the votaries of Islam [. . .] . Furthermore, most of our clerks cannot speak Arabic and are consequently incapable of exercising control over documents written in this language.[18]

This suggests that the selection of French as a unifying regional language was informed less by its status as the sole alternative than by the exclusions to the colonial administration presented by Arabic as a linguistic contender—much as the problem of facing "too many dialects to master" challenged the native speaker less than the aspiring master.

As Ponty's circular suggests, the spread of the French language was also envisioned as an ideal antidote to the potentially radicalizing influences of the Arabic language as a religious medium. The long shadow cast by earlier theorizations of ideological containment in connection with the curbing of Arabic, as discussed in a previous chapter, is apparent across comments by colonial agents in the years leading up to World War I.[19] Following the alleged assassination of a colonial administrator by an Islamic cleric in Futa Jallon, for example, the inspector general of the colonies, M. Phérivong, suggested to superiors that the administration's dependency on a potentially hostile class of Arabic interpreters needed to be urgently remedied given the "existence of an Islamic problem" in the AOF. By his estimation, the spread of the French language was "the best method of combatting the activities of the marabouts about whom we are poorly informed since between them and us there is no contact except through interpreters who are their own pupils."[20] In documents dating from 1910, Mariani, the inspector of Muslim education in the AOF, wrote in a similar vein to Governor Ponty, stating that "[k]nowledge of the French language is the best possible antidote against the danger of a retrograde Islam."[21] In a statement mirroring Alfred Le Chatelier's earlier claims, he added: "The study of a living Christian language is the most effective remedy to Muslim fanaticism . . . The Mahommetans who know French or English are less fanatical and less dangerous than their co-religionists who can only speak Arabic, Berber or Turkish."[22] In addition to this characterization of French as an antidote to Islamic "fanaticism," a strategy of containment was later proposed by the Islamicist Paul Marty (a protégé of Alfred Le Chatelier's), who recommended not only that Qur'anic schools be denied access to animist regions but also that the use of Arabic script be bypassed with the transcription of local languages into the Latin alphabet.[23]

Thus, following the establishment of the AOF in the 1890s, a period in which the colonial administration sought to replace outright military conflict with alternative modes of control, colonial records suggest the extent to which linguistic competition was seen to translate antagonistic relations of force. Reforms initially aimed at an elite class of local interpreters—prompted by a feared overdependency on Arabic translators for official correspondence—extended to a broader language policy, with the spread of French envisioned under the Ponty administration as the most significant front to advance France's "civilizing mission" among a general public.[24] In this light, Ponty's 1911 circular banning the use of Arabic in official correspondence in the AOF also expressed the need "to accelerate the diffusion of our language" and to encourage enrollment of "native children [in] our schools in greater numbers."[25] Declaring that popular knowledge of the French language was "the primordial condition of our success and its longevity," without which "the most praiseworthy intentions of our administration and our justice risked being misunderstood," Ponty argued that through "schools of language where the children learn to understand and speak French," French influence would "insinuate itself among the masses, penetrate and envelop them like a thin web of new affinities."[26]

Education policy during this time "became the litmus test of French attitudes towards Islam in the colony," and "in no case was the political aspect of education reform more clear than in the question of Muslim Education," as noted by historian Christopher Harrison.[27] Not only was Arabic banned from official correspondence under the Ponty administration, but attempts were also made to reform, limit, and monitor Qurʾanic schools and to displace them with French alternatives. In the words of Mariani, director of Islamic education under Ponty, the French set about to "laicize," restrict, and control Islamic education by licensing marabouts, limiting enrollment to students already attending French schools, introducing French language pedagogy in Islamic institutes of higher education, and experimenting with Franco-Islamic *medersas*.[28] Although many of these French efforts to control Qurʾanic education were later considered ineffective, the traces of these aggressive policies nonetheless throw into relief the emerging linguistic front lines of two competing spheres of influence. French was the principal language for official brokering in the public domain, while Arabic dominated the increasingly segregated realm of "private" religious worship and education.

As these policy trends suggest, while the Arabic language continued to be upheld as a form of unrivaled symbolic capital and as a status language among Muslims in French West Africa, French was beginning to assume an ascendant position as a public, official acrolect around the turn of the twentieth century. In the course of tracing Bamba's defense of Arabic at the height of French retrenchments in West Africa in the remainder of this chapter, the following connection between French colonial documents and Bamba's writings deserves emphasis. The French administration eventually developed a policy of "accommodation" with the Murid leadership in the years leading toward World War I, in part spurred by racialized ideas taking root among French colonial agents in connection with the ethnographic codification of a sub-

Saharan, West African "black Islam" (*Islam noir*).[29] "Black Islam" was by this logic considered a subordinate, more malleable, less radicalizing force than its "white" Moorish counterpart, *Islam maure*. Central to these efforts were the ethnographic surveys of Paul Marty, the French Islamicist whose policy recommendations largely determined late colonial policy on Islam in the AOF after his appointment in 1912. According to Marty's inaugural scholarship on this racial distinction internal to Islam, *Islam noir* tended to heterodoxy and ideological corruption but had the "advantage" of therefore being more ideologically pliable than its North African and West Asian counterpart.[30] "White Moors" north of the Senegal River, due to their "strong proportion of Semitic blood" and "identical conditions" to Arab communities of the "Orient," he generalized, have "conserved" an Orthodox Islam in contrast to their black Senegalese counterparts.[31] This pattern, Marty claimed, citing Orientalist contributors to the 1901 *Questions Diplomatiques et Coloniales* inquiry on the "future of Islam," follows a general trend across Islam's African and Asian expansion: As Islam "grows distant from its cradle, toward the East as West, as races and conditions change, it becomes increasingly deformed," whether among "Malays [. . .] or Nigritic races."[32]

In support of such assertions, Marty alleged the general inability of black Africans to grasp the complexities of the Arabic language and to effectively adapt to Arabic ritual and orthodox Islamic practice.[33] He claimed that "religious education" in black Africa was "purely mechanical," bearing "no effect on the intellectual development" of the local populace, and cited the impoverishment of Qur'anic institutions and the poor training of Qur'anic school instructors as advantageous to French colonial interests.[34] A sense of linguistic competition is clearly inscribed in Marty's writing: "The veneer of Islam and Arabic that cover this faith [in black Africa] . . . is extremely superficial. Except for a few scholars whose intellectual achievements are quite impressive total ignorance dominates everywhere. [. . .] The result is perhaps deplorable from an Islamic point of view but it is excellent from the French point of view."[35] Marty's ethnographic codification of *Islam noir* was not only notable for its ideological tempering of a perceived threat among Senegalese Muslims, enabling more normalized relations between colonial agents and Muslim clerics of the Senegalese interior during his tenure (including the Murid leadership); it also involved the colonial French translation and adaptation of endemic prejudices within the scholarly community of the Senegalo-Mauritanian region, prejudices that elevated "white" Moorish communities (*bayḍān*) north of the Senegal River over the "black neophytes" to their south.[36] As will be discussed later, Marty's ethnographic constructions were highly informed by the discriminatory views of Mauritanian (*bayḍān*) Muslim elites such as Cheikh Sidiyya Baba: a close French collaborator, former teacher of Bamba in the Qadiriyya order, and co-architect of colonial Mauritania, itself a racial construct segregating Mauritanian *bayḍān* (whites) from their alleged inferiors among the Senegalese *sudān* (blacks).[37]

Upholding Arabic

In light of the foregoing observations, Bamba's writing on parity between "black" and "white" gains gravity when viewed through the convergence of both colonial and regional racism in French West Africa. Foregrounding his foundation of his own Sufi order, his poetry projected his equal status among an erudite Muslim community of Mauritanian *bayḍān* (white) scholars while challenging his early marginalization by a French colonial surveillance state in formation. Bamba considered his poetry a divine benediction—a blessing that facilitated his Arabic erudition and linguistic "passing." Poetry served as a medium that elevated him as a black poet across an interethnic arabophone community, neutralizing his own experiences of prejudice across lines of color and linguistic difference (between *sudān* and *bayḍān*, *ʿarab* and *ʿajam*). Bamba's writing on his colonial exile to Gabon, a period in which he claimed to have reached a linguistic mastery unrivaled by other non-native speakers, illustrates how the poet viewed his own writing as a form of sanctuary during a period of trial, imagining himself capable of transcending French efforts to limit his influence in his native Senegal through his devotional Arabic verse.

Ahmadu Bamba first rose to public prominence as a young man in 1882–83 for objecting to the enslavement of fellow Muslims at the court of Lat Joor Joop, the Wolof regent of Kajoor, who had gifted enslaved Muslims to Bamba's father, the cleric Muamar Anta Sali. After Lat Joor's victories over a fellow archrival, the Madiyanké jihadist Amadu Sheikhu, and amid the enslavement and distribution of Sheikhu's defeated followers as war captives, Bamba publicly argued that it was unlawful for Muslims to enslave fellow Muslims as "apostates" and found himself challenging on these grounds an older generation of clerics at the Wolof court (including his former teacher Majakhate Kala). The sequence of confrontations that followed influenced Bamba's ultimate decision to distance himself from Lat Joor's court.[38] His growing alienation from traditional rulers, however, worked against Bamba at a time when

French agents sought to employ segments of a weakened local aristocracy as intermediaries and interpreters. Growing tensions between Bamba's followers and traditional African chiefs in Kajoor gave rise to the first appearance of Bamba's name in colonial documents in 1889. Although the circumstances leading to his first arrest and exile by colonial authorities in 1895 remain poorly documented, the French verdict appears to have been based on distorted or falsified intelligence information on Bamba's amassing of weapons in preparation for an open declaration of jihad against the French. As noted by historian Cheikh Anta Babou, despite Bamba's estrangement from Lat Joor's court, his early association with the Wolof regent through his father was ironically held against him as evidence of his guilt and became grounds for his exile to Gabon.[39]

The following anecdote, detailed by his hagiographer Sëriñ Muusaa Ka in a poem entitled "Odyssey by Sea" ("Yoonu géej gi"), illuminates Bamba's reaction to his exile.[40] As Bamba awaited his forced boarding of a ship to Gabon in St. Louis after his sentencing by a French tribunal, he learned that a newly appointed governor of the AOF, Jean-Baptiste Chaudié, had arrived in St. Louis. Although Bamba began drafting a letter of appeal to the new governor on the urging of an acquaintance, he subsequently regretted and abandoned this initial pursuit. He then penned a poem affirming his trust in God. What had opened as a draft letter of appeal to the French governor was thus displaced by a devotional Arabic poem appealing to a higher authority, a poem in which the poet reinterpreted his fate in Gabon as a form of sacrifice, as a challenge presented by God, through which the French became mere instruments of a higher power.[41]

On multiple occasions in his writing, Bamba underscores the profound religious significance of his exile and reconceives of the event as a test of faith, drawing parallels to the exile of the Prophet Muhammad to Mecca.[42] One of his most celebrated poems, "Asīru maʿa al-Abrār" ("I Walk among the Righteous"), for example, reconceives of his entrapment among the French as a form of religious bondage. Bamba's play on the Arabic terms for slave and captive—*ʿabd* and *asīru*—subverts the notion of the poet's surrender to colonial hands:

أسيرُ مع الابرار حين أسيرُ
وظنَّ العدى أنّي هناك اسيرُ

مَسيرُ مع الاخيار للهِ بالنّبي
وما لي لغير الله عوضُ مسيرُ

أسيرُ إلى ذى البرِّ والبحرِ عابداً
ولستُ إلى الفُجّارِ عوضُ أسيرُ

I walk among the righteous when I walk [*asīru*]
Though the enemy thought me captive [*asīru*] as they stalk

My path is with those chosen for God by the Prophet
And none but God could alter to Him my path

I walk to the Possessor of land and sea in bondage [or worship, *ʿābidan*]
Not to the ungodly do I divert my step[43]

The poet relies on Arabic terms that sound identical but carry opposing meanings, ultimately revealing an emancipatory message. Such diction illustrates the ambiguity of Bamba's status as a figure who appears constrained but who believes he is actually free. The poet employs a certain ingenuity when pairing and rhyming the term "captive" (*asīru*) with the homonymous phrase *asīru* ("I walk" or "I move"), as he compares his worldly captivity with an illusion dispelled by his free movement as "God's bondsman." These key lines of the poem also reframe the stakes of his captivity among French authorities by playing on the dual meaning of the Arabic term *ʿabd,* which can mean both "worshipper" and "slave"—the latter a status the poet accepts only in subordination to God. As Bamba proclaims elsewhere in the poem, "[M]y fate [*maṣīr*] is to become God's slave, the Prophet's servant." He plays here on the terms for "path" and "fate," *masīr* and *maṣīr,* which are near homonyms ("maṣīrī kawnī ʿabdahu khādim al-nabī").[44]

Bamba's poems further suggest that his pious study of Arabic in isolation lent meaning to his arrest and exile, resulting in a mastery of Arabic that he viewed as a divine benediction.[45] A second poem written after his return from Gabon, "Jāwartu" ("I Adjoined [My Lord]"), illustrates this characterization of his eloquence as a reward for piety:

جاورت ربّي بلسان العربِ
بلا نهايةٍ وطابت قُرَبِ

نَزَعَ لي الاسلام عند غُربَتي
لدى الجزائر مُنيرُ تُربَتي

نُزِعَ لي نورُ اللّسانِ والكتابِ
ازمانَ خِدمتي لدى اهل الكتابِ

I adjoined my Lord through the language of the Arabs,
Without end may my closeness be!

Wrested, I inclined to Islam in my island exile
Through the One who illumines my homeland

Emanating to me the light of the tongue and the book
In my time of service beyond men of my faith[46]

By the poet's own claims across his corpus, Bamba's facility in Arabic gained through isolated study during his eight years of seclusion in Gabon bestowed on him the esoteric power of a divine message privately accessed; as a result, his postexilic eloquence in Arabic is often interpreted within Murid sources as the poet's *karāma* (saintly miracle), the precondition of his establishment of the first Sufi brotherhood in sub-Saharan West Africa independent of its North African lineage.[47]

In "Masālik al-Jinān" ("Paths to Paradise"), a poem originally penned before his exile but rewritten after his return from Gabon, Bamba claims that it was during his isolation in Gabon that, as Cheikh Anta Babou has said, "he acquired an understanding of the Arabic language never achieved by a non-native speaker."[48] To the extent that imitation of the Prophet is considered an act of piety, Bamba imagines his own eloquence to be a divine blessing and an extension of the Prophet's miraculousness. In a second poem revised after his return, "Jadhb al-Qulūb" ("The Heart's Attraction"), Bamba presents cultivation (*adab*) as a means of prophetic guidance, rendering poetry a genre of illumination for the poet himself. A certain mimesis or reflection of the Prophet and his transcendence is suggested through the following lines:

هب لي كون قلمي بشارة المُقَدَّمِ
واكتب به تَقَدُّمِ بلا أذى او ألمِ
صلّي على خير النبي قدا الورى بالأدبِ

Grant me, make of my pen an annunciation favored by he who is foremost [*al-muqaddam*]
That I may write the foremost [poems] [*taqaddum*] by his grace without anguish or pain
Pray for the greatest of prophets who guides men by their cultivation [*adab*][49]

With the doubling of the motif of precedence (*al-muqaddam/taqaddum*), the Prophet's supremacy as a benefactor is mirrored through the supremacy of the poet's verse as a benediction. This devotional poem seeking the Prophet's blessing, in other words, reflects the supremacy of the Prophet through a verbal chiasmus, as the poet's lines of verse unfold as though evidence of an answered prayer: Uncommon eloquence becomes a reward for uncommon piety.

An excerpt from a second poem, "Mafātīḥ al-Jinān" ("The Keys to Paradise"), further demonstrates this self-referential understanding of linguistic and poetic mastery as a mimetic sign of benediction:

> Toward me God grants that which I desire: knowledge beyond learning.
> *My miracles* [*karāmāt*] *are the verses I trace,* in the service of he that I serve,
> I have become the bliss of my era, by my deeds and by my speech.[50]

Mediating a mystical experience for Bamba, the act of writing here becomes an act of gnosis through which the poet's ego or subjectivity seems displaced by a divine force. By virtue of this displacement, the very notion of the poet's selfhood is troubled, as the ode becomes a medium of transcendence, a mimetic field (in imitation of the Prophet) that is not without its ambiguity—a posture of self-abnegation and self-instrumentation that resembles a kind of supremacy.

Another eulogy of the Prophet, "Nūru al-Dārayni" ("Light of Two Hearths"), further illustrates this dynamic:

> Would that my poetry from hereon transcend the status of prayer and fast,
> And unveil by these lines the hidden realms of you that know all, you the greatest, the all-knowing. [...]
> Would that my writing direct me toward you, and that my life direct me toward him [the Prophet]
> May the all-powerful grant me ease where others toil, showing me the path of the righteous.
> By the immense power of the Prophet, may my poem be the greatest subject of your satisfaction. [...]
> May my writings equal the pilgrimage, the fast, and the prayer, saving my people.

Make of my life an enduring worship, bearing the message of the Prophet,
And elevate toward your sacred throne this ode, by your sacred name.[51]

As this last excerpt suggests, poetry elevates Bamba but extends beyond the luminary figure of the individual speaker, with the poet's prayerful request for collective salvation on behalf of "my people." Given his restriction to a space of devotion in exile, the poet's request—that his writing "equal the pilgrimage" to Mecca as a devotional act—gains further poignancy when read against colonial French constraints on Bamba's movements.[52]

Linguistic Mastery as Social Capital

Bamba's first exile to Gabon was followed by a second in Mauritania (1903–7), an exile that he viewed as continuous with the first in a divinely ordained plan in which French colonial agents were again mere instruments of a higher power. If his forced sojourn in Gabon was, he claimed, a divine test of isolation from fellow Muslims, he considered his exile in Mauritania a reward for having surpassed this test of piety in seclusion.[53] Bamba's writing on his time in Mauritania, however, during and prior to his exile, illustrate that his Mauritanian experiences posed their own hardships—marked by prejudice against him as a Muslim *sudān* among *bayḍān* (a "black" among "whites"). Amid these challenges, he viewed his own erudition in Arabic as a way of overcoming forms of linguism and colorism espoused by fellow (Mauritanian *bayḍān*) Muslims; Bamba's poetry elevates his use of Arabic not only as a sign of transcendence beyond colonial French impositions but also as a unifying medium, neutralizing his own experience of prejudice within interethnic communities of Muslim scholars across Senegal and Mauritania. Evolving from an aspirant seeking benediction (*baraka*) through Mauritanian teachers during his youth in the 1880s to the prominent leader of an independent Sufi movement upon his return from Gabon, Bamba became recognized for his poetic eloquence across racial lines between Senegal and Mauritania; his eloquence assumed a paramount form of symbolic capital in Mauritania when the black poet became the subject of eulogies composed in his honor by (white, Moorish) disciples from among the Banu Dayman (a lineage of prestigious Moorish clerics), a veneration emphasized within hagiographic *ʿajami* Murid sources.[54]

This acknowledgment of the black poet's erudition and poetic excellence among *bayḍān* Muslims can be considered all the more significant given the early years of racism Bamba allegedly suffered as a student of the Qadiriyya scholar Cheikh Sidiyya Baba in Mauritania.[55] These early experiences of racism in Mauritania prompted him to begin one of his most renowned poems—which I used as this chapter's epigraph—with an assertion about the indifference of erudition to ethnicity or skin color:

فكلما فيه صحيح اثبتا   فحسّ الطرّ به اثبتا
ولا يصدّد مدى الازمان   عن اخذه كوني من السوداء
اذا اكرام العباد عند الله   اكثرهم تقوى بلا اشتباك

All that is in this [poem] is right and steady / so hone yourself with it readily [. . .]
And turn not away from its acceptance / for the blackness of my skin [literally: "for my being one of the blacks"]
As the greatest of God's devotees [*ʿibād*] are the greatest in piety [*taqwā*], worshipping with detachment[56]

These lines invoke for their moral authority hadith traditions on the Prophet Muhammad's last sermon, which proclaim the equality of *ʿajam* and *ʿarab*, *sudān* and *bayḍān*, distinguished only by their individual piety (*taqwā*). They equally invoke verse 49:13 of the Qurʾan, a verse that also claims the parity of peoples and tribes, differentiated only by piety (*taqwā*): "We have made you into peoples and tribes that you may come to know one another; truly, the noblest among you before God is the most pious [*atqā*] among you." Vital for understanding the stakes of Bamba's plea is the poet's emphasis on piety over differences in skin color. His characterization of God's devotees as a community of *ʿibād*—meaning both "worshippers" and "servants" or "slaves"—lends further poignancy to his claim of piety as a leveling force. Bamba's diction gains even greater gravity when read with the understanding that the Arabic term *ʿabd*, rendered in plural form as either *ʿibād* or the more pejorative term *ʿabīd*, was—and remains—a derogatory epithet used against darker-skinned peoples of sub-Saharan African descent in North African and West Asian Arab contexts.[57]

Although Bamba had been a disciple in Mauritania of Cheikh Sidiyya Baba, the black poet's claims to religious erudition caused persistent tension for him among many Mauritanian scholars, who continued to view themselves as Bamba's racial superiors. According to Babou, it was for many of his Mauritanian acquaintances "not easy to acknowledge the intellectual and spiritual authority of a 'black' over a 'bidan.'"[58] On one occasion, Sidiyya Baba, Bamba's former teacher, expressed in writing "his scorn for the uncivilized 'little black kinglets' of Senegal who did not deserve the attention the French gave them."[59] Mauritanian disregard for black fellow Muslims was notably observed by French colonial officials—including those who penned the earliest French ethnographies distinguishing between an allegedly "black Islam" and "Moorish Islam" (*Islam noir* and *Islam maure*). Paul Marty, for example, the first colonial agent to codify this distinction (through surveys conducted between 1912 and 1917), is known to have cited as evidence an unspecified work authored by Baba in which the latter wrote of the general superficiality of "black" conversion to Islam:

> The Blacks think of themselves as Muslims, however the majority among them do not have the slightest correct notion of what Islam is really about, they ignore the Islamic ethic, its law and principles. But we [the Moors] in our capacity as teachers and guides] have a lot of responsibility to bear in this situation.[60]

Through such citational practices, Marty's ethnographic writing on *Islam noir* records and adapts regional forms of colorism and linguism that elevated "white Moorish" Muslims over their "black" counterparts across the Senegal River, the latter allegedly adherents of a "debased" and "simplified" form of Islam remote from its "Semitic" origins.[61] Framing black Arabophones at "the margins of classical orthodoxy," Marty mentions in evidence the ritually accented or garbled Arabic of black Muslims as a general populace.[62] In one exemplary passage on "black Islam" (in which Marty transcribes common mispronunciations of the Arabic *fātiḥa* among Wolofs), he contrasts the accented quality of black Muslim prayers with the grammatical and elocutionary fastidiousness of superior Mauritanian sheikhs, noting that "black slaves" among the Mauritanians are notorious for retaining their accents and that Wolof lacks fifteen of the twenty-eight letters required to pronounce Arabic, leaving Marty to cynically remark: "[I]f truly God hears only Arabic, and a well-pronounced Arabic, the prayers of our Senegalese marabouts surely rise not to his throne."[63] "The Moors," as "agents of Islamization and spiritual directors of the blacks, bluntly declare that a black mind is entirely resistant to Muslim doctrine," Marty notes while asserting that grammatical Arabic mastery demands a "subtlety beyond the intellectual attainment of the blacks."[64]

These colonial adaptations of regional "Moorish" prejudice lend poignancy to Bamba's claims of eloquence as a non-native, black speaker. Self-referential dimensions of Bamba's writing, which draw attention to the poet's Arabic mastery, gain significance against this historical convergence of intersecting hierarchies. Bamba's writing on his isolation in Gabon, where he attained an uncommon fluency for non-native speakers, served the poet in the following sense: It tempered his displacement by a French colonial surveillance apparatus while justifying his rise as an equal to his Mauritanian *bayḍān* counterparts within an erudite arabophone community. As historian David Robinson has argued, Ahmadu Bamba as a charismatic founder of the Murid movement in effect converted a form of symbolic capital—his devotional corpus and exceptional linguistic facility in Arabic—into social capital; with the growing number and prominence of Bamba's followers, French colonial authorities faced increasing pressure to reconcile with the exiled poet as a charismatic religious figure with an indispensable following. The basis of Bamba's eventual authority as a regional religious leader, the development of his non-native linguistic mastery and erudition, in other words, not only foregrounded his religious prominence in Senegal as the founder of the Murid movement but also paved the way for an eventual conciliation (or, to use Robinson's term, "accommodation") brokered between the Murid founder and French colonial authorities.[65]

Although Bamba was permitted to return to Senegal in 1907 after his exile in Mauritania, close surveillance became a precondition for normalized relations between French authorities and the Murid leader, who was kept under house arrest in the remote semidesert between Jolof and Waalo upon his return.[66] Troubled nonetheless by the continual flow of disciples to this remote location, the French limited his visitors, closed Murid schools near him, and repeatedly relocated him to new sites to discourage aspiring devotees. Despite these efforts to remove the sheikh to ever more remote locations, the sequence of Bamba's displacements came to form the basis of a sacred geography for the growing number of Murid followers in Senegal, with Bamba's deportation to Gabon compared by devotees with the Prophet Muhammad's *hijra*, or forced migration from Mecca to Medina.[67] With a certain irony, then, practices intended by the French to curb Bamba's influence contributed to his movement's rise, owing in part to the perceived martyrdom of the founder in exile.[68]

Among the most significant aspects of Bamba's legacy is the corpus of didactic Arabic verse that he composed for his followers, which came to inspire a rising generation of vernacular language poets who sought to translate and disseminate his ideas within an *ʿajami* (Arabic script) writing tradition in local languages (principally Wolof and Pulaar).[69] One of the sustained features of many Murid communities of interior Senegal continues to be a devotional attachment both to the Murid founder's Arabic poetry and to the *ʿajami* writing traditions his movement fostered. Along with these transgenerational attachments is a self-conscious aversion to French language use, still viewed by many in the Murid community as a hostile colonial vestige.[70] According to historian Cheikh Anta Babou, "One of the biggest challenges that the Murids faced was keeping French schools out of their sacred space," leading Bamba himself to openly challenge the colonial commandant of Diourbel in 1914 to justify the policy of forcing his Murid followers to study the French language; in the process, Bamba reportedly asked the commandant "how he would have felt if he was compelled to study Wolof."[71] The concern of the Murid leader, who rarely sought open contact with the French, reflects his own conviction in the potency of education for rising generations—of which he stated in one of his poems, "Nahju Qaḍāʿi al-Haji" ("Path to the Satisfaction of Needs"): "[T]eaching the youth is like inscribing on stone, teaching the old is like writing on water."[72]

Postcolonial Segregations: Digraphia, Invisible Literacies, and Vernacular Rifts

Policies of accommodation between the French colonial administration and the Murid order had a linguistic analogue: A symbiosis arose between French control of public office in Senegal and the Murid leader's belief that his charismatic influence derived from a higher realm—a realm in which the esoteric mastery of Arabic was understood to be an unrivaled form of symbolic capital. Though initially viewed by French colonial agents as linguistic and ideological competitors, the French and Arabic languages eventually reached a symbiotic coexistence as discrete (and segregated) acrolects in Senegal. The coexistence of Arabic and French, however, left the public standardization of Senegalese vernaculars a matter unresolved at the front lines of both languages.[73]

In the wake of Bamba's death in 1927, poets and hagiographers writing in Wolof *ʿajami* (Wolof in Arabic script) continued to promote translations of his work into Wolof, not only contributing to the greater accessibility of Bamba's teachings but also promoting a less purist stance on the Arabic language as a medium for devotional poetry. Whereas Bamba had principally chosen to write in Arabic, he nonetheless fostered among his followers a generation of poets who embraced the writing of devotional verse in local languages. Murid *ʿajami* figures claim that Bamba encouraged this practice.[74] One of Bamba's hagiographers, Sëriñ Muusaa Ka, recalls in defense of his own *ʿajami* writing that the Murid founder was known to proclaim before a mixed audience of Moorish and Wolof listeners: "Nobility is neither the property of Arabs nor of non-Arabs [*ʿarab* and *ʿajam*]. It is the property of the most God-fearing and the most righteous."[75] Ka himself wrote of his own chosen language of composition:

> Wolof, Arabic, and all other
> languages are equally valuable:
> All poetry is fine, that
> aims at praising the Prophet.[76]

As with Bamba's poetic legacy, Ka's claims align with traditions of parity between Arab and non-Arab languages and peoples—the latter distinguished only by their piety. A comparable claim on parity and the sanctity of heteroglossia appears in another renowned poem by Ka, "Taxmiis bub Wolof" ("The Wolof Quintains"): "I will say things that Arabs do not know. It is because of divine mercy that there is ethnolinguistic diversity."[77] The poem (appearing to invoke Qurʾanic verse 30:22) was written in response to a Tijani scholar, Aadi Ture, who had declared that "Arabic is superior to Wolof" and "Arabs are gold and Wolof are copper."[78]

If Bamba's promotion of Arabic and Arabic script literacy in Senegal remained limited to a close following of immediate devotees (such as Ka, capable of writing in Arabic script but mediating for an illiterate or semiliterate following), so too was the early twentieth-century French goal of widespread pedagogical reform in Senegal. As Conklin observes, if colonial ambitions to reinvent rural education failed, resulting in an eventual French literacy rate in Senegal of merely 20 percent toward the end of colonial rule, France's stated objective for public education ("creating a class of literate [francophone] auxiliaries") nonetheless left an indelible mark on the future of cultural politics and language debates in the region.[79] A year after Bamba's passing in 1927, the future first president of independent Senegal, Léopold Sédar Senghor, would begin his inaugural voyage from Senegal to France. As one of the first native-trained graduates from the AOF to earn a scholarship for higher education in France, he would later emerge as one of the most influential arbiters on language questions in his native country. In contrast with the linguistic orientations of his arabophone predecessors in Senegal, Senghor's eventual orientation as a linguistic policy maker was relatively Gallocentric, promoting the notion (or prejudice) that French was the only possible contender for an official language of state in the region. The colonial-era fate of Arabic is deeply intertwined with the fate of local-language literatures, with their transcription and their textual transmission—or absence thereof. A logical inference follows from this observation. To the extent that a familiarity with Arabic complemented the transmission of vernacular literatures written in the Arabic script, French efforts to displace Arabic literacies had an adverse effect on the continuity and visibility of this *ʿajami* tradition. As we will see in subsequent chapters, later generations of francophone authors sought to recover the literary inheritance of vernacular languages from which they were textually estranged and to experimentally transcribe local vernaculars in the Roman alphabet. Their efforts suggest the extent to which the perception of textually orphaned local languages may have been an indirect and historically aberrant by-product of aggressive colonial language policies in French West Africa. This condition may in part explain the extreme emphasis placed by subsequent generations of francophone authors on oral traditions; oral traditions, when their transcribed alternatives in Arabic were publicly diminished, were what remained accessible for the literate writer after the institutional expansion of French and its Latinate orthography.

Given that official efforts to codify and standardize the transcription of native languages through the Roman alphabet did not begin until 1968 and in some cases continue unresolved in Senegal, the following conditions deserve emphasis—especially in connection to rising generations of early francophone authors who gained prominence by the mid-twentieth century.[80] Colonial policies that meant to limit Arabic literacies as a potentially radicalizing force, and to promote Europeanized alternatives in their stead, altered the way local illiteracies were publicly framed; native-language literacy was increasingly characterized as a virtual illiteracy, just as Arabic or Arabicized literacies became increasingly irrelevant or underacknowledged within the public domain among literate circles of twentieth-century writers, as noted by historian Ousmane Kane and sociolinguist Fallou Ngom.[81]

This observation should nonetheless be considered with the following qualification. The colonial redefinition of native and Arabicized literacies as virtual illiteracies—and the perception of native vernaculars as textually orphaned languages by rising generations of francophone authors—was largely relevant for those interpreters and writers who, if not schooled in French, might have instead been educated more exclusively in Arabic and in *ʿajami* traditions (native languages transcribed in Arabic). For this community of francophone writers, the disconnection between postcolonial practices of transcription (in French or Latin script) and their ambitions to represent vernacular literary traditions was a decisive condition of their work.

Another qualification should be made in this connection. The discontinuity in native-language literacy does not apply to writers who (affiliates of autonomous, religious communities such as the Murid order) continued to be sufficiently well versed in the Arabic script to sustain and transcribe native-language literatures without interruption. It is in this light that the following disparity can be seen. Whereas francophone authors grappled with their choice of the French language, experimented with the informal romanization of native languages, and sought alternative media such as cinema to address their perception of a textually orphaned vernacular language, authors versed in Arabic (though less publicly visible, less frequently published and circulated in formal print) continued writing native-language literatures in Arabic script without interruption.

Major francophone authors—such as Léopold Senghor and Ousmane Sembene, examined in later chapters—were plagued by the problem of vernacular language transcription and by questions of vernacular literary representation; they generally eschewed writing in their native Serer and Wolof and developed in response an alternative poetics of *négritude*/Francophonie (in Senghor's case) and an oral poetics of the cinematic medium (in Sembene's case). In contrast, the Murid community and its autonomous pedagogical apparatus—established by Bamba, who himself included lines of Wolof in certain poems—produced two of Senegal's most prolific poets of Wolof in the twentieth century, Sëriñ Muusaa Ka (a near-contemporary of Senghor) and Sëriñ Mbay Jaxate, whose work has since become widely known and sung (effectively disseminated among a textually illiterate audience in Senegal).[82]

Dismissing Arabic and Arabic script writing as a private and predominantly religious practice mistakenly naturalizes what had originally been a process of literary segregation: Arabic was circumscribed as a nominally "religious" medium, rendered "private" and unofficial, in contrast to its historical vocation as a regionally transactional language and script. Countering such tendencies, West Africanist historians and linguists have noted the exceptional range of regional *ʿajami* writing beyond religious concerns, extending from medieval pharmacological works to condemnations of the Axis powers by Senegalese *tirailleurs* in World War II.[83] The gap between francophone speakers of Wolof and Wolof writers in Arabic script has only recently been addressed, as linguist Arame Fal notes, through informal initiatives in the last decades of the twentieth century. These include, for example, the transcription (into Latin orthography) of Ka's poetry and the circulation of recordings of his verse.[84]

Bamba's didactic Arabic poetry and defensive attachment to Arabic sheltered a generation of vernacular poets writing in their native languages in Arabic script at a time when francophone authors, estranged from the textual transmission of their native languages and initially challenged by the transcription problem, sought refuge in an alternative poetics of cultural translation. Literary parallels shared across this linguistically segregated regional corpus have yet to be fully explored, though subsequent chapters offer a point of departure: Distinctive visions for an emancipatory and more equitable future in the wake of French colonialism were expressed across languages both "sacred" and "vernacular."

4

Arabic as a Counterimperial Symbol

The difference of language and skin is not something that can be erased, for the appearance of these differences makes evident a tribe, makes evident a nation. [. . .] All of this is recognized by the faith of Islam. [. . .] By God, there is no difference between non-Arab and Arab [*ʿajam* and *ʿarab*], between those of white skin and those of black skin. The highest by His side is only who to Him is most devoted.

—HAMKA, "ISLAM DAN KEBANGSAAN"

THE INDONESIAN WRITER and politician Hamka wrote in his memoirs of linguistically passing among Arabs and experiencing their generous hospitality during his pilgrimage to Mecca in 1927, while bearing witness to the scorn directed against ethnically Malay (Jawi) pilgrims who failed to assimilate during their sojourn.[1] Fellow travelers unable to acculturate were perceived by some of their Arab hosts as culturally subordinate and ethnically inferior—as second-class citizens within a shared community of faith. For Hamka, as for Bamba in West Africa, fluency in Arabic was a sign of distinction, key to elevating and integrating oneself within an arabophone community of shared belief. Such forms of arabophone pride, however, were tempered by Hamka's own assertions of interethnic parity between *ʿarab* and *ʿajam*, black and white—as my epigraph drawn from a political essay in 1939 suggests.

The trilingual Sumatranese author known locally in Indonesia as Hamka occupied an exceptional position as a writer who gained prominence as the Arabic language and script were abandoned for popular publishing in the Dutch East Indies in the 1920s.[2] His descent from a formidable line of Islamic scholars in Sumatra, and his proficiency in both Arabic and Latin scripts (*jawi* and *rumi*), placed him in a unique position as a writer whose career adapted to the changing tides of Indonesian print and the shifting contours of local debates on language politics and Indonesian nationalism until his death in 1981.[3] Although Hamka largely disused Arabic for publishing by the 1930s, he continued to inscribe in his work an enduring arabophone pride, which he equated with a sense of pan-Islamic community across the Indonesian archipelago and Malay Peninsula. Traces of Hamka's arabophone attachments resurfaced in his romanized writing as he sought "to reconcile Islamic activism within the new frameworks of the rumi [romanized] press and the Dutch colonial state"—and, later, within the independent Indonesian state that emerged in its wake.[4]

As a leader of one of Indonesia's largest movements of Islamic reformism, the Muhammadiyah, Hamka held an unrivaled position in twentieth-century Indonesian history as an intermediary between two fields often deemed mutually exclusive by the region's more conservative Islamic scholars.[5] As aptly stated by the Indonesian literary critic Farchad Poeradisastra, "[I]t would be easy to find clerics more learned, better writers abound, but there is no comparable figure in Indonesian history (with even half his talents) who attempted to bridge the literary and religious realms."[6] It is not only Hamka's multilingualism—his fluency in Arabic, Indonesian Malay, and his regional Minang dialect—but also his self-conscious mediation among Indonesia's literary, religious, and political domains that render him an unparalleled subject for tracing the controversies provoked by the coexistence of Arabic, colonial, and local languages in the region of Indonesia.

Hamka was born in the Minang highlands of West Sumatra in 1908, the child of a prominent Muslim scholar and editor of *jawi* (Arabic-script) newsprint. Although Hamka received a traditional religious upbringing, his exposure to popular Indonesian and Arabic fiction was the result of autodidactic efforts (and rebellious treks to local bookstores despite his father's disapproval) rather than due to any formal training, making his eventual literary prominence in Indonesia the more remarkable. After returning from the Hajj pilgrimage at the tender age of nineteen, he worked as a journalist and editor of Islamic periodicals in Sumatra and became a writer of Indonesian popular fiction through the 1930s. Hamka grew increasingly involved in electoral politics in the 1940s, writing frequently on political subjects as a member of the newly established Islamic political party Masyumi after Indonesian independence. His career took a more conservative turn after Indonesian independence, as he came to express his disenchantment with the relatively secular direction of emerging constitutional reforms under the presidency of Ahmed Sukarno. Hamka's literary legacy—which relied in part on Indonesian literary adaptations of Arabic source texts—also became embroiled in some of Indonesia's most vitriolic culture wars, when his adaptations were mistaken for plagiarisms.[7] After a public falling out with Sukarno, he was rehabilitated by Sukarno's successor and usurper, General Suharto, as the first head of the "New Order" government's advisory council of Islamic scholars (Majelis Ulama Indonesia), a position he held until his passing.

Hamka's shifting positions on language politics during his career add layers of complexity to any analysis of his writing. Across both his earlier, more liberal writing before the Indonesian Revolution and his more politically conservative turn after independence, he experimented with different tactics to realign Indonesian literature and public culture with Arabic. Prior to independence, Hamka explored the coexistence of Arabic and romanized Indonesian for a future nation-state through forms of literary adaptation and narrative experimentation in popular fiction. In the wake of the independence struggle, however, he argued in more ideologically purist ways that the Indonesian language needed to abandon the Latin script and "return" to Arabic orthography as a mark of decolonization.[8]

The present chapter continues to explore Arabic-Islamic ideals of ethnolinguistic parity defended by arabophone writers across colonial practices of "divide and rule." Writers such as Hamka, like Bamba of an earlier generation, drew on these ideals to directly challenge the racialized hierarchies imposed by Western European empires within an African and Asian expanse.[9] Like the literary corpus of Bamba, Hamka's writing can also be seen to challenge intersecting Eurocentric and Arabocentric hierarchies that he witnessed during his career as a writer. First active as Indonesian nationalism was gaining momentum in the interwar period, Hamka invoked long-standing Islamic traditions of parity—between black and white, Arab and non-Arab (*ʿarab* and *ʿajam*)—in his early writing to legitimize an Indonesian nationalist movement emerging against Dutch rule in the 1930s and early 1940s.[10]

I also explore Hamka's attachment to such ideals of parity as they complement his envisioned coexistence of Arabic and nationalized Indonesian. Emerging ideas about this linguistic coexistence, however, were impacted by the politicization of both Arabic and Indonesian Malay by Dutch colonial agents, resulting in polemical reactions from subaltern writers like Hamka. To explain such dynamics, the present chapter reconsiders the local fate of Arabic literacies as they were marginalized in the late colonial period—a consequence, as in French West Africa, of colonial ambitions for Islam's containment. Such efforts provoked a symbolic defense of Arabic in Indonesia, as shown through Hamka's writing at different points in his career.

We will begin with an overview of late colonial policy trends in the Dutch East Indies, which contributed to the public marginalization of Arabic in Indonesia. In the process, I illustrate how colonial support to curb Arabic literacies contributed to the linguistic conditions and constraints that an arabophone writer such as Hamka faced early in his career, as romanization was gaining momentum in local print during the 1920s and 1930s. After introducing these dynamics, the chapter illustrates how Hamka anticipated the coexistence of Arabic and Indonesian for a future independent state through experiments in popular fiction. I foreground this by illustrating how he defended this coexistence in national terms through interwar journalistic and political essays in which he cited Islamic intellectual traditions on ethnolinguistic parity. The chapter then turns to Hamka's changing ideas on language politics in a decolonizing Indonesia after independence. Amid his growing disenchantment with the relatively secular leadership of the newly independent Indonesian republic during the 1950s, he advocated for a return of Indonesian national culture to its allegedly more Islamic and Arabic origins with the revived use of the Arabic script. He also expressed a hostility to romanized print standards as a colonial vestige. A counterimperial affiliation with Arabic emerges within Hamka's writing, persisting even after the rise of romanized Indonesian Malay as a print medium and intensifying across national language debates in the wake of Indonesian independence.

I end with a final note on the stakes of this chapter, given those that precede and follow. Evidence here challenges mistaken claims that local "print vernaculars" would displace ritual Arabic in the model of nationalized European vernaculars with the decline of Church Latin. To read evidence from the most populous Muslim-majority republic that emerged in the wake of World War II, Arabic's symbolic value had not corroded but evolved under the pressures of European colonization: No longer only a sacred symbol in Indonesia, it had become by the mid-twentieth century a counterimperial one.

Curbing Arabic Literacies: Colonial Parallels in the Dutch East Indies

Efforts by colonial Dutch officials to limit the use of Arabic among rising generations of Indonesians by the late nineteenth and early twentieth centuries provoked a local defense of the language among arabophone intellectuals like

Hamka.[11] Such politicizations of Arabic parallel those observed in the previous chapter, which retraced how major colonial agents in French West Africa—like their Dutch counterparts—sought to curb Arabic literacies, provoking a defensive reaction by influential arabophone writers in connection to Arabic. Despite this general similarity, there is a major difference between the patterns traced in the previous and present chapters. The forms of Europeanized literacies promoted in each region differed. In contrast to the French, who spread their own language to restrict the influence of Arabic, Dutch agents promoted the use of Latin orthography for local-language writing to weaken attachments to Arabic. Colonial Dutch support for romanization would foreground how later debates on orthography—which pitted Latin script use against Arabic for local languages (such as nationalized Indonesian Malay)—became intensely controversial in the wake of Indonesian independence, as observed in Hamka's essays on the politics of script noted in this chapter's conclusion.

Dutch language practice was aberrant when compared with that of the Portuguese, Spaniards, and French, who tended to promote their own languages among their colonial subjects. The Dutch, in contrast, largely withheld use of their language in the Dutch East Indies and instead reverted to Malay for administrative purposes from the seventeenth through the nineteenth century.[12] The reasons for this trend are a point of controversy. Certain scholars suggest that Dutch colonists sought to preserve their language as an exclusionary, high-status medium in their colonies, though more influential factors may have been the failure of Dutch language pedagogy in early missionary schools, the perceived sufficiency of Malay for early Christian missionary work, and the challenges confronting Dutch officials when trying to master the principal court languages and scripts of the archipelago—Sanskritized Javanese and Arabic-script Malay (also known as *jawi*).[13]

The common reversion to Malay as an interpretive medium corresponded with a crisis of transcription by the mid- to late nineteenth century, as colonial officials within the region became increasingly convinced that the Arabic script in which Malay had been widely transcribed since the thirteenth century was linguistically inadequate and ideologically suspect.[14] Contributing to this suspicion was an anti-Semitic bias in the study of the region's indigenous languages espoused by the British colonial official John Crawfurd in his *History of the Indian Archipelago* (1820) during the region's British interregnum.[15] Crawfurd's work inaugurated a tendency among later Dutch administrators in the region to favor Indic dimensions of indigenous languages and to elevate the Sanskritized Javanese script over the supposed corruptions of its Semitic Arabic alternative. This hierarchical division between Indic and Semitic scripts was defended through reference to an emerging philological bias, according to which the faithful correspondence between transcription and the spoken word was seen as a sign of linguistic refinement.[16] The absence of voweling in Arabic-script Malay (*jawi*) was thus considered a mark of inadequacy when compared with the more exact correspondence of transcribed Javanese.[17]

Arabic orthography for Malay not only was dismissed for its lack of voweling but was also marginalized for the convenience of Dutch colonial agents. As in French West Africa, the difficulty of mastering Arabic and of surveying *jawi* materials for Dutch officials was a factor, as it became "increasingly clear that teaching the natives to write in roman script would be far easier for the Europeans than learning the rules of *jawi* Malay in Arabic script themselves."[18] The problem of finding reliable interpreters added to a general sense of insecurity that culminated in the identification of Arabic as a possible conduit for Islamic fanaticism.[19] The mastery of Malay in Arabic script presupposed a command of the Arabic language, familiarity with the Qur'an, and the danger of Islamic militancy, as argued in one exemplary statement in the 1860s by Jan Pijnappel, a Malay language instructor for colonial administrators at the Delft Academy.[20] By his estimation, use of Arabic orthography for Malay applied to a local demographic "the pressure of an unwholesome leaven of fanaticism personally acquired by all those who, through knowledge of Arabic script, had access to Arabic culture and the Koran."[21]

The latter half of the nineteenth century witnessed the most direct colonial interventions in the realm of local pedagogical and print languages, as colonial agents continued to favor Sanskritized Javanese influences over the Arabic script for local-language writing. In keeping with Arabic's conflation with the threat of Islamic radicalism, the Dutch advisor for native affairs, Karel Frederik Holle, appointed to the Indies in 1871, sought to regulate religious influence "without explicitly encroaching on the domain of religion" through the modification of local orthographies.[22] Offering a dramatic solution to the Arabic transcription "problem" in West Java, Holle developed an artificial variety of Sanskritized Javanese script to bypass the more customary use of Arabic orthography for the publication of agricultural brochures and a popular monthly in West Java.[23] "The conservation of the Arabic script, if necessary," he explained, "might safely be left to *pesantrens* [religious schools] and *langars* ["chapels" for elementary Qur'anic recitation]."[24]

Holle's efforts anticipate those of Christiaan Snouck Hurgronje, the most influential architect of Dutch Islamic policy toward the turn of the twentieth century (and a figure who featured in our opening chapter). Upon his appointment as advisor for Islamic affairs in the Dutch East Indies in 1889 during the Dutch expansionary war in Aceh, he initiated a policy of ruthless suppression within North Sumatra's clerical community and promoted cultural solutions to Islamic hostility against Dutch colonists. Snouck Hurgronje argued that the expansion of secular or Westernized education in the Dutch East Indies—and the local use of romanized writing as its armature—was among the "surest means of reducing and ultimately defeating the influence of Islam in Indonesia."[25] Eventually falling under the policy front of cultural "Association" with Europe, his advisements after the Aceh War were for the widespread depoliticization of Islam in the Dutch East Indies. This involved a twofold tactic of outward religious neutrality on the part of Dutch agents (as devotional Islam, he claimed, posed no inherent threat) and the vigilant suppression of early signs of political incitement among local clerical communities.[26] Snouck Hurgronje equally argued that a "spiritual annexation" had to follow subjection "by force"—through policy advisements whose influence extended to the realm of local literacies.[27] His suggestions translated into enduring Dutch support for the least religiously radical elements of indigenous society, with the courting of the Javanese aristocracy, *adat* leaders, and customary chiefs from outer islands.

In an extension of Holle's logic, Snouck Hurgronje also promoted the romanization of the Acehnese and Malay languages.[28] A push to displace the use of Arabic occurred under Snouck Hurgronje's counsel with an official circular in 1894 "urging all *penghulus*" (district leaders and religious officiants supported by the Dutch government) "to employ the Latin script" instead of Arabic.[29] In the same year, Snouck Hurgronje promoted the adoption of a standardized system of romanized orthography for archipelago-wide Malay, designed by Dutch linguist and school inspector Charles Adriaan van Ophuijsen.[30] Van Ophuijsen's standard for written Malay (known locally as "Ejaan van Ophuijsen") eventually became a colonies-wide norm for regional print until the end of Dutch colonial rule. Snouck Hurgronje's recommendations were meant to reorient native masses toward European civilization through the secular, Western education of *priyayi* and *adat* aristocrats, greater assimilation of Indies natives into the civil administration, and the development of a more extensive pedagogical infrastructure for the indigenous populace.

Dutch policies of "Association" strikingly compare with parallel developments in French West Africa, where colonial agents promoted European literacies on similar grounds, under the cause of a French colonial *mission civilisatrice*. Of particular note is Snouck Hurgronje's possible influence on this regionally distant process by the turn of the twentieth century: Upon his return from Sumatra, his exposition of Dutch Islamic policy through lectures and publications across Europe was carefully followed by key French scholars and colonial administrators with connections to French West Africa. His lectures on the topic, as noted in earlier chapters, were translated and published in policy-oriented French colonial journals—at roughly the same time that colonial French policies of "Association" were envisioned to moderate and displace an earlier French policy of "Assimilation" (including by former French Indochina–based officers such as Jules Harmand).[31] Also striking is the coincidence of the 1911 French colonial translation and publication of Snouck Hurgronje's Islamic policy recommendations with the decision in French West Africa to prohibit the official use of Arabic within colonial courts and for administrative purposes, despite digraphic French and Arabic having been conventionally employed until then.[32] It again deserves emphasis that the final policy outcome of European policies of "Association" differed in both cases. The French language spread through France's West African colonies, and the Dutch promoted romanization, though both colonies shared a common interimperial concern: that Arabic literacies might become an unchecked conduit for Islamic fanaticism or anticolonial incitement.

The rise of romanized "van Ophuijsen" Malay as a textual standard in the Dutch East Indies bore several implications. Since vowels were not uniformly transcribed in Arabic script and because dialectal differences in Malay are carried through vowel pronunciation, the transition from Arabic to romanized orthography meant selecting a single Malay dialect as a written model for transcribing vowels. In the process, dialectal differences were elided, corresponding to the perception of script unity across arabographic Malay-speaking regions, conjoining present-day Indonesia and Malaysia. In the process of romanization, a system of dialectal unity in Arabic script gave way to the upholding of a single dialect as a romanized model for the proto-Indonesian language in regions controlled by the Netherlands. A final implication follows, as Benedict Anderson explained: "[C]ertain dialects inevitably were 'closer' to each print-language in which an emerging nationalism was expressed," in contrast to "their disadvantaged cousins."[33]

Although Dutch officials envisioned the use of romanized Malay as a colonial asset in the nineteenth century, interinsular Malay was increasingly recast as a unifying medium to challenge the legitimacy of colonial Dutch interests in the early twentieth century. It was renamed the "Indonesian language" (*bahasa Indonesia*) and was envisioned as a nationalist symbol by youth movements of the interwar period—a subject with greater implications explored in the next chapter. The Dutch choice, however, of a model for romanized transcription—falling on the Sumatranese Minang dialect—would have important effects on the beginnings of Indonesian and proto-Indonesian literature, as romanized van Ophuijsen Malay became a pedagogical norm and colonial standard for literary print in the Dutch East Indies (until after independence in 1947, when the orthography was slightly modified).[34] With the establishment of the Dutch colonial publishing house Balai Pustaka—the largest in the colonies when established in 1908 and later transformed into the printing press of independent Indonesia's National Ministry of Education and Culture—ethnic Sumatranese from the Minang region, a minority within the Indies archipelago, came to dominate local publishing by the early 1920s and, as Jeffrey Hadler notes, "in many ways defined official, proto-national Malay."[35] As Hadler describes this process, "[T]hrough literature and the fixing of a protonational language, the [ethnic] Minang Kabau of *Balai Pustaka* saw their best chance to inject aspects of their home culture onto that of the colony."[36]

As a Sumatranese Minang author who published with Balai Pustaka, Hamka wrote with pride in the 1930s of the pioneering role assumed by Sumatranese writers in forging a nationalized Indonesian language through romanized literary platforms. However, in his postindependence accounts of colonial-era linguistic change, he characterized the emergence of romanized Malay as a purely Dutch imposition, without acknowledging the trade-off involved for the Sumatranese Minang with this shift to romanization.[37] His later faulting of Dutch agents for single-handedly de-Arabizing and romanizing the region as a top-down process, therefore, likely attributes to Dutch bureaucrats more power and agency than they deserve. Balai Pustaka played a major catalyzing role in the romanization process, but the commercial calculus of multiple agents in an emerging, regional print market lent such initiatives their necessary momentum for widespread change. The decision by publishers of Islamic periodicals to begin digraphic print in the 1920s (in both Arabic and Latin scripts) likely dealt Arabic a fatal blow as a fading print medium in the region, as Michael Laffan suggests.[38] As romanized Malay gained ground over Arabic-script Malay (*jawi*), agents within the Islamic press, and Hamka as a prominent editor of a leading Islamic journal in Sumatra, were arguably complicit in this process—despite Hamka's eventual arguments to the contrary. Across these regional changes, however, the terms through which ritual Arabic and the romanized Indonesian Malay language would coexist remained a persistent matter of controversy.

Nationalism against Empire: An *ʿAjami* Lineage

When the first natively organized conference on the Indonesian language was held in 1938, a conference that elevated romanized Indonesian as a rising print language and nationalist symbol, Hamka was working in the North Sumatranese capital, Medan, as the chief editor of the popular Islamic periodical *Society's Compass* (*Pedoman Masjarakat*).[39] Hamka was quickly emerging on the North Sumatranese publishing scene as an influential commentator, mediating among his magazine's diverse readers. This readership included the charismatic, nationalist firebrand and eventual first president of independent Indonesia Ahmed Sukarno, a family friend of Hamka's. Issues of the journal were personally sent to Sukarno during the politician's imprisonment for counterimperial agitation (in Bengkulu, West Sumatra).[40] In his editorial role in the late 1930s and early 1940s, Hamka challenged accusations of apostasy emerging against Sukarno in the Javanese Islamic press, after the publication of Sukarno's own controversial essays promoting a future secular republic over a regional Islamic state to countervail Dutch rule (a debate traced more closely in the next chapter).[41]

Hamka's writing in the course of these formative debates ultimately disavowed support for a formally Islamic state, advocating instead for the development of an "Islamic society" to "fill the vessel" of a representative, regional democracy.[42] To defend the pluralist and relatively secular direction of Indonesia's rising nationalist movement, he claimed the alignment of Indonesian nationalism with Islamic precepts on interethnic parity and the complementarity between nationalized Indonesian Malay and the sustainment of devotional Arabic for most Indonesians in a future nation-state. The pages of Hamka's *Pedoman Masjarakat* featured a series of editorials, "Islam and Nationalism" ("Islam dan Kebangsaan," 1939–40), in which Hamka argued that no conflict existed between Indonesian nationalism and the regional sustainment of Islamic forms of ritual practice.[43] In arguments Hamka would later develop during the revolutionary struggle (in monographs published under the titles *Negara Islam* and *Islam dan Demokrasi* in 1945–46), he explained that a caliphal state was not expressly mandated by the Prophet Muhammad, nor was it a model deserving emulation, given past excesses committed in its name.[44] The true key to an emancipated future was nonetheless to be found in ideals that had taken root within the history of Islam itself, through teachings on equality and liberty—even if they were not universally adhered to by leaders claiming the mantle of Islamic statehood. Hamka, for example, cites in illustration of such principles a historical anecdote (hadith) recounting the punishment leveled by the caliph ʿUmar against the Arab commander of Egypt, ʿAmr ibn al-ʿĀṣ, for failing to check the arrogance of his own son for gratuitously assaulting a subaltern Egyptian Coptic Christian and for "treating a free man as though a slave."[45]

On the grounds of such narrative inheritances and of principles embedded within the Qurʾan and hadith, Hamka claimed, Islamic teachings had anticipated the globally equitable formation of new nation-states on the basis of democratic ideals and principles of religious pluralism.[46] "In truth," he wrote, "there is no conflict between the National and Islam, just as there is no conflict between the tree and its branch, for Nationalism is one among the branches of the Islamic faith."[47] In an illustrative translational moment between Arabic- and European-language terms amid the debate over what would become the world's largest Muslim-majority democracy, Hamka advanced the following argument—cited in this chapter's epigraph—with final reference to the Prophet Muhammad's farewell sermon and verse 49:13:

> The difference of language and skin [*bahasa dan koelit*] is not something that can be erased, for the appearance of these differences makes evident a tribe, makes evident a nation [*natie*]. [. . .] All of this is recognized by the faith of Islam. [. . .] By God, there is no difference between *ʿAjam* and *ʿArab* [non-Arab and Arab], between those of white skin and those of black skin. The highest by His side is only who to Him is most devoted [*taqwā*].[48]

Hamka cites the Dutch term for "nation" (*natie*), but the concept is realigned—not with a European precedent or intellectual genealogy but with Arabic-Islamic notions of equality between *ʿajam* and *ʿarab,* across differences of "language and skin." References to the Prophet Muhammad's last sermon (on the equality of *ʿarab* and *ʿajam*) and Qurʾanic verse 49:13 (on the parity of "tribes" and "peoples") offer by Hamka's logic the grounds of an emergent, democratic republic on an international stage. Hamka derives the task of establishing Indonesia as a nation from the reciprocal Arabic imperative *taʿārafū*, of "knowing and being made known" among peoples, suggesting that the pursuit of a global politics of mutual recognition is an Islamic injunction: "Nationalism [*kebangsaan*] is acknowledged by Islam, with the utterance of God [49:13]: 'And we have made of you peoples and tribes that you may know one another, and to one another be known, for indeed the greatest among you by God's esteem is among you the most devout.'"[49] A Qur'anic verse sanctifying polyglossia—the diversity of "your languages and your colors" (*alsinatikum wa-alwānikum*)—is equally cited by Hamka to defend nationalism as the consequence of God's variegation of human languages and "colors" (verse 30:22).[50]

Scholars of Arab nationalism may be tempted to dismiss such arguments as derivative—as claims already well rehearsed in emerging West Asian and North African debates on nationalism in the late nineteenth and early twentieth centuries.[51] To dismiss Hamka as a peripheral writer, however, misses how his own invocations of parity gain gravity in the context in which he was publishing—at the alleged "margins" of a colonized "Muslim world." Lending poignancy to Hamka's reinterpretation of these Arabic-Islamic traditions of parity is its historical timing and location: emerging in the wake of an Orientalist and colonial precedent of reading these same Islamic traditions on parity as either "religious propaganda" or liberalism within the Muslim world's African and Southeast Asian frontiers (as noted in chapter 1). Writers such as Hamka—like Bamba before him at another continental extreme—referenced this shared inheritance to challenge the racialized global hierarchies taking root in a colonized African and Asian expanse, just as these Islamic traditions (i.e., on difference and parity) were cited by Hamka to defend the religious legitimacy of an emerging pluralist republic. Through Arabic as a shared contact language, these Arabic-Islamic teachings connected figures across sites as distant as the colonial Dutch East Indies and French West Africa. Another contextual dimension of such statements deserves emphasis. Defying colonial support for the marginalization of Arabic, Hamka drew on his own literacy in Arabic to reinforce his arguments on the coexistence of Islam and counterimperial nationalisms—and, by extension, to reinforce his claims on the local complementarity of ritual Arabic and a nationalized Indonesian "vernacular" within a future independent state.

In the late 1930s and early 1940s, Hamka not only supported the promotion of Indonesian as a language of unity for the nationalist cause but probed the terms of its coexistence with Arabic as a sustained cultural force and symbol of pan-Islamic unity for a nationwide reading public. Prompted in part by letters sent to Hamka's journal by concerned readers, the pages of *Pedoman Masjarakat* published editorials and popular advice columns to address emerging public debates on the use of the newly nationalized language in the domains of ritual, prayer, and sermons and for the translation of the Qur'an itself.[52] Hamka and his father, also a prominent religious scholar, emerged as influential commentators on the lines of demarcation being negotiated between Arabic as a ritual medium and the recently nationalized Indonesian language (*bahasa Indonesia*).

In response to readers' concerns, Hamka defended sustaining Qur'anic Arabic as a scriptural medium, arguing against the displacement of Arabic by nationalized Indonesian for the reading of the Qur'an as a sacred text; Indonesian was still a historical novelty, he argued, unsuited to this translational task.[53] To defend the use of Arabic as a ritual language in Indonesia, he drew comparisons between Indonesian and colloquial Arabic speech, noting the disparity between a more "bookish" scriptural Arabic and the spoken language of most native Arabic speakers in Arab countries themselves.[54] Even among native Arabic speakers of the Middle East, he claimed, Qur'anic Arabic was confined to sacred ritual or textual reading. Differences between a spoken language and Arabic texts or scripture, Hamka argued, were the norm even in historically custodial centers of Arabic learning and religious sciences; Arabic's coexistence as a religious acrolect with Indonesian, therefore, would not alter the fundamental character of Indonesian nationalism. In a claim likely intended to disarm counterarguments by Dutch-educated secular elites against the religious use of Arabic in Indonesia, he asserted: "Occasional use of the language of the Qur'an will not cause our nationalism to change."[55]

This is a claim that Hamka dramatically revised in the postindependence context, when he insisted that Arabic lexically and orthographically offered the true basis of nationalized Indonesian Malay and of decolonized Indonesian culture. Before drawing attention to this shift, however, I first illustrate how his pre-independence literary writing engaged in experimental conciliations between Arabic and romanized print. Despite the transition to romanized print for his fiction by the 1930s, Hamka's own work continued to be imbued with an arabophone and *jawi* affiliation. Here, I illustrate how his literary experiments shifted with the changing ideological currents prevailing in the late colonial Dutch East Indies, as the region moved toward a future and independent nation-state.

Nostalgia for Arabic in Romanized Print

Hamka's claims on the cultural complementarity of Arabic and Indonesian for a future independent state were anticipated through his own forms of literary adaptation and narrative experimentation during the 1930s. Arabophone solidarities emerge through multiple dimensions in his writing, gesturing to nested or imbricated affinities connecting an emergent Indonesia to a transregional arabophone community. Attachments to both a classical Arabic literary past and the Hijaz as a charismatic space surface in his early work, in his manipulation of readerly affect through the genre of the early Indonesian sentimental novel. Mecca is portrayed as a cosmopolitan religious space for Southeast Asian Malay pilgrims, appearing as a refuge from the constraints of provincial Sumatranese *adat* (customs) in one of his major early novels. Marking the intensification of the Indonesian nationalist movement in the late 1930s, however, Hamka's later fiction characterizes a modern nation as an additional sanctuary: an emergent nation gaining sanction through an interinsular print community, offering new social freedoms to protagonists escaping Sumatranese provincialism.

As I illustrate through his major literary texts, Arabic may have lost its status as a widespread print medium in the region by the 1930s, as attested by Hamka's own publishing choices; it nonetheless retained its status as a symbol and source language for Indonesian literary innovations during this nationally formative decade. Translational dynamics and trace elements of Arabic within his early literature demonstrate this clearly, suggesting that romanized print and Arabic literacies—*rumi* and *jawi*—were less oppositional than his more polemical arguments after independence would suggest. In illustration are Hamka's early works, which include adaptations into Indonesian Malay of the "Arab tale" *Laila Madjnoen* (*Majnūn Laylā*) and of the Egyptian *nahḍawi* author Luṭfī al-Manfalūṭī's Arabic fiction. Hamka might thereby be seen as a translational figure at the nexus of two literary movements: working between the translations of the literary *nahḍa* in Egypt and the development of Balai Pustaka in the Dutch East Indies, with which he published the novels here considered.

Hamka began writing poetry and minor prose works in Arabic and Arabic script in the 1920s, before shifting to romanized print in the 1930s. After this transition, he sustained a connection to Arabic literature as an influence and inspiration for his Malay fiction. Among Hamka's Arabic-script (*jawi*) writing in the 1920s is a lost work, banned by Dutch authorities, whose contents might nonetheless be inferred by Hamka's postindependence publications. The prohibited work, a semipolitical tract entitled *Minangkabau Traditions and the Religion of Islam* (*Adat Minangkabau dan Agama Islam*, 1929), was likely critical of a decadent Minang aristocracy in his native Sumatra, a local elite supported by colonial Dutch rule.[56] Against provincial forms of classism, Islam was likely presented as a countervailing force—a force to which Hamka pledged allegiance throughout his fiction, in keeping with his stated aim (in his inaugural *Pedoman Masjarakat* editorials) to "spread Islamic Art, the Literature of Islam and the Culture of Islam."[57] In the close readings that follow, I consider how diglossic patterns in Hamka's romanized Malay adaptations of Arabic fiction advance this objective, by reconciling an arabophone Malay (*jawi*) cultural inheritance with locally ascendant romanized print.

Hamka's *Laila Madjnoen* (1932) rewrites the classical Arabic love story of the ʿUmayyad-era poet Qays, driven to a state of insanity when his beloved is promised to another suitor in marriage. Hamka advertised his adaptation as a faithful translation of an authentic "Arab Tale" (*Ceritera di Tanah Arab*), though his rendition was an evident expansion of an abridged (two-page) gloss originally published in Arabic.[58] The text of *Laila Madjnoen* at times reads like a stark exchange in dialogue, interwoven with translations of Arabic poetry attributed to the poet-protagonist, Qays. Hamka, however, adds an ethnographic dimension to his narrative, to call attention to its status (or pretension) as an "authentic translation," usually footnoting transliterated Arabic terms.[59] In the opening pages of the text, the narration first slows to translate the exotic, to adapt to a local sensibility and language the foreignness of a desert landscape: to name by reference to Indies foliage the precise shade of the purebred Arabian horse on which the protagonist rides or to translate elements of his desert costume. Laila is described as bearing "typically Arab" feminine features, a moon-shaped face and dark hair contrasting with her pale skin.[60] The Malay narrative breaks into bilingual patterns and transliterated Arabic with the engagement rites of the female protagonist, offering Malay translations of customary Arabic phrases of hospitality.[61] The text reaches a descriptive crescendo with another ethnographic interlude, as the narration slows to translate for a local audience the details of Laila's tragic wedding, with the customary isolation and preparation of the bride, the collection of the *walimatul ʿurs* (an Arabic term for the tools or possessions of the bride and groom), and the grand procession of slaves and horses bearing the *sukduf* (Arabic for "bridal carriage") to Laila's groom.[62]

The story's narrator characterizes himself as an arabophone Malay interpreter with privileged access to "Arab lands." Calling attention to the position of the narrator (or author) as an arabophone guide for the Malay reader are phrases in which he draws attention to the limits of his own translation. Without conveying the exact exchange of the two ill-fated protagonists in their first amorous professions, for example, the narrator suggests his unique access to an original Arabic version of the story through bilingual patterns that compare an indescribable Arabian landscape with a love that cannot be conveyed in speech, an experiential (and aesthetic) boundary for the non-arabophone reader: "The inconstant winds of Arab lands are at times intense and scorching, at times of *indescribable* cold—like the hot winds of ***samum*** during the season of ***shaif*** (summer), which became like love's raging fire between those two youths."[63] Or elsewhere: "If the vast and strange natural beauty of the desert became poetry and melodious speech to them, none know its sweetness and pleasure but those who have also grown accustomed to life observed among the Arabs."[64] Such passages perform the narrative subordination of Malay to a more authoritative Arabic, the latter presented as though a language that resists translation—a language drawn from a region beyond compare. Such passages also privilege the status of the arabophone narrator over the less literate or non-arabophone reader and elevate the Jawi pilgrim to "Arab lands" over his more provincial counterparts.

The text's assertion of Arabic superiority is nowhere more direct than in a didactic statement voiced by the poet-protagonist, Qays; in the course of the novel, he claims to defend Arabic as a poet against "Roman" and "Persian" incursions and identifies "Arabic sciences" and Arabic poetry ("the sciences of language" and "the craft of composing poetry") as cultural riches to be defended from the interference of other languages. With the introduction of Qays, the narration suggests a moral equivalence between his linguistic purism and religious devotion, defending through his poetry the Prophet Muhammad's native tongue, as Qays tells Laila:

> Surely you know that our people fear the destruction of our language, as we have already much mingled with the Persians and the Romans [*Parsi dan Rum*], who have only just become subject to Islamic governance. Against this destruction the caliph guards, and for this reason do I study the various sciences of language, and above all, the craft of composing poetry.[65]

One might read this passage less as a fictionalized statement on early Muslim Arabia and more as an expression of contemporary anxieties on the future of a once-Arabicized East Indies Malay. The cultural dominance of Sanskritized Javanese and growing Dutch influences in the archipelago might be understood as the true forces behind this "feared" "mingling" or interference.

Hamka's second major fictional work of this period (1936–37), *Beneath the Sanctuary of the Kaʿbah* (*Di Bawah Lindoengan Kaʿbah*), is also set in the Hijaz. Its plot unfolds, however, in the wake of the Saudi takeover from Sherif Hussein, after which the rate of Malay pilgrimages to Mecca rose dramatically. The narrative traces the pilgrimage of an impoverished protagonist from Sumatra to Mecca, in the melodramatic style of *rantau* Malay novels: The novel features a stillborn romance between a humble and devout protagonist and the higher-born object of his affections. Hamka employs this star-crossed plot to launch a reformist critique of traditional Sumatranese customs, condemning the materialism of matriarchal marriages brokered between pedigreed families. Mecca emerges in contrast as an idealized space at once egalitarian and otherworldly: a religious cosmopolis offering a more just counterpart to worldly inequities and an alternative to the provincial class consciousness of the protagonist's native Sumatra.[66] The sentimental novel ends with the sudden illness and premature death of the protagonist and his beloved, in the midst of his pilgrimage rites—but with a melodramatic final turn.

As in *Laila Madjnoen*, the strength of the text as a contemporary social critique borrows its moral authority from the narrator's arabophone affiliation with the Prophet Muhammad and his native Hijaz (also shown through diglossic patterns and code-switching in the text between Arabic and Malay).[67] A second narrative pattern advances this affiliation between the Hijaz and the Indies. Temporal progressions are marked in *Sanctuary of the Kaʿbah* through epistolary chronotopes for measuring the passage of time: Delays in sending and receiving news of crucial plot events between the Hijaz and the Indies are central to the tragedy of the novel. The narrative, in other words, renders in tragic form the contrast between a profane, worldly temporality—marking the insurmountable separation of the protagonist from his beloved—and the more utopian and eternally sacred space of Mecca. It is only "in the shadow of the Kaʿbah" where the two lovers unite in a final dreamlike sequence, transcending the earthly division between the Indies and the Arabian Peninsula.[68]

These earlier texts precede a general shift in Hamka's orientation (evident in his writing by 1938), as the Indonesian nationalist movement gained momentum and the Indonesian language became a cultural symbol for rising nationalist sentiments.[69] Hamka's literature appears to mirror this evolution, as it shifts in emphasis from a transregional and pan-Islamic sense of scale to narratives of a more local nationalist sensibility. Hamka's novel *Tenggelamnja Kapal "Van der Wijck"* (*The Sinking of the* Van der Wijck *Ship*) attests to this shifting orientation while engaging a narrative style that still sutures worldly events to a sanctified sense of destiny or fatedness. Adding further dimensions to the text is its status as an Indonesianized adaptation of an Egyptian novel by Luṭfī al-Manfalūṭī's, suggesting Hamka's continued aspiration to align his Indonesian writing with Arabic source texts and charismatic cultural sites in arabophone West Asia or North Africa.[70]

In *Tenggelamnja Kapal "Van der Wijck"* bilingual patterns depend less on the translation of Arabic to Indonesian Malay and more on the translation of the regional Minang dialect into Indonesian. This shift in orientation is ushered into the text with the introduction of *Van der Wijck*'s bi-ethnic protagonist: Half-Makassarese (from the island of Sulawesi), half-Minang (from Sumatra), he finds himself linguistically alienated and culturally orphaned by the conflicting traditions of the matriarchal Minang and patriarchal Makassarese. As an émigré (or internal pilgrim) escaping Sumatra to the island of Java, he shelters in the promise of the national, taking refuge in the emerging contours of the nationalist movement.[71] Hamka's linguistic reorientation toward the national reaches its climax in the novel's final chapter, where the beginnings of modern Indonesian literature are self-referentially portrayed: It features the success of young Sumatranese writers in Java, as the protagonist gains fame for his novel *Terusir* (*Cast Out*)—the title of one of Hamka's own fictional works.[72] Gaining prominence as a writer of Indonesian Malay, the protagonist becomes a leading member of the "Club Anak Sumatera" (Children of Sumatra Club)—a name that evokes the historical Jong Sumatranen Bond, a protonationalist Sumatranese youth movement that famously promoted the Malay language and its literature as a unifying national force for an emerging Indonesia in the 1920s.[73]

Although Hamka borrows central plot elements and epistolary passages from al-Manfalūṭī, he adds a new framing narrative to foreground the local, ethnic origins of his protagonist. He equally embellishes his Indonesian Malay prose with Minang proverbs and traditional poems (*pantuns*), along with extended autoethnographic passages that introduce and critique Minang traditions for an interinsular (Indonesian) audience. When comparing this with al-Manfalūṭī's Arabic version (*Majdūlīn*), it becomes apparent that the bi-ethnic protagonist and interinsular "pilgrim" is Hamka's innovation. Advanced through bilingual passages between Minang and Indonesian, the ethnographic aspect of Hamka's *Van der Wijck* gives his adaptation a narrative arc that is entirely absent from its Arabic counterpart.[74]

Despite Hamka's shift in emphasis from a transregional, pan-Islamic affiliation to an interinsular, proto-national scale between *Kaʿbah* and *Van der Wijck*, one might see a continuity between the two novels in their alignment of worldly plots with a sense of divine destiny. In *Van der Wijck*, this sense of fatedness is facilitated through reference to an event that gave the novel its name: the sinking of the Dutch *Van der Wijck* ship in 1937 in its passage between the Indonesian islands of Java and Sumatra, an event well documented in the local press. If *Kaʿbah* dramatized the tragedy of profane distances from a sacred space (the tragic distance between the Indies and Mecca), it is the interinsular Indies that appears as a hallowed site of shared tragedy in *Kapal "Van der Wijck."*

In making a contemporary event the object of his narration, Hamka translated the tragedy from one of historical unfolding into one of prophesy and fulfillment. Marked by an epistolary format connecting his protagonist to a beloved Sumatranese passenger on the sinking vessel, Hamka's novel projects a sense of fatedness onto a temporally progressive narrative, given his readers' foreknowledge of the event that concludes the tale. The narrative capitalizes on the formation of a proto-national print readership contemporaneous to the sinking of the *Van der Wijck*, as the novel's sentimental effects depend on the local print public's knowledge of this tragedy. Indeed, Hamka's *Van der Wijck* is an example of how the success of early Indonesian novels depended on the journalistic rise of a nationalized print vernacular (as Benedict Anderson suggested in *Imagined Communities*). In Hamka's narrative handling, however, traces of a cosmological sensibility—the attribution of events to providence—feature prominently in the text. The tale proceeds not merely through a secular, progressive temporality but through a sense of destiny and hallowed time—contrary to Anderson's assumptions when interpreting the early Indonesian novel as a purely secular genre.[75]

As we can see in these novels by Hamka, early Indonesian sentimental fiction adapted to the demands of cultural influences often colonially framed as antagonistic. His literary work inscribed the traces of competing languages and scripts while sustaining a connection to pan-Islamic and emerging national sensibilities in literary form. Despite Hamka's gradual, interwar disuse of Arabic orthography, romanized Malay print offered him, as a Sumatranese writer, a literary platform of unprecedented reach, even if it meant abandoning on the surface a *jawi* (Arabic script) tradition. Indies-wide, romanized print in this way allowed Sumatranese authors to represent Sumatranese customs to an interinsular audience and to sustain an arabophone Malay sensibility in adapted forms.

This exemplifies where Benedict Anderson was correct, while demonstrating the limits of his premises on the Indonesian novel and print vernaculars in *Imagined Communities*: The contours of Indonesian nationalism were indeed envisioned through complementary forms of newsprint and the novel, as he argued, but these visions arose amid the sustained elevation of Arabic as a charismatic language in the Indies, contrary to his assertions. Early Indonesian novels as representational sites for imagining the nation were not merely literary innovations in vindication of a lost religious cosmology, eroded through the decline of a devotional (Arabic) language. They were instead viewed by one of Indonesia's most prominent writers as a medium through which the enduring contours of religious identity could be reinvented within an ascendant print language and print market.

Script as Symbol: Arabic in Indonesia

In the 1930s, Hamka defended the complementarity of Arabic as a ritual language and nationalized Indonesian, but his emphases shifted in the wake of Indonesian independence, after a turbulent decade that witnessed the region's subjection to Japanese occupation during World War II (1942–45) and the overthrow of Dutch rule during a violent postwar revolutionary struggle (1945–49). Hamka increasingly challenged what he believed was the excessive Javanization and Indic-Sanskritization of postrevolutionary Indonesian national culture. His publications during the 1950s became marked by a nostalgic regret for the widespread disuse of Arabic orthography in Indonesian print. The decolonized future of Indonesian culture had an orthographic analogue, he now asserted. Arabic script forms and loanwords deserved a national revival; only with its re-Arabization could the Indonesian language be classed as a truly decolonized medium.[76] Observing the sustained use of Arabic script in the adjacent region of British-controlled Malaya, Hamka argued that a regional arabophone community within Malay Southeast Asia had been artificially partitioned through colonial boundary-drawing, resulting in the separation of Dutch and British domains of influence in the nineteenth century. Romanization in Indonesia, he claimed, was therefore a historic affront to this arabophone (and arabographic) Malay community.

Although Hamka had argued prior to independence that Indonesian nationalism would remain unchanged by the sustaining of Arabic as a ritual acrolect, he reversed this position after Indonesian independence.[77] By the

1950s, he insisted that Arabic offered Indonesian nationalism its most authentic cultural roots, given the entrenchment of Islamic religious education in Indonesia's rural regions. An attention to questions of class informs Hamka's postindependence defense of Arabic as a representative source of Indonesian national culture; European lexical borrowings and code-switching in Indonesian print, he claimed, were exclusionary and unrepresentative practices favored only by elites in more European-oriented urban centers.[78] The greater proximity of Indonesia's rural Muslim masses to Arabic (through continuous, if informal, Islamic schooling) was reason enough for a national return to Arabic orthography and for the enrichment of nationalized Indonesian with Arabic terms.

At this point in his career as a public figure, Hamka characterized Balai Pustaka as an exclusively colonial incursion—notwithstanding his former status as an author whose most popular works were published by the Dutch publishing house in the 1930s.[79] Through Balai Pustaka Arabic literacies became publicly invisible, he argued, amounting to a virtual illiteracy:

> The Arabic script [*huruf Arab*] was no longer accorded importance after Balai Pustaka was established. Since then, the life of the Arabic script was no longer in the domains of the government. We had to accept the reality that Latin script was the script that we were obliged to use—to the point that the sentiment arose that <u>those uneducated in Latin script were deemed illiterate</u>. [. . .] After the Nationalist Youth Congress of 1928 officially changed the name of the Malay language into Indonesian, the Arabic script became even more remote. [. . .] Previously, the Arabic language lent the Malay language its greatest, most flourishing qualities. But the New Indonesian language grows not from Arabic but, rather, is propped up by the Dutch language, is infused by the Dutch language.[80]

Frustrated by the long shadow of Dutch influence on Indonesian print, Hamka envisioned counterimperial progress as a return to what he imagined was a purer Malay, more closely aligned with Arabic. He now viewed Indonesia as a fundamentally Islamic and arabophone state, which deserved to extend its cultural solidarities—if not its postindependence borders—to Malaysia, a former British colony that had retained its orthographic use of Arabic through the 1950s.

Hamka wrote his most controversial publication on language politics after independence on the occasion of Malaysian independence from Britain in 1957, a work entitled *Kenang-Kenangan ku di Malaya* (*My Memoirs of Malaya*).

A nostalgic and polemical work, his *Memoirs of Malaya* argued that the historical patrimony of pan-Malay, arabophone identity conjoined insular Indonesia and peninsular Malaysia (separated as Dutch and British colonies in the nineteenth century).[81] Reverting to the Arabic script for this publication, Hamka praised the sustained Malaysian use of Arabic orthography relative to its mass abandonment in Indonesia (expanding on a view first expressed in the early 1950s): "[T]he path of the Indonesian language has increasingly deviated from the spirit of Islam. Not like the Malay language in peninsular Malaya that still employs the Arabic script."[82] Indonesian writing, he argued, had become beset with the "rootlessness" of the Indonesian language, a language "now beginning to waver beneath a wind that moves in every direction."[83] Hamka's unusual decision to publish in Arabic orthography and to first release his book overseas in Malaysia (through a Singaporean publisher) positioned the publication as a challenge to dominant market trends in Indonesia. This decision also allowed him to critique contemporary Indonesian language practice to an audience comfortably removed from Indonesia's increasingly polemical debates on Arabic and nationalized Malay.[84]

Hamka's linguistic claims regarding the importance of arabophone writing to a sense of unity across Malaysia and Indonesia had a political analogue. Since the difference, he argued, between a historically arabographic *bahasa Melayu* (Malay language) and a romanized *bahasa Indonesia* (Indonesian language) was negligible and colonially imposed, the political and cultural difference between *kebangsaan Melayu* (Malay nationality) and *kebangsaan Indonesia* (Indonesian nationality) was equally arbitrary. This argument provoked Sukarno's suspicion at the height of Indonesia's confrontation with British-controlled Malaysia in 1957. According to Hamka's later interviews (in the 1970s), his desire for a cultural rapprochement with Malaysia, advanced by his arguments on the arabophone patrimony it shared with Indonesia, contributed to his imprisonment by Sukarno. During his imprisonment, Hamka penned a de facto translational work of Qur'anic exegesis (*tafsir*) as a source of personal solace and devotional labor.[85]

Hamka's polemical contributions to language debates in Indonesia illuminate the stakes of Indonesia's acculturation within a territorially and ideologically ambiguous arabophone community; for Hamka, Arabic's status as a cultural force challenged the very legitimacy of colonially inherited boundaries. His legacy illustrates (contrary to Benedict Anderson's suggestion in *Imagined Communities*) that Arabic was not a medium in unilateral "decline" as the political and cultural boundaries of Malay Southeast Asia were reassessed in the mid-twentieth century; it had its defenders as a counterimperial symbol in the wake of Indonesian independence. The nature of Arabic's coexistence with Indonesian, however, remained a controversial issue across the twentieth century—an issue pursued in subsequent chapters on literary innovations generated by language debates in postindependence Indonesia.[86]

Vernacular and Sacred: Enduring Coexistence

Six centuries of Islamization in the Indonesian region contributed to the adoption of the Arabic script for Malay transcription. This adoption of Arabic script inaugurated a pattern of diglossia in religious pedagogy, according to which Arabic became "the authoritative language of learning" and Malay became a "language of popular exposition," as historian A. H. Johns makes clear in his introduction to Qur'anic exegesis in Malayophone Southeast Asia.[87] The regional introduction of the Latin script and gradual romanization of local print nonetheless radically altered the relationship of most Indonesians to the Qur'an as a sacred text. With the rise of romanized literacies, a new equilibrium had to be negotiated between a Malay progressively transcribed in Latin orthography and Arabic as a religious acrolect whose status suffered, by Hamka's estimation, from lower literacy rates in the postindependence context. Despite this growing encroachment of Latinate literacies, a trade-off might nonetheless be discerned within the devotional realm. Increased literacy rates in the region—even in romanized form—meant greater access to the textual experience of the Qur'an for most Indonesians; its translation and publication in Latin-script Malay as opposed to *jawi*, however, meant an added degree of removal from the original text. To read figures like Hamka on this process, the widespread adoption of romanized Malay for Indonesian Muslims resulted in a linguistic and literary crisis that remained insufficiently resolved by orthodox Muslim scholars. As Hamka later claimed when commenting on New Order translations of the Qur'an into Indonesian, Islamic scholars as a group had failed to address the aesthetic demands of Qur'anic translation and exegesis for a contemporary reading public.[88]

In Hamka's contributions to language debates in Indonesia, the continued influence of Arabic in insular Southeast Asia with the rise of Indonesian nationalism is uncontestable. Taking exception to Benedict Anderson's counterargument that romanized print in Indonesia merely "replaced a 'dead' language of the divine," Michael Laffan contends that

> the Arabic script was an important signifier of alterity and nationhood not so readily erased by the modern newspaper. Indeed, in the early twentieth century, the Jawa [an Arabic ethnonym for Malay Southeast Asians] had recourse to two ecumenical languages—Arabic and Malay—each able to be written in the one sacred script making Anderson's [. . .] view, for that time at least, a gross overstatement. [. . .] Although the *jawi* [Arabic-script] variant of Malay did ultimately fade in Indonesia, the shift from sacred to vernacular involved more a bifurcation of communalisms than the assertion of one over another. [. . .] Arabic continues to retain sacred force for all Muslims as both revealed and enunciated speech, while Malay continues to unite members of the largest Muslim nation in the world.[89]

Laffan identifies the relationship of sacred and vernacular communalisms more accurately—as a linguistic bifurcation rather than an assertion of the vernacular over the sacred—but his examination of these dynamics does not extend beyond the first decades of the twentieth century. As such, his observations on the impact of the Arabic script as a "signifier of alterity and nationhood" generally conclude with the decline of the *jawi* press in the 1910s and 1920s, though the specter of a *jawi* (Arabic script) legacy in insular Southeast Asia nonetheless continued to impact Indonesian print culture and to challenge local projections of secular nationalism in Indonesia after the 1920s. There is reason for Laffan's conclusions to be explored and extended beyond the parameters of his own evidence.[90]

In the Indonesian case, Hamka's writing through the 1950s exhibits the traces of this "bifurcation of communalisms." His work demonstrates that the Arabic script became a nostalgic emblem for an arabophone, pan-Malay (Jawi) community, even after the 1920s, when the number of Arabic-script periodicals in the Dutch East Indies had decreased.[91] As we have seen, Hamka's positions—and his approach to these communalisms—shifted dramatically over the course of his career, in line with the changing contours of national language debates within Indonesia. In his earlier literature of the 1930s, he sought to reconcile these two communalisms ("sacred" and "vernacular") in ways that adapted arabophone Muslim sensibilities to emerging *rumi* print networks.[92] Though Hamka used the voice of his protagonist to protest the perceived contamination of Arabic culture with "Roman" influences in his colonial-era adaptation of *Laila Madjnoen*, it was not until the rise of language debates after independence that his protests against Europeanized literacies gained their greatest force. As his legacy attests, even within predominantly romanized Indonesian/Malay print, the Arabic language and script retained their significance as symbols of pan-Malay Islamic community in the twentieth century, at times rivaling more Java-centric and secular visions for an Indonesian national future.

Whereas the present and preceding chapters focused on colonial-era dynamics, the second section of this book more specifically considers developments after World War II with the rise of emerging nationalisms. It moves in roughly chronological order, tracing how counterimperial nationalisms were anticipated and evolved in the mid-twentieth century across several sites. We shall first revisit Indonesian cultural debates from World War II through the Bandung Conference, before transitioning to postrevolutionary Egypt after Bandung and amid the nationalization of the Suez Canal in the mid-1950s. Controversies in the late 1950s and early 1960s over pan-Africanism and emerging nationalisms are then followed through a chapter on Senegal—the site of French West Africa's colonial capital and a country that risked losing its regional prestige after French West Africa's dissolution into constituent nation-states.

SECTION II

Vernacular Difference and Emerging Nationalisms

5

Vernacular Revolutions

THE FIRST ASIA-AFRICA CONFERENCE of newly independent states, held in Bandung, Indonesia, in 1955, was hailed by sympathetic observers as an event as historically significant as the European Renaissance.[1] The renowned African American novelist and journalist Richard Wright, a leading and frequently cited informant on the conference proceedings, noted that Ahmed Sukarno, the hosting Indonesian president, used a cartographic image in his opening remarks to justify this otherwise disparate gathering. According to Wright, Sukarno "placed his finger upon the geographical gateway" of colonial entry to Asia, a gateway Sukarno identified as "the life line of imperialism," running "from the Straits of Gibraltar, through the Mediterranean, the Suez Canal, the Red Sea, the Indian Ocean, the South China Sea, and the Sea of Japan."[2] Sukarno's rhetoric on this occasion transformed an enormous stretch of the global map into a visceral image of common grievance. "For most of that enormous distance," Sukarno proclaimed, "the territories on both sides of this line were colonies, the people were unfree, their futures mortgaged to an alien system. Along that life line, that main artery of imperialism, there was pumped the lifeblood of colonialism."[3]

Sukarno characterized the regions of Asia and Africa through two grievances. The first was their shared history of colonial "unfreedom"; the second (which was unremarked upon by Wright) was that mutual ignorance had overtaken both continents as geographically proximate but imperially divided sites. Sukarno explained: "Relatively speaking, all of us gathered are neighbors. [. . .] Many of us have a common religion. Many of us have common cultural roots. We have so much in common. And yet we know so little of each other."[4] Despite efforts to correct this dilemma after the Bandung Conference, the iconic gathering left open the question of how to resolve the challenge of mutual ignorance across Asia and Africa's linguistic diversity and through both continents' shared languages of historical contact.

The littoral routes identified by Sukarno as the "main artery" of European colonialism, drawing together regions from northwest Africa to the Strait of Malacca and beyond, were notably the same spaces through which Arabic speakers could venture without a translator before the rise of European empires. Notwithstanding the linguistic diversity of this transcontinental space, Arabic was the only medium for such widespread contact until the colonial introduction of European languages and Latinate scripts. In the wake of imperial British naval ascendancy in the Indian Ocean region, and then the Allied victories in World War II (ushering forth an era of Anglo-American global hegemony), observations about the dominance of European languages at the Bandung Conference suggest the direction in which these changes were moving globally. As Richard Wright noted, one curiosity of the Bandung Conference was that delegates widely used English to proclaim a common counterimperial cause.[5] At the highest levels of diplomatic brokering and political exchange, Arabic, a once-unparalleled language of transcontinental contact and diplomacy across coastal Asia and Africa, had been displaced by a rival contact language by the mid-twentieth century. Given Bandung's aspirations to recognize anew the historical connections shared across an Asian-African space, what did the displacement of Arabic by colonial contact languages imply for the politics of culture and of mutual recognition among emerging Asian-African states in the mid-twentieth century?

For his part, Wright was unequivocal when interpreting the dominance of English at Bandung: He concluded that the conference proceedings were gesturally directed to a former colonial and European/American audience.[6] But rather than perceiving English as a self-alienating choice for non-native Asian and African speakers (who likely had few alternatives at Bandung), Wright discerned a poetic justice in their acts of linguistic appropriation, seeing them as a rejoinder to earlier revolutionary calls for equality only partially fulfilled by Europe and America's own revolutionary precedents.[7] By Wright's estimation, English was being tested in unprecedented ways with this Asian-African gathering, as the language was gaining "a new extension of feeling, of moral knowledge," through a rising preponderance of non-native Asian and African speakers and through their counterimperial claims.[8]

The dominance of English at Bandung and the forms of moral knowledge it presumably conveyed, however, generate several open questions, not least regarding the global legacy of alternatives to English as an Asian-African contact language. The delegates at Bandung predominantly spoke (or were translated into) English as they pronounced a common cause. Moving beyond the metropolitan-centered projections of Bandung's pronouncements—and out of English—into the linguistically diverse, "Babelian" contexts that the Bandung front allegedly represented, in what languages of mutual recognition would that common cause endure? What nuances remained untranslated into English in the call for Asian-African solidarities and forms of cultural recovery, unobserved by an anglophone figure such as Wright? What fell beneath the translational thresholds that informed Wright's ruminations on the long arc of liberationist struggles bending finally toward justice, ascending to a broader audience of global recognition?

Wright intuits—but fails to fully discern—how Bandung as a counterimperial front gathered statesmen possessing uncommon eloquence in their native tongues. Observing the hosting president Sukarno from the sidelines of the conference, Wright concluded that Sukarno was a master orator and charismatic wordsmith. He inferred that "this man had done nothing all his life but utilize words to capture the attention and loyalties of others."[9] Speaking for and among "the voiceless" and "unregarded," a community of "little physical power" incapable of "indulging in power politics," Sukarno proclaimed that "the peoples of Asia and Africa, [. . .] far more than half of the population of the world, [. . .] can mobilize what I have called the *Moral Violence of Nations* in favor of peace."[10] Wright developed an unmistakable impression of what unified this otherwise disparate gathering of Asian-African delegates across a common defensive front by observing Sukarno's oratorical tactics:

> [A]s I sat listening, I began to sense a deep and organic relation here in Bandung between race and religion, two of the most powerful and irrational forces in human nature. Sukarno was not evoking these twin demons; he was not trying to create them; he was trying to organize them [. . .]. The reality of race and religion was there, swollen, sensitive, turbulent [. . .].[11]

Such passages indicate that Sukarno represented for Wright an Asian-African "color line," which Wright conflated with a defensive, subaltern religious posturing. This understanding compelled Wright to conclude his account of the Bandung Conference with the question of whether "racial and religious feelings [were] already set in so deeply in Asia and Africa that it would be impractical to transform and attach them to secular and practical goals."[12] (In such assertions by an American observer, one might discern the uneasy identification of Asia and Africa's newly independent states with a vestigial religious alterity derived from a colonial past—as though the aura of a once-colonized "Muslim world" endured in Bandung.)

As the materials examined in this chapter suggest, however, Wright was not entirely attuned to the strains of political pragmatism that informed Sukarno's rhetoric at Bandung or to Sukarno's pragmatic modulation of "racial and religious" feelings in an Indonesian language context. A prominent nationalist politician since the 1920s and 1930s, Sukarno was known in Indonesia for insisting that "in a future Indonesian state, there are only two alternatives politically: unity of religion and state without democracy, or democracy with the state separated from religion."[13] Promoting the latter alternative on the Republican Turkish model, as head of state Sukarno sought to reconcile rival branches of Indonesia's emerging independence movement, branches that he characterized throughout his political career as "Nationalism, Islamism, and Marxism."[14] His postindependence political brokering also coincided with forms of outreach across the archipelago's islands (after a Japanese occupation during World War II). Hailing from Indonesia's most populous island of Java, Sukarno built close alliances with politicians from Sumatra, the region's next most populous island, appointing as his first prime minister the Sumatranese Socialist politician Sutan Sjahrir in 1945.

An additional protagonist within this chapter—a politically enigmatic and now culturally iconic figure—factors into Sukarno's relationship with his first Sumatranese prime minister: Sutan Sjahrir's nephew Chairil Anwar. Chairil (as he is known in Indonesia) would eventually become Indonesia's most iconic poet during the nation's independence struggle. At the close of Japan's occupation of Indonesia, it was Chairil who spread word of Japan's surrender to his peers within Indonesia's nationalist youth movement (*pemuda*)—a movement whose leadership then pressured Sukarno to formally declare Indonesia an independent state. Although Sukarno had been reluctant to declare Indonesian independence due to the widespread presence of occupying Japanese troops in 1945, this pressure eventually forced his hand in declaring independence on August 17 of that year—a matter of days after Japan's capitulation to Allied forces with the bombings of Hiroshima and Nagasaki.[15] Chairil Anwar famously commemorated this historic declaration through his poetry.

Moving from political rhetoric to poetry in the Indonesian language during the formative years surrounding the national independence movement, the balance of this chapter engages in connected readings between Sukarno's rhetorical motifs as a revolutionary leader and a secular visionary for a future

Indonesia and poetry by Chairil derived from Sukarno's speeches. I begin by considering how Sukarno elevated forms of Indonesian nationalist rhetoric to an international stage at Bandung, when he lent poetic form to idealist political abstractions of interreligious parity and secular pluralism on a global scale. I pivot out of Sukarno's English rhetoric at Bandung to his Indonesian speeches, to draw the following connection: Poetic motifs and forms of linguistic code-switching in his English and Indonesian speeches subtly reflect the historical controversies surrounding Indonesia's future as an emerging secular or pluralist nation-state.

I examine how the imagined stakes of national belonging culminate with one of Chairil's most iconic poems, which envisions a symbolic "pact" with Sukarno at the point of Indonesia's declaration of independence. I demonstrate that this poem draws on a specific set of motifs employed by Sukarno to characterize the spirit of revolutionary change as "flood" or "fire." Through such motifs, Chairil's poetry invoking Sukarno appears connected to broader political debates on the secular future of the emerging Indonesian republic. On these grounds, I consider the stakes and fracture points of national belonging through selections of Chairil's poetry, examining the tensions between a speaker's sense of collective consciousness and individual skepticism.

This chapter's principal argument derives from the position of *bahasa Indonesia*, the nationalized language of Indonesia, as a radical cultural experiment for national unity, a language ideologically and formally malleable at the foundations of an emerging nation in the 1930s and 1940s. Building from previous scholarship on Indonesian as a unifying cultural force, I consider in novel ways how lexical enrichments and poetic experiments in the language were connected to specific motifs in currency among Indonesia's nationalist leadership in the 1930s and 1940s. These include translational motifs that reflected the agonistic pressures of both Arabic and European cultural influences on Indonesian as a literary and political medium, illuminating potential fracture points for the language as a unifying force. I highlight specific metaphors shared between Indonesian revolutionary poetry and political rhetoric of the period and view them in connection to broader questions about the communal boundaries and pluralist future of an emergent Indonesia. In this way, we can see how the vital influences on Indonesian of historically sacralized languages such as Arabic were evident through national print platforms and through a poetic corpus that emerged with Indonesia's foundations as an independent republic.

Indonesia as Paradigm for Asia-Africa: The Meanings of Bandung (beyond English)

Limited to Sukarno's Bandung speeches in English, Richard Wright missed the implications and nuances of Sukarno's oratorical tactics in Indonesian terms. He misread, to some degree, what Sukarno foundationally stood for on an Indonesian political stage in the formative years of the Indonesian republic and overlooked how Sukarno's relatively secularist ideas were rechanneled within his Bandung address as a political pragmatism in the service of an emerging Indonesian state. Wright seems equally unaware that Sukarno recurrently had to defend himself against charges of apostasy within Indonesia's more conservative Muslim circles after his rejection of an Islamic religious constitution for a newly independent Indonesia.[16]

Wright, in other words, overlooks the position of Sukarno as a doubly embattled figure on the Bandung stage, implicated in a two-front struggle for both international recognition and internal legitimacy. On the one hand, Sukarno was speaking back to largely "racial" and "religious" others within metropolitan European and American circles; on the other, he was speaking defensively across internal front lines against more Islamocentric challengers on the future and ideological legitimacy of a religiously pluralist Indonesia. Sukarno's rhetorical finessing and international branding of an independent Indonesian state was defined not only against a colonial European predecessor but against ideological challengers within (post)revolutionary Indonesia. His political rhetoric, forged at the convergence of colonially inflected European and Islamically inflected Arabic literacies, more broadly reflects this situation, although it falls beneath the thresholds of anglophone visibility as Wright discerns them.

The terms of a delicate and improbable solidarity for the fledgling Indonesian republic despite its internal diversity were not a matter of mere rhetorical abstraction but addressed the dilemma of collective survival in the minds of Indonesia's rising nationalist leadership. Implicated were the grounds of interconfessional solidarity and interethnic coexistence, as the new nation-state, Sukarno repeatedly argued, could not survive as a religious republic that threatened to alienate its many religious and ethnic minorities.[17] Sukarno was openly fighting an Islamist insurrection (Darul Islam Indonesia) and factionalist splinter groups in parts of Sumatra and Java at the time of the Bandung Conference, a fact that also seems to have fallen beneath Wright's purview, though in his account he notes what he calls the "mysterious presence" of "Indonesian bandits" wreaking havoc across the countryside.[18]

What appears for Wright to be Sukarno's (and Indonesia's) promotion of a racialized religious front deserves to be tempered by counterevidence subtly projected onto the Bandung stage through Sukarno's own speech—with Sukarno's vision of a "practical" solution to the "problem" of interethnic and interreligious solidarities within Indonesia and across an Asian-African expanse (to reuse Wright's own terms).[19] It is in this light that one might understand Sukarno's description of the Indonesian archipelago as a paradigm for Asia-Africa itself. As Sukarno proposed:

> Indonesia is Asia-Africa in small. It is a country with many religions and many faiths. We have in Indonesia Moslims, we have Christians, we have Civa-Buddhists, we have peoples with other creeds. Moreover, we have many ethnic units, such as Achehnese, Bataks, Central-Sumatrans, Sundanese, Central-Javanese, Madurese, Toradjas, Balinese [. . .] . But thank God, we have our will to unity. We have our Pancha Sila. We practice the "Live and let live" principle, we are tolerant to each other. Bhinneka Tunggal Ika—Unity in Diversity—is the motto of the Indonesian state. We are one nation.[20]

Notwithstanding Sukarno's praise in his Bandung speech of Asia-Africa as the birthplace of many of the world's "great religions," his ultimate emphasis on the common need for the emerging states of Asia and Africa to transcend religious attachments reflects his ambivalent gestures to Asian-African religiosity as both a source of solidarity and a potential fracture point. Wright accurately noted Sukarno's characterization of "the East" as a common ground for religious communities in historical formation.[21] But Sukarno qualified the political impact of religiosity in public life. "Must we be divided by the multiformity of our religious life?" he asked in his speech, treading the tenuous grounds of solidarity extended toward theocratic regimes represented at Bandung while advancing an antitheocratic argument in broader terms.[22]

It is in this light as well that Sukarno referenced a line of Javanese poetry—*bhinneka tunggal ika*—that yielded the Indonesian nationalist motto ("Bhinneka tunggal ika," or "Unity in diversity").[23] Whether Wright sees it or not, this invocation of a fourteenth-century poem in twentieth-century politics frames the threat of religious or sectarian conflict as a perennial political problem. Composed by the Buddhist Javanese poet Mpu Tantular during the

Majapahit Empire, the line "bhinneka tunggal ika tan hana dharma mangrwa" ("there is unity in diversity, for there is no duality in truth") was adopted as a nationalist slogan for the fledgling Indonesian republic, rising to a principle of "unity in diversity."[24] But the lines were borrowed from the poem's originally prayerful invocation against the world's destruction after a period of strife between Javanese Buddhists and Hindus, in lines of verse that had once imaginatively redressed historically Shaivist and Buddhist tensions on the island of Java before the region's widespread Islamization.[25] Within the mid-twentieth-century politics of an emergent Indonesia, these fourteenth-century lines of Javanese verse were repurposed by ascendant nationalist circles as a principle of interreligious (and interethnic) coexistence within an evolving republic—translationally glossed by Sukarno at Bandung as a principle of "unity in diversity" and "live and let live."[26]

The meanings of this invocation are clarified by Sukarno's claim that religious diversity and equal rights across religious differences not only were a matter of Indonesia's national survival but must be recognized across "Asian-African" regions and former colonial territories as the grounds of a new universal value:

> Unless we realise that all great religions are one in their message of tolerance and in their insistence on the observance of the principle of "live and let live," unless the followers of each religion are prepared to give the same consideration to the rights of others everywhere, unless every State does its duty to ensure that the same rights are given to the followers of all faiths, unless these things are done, religion is debased, and its true purpose perverted. Unless Asian-African countries realise their responsibilities in this matter [. . .] the very strength of religious beliefs, which should be a source of unity and a bulwark against foreign interference, will cause its destruction, and may result in destroying the hardwon freedom which large parts of Asia and Africa have achieved by acting together.[27]

This was not quite the adaptation of European liberal ideas to an Asian-African context, Sukarno argued (claiming in the process that a European-derived "Liberalism" "is obsolete"), but, rather, a matter of political pragmatism for Asian-African survival.[28] Across a bicontinental expanse, the state-sanctioned enshrinement of equal rights despite religious differences was a fundamental safeguard against foreign re-interference, he claimed. Sukarno here implied the value of reconciling and transcending differences of race and religion, without which the ethnically and religiously diverse Indonesian archipelago would politically balkanize. As Sukarno emphasized of both Asia and Africa, and of Indonesia as their paradigmatic microcosm, embracing the notion of unity in diversity—*bhinneka tunggal eka*—was a matter of survival for this newly independent bloc of states. These states otherwise risked the intrusion of external forces that could capitalize on Asia-Africa's religious and racial diversity to weaken their sovereignty. As much as he lauded the religious inheritance of "Asia-Africa," Sukarno forewarned that such foreign manipulations risked staging within Asia and Africa a resurgent neocolonial future of imperial division and reconquest.

The Political Life of Poetic Language: Code-Switching and Secularist Rhetoric

In both his Bandung address and his major speeches surrounding the independence struggle, Sukarno took poetic liberties by drawing controversial European linguistic figurations into his rhetoric. These poetic liberties illuminate Sukarno's position as an embattled secularist figure in Indonesia. Local responses to his use of such figurations were influenced by two mutually informed debates that coincided with the Indonesian independence movement: debates on the scriptural parameters of national culture and the religious contours of an independent Indonesia.[29] In these debates, the nationalized language of Indonesia became a virtual battleground and an embattled symbol, where European lexical borrowings or code-switching in the mouths of politicians could be interpreted as a neocolonial sign.

Indonesia had been a Dutch colony until the region's Japanese occupation from 1942 to 1945 and was among the first of Europe's colonies to declare independence in 1945. Following the immediate postwar situation, the fledgling nation struggled to build solidarities across an archipelago of several thousand islands. In the wake of the Japanese occupation and surrender to Allied forces after the war, the question of whether Dutch forces would reoccupy the region persisted, as did the question of what form the new independent nation would take should that reoccupation fail. Which islands of the former Dutch Empire would the new nation-state encompass? What role would its predominantly Muslim communities play in the new republic? Would Indonesia transform into an independent Islamic state, or would it become a pluralist republic to accommodate its many religious and ethnic minorities? The internal foundations and external boundaries of an independent Indonesia were in question at the onset of the revolutionary struggle that began in 1945.

These open questions were reflected in evolving debates on the languages of national unity and the cultural grounds of an emergent solidarity. What had once been known as *pasar Malay* ("bazaar" or "market Malay," the maritime lingua franca of the archipelago) was evolving into a new political language during the interwar period and in the course of the revolutionary struggle. A rising nationalist leadership saw the language as more equitable than alternatives such as Dutch (limited to colonially trained elites) and Javanese (the native language of Indonesia's largest ethnic population but marked by hierarchical registers indicating a speaker's social rank).[30] Envisioned as a medium of proto-national unity as early as 1928, the Indonesian language (*bahasa Indonesia*) was not, however, fully formalized as the language of the emerging nation-state until after the Japanese occupation, a period when the former colonial Dutch language was prohibited.[31]

Indonesian was a medium built heavily from borrowings from other languages—such as Javanese, Dutch, Arabic, and Sanskrit—by virtue of its multilingual language planners and nationalist leadership. By 1966, some fifteen years after Indonesian independence and a decade after the Bandung Conference, European- and American-based observers of Indonesian politics were claiming that Indonesian had developed into a strange synthesis of different influences by virtue of its borrowings from other languages. Rather than condemning Indonesian for its inauthenticity, Indonesianist historian Benedict Anderson (more generously than his colleagues Clifford Geertz and Herbert Luethy) considered the newly nationalized language a generative cultural experiment, claiming that it "represented a project, an aspiration to unity and equality, a generous wager on the future," and an exceptional logistical feat, given the nation's extreme internal diversity.[32] The late Dutch colonial era, he argued, had in effect fostered a cluster of segregated literacies across the archipelago, leaving politicians of the fledgling nation-state of Indonesia with the exceptional challenge of mediating across these segregations.[33]

Anderson presciently offered other reasons not to dismiss the language as a political force, noting that—once consolidated pedagogically—it would orient a rising generation of Indonesians, including an ascendant political class for whom it would serve as a virtually native medium. For the nationalist intelligentsia in the interwar and revolutionary period, however, the Indonesian language was a novelty whose adoption involved an incessant bilingual (if not multilingual) code-switching—what Anderson calls a "two-mindedness."[34] Sukarno, for example, like many nationalist elites of his generation, was a

Dutch-trained polyglot with partial literacies in at least three or four languages, and he drew from multiple sources when navigating the fault lines of Indonesia's emerging language debates. Sukarno and the poets who imagined themselves his public interlocutors might therefore be considered translational figures in their innovative framing of a new nationalist rhetoric.[35]

A rising generation of European-trained nationalist politicians expressing themselves in the Indonesian language (including Sukarno) needed to be relentless internal translators, treading various fault lines as they probed the ideological terms of the new language's orientation. Lexical borrowings and infelicitous turns of phrase that suggested an overreliance on European collocations risked appearing tethered to a colonial past. And yet, Sukarno's generation of politicians needed to integrate European influences into the new language (as a sign of vernacular elevation against European-styled notions of progress), even as they distinguished the language from such influences (as a sign of counterimperial distinction). Arguments about translational borrowings and infelicities—particularly as they surfaced in the rhetoric of revolutionary nationalist leaders, such as Sukarno—reflected this cross-sectional history of a language in flux.

It appears to have been one of Sukarno's bicephalist or "double-minded" idiosyncrasies to translationally rely on controversial European figurations to defend a secular future for Indonesia and to envision "modernized" Qur'anic literacies and interpretive practices within a future Indonesian republic.[36] To read Sukarno in the 1930s and 1940s, the ideological or religious legitimacy of an emerging nation-state beyond a caliphal system or standard depended on the spread of more progressive, "elastic" scriptural and religious literacies beyond Arabic source texts to build popular consensus and legitimacy.[37] To this end, he drew liberally from the *marxisant* vocabulary and turns of phrase of his European intellectual forebearers (notably from Jean Jaurès on laicism and social democracy), in a borrowing that then became a characteristic turn of phrase in Sukarno's Indonesian rhetoric on Indonesian Islam.[38]

The French socialist politician Jean Jaurès (whose collected speeches of the late nineteenth and early twentieth centuries Sukarno privately admired and studied) promoted secularism as the most authentic embodiment of French republican ideals and employed a metaphor that Sukarno liberally borrowed.[39] In his collected parliamentary speeches, Jaurès addressed his detractors by claiming that he and his socialist allies had captured "the flame" (*la flamme*) of republican principles, whereas his opponents had merely grasped their "ashes" (*la cendre*)—a turn of phrase that Sukarno translated and reconfigured in Indonesian terms to promote his vision for a more secular Indonesian state on the basis of *api Islam* (the fire of Islam).[40]

Sukarno first employed the metaphorical term "soul-fire of Islam" (*jiwa-api Islam*) and what he called the "fire" or "flame" of the Qur'an and hadith to call for more dynamic, "elastic interpretations" of scripture through "a basis of general knowledge" rather than "purely theological expertise."[41] He also used these metaphors to promote a progressive, historically informed approach to the reading of scripture that legitimated systems of political change beyond the emulation of Islam's earliest caliphal systems. As first expressed in an argument that he would controversially restate in later speeches and articles published in Indonesia's burgeoning Islamic press:

> Islam is progress. [. . .] Why in spite of this do Muslim politicians here always advocate a political system "like that of the times of the great caliphs"? *The fire* of the age of the "great caliphs"? [. . .] [D]o we forget that it was not *they* who discovered that fire, not *they* who invented it, not *they* who wrote of it? [. . .] That they merely "extracted" that fire from something *which we too also possess today*, namely from the Word of Allah and the Sunnah of the Prophet? But what have we extracted from the Word of Allah and the Sunnah of the Prophet? Not *the fire*, not *the light*, not *the flame*, but *the ashes, the dust, the cinders.*[42]

The recurrent phrasing that Sukarno employed—to "capture the fire, the flame" of Islam "rather than its smoke and its ashes alone"—came to have two complementary meanings.[43] On the one hand, seizing this captive fire meant "seeing the 'soul of the letter' in scripture," "freeing Islam from the conflict of letters" or "the casuistry" of limited (jurisprudential) interpretations of Qur'anic scripture.[44]

As he would argue on a second level of interpretation, capturing the fire of Islam over its ashes also meant legitimating a religious "dynamism" that accommodated radical political reforms (often in the secular Turkish model).[45] This would, in his words, allow the "spirit" of the faith to "burn because of its own strength," rather than through what he tactically called an emasculated dependency on state protections. ("Islam," he suggested controversially, must be "weaned" from the state.)[46] His claims were frequently expressed along the following lines:

> When the Islamic spirit of the people burns, it is certain that their parliament will be flooded by the spirit of Islam. [. . .] If the Islamic spirit burns,

> that is the true spirit of Islam, which [. . .] burns because of *its own strength, its own élan, its own endeavor* [. . .] without the care of the state, without the support of the state, without the protection of the state.[47]

> Islam does not ask a formal declaration that the state is an Islamic state, it calls for a state that truly flames with the fire of Islam in the hearts of the community. The fire of Islam truly flaming throughout the whole body of its people—this is what makes a state an Islamic state, and not a statement on a scrap of paper that "the state is guided by religion." For what reason are we afraid of an act of constitutional discretion that the state "is separated from religion"?[48]

By this means, Sukarno argued that it was possible to observe the presence of Islam within political life without recourse to a formal religious constitution. This argument resolved, at least on a figurative register, the quandary of how a secular (or religiously pluralistic) republic might coexist with the Islamic informants of Indonesian nationalism.[49] Islam as an animated, regenerated faith, he suggested, would mean that Islam would appear on the international stage "as a living religion, [. . .] a living creed, a living guide for the soul—a living fire of the spirit! [*Islam sebagai api-jiwa*]," rather than being limited to "just a collection of precepts" or "a mere 'formal system.'"[50] These were positions that earned him the suspicion and scorn of certain religious circles, as Sukarno would admit in his own writings. Prominent Islamic scholars charged him with not only scriptural illiteracy and a lack of moral and political authority but even a heretical factionalism and a divisive tribalism, if not outright apostasy.[51]

If one traces the origins of Sukarno's figurative language on the *fires of Islam* to its earliest written instantiations (personal letters from Endeh prison in the mid-1930s), it is clear that his earliest usage aimed to challenge the conventional limits of what passed for scriptural literacy and theological expertise among contemporary circles of religious scholars, particularly those claiming to distinguish communities of faith from apostasy or heresy (*takfir*).[52] As evident from Sukarno's own writings, the question of who could claim the moral authority to arbitrate these controversies bore stakes no less vital than the eventual character (and religious legitimacy) of an envisioned Indonesian constitution, the rapport between Islamic movements and a representative parliament, and the national accommodation of religious minorities within an eventual republic.

Some of his political skeptics coyly responded with figurative variations on Sukarno's rhetoric. In an early rejoinder, for example, the prominent nationalist politician Dr. Tjipto Mangunkusomo played on the ambiguous meaning of *api Islam* as passion or hellfire, by remarking that it was Marxism rather than Islam that was "burning Sukarno's soul."[53] The Islamic scholar and politician Mohammad Natsir protested that separating Islam from an eventual Indonesian state in the Turkish model was a flirtation with anarchy—a political chaos comparable to a kind of drowning. This was a clear play on Sukarno's own rhetoric comparing ideological dynamism with a cathartic flood or an inescapable, rising tide—a "current," as Sukarno had argued, destined to "wash away" the vestiges of "conservatism and orthodoxy" across global Muslim communities.[54] As Natsir pronounced in a sequence of articles protesting Sukarno's praise of Turkish secularism: "To the clan of Kemalist defenders in Indonesia, we have this to say in response. There's an adage that rings true: 'A drowning man will grab anything, even if it's the toe of his own foot.'"[55] This statement is notably embedded in an article in which Natsir, while excoriating Sukarno's Kemalist inclinations, also criticized his and his supporters' lack of literacy in Arabic—leaving them free to desperately "grab" and selectively misquote, for their own ideological ends, translated Arabic texts on the nature of Islam and on Islamic political statecraft glossed by European Orientalists.[56]

Such rhetorical flourishes reflect the imaginative projections of an Indonesian nationalist movement searching for the terms of its own unity. Sukarno's statements on this are instructive. In an implied defense of his code-switching between Indonesian and European languages, he attacked those who defensively (and vehemently) rallied behind Arabic in purist ways as a counterimperial tactic, claiming that they had embraced a regressive, "defensive fanaticism" to distance themselves from an imperial enemy.[57] Equally excoriated by Sukarno were clerical figures (*kaum fiqh*) who labeled as apostasy (*takfir*) any behaviors appearing Western—including use of the Latin script or "any effort at dis-Arabizing."[58] This fury of political exchange in the early 1940s was catalyzed by debates among politicians on whether Islam had lost its appeal for a rising generation of young Indonesians—among whom the young poet Chairil Anwar was to become a cultural icon.[59]

The Animus of Revolutionary Poetry

Chairil Anwar, the Indonesian poet most often associated with the foundations of Indonesian nationalist poetry, came of age during the Japanese occupation and Indonesia's subsequent independence struggle. A figure central to an emerging literary canon in the 1940s, Chairil benefited from the fact that his native Sumatranese dialect, by a convergence of historical accidents, was relatively close to the romanized print standard that came to be nationalized in postindependence Indonesia. In the wake of independence, his poetry was critically acclaimed for advancing formal innovations that distinguished him from his compatriots, with major Indonesian critics claiming that he imparted a new "modernist" sensibility to the Indonesian language through his poetic concision, free verse innovations, and distinctive style that elevated colloquial modes of speech.[60] He characteristically relied on relatively colloquial, vulgar pronouns to dramatize modes of address in nonhierarchical forms, using the first-person Malay pronoun *aku* rather than the more refined and deferential *saya*.[61] Through this distinctive style, Chairil poetically conjured and addressed Sukarno in a poem composed during one of the most perilous years of the independence struggle—and a matter of weeks before Sukarno's kidnapping by Dutch forces, as the independence movement threatened to fail through internal splintering.[62]

As implied by Chairil's poetic characterization of him, Sukarno as a public speaker gave poetic form to idealist political abstractions—of progress, parity, and pluralism—through his rhetoric on revolutionary change as a leveling, natural force. Capable of mesmerizing crowds across the archipelago in Indonesian, Sukarno fashioned himself the mouthpiece of the popular masses.[63] It is in this capacity—as a controversial and charismatic "solidarity maker" for the fledgling nation—that he was poetically invoked by Chairil Anwar at a time when the revolutionary struggle was threatening to fracture.[64] In part through Chairil's poetic enshrinement of Sukarno in the newly nationalized language, Chairil himself came to be nostalgically associated in postindependence Indonesia with the revolutionary struggle as a cultural icon.

Composed in 1948, Chairil's poem entitled "A Pact with Brother 'Karno" ("Persetujuan dengan Bung Karno") restages and commemorates Sukarno's declaration of Indonesian independence on August 17, 1945, and resurrects Sukarno as a monumental figure of revolutionary change. The poem begins with an irreverence characteristic of Chairil's verse that gives way to an oath of self-dedication, as the poetic speaker merges with his addressee and the poem assumes a devotional turn through the term *zat* (a Malay word taken from the Arabic *thāt*, meaning "essence" or "innermost self" and often assuming in religious contexts a mystical inflection).[65] The poem in full shifts in scale as the individual speaker dissolves into a collective sense of self through a symbolic political pact with the revolutionary leader:

Ayo! Bung Karno kasi tangan mari kita bikin janji
Aku sudah cukup lama dengan bicaramu, dipanggang atas apimu,
Digarami oleh lautmu

Dari mula tgl. 17 Augustus 1945
Aku melangkah kedepan berada rapat disisimu
Aku sekarang api aku sekarang laut

Bung Karno! Kau dan aku satu zat satu urat
Dizatmu dizatku kapal-kapal kita berlayar
Diuratmu diuratku kapal-kapal kita berlayar
Diuratmu diuratku kapal-kapal kita bertolak & berlabuh

Hey! Brother 'Karno, give me your hand, let's make a deal
I've heard enough of your speeches,
been roasted by your fire [*apimu*],
Been salted by your seas [*lautmu*]

From 17 August 1945, the day this country set itself free,
I've marched along front, right next to you
Now I am fire, now I am sea.

Brother Karno! You and I are one essence [*zat*] one flesh [*urat*]
in your essence in my essence [*Dizatmu dizatku*] our ships set sail
In your flesh in my flesh [*Diuratmu diuratku*] our ships set sail
In your flesh in my flesh our ships leave and anchor.[66]

The poem invokes Sukarno as a revolutionary orator, and it is on these grounds that Chairil's performative exchange with Sukarno is still commemoratively recited in annual celebrations of Indonesian independence. The poem has in this way sustained the memory of Sukarno as a public speaker long after the raw polemics surrounding his ideological rhetoric in the 1930s and 1940s receded into vague impressions of a historical past. The poem nonetheless dramatizes the tension between individual skepticism and a sense of revolutionary belonging among members of Sukarno's listening public of the 1940s, by performing a moment of personal transformation catalyzed by Sukarno's own rhetoric.

When considering how communities are imagined in literary form, and how vernacular literatures scaffold an emerging national consciousness, we can make a number of related observations on Chairil's poem. A minority of the Indonesian public read Sukarno's speeches in the limited print journals circulating through the archipelago during the 1930s and 1940s. The great majority heard Sukarno's rhetoric through his broadcasts via the network of radio propaganda set in motion under the Japanese occupation and redeployed in the mid-1940s by an Indonesian revolutionary leadership for the Indonesian nationalist cause.[67] The poem, in effect, attests to this audial sensibility of a nation in formation. It is as much a portrait of an individual speaker fatigued with the rhetoric of a rising nationalist leadership as a reflection of Sukarno as a revolutionary speechmaker, peddling ideas to an ambivalent public. As a portrait of public persuasion, the poem illustrates the tensions between individual distinction and collective belonging that characterize much of Chairil Anwar's revolutionary verse.

In more formal terms, the poem begins with a brash address of the nationalist leader, transforming what seems like a truce ("give me your hand") and a dismissal ("I've heard enough of your speeches") into something more closely resembling a performative pact. Stylistic choices and forms of diction reinforce tensions within the poem between collective belonging and the speaker's sense of individual distinction. Representative of the poet's style are egalitarian forms of colloquial address and locution, as the speaker reckons with the revolutionary leader through the coarse first-person pronoun *aku* rather than the deferential *saya*. Amid the poem's concision and economy of expression, a characteristic feature of Chairil's poetry, its colloquial style is elevated through its free verse form, bringing a sense of spoken verisimilitude to the poem as an imagined dialogical exchange between a politician and a member of his listening public. Motifs borrowed directly from Sukarno's revolutionary-era rhetoric lend atmosphere to the short poem while dramatizing a moment of personal persuasion.

Chairil's pairing of metaphors at first makes a triviality of Sukarno's oratorical passion and charisma, leaving the speaker among Sukarno's listening masses "roasted and brined" by the orator's "fire" and "seas," like a peddler's street-side morsel. This initially irreverent tone, however, gives way to a declaration of unity between the speaker and his addressee. The metaphors of fire and flood gradually mediate a transcendent unity, coinciding with the dissipation of the speaker and tempering the hierarchies implied by the poem's opening lines. Though the poem begins with an irreverent tone, it takes a devotional turn with the insertion of the monumental date on which Sukarno declared Indonesian independence: August 17, 1945. This devotional gesture approaches the mystical through the transformative metaphors of fire and sea, describing the dissolution of the speaker into a greater immanence (in motifs arguably reminiscent of earlier traditions of Malay Sufi poetry).[68] The initial grilling of the speaker, then, transforms into a more sacrificial conflagration unifying speaker and addressee.

Such metaphors, however, also conjoin the poetic to the political, for Sukarno as a public speaker recurrently gave poetic form to idealist political abstractions through his rhetoric on revolutionary change as a leveling, natural force (like fire and flood or sea). Chairil's poetic invocation of Sukarno's rhetorical motifs, especially of "fire," therefore, is all the more poignant as a vindication of Sukarno, given the accusations leveled against him within the Indonesian Islamic press in the years preceding and following the revolution.

In addition to championing an *api Islam*, the "fire of Islam," Sukarno also invoked Heraclitus in Greek, *panta rei*, to claim that everything flows forward and that conservative ideals "will break under the strength of the flood of new ideology"—a secular or pluralist Indonesian nationalism (*kebangsaan*).[69] By his translation, *panta rei* rendered time itself a liberalizing force, a current washing away the vestiges of "conservatism and orthodoxy" across global Muslim communities; by its power, "even a hundred ideologies as hard as the wahabist ideology will be powerless to stop the flow of the river which is called time," Sukarno claimed.[70] Lending poetic language to his vision of ideological regeneration and secular progress through another figuration, he argued that Indonesians must "burn with the fire of Islam" rather "than cling to its ashes."[71]

If Sukarno metaphorically intended the "*fire* of Islam" to mean a religious fervor or passion, the semantic dangers of this unorthodox metaphor are evident, given what local critics in the Islamic press claimed was its untranslatability into scriptural Arabic terms. The Arabic term for "fire," *nār* (pl. *neirān*), recurs in the Qur'an as a metonym for hell and eternal damnation. As one critic noted, *nār* unambiguously represents in scripture the forces of "destruction and obliteration, vice and depravity," through such stock expressions as "the fires of war," "the fire of rage," and "the fire of oppression."[72] Sukarno's use or misuse of fire as a metaphor for religious passion contributed to perennial controversies about his rhetoric within the Indonesian Islamic press, which began in the late 1930s and early 1940s and persisted in the wake of independence during the 1950s.[73] As one critic claimed, "None of us have ever heard the existence of the [Arabic] phrase '*niranul Islam*.'"[74] Such errors, he claimed, played into the hands of European colonists and hostile Orientalists in their portrayal of Islam as a destructive creed. To Sukarno's challengers, the inscrutability of his figurative language and his poetic license demonstrated not only the limits of his scriptural literacy but also the distortive risks of a nascent political rhetoric unmoored from scriptural standards and oriented toward European figurations.[75]

In this light, Chairil's poem can be seen all the more to play with the thresholds between devotion and irreverence, in an apparent reclamation of Sukarno's own figurative language and poetic license. Uniting with Sukarno meant embracing "the flood of [a] new ideology" in his branding of Indonesian nationalism (over a rigid traditionalism or Salafism).[76] Where Chairil conveys the consequences of being moved by Sukarno's speech, the poem also dramatizes the stakes of a historic choice at the thresholds of Indonesian independence: to burn with brother 'Karno in the revolutionary claim to national unity, whether that be in glory or in hellfire.

Bearing in mind the controversies surrounding Sukarno's rhetoric, then, allows us to reread Chairil's poetic address of Sukarno against the gravity of the politician's claims, appreciating it through its historic dimensions as the textual trace of controversial and seismic political transformations. Chairil's speaker in "A Pact with Brother 'Karno" appears either willingly aflame or immersed—anchored and setting sail—in the waters that Sukarno rhetorically evoked, rather than desperately drowning in Sukarno's "seas" (as Natsir implied of Sukarno's followers). Chairil's imagined rejoinder to Sukarno in "A Pact with Brother 'Karno" might be understood as the response of a young poet reckoning with Sukarno's claims, speaking for a rising generation at the onset of a revolution beset by the risks of internal dissolution. The speaker's ultimate accord with Sukarno, his vision of a final unity with Sukarno, then, deserves to be read in these terms: as the dramatization of a listener initially exhausted by Sukarno's rhetoric (*bicara-mu, api-mu, laut-mu*—"your talk," "your fire," "your seas") but ultimately moved by Sukarno's claims. Chairil's poem conveys the stakes of what it meant to witness the controversies over Sukarno's rhetoric and yet to "throw one's lot" with Sukarno's revolutionary movement, not only to "fall in step" but to be virtually one with Sukarno, as "one essence, one flesh."[77]

The Savor of Freedom and Language Reborn

In a manifesto broadcast during the struggle for Indonesian independence in December 1945, Chairil imagined his nation's emergence from the Japanese occupation and the Dutch Empire preceding it as the rebirth of what he called *Kata*—of "speech" or "the Word" breaking free from the strictures of either political propaganda or the sentimental traditionalism of late colonial writing:

> And now: Hoppla! A jump great enough to fulfill the promise of this young nation of ours. After the rebellion against the Word [*Kata*], we forgot that the Word spreads its roots, lives from era to era [. . .]. The price of the spirituality [*kerohanian*] we've destroyed is that we must grope our way back in the best style possible. When it loses the fullness of its freedom, the world—ourselves most of all—enjoys recovering the savor of freedom.[78]

Protesting the occupation's transformation of young artists "into disciplined shock troops," Chairil's 1945 manifesto envisioned a future of absolute artistic freedom—of artistic speech poised to defy the silence of writers overtaken by imperial and fascist directives during World War II.[79]

Although Chairil's voice became closely associated with the Indonesian revolutionary struggle through radio broadcasts of his poetry marking the end of the occupation, certain paradoxes attach to his canonization as a "revolutionary" poet. While he spoke powerfully of the freedom of "this young nation of ours," Chairil was remembered by his contemporaries as politically noncommittal and personally irreverent. He was frequently accused (most notably by leftist critics) of holding no firm convictions at all.[80] But judging from his radio manifesto, it is precisely the brutality of an occupying power during World War II and its efforts to form art to the mercenary needs of propaganda that offers the logic of understanding Chairil's poems and legacy through their political ambivalence: embodying the spirit—or urgency—of revolutionary change but defying the imperatives and strictures of politics. "An era of 'isms,'" he once scrawled on paper, "is a one-sided party for one-sided dancers. What I admire is the violence, the passion with which they brawl!"[81]

Despite his self-description as the admiring spectator of a violent, ideological arena that implicitly pitted Indonesians against fellow Indonesians, in present-day Indonesia Chairil's poems are now channeled into untroubled gestures of revolutionary nostalgia and iconic pageantry celebrating the nation's established unity against a common former enemy. Politicians and schoolchildren frequently recite his poetry during annual commemorations of Indonesian independence as a form of patriotic performance, often with little appreciation for the conditions that informed his writing: his distaste for verse that resembled political propaganda, and the uncertain future of an independent Indonesian state in the 1940s. As the urgency of those nationally formative ideological "brawls" would fade into a historical past, Chairil's poems and the reflections he would dash off in private nonetheless attest to the existence of old antagonisms that fashioned the era in which he wrote.

As a condition for appreciating his poetry, what, then, would it mean to dignify Chairil's self-description as a witness (from the early 1940s until his death in 1949) to the ideological infighting that formed Indonesia's struggle for independence? Rather than reading his poetry as a canonical fait accompli for modern Indonesia, what would it mean to aesthetically recover a sense of the raw political contests and the work of solidarity-building that formed the era in which he penned his verse? By revisiting the contested ideological orientations of the newly nationalized Indonesian language in which Chairil composed—a nationalized literary vernacular formed through the pressures of colonial influences, sacralized Arabic, and a local dialectal diversity—I suggest how the poet may have subtly tested emerging constraints on artistic liberties and poetic license during a formative era of ideological infighting, as debates on the secular or religiously pluralist future of an independent Indonesia intensified during the height of the nationalist movement and independence struggle.[82]

In the wake of national independence, Chairil's poetry became closely associated with the Indonesian Revolution. Major Indonesian literary critics of the 1950s designated him posthumously as the leading poet of the "1945 generation," associated with the year Indonesia declared independence.[83] This reputation would persist across Indonesia's successive regime changes, as his poems assumed a transgenerational afterlife (following the post-1965 "New Order"). A protean legacy nonetheless attaches to Chairil's persona, with many (including those who knew him personally) associating his poetry with an extreme irreverence and impenitence. Often cited in evidence, his poem "Dimesjid" ("At the Mosque"), for example, turns a space of quotidian worship into a mutually destructive arena. The speaker hollers and wrestles God down from His heights, as they move into an endless conflict of mutual destruction and victory deferred, with God and speaker "[d]estroying each other / One hurling insults, the other gone mad":

Kuseru saja Dia
Sehingga datang juga
Kamipun bermuka-muka.
Seterusnya Ia bernyala-nyala dalam dada.
Segala daya memadamkannya

Bersimpah peluh diri yang tak bisa diperkuda
Ini ruang
Gelanggang kami berperang
Binasa-membinasa
Satu menista lain gila.

I shouted at Him
Until He came
We met face to face.
Since then He's burned in my breast.
I've struggled with all my strength to extinguish Him
My body, which won't give in, is soaked with sweat
Here, this very space,
Is where we fight
Destroying each other
One hurling insults, the other gone mad.[84]

The incendiary presence of an antagonist referred to in the third person, subtly personified as an internal burning and an indomitable enemy (*Dia*—Him), allegorizes the private forces of ambivalence in this account; weighing in the balance are the savage will of the speaker to destroy his divine interlocutor and the brute inability of the speaker to "extinguish Him." Often read as a poem of straightforward irreverence (a sign of the poet's "atheism"), the poem itself does not foreclose this possibility or overdetermine this conclusion, as the struggle appears endlessly deferred. (Chairil's poem "Sorga" ["Heaven"], however, in which the speaker doubts the superiority of heaven's pleasures to the worldly temptations of earthly ports, more clearly supports such characterizations of Chairil's irreverence.)[85]

Contributing to Chairil's protean legacy, however, are Indonesian critics and commentators who privilege devotional dimensions of his verse, rallying his image in the service of more reverential religious claims. A New Order pamphlet championing Chairil Anwar as a nationalist poet, for example, highlights the poem "Doa" ("Prayer") over alternatives that would suggest a more multifaceted and ambivalent quality to Chairil's verse. Dedicated "Kepada Pemeluk Teguh," "To a Devout Believer," this sparse poem evolves through a confessional address. The poem opens with a divine invocation (to "Tuhanku," "My Lord"), often read as a form of repentance—partially excerpted below:

cayaMu panas suci
tinggal kerdip lilin dikelam sunyi [...]
aku mengembara di negeri asing [...]
Aku tida bisa berpaling.

Your warm pure light
Remains a flickering candle in the lonely darkness [...]
I wander in strange lands [...]
I cannot turn away[86]

The poem moves through the voice of a repentant sinner and has engendered an entire tradition of reading it as a sign of internal conversion, a tradition evident in pastiches of Chairil's verse by Islamic school students and in clerical sermons published after Chairil's death.[87] Hamka, for example, the eventual head of the Indonesian council of Muslim clerics whose work featured in the preceding chapter, cited the poem "Prayer" in a sermon in the early 1960s as a kind of memento mori—a reminder of death itself, invoking Chairil as a "godless" but ultimately repentant figure. His reference to Chairil offered him a pretext for sermonizing on the Qurʾanic concept of *barzakh,* an isthmus or a barrier separating the living from the penitent dead.[88] It is this protean quality of Chairil Anwar's verse and legacy, this remembrance and portrayal of the poet in popular culture as an ambiguous and vitalist figure, that should be considered when reading his poetry. Like the poems he composed with directly religious overtones, "A Pact with Brother 'Karno" vacillates between devotion and irreverence, as revolutionary fervor appears legible as both an indomitable fire and an illumination that converts the ambivalent nationalist.

Chairil Anwar passed away almost fifteen years before Sukarno's reign would end through a military coup in 1965.[89] Marking the end of Sukarno's presidency, Indonesia's self-declared "New Order" under General Suharto claimed to correct the ideological missteps of its revolutionary predecessor, as ordinary citizens sympathetic to the nation's political Left—and many simply caught in the cross fire—fell under suspicion of mass irreligiosity (along with Sukarno, who would face accusations of straying toward a supposedly godless communist path toward the end of his presidency). Amid the "brawling -isms" of Indonesia's New Order, defenses of Indonesia's Muslim patrimony gained currency at the height of the Cold War, eventually touching one of the champions of Chairil Anwar's poetry, a major Indonesian literary critic of the 1950s,

H. B. Jassin. Charged with blasphemy and sentenced to prison for publishing a short story in which God was crudely personified, Jassin would engage in devotional forms of translation as a matter of personal penitence, publishing what he considered the first poetic translation of the Qur'an into Indonesian (in 1977).[90] No sooner was it published than the translation proved controversial along the lines of earlier polemics. Jassin's secular formation as a Dutch-trained critic and his relative illiteracy in Arabic were cause for skepticism among more fluently arabophone compatriots and conservative religious ideologues. His reliance on English translations of the Qur'an for his own poetic rendering was equally controversial.[91] Again, the politics of language and culture in Indonesia might be understood through the entwining of the vernacular and the sacred, as the linguistic cross-threads informing Indonesian poetics seem to strain with the anxieties of transmission associated with charismatic texts in Arabic.[92]

Conclusion

As romanized print was overtaking much of the country's publishing landscape by the mid-twentieth century, the nascent orientations of what might be considered Indonesian "vernacular" culture were shadowed by the polemical front lines of colonial languages and scriptural Arabic. Nationalized Indonesian continued to be riven between European imperial vestiges and defensive attachments to Arabic as a counterimperial symbol, as Arabic literacy continued to signal interpretive authority and religious piety for those claiming its mastery. These rifts were evident in the controversies surrounding Sukarno's own rhetorical choices in Indonesian on the secular future of the new republic.

Against these dynamics, early assertions of revolutionary Indonesian poetry appear haunted by the polemics of scriptural literacy in ways that transform an otherwise simple poetic pledge into an ambiguous political statement, playing on its status as a declaration of religiously inflected devotion or irreverence. Among the pleasures of rereading Chairil Anwar's poetry—with its invocations of Sukarno's controversial rhetoric—is therefore to discern how it subtly records the aesthetic and political valences of a nationalized (or nationalizing) language in formation in the 1940s, a progressively unifying vernacular whose ideological orientations were as yet rhetorically untethered and ambiguous.

The poetic and political controversies attached to the Indonesian language from the 1930s through the early 1950s attest to the ideological openness and linguistic indeterminacy that characterized Indonesian decolonization, as Indonesia negotiated new forms of cultural solidarity and political autonomy across a vast territorial dispersion. It is vital to recall that the medium upheld as a revolutionary national language—and used to unify the diverse islands of the former Dutch East Indies—was itself a novel political experiment. It was a medium in dynamic flux, subject to the controversies of meaning associated with its status as a relative orthographic novelty (given its recent romanization in the late nineteenth century) and with its modes of internal enrichment, borrowing lexically from a range of dialects and languages by virtue of its polyglottic speakers (Arabic, Dutch, Sanskrit, and Javanese, among others).[93] It is on these grounds that the remarkable political and poetic experiment known as the Indonesian language can be appreciated, in its movement across an exceptional degree of ethnolinguistic diversity, managing its status as a non-native and interconfessional language across a myriad of potential fracture points. As noted by Benedict Anderson in *Imagined Communities*, at the time of Indonesian independence "almost no Indonesian spoke *bahasa Indonesia* as his or her mother-tongue; virtually everyone had their own 'ethnic' language and some, especially people in the nationalist movement, *bahasa Indonesia/dienst-maleisch* as well. Today there are perhaps millions of young Indonesians, from dozens of ethnolinguistic backgrounds, who speak Indonesian as their mother-tongue."[94] The subtle connections between Sukarno's speeches and Chairil's imagined rejoinder attest to the rhetorical and poetic innovations that contributed to the evolution of the Indonesian language as it became a nationalized medium with distinctive political and aesthetic valences, a process in which both Chairil as a revolutionary poet and Sukarno as a public orator played a vital role.

6

Between Pride and Humility

قلت للطوب انت فرحان قال لي إسمع
الحمامة البيضا من باندونج تسجع
رقص الضي على جناحها و شعشع
اللمون و البرتقان
قلت حانزل زي ما بتنزل و حاطلع
زي ما بتطلع و اقلدها و ابدّع
في الغنا والطيران

I asked the bricks of their joy, and they said, listen:
The white dove of Bandung coos
Light dances upon her wings and spreads
Through lemon and orange groves
I said: I will fall as you fall and rise
As you rise in imitation, creating
In song and in flight.

—FU'ĀD ḤADDĀD, "FARḤA," 1956

PUBLISHED AT THE ONSET of the Suez Crisis in 1956, a year after the Bandung Conference, the colloquial Egyptian poem "Farḥa" commemorates the Asia-Africa conference in ways that intertwine its legacy with the territorial claims of an independent, postrevolutionary Egypt. The poem lauds the nationalization of the Suez Canal and the building of the Aswan High Dam as signs of Egyptian autonomy under the leadership of Gamal Abdel Nasser—Egypt's president and Bandung delegate. The most prolific colloquial Arabic poet of mid-century Egypt, Fu'ād Ḥaddād (1927–85), composed the poem following his release from prison as a communist political prisoner from 1953 to 1956. This was a period—coinciding with the Bandung Conference and the formative years of the Non-Aligned Movement—when Nasser was consolidating power in the wake of the "Free Officer's Revolt" and when thousands of members of the Egyptian Communist Party like Ḥaddād were subject to a first wave of postrevolutionary suppression. Marking the efforts of a poetic class reconciled to a regime progressively quieting or co-opting its political opposition in the 1950s, the poem also attests to the ambiguous nationalist rebranding of Asian-African solidarities in mid-twentieth-century Egypt.[1]

Fu'ād Ḥaddād is often considered the pioneering founder of the Egyptian colloquial verse movement that began in the 1950s and 1960s (known as the *shiʿr al-ʿāmmiyya* movement).[2] As exemplified by his eulogy of the Bandung Conference, "Farḥa," Ḥaddād's poetry intertwined the sensibilities of a revolutionary pan-Arabism with broader subaltern solidarities, imaginatively aligning mid-twentieth-century Egypt with counterimperial resistance movements across Asia-Africa. Exploring the foundations of Egyptian national selfhood was central to his writing, as his poetry sought to dignify common Egyptian speech forms in formally groundbreaking ways. His poetic corpus explored the contours of Egyptian collective identity, often exalting historic sources of Egyptian Arab pride while gesturing sympathetically toward the universally oppressed in recognition of Egypt's own history as a culturally hybrid region of successive conquests. To this end, Ḥaddād privileged a subaltern Egyptian and Islamic sensibility through his verse, a sensibility reinforced by his choice of a lower linguistic register (*ʿāmmiyya*) for his poetry. By forgoing the prevailing standard of written Arabic (*fuṣḥā*) in Egypt, Ḥaddād, as characterized by literary scholar Marilyn Booth, "fashioned a dialectic, confrontational poetic voice," drawing from Egyptian folklore and popular culture to "celebrate and probe ideologies of collective identity" in Egypt.[3]

Born in Cairo to an upper-class family of Lebanese Christian origin, Ḥaddād became a devout Muslim after converting as a young man. He became a communist political activist in his youth, an affiliation he sustained throughout his life, suffering two periods of arbitrary imprisonment under the Nasser regime (1953–56 and 1959–63). The poet's imprisonment was personally and stylistically transformative. During his incarceration, he shared close quarters with prisoners among Egypt's rural lower classes, an experience that reoriented him toward Egyptian folkloric and colloquial influences. Initially immersed in an elite francophone literary milieu, he ultimately rebelled against his early French education, increasingly convinced that Arabic

ʿāmmiyya in Egypt occupied an unrivaled position as the language of the common masses.

Ḥaddād's writing of the 1940s and early 1950s included anti-monarchist protest poems, and he sustained a concern with anti-elitist themes throughout his prolific corpus. His early poems immediately marked him as a figure of exceptional innovation. Whereas *ʿāmmiyya* verse had long been associated with light comic fare and satirical ditties when appearing in Egyptian newsprint through the 1940s, Ḥaddād's repertoire, which gained prominence after World War II, showed that *ʿāmmiyya* poetry could probe a full range of stylistic expression and complex subjects. His poetry was considered stylistically revolutionary for being both "simple and profound" (*basīṭ wa-ʿamīq*).[4]

Despite Ḥaddād's innovations, his use of Egyptian colloquial Arabic (*ʿāmmiyya*) over classical or literary Arabic (*fuṣḥā*) consigned his poetry to a critically marginal status.[5] As with other poets associated with Egyptian colloquial writing after World War II, Ḥaddād occupied a liminal position relative to Egyptian national culture and a national poetic canon in formation. His work in many ways remained peripheral within a literary corpus dominated by *fuṣḥā*, but it was central to mass media forms of public commemoration and national imagining, with many of his poems gaining iconic status in Egyptian popular culture as song lyrics.

This chapter builds on scholarly initiatives that have begun to redress Ḥaddād's critical marginality within studies of Arabic literature, and I offer new comparative grounds for appreciating his stylistic innovations as a poet of Egyptian colloquial Arabic.[6] Ḥaddād's poetry marks him as a master of verbal play, a skill he often deployed to challenge intersecting hierarchies of class, race, and language in postcolonial Egypt.[7] Egalitarian themes within his poetry are significant not only within the field of Arabic literary studies but for comparative approaches to postcolonial writing across Arabic-Islamic contact zones.

This chapter illustrates how the corpus of a major pioneer of Egyptian colloquial poetry disarmed some of the biases against the literary use of *ʿāmmiyya* amid the print dominance of *fuṣḥā* as a literary and ritual acrolect. Ḥaddād's poetry self-referentially dramatizes how vernacular, colloquial, or dialect writing, if elevated to a literary standard, vitally complements *fuṣḥā* rather than displacing it as a textual medium associated with Qurʾanic scripture, orthodox ritual, and pan-Arab print. Gesturing to an imagined arabophone realm, the poet also presents *ʿāmmiyya* poetry as a medium of broad solidarities across lines of both race and class, yielding visions of arabophone solidarity that go far beyond the territorial confines of Egypt itself.

In a medium that potentially forfeited a regionally expansive (extranational) public, Ḥaddād's poetry suggests how the contours of *ʿāmmiyya* or vernacular writing can be locally inclusive across lines of class. Moreover, his poetry extends this egalitarian sensibility not only to Egypt's underclass; it extends it to the non-Arab (*ʿajami*) subaltern as well, by emphasizing the historical solidarities of Egypt as a region that was itself once conquered and Arabized. To illustrate this general pattern across Ḥaddād's work, this chapter explores how Ḥaddād's poetic corpus—canonically marginalized for its *ʿāmmiyya* register and therefore allegedly provincial public compass—bears its own vision of an imagined community of broad solidarities, a vision that surfaces through intertwined scales of affiliation. It aligns Egyptian nationalist solidarities with a counterimperial Asian-African and pan-Arab cause across confessional lines. Ḥaddād's vision also aligns a transregional arabophone *umma* with the interconfessional and historically hybrid constitution of an Egyptian past.

Focusing on key instances of linguistic self-referentiality within several of his poems, my analysis moves toward the following conclusion: Ḥaddād's poetic corpus, which speaks to the coexistence of the sacral (ritual Arabic) and the positionally vernacular (*ʿāmmiyya*), exhibits the tensions between an ethnolinguistic Arabocentrism and Islamically derived claims to parity between "Arabs" and "non-Arabs," or between (as Ḥaddād describes it) *kāfat al-ajnās*. This is a phrase that translates (with ambiguities by the mid-twentieth century) as "the totality of races" or "the totality of humankind" (*jins* or *ajnās* here legible as an Arabic cognate for the Latin *genus* or Greek *genos*).[8]

I will begin by clarifying the stakes of Ḥaddād's choice to compose poetry in Egyptian colloquial Arabic as a positionally subaltern and egalitarian medium. I first present an overview of how the colonial-era and protonational polemicization of diglossia in Egypt conditioned and constrained *ʿāmmiyya* as a written standard and a literary medium by the mid-twentieth century.[9] I then consider the representational stakes of *ʿāmmiyya* writing as portrayed in some of Ḥaddād's most iconic poems from the mid-1950s through the late 1960s. The chapter's final close readings show how Ḥaddād's poetry challenges ideological or linguistic biases that associate writing in Egyptian colloquial Arabic with a narrow territorial or national provincialism. The poems I examine proclaim in colloquial verse Egypt's historic solidarities with an Arab Levant, and they align Egypt's struggles during the Suez crisis with counterimperial resistance movements across Asia-Africa. Ḥaddād's corpus, in this way, appears to grapple with what Nasser during the Bandung era claimed were Egypt's concentric solidarities as a liberated region—given Egypt's position as at once "Arab," "African," and predominantly "Muslim."[10]

Building from these readings, the chapter's conclusion attests to the paradoxes of public language use in revolutionary and postrevolutionary Egypt of the 1950s. One of the peculiarities of the decade was that the public sustaining of *fuṣḥā* and the sidelining of *ʿāmmiyya* in print and literature prevailed, even though a new political leadership was giving informal sanction to Egyptian *ʿāmmiyya* as a pan-Arab political force and a charismatic medium of public oratory. The speeches of high officials such as Nasser tended to be uniformly redacted back into a formal standard of *fuṣḥā* in journalistic print, with *ʿāmmiyyāt*, or colloquialisms, generally excised.[11] This paradox in part explains the liminal status of Ḥaddād's colloquial poetry, which was poised at both the center and the periphery of the national. Critically marginalized as written poetry, his poems rose to the fore as song lyrics on Egyptian national and regional pan-Arab platforms: Iconic Egyptian singer Sayed Mekawy put poems from Ḥaddād's *misaḥḥarātī* collection as well as poems such as "The Earth Speaks Arabic" to song. Even ordinary Egyptians who may not know his name as a literary figure often know something of his work, especially his *misaḥḥarātī* poems, which were annually broadcast on Egyptian radio stations during the month of Ramadan.[12]

An Embattled Medium

To fully appreciate the liminal status of Ḥaddād's poetry and the stakes of Ḥaddād's choice to compose poetry in *ʿāmmiyya*, it is necessary to understand how the colonial-era politicization of "classical" Arabic and the Egyptian "vernacular" contributed to the marginalization of *ʿāmmiyya* as a written standard and literary medium by the mid-twentieth century. Underscoring the measure of Ḥaddād's innovation as a poet of Egyptian colloquial verse, the genre he championed, *shiʿr al-ʿāmmiyya* (*ʿāmmiyya* poetry), was considered an oxymoron when Ḥaddād's close associates coined the term in 1961.[13] The Arabic term for poetry (*shiʿr*) conventionally denotes an elevated genre associated with compositions in high (or classical) literary Arabic. As such, *shiʿr al-ʿāmmiyya* was a subversive designation for a new poetic form, conjoining the term for relatively base varieties of common speech (*ʿāmmiyya*) with the most elevated genre of an Arabic literary canon (poetry, or *shiʿr*), a canon from which "common" verse forms had been excised in the course of its classical anthologization.[14] Ḥaddād's struggle to elevate *ʿāmmiyya* poetry as a genre of literary value and cultural prominence indirectly reflects the transgenerational constraints on poetic form of certain language biases and controversies that intensified in late nineteenth- and early twentieth-century Egypt, among other former Ottoman Arab provinces, as traced in a previous chapter. The stakes of Ḥaddād's poetic innovations—which unsettle the divisions between Egyptian provincialism and transregional pan-Arabism and between colloquial Egyptian speech and high ritual Arabic—gain gravity when understood against this controversial history.

Colonial-era language debates, which intensified in Egypt during the British occupation after 1882, cast a long shadow across the late nineteenth and early twentieth centuries and contributed to the local defense of high literary Arabic as a print standard at the expense of Egyptian colloquial Arabic. The British occupation generally proceeded as a "holding operation" to defend British naval access to South Asia, and its policy architects were uninterested in extensive forms of social engineering beyond what was necessary for the execution of British strategic interests.[15] At the onset of the occupation in the 1880s and 1890s, however, several prominent colonial officials advocated the use of the Egyptian vernacular over classical or Qur'anic Arabic as an administrative and pedagogical standard. Such proposals in favor of *ʿāmmiyya* elicited a defensive backlash among local (and often elitist) intellectuals who protested the colonial promotion of an allegedly coarser or more vulgar standard of spoken Arabic.[16] As Egypt was a semiautonomous Ottoman province occupied by Britain, its position as an interimperial or doubly colonized space in the nineteenth century further contributed to the growing public attachment to *fuṣḥā* over *ʿāmmiyya* as a dominant print standard in the late nineteenth and early twentieth centuries. Republican Turkey's divestment from the Arabic script after 1928 gave further momentum in Egypt to defensive attachments to classical or high literary Arabic and to the sustaining of Arabic orthography as a public standard.[17]

The dissolution of the Ottoman Empire lent political urgency to debates on how Arabic as a transregional lingua franca might sustain the cultural patrimony of the former Ottoman Empire's Arab provinces. The classical Arabic language, it was frequently argued, deserved promotion as a regionally unifying medium to rebuild historical solidarities lost to this dissolution. Given the persistent infrastructural supports for *fuṣḥā* across every Arabic-speaking Ottoman province through long-standing Muslim religious institutions, the emerging consensus of interwar and mid-twentieth-century language debates was that sustaining classical Arabic as a unifying language was more viable than the regional extension of a provincial dialect (such as Egyptian *ʿāmmiyya*) to other Arabic-speaking nation-states. Concerns that the elevation of Egyptian *ʿāmmiyya* writing would culturally balkanize regions (and print markets) historically united by *fuṣḥā* also prevailed across early to mid-twentieth-century language debates. Pro-*ʿāmmiyya* reforms, it was further argued, threatened to culturally weaken the region, divide Muslim communities from their sacred language, and disinherit Egyptian youth of an Arabic-Islamic intellectual lineage historically transmitted in *fuṣḥā*.[18] Amid defenses of literary Arabic as a regional print standard with broad political sanction in former Ottoman Egypt, *fuṣḥā* came to be associated with literacy in formal literary terms (increasingly defined through "modern" print textualities), as *ʿāmmiyya* literacies were recast as virtual illiteracies (*ʿummiyya*), as Hoda Yousef observes.[19]

In the wake of the Free Officers Movement, which overthrew the Albanian Ottoman dynasty of King Farouk I and demanded the expulsion of British troops from Egypt in 1952, military officers originating from Egypt's lower middle classes, such as President Nasser, engaged in speechmaking dominated by Egyptian *ʿāmmiyya*. Their speeches were broadcast through new media technologies such as radio and television.[20] Through this process, Egyptian *ʿāmmiyya* became a de facto pan-Arab and nationalist medium in sound rather than print.[21] This is a development that Ḥaddād's poetry self-referentially records through oblique references to Nasser's oratory as a source of inspiration for several of his poems of the 1950s, including his poem on Bandung.[22] As reflected by Ḥaddād's corpus, a new political leadership was giving informal sanction to Egyptian *ʿāmmiyya* as a pan-Arab political force and a charismatic medium of public oratory in revolutionary and postrevolutionary Egypt of the 1950s. This was the case even though *fuṣḥā*, a literary Arabic more closely aligned with Qurʾanic standards of eloquence, continued to be promoted as an official print standard and patriotic medium.

Vindicating literary traditions and colloquial forms associated by the mid-twentieth century with the unlettered masses, Ḥaddād's critically underexamined corpus of poetry allows us to reassess how language controversies gave rise to poetic innovations in Egypt.[23] The following demonstrates how Ḥaddād as a pioneering colloquial poet confronted two biases against *ʿāmmiyya* that dominated Arabic print in mid-twentieth-century Egypt: first, by challenging the public association of *ʿāmmiyya* literacies with the fracturing of pan-Arab solidarities and, second, by opposing *ʿāmmiyya*'s polemical association with the thresholds of religious decadence and disinheritance.[24] Ḥaddād was nonetheless reckoning with a formidable centuries-old bias in his efforts to distance literary *ʿāmmiyya* from its association with religious dissolution. As an example, one of the earliest classical anthologists of *ʿāmmiyya* poetry, Ṣafī al-Dīn al-Ḥillī (d. 1349), evocatively characterized *ʿāmmiyya* and the liminal status of *ʿāmmiyya* poetry in the following way: Conventional standards of eloquence in Arabic (*maʿyār al-faṣāḥa*) divide poetic language along a spectrum between "paradise and [hell]fire" (*jinna wa-nār*), leaving *ʿāmmiyya* (solecistic, grammatically aberrant) verse as though stranded on an interstitial isthmus, a *barzakh* (barrier separating the living from the dead).[25] Colloquial Arabic (*ʿāmmiyya* or *malḥun*) verse by this logic occupies a kind of limbo, awaiting reform against a divine standard. Such classifications of poetry as *barzakhī* implicate not merely the stratification of language forms but the stratification of their human users, as literary critic Sayyid Dayfallah notes, confining them to a matrix of refinement and vulgarity and, by association, of pious "gravity" and "dissolution."[26] While the notion of *ʿāmmiyya* verse as *barzakhī* frames it as a liability for poetry, Ḥaddād portrays *ʿāmmiyya*'s liminality as an asset, characterizing it instead as the transcendent convergence of nominally "high" and "low" devotional forms.

Before moving forward, we should note the ambiguities associated with translating the concept of *ʿāmmiyya* into English. The term *ʿāmmiyya* is often translated as "dialect," "vernacular," or "colloquial"—the three terms often assumed to be synonyms, though, as Shaden Tageldin notes, they problematically bear "non-synonymous" and nonidentical meanings.[27] (One might gloss these differences by suggesting that "vernacular" implicates the linguistic habits of a particular cultural or regional subgroup, "dialect" designates the variant form of a dominant standard, and "colloquial" designates the spoken over the written.) This translational quandary is all the more problematic given the ideologically freighted history through which the concept of the "vernacular" and Eurocentric paradigms of "vernacularization" were first translated into Egyptian Arabic contexts in the course of the late nineteenth century (as traced in a previous chapter). Tageldin suggests that, given its historically interstitial status, "perhaps *ʿāmmiyya* should not be translated as *vernacular* at all, but reinterpreted as *medium* in every sense: a language at once 'common' and 'pure,' ordinary and originary (thus mythic, and so extraordinary), unruly and rule-bound, within and beyond system."[28]

Tageldin's insight is useful for framing what Ḥaddād defends in his poetry: the status of Egyptian *ʿāmmiyya* poetry as a mediating form, as a medium "in every sense" that exists between elite and common publics (between *khāṣṣa* and *ʿāmma*), generating a spectrum of innovations across Arabic's high and low registers. This is a dynamic that Ḥaddād allegorizes through the self-characterization of the Egyptian listener and speaker of Arabic as *hagīn*—as a hybrid or cross-bred figure—a notion that is self-referentially animated in various ways throughout his poetry. The protean vocation and hybrid status of the speaker of Egyptian colloquial Arabic, Ḥaddād emphasizes, extends the sensibilities of the colloquial poet laterally—across lines of nation, region, race, and class. Challenging the common bias against vernacular or dialect poetry as territorially provincial, Ḥaddād's poetry advances a front for broad solidarities in both pan-Arab and Asian-African terms. Where a translational slippage occurs throughout this chapter, designating *ʿāmmiyya* variously through the anglophone terms "dialect," "vernacular," and "colloquial," this corrective sense of *ʿāmmiyya* as a fundamentally spectral form and hybrid medium bears emphasis as an important point of qualification and translational nuance.

Arabness between Pride and Humility

Ḥaddād affirms the complementarity of sacred and colloquial language forms in a sequence of poems voiced through the persona of the *misaḥḥarātī*.[29] In medieval contexts, the Egyptian *misaḥḥarātī*—a figure who traditionally roamed the streets striking a drum to awaken devotees for the morning prayer—sang colloquial verse forms (known as *qūmā*). Ḥaddād poetically resurrects this traditional figure to reimagine the meanings of keeping vigil on an Egyptian national stage. His colloquial summons to the predawn Ramadan meal and prayer attest to the coexistence and mutual regeneration of Arabic in high and low registers, circulating in common spaces between the erudite elite (or the *khāṣṣa*) and the common masses (the *ʿāmma*). Ḥaddād's collection of *misaḥḥarātī* poems symbolically elevates an Egyptian underclass, by writing in the voice of a devotional figure central to the continuities of religious ritual in Egypt but socially marginal for engaging in a trade close to mendicancy.[30] The persona of Ḥaddād's *misaḥḥarātī* stands against purist associations of *fuṣḥā* with Muslim piety and colloquial speech with the corruption of a ritual standard. This figure's devotional, colloquial poetry resonates with the sacred, representing a devout, "awakened" underclass.

By presenting the status of colloquial verse at the convergence of "high" and "low" (or "sacred" and "worldly" forms), Ḥaddād's poetry disarms ideologically religious biases against *ʿāmmiyya* as a corrupted or debased literary medium, challenging the notion that *ʿāmmiyya* or vernacular poetry introduces divisions between devotional Muslims and *fuṣḥā* as a medium of orthodox ritual and charismatic transmission. The poet accomplishes this by positioning vernacular poetry at the thresholds between ritually charismatic texts and their popular reception and circulation among an Egyptian common public.

Ḥaddād's inaugural poem of the genre, entitled "Yā Hādī," or "The Guide" (one of the descriptive names of God in Islamic tradition), was published for the month of Ramadan in 1964. The poem self-referentially draws attention to the *misaḥḥarātī* as a figure who reconciles the ritual call to prayer (*ʿadhān*) with its common reception in an Egyptian Arabic vernacular. The poem also reconciles the coexistence of vernacular orature with high Qurʾanic and literary Arabic by subtly portraying Arabic poetic supremacy and Arab Egyptian ethnic identity in ambiguous terms, associated with the coexistence between "high" and "low" art forms as matters of hybrid inheritance after the Muslim Arab conquests of Egypt in the seventh century. To this end, it speaks with deference of what was brought to Egypt by the *fatḥ*, or Arab Muslim conquests—the Arabic language, a progressively dominant faith, and the self-identification of Egypt with Arabness—with such lines as "sweet the country after she tramples upon idols" or with the speaker's opening praise of the call to prayer brought to Egypt by the "winds of Hijaz." As marked, however, through a sequence of subtle self-referential signs within the poem that portray the *misaḥḥarātī*'s language and lineage as cross-bred—as marks of both pride and humility—the *misaḥḥarātī* himself appears the ambivalent heir to the Arab conquests of Egypt (and its bequest of the call to prayer in high ritual Arabic). This sharpens the ambiguities that conclude the poem, which seem to subtly position Egyptian Arabic poetry itself as a cross-bred form that mediates, domesticates, and acculturates the sacred, the call to prayer, and its vernacular resonances.

Marking the nexus between orthodox ritual and a common public, the *misaḥḥarātī* appears within the poem as a devotional figure who translates into colloquial terms the sensibilities of the *ʿadhān*, or call to prayer, in *fuṣḥā*. After its opening lines, borrowed from common *misaḥḥarātī* street calls ("Awaken, Oh, sleeper, and witness the eternal"), the poem builds through a rapid meter, as though to mimic the rousing drumbeats of the awakener's trade.[31] As it develops a vernacularized summons to pray, the poem introduces a connection between a collective public addressed by the *misaḥḥarātī*'s Ramadan poems (the "we" or "us" invoked by the speaker) and their (or "our") relationship to the call to prayer bestowed by God upon Egypt through "the winds of Hijaz." The opening lines of the poem compare the call to prayer to a divine summons brought by the Hijazi winds, before it moves into lines that liken the Egyptian *misaḥḥarātī* himself to a figure of embodied verdancy or efflorescence, revocalizing and resonating with the terms of the call to prayer in ways that play on the notion of flourishing, thriving, or salvation (*falāh*)—a term central to the *ʿadhān*, which culminates with the lines: "ḥayya ʿalā al-ṣalā, ḥayya ʿalā al-falāḥ" ("hasten to pray, hasten toward salvation [or "to flourish"]").

Ḥaddād writes:

اصحى يا نايم
وحدّ الدايم
وقول نويت
بكرة ان حييت
الشهر صايم
والفجر قايم
اصحى يا نايم
وحدّ الرزاق
رمضان كريم

مسحراتي
منقراتي
بعد الصلاةِ
على نبينا
باقول يا هادي
العقل زينه
الله هادينا
ع الندهة جينا
على ريح
حجازي
سقنا الهجينة
الله يجازي
اللي يهاجينا
أنا قلب نخلي
أحسن مناخ لي
[. . .]
حمام بلدنا
زغلول بلحنا
فرد جناحنا
على وادينا
وكان فلاحنا
دنيا ودينا

Awaken, Oh, sleeper
Witness the Eternal
And say you intend
Tomorrow, should you live,
for the month to fast
and at dawn to rise [to pray the *fajar*],
Awaken, Oh, sleeper
Unite in the Sustainer [*al-Rizzāq*]
Ramadan is generous

Misaḥḥarātī
[hear] the beat of my drumming
After praying
for our Prophet
I say, "Oh, guide supreme!" [*Yā, Hādī*]
Insight is an ornament
God has guided us
To His call we came,
[a call] on the winds
Of Hijaz
We rode the *hagīna* [meaning either "half-bred steed" or "rapid steed"]
Allah rewards [or "punishes"]
The one that rouses us [or "mocks us," *yehāgīnā*]
[Like] the heart of my palm tree
[Egypt is] the best climate for me [. . .]

The pigeon of our country
Our prized young pigeon [*zaghlūl*]
Stretched our wings
Across our oasis
And our salvation [*falāḥnā*] became
Worldly and religious [*dunyā wa-dīnan*][32]

The images that poetically follow are of a festive levity and verdancy engendered by the voice of the *misaḥḥarātī*, with a line that implicitly equates the salvation (*falāḥ*) of a hearing public with the elevation of a laboring underclass (*fallāḥin*) through a vision of earthly prosperity: "[O]ur salvation became worldly and religious" ("falāḥnā dunyā wa-dīnan").[33] Forms of wordplay and double entendre in the poem further implicate a connection between the awakener beating his drum and historic forms of national vigilance. A comparison of the heart of the *misaḥḥarātī*, for example, with a generous date palm yielding clusters of fruit leads to a vision of a *zaghlūl*, or a "young pigeon," whose wings are described as spreading over "our oasis"; this is an image that plays on the name of the pioneering nationalist leader of the interwar period, Saʿd Zaghlul, head of the Wafdist movement, which first demanded an end to Britain's occupation of Egypt.

While portraying Egypt as a region of postcolonial prosperity and salvation, the poem's opening lines also characterize Egyptian identity through an oppositional tension between historic pride and humility, between Egyptian territorial attachments and the movements of an invading cavalry during the Arab Muslim conquests. Self-referential details within the poem's opening, for example, compare the speaker with both a figure rooted in Egyptian soil, thriving in its oasis climate like a palm tree yielding fruit to his listening public, and a figure of movement affiliated with the Hijazi winds and a rapid (or mongrelized) cavalry. Ḥaddād's poetic ingenuity is exceptional in presenting this tension between Egyptian pride and humility. His simple pairing of terms and end rhymes builds on the ambiguous Arabic term *hagīna* (*fuṣḥā*: *hajīna*), which can mean both a mongrelized steed (an object of underclass shame and mockery) and, more archaically, a rapid steed (an object of boastful pride for an exultant, victorious cavalry).[34] On this basis, and due to the ambiguities associated with the verb *yehāgīnā*, which can mean (depending on interpreted etymology) "to mock" or "to rouse," the same lines can be understood as inviting two contrary meanings. The lines in which these rhymed terms (*hagīna*, *yehāgīnā*) are embedded can be interpreted as either "We rode the half-bred (mongrelized) steed / [and] God punishes / The one that mocks us" or "We rode the rapid steed / [and] God rewards / The one that rouses us."[35] Given that the *misaḥḥarātī* awakener was a traditionally humble, underclass figure occupying a trade close to mendicancy, these lines carry a poignancy in their assumption that "God rewards those that rouse us" (from sleep) and in their proud affiliation with a rapid cavalry (running parallel, in the lines of the poem, with the call to prayer brought by the "winds of Hijaz"). While these lines carry within them the *misaḥḥarātī*'s implicit boast, elevating his status as a worldly guide who summons the prayerful on behalf of a guide supreme, they also carry an implicit rebuke to those who would mock him on the grounds of class—or potentially of (mixed) lineage or race.

Where the *misaḥḥarātī* as a worldly guide describes himself as a figure bridling, guiding, or driving forth a half-bred steed (*suqnā al-hagīna*), another comparison appears possible for characterizing his status as a mediating figure. In Egyptian colloquial Arabic, the term *hagīn* or *hagīna*, while commonly referring to hybrids and crossbreeds, was also historically a designation for individuals born of a lower-status (non-Arab) mother and a higher-born (Arab) father, a concept associated in early Muslim communities with the half-caste *muwalladūn*, eventually yielding in the Spanish Iberian context the term *mulatto*.[36] Within the poem, the Egyptian colloquial term for this *mulatto* crossbreed or "half-breed" underscores the ingenuity of the poet's end rhyme, pairing in alternating lines the terms *hagīna* and *yehāgīnā*, rhyming the term for an implied "half-breed" driven on by the *misaḥḥarātī*, in one possible interpretation, with the work of "collectively rousing" an implicitly hybrid public. In one interpretation of the poem's opening lines, then, the notion of a mixed lineage is intertwined with the legacies of the Arab conquests in Egypt as a source of both humility and pride. This is equally suggested by the poem's intermedial lines, where the speaker proudly eulogizes the Arab Muslim conquests while illustrating his own qualified deference in their wake:

وعرب فوارس
نقول فتحنا
فتحاً مبينا
أنا قلت سجدة
للهِ سجدة
لعدوى سَكْته

And the Arab cavalry
we call it our conquest,
triumphed a clear victory
I said: prostration [to God]
For God alone, prostration
For my enemy, a silencing blow[37]

After referencing the "coming" of the call to prayer to an Egyptian collective in its opening lines, the poem sustains its historical allusion to the Arab Muslim conquests of Egypt in the penultimate lines. Toward the poem's conclusion, a sense of Arab pride is conveyed through a vision of both military prowess and poetic supremacy, a pride that Dayfallah aligns with a tradition of *jāhilī* (pre-Islamic tribal) Arabic boast poetry (*fakhr*).[38] Eulogizing the sweetness of the country "after her trampling of idols," these culminating lines clearly describe through their diction and through reference to a victorious Arab cavalry the Arab Muslim conquests (or the *fatḥ*) of Egypt in the seventh century. A self-consciously Arab pride, in this regard, distinguishes an Arab military and cultural supremacy from non-Arab others, as the poem insists on the humanity of the speaker against emergent hierarchies in Egypt after the conquests (implicitly privileging Arabs over non-Arabs):[39]

في عينى إنسان وفي عيون البلد إنسان
حلوه البلد بعد ما داست على الأوثان
حلوه البلد شهداءها قدّموا العرسان
حلوه البلد يا أحن قلوب وأوفى لسان
غنى الأمل يا حبيب والفتح يا حسان
ما سمعت الدنيا أمثال العرب شُعَرَا
ولا رأت مثل فرسان العرب فرسان

> In my eyes [I am] a person and a person in the eyes [*ʿuyūn*] of the land
> Sweet is the land after her trampling of idols [*awthān*, pronounced *awsān*]
> Sweet is the land whose martyrs yield bridegrooms [*ʿursān*]
> Sweet is the land, Oh, tenderest of hearts and most loyal of tongues [*lisān*]
> Singing hope, Oh, beloved, and conquest [*fatḥ*, or "victory"], Oh, beautiful [*ḥussān*],
> The world has not *heard* the *likes* [or "the *proverbs*," *amthāl*] of the Arabs as poets [*shuʿarān*]
> Nor seen a cavalry like Arab horsemen [*fursān*][40]

These culminating lines of the poem rally to the cause of Egyptian Arab pride a sense of military prowess and poetic supremacy, a pride deriving from the Arab Muslim conquests (and, as Dayfallah contends, aligned with practices of pre-Islamic tribal boast poetry foundational to a classical canon in *fuṣḥā*). In so doing, however, they destabilize the terms of what culturally and linguistically passes for "Arabness," by slipping into the poem elements of ambiguity regarding what generically constitutes the apex of Arabic poetic achievements.

Double meanings and puns within these lines subtly elevate the colloquial and the folkloric as the material of Arab cultural supremacy, implicitly raising *ʿāmmiyya* to the culturally sanctioned status of "high" poetry in *fuṣḥā*.[41] Where the poem describes Egypt after the Muslim conquests as a site of "the most loyal tongues" or "languages" (*lisān*, meaning both "language" and "tongue"), it leaves open the question of what amounts to linguistic allegiance in diglossic Egypt or what represents a "loyal tongue" when spoken on behalf of Arab poetic supremacy. The poem also leaves ambiguous what qualifies as "superior" poetry through a pun on the term *amthāl*, which can mean both ideal "paragons" and folkloric "proverbs." As such, a single line yields two potentially divergent meanings: "The world has not *heard* the *likes* [*amthāl*] of the Arabs as poets [as paragons]" and "The world has not *heard* the [superior] *proverbs* [*amthāl*] of the Arabs as poets." In the latter case, the term *amthāl* is associated less with the poetic than with the folkloric, the common, the idiomatic, and often the vulgar in colloquial or dialect form. The poem's central assertions, then, on the incomparability of "Arabs as poets"—whose "likes" or whose "proverbs" "the world has not *heard*"—elevates the colloquial as the poetic speaker cunningly challenges the marginality of his own medium (*ʿāmmiyya*) by praising a generic hybrid of high and low culture (poetic proverbs).[42]

Egyptian claims to Arab supremacy are, then, held in tension with a sense of subalternity relative to high literary Arabic in a poem that insists on a hybrid (Egyptian Arab) speaker's humanity in the "eyes" of "the land." Egypt appears in Ḥaddād's poetry as a historically subaltern region after the Arab Muslim conquests and is yet lauded as the proud custodial embodiment of Arabic-Islamic values. These values, especially in his poetry after the Naksah or defeat of 1967, encompass an ideal of cultural parity that enjoins Egyptians to level racial or ethnolinguistic hierarchies in the name of Islam. Through such portrayals of Egyptian cultural hybridity, Arabness appears to transcend historical divisions between Arab Muslim peripheries and centers, as Egypt itself is characterized as a liminal site through which sympathies extend from Arab communities to the universal subaltern.

Parity Between *ʿArab* and *ʿAjam*

Following the War of 1967 (or Naksah), Ḥaddād wrote a poetry collection that explored the vantage point of an Egypt whose status historically shifted between conqueror and conquered. Within this collection, a cycle of *misaḥḥarātī* poems published in 1968, the poet reconciles the grounds of Arab ethnic or racial pride with an egalitarian sensibility—here analyzed in two poems, "The Summoner" ("Ṣāḥib Nidā") and "Heart of the Believer" ("Qelb Muʾmin").

Ḥaddād's poems stage in *ʿāmmiyya* verse a conciliation already evident within an emerging corpus of Arabic literature in *fuṣḥā* during the nineteenth century. These poems exhibit a tension between Arabic as a charismatic language aligned with a particular sense of ethnolinguistic belonging and Arabic as a language of interethnic and aspirationally universal vocation in Islamic religious terms. Arabic is described within Ḥaddād's corpus as an unrivaled language, one aligned with a charismatic Arab Muslim messenger (the Prophet Muhammad); and yet, it is a medium historically associated with a message whose singularity appears tempered by two dynamics that unsettle its status as a prestige language. The first is the coexistence of a "pure" register of Arabic (*fuṣḥā*) with a more vulgar *ʿāmmiyya*; the second is the ritual vocation of Arabic as a medium that crosses the thresholds between "Arabs" and "non-Arabs"—between *ʿarab* and *ʿajam*. Ḥaddād's post-Naksah *misaḥḥarātī* corpus addresses this polycentric matrix that defines Arabic as a contact language. His poems in the collection mark the tensions between Arabic's nativist and interethnic guises—bearing a historically Islamic role, as a language of conquest from West Asia to North Africa, and informing the historical (af)filiations of a hybrid Egyptian populace.

The self-referential aspect of "The Summoner" is striking for its claim that the figure of the *misaḥḥarātī* possesses an instrument (a *ṭabla*, or drum) that is itself personified as a faithful reciter of the Qurʾan, a *ṭabla mujawwida*—coming from the term *tajwīd*, meaning "to recite the Qurʾan in linguistically sanctioned form," though the term *mujawwida* can also mean "well-crafted," in another example of verbal play. The poem presents a vision of the drumming *misaḥḥarātī* as a colloquial or vernacular figure of ritual resonance, one that resolves a certain paradox: If he expresses himself through corrupted forms of speech when compared with a more purified, ritual standard of Arabic, he nonetheless contributes to a devotional soundscape central to sustaining orthodox ritual (prayer) and to the mass reception of sacred verse.

The opening lines of the poem reinforce this notion, building through an end rhyme that resonates with the Arabic term for a summons (*nidā*) or call: *munshida, ṣadā, mujawwida, shadā,* connoting "to chant," "to echo," "to recite," "to warble." Each end rhyme conjures scenes that animate the environs of the Nile valley in its response, intertwining the *misaḥḥarātī*'s call to awaken and pray with a eulogy of Egypt as a monumental and ritually charismatic site. To this end, the poem advances its praise of Egypt not only as the locus of history's earliest embodiments but also as "ḍammiyat al-Azhar wa-l-Sayyeda Zaynab," guardian of the mosques of al-Azhar and Sayyida Zaynab, sites defended by "a thousand minarets, hand in hand," shielding "a unified *umma*":

مسحراتي صاحب ندا
منقراتي كدا كدا
في إيدي طبلة مجوّدة
امشي على ريحة الندى
و النسمة في الجوّ مُنشدة
توالي موالي والحدا
يا مصر يا واحة مسعدة
نطقت والفجر كان صدى
حتى الشجر فى الحجر شدا
لما بدأت التاريخ بدا
لِحمه وطول الزمن سِدى
إنتِ الأميرة المجاهدة
الإنسانيّة أم الفدا
أم الحضارة يا والدة
ضميتِ الأزهر والسيدة
وألف مادنه يدأ يدا
سياج لأمة موحدة

Misaḥḥarātī, Hear my summons [*nidā*]
Munaqarātī, striking, striking [*kida, kida*]
In my two hands, a drum recites [*ṭabla mujawwida*]
As I walk on the winds of dew [*nadā*]
The breeze through the air chants [*munshida*]
the measure of my *mawwāls* [poems]
Oh, Egypt, oh joyous oasis [*wāha musaʿada*]
You spoke and dawn was your echo [*ṣadā*]
Even the trees in the stones warbled [*shadā*]
When you began history began [*badā*]
to embody itself and across time prevail [*sidā*]
you princess who strives [*mujāhida*]
for humanity, mother of redemption [*al-fidā*]
mother of civilization, Oh, mother [*wālida*]
of al-Azhar and al-Sayyeda
and a thousand minarets hand in hand [*yedan yedā*]
shields for a unified *umma*[43]

After this description of Egypt as the guardian of a defended *umma*, the culminating lines of the poem address the terms of this defense, its "surety," with the following lines, building from an implied ethnolinguistic association with the Prophet Muhammad: "We are Arabs and the Prophet is Arab" ("iḥnā ʿarab wa-l-nabī ʿarabī"). To this end, the speaker invokes the notion that "Arabness" encompasses both "us" (a listening public) and "the Prophet," correlating "Arabness" with a charismatic guarantor or figure of protection:

صوموا و قولوا آمنا يا عباد الله
كونوا قلوب مطمئنة يا عباد الله
النصر فينا ومنّا يا عباد الله
احنا عرب والنبي عربي وضامنّا
ما ينكسرشى يميننا يا عباد الله[44]

Fast and speak peace, oh servants of God
Be with hearts reassured, oh servants of God
For victory is within us and for us, oh servants of God
We are Arabs and the Prophet is Arab and our guarantor
Will not break faith with us, oh servants of God[45]

In these penultimate lines of the poem, an association between a listening public and the Prophet—unified in Arabness—reassures those humbled by their devotion or servitude to God (*ʿibād Allah*). Such claims of what might appear legible as Arab racial or ethnic pride are nonetheless qualified by a virtual counterclaim also evident in Ḥaddād's poetry within the same cycle of *misaḥḥarātī* poems, composed for the month of Ramadan in 1968.

In this respect, Ḥaddād's corpus also encompasses and intertextually references an egalitarian pride aligned with Arabic-Islamic teachings, albeit advanced by an Arab prophet within an "Arabic" language (rather than a non-Arabic or *ʿajamiyya* one). In a second poem within the cycle, the notion of Arab distinction is very explicitly held in tension with egalitarian injunctions as they pertain to a defeated populace, whether in Egypt during the Arab conquests of the seventh century or in a contemporary Egypt after the Naksah of 1967. The poem in question, "Qelb Muʾmin," meaning "Heart of the Believer," begins with a sequence of lines mourning the dead in the wake of defeat, as the vigilant beating of the *misaḥḥarātī*'s drum is described as mimicking the restless heartbeat of the *misaḥḥarātī* himself. The poem then addresses the "heart of the believer," intertwining a sense of loss for the departed with the consecration of Egypt's wartime dead as a matter of sacrifice, sanctified as the speaker concludes that the highest authority over both victor and defeated is that of *al-ṣamad*, "the everlasting," an epithet of God:

مسحراتي
منقراتي
لا قلبي ريّح
ولا رقد
دارت رحاية
على الضحايا
فجرى وضُحايا
دم وجسد
والأرض حاضنة
[. . .]
احنا اتحدنا
يا جيش بلدنا
على كل مادنة
الله أكبر
على كل منبر
الله أحد
أرض العروبة
لمن سجد

Misaḥḥarātī [Hear my summons]
Munaqarātī [The beat of my drumming]
My heart does not rest
awake in my breast
with the outbreak [of war]
for the slaughtered, mourning
To forenoon from morning
body and blood
in the embracing earth [. . .]
We are united
Oh, troops of our country
Upon each minaret
God is greatest [*Allahu Akbar*]
Upon every pulpit
God is one [*Allahu Aḥad*]
The Land of Arabness [*al-ʿurūba*]
Is for those who bend [prostrate in prayer] [*liman sajad*][46]

After a line claiming that "[t]he Land of Arabness [*al-ʿurūba*] / Is for those who bend" in prayer, the poem builds on the motif of bending or inclining both as a prayerful movement and as the embodiment of an ethical sense of humility. Through the poem's central tensions, it indirectly contrasts a contemporary victor after the Naksah with the implicit humility of an Arab people; the latter, within the evolving logic of the poem, exhibit humility whether in times of victory or defeat, as the poem describes through oblique references to the early Muslim Arab conquests across West Asia and North Africa. To this end, the speaker claims in the poem's penultimate lines:

وما قالش لكبيره يابا وعظم الإحساس [. . .]
ولا تبنّى ولا هزّ الهلال السمح [. . .]
والعرب عدلوا
—ولا حد قبل العرب—بين كافة الأجناس

Our enemy does not bend [or "incline," *inʿaṭafa*] for mankind
Saying not "oh, father" [*yā ābā*], to his elder out of grandeur of feeling [*ʿaẓm al-iḥsās*] [. . .]
Nor does he bear the crescent of liberality [or "forgiveness and generosity"] [*lā hazz al-hilāl al-samḥ*] [. . .]
And the Arabs equalized [or "did not discriminate"]
—and none before the Arabs—between the entirety of races [*kāfat al-ajnās*][47]

The poem culminates with these lines, which fold within themselves a certain paradox: an assertion of Arab *moral* superiority on the grounds of an indifference to Arab *racial* superiority, as "the Arabs did not discriminate [or "equalized"]—and none before the Arabs—between the entirety of races [or "kinds," *ajnās*]." Here, then, a sense of contemporary defeat appears tempered by an assertion of moral authority in egalitarian terms—but bearing a certain internal contradiction, as assertions of Arab moral authority (or superiority) depend on what is designated an "Arab" indifference to racial hierarchies. In other words, a claim to moral righteousness named as a liberality or magnanimity historically aligned with "Islam" or the "crescent" of "generosity" derives from claims of a radical and historically unprecedented indiscrimination between Arabs and *kāfat al-ajnās*, "the totality of humankind." This term, however, the plural of *jins*, might equally be interpreted as the totality of *races*, of *strata*, of *kinds* (as cognates for *genus*, *jins* being also the root of *jinsiyya*, the Arabic translation for *citizenship*).

The poem's emphasis on the interiority of the faithful (the "heart of the believer") and these final, stanzaic lines subtly align with Islamic precepts proclaiming an equality between "peoples" and "tribes" (*shuʿūb wa-qabāʾil*), or between "Arab and non-Arab" (*ʿarab wa-ʿajam*), precepts that suggest a leveling between peoples distinguished only by their internal states of devotion. Although the final lines of the poem may be read as a claim to equality across racial or ethnic differences (depending on one's translation of the term *ajnās*), they may be equally read as a claim to equality across differences of class, given that *ṭabaqāt al-ajnās* (strata of *ajnās*) had equally designated differences between elites and commoners in classical Arabic contexts.[48] Here, then, the poem seems to culminate with an argument on parity that is a matter not just of "justice" (*ʿadl*) in racial or ethnic terms but of class within a shared community of faith. This is particularly poignant given that Ḥaddād's *misaḥḥarātī* corpus challenges the marginalization of *ʿāmmiyya* as it associates a less textually literate underclass with decadence or dissolution in speech, as noted by Dayfallah.

At a time of Egyptian national mourning after the 1967 conflict, in his November 1968 Ramadan poems, Ḥaddād's poetry seems to present to its readers or auditors the following claims as a matter of consolation: first, that "[w]e are Arabs and the Prophet is Arab" ("iḥnā ʿarab wa-l-nabī ʿarabī"), asserting a sense of Arab (af)filiation with the Prophet Muhammad. And yet, as another tactic of consolation, Arabness is associated with a morally superior leveling of racial hierarchies, as though to gesture to Egypt's hybrid constitution and subaltern position as a region historically Arabized (with claims such as "al-ʿarab, wa lā aḥad qablihim, ʿadalū al-ajnās"). This poetic sense of national pride amid defeat occasions a humility that moves the speaker—embodied by the figure of the *misaḥḥarātī*—in two directions: inward, toward an introspective and nostalgic quest for historic forms of pride, but also toward an extension of broadened sympathies, through an inclination or *bending* (*inʿiṭāf*) toward what Dayfallah calls the universally oppressed or marginalized in mutual recognition.[49] As Dayfallah considers more broadly of Ḥaddād's corpus, Ḥaddād's poetry (within the *misaḥḥarātī*) progressively moves toward an enlargement of the collective self, moving away from a tribalist (*qabalī*) sensibility to a more layered sense of "the people's" (*al-shaʿab*'s) internal diversity.[50]

Such arguments are reinforced by the association of the speaker in Ḥaddād's inaugural *misaḥḥarātī* poem (of 1964, "Yā Hādī") to the cross-bred or half-bred mulatto—*hagīn(a)* in Arabic—along with his reference to Arabic-Islamic ideals of indiscrimination among the totality of humankind (*kāfat al-ajnās*). Here, one might recall the Islamic hadith of the punishment exacted by the caliph

ʿUmar upon the Arab commander of Egypt ʿAmr ibn al-ʿĀṣ and his son for presumptions of Arab racial superiority over conquered Egyptians in the seventh century, an anecdote cited by Egyptian and Indonesian authors noted in preceding chapters on Islamic ideals of parity in Egypt. Historic assertions of Arabness, in other words, are intertwined in such Islamic traditions with the memory of Egypt as a formerly non-Arab (or *ʿajam*) space. The shifting grounds of Egypt's identification with Arabness emerge in Ḥaddād's poetry, as the value of Egypt's Arab self-identification seems to vacillate between affiliation and disavowal, pride and indifference, as a moral or ethical imperative.

"The Earth Speaks Arabic"

In another important sequence of poems written on the history of Cairo in 1968, Ḥaddād enshrines the aural traces of Cairo's past from the Arab conquests of Egypt to the rise of counterimperialism in the twentieth century. In the process, he portrays *ʿāmmiyya* verse again as a mediating form between the provincial and the transregional, between sanctioned Qurʾanic recitations (or *tajwīd*) and their reception among a common, listening public. This is further evident within Ḥaddād's iconic poem "The Earth Speaks Arabic" ("Al-Arḍ Bitetekelem ʿArabi"), which imaginatively conjoins Egypt to the Levant through a shared soundscape. It is spoken in the voice of a traditional Egyptian bard, a *ḥakawātī*, who recounts Egypt's layered past. By illustrating the conditions of its own genesis, the hearing or reception of a Qurʾanic recitation from the minarets of Cairo, the colloquial poem portrays the generative coexistence between colloquial poetry and sacralized speech. "The Earth Speaks Arabic" is widely considered a poem of national solidarity and consolation written after the Naksah, the "setback" or defeat after the 1967 war between Egypt and Israel, in which Egypt lost the Sinai Peninsula and failed in its aspirations to wrest Palestinian territories from Israeli control. The territorial ambiguities associated with Arabic and the shifting boundaries of pan-Arab solidarities are implicated in the poem's opening lines, invoking "one country"—unnamed, territorially undefined, but reflecting "a single sky." The poem conjures a national audience ("children of one country"), but it is a public conjoined by the common act of listening, rather than reading:

يا سامعين أبناء بلد واحدة
تحت السما الواحدة [. . .]

> Oh, you who listen, children of one country
> beneath a single sky [. . .][51]

The poem's subject, then, appears to be a country defined by territorial ambiguities: an arabophone country grounded but limitless, defined by transcendent horizons, as the poem personifies "the Earth" as a speaker of Arabic. The poem, however, self-referentially leaves open *which* Arabic the personified Earth speaks—in effect eliding the controversial division between *ʿāmmiyya* and *fuṣḥā* that haunts registers of Arabic speech, a division often associated with the risks of cultural fragmentation across transregional arabophone communities.

Through these opening lines, the poem nonetheless indirectly dignifies as its subject the colloquial or vernacular—an Arabic that is "spoken" and "heard," rather than written and read. It implies that Arabic speech attaches to both a terrain and a limitless transcendence for those who hear it. In addition to emphasizing what is aurally shared by its addressees, children of a single country, the poem consecrates Arabic as though arising from a natural terrain:

الأرض بتتكلم عربي
رد على قدس فلسطين
أصلك مَيّة وأصلك طين
الأرض بتتكلم عربي

الأرض بتتكلم عربي سَبَل وكروم
تجرى اللقمهة على المحروم
ما تثبتش حصون الروم
الأرض بتتكلم عربي

[. . .]

الأرض بتتكلم عربي بوَجْد وشوق
الفرع اللي يهم لفوق
لاجل الجدر يشم الضوء
الأرض بتتكلم عربي

الأرض بتتكلم عربي جدورها جدود
مد اتوسّع زيّ العود
انت الباكر والمولود
الأرض بتتكلم عربي

The Earth speaks Arabic
Answering the *Quds* of Palestine,
You come from water, you come from clay,
The Earth speaks Arabic

The Earth speaks Arabic through its stalks and vines
Running morsels to the deprived,
Unsettling the fortresses of Rome [Byzantium],
The Earth speaks Arabic

[...]

The Earth speaks Arabic with passion and longing
[Like] the branch that favors the heights
And for the sake of the roots smells the light
The Earth speaks Arabic

The Earth speaks Arabic, her roots ancestral,
extending, widening, reaching like canes,
You are the first shoots stirring,
The Earth speaks Arabic[52]

Arabic is here envisioned as a medium inextricable from a message of territorial belonging but associated with the transcendence of man-made boundaries embodied by "the fortresses of Rome." Lines from the poem suggest an equivalence between the land and those who live from it, those who arise from and return to the earth, claiming of a listening populace that "[y]ou come from water, you come from clay, / The Earth speaks Arabic." Here a Qur'anic or biblical resonance might be read within these lines as a memento mori, evoking the Qur'anic notion that humanity derives from clay (*min al-ṭīn*).

As the poem unfolds, claims to the land as an arabophone site are also reinforced. The personification of the land as a speaker of Arabic resurfaces through the poem's recurrent refrain ("The Earth speaks Arabic"). It is a refrain, however, progressively intertwined with historical invocations that naturalize the association between arabophone speech and territorial attachment. As such, the poem begins with a remembrance of Salāḥ al-Din al-Ayyubi, who employed the hills of Muqattam in Cairo as a defensive seat from which to retake Levantine territories from Christian Crusaders in the twelfth century.[53] Notwithstanding such references to the Crusades, the poet envisions the "land that speaks Arabic" as an imagined community religiously sanctioned rather than religiously derived. The poem references the history of medieval conflict between Muslim and Christian armies, but the scales of an imagined justice, arbitered by the Earth "herself," is envisioned in cross-confessional terms:

والأرض هي الحَاكِمَة بالعدل
بين ابنها والمستبد الغريب
الجبارين اللي احتموا بالصليب
داسوا على عيسى وكتاب المحبة
عملوا الدمار والقتل والتخريب

And the Earth [the land] is the governor of justice
Between her children and strange tyrants,
Strongmen that took shelter by the cross
Trampling upon Jesus and the beloved book
Enacting destruction, slaughter, and devastation[54]

Reference to the Crusades addresses lines of enmity between "foreign tyrants" and "children of the land" or earth, rather than antagonisms drawn across religious lines. Here, the victories of Salāḥ al-Din are imagined as antagonizing not Christians (*masīḥīyyun*) but, rather, Christian pretenders (*mutamasīḥīyyun*), inviting the possibility of interpreting Salāḥ al-Din's counter-Crusades not as an aggression against Christianity but as a vindication of it. Here we might see Ḥaddād, himself a Christian convert to Islam, distinguishing between feigned and authentic representatives of a religious faith—a pattern that some critics have generalized across his work, contrasting subaltern figures of religious conscience from politically empowered religious pretenders.[55] Written in the wake of a devastating national defeat in 1967, the poem offers in contemporary consolation the memory of a past triumph. Recounting the history of Salāḥ al-Din, the speaker consoles his listeners with the assertion that, in the absence of victory, "truth" reigns victorious. To this end, the poem advances a retelling of the past, a "dawn that pains the eyes of the powerful, of mighty tyrants," by glorifying what the speaker describes as a misnamed era of past triumph, mistaken by *al-gharb* (the West) as an "age of darkness" or the Middle Ages. The culminating lines of the poem reinforce this notion—even as the poem seems to consecrate as a matter of divine ordainment the mysteries of "victory" and "defeat"—with the final, Qur'anic claim that "victory is from God."

By its final stanzas, the poem reveals itself to be a form of rumination, as it dramatizes its own catalysts through the intertwining of a contested landscape and soundscape from Cairo to al-Shām—the Levant, a region encompassing Syria and Palestine. With the redirection of the speaker's attention skyward, an echo of the poem's opening lines appears at the end, moving toward an ambiguous and potentially endless horizon, as though resonant with the opening image of the poem ("a country / beneath a single sky"). A sense of auditory soundscapes shared by an imagined community of hearers is emphasized, as the ambiguous borders of the "one country" first invoked in the poem return to the immaterial, to sacred sounds carried by Cairene winds.

In its final stanzas, the poem stages the conditions of its own genesis—an attestation of the triumphs of Salāḥ al-Din, in the wake of whose victories minarets continued to stand from Egypt to the Levant. The speaker concludes the poem with a description of his own hearing of voices from these minarets. It is these historic traces in the soundscapes of Cairo, the aural resonance of Qur'anic Arabic from the city's minarets—"[t]he voice of the reciter in the verses of light"—that stir within "the imaginings of the poet" an inspiration for the poem itself, returning the speaker's attentions to the horizons between earth and sky:

والأرض صنعتها الأمل والبشاير
والشمس دوّارة عليها تشاور
تاخد وتدي في خيال الشاعر
تلقاه عجب في الدنيا هلّل وراج
في الشام ومصر تنادت الأبراج
الفتح تم في ليلة المعراج
صلّوا على طه الرسول الحبيب
أفتح إيديَّ لفوق الاقي المجيب
يا قاهرة نجومك ملاليّه
فيها الهداية لآخر المعمور
أما رياحك حامِلَة ليَّه
صوت المرتّل في آيات النور:
"و نصرٌ من اللهِ و فتحٌ قريب"

And the Earth's labors are hope and good tidings
As the sun encircles her in gesture
Taking and giving in the imaginings of the poet
Whom she meets as a wonder in the world, exultant and resonant
In the Shām [the Levant], in Egypt, the turrets call to each other
Victory persists in the night of ascent [*miʿrāj*]
As they pray on the name [*Ṭāhā*] of the beloved Prophet
I open my hands upward and meet the One who answers
Oh, Cairo, your stars glimmer
Bearing guidance to the last world
For your winds carry to me

The voice of the reciter in the verses of light:
"And victory is from God and a conquest near"[56]

By renarrating a scene of call and response—with God evoked as *al-Mujīb*, "the One who answers"—the poem animates a sense of the sublime, of the generative wonder or awe (*ʿajab*) that arises through the convergence of sacralized speech and colloquial poetry. The poem invokes one of its own catalysts amid minarets that form part of a common terrain and soundscape: a Qurʾanic verse that "speaks" in consolation to the present in a time of defeat. As such, one can read the act of the speaker's prayer—"I open my hands upward and meet" the response—as a staging of the *ʿāmmiyya* poem's genesis itself, legible as a response to the *tajwīd*, the orthodox recitation of Qurʾanic scripture, echoing forth from the minarets of Cairo.

The ultimate impression left is one of the lived coexistence of *ʿāmmiyya* poetry and sacralized speech. The poem, then, vividly projects a vision of Arabic linguistic unity in a colloquial register while eliding the contemporary fact of its own marginality by virtue of its colloquial form. The claim of arabophone unity persists, notwithstanding the poem's own peripheral position as part of a colloquial literary corpus. This is all the more poignant given the elevation of several lines of the poem to iconic status as lyrics, recirculating within arabophone soundscapes nationally and transnationally when they were famously sung by Sayed Mekawy.[57]

"The Earth Speaks Arabic" elevates Arabic speech as an object of Arab pride, but the poet, while composing in *ʿāmmiyya,* again refuses to directly specify which Arabic the refrain fundamentally represents—as though eliding those historical polemics that gave rise to the marginality of Ḥaddād's own choice. The poet instead stages as a quotidian inheritance the coexistence and mutual regeneration of *fuṣḥā* ritual and *ʿāmmiyya* verse, without privileging those language ideologies that opposed them in agonistic terms. Ḥaddād's iconic poem presents a kind of transcendence of these polarizing controversies, presenting *ʿāmmiyya* poetry as a medium of religious transcendence, of historical retrieval and self-knowledge, and of lateral mediation for subaltern solidarities "beneath a single sky."

In Praise of Bandung

Amid the broader cause of pan-Arab unity, Ḥaddād's poetry memorialized critical moments of postrevolutionary imagining for an Egypt perennially embattled: engaging in boundary wars over the Suez, struggling to control its

Nilotic waterways, and negotiating its solidarity with Palestine. The poem "Farḥa" interprets Egypt's victory after the Suez crisis and its independent construction of the Aswan High Dam without Anglo-American or foreign financial backing under Nasser as a sign of counterimperial sovereignty. As such, the imagined call of "the white dove of Bandung" functions within the poem as an aural refrain, interwoven with a sequence of poetized vignettes on the collective mobilization of an Egyptian populace—of laborers indirectly portrayed through images of bricks rising, of arms lifting to "build the dam at the head of the canal," as though raising a "new dawn" of sovereign prosperity. As the white dove of Bandung coos, visions of mass labor are reimagined as forms of collective self-possession, overturning associations of these sites with older regimes of colonial (and khedival) coercion, given that their construction was once built on the backs of a corvée system of forced Egyptian labor:

قلت للطوب انت فرحان قال لي إسمع
الحمامة البيضا من باندونج تسجع
رقص الضي على جناحها و شعشع
اللمون و البرتقان
قلت حانزل زي ما بتنزل و حاطلع
زي ما بتطلع و اقلدها و ابدّع
في الغنا والطيران

I asked the bricks of their joy, and they said, listen:
The white dove of Bandung coos [or "composes in rhyme," *sajʿ*]
Light dances upon her wings and spreads
Through lemon and orange groves
I said: I will fall as you fall and rise
As you rise in imitation, creating
In song and in flight[58]

The poem in subtle ways suggests its aural catalysts through images of collective movement, as it invokes the conditions of its appearance as a response to the iconic lines of a speech broadcast by Nasser in July 1956 announcing the nationalization of the Suez Canal, a symbol of Anglo-French expropriation in Egypt. The impression is one of a populace mobilized and elevated by their own voices, as part of a call and response both to the "white dove of Bandung" and to Nasser's speech. The poem describes a radio broadcast that rides "upon the waves of Alexandria," whose "summering breezes have called gently forth / What forty generations have awaited." The broadcast was met with festive street cries across Egypt, cries that surface in the poem: "We have nationalized the Canal" ("iḥnā amimnā al-qanāl"). The speaker characterizes this rallying cry as "[w]ords every Egyptian knows by name," sating "[t]he yearnings of every era" amid the cooing of "the white dove of Bandung":[59]

والحمامة البيضا من باندونج تسجع
لما ترفع جناحاتها البيضا ترفع
السنابل والكيزان [. . .]

انا مش قادر أقول سحر الليلادي
وقفت الدنيا عشان تسمع بلادي [. . .]

طير يا راديو على موج اسكندرية
على نسمة مصيّفة نادية طريّة
أربعين جيل في انتظار الكلمة ديّه
كل أشواق الزمان
والحمامة البيضا من باندونج تسجع
ترتوى العطشانة والعطشان وتشبع
الجعانة والجعان

غنّوا في ضلوعي يا أهلي ويا رفاقي
زي ما بيغنّي نيلنا في السواقي
وانا قلبي يجيب نشيد أرضي وسمائي
قبل ما تجيبه الودان
والحمامة البيضا من باندونج تسجع
"إحنا أممنا القنال" ما اعرفش أروع
منها كلمة ع اللسان
كلمة تعرف كل واحد مصري باسمه [. . .]

[A]s the white dove of Bandung coos:
the lift of her wings raises
the crops and the corn [. . .]

I am powerless to speak [the charms of] these nights
The world has stopped to hear [the voice of] my country [. . .]

Fly oh, radio [sounds] upon the waves of Alexandria
the summering breezes have called gently forth
What forty generations have awaited by this speech[60]

The yearnings of every era
And the white dove of Bandung coos,
Saturating thirsts and sating
Hunger after hunger

Sing within my ribs, oh, my kin, my companions,
Like our Nile sings as it turns in the waterwheels
My heart replies with a chant to my land and sky
Before listening ears reply
And the white dove of Bandung coos,
"We have nationalized the Canal"—I know no more marvelous
Words than these upon the tongue
Words every Egyptian knows by name [. . .][61]

The poem plays on the notion of a call and response—between that which is heard and that which is inspired in response, implying an equality between revolutionary laborers and soldiers, between "those that work with their hands and those that possess by their hands." Within an imagined "world" listening to and stilled by the voice of "my country," the speaker enjoins his public to sing "[l]ike our Nile sings as it turns in the waterwheels."

The poem as eulogy arguably subverts its classical precedents, recentering an older court tradition of praise poetry upon an image of Egypt's popular masses as the more authentic patrons of (postrevolutionary) Egypt.[62] To this end, the poem embeds an anti-monarchist vision within a counterimperial one. It recurrently centers on a collective while alluding to Nasser as an animating source of popular inspiration. In the third stanza Ḥaddād introduces a eulogistic wordplay on the meaning of *Gamāl* (Nasser's first name, which also means "beauty" in Arabic), proclaiming that "Egypt delights in the beauty [*gamāl*] of her realized hopes," embedding a reference to Nasser, Egypt's Bandung delegate, with an assertion of Egypt's "self-realization":

مصر فرحانة بجمال حقق أملها
ورفع صوتها وأحلامها وعضلها
وبنى لها سد من أول قنالها
صبح البر أمان
والحمامة البيضا من باندونج تسجع
غنوه فوق النيل وفوق شطْآنه تجمع
القلوب رقة وحنان

Egypt delights in the beauty [*gamāl*] of her realized hopes
And raises her voices and dreams and strength
To build the dam at the head of the canal
Securing the land
As the white dove of Bandung coos
Her song above the Nile and its shores gather
Hearts gentle and tender[63]

The speaker in another instance describes a contemporary Egypt "stronger than kingdoms," indirectly praising the overthrow of Egypt's former monarchy at Nasser's hands, in a stanza that describes a populace elevated for having glimpsed the "beauty [*gamāl*] of freedom." It is a beauty compared with the epic heroine ʿAbla, as the listening public is compared with the cavalry of her suitor, the folk hero ʿAntar, whose "gathered spears glisten." "Neither Paris nor London will rule us / Like Washington rules over them both," the speaker proclaims, with a concluding image of defiance that conjures the festive "canons of Ramadan"—ambiguously accompanied by the cooing sounds of the "white dove of Bandung":

إحنا يا حرية أقوى من الممالك
كلنا بنرمح عشان نلمح جمالك
فوق حصان عنتر يا عبلة بنت مالك
وانتِ تسقي لنا الحصان
والحمامة البيضا من باندونج تسجع
والرماح اللي ركزناها بتلمع
واقفه زي الديدبان

مش باريز اللي حتحكمنا و لندن
زي ما بتحكم على الاتنين واشنطن
عرب الحرية بنحيى و نحضن
الحبايب والجيران
والحمامة البيضا من باندونج تسجع
حلوة بتقول مش حيفضل بكرة مدفع
إلا مدفع رمضان

Oh, freedom, we are stronger than kingdoms
We are transfixed by the glimpse of your beauty [*gamāl*]
Above ʿAntar's steed, Oh, ʿAbla daughter of Malik
You quench the thirst of our horses

As the white dove of Bandung coos,
And our gathered spears glisten
Standing like vigilant guardsmen

Neither Paris nor London will rule us
Like Washington rules over them both
Arabs of freedom, we greet and embrace
Our beloved and neighbor
As the white dove of Bandung coos,
Saying sweetly: tomorrow we fire no canons
But the [festive] canons of Ramadan[64]

The poem captures the raw, festive spirit—or *farḥa*—of a transformative, nationalist moment, enshrining in poetic form an episode of public celebration. The poem forms part of a broader collection entitled *Ḥanibnī al-Sadd* (*We Shall Build the [Aswan] Dam*), a title itself taken from street cries and public soundscapes emerging immediately after Nasser's Alexandrian speech.[65]

The circumstances through which Ḥaddād captured this festive spirit, however, were not without their ambiguities: The collection of poems reflects the high points of Nasser's Egypt while marking the poet's reconciliation with Nasser's regime after a period of imprisonment.[66] During Ḥaddād's imprisonment, his approach to his poetry transformed under the influence of fellow prisoners drawn from Egypt's rural underclass. Despite Ḥaddād's elite background and (French) education, the experience attuned him to the colloquial legacies of Egyptian folkloric traditions and to the hardships of Egypt's rural poor.[67] His poetic invocation of Bandung may therefore be legible as a sincere elevation of Egypt's laboring masses, as an alignment of these masses with an emancipated Asia-Africa, and as a politically usable literary text. The poem therefore indirectly records the struggle of radical leftist poets who were forced to reconcile with an increasingly authoritarian postrevolutionary regime, one that progressively quelled political opposition in the 1950s. In this way, as previously noted, Ḥaddād's poem in praise of Bandung ("Farḥa") documents the ambiguous nationalist rebranding of Asian-African solidarities in mid-twentieth-century Egypt.

Ḥaddād's invocation of Bandung translates into localized poetic form a sense of transregional solidarities, imagining its implications on a national stage at the onset of the Suez crisis—a high point in the vicissitudes of pan-Arabism under Nasser's leadership. This occurred notwithstanding the possibility that such invocations of Bandung in Egyptian colloquial Arabic were less likely to reascend to international platforms of recognition in print than poems written in *fuṣḥā*. The first journal of Afro-Asian writing (later renamed *Lotus*), for example, was an indirect outgrowth of publishing platforms that arose from the Bandung gathering beginning in the late 1960s and the 1970s. It took recourse to three languages of broad transregional reach for publication—French, English, and Arabic—but, as Hala Halim notes, it employed Arabic in *fuṣḥā* rather than in dialect forms. Relatedly, its features on Arabic literature during the late 1960s and 1970s (when Ḥaddād was actively publishing) tended to focus on writers in *fuṣḥā* rather than *ʿāmmiyya*—a reflection of the general state of Arabic writing and critical circles in the mid- to late twentieth century.[68]

Although *ʿāmmiyya* poetry deserves greater visibility within comparative Asian-African literary criticism, a caveat here is needed. The redemptive appeal of the vernacular as a concept and cultural front for broader South/South comparisons must be assessed, as Shaden Tageldin has argued, against its deployment and distortion in the wake of colonial interference, colonially engineered literacies, and the local impact of colonial-era taxonomies. This renders the term "vernacular" itself a problematic concept for capturing the most radical impulses and nuances of anticolonial writing. As she observes:

> The currency of the vernacular cannot be disarticulated from the rise of modern regimes of literary comparison in the shadow of nineteenth-century imperialism. Indeed, the translation of non-Europhone terms like *ʿāmmiyya* into the English term *vernacular* and its European analogues homogenized those terms and their complex semantic fields in the name of North/South comparability. Rather than re-homogenize their differences in the name of new East/South comparatisms, we might take these as theoretical lines of flight, reimagining as *mediation* what ideologies of the vernacular typically construct as binary oppositions between orality and writing, commons and elites, nature and artifice, living and dead, native and foreign.[69]

Ḥaddād's poetry employs *ʿāmmiyya* verse as a mediating form between orality and writing, native and foreign, commons and elites. His poems, which invite comparison across historically subaltern languages, unsettle such binaries for the sake of an egalitarian idealism. Writing such as Ḥaddād's answered Bandung's "call" for lateral Asian-African exchange and recognition, even as its colloquial register constrained its recirculation within Asian-African print and scholarly circuits still dominated by European languages and, within Arabic studies, by *fuṣḥā*. Tracing egalitarian patterns in Ḥaddād's work (patterns uneasily attached to the "vernacular" as a translational concept) allows us to redress a Bandung-era grievance voiced by Sukarno in 1955 across Asia-Africa's linguistic diversities. As we trace these patterns across language debates and literary form, a shared idealism becomes visible as a "line of flight" that crosses Asia-Africa's enduring problem of "mutual ignorance."[70]

7

After Empire: Segregations

IN 1959, on the eve of colonial French West Africa's fragmentation into several independent nation-states, the poet and statesman Léopold Sédar Senghor published a striking characterization of the Bandung Conference before his rise to the Senegalese presidency. He began by lauding the unprecedented character of the gathering, hailing it as a "moral victory" for Europe's former colonies in Asia and Africa.[1] Despite this initial praise, he went on to warn about the effects of the conference in its sanction of new forms of hegemony under the guise of anticolonial nationalisms. Although not a direct participant in the gathering, Senghor wrote from a lateral position both sympathetic toward Bandung's cause and critical of its potential impact. Of the conference's final communiqué, he observed that Bandung's motivation and legacy derived not from a common counterimperial racial consciousness across Asia-Africa but from an overreliance on nationalism as a potentially coercive front. "The conclusions of the Bandung Conference," Senghor wrote, "referred not to homeland [*patrie*], or to race, or even to the people but to the nation. The men of Bandung appropriated for themselves the myth that Europe had transmitted to them."[2] Senghor explained this process in the following terms:

> It is in effect on the model of Europe that the peoples of color constitute themselves as nations and battle for their independence. They confiscate, first, race, language, religion, morals, culture—to use them, as needed, *against* a particular race, a certain language, a certain religion, a particular set of moral beliefs, a certain culture of the country. [...] It is the Sudan that wishes to Arabize and Islamize the black animists of the south; an India that would impose an Aryan language upon Dravidians; a Tunisia that would abolish polygamy; a Turkey that makes itself secular and adopts the

> Latin alphabet; an Egypt that revendicates the Sudan, Morocco, Mauritania; it is the nation that makes itself a state, and, to assimilate, secretes an interior dictatorship, an exterior imperialism.[3]

Casting a glance over the expanse of Asia and Africa, Senghor located the earliest Asian entrenchments of the "national idea" in Turkey, before its extension elsewhere as a counterimperial "oppositional nationalism" (*un nationalisme contraire*) across the Asian and African continents.[4] Senghor expressed his apprehension that as an emergent nation becomes a state, it "makes of itself Religion," tending, "in its highest epoch of fervor," to dangerously "inquisitional and iconoclastic" ventures for the sake of "assimilation" and "*uniformization*. [. . .] Assimilative in the interior, the Nation is *imperialist* toward its exterior."[5] The Bandung Conference, he argued, advanced a call to shared independence that bore the risk of nationalist exploitations in the name of lateral solidarity, exploitations that proceeded in the name of emancipation but threatened to promote new forms of colonization.

Critical of provincial nationalisms, Senghor initially promoted a postindependence federalist arrangement to unite France's former West African colonies through French as a common language and on the grounds of civic parity with France, an effort that remains one of the greatest controversies of his legacy as a politician. He faced perennial accusations of harboring neocolonial sympathies; he was charged with indifference to more locally authentic, national forms of cultural representation.[6] Senegalese compatriots and political challengers frequently accused him of promoting policies of cultural uniformization—not in the name of Senegalese nationalism but, rather, in the name of French as an emblematic but false bearer of cultural parity between Senegal and France as a former imperial metropole. Central to the controversy were Senghor's frequent claims that French could be transformed from a colonial language into an emancipatory medium in Senegal, a view that his critics argued simply extended the violence imposed by a colonial past on local culture, contributing to the postindependence marginalization of Senegalese vernaculars.

As head of state, Senghor justified his choices through his aspiration to build shared solidarities across France's former colonies. But how did his decisions as a poet and statesman seek to avoid surrendering to assimilative neoimperial practices for the sake of counterimperial freedoms? How did debates over language and representation factor into this perennial balance for Senegal's formation as a unified but culturally diverse nation-state with broad lateral solidarities?[7] Given Senghor's status as a poet and politician, how did the language of his poetry and public rhetoric give form to the idealist political abstractions of parity and pluralism?

Like the Dutch in Indonesia and the British in Egypt, France left behind in postcolonial West Africa a populace beset by segregated literacies. Figures such as Senghor, a trained linguist who assumed the helm of independent Senegal as president in 1960, were responsible for reconciling these segregated literacies. As we will see, Senghor's writing offers a vital lens through which to interpret the effects of the late colonial rift between European and Arabic language literacies in Senegal, with important implications for vernacular forms of representation in the wake of national independence. His legacy offers unique insights into how vernacular writing and literary sensibilities in French West Africa were riven between French (Latinate) and Arabic orientations and writing systems, which remain largely unreconciled in Senegal.[8] He nonetheless envisioned emancipatory connections across these rifts, as I illustrate throughout this chapter.

Senghor first entered electoral politics at the end of World War II, winning a seat on the French Socialist ticket as a Senegalese deputy to the French National Assembly in 1946. Among his earliest objectives was to address the unequal extension of French citizenship rights to Senegalese subjects, who were divided across a segregated legal system that favored Senegal's urban coasts over its rural interior and preferentially treated Christian over Muslim subjects. In speeches Senghor mentioned that this was a personal issue for him, as his own family included both Christians and Muslims.[9]

Hailing from Joal, south of Dakar, Senghor (born in 1906) was raised by a Serer father who had converted to Catholicism and by a Fulani Muslim mother, whom Senghor often described as an animist.[10] Though Senghor himself was a devout Catholic and attended French Catholic schools, several of his siblings remained practicing Muslims. Earning a scholarship to study in Paris in the 1920s and 1930s, Senghor became active in Caribbean and African diasporic literary circles, building close relationships with many fellow writers who would become prominent statesmen in France's former colonies. Among them was the Martinican poet and future politician Aimé Césaire, with whom Senghor cofounded the pioneering student journal *L'Étudiant noir* (*The Black Student*) and promoted the cause of black cultural consciousness under the auspices of (what came to be called) an emergent *négritude* movement.

Senghor continued to write poetry in French through the 1970s and was a prolific essayist throughout his political career. He became president of independent Senegal in 1960, after trying unsuccessfully to broker a federalist future for the country along with other territories across former colonial French West Africa. He continued to promote the French language and a common regional currency within West African francophone territories when his federalist efforts failed. Surviving an attempted coup in 1962, after which he imprisoned many political opponents and controversially embraced single-party rule, Senghor remained president of Senegal until his retirement from office in 1980.

This chapter begins by exploring egalitarian motifs in Senghor's poetry during the 1940s before examining his evolving statements as a politician and public intellectual on local language debates in Senegal. It shows how Senghor envisioned the French language as an emancipatory and egalitarian medium in his poetry—with regard not only to colonial racial hierarchies but to precolonial West African hierarchies of caste and ethnolinguistic difference. As evident through connections between Senghor's poetry and political rhetoric, his claims to Senegalese distinction challenged a series of intersecting hierarchies beyond French colonial centers of cultural recognition, including Arabocentric hierarchies among Senegal's largely Muslim populace. After focusing on French as an acrolect, this chapter traces Senghor's characterization of Arabic as a prestige language in West Africa; I argue that Senghor discerned egalitarian parallels between arabophone and francophone Senegalese writers in order to bridge literacies segregated through a colonial past. Notwithstanding these parallels, Senghor's ambivalence to Arabic as a medium ambiguously African demonstrates his evolving approach to the contours of Senegalese nationalism. Senghor's shifting approach, as we shall see, also reflected his changing visions for pan-Africanism and Asian-African solidarities.

Caste and the Subversion of Vernacular Orature

Senghor's legacy as a poet and public intellectual has been largely identified with his promotion of *négritude*, a concept that Senghor reinterpreted throughout his career but which he frequently defined as a racialized (black) essence or creative genius and as an ideal counterpart to the French language.[11] Lending its name to a pioneering movement of Caribbean and African francophone poets of the 1930s–50s, *négritude* was a neologism originally coined by Aimé Césaire to describe an emergent sense of "racial consciousness and social revolution" in 1935 in *L'Étudiant noir*.[12] Senghor, a central figure of the movement, borrowed and redefined the term throughout his career in multidimensional ways, considering it a front for political and social change in Senegal and an instrument of nostalgic recovery for a "negro-African" culture colonially eclipsed.[13]

Generally overlooked in scholarship on *négritude*, however, is how Senghor's poetry advanced egalitarian sensibilities not only in racial terms but through an attention to West African caste systems that predated European imperialism.[14] The following pages offer a reading of Senghor's poetry as subverting the enduring legacies of provincial West African caste systems and their unique manifestations in West African speech communities. Senghor's subversion appears through vernacular stylistic borrowings and through innovations in his French-language poetry. Although I offer a sympathetic reading of caste in Senghor's poetry as liberationist, it is also possible to interpret his treatment of the lower-caste bardic figure (or *griot*) as caste minstrelsy, a practice in which a poet superficially adopts the persona of a "casted" bard as a performative device that can be donned and discarded—a practice detached from the real social constraints of actual *griots*.

Senghor's ability to poetically impersonate this underclass figure could be read as a sign of Senghor's privilege: Caste minstrelsy, in this sense, might be understood as the mark of an elite poet's distance from a "casted" bard's inherited social limitations—limitations that authentic *griots*, born into endogamous families of traditional praise singers in Senegal, may not so easily or performatively discard. I should also note that even if Senghor's poetry indeed subverts caste hierarchies, as a politician Senghor's stance toward caste was more ambivalent, a complication taken up in the chapter's conclusion. Even though it is certainly possible to see Senghor's poetry as engaging in caste minstrelsy, I lean toward a liberationist reading because it aligns Senghor's verse with the idealism of his broader poetic corpus during this pre-independence period, a corpus that addressed the twinned hardships of colonial-era racism and classism.

In my more generous reading, Senghor's deployment of *négritude* challenged intersecting hierarchies not only of race and language but of caste or class, challenging multiple forms of cultural stratification and traditional axes of social exclusion passed down through vernacular literary forms. In his invocation of a vernacular precedent in orature, Senghor does more than sentimentally or nostalgically ornament his poetry with vernacular references and forms of code-switching, as some critics have claimed. He instead dissociates himself from older lines of patronage, from inherited social hierarchies and poetic conventions according to which eulogistic speech appears to be a sign of social subordination for the bardic speaker in West Africa (the *griot, gewel,* or *djeli*), traditionally born to laud his nobler patrons and social superiors.

The figure of the bardic *griot* has been much examined in Senghor studies, inviting controversy over the authenticity of his references to traditional oral poetry.[15] Existing criticism on this motif, however, tends to overlook the caste contrasts that dominate Senghor's reference to oral traditions of bardic oratory, particularly with regard to eulogistic practice. Senghor frames *négritude* not merely as a generic (oratory) complement to the French language but also as the mediation of an emancipatory call through its implied transformation of the speaker. He depicts a process of liberation that redefines the nature of freedom itself, not as a status (opposing the noble to the "casted") but as a right that privileges self-creation over an inherited nobility. The gesture of a highborn figure trading his lance for bardic instruments, a prominent motif within Senghor's poetry, can be best understood against this background, given that the performance of bardic discourse by a "noble" would have been traditionally considered a social demotion incompatible with such a high rank.[16] Tropes of caste disavowal and ancestral forgiveness characteristic of Senghor's poetry gain value from this contextual background, as the imagined chagrin of a speaker's ancestral forebears is tempered by a speaker's heralding of egalitarian claims.

References within Senghor's poetry to local traditions of praise oratory as performed by an underclass (or lowborn) bardic caste are central to understanding Senghor's challenge to caste dynamics in Senegal. To begin, a few points of conceptual clarification are required on the caste system in West Africa and its relationship to socially stratified traditions of vernacular praise oratory. As explained in prevailing ethnographic literature on the topic, caste in West Africa might be understood as "a series of ranked, endogamous occupational groups," including professional bards tasked with performing eulogistic praise oratory (*woy* in Wolof, *gim* in Serer) for higher-born patrons during family celebrations and "life-crisis" events.[17] Caste institutions and their associated patronage systems persist within Wolof, Serer, and Fulani ethnic communities.[18] Senghor, born of a higher-ranking, noble family (*guelwar*) of mixed Serer and Fulani heritage, was raised among these communities within the Senegambian region of West Africa.

Vital to understanding the egalitarian stakes of Senghor's poetry are hierarchies that separate "noble"-born communities from lower-born "bardic" castes, yielding a particular speech register for bardic forms of praise oratory.[19] As the anthropologist Judith Irvine describes this dynamic: "Caste differences are culturally associated with differences in speech style. A [more reserved, taciturn] style connected with high rank (*waxu géér*, 'noble speech') contrasts with a style connected with low rank (*waxu gewel*, '*griot* speech'), so named after the bardic caste which in some respects is said to epitomize low-ranking groups."[20] As Irvine explains, bardic speech or "*griot* speech"—considered "loud, high pitched, rapid, verbose, florid, and emphatic"—is both the mark of an underclass and the speech register in which praise oratory for upper-class patrons is performed.[21] The contents of bardic praise songs are often "genealogical eulogies," which involve naming the ancestors of higher-born patrons, "connecting them to kings or village founders or other heroic figures" through songs that praise an addressee's character and elaborate a patron's qualifications for higher social rank due to a distinguished bloodline.[22]

Within West African caste traditions, bardic eulogy confers status on the pedigreed while reinforcing social hierarchies that mark bardic poets as underclass figures destined to praise their social superiors. Egalitarian dimensions of Senghor's poetry can be understood on these grounds: as a subversive, hybrid adaptation of vernacular sensibilities ("*griot* speech") within his French-language poetry. Through self-referential patterns in Senghor's poetry, the self-nomination of the speaker as a bardic poet or eulogist is legible as a disavowal of the caste system, often through poems that allude to the transformation of the speaker from a noble to a self-designated member of the orator caste. Poetized self-transformations of the speaker as *griot* animate a dominant trend or concept in Senghor's work: the transmutation of force into choice, of an inherited status into a chosen one, a persistent vision of liberty within scenes of ultimate entrapment. Where the term *négritude* first appears in Senghor's poetry as a resolution to contradiction (in the poem "To the Music of Koras and Balaphon," for example), its employment transforms an exclusionary axis into an inclusive one. *Négritude* translates the terms of disenfranchisement into those of empowerment—with regard not only to colonial forms of linguistic coercion and racial prejudice but to more local axes of exclusion on the basis of caste or class.[23]

Although eulogistic overtones dominate his poetry on a traditional nobility (*guelwar*), Senghor's dignification of a native hereditary class is coupled with a poetics of renunciation, with Senghor's speakers relinquishing their birthright status as noble *guelwar* in favor of the humbler orator's role (*gewel* or *griot*). Controversially, Senghor imagines this caste transformation as one catalyzed under the aegis of the French tricolor and the French language. Senghor's chosen language of composition (French) in this regard appears recurrently poised as the "natural" vessel of revolutionary or enlightenment ideas on liberty and equality, a posture that is significantly developed through the reflexive theme of class or caste inversions and renounced nobilities.

The motif of caste renunciation is most pronounced in Senghor's 1948 collection of poems, *Hosties noires* (*Black Hosts*). But this motif also resumes and resolves the tropes of schismatic fealty that dominate Senghor's first collection of poems, *Chants d'ombre* (*Songs of the Shadows*, 1945), including the collection's fixation with the figure of the prodigal son and jealous ancestral gods. A prime example of this rhetorical strategy is found in the inaugural poem of *Hosties noires*, which revisits the theme of the prodigal son to dramatize the speaker's renunciation of noble entitlements. In "Poème liminaire," as Senghor's speaker renounces his noble status, becoming an orator in an act of humility, he eulogistically refashions the virtues of his original lineage while "trad[ing] his lance / For the sixteen beats of the *sorong*."[24] By favoring the power of speech over the traditional glories of his warrior forebearers, he both relinquishes and regenerates the virtues of his noble lineage, privileging oral poetic traditions as a natural complement to the assumption (or imposition) of the French language. As the poem progresses, the speaker couples his renunciation with a reinvention of the caste system. In the poem's final lines, he heralds a "new nobility," whose role is

> not to dominate our people, but to be their rhythm and their heart
> Not to feed upon the land, but to rot like millet seeds in the soil
> Not to be the people's head, but their mouth and their trumpet.[25]

> non de dominer notre peuple, mais d'être son rythme et son coeur
> Non de paître les terres, mais comme le grain de millet de pourrir dans
> la terre
> Non d'être la tête du peuple, mais bien sa bouche et sa trompette.[26]

Embodying a new, hybrid class of (what might be called) the "noble *griot*" (traditionally an oxymoron), the speaker of "Poème liminaire" nominates himself the elegist of fallen West African sharpshooters (*tirailleurs sénégalais*) and opposes his orature to the exclusions of traditional nobility and to the omissions of bureaucrats and colonial, continental poets who sing of "heroes," but none with "black skin."[27]

In a second example, Senghor employs the European trenches of World War II as a setting for dramatic class inversions in his poetry, as he subverts hierarchical Senegalese traditions of address in vernacular orature and eulogy.

Senghor's poem "Taga de Mbaye Dyôb" ("Ode to Mbaye Dyob") exemplifies this reinvention, as a poem that contrasts the valor of commoners or "lower-born" sharpshooters to the relative humility of the nobly born *guelwar*-turned-eulogist. Beginning with a traditional gesture of oral praise poets in Senegal, the repetition of a patron or addressee's surname, the speaker relinquishes his superior birthright status by designating himself the eulogist (*gewel*) of a commoner, conferring upon a soldier of unknown lineage the traditional glories of a warrior class:

Mbaye Dyôb! je veux dire ton nom et ton honneur.
Dyôb! je veux hisser ton nom au haut mât du retour, sonner ton nom
comme la cloche qui chante la victoire
Je veux chanter ton nom Dyôbène! toi qui m'appelais ton maître [...]
Dyôb! qui ne sais remonter ta généalogie et domestiquer le temps
noir, dont les ancêtres ne sont pas rythmés par la voix du tama [...]
Dyôb!—je veux chanter ton honneur blanc.[28]

Mbaye Dyôb! I want to say your name and your honor.
Dyôb! I want to hoist your name to the tall returning mast,
Sound your name like the bell clanging victory
I want to praise your name Dyôbène! You who called me
Your master [...]
Dyôb! You may not know how to recite your lineage
Or tame the darkness, you whose ancestors do not keep time
To the *tama* drums. [...]
Dyôb!—I want to praise your white honor.[29]

Having granted his subject the privileges of a noble, the speaker completes this caste or class inversion by further prophesying for his subject the traditional honors of a warrior class: a virgin chorus beyond the battlefield ("les vierges du Gandyol"), singing his praises as an ennobled commoner.[30]

Senghor's elevation of the commoner and humble transformation of a noble speaker move to egalitarian and semi-messianic extremes in his poem "At the Call of the Race of Sheba" ("À l'appel de la race de Saba"), written in the wake of the Italian invasion of Abyssinia. Presenting a battlefront scene, the poem moves from an opening eulogy of the speaker's *guelwar* ancestors to his ultimate abandonment of his highborn status. Although the poem begins with a remembrance of traditional eulogists, with the scene of the speaker's noble father patronizing and "surrounded by *griots* and *koras* [string instruments]," the speaker envisions himself an orator who transcends caste, class, and race, "forging his mouth" into a "trumpet of liberation."[31] In this self-designated role, the speaker pronounces a casteless prophecy, a "day of liberation" (*le jour de libération*) under the banner of the Marseillaise, "jaillie des cuivres de nos bouches, la Marseillaise de Valmy."[32] Here, Senghor poetically reconfigures notions of transcendence and liberty by recasting his chosen language as an intrinsic expression of liberty—a medium heralding an egalitarian future:

> Ni maîtres désormais ni ésclaves ni guelwars ni griots de griot
> Rien que la lisse et virile cameraderie des combats, et que me soit égal le fils du captif, que me soient copains le Maure et le Targui congénitalement ennemis.[33]

> From now on neither masters nor slaves, Nor *guelwars*, nor *griots* of *griot*,
> Nothing but the smooth, virile camaraderie of battle, And I become the equal of the son of slaves, and am friends now
> With the Moors and the Tuaregs, lifelong enemies.[34]

The concluding stanzas of the poem further contrast the social distinctions of the speaker's forebearers—his father distinguished as a warrior-athlete among rivals—to the speaker's increasingly diffuse sense of self, subsumed within an egalitarian collective.

Senghor is often criticized for an excessively laudatory and even bombastic tone in his praise of an African past. But if one reads closely Senghor's inaugural use of the neologistic term *négritude* in light of his rebaptism of the African oral poet as a *noble griot*, the transcendence that he grants to *négritude* (or a black racial consciousness) is not just a function of French language use but also a transcendence of the class hierarchies through which the West African bard traditionally speaks. In this light, in Senghor's poem "Que m'accompagnent kôras et balafong," one can read his first use of *négritude* not only as a function of the French language, as a response to colonial forms of linguistic coercion, but as a vindication of the bardic poet as a figure of transcendence, imagined as the descendant of both the enslaved and the noble born. Here the poet transforms the terms of an ancestor's capitulation and surrender into those of sacrifice. He tempers the theme of historic defeat with the promise of salvation, of *négritude* later conveyed in redemptive terms as a form of transcendence—"melting away all contradictions" of race and class.

The poem culminates with a violent illustration of a translated Mandinka proverb embedded in the sixth stanza ("On nous tue, Almamy! On ne nous déshonore pas"—"They kill us, Almamy! They dishonor us not").[35] The speaker, on the verge of defeat, after sixteen years of warfare, at the fourteenth-century battle of Trubang, transforms the objects of potential pillage and capitulation into offerings of sacrifice, burning treasures on a pyre in a final exercise of liberty.[36] In a self-reflexive portrayal of the speaker's voice—equated with what had been spared from ancestral pyres after conflicts that pitted Africans against Africans—the poem contrasts the transient marks of social nobility to the endurance of poetic speech, a voice carried by blood: "But saved is the Voice [*la Chantante*], my pagan sap that mounts and stomps and dances."[37]

The implied contrast between the poet's voice as an immaterial treasure (carried in the blood) and the "powdery" marks of noble status (destroyed within a pyre) introduces the notion of redemptive equality into the poem carried through the poet's own speech. Here Senghor naturalizes the unity of lineage and orature elsewhere resolved in his verse through the conceit of the *guelwar* become lower-born bard. It is a resolution emphasized in the poem's most iconic lines with interreligious evocations. The motifs of the "voice" (a power conveyed in blood) and the "muted trumpet" are borne through the promise of salvation beyond enslavement, underscored through the poem's vital third stanza. This stanza dramatizes the speaker's choice of orature as a form of transcendence:

Mais s'il faut choisir à l'heure de l'épreuve
J'ai choisi le verset des fleuves, des vents et des forêts
L'assonance des plaines et des rivières, choisi le rythme de sang de
  mon corps dépouillé
Choisi la trémulsion des balafongs et l'accord des cordes et des cuivres
  qui semble faux, choisi le
Swing le swing oui le swing!
Et la lointaine trompette bouchée, comme une plainte de nébuleuse en
  dérive dans la nuit
Comme l'appel du Jugement, trompette éclatante sur les charniers nei-
  geux d'Europe
J'ai choisi mon peuple noir peinant, mon peuple paysan, toute la race
  paysanne par le monde.
"Et tes frères sont irrités contre toi, ils t'ont mis à bêcher la terre."
Pour être ta trompette![38]

But if one must choose in the final hour
I have chosen the verse of the rivers, of winds and of forests
The assonance of the plains and the streams, chosen the rhythm of
blood in my fleeced body
Chosen the tremor of the *balafongs*, the harmony of strings and brass
that seem false, chosen the
Swing the swing, yes, the swing!
And the distant muted trumpet, like a nebulous cry of mourning in
the night
Like the call to Judgment, thunderous trumpet upon the snowy graves
of Europe's slaughter
I have chosen my black toiling people, my peasant people, all the
world's peasant race.
"And your brothers are angered by you, they have made you till
the soil"
To be your trumpet![39]

Through these lines, the speaker imagines a sonic solidarity carried through the histories of transatlantic slavery—between the "distant trumpets" of American "swing" and the subaltern songs of the African *griot*. With its reference to the biblical curse of Canaan (a historical apology for slavery), the stanza foreshadows later climactic scenes of enslavement and sacrifice and underscores the central conceit around which these scenes revolve. The conceit gives rise to the problem of "forced choice" (*s'il faut choisir*—"if one *must* choose"), which is resolved only by an imagined transcendence amid coercion. It is in this light that the poet's first use of *négritude* as a redemptive, transcendent unity should be read as a form of deliverance to the speaker himself in his eulogy of the African night, a medium of near-mystical synthesis: "Night that melts all of my contradictions, all contradictions in the primal unity of your *négritude*, / Receive the child ever the child that twelve years of wandering have not aged."[40]

Négritude as Double Transcendence: Parallels from French to Arabic

When read alongside motifs of class or caste subversion within Senghor's corpus, *négritude* appears to be not just the smooth transposition of a black, indigenous poetic sensibility into French but a challenge to local practices of stratified speech between African bards and their African publics. Thus, *négritude* bears an egalitarian claim to what the reinvention of vernacular orature and eulogy could resemble. To reference again Césaire's original definition of the term in 1935, Senghor's sense of *négritude* here appears as a matter not only of "racial consciousness" but of caste upheaval. If one rereads Senghor's inaugural poem on *négritude,* it is clearly born of a poignant sense of African history, of the poet's legacy forged in the violence of Africans against Africans, with gestures to its tragic transatlantic effects. Far from merely "speaking back" to the French in French, in other words, the terms of vernacular orature in which Senghor speaks suggest that his choice of French not only tempers racial hierarchies across an African-European divide but also redefines traditional class divisions subordinating the lower-born West African poet to higher-born African patrons. French to some degree functions for Senghor as a positional sanctuary from native speech forms freighted with distinctive registers of class or caste, as an alternative to forms of locution that generically subordinate one speaker to another (in the way, perhaps, that Indonesian Malay had functioned for many Javanese writers, to gesture to lateral comparisons in the "Bandung spirit").

Négritude might here appear to be a neologistic invention that speaks to a plural audience: It addresses the status of poetry as itself a liberationist sanctuary against intersecting social hierarchies in West Africa. In Senghor's vision, poetry socially positions the speaker as "the equal of the son of slaves" and of the low-class *gewel* or *griot.* The speaker is also poised, as Senghor claims in his poem on the "race of Sheba," as the "friend" and equal of "lifelong enemies" "the Moors and the Tuaregs." Given that *négritude* was first born as an idealized resolution to contradiction, its employment in his poetry and linguistic pronouncements conceptually transforms an exclusionary axis into an inclusive one, translating the terms of social disenfranchisement into those of empowerment across a complex matrix of class or caste and racial differences. Senghor's reference to *négritude*—as a reflection of "black racial consciousness"—here appears a multidimensional, discursive term for intuiting the horizons of a more inclusive humanism, an egalitarianism that tempers intersecting histories of linguism, colorism, and class prejudice in West Africa.[41]

This vision of *négritude* appears all the more poignant given that Senghor as a statesman employed the term to frame parallel innovations between francophone and arabophone African poets later in his career (in the 1960s and 1970s), challenging the intersecting legacies of Eurocentrism and Arabocentrism in Muslim West Africa. In ways comparable to African francophone poets' reclamation of French, African poets of Arabic had, he claimed, elevated black aesthetic values in ways that turned their chosen language of composition into an egalitarian instrument, a tactic that since the 1930s Senghor had long associated with poets of the *négritude* movement in French. Through forms of literary innovation in Arabic and Arabic-script poetry (*ʿajami* verse), non-native, black African speakers of Arabic, he argued, laid claim to a poetics of "black African" distinction and cultural parity with native Arabic speakers, leveling long-standing precolonial hierarchies between Arabs and non-Arabs across Muslim African contexts. In their own distinct linguistic tradition, in other words, they, too, were *négritude* figures of "racial consciousness" and "social revolution" in the wake of French imperialism.

A shift in focus from Senghor's French-language poetry back to his historic role as a politician allows us to see his broader concern with plural (and intersecting) forms of intra-African hierarchy, beyond those that divided Senegal from French colonial centers of prestige. Continuities between his poetry and his political rhetoric further illustrate how Senghor as a public figure and statesman sought to give form to idealist political abstractions of parity and pluralism through the language of poetry, encompassing multiple scales of solidarity beyond a metropolitan colonial center. During his presidency, Senghor increasingly characterized the Senegalese terms of pan-African solidarity as a movement toward a universal humanism from a West African basis of *négro-arabo-berber* cultural symbiosis.[42] In illustration, the following discussion draws attention to how Senghor not only challenged precolonial caste hierarchies through his early French-language poetry but, as a public intellectual, extended such challenges to other social hierarchies within arabophone Africa, using *négritude* as a multidimensional point of convergence and comparison.

To this end, Senghor would proclaim on multiple occasions in the 1960s and 1970s that egalitarian parallels existed between French poets of *négritude* (like himself) and their arabophone counterparts. These counterparts included, according to Senghor, the Malinke *ʿajami* poet Sitokoto Dabo, in his appropriation and mastery of a "foreign" language or script (Arabic), and Ahmadu Bamba, the arabophone Wolof poet we have previously examined. A speech given by Senghor in 1979, for example, lauded Dabo for "employ[ing] Arabic characters to express his négritude, using his own poetic license for greater melody to excellent effect."[43] Such claims were equally sustained in Senghor's public eulogies of Ahmadu Bamba, whom Senghor claimed had domesticated and acculturated not only Arabic poetry in Senegal but Islam itself as an allegedly foreign presence in black West Africa. At the inauguration of the principal Murid mosque in Touba (a building project that Senghor's government cofunded), Senghor acknowledged the social impact of the Murid founder and declared him an iconic figure of "negrified" Islam.[44] He proclaimed the racial contours of Bamba's legacy in the following terms: "What Ahmadu Bamba, once again, wanted was to entrench ["to root," *enraciner*] Islam in black lands, by Africanizing it—dare we say, by negrifying it [*en le négrifiant*]."[45] Bamba, according to Senghor, had in this way "revolutionized" Islam in Senegal by indigenizing and assimilating the faith, by making a "religion of nomads" into a "religion of peasants" (in apparent reference to dedicative forms of agricultural labor associated with the Murid order).[46] Refashioning what had once been a pejorative term in French Orientalist texts into a source of pride, Senghor claimed that Bamba was a culturally revolutionary figure who had "made of black Islam [*Islam noir*] an instrument of political and, above all, spiritual liberation."[47]

In Senghor's statements on his arabophone counterparts, then, *négritude* as a "negro-African" aesthetic embodied a quality of local distinction in a foreign medium. It translated into the Arabic language and script an aesthetics of "negro-African" singularity, rendering black arabophone poetry (like its black francophone counterpart) a culturally hybrid form. Through such statements, Senghor implied that across the segregated realms of literacy left behind by French imperial policies—policies that privileged French over Arabic—both francophone and arabophone West African poets expressed a sense of local distinction through "borrowed" languages and writing systems. In this way, Senghor's public pronouncements after his rise to the presidency in 1960 project a vision of egalitarian idealism that connected vernacular "black African" sensibilities across two acrolects in Senegal.

Although Senghor tried through such pronouncements to overcome linguistic segregations that were colonially inherited, he himself was a product of those segregations. He therefore faced considerable limitations in his own efforts—not least through his inability to read Arabic (a status he regretted in his speeches of the 1960s). Senghor's public statements on arabophone poets can be understood as largely symbolic, inferring the existence of parallel "black" or "indigenous" sensibilities across French and Arabic Senegalese poetry, rather than presenting a direct exposition of those parallels. In the absence of Senghor's own analysis, then, what would it mean to take seriously Senghor's inference of similarities across colonially fostered segregations between French- and Arabic-trained elites in West Africa—to pursue unexplored lines of connection between the historically divided francophone and arabophone orientations of Senegalese poetry in the wake of colonial rule?

Building from Senghor's symbolic assertion of Ahmadu Bamba's status as an arabophone figure of "negrified" Islam, conclusions drawn from the previous chapter on Bamba's West African Arabic poetry offer lines of comparison. These include comparable dynamics in Senghor's and Bamba's poetry that challenge the intersecting hierarchies of race and class (or caste) in Senegal and that draw attention to the politics of "black" Senegalese writing in nonnative languages as a matter of "racial consciousness."[48] As historians of the Murid founder have noted, Bamba's doctrinal emphasis on Islamic traditions of equality before God encompassed ideals of racial parity not only between *bayḍān* and *sudān*—"white" and "black"—but between casted and noble in traditional Wolof society.[49] This was an emphasis that attracted significant numbers of Senegal's lower-caste followers to the Murid order and offered the promise of social elevation to members of a traditional underclass in the late nineteenth and early twentieth centuries.[50] Bamba's poetic critique of traditional West African hierarchies of caste extended to his poetry, appearing in poems such as "Nahju Qaḍāʿi al-Ḥāji" a didactic poem intended for his disciples on requisite codes of conduct (or *adab*):

النّاسُ من جهة التّمثيل أكفاءُ
أبـوهُـمُ آدَمٌ والأمُّ حـوّاءُ
فإن أتيتَ بفخرٍ من ذوي حَسَبٍ
يُفاخرونَ بـهِ فالطيّن والماءُ
ما الفَخَرُ إلّا لأهل العِلم إنّهُمُ
على الهُدى لِمَن استهدى أدلاءُ
وقَدْرُكلِّ امرئٍ ما كانَ يُحسِنُه
فالجاهلونَ لِأهل العِلمِ أعداءُ
فَفُزْ بِعلمٍ تعِشْ حيّاً بـهِ أبـداً
النّاسُ مَوتى وأهلُ العلمِ أحياءُ

All peoples, compared, are equal [*akfāʾ*]
Their father is Adam, their mother Eve,
If you bear pride of lineage [*min dhawī ḥasab*, literally
 "from inherited merit"]
That pride is but clay and water.
For what is pride to followers of knowledge [*ahl al-ʿilm*]? It is they
To whom guidance is given as seekers in signs.

The rank [*qadr*] of every prince did not better his kind,
And the ignorant are an enemy to those who know,
So victor in knowledge, living ever by it revived:
All peoples die, though knowledge's kin will live [*ahl al-ʿilm aḥyāʾ*].[51]

Such lines undercut genealogical or inherited pride derived from class or rank, leaving notions of prestige and kinship realigned instead with knowledge as a medium of transcendence and immortality. *Ahl al-ʿilm*—the peoples, kin, or followers of knowledge—supersede, to the limits of life itself, the pride of all others destined to death. Such lines gain gravity against the realities of a West African caste system that still endures. And yet, these lines affiliate—in their censure of pride through "inherited merit" (*ḥasab*)—with long-standing poetic and exegetical traditions in Arabic, which challenge social presumptions on the basis of lineage.[52] Bamba's teachings and didactic poetry emphasized that legitimate social status is conferred by erudition as a mark of piety, with "knowledge and faith" prevailing over "eminent descent" as sources of social distinction.[53] His teachings had a major impact on devotional praise poets and poetic genealogists among his Murid disciples, including rising generations of twentieth-century arabophone and *ʿajami* poets whose status came to be associated with religious erudition (rather than, it might be presumed, with the social inferiority of a traditionally bardic underclass in West Africa).[54]

To consider Bamba and Senghor's standing in Arabic and French comparatively, then, it is possible to discern within their poetic corpus intersecting visions of parity unique to a continental West African social context, as they brought to their poetry and public legacy an intersection of race and class consciousness across their linguistic differences. Their poetic work also illustrates parallel trends in the adaptation of a foreign language through which ethnolinguistic or racial hierarchies were historically implied. In each case, the poet's linguistic competence in his adopted language is projected as a sign or herald of equality, as his adopted language becomes a vessel of transcendence beyond racial difference and class hierarchies, toward a sense of the universal, whether secular or divine. The writings of Bamba and Senghor can thus be seen as divergent poetic responses to disempowerment, responses through which linguistic choice can be read as redefining the nature of freedom itself.

The notion that language becomes a medium of emancipation is recurrently conveyed in the writing of each poet and can be compared on redemptive grounds, as each language is reflexively portrayed as a form of deliverance to the poet himself. As we have previously seen, Bamba portrayed his mastery of

Arabic as a non-native language in West Africa as a sign of egalitarian transcendence and religious authority in his poetry—an authority that surpassed the worldly, French colonial agents who condemned him to exile for alleged counterimperial agitation. Despite the colonial segregation of their two linguistic traditions, then, Senghor's and Bamba's poems serve as apologistic defenses of their choice of language, recasting its use as a sign of transcendence. Writing under historical conditions of colonial prejudice, both poets inscribed in their poetry challenges to social and ethnolinguistic hierarchies that were both colonial and continental. For Bamba, this axis was signified by the difference between *bayḍān* and *sudān*, between the native and non-native speaker of Arabic, whereas for Senghor this meant a parallel hierarchy of the French European over the francophone black African.

Senghor's intuition of such parallels, however, and his public lauding of arabophone elites as figures of *négritude* distinction, occurred quite late in his career as a public intellectual. An important factor that explains this shift and its timing deserves mention, as Senghor had tactical reasons beyond mere idealism for such rhetorical gestures after his assumption of the Senegalese presidency in 1960. Instrumental to his political rise as a Roman Catholic in predominantly Muslim Senegal were his alliances with Muslim clerical elites, especially within the Murid brotherhood (and with Bamba's son, Falilou Mbacké)—a brotherhood that Senghor claimed in his Touba inauguration speech had "adopted him" as "one of their own."[55] The force of such alliances was particularly critical in the midst of the elections and constitutional crisis of 1962–63. During this period, Senghor relied heavily on the support of an influential Murid leadership to sustain his presidency over more radical anticlerical challengers.[56] Senghor notably made his most significant pronouncements on the arabophone Bamba as a revolutionary figure of "black Islam" during the political tensions of 1963, in a speech characterizing the nature of Senegalese "laicism" not as a form of state-sanctioned antireligious practices inherited from French colonial predecessors but as a mutual accommodation between the Senegalese state under his leadership and the cultural force of the nation's religious communities. These communities included an autonomous constellation of powerful Sufi brotherhoods in Senegal whose moral suasion regularly influenced a broad electoral base.[57] Such forms of accommodation and co-legitimation between the Murid brotherhood and the Senegalese state—which many historians consider an inheritance of French colonial practices since the 1920s and 1930s—have been equated with the "vernacularization of democracy" itself within an "Islamo-Wolof" context.[58]

Senghor's rhetorical tactics in the 1960s–70s, then, reflect how his early poetic idealism was evolving and translating into new forms of political pragmatism, with Senghor's symbolic conciliation of francophone and arabophone literary divisions and, relatedly, with his brokering of local alliances between secular and religious elites (a legacy of his presidency critiqued by his more radical leftist opponents, as explored in the next chapter). It is on this basis that we might understand Senghor's positive characterization of Arabic as a prestige language and a medium of symbolic authority in Muslim West Africa, notwithstanding its marginalization by the French colonial state as a written standard during the late nineteenth and early twentieth centuries. Senghor's public embrace of Arabic poets and literacies in Senegal—as with French as a historical imposition—was nonetheless a position he gradually arrived at later in his career. This belated embrace of Arabic and *ʿajami* writing traditions occurred despite Senghor's early ambivalence or even hostility to the presence of Arabic as a prestigious cultural force in West Africa in the 1940s. Attesting to his evolving vision for the pan-African alignments of independent Senegal, his positions gradually shifted across his career, moving from early protests against the dominance of French and Arabic over local vernaculars to a more conciliatory embrace of French and Arabic as cultural complements to local languages.

Senghor's Ambivalence toward Arabic

As a native speaker of Serer who chose to write in French, Senghor occupied the margins of the arabophone communities over which he presided as head of state. Nevertheless, because perennial controversies over whether indigenous languages could be formalized as national standards were ultimately tied to transcription issues and writing systems, the status of Arabic as script and medium in West Africa also became a matter over which Senghor was obliged to pass judgment, even though he himself was not literate in Arabic. Senghor was one of several intellectuals of his generation to engage with these controversies. However, because of his long and prominent public career—writing as a scholar of linguistics since the 1930s, gaining prominence as a francophone poet and politician, and serving as a linguistic policy maker as Senegal's first president—his personal legacy uniquely addresses the polemics of vernacular representation in Senegal over several decades.[59]

Senghor's writing therefore offers a lens through which to discern the transgenerational impact of the late colonial segregation of European and Arabic literacies. Although he tried to overcome imperially segregated writing practices as president, he himself was a product of colonial-era policies that elevated a rising generation of francophone West African elites over their arabophone counterparts. As a result, his attitudes were often ambivalent regarding both French and Arabic as prestige languages, particularly as they overshadowed local forms of vernacular or indigenous writing. At times in self-contradictory ways, Senghor would change his position about whether Arabic was antagonistic or complementary to indigenous languages where politically convenient, often slipping back into colonial-era taxonomies to characterize the coexistence of Arabic and local vernaculars. In the process, he moved from relatively purist ideas about vernacular representation early in his career toward the promotion of an idealized cultural hybridity, often relying on concepts borrowed from French Orientalist taxonomies that divided black African and Arab subjects for framing his own evolving political alignments.

Senghor has been known (and excoriated) for his eventual claim that French and vernacular sensibilities (associated with "black cultural values" or *négritude*) were ultimately complementary, opening him to charges of a neocolonial Gallocentrism among his critics. Fewer scholars have noticed, however, that Senghor also engaged with arguments later in his career as a statesman on the ultimately symbiotic relationship between Arabic and local vernaculars as former rivals and aspirational complements. Senghor modified these views with his changing public status, as Arabic became by his estimation in the 1960s a vital tributary for pan-African solidarities. In key statements in the 1960s, Senghor appeared to resolve his earlier ambivalence about Arabic in the wake of Senegalese independence. Although he generally considered Arabic to be a foreign presence in the region—and compared it, in some respects, with French as a medium that introduced or reinforced racial hierarchies within sub-Saharan Africa—he argued that Arabic could be co-opted for egalitarian ends.

Senghor's early writings on African literature, however, aggressively advocated for the "defense" of sub-Saharan African languages against the incursions of French while minimizing the importance of an arabophone precedent for the transcription of local languages. In an early public address dating from 1937, for example, Senghor portrayed the French language as an inescapable aggression, in light of which marginalized local languages must be revalued and transcribed. But the question of the script or writing system for indigenous languages—Latinate, Arabic, or a third alternative—remained open and unaddressed in claims such as the following:

> Intellectuals have a mission to restore *black values* in their truth and excellence, to awaken their people to the taste of bread and the games of the spirit, by which we are *Men*. By writing, above all. There is no civilization without a literature that expresses it, and that illustrates its values, as for the jeweler the crown jewels. And without a written literature, there is no civilization that moves beyond a simple, ethnographic curiosity. *For, how is it possible to conceive of an indigenous literature that is not written in an indigenous language?* [. . .] There is a certain taste, a certain odor, a certain accent, a certain black timbre that is inexpressible with European instruments.[60]

Several assertions within this statement deserve emphasis. Senghor here conflates literature with the textual and transcribed; alternatives to written literature are dismissed as a mere "ethnographic curiosity," and French is equally dismissed as a foreign medium incapable of conveying indigenous sensibilities. On each of these points, Senghor would directly contradict himself later in his career. Such claims nonetheless underscore how the question of indigenous forms of linguistic representation was inextricably linked to the problem of a written standard for vernacular languages—indigenous languages that appeared textually orphaned in the wake of Arabic's marginalization by French colonial agents in West Africa by the earliest decades of the twentieth century.[61]

In a key statement that illustrates Senghor's self-contradictions (published in 1945), he modified his claims about local vernaculars, stating that the indigenous literature of "black Africa" is not a genre in search of a written medium or script but, rather, one that, when historically written in Arabic, was an inauthenticity, a kind of rhetorical fabrication, a cultural entanglement from which the "truest" forms of black African literature deserved to be extricated.[62] In such statements, Senghor folded into his claims an acknowledgment of *ʿajami* writing—of vernacular or indigenous writing in Arabic—but characterized Arabic as a medium contaminating an allegedly authentic sense of blackness. Self-consciously responding to colonial proponents of a "negro-African tabula rasa," "who do not wish to perceive in our great states of the Medieval Age and of the modern era more than a creation of Islam," Senghor highlighted the presence of an Arabic-influenced local textual literature but suggested his preference for an oral tradition, which he deemed a more authentic expression of *l'âme noire* (the black soul).[63] Europe's great Africanists, he wrote,

> will tell you that black Africa possesses supple, rich languages, capable of expressing even abstractions, although in a manner entirely African, full of

imagery, and poetic. They will tell you that she possesses a certain number of written languages. *Nonetheless, I prefer, to her written literature, influenced most of the time by Arabic, and leaving the imprint of rhetoric, the oral literature of the griots,* our troubadours, who take no leave of erudition while expressing the "emotional warmth" of the black soul.[64]

Though Senghor in his 1945 article challenged Arabic's ability to authentically convey *l'âme noire* and to embody the emotional vibrancy of vernacular oral poetry, in his later writings on the ultimate syncretism of *négritude* and French he nonetheless promoted an alternative "foreign" medium through his choice of French. Senghor justified his choice of French with arguments on the primacy of cultural "bicephalism" and *métissage* (hybridity), according to which French appears to be the intrinsic complement to and ideal textual vessel for the local, authentically African oral tradition that preceded a written French one—paying little or no attention to the Arabic or Arabic-influenced African textual tradition that French print culture eclipsed in the early twentieth century.

To juxtapose this statement in 1945 with those Senghor expressed in 1937, a hierarchy appears evident in his early writing that is distinctively and vestigially colonial in tenor, even as it seeks to usurp French colonial sensibilities in favor of the vernacular and indigenous. According to this colonial logic, literature must be definitively understood as written text for it to be culturally relevant, but "Africa's written literature" is deficient if it is conveyed or "influenced by Arabic." Senghor's statements here suggest, in other words, that cultural forms must be transcribed to be understood as "literary" but that indigenous orature is preferable to written literature if the latter is transcribed in a culturally contaminated (or contaminating) Arabic. It is in this light that his idealized poetic symbiosis of French and "negro-African" vernacular sensibilities can be seen as arising from a colonially inflected sense of Arabic as a decadent foreign presence and cultural hegemon in black West Africa, a position resulting from Senghor's indignation that black Africa might be considered a civilizational nonentity without an Arabic-Islamic cultural "leaven."[65]

When Senghor assumed control of Senegal as head of state in 1960, he adjusted his views as a matter of broadened horizons and as a matter of political expediency: The relationship between indigenous African languages and Arabic, once viewed by Senghor as relatively stratified and antagonistic, appeared to him more complementary and symbiotic by the 1960s. As we have seen, in several key statements in the 1960s and 1970s he came to recognize both Arabic and French as local acrolects in West Africa, but he now understood their literary use by non-native speakers as parallel gestures of egalitarian subversion or hybrid adaptation rather than as signs of cultural contamination or decadence.[66] It is on these grounds that he would characterize arabophone figures such as Dabo and Bamba as "negrified" poets of Arabic and *ʿajami* writing, shifting away from relatively purist attitudes about language toward an idealization of cultural hybridity in the name of a "negrified" arabophone poetic corpus.

In the wake of Senegalese independence and in the search for continental African solidarities after French West Africa's fragmentation, Senghor's address of Arabic's presence both locally in Senegal and continentally (as a foundational contribution to Africanness) appears modulated by new political alignments. Such alignments are suggested by his lauding of Sitokoto Dabo and of Ahmadu Bamba's legacy in Touba (intranationally) and by a major diplomatic speech on Arabness and *négritude* in Cairo (internationally) in 1967. In his 1967 speech, Senghor explained that his growing interest in the Arabic language as part of an African "patrimony" dated to the constitutive conference of the Organization of African Unity in 1963, when he came to recognize the influence of Semitic Berber languages on vernacular ritual and religious terms in West Africa, extending to an influence even within Christian communities in Senegal.[67]

On the occasion of his Cairene speech in February 1967, marking a major shift in his thinking, Senghor paid a diplomatic visit to Nasser at the height of Nasser's popularity in the months prior to the Naksah. During this visit, Senghor presented an extensive and erudite speech on the "foundations of African unity," or what he termed (with characteristic neologism) its constituent grounds, *négritude* and *arabité*. While the address, given in French, ranged broadly from the continent's Neolithic beginnings to the emergence of language and artistry in continental Africa, pride of place was given to the historical commingling of Arabness and "negro-African" culture, a shared patrimony moving toward what Senghor rhetorically termed the "unity in diversity" (*unité dans la diversité*) of African civilization.[68] Signs of this unity in diversity and cultural commingling, he argued, could be seen in the continent's spectrum of languages:

> In truth, there are, again, between Arabic, on one hand, and languages of the *Bantu* and *Sudanese* groups, on the other hand, a series of intermediate languages that, upon examination, reveal themselves to be *mixed languages*

> [*langues métisses*]. [. . .] These are Ethiopian languages, Ancient and Coptic Egyptian, Berber languages, and, finally, Cushitic languages. *There have been, from these two sides—Arabo-Berber and negro-African—assimilation and, at the same time, reciprocal reaction to the other.*[69]

Notwithstanding this linguistic chain of kinship, the rifts between what he called "Arabo-Berber" and "negro-African" orientations of the continent remained the most important challenge to African unity, he argued, with linguistic divisions between former anglophone and francophone colonies a close second.[70]

By characterizing African culture or civilization as a continuum of mutual influences, Senghor aimed to overcome imperial taxonomies that symbolized colonial-era continental rifts across North and sub-Saharan Africa.[71] And yet, such efforts to overturn imperial or colonial-era divisions appear attenuated by his ambivalent position as the cultural product of that segregation in Senegal. This tension between Senghor's colonial education and his counterimperial aspirations gave rise to apparent self-contradictions and irresolutions within his 1967 Egyptian speech, among others, about the conditions of continental African unity as informed by "negro-African" and "Arabo-Berber" cultural forces—not least on the question of which languages best mediated the twentieth-century horizons of African unity and counterimperial autonomy and the taxonomic nature of these colonially inflected divisions (Arabo-Berber and negro-African).[72]

Senghor's claims about continental Africa's Arabic or "Arabo-Berber" orientations were notably informed by a host of French metropolitan texts rather than through sub-Saharan Africa's long-standing circuits of Arabic and *ʿajami* scholarship. One peculiarity of his speech was the absence of any direct reference to Senegal's own corpus of Arabic and *ʿajami* (Arabic-script) poetry. Given Senghor's position as a poet, linguist, and literary critic whose comparative scope and omnivorous interests ranged from Latin to Dravidian languages and whose speech in Cairo on African unity extended to esoteric comments on Arabic poetics, the absence of any citation of Senegal's poetic traditions in Arabic is itself instructive. This absence suggests either a conscious omission or, more likely, the institutional mutual exclusivity of the francophone literary canon that he himself represented and the arabophone West African one that he failed to cite. He instead directly culled references from a French "colonial library" to inform his characterization of a hybrid pan-Africanism, even as those citations were intended to serve a counterimperial project: scaffolding and envisioning in intellectual terms the cultural (and political) grounds of continental African unity and reciprocal exchange.[73]

Through his ambivalent uses of colonial-era concepts (on race and the racialization of Arabic), Senghor's public statements offer a lens through which to interpret the effects of late colonial practices and policies of cultural segregation during the late nineteenth and early twentieth centuries. This segregation involved both the promotion of French and displacement of Arabic in the public realm in French West Africa and the racialized, ethnographic and linguistic distinction between a more orthodox, Islamized "Arab" North Africa and "black" sub-Saharan African region with tenuously Arabic-Islamic orientations. Senghor inherited the results of that continental division and those segregated literacies and negotiated them as public intellectual, poet, and trained linguist before arbitering over them as politician and head of state. As president, he sought to bridge and in effect repoliticize those divisions for the new exigencies of an emergent, postindependence nation-state. Among the consequences of this repoliticization is that Senghor drew master terms and concepts, even pejorative ones (such as the French Orientalist term *Islam noir*), from a French colonial context and reused them in defiant and unexpected ways, entwining them with egalitarian assertions about two historically prestigious languages in Senegal: French and Arabic.

One can thus see how French colonial ideologies of language and race resurface and are at times idiosyncratically reinterpreted in Senghor's rhetoric on African unity. Senghor in effect refashioned racialized French terms (such as the pejorative term *nègre*) to interpret histories of Arabic and Arabic-Islamic acculturation across ethnolinguistic lines, by redefining such terms as "negro-African," *négritude*, and *négrifiant* (blackening) against the "Arab" or "Arabo-Berber."[74] Through notions of "negro-African" distinction relative to Arabo-Berber alternatives, or to *negrified* Islam as a matter of pride attached to arabophone Senegalese poets, Senghor subverted the meaning of racialized French characterizations of sub-Saharan African Islam. He did so by implying that "Africanizing" and *negrifying* Islam—and Arabic as its charismatic, ritual medium—historically added to their value rather than detracting from it. It is on these grounds that arabophone Senegalese poets appear comparable to their francophone counterparts for Senghor, advancing across two linguistic orientations and "scriptworlds" a shared project of black consciousness and social revolution, unsettling intersecting hierarchies in continental Africa.[75]

Senghor's Legacy

As I hope to have shown, *négritude* for Senghor became the "arbiter of an alliance between African traditions and contemporary political struggles," surfacing in his poetry and political rhetoric "as a tool for forging a new supranational and national sense of being and belonging" (to borrow Elizabeth Harney's apt description).[76] To gesture again to transregional comparisons in the "spirit of Bandung," Senghor's diplomatic invocations of *négritude* across Southeast Asian and North African contexts illustrate the term's protean contours as a counterimperial front for political transformation. His application of the term appeared to his advocates and critics, however, at turns as radically progressive or as misguided and reactionary, depending on regional and former imperial contexts. In the name of *négritude* and black diasporic solidarity, for example, Senghor denounced the violence, racism, and linguism of ethnic Indonesian Malays against black Polynesians in West Papua and East Timor in the 1960s and 1970s—the by-products of military conflicts that Sukarno and Suharto's governments had framed as an extension of emancipatory struggles against former colonists in the archipelago (the Dutch and the Portuguese).[77] But if Senghor supported Timorese and Papuan independence against Indonesia, he withheld his support from Algeria's earlier national independence struggle against colonial France—leading Frantz Fanon, in his renowned criticism of Senghor on the Algerian struggle, to claim it impossible to support "African-Negro culture" and "the cultural Unity of Africa" without giving "practical support to the creation of the conditions necessary to the existence of that culture" through the political "liberation of the whole continent" in national terms.[78] Senghor's legacy in connection with *négritude* as a liberating front appears less certain, in other words, when its frame of reference shifts from Southeast Asia to North Africa, particularly in the context of former French (as opposed to British or Dutch) colonies.

Senghor's legacy with regard to caste is also ambiguous. Although my reading of caste in Senghor's poetry is relatively generous and sympathetic, I acknowledge an alternative and more critical approach to his poetic invocation of caste: as an opportunistic cultural borrowing rather than a fully liberationist one. For Senghor's poetic idealization of a "noble" *griot* or a bardic underclass did not translate into clear policies for social reform during his career as a politician. Although the archive on this subject is sparse, Senghor's nonliterary writing on the West African caste system in the 1940s notably fails to advocate for its transformation. Senghor's most direct overview of the caste system (*nyêni*) in West Africa appeared in his 1945 essay "Vues sur l'Afrique noire ou assimiler, non être assimilés," where his address is limited to uncritical ethnographic descriptions that skirt the issue of immediate social reform.[79] It is also unclear whether Senghor's exclusively poetic vision for caste subversion extended to his eventual management of state-sponsored forms of artistic patronage in Senegal (which would have implicated many members of a traditionally underclass, artisanal caste).[80]

Perhaps the most damning evidence of Senghor's political ambivalence regarding caste hierarchies, however, is in recollections of his reliance on bardic praise singers who eulogized him as a politician—apparently as a matter of public strategy to manufacture an appearance of consensus around his presidential policies.[81] As recalled by literary critic and publisher Ulli Beier, for example, Senghor's address to the Senegalese National Assembly in 1971 involved accompaniment by a group of traditional *griots* "strategically placed" in the assembly hall "to shout the President's praises" and punctuate his speeches in what Beier calls a "piece of perfect theater."[82] When viewed against claims of caste inversion in Senghor's poetry, such scenes of the "noble" Senghor surrounded by underclass bards in eulogistic chorus gain a certain irony—especially given Senghor's self-promotion as an ardent socialist.

Given this ambiguity, and in the absence of more evidence to the contrary, an open question endures in connection to Senghor's legacy in West Africa. What do we make of politicians such as Senghor whose rhetorical and cultural use of caste appears disconnected from their policies on social change? Perhaps Senghor's poetic use of the motif amounts to a kind of caste minstrelsy, given his status and later political posturing as a pedigreed politician. Or perhaps Senghor's poems should be read as transient but idealist statements, imagining a social future where caste hierarchies would be subverted. But it cannot be denied that, on the plane of social and political praxis, Senghor fell short of any such transformation. Given the contradictions he embodied, one might ask whether such an envisioned end to traditional caste systems paradoxically fostered alternative hierarchies in their place. (This might be implied by the scene of an elite poet-turned-politician surrounded by underclass bards praising his ostensibly socialist policies.)

To more accurately situate Senghor's shifting positions (and literary innovations) as they emerged with the process of decolonization means to bracket the nation-state as the necessary horizon of a decolonized future, as Gary Wilder has argued.[83] Such insights offer an important basis to understand Senghor's changing visions for an emancipated future, arcing not toward a directly nationalist and nationally vernacular horizon of representation but toward a more hybrid vision of polycentric solidarities advanced by claims of cultural parity. This equally explains Senghor's validation of supranational solidarities as expressed in languages historically foreign to West Africa, including French and Arabic. We might therefore suspend the vernacularized nation-state as the imagined end of a counterimperial process of self-determination anticipated in literary form when assessing his legacy.[84]

Envisioning Senegal's postcolonial future, Senghor's 1959 statements on the Bandung Conference illuminate his initial promotion of a broader French African (or "Eurafrican") federalism and his suspicion of nation-states as an emancipatory horizon. There was a certain pragmatism in this. The balkanization of the former colony of French West Africa risked a comparative loss in regional influence and prestige for Senegal, the site of French West Africa's colonial capital. Independence in isolation, Senghor would frequently claim, was not independence at all but, rather, an invitation for isolated nation-states to be divisively re-exploited by neocolonial forces.[85] At stake in the brokering of a decolonized future for mid-twentieth-century Senegal were the differences between formal independence and substantive freedoms, which, he claimed, could not be guaranteed by simply refashioning former colonies into individual nation-states.[86] This point helps us to understand Senghor's ambivalence toward a provincial sense of Senegalese nationalism, as well as his promotion of a broader federalism as a statesman in the twilight of France's West African empire.

On this basis, one might also understand Senghor's tendency to advocate for transnational solidarities as the first president of independent Senegal when those federalist initiatives failed. One way that he pushed for such solidarities was by promoting the French language in West Africa as a common cultural currency. Another was by gesturing to a certain vision of pan-Africanism, emphasizing modes of continental hybridity and civilizational reciprocity across North African and sub-Saharan regional lines (or "Arabo-Berber" and "negro-African" divisions during the 1960s and 1970s).[87] Such efforts reflect Senghor's changing positions on the politics of language and offer a lens to interpret West Africa's shifting political solidarities as he imagined them. Senghor first envisioned continued solidarities between France and its former African colonies amid Senegal's transition to independence. In the wake of independence, he then imagined solidarities that would bridge both the regional schisms between North and sub-Saharan Africa and the cultural schisms within Senegal itself.

Senghor's inability during his presidency to fully resolve or bridge segregated literacies and writing systems in Senegal would haunt him throughout his political career. Demands for him to confront his failures surfaced by the 1970s, not least in the foundational pages of the first vernacular-language journal published in Senegal (1971–78), *Kaddu*. To read his critics within the journal's pages, Senghor's rhetorical tactics and language policies after independence were neither egalitarian nor sufficiently representative of vernacular forms of local culture.

Although delegates from French West Africa were not present at the Bandung Conference, it is clear that French West African subjects had been inspired by its agenda and engaged in initiatives that directly challenged Senghor's own more conservative positions. The Fédération des étudiants d'Afrique noire en France (Federation of Black African Students in France, FEANF), for example, published a pamphlet in 1958 entitled *Le sang de Bandoeng* (*The Blood of Bandung*) in support of the struggle for Algerian independence.[88] In keeping with the spirit of the times, and to challenge French as a hegemonic presence in Africa, Senegalese members of FEANF in the same year developed *Ijjib Volof*, one of the earliest romanized syllabaries for Wolof, Senegal's spoken lingua franca.[89] This was an initiative that prefigured the founding of *Kaddu* by many former associates of FEANF nearly a decade later. Scholars frequently gloss over this publication, assuming that it was a humble pro-literacy initiative; but this foundational journal, as we shall see in the following chapter, significantly illustrates the existential struggle of Senegalese print vernaculars against the prestige of both Arabic and colonial acrolects in the projection of Senegalese national consciousness.

Focusing on the final decades of the twentieth century, the book's next section uncovers parallels between Senegal and Indonesia, two regions colonially associated with the "peripheries" of the "Muslim world." It shows how writers within these regions challenged Eurocentric and Arabocentric forms of prejudice in comparable ways, before considering how these parallels extend to Egypt, a region colonially politicized as a center of Arabic print and as a cultural vanguard within the Muslim world.

SECTION III

Connected Histories and Competing Literacies

8

"Margins" of a "Muslim World"

DESPITE THEIR PARALLELS AS languages that mark the African and Asian extremes of a global Muslim community, or *umma*, Wolof and Indonesian are rarely compared. Historically transcribed in the Arabic script, both were coastal languages of colonial contact whose fates were intertwined with Arabic's fortunes.[1] The expansion of Wolof and Indonesian Malay, as major languages of coastal trade and informal religious exposition, among non-native speakers accompanied two coinciding processes in West Africa and insular Southeast Asia: the regional spread of Islam and the consolidation of colonial empires.[2] The twentieth-century backlash against European literacies as instruments of empire gave rise to the counterimperial promotion of each language among local writers. The indebtedness of each language to Arabic influences, however, has remained a matter of controversy in postindependence Senegal and Indonesia.[3]

This chapter compares the literary innovations of two of Senegal and Indonesia's most renowned authors of the mid- to late twentieth century, Ousmane Sembene and Pramoedya Ananta Toer. It illustrates how they each promoted ideals of ethnolinguistic parity through vernacular print initiatives and historical fiction in Wolof or Indonesian. Through their efforts to elevate vernacular publishing and literary narratives, both Sembene and Pramoedya responded to the effects of European colonial policies of "Association" established in the late nineteenth and early twentieth centuries. Such policies, which evolved through interimperial policy-sharing that directly connected Dutch and French colonial agents, sought to spread Europeanized literacies among colonized elites as Arabicized alternatives were being marginalized.

Sembene and Pramoedya each advanced subaltern forms of historical literacy for local readers against Eurocentric and Arabocentric alternatives. The two writers promoted regional histories written "from below" (to paraphrase Pramoedya),[4] challenging in the process the local prestige of Arabic and the scholarly prestige of European languages such as French, Dutch, and Portuguese for chronicling an Indonesian or Senegalese past. Sembene and Pramoedya also defended the right to ethnolinguistic difference and the value of plurilingualism as a matter of global parity. Their fictions portrayed ideals of cultural equality and pluralism as values locally derived rather than arising from liberal European influences.

The focus by both Sembene and Pramoedya on vernacular language in their revisionist historical fiction and other writing reflects their common conviction that linguistic dynamics translate historical relations of force. Their historical fiction explores the rise of intersecting Arabocentric and Eurocentric hierarchies in their native regions, hierarchies that, they claimed, rendered local languages doubly marginalized with the consolidation of European empires and with the spread of Islam in West Africa and Southeast Asia. Both authors controversially portrayed these regional processes—Islamization and European colonization—as interdependent. And both suggested through their fiction that precolonial religious tensions left each region vulnerable to foreign exploitation and colonial rule.

Sembene and Pramoedya also viewed informal vernacular print networks and their historical revitalization as a crucial way to bridge the segregated literacies bequeathed by European empires. Both writers claimed that the authentic beginnings of nationalized culture in Senegal and Indonesia arose through developments beyond the direct orbit of colonial print. For Pramoedya, the first stirrings of Indonesian national consciousness appeared through independent vernacular print at the turn of the twentieth century, rather than through the literary workings of the colonial Dutch publishing house Balai Pustaka. The genesis of Indonesian national culture therefore appeared in an unstandardized vernacular "people's Malay," deemed an unruly, "wild" print form by colonial officials.[5] For Sembene, the Eurocentric legacies of the French colonial state in West Africa left unfinished the work of establishing a vernacular Senegalese press after independence. These conditions motivated Sembene and the Senegalese linguist Pathé Diagne to cofound Senegal's first native-language journal, *Kaddu*, in a nonofficial orthographic standard.

Although vast distances separated these two authors in Indonesia and Senegal, their itineraries crossed on at least one occasion at the inaugural Afro-Asian Writers' Congress in Tashkent in 1958, a gathering inspired by the Bandung Conference. Although evidence of their direct contact has yet to be found, their joint participation in Tashkent attests to their imbrication in emerging networks of Asian-African literary exchange after Bandung.[6] Whereas Sembene gained international prominence through his continued engagement with the Afro-Asian Writers movement, Pramoedya's participation in Afro-Asian literary exchanges was cut short by his arrest and incarceration after an anti-communist coup in Indonesia in 1965.

Pramoedya (1925–2006) had become an affiliate of the leftist Indonesian cultural organization Lekra by the time of the Tashkent gathering, working as a journalist and literary editor during the 1950s and early 1960s for the nationalist paper *Bintang Timur*. Along with many fellow Indonesian leftists, Pramoedya was a victim of the mass violence that overthrew the Sukarno regime in 1965. Forbidden pen and paper during his brutal first years of imprisonment on the carceral island of Buru, he entertained his fellow prisoners by recounting from memory the stories he had lost during his arrest, when his working manuscripts were destroyed. Among those he retold are the novels examined in this chapter (published after his release from prison), *Arus Balik* and the four novels of the *Buru Quartet*.

Sembene (1923–2007), in contrast, enjoyed relative freedom as a writer and filmmaker during Senghor's presidency, despite his arbitrary censorship by Senghor for political reasons (as we shall see). Sembene, originally from a Wolof-speaking family in the Senegalese region of Casamance, migrated to France as a dockworker after World War II, before becoming a prominent union activist. He joined the French Communist Party before Senegalese independence and remained an ardent leftist throughout his postindependence career in Senegal, publicly opposed to Senghor's increasingly authoritarian tendencies and to his promotion of French as an official language. Sembene's concerns about the dominance of French in West Africa led him both to cofound *Kaddu* and to experiment with vernacular-language filmmaking to reach audiences illiterate in French.

The chapter opens with an illustration of how *Kaddu*, the journal cofounded by Sembene, elevated Wolof relative to French and Arabic acrolects. I then analyze Sembene's allegorical film *Ceddo* as a complement to his print activism, before exploring the film's parallels with Pramoedya's historical novel *Arus Balik*. After considering the satirical portrayal of politically exploitable "truth languages" in *Arus Balik*, which resonates with Sembene's controversial legacy, I revisit the colonial-era history of vernacular "people's Malay," portrayed as an egalitarian medium in Pramoedya's historical novels making up the *Buru Quartet*.

Sembene and Pramoedya explored the terms of a pluralist and egalitarian future for postindependence Senegal and Indonesia. Both writers' fictions suggest that liberty against a foreign power can only be ensured through regional unity across religious differences, rather than through a coercive political unity on the basis of Islam as a state religion. When compared in tandem, their legacies—at the regional extremes of a once-colonized "Muslim world"—jointly challenge Eurocentric and Arabocentric claims to cultural precedence. Their desire to undercut both Eurocentric and Arabocentric cultural claims led them to recover the subaltern foundations of vernacular print—another important dimension of their legacies that, in Sembene's case, remains critically underexamined.

Kaddu's Print Activism

The journal *Kaddu* is often glossed in Sembene scholarship as a pro-literacy publication for an illiterate audience. This impression, however, is contradicted by the journal's opening editorials, which reflect a more complex reality in which presumed readers occupied a spectrum of mixed and partial literacies across a multitude of languages and pedagogical influences. One of the journal's early editorials, for example, assumes that *Kaddu*'s implied reader was partially literate in at least two, if not three, languages: The journal's readers, the editorial claims, were likely schooled for almost a decade in French or Arabic, in either "foreign" schools or religious schools, without mastering either of these languages.[7] This was a tragedy compounded, according to the editorial board, by the enduring dilemma that their readers' own native languages remained textually unstandardized, institutionally overlooked by the Senegalese state as a vital repository of information.

Kaddu, in other words, was not quite addressing pure illiteracies but, rather, partial literacies and segregated literacies in postindependence Senegal. In several editorials, the journal's founders and contributors viewed themselves as bridging a complex set of intranational literacies, aspiring to complete an urgent task they believed Senghor's regime had failed to begin.[8] Boasting a regular column published in Pulaar and Mandinka, and with stated (but never realized) plans to publish complementary titles in several more of Senegal's vernacular languages (beyond *Kaddu* in Wolof), the journal's editors sought to redress the strange asymmetries imposed by the Gallocentric policies of a former French colonial state, partially sustained by the pro-francophone policies of Senghor as its postindependence successor.[9] As remembered by Seydou Nourou Ndiaye, the owner of the publishing house that printed *Kaddu* (Éditions Papyrus), the motive behind the journal's establishment was to demonstrate the feasibility of developing print media in local languages in spite of the dominant use of French.[10]

The pages of *Kaddu*, however, also illustrate the existential struggle of Senegalese vernaculars relative to a Qur'anic Arabic acrolect and Arabic script. In the final volume of *Kaddu*, the journal's editorial board appears to have grappled with the problem of digraphia—evincing a sense of the region's vernaculars historically suspended between two (allegedly foreign) scripts. Beginning with its earliest volumes, the journal published informal transcription tables (*ijji*) in each issue to guide its readership through the journal's newly inaugurated (but officially unsanctioned) Latin orthography for Wolof.[11] Attuned to the issue of script as symbol, however, the editors not only experimented with publishing an Arabic and Latin syllabary by their final issue; they included a syllabary or transcription table for a third, invented script created by the linguist Pathé Diagne—a symbolic dissociation from nominally foreign spheres of literary influence.[12] Alongside such experiments, however, the final page of the journal's last issue concluded with an *ʿajami* poem composed by Diagne in Wolof and transcribed in Arabic script. The poem ("Bind ci sa lakk," or "Writing in Your Language") proclaimed the value of writing in local vernaculars, whether in *haraf tubab* or *haraf Arab* (Latin or Arabic scripts).[13]

The pages of *Kaddu* reveal how the beginnings of vernacular print in Senegal contended not only with the legacy of French as an official language but with Arabic as a medium of religious prestige and interpretive authority for Senegal's Muslim majority. In this connection, controversies editorially covered during the journal's publication reveal the imbrication of debates that persisted after Senegalese independence, on the religious contours of an independent Senegal and the Arabic informants of an emergent national culture. The political parameters of these debates were especially marked in an early set of editorials and articles on legal reforms to the Senegalese family code—a debate taking root in 1972, when religious leaders protested sustaining French family law without due consideration for Islamic precepts.[14] In *Kaddu*'s coverage of this controversy, the journal identifies two rival cultural hierarchies and juridical models by shorthand, with a line in one of its editorials that reads: "Napoleon or Arabic?" to which the journal's response is: "*[N]either!*"[15] It was a distinction that *Kaddu* explored (in editorials written under pseudonyms) by claiming that one had to differentiate between universal articles of faith and the provinciality of regional customs.[16]

The journal's positions on the controversy might be summarized as follows: "Arab customs" are a matter of regional differences rather than articles of faith; religious guides must know the difference and be enjoined to interpret the Qur'an rather than merely memorizing it, so as to adapt it to Senegalese realities and customs, translating its precepts in vernacular languages to make the faith more accessible.[17] In direct provocation of more conservative religious circles on questions of scriptural interpretation, the journal claimed:

> Those who cannot translate the Qur'an or Bible to make them accessible for the present times, those who do not recognize that a religious belief and traditions are not the same, you are similar to those who only know or focus on French law and who merely reference Napoleon's codes. What is difficult to find in Senegal is a real religious guide who can get to the essence of what is said in the Qur'an or Bible, and who does not just memorize them [. . .] .[18]

Notably, Sembene's cofounder of the journal, the linguist Pathé Diagne, engaged in such translational work, claiming to have been the first to translate the Qur'an into romanized Wolof to serve this purpose.[19] The journal's editorial choices—experimenting with the use of both Arabic and Latin script within its pages, while debating the *defrancisation* and *desarabisation* of Senegalese culture—throw into relief the existential struggles of a nationally emergent Senegalese vernacular culture relative to both ritual Arabic and colonial alternatives.[20]

To this end, *Kaddu*'s contributors also justified the promotion of African vernaculars relative to high ritual Arabic by highlighting the issue of Arabic diglossia in North Africa and West Asia, claiming the existence of parallel trends toward vernacular language representation in custodial centers of Islamic learning.[21] Even among native Arabic speakers, the journal claimed, attention is given to the issue of transcribing *Arabic* dialects or vernaculars among the region's illiterate masses, who speak in ways distinct from "university" standards of the written Arabic language.[22] *Kaddu*'s editorial contributors, in other words, asserted the following: If, as some of Senegal's clerical elites and religious conservatives allegedly argued, Arab North Africa and West Asia should be emulated as cultural leaders on language forms and interpretive practices, the privileging of Senegalese vernaculars should prevail whether one justifies it as an end in itself or as an emulation of these trends in North Africa and West Asia.

If the pages of *Kaddu* highlighted the existential struggles of literary vernaculars against a Qur'anic inheritance and within a historically arabophone cultural space, the publication's efforts were not necessarily intended to erode Muslim religious solidarities—at least of a certain orientation. Amid *Kaddu*'s editorial calls for the distinction between Islam as a matter of faith and Arabism as a question of cultural affiliation, its pages also sought to reconcile Senegalese vernacular cultures to transregional Muslim solidarities in qualified ways. Although its articles on Senegalese history challenged the notion that West African cultural memory began with the advent of Islam in the region, the publication nonetheless commemorated figures of anticolonial religious resistance to French rule and highlighted transatlantic Muslim solidarities for the paired causes of anticolonialism and black racial pride. In this light, the pages of *Kaddu* not only revisited the histories of anticolonial jihadists such as Samori Toure and al-Hadji Omar Tall; they featured praise poems in Wolof of figures such as Malcolm X.[23] The death of Nkrumah, in another example, occasioned an extraordinary feature in the pages of *Kaddu*, with a commemorative article that urges readers to understand Nkrumah's life like a *saar*, the Wolof term for a sura or verse in the Qur'an: "[H]is life should be read like a *saar*—it should not only be memorized, but emulated."[24] This line offers an illuminating glimpse into the journal's implied reader, who might be presumed to read the Qur'an as a source of memorization and moral emulation but could be enjoined to embrace secular paragons (such as the non-Muslim Nkrumah) with reverence.

As suggested through these features, the journal's characterization of African history and the defiant editorial tone of many of its articles in Wolof (irregularly published from 1971 to 1974, with a final issue appearing in 1978) suggest that the contributors viewed themselves as committed to an unfinished revolution across a complex set of affinities—political, (inter)religious, and racial. Early literary contributions to the journal, including anonymously written praise poems for Miriam Makeba (upon her visit to Dakar from South Africa), as well as eulogies of Malcolm X (adapted from an Amiri Baraka poem), reveal the editors' support for unfinished liberation movements not only in continental Africa but within an African American diaspora.[25]

Inaugural volumes of the journal also frequently addressed how continental African history might be vindicated beyond the institutional dominance of the colonial French language in Senegal. In light of these initiatives, *Kaddu*, which itself means "voice" or "vote" in Wolof, sought to give expression to an imperially obscured or distorted past, to reconnect its readership with historical inheritances whose transmission seemed troubled by broken lines of linguistic filiation. In its efforts to reestablish these connections, *Kaddu* emphasized the longevity of African histories whose imperial reach and precedence to European empires denaturalized European colonial claims to unrivaled cultural supremacy; the journal equally unsettled notions that sub-Saharan African history began with Arabic-Islamic practices of chronicling. Particularly notable, in this regard, was the indirect editorial restatement of a thesis controversially popularized by the Senegalese Egyptologist Cheikh Anta Diop (a political and intellectual rival of Senghor), who asserted the black, sub-Saharan origins of pharaonic civilization in Egypt and implied that any indebtedness of Hellenic Europe to pharaonic Egypt was therefore an indebtedness to sub-Saharan Africa.[26] Rallied in the editorial pages of *Kaddu* within this *longue durée* framing of continental African history were references to African polities whose formation preceded the more recent wave of European colonization in Africa, including the empires of Ghana, Tekrur, and Mali under Mansa Moussa in the fourteenth century.[27] These editorial references project a sense of continental history that not only predates Europe's imperial rise but presages the decline of European empires in the twentieth century—empires that in the longer arc of African historical time appear as recent and transient phenomena.

In its coverage of African history, the journal also featured commemorative articles on nineteenth-century West African figures of resistance to European colonial and commercial expansion. Samori Toure, for example, the anticolonialist subject of Sembene's final unfinished film, features in a commemorative volume published on the anniversary of Senegalese independence.[28] Pride of place in this special issue is also given to the Tijaniyya jihadist al-Hadji Omar Tall (Cheikh Omar Tijaniyya) and to Lat Joor Joop, who resisted the French colonial establishment of a railroad into the Senegalese interior—a railroad that forms the principal setting of Sembene's novel about a workers' strike, *Les bouts de bois de dieu* (*God's Bits of Wood*).[29] As one might expect of a publication founded and sustained by leftist activists (as Sembene and Diagne were), these features on African historical figures also challenged the maintenance of social hierarchies on the basis of charismatic lineage or alliance.

In this light, the journal's editorials demanded that such historical figures be remembered "for their actions" rather than for their social status, revered for their championing of African independence rather than their status as regents or courtly allies.[30] The claim appears leveled against unnamed contemporary targets, disarming associations between religious authority and presumptions of social prestige and material entitlements. Also notable in this connection is an editorial reference to al-Hadji Omar Tall as an anticolonial figure whose legacy serves as an indictment to religious clerics indifferent to presumably neocolonial practices in the "present" of the journal's publication. A contribution devoted to al-Hadji Omar, for example, concludes with the cryptic statement: "It is important to remember al-Hadji Omar especially for those [religious leaders] who hide."[31]

Across these historical features, the complementarity of the journal's didactic efforts and several subjects explored in Sembene's historical films and fiction are apparent. This convergence is particularly salient in the journal's coverage of *Ceddo*, Sembene's allegorical film on the regional spread of Islam—a controversial film censored by Senghor for its anticlericalism, the outcome of an ideological controversy fronted by a linguistic one. The reason publicly given by Senghor for the film's prohibition in Senegal was the mistranscription of the Wolof term *ceddo*, roughly meaning "rebel" or "the one who refuses."[32] (In the case of the film, the term designates a populace that refuses conversion to Islam.) The censorship generated fierce public debates about whether the title should be rendered, as the director claimed, with a doubled consonant (*Ceddo*) or, as President Senghor asserted, with a single one (*Cedo*). The pages of *Kaddu* attest to these debates, which pitted the film's director against the president on linguistic grounds, with *Kaddu* protesting against Senghor's misjudgment.[33] The question of how a vernacular Wolof term should be transcribed or transliterated into romanized text, and the question of who had the moral right and institutional authority to sanction its transcription (Sembene as a native Wolof speaker or Senghor as a French-trained Serer linguist), factored into this controversy.

Notwithstanding the linguistic parameters of the debate as marked in *Kaddu*'s pages, common consensus was that the film's contents were politically incendiary, and President Senghor's sensitivities to the unflattering portrayal of clerical figures within the film led to its censorship. As Tobias Warner and Mamadou Diouf have noted, the general pretext of the film, though historical, was critical of contemporary Senegalese politics and appeared to satirize the undue influence and perceived interference of clerical authorities and religious elites within the affairs of the Senegalese state under Senghor.[34]

As Sembene himself suggested in interviews, *Ceddo* traces Senegalese dynamics that may have arisen in a colonial past but "are still occurring."[35] A close viewing of the film, especially when read against the editorial concerns of the journal he cofounded, implies what he may have intended by such statements: a critique of what some scholars of African politics have called the dynamics of informal brokering between religious elites and secular state representatives in Senegal.[36] On these grounds, the editorial positions of *Kaddu*—in its critical coverage of the family law controversy of the 1970s, for example, and in its veiled rebuke of unnamed clerical figures too close to centers of power and tolerant of culturally "neocolonial" practices under Senghor—appear to complement the didactic message of *Ceddo* as a satirical and allegorical film of both historical and contemporary importance.

Ceddo's Diminishing Freedoms

Sembene's historical film *Ceddo* allegorically portrays the displacement of traditional systems of authority by Islamic religious alternatives and controversially posits the interdependency of the transatlantic slave trade and religious wars of forced conversion to Islam in West Africa. Dramatizing the problem of political succession for a fictional Wolof kingdom after the king's conversion to Islam, the opening sequence of the film questions the basis of dynastic authority in the kingdom with Islam's introduction.[37] Through early scenes where patterns of royal inheritance and political succession are debated among heirs to the fictional throne, the film sets in opposition orally inherited precedents mandating matriarchal lines of succession against a patriarchal alternative promoted by the kingdom's new imam. The fictional king, deciding to favor his imam's invocation of Islamic precepts over a traditional alternative, unwittingly justifies his own overthrow: The king's denial of his nephew's matrilineal succession nullifies the basis of his own authority as a matrilineal heir, leaving his kingdom in a heightened state of civil war. As though to aurally foreshadow the transatlantic displacements that result from the religious violence to follow, African American gospel music poignantly accompanies the film's scenes of pillage and enslavement, strangely contrasted with the muteness of European merchants and Christian missionaries to whom non-Muslim war captives are bartered for arms and alcohol. The world envisioned by the film implies that religious coercion and inequities between Muslims and non-Muslims paved the way for foreign exploitation of the gravest forms, an exploitation augured by the symbolic presence of marginal European figures in the film: A colonial tradesman and missionary priest appear to silently prey on the populace of this weakened kingdom.

Plotlines showing the kingdom's dynastic transformation further suggest how linguistic relations reflect relations of force. The kingdom's changing norms after the regent's conversion result in the gradual shunning from the royal court of the king's *griot,* whose public orations advance in aphoristic Wolof proverbs. Sembene's choices in cinematography underscore this transformation while marking the rise of a new religious and linguistic authority within the kingdom. In contrast to the *griot*'s gradual exclusion from court, the king's new imam (and eventual usurper) seals his position of authority by ritually renaming his subjects with Arabic names that evoke the charismatic lineage and companions of the Prophet Muhammad.

In the film's final scene, however, the imam is assassinated in the midst of this ritual renaming by the daughter of the original king; this denouement corresponds to a tentative act of restoration on behalf of the kingdom's outcast subjects who refused conversion, the *ceddo*. The film's final shot of the princess, walking away from the deceased imam as though to face her subjects as the new claimant to the kingdom's throne, coincides with a break in filmic patterns; the princess turns away, but what follows is the absence of a corresponding, orienting shot to designate the scene—or public—she faces. The effect of the scene is to leave the viewing audience with the impression of their own confrontation by this final female protagonist, as the filming camera conflates the viewer with the princess's embattled subjects.[38] As film critic Philip Rosen writes of *Ceddo*'s ultimate effects, "This theater has two publics: the diegetic audience within the film, which is the Wolof nation defining itself through all the speech it witnesses, and the film-going public which, if African, is constructed as a collective in some way continuous with the first."[39]

On the level of cinematography, Sembene's formal choices imply a suturing of the film's diegetic and nondiegetic audience through the director's insertion of the camera into the role of the *griot,* whose traditional functions include the work of court interpreter and genealogist. Sembene's cinematic *griotage* translates a traditional experience of circular, performative space into a visual continuity throughout the film, orienting panoramic shots and cuts between characters around a circular center marked by an emblematic prop; this central position is often occupied by the figure of the *griot* during moments of courtly address but is marked early in the film by a *samp,* the ceremonial staff of a non-Muslim *ceddo* refusing conversion, proffered to the king in protest against mounting pressures on his populace to convert.[40]

By this method, Sembene cinematically inserts his camera into the *griot*'s narrative role, visually emphasizing the gradual displacement of the traditional orator from a fictional center of power while poising the camera and the cinematic screen as a recuperative medium. From its central position, the camera traces the eventual banishment of the king's *griot* by the imam from within the court's oratory space. In the process, a traditional interdependency between king and *griot* is displaced by a newly brokered dependency between king and imam, before the king's death (or secret assassination) and replacement by the cleric himself. In a late scene in which the imam installs himself as a new theocratic regent, Sembene symbolically maintains the central position of the camera but uses longer shots to exaggerate the perceived distance between the imam and his subjects, the latter crowding the screen as a growing mass of forced converts.

Whereas early scenes emphasize the centrality of the Wolof *griot* as a political orator and interpreter within the traditional court, the film traces the *griot*'s displacement by the king's imam as a usurper, a figure whose authority appears progressively linguistic and translational. The imam characterizes himself in climactic scenes as a translational master of Arabic, described by the imam as the "beautiful language" (*lakk rafet*) of the Prophet Muhammad. In a scene where the imam promotes his own ascendant position among followers, his Wolof designation for the Prophet translates as "the proprietor of speech," *boroom wax*. Asserting his unique interpretive authority as a translational figure, the imam characterizes religious wars as a benevolent necessity, promotes the conversion of animists, and defends the prejudicial treatment of nonbelievers who persist in their disbelief. On the grounds of his linguistic mastery, he equally claims the power to rename his subjects among recent converts as a matter of integration within the faith.

Countering the imam's claims is the late king's nephew, who characterizes the imam as a foreigner of questionable authority and provenance and who is ultimately shunned from court as an apostate. Ethnocentric attachments on the part of both figures are legible in their mutual antagonism, as the king's nephew scorns the imam as a "foreigner," an Arab or Arabized figure of paler complexion and apparently mixed background—all pretexts through which the imam appears to pride himself as the social superior of his Wolof followers. The confrontation between the imam and the king's nephew generates a series of debates about the conciliation of Islam with local *cosaan* (traditions). Palaver scenes of public controversy that dramatize the conflict between the king's nephew and imam also trace the gradual marginalization of the unconverted.

A visual continuity across these scenes is persistently marked by the ceremonial staff (*samp*) of a non-Muslim *ceddo* presented to the king to symbolize a singular demand: that the kingdom's community of non-Muslims be exempt from inequities, forced labor, and forced conversion.[41] The film traces these developing controversies through the perspective of progressively minoritized non-Muslims or *ceddo*, the "people of refusal," who by the end of the film are ultimately constrained: facing the impossible choice of conversion under duress, exile, or bartering for arms to rebel in complicity with European slave traders. If there is a didactic message within the story, it appears to be voiced on behalf of these marginalized figures, as stated by one of their elders and early plaintiffs to the kingly court: No religion (*ay dine*) is worth the loss of human life.

Sembene's film presents the constraints imposed on a proudly unassimilated and gradually minoritized non-Muslim underclass in a progressively Islamized, fictional Wolof kingdom. Through the plight of Wolof *ceddo*, tensions between Arabic-Islamic acculturation and non-Arab cultural distinction are allegorically portrayed at the thresholds of a growing Muslim community in West Africa. This subtext alludes to open questions about the terms of interreligious coexistence and Muslim acculturation in Senegal. Particularly when understood against many of the editorial positions published in *Kaddu*, the journal Sembene cofounded, *Ceddo*'s allegorical challenge to Arabocentric and Islamocentric hierarchies suggests that, as Sembene himself admitted, the film indirectly addressed forms of historical stratification that continued to be controversial in twentieth-century Senegal, encompassing debates on Arabic as a cultural force and ritual acrolect relative to local vernaculars.

On these grounds, Sembene's film warrants comparison to Pramoedya's historical novel *Arus Balik*, as both imagine the experiences of a minoritized non-Muslim underclass amid the twinned historical processes of cultural Arabicization and Islamization in a region peripheral to native Arabic speech communities and to earlier regions of conversion in West Asia and North Africa. Both authors portrayed these transformations through allegorical narratives of political succession, restaging debates on the grounds of interreligious coexistence and Islamic acculturation in allegorical and (proto-)national terms. The historical processes of regional Islamization and European colonization were also portrayed by both authors as interdependent in their fiction, controversially suggesting that interreligious conflicts rendered each region vulnerable to foreign exploitation and colonial rule.

Toward a Colonial Future: Religious Violence and "Truth Languages" in *The Current Reverses*

Though not the first novel published upon his release from a "New Order" prison, the first manuscript that the embattled Indonesian author Pramoedya Ananta Toer attempted in the Buru island gulag after he was permitted paper to write was *Arus Balik* (*The Current Reverses*), a novel that retraced the sixteenth-century decline of the Majapahit Empire, the last Indianized kingdom in Eastern Java. The Majapahit Empire was a former maritime power weakened by Portuguese naval incursions and beset by the foundation and expansion of adjacent Muslim principalities and kingdoms. As with other fictional narratives Pramoedya composed in Buru, the choice of a historical subject was tactical for the imprisoned leftist writer, as a focus on ancient empires and remote histories appeared less controversial than topical subjects. His historical fiction nonetheless bore contemporary implications for a twentieth-century readership, as it engaged with historiographical controversies that emerged in Indonesia before his imprisonment. From the late 1950s through the early 1960s, Pramoedya was openly pursuing archival research on the Majapahit period and preparing revisionist scholarship through notes that would eventually be confiscated or destroyed upon his arrest, leaving him to reconstruct from memory in prison the vestiges of his earlier research.[42]

Pramoedya's historical fiction on precolonial empires was informed by national debates concerning the grounds of Indonesia's territorial integrity, the nation's ideological roots within ancient empires and kingdoms (including the empire of Majapahit), and the nation's interimperial genealogy. His own sympathies aligned with an emerging trend in leftist historiographical writing that emphasized the interdependency of precolonial forms of feudalism and the rise of European colonialism.[43] This line of revisionist scholarship—which was cut short by the "New Order" regime in 1965—implied that the political process of decolonization in Indonesia left unfinished the task of dismantling precolonial social inequities. Such inequities, Pramoedya believed, were reinforced by the Dutch colonial state and came to persist in postcolonial Indonesia.

Pramoedya's *Arus Balik* therefore challenges as ahistorical the postindependence glorification of a precolonial past often seen in more conservative forms of nationalist historical writing. As Pramoedya emphasized in interviews, he chose in his fiction to narrate past dynastic chronicles from the position of "common" characters in order to distance a collective Indonesian imagination from the "cage of legends."[44] Precolonial and imperial histories, he claimed, deserved to be rewritten through fiction that would elevate the subaltern vantage points excluded from colonial archives or classical chronicles. Pramoedya thus intended for his own realist fiction to undercut the idealized epic narratives that enshrined Indonesia's imperial (and interimperial) past in collective memory.[45] By privileging common and underclass histories, Pramoedya also sought to demythologize the languages of social and political privilege through which Indonesia's precolonial history was recorded (including Sanskrit, courtly Javanese, Arabic, and *jawi*).

Across their regional distances and distinctive media, the similarity of *Arus Balik* to Sembene's *Ceddo* lies in their allegorical portrayal of Islam's historical expansion at the thresholds of a colonized "Muslim world." Both works portrayed regional histories of interimperial and interreligious conflict (including wars of conversion) amid a growing European commercial presence. Through the perspective of a progressively minoritized, non-Muslim underclass in sub-Saharan West Africa and Southeast Asia, through rebelling *ceddo* and non-Muslim Javanese commoners, Sembene and Pramoedya critiqued Islamocentric and Arabocentric forms of social stratification and discrimination. In this way, *Arus Balik* traces the dynamics through which Java (and the Indonesian archipelago) underwent two coinciding transformations with the decline of the Majapahit Empire: the growing Islamization of the region and its growing vulnerability to waves of European merchants and commercial monopolies after the sixteenth century. In allegorical ways, the novel upholds as a matter of regional autonomy the ideal of a religiously pluralist state with maritime supremacy, as opposed to a polity with a single state religion.

Set among divisive wars of religious violence and forced conversion, *Arus Balik* reimagines the decline of the Majapahit Empire with the entrenchment of Islam in northern Javanese coastal kingdoms of the late fifteenth and sixteenth centuries (Tuban and Demak). Amid this backdrop, *Arus Balik* identifies the terms of interinsular coexistence for both a historical and a contemporary Indonesia. Ominous lines interwoven in the text foretell that interreligious conflict across the archipelago will lead to foreign exploitation and a lost regional autonomy. Like Sembene's *Ceddo*, the narrative opens after a king's recent conversion in Tuban, the main vassal port of the Majapahit Empire and the earliest commercial port through which Islam is believed to have spread to Java, Indonesia's most populous island.[46] In ways that parallel *Ceddo*, the political backdrop of the novel explores dynamics of conversion, religious discrimination, and new forms of social hierarchy associated with the early Islamization of Java. Through a drama of dynastic succession and displacement, the novel explores the grounds of political legitimacy in a time of uncertainty amid Europe's growing commercial presence in the region. Pramoedya reinterprets the legacy of two historical Muslim kings of the northern Javanese Sultanate of Demak (for which Tuban was a vassal port) to develop his own didactic narrative. He contrasts the accomplishments of Sultan Unus, who led a naval fleet against the Portuguese in Malacca in a failed attempt to expel them from the region, to the ambitions of his successor, Trenggono, a figure who conquered neighboring coastal cities of Java (Tuban and Sunda Kelapa) and subdued Hindu resistance to his rule in Central Java. Through this coastal microcosm, the drama of the novel vacillates between two options of a recurrent choice. One involves strategic naval unification across religious divisions and against a common enemy, to protect interinsular free trade. The second alternative is a unified Islamic state, advanced through religious wars, coercive forms of conversion, and questionable alliances with a new, exploitative Portuguese presence; this alternative comes at the expense of maritime independence.

Pramoedya's portrayal of these two historic leaders favors the tactical defenses of Unus, recurrently depicted as a leader who overrides religious differences for political unity against the Portuguese. Trenggono, who, in the fiction of the novel, overtakes neighboring Javanese kingdoms for personal gain, is more negatively portrayed for prioritizing land conquests to establish a greater Islamic empire on the island of Java while losing in the process the naval independence upon which his kingdom is based. The tragedy at the heart of the work lies with Trenggono's ultimate decision to favor religious conquests over maritime alliances that transcend religious difference, disregarding the prophecy of his mother, Ratu Aisah, who warns that "those that lose the seas will lose the land."[47]

Amid Trenggono's decision to favor wars of religious conquest over interconfessional alliances, the narrative follows the personal tragedies of a progressively minoritized non-Muslim commoner, Galeng, a figure with ambiguous Hindu and Buddhist orientations in Islamizing Java.[48] The novel depicts Galeng's growing awareness of the failure of interreligious resistance to imperial Europe.[49] Comparing himself to a handful of sand, *secauk pasir*, Galeng proclaims his tragic inability "to make kings and sultans conscious" of the dangers of the Portuguese arrival from the north.[50] Galeng transforms by the novel's end into the obscure hero of a failed rebellion against the Portuguese, a minoritized (Hindu/Buddhist) figure in a region historically beholden to competing claims of religious supremacy.

Galeng's final position as a tragic figure leaves the impression of a lost opportunity for regional independence in the unmet idealism of Pramoedya's novel. This "positive hero" of *Arus Balik* remains unsung, praised only in the collective but transient memory of local survivors of the Portuguese incursions to Malacca and northern Java and marginally detailed in the journals of Portuguese sailors.[51] In this way, the conclusion of the novel highlights its overall purpose as a recuperative work of historical fiction: It imagines the subjectivities of commoners among the historically vanquished, the religiously minoritized amid the shifting commercial tides of insular Southeast Asia, figures who remain eclipsed in colonial archives and in popular epics that selectively lionize only the victors and elite dynasts of empires past. The novel equally speaks to history's dependency on languages of political prestige rather than those "positionally vernacular,"[52] tracing the disempowerment of Javanese commoners in ways that parallel the fate of the underclass *ceddo* and court *griot* in Sembene's historical fiction.

Narrative vignettes illustrate the commercial leverage and symbolic capital of new acrolects in *Arus Balik* with the decline of the Majapahit Empire, as new social hierarchies and commercial monopolies lend an increasingly coercive force to the growing adoption of Portuguese and Arabic literacies among the archipelago's inhabitants in Java (for whom the positionally "vernacular" is implicitly Javanese). The hypocrisies of a Portuguese Empire that expels Iberian Muslims from its post-*reconquista* territories only to exploit their translational services in the Indonesian spice islands surface in the novel in this context: An Iberian Arab Muslim refugee in the Javanese port of Tuban facilitates local trade with the Portuguese as the Javanese regent's new harbormaster, or *syahbandar*.[53] As incisively noted by Christopher GoGwilt, "The harbor master's power—and hence the [novelistic] reader's sense of global political power—is significantly grounded in his command (or claim to command) of a particular set of languages and scripts," including Malay, Arabic, and Portuguese.[54] As such, the rise of the Iberian Arab *syahbandar* foregrounds "the role of translation in the competing forces of global and local power," as his ascent marks the rising value of European and Arabic literacies against their Indic and Javanese others in both global and local terms.[55]

These changing fortunes appear through the dramatic clash of two *syahbandars* of rival linguistic competence in the strategic port of Tuban.[56] Through an initial rivalry between these competing harbormasters—a Bengali Muslim and the Iberian Arab—the novel satirizes the connection between religious authority, charismatic lineage, and the native mastery of Arabic as a locally ascendant language with Islam's expansion. As each rival scorns the other for his presumption to religious authority—the Bengali mocking the Iberian Arab for his unlikely descent from the Prophet Muhammad, the Iberian scorning the Bengali Muslim for his religious airs as a non-Arab and non-native speaker of Arabic—the novel juxtaposes their mutual disdain to offer a double parody of both characters. Amid this double parody, the displacement of the non-Arab Bengali by the Iberian Arab occurs according to the new commercial and translational needs of the regent of Tuban. The excessive pride of the new Iberian *syahbandar* in his native mastery of Arabic, his disregard for non-Arabic languages (i.e., Javanese) commonly spoken in the archipelago, and his scorn for the solecisms of non-native speakers of Arabic are further ironized by his inscrutability among his own Javanese subordinates, who privately disdain him for his incomprehensibility in their own language.[57] The Arab harbormaster's religious pride and prejudicial contempt for non-Arabic languages are also ironized by their context in Java: Where successful across the archipelago, the peaceful spread of Islam is illustrated in the novel through its indebtedness to non-Arabic forms of linguistic transmission, translation, and literary or oral mediation.

Arus Balik portrays noncoercive forms of mass conversion to Islam in Java as dependent on the vernacularization of religious instruction and forms of charismatic transmission, tempering the unrivaled dominance of Arabic as a sacralized language and script among a populace progressively converting to Islam. Islam's dependency on non-Arabic circuits of transmission and translational exposition is portrayed through contrasting pedagogical styles among Muslim proselytizers, with mass conversions in the region coinciding with the formation of transcultural Islamic traditions in Java. A filial attachment to local, Indic Javanese orthographies among the unconverted informs this pedagogical contrast, dramatized through the limited impact of a Muslim proselytizer known as Muhammad Firman, who tries to convert the Hindu masses of Java's interior:

> The village folk were astonished that worship was not taught in Javanese writing [in Devanagari *kawi* script], and wondered what it would mean if the children, once grown, knew nothing about the teachings of their ancestors? [...] These hardships began to confront Pada [Muhammad Firman,

> the proselytizer]. The Arabic script that he taught was too difficult to be used and spoken. And the attrition of his students began one by one. He was in the process of facing failure. [. . .]
>
> He began to write *tembang* [versified poetry in a traditional Javanese style] in the Arabic language and script about the stories of the Prophet of God. His students (of which there remained few) spread those *tembang* throughout the village of Awis Krambil, and he was pleased with his success. He heard his writings sung upon the backs of buffalos in the fields, or in lonely nights when the moon failed to rise, in homes scattered across vast distances. And yet, the ranks of his students did not rise.[58]

The local beginnings of an Arabic manuscript culture are envisioned through such passages, although the novel also portrays its limits among a Javanese populace attached to older cultural inheritances. In the face of his failure to proselytize in Arabic and Arabic script, the proselytizer begins to teach in Javanese and to translate his religious teachings into Javanese poetic forms. In contrast to the limited success of Muhammad Firman and the inscrutability of other arabophone proselytizers (Hayatullah) portrayed by the novel among a Javanese populace, Raden Said (a historical prince of Tuban and a sanctified figure of local legend known by his religious name, Ki Aji Kalijaga) offers a positive example of vernacular proselytization and peaceful conversion.[59] Wandering humbly through the Hindu interior of Java, Kalijaga gains converts through oral narration in vernacular Javanese, rather than through adherence to Arabic as an untranslated "truth language."[60] Moving from *desa* to *desa*, Kalijaga is depicted as an itinerant sage, sitting beneath trees in the villages of the Hinduized interior. Narrating stories of the Prophet, Kalijaga regales the children of commoners, who are joined by their mothers and then by the village masses, as he increasingly gains converts through Javanese.[61]

In Pramoedya's novel, ruling elites are the first and most influential figures to convert to Islam in the region. The plot follows the fortunes of commoners after their rulers have converted. The ways in which the common masses adapt to new social hierarchies with the introduction and uneven spread of Arabic as a ritual medium form part of the novel's drama—a narrative dimension that parallels Sembene's storyline in *Ceddo*. Passages in *Arus Balik* trace the growing realization among a Javanese underclass that languages are politically exploitable as symbols of authority and religious prestige regardless of which language (Sanskrit or Arabic) is sacralized.[62] Through such conclusions on the corruptions of political regents regardless of their religious identity, the novel challenges theocratic norms and the social divisions they sow. It portrays such norms and divisions as the preconditions of foreign rule.

Arus Balik cautions its postindependence readership against re-creating precolonial conditions of vulnerability to foreign rule, correlating early Portuguese incursions with a time of disunity in which new ethnolinguistic hierarchies and interreligious tensions were introduced to the region and divided its populace. At another continental extreme, *Ceddo* resonates with a comparable warning for a West African audience. A rejection of theocratic norms allegorically appears in both works as a matter of locally contingent and tactical necessity rather than as a form of "secularism" with a European and vestigially colonial origin. In allegorical terms, both Sembene's and Pramoedya's fictions suggest that the sole basis through which liberty against a foreign power can be ensured is through regional unity across religious differences, rather than a coercive political unity on the basis of Islam as a state religion. Pramoedya's *Arus Balik* suggests that religious pluralism forms the natural complement to political freedom in the Indonesian archipelago, in keeping with the choice between a religiously pluralist thalassocracy and a landlocked Islamic state vulnerable to foreign interference. This notion is reinforced through didactic statements within the text, conveying a pluralist message that resonates with that of Sembene's *Ceddo*.

As evident in their allegorical portrayals of the spread of Islam in the two regions, Pramoedya's and Sembene's fictions uphold an ideal of cultural parity across two scales of affiliation: within multiethnic communities of Muslim belonging and within a nationally emergent political space in which conciliations were historically negotiated between Muslims and non-Muslims. Their work in tandem imagines distinct local lineages for these egalitarian ideals, though their conclusions align with a transhistorical Muslim genealogy of idealized parity between Arabs and non-Arabs (*ʿarab* and *ʿajam*), as explored in previous chapters. Subtle traces of *ʿarab* and *ʿajam* ethnolinguistic tensions resurface amid questions of religious assimilation and cultural distinction with the expansion of Islam; such tensions impact the way that histories of European imperial contact are imagined in fictional form.

In other ways comparable to Sembene's concerns on cultural pluralism and competing literacies in West Africa, Pramoedya's novel probes the contested linguistic inheritances that gave rise to its own emergence in literary form. The contested cultural genealogy of the twentieth-century Malay Indonesian novel surfaces within *Arus Balik* through the agonistic struggle it portrays between languages and scripts, as Christopher GoGwilt suggests, implicitly marking the novel's own emergence as a hybrid, romanized form arising from the crucible of past empires.[63] In Pramoedya's later writing on the early twentieth-century Indonesian print culture amid these linguistic crosscurrents, he would continue to privilege the "positionally vernacular," noncolonial beginnings of what would become romanized Indonesian as a literary medium, envisioning its changing fortunes as it bridged the imperially segregated literacies engendered by the Dutch colonial state.[64]

"People's Malay" and Counterimperial Print

Among the manuscripts Pramoedya was developing that were permanently destroyed upon his incarceration as a leftist political prisoner in 1965 was an extended scholarly work entitled *A Preliminary Study of the Indonesian Language* (*Studi Percobaan tentang Sejarah Bahasa Indonesia*).[65] While the manuscript itself was never recovered, articles Pramoedya wrote in the early 1960s suggest his evolving conclusions on the subject. By the 1950s, the subject had already become controversial, with different parties contesting the roots of the nationalized language as a Malay vernacular relative to both Arabic writing systems and colonial standards of romanization (van Ophuijsen's orthography, "Ejaan van Ophuijsen"). Between September 1963 and April 1964, Pramoedya published a series of articles on the history of the Indonesian language in "Lentera," the cultural page of the Indonesian nationalist (and increasingly leftist) newspaper *Bintang Timur*. In these articles, he traced the authentic beginnings of the proto-national, Indonesian language as a medium of independent political association beyond the reaches of the Dutch colonial state.[66]

Within this series of articles, Pramoedya characterized the precolonial history of Malay through a vital distinction between courtly "palace Malay" (*Melayu istana*) and a more egalitarian "people's Malay" (*Melayu rakyat*), the latter representing the most authentic origins of Indonesian as an interinsular and interethnic language.[67] Courtly Malay, Pramoedya argued, was an elite language privileged by a Malay aristocracy centered in Sumatra's provincial kingdoms, which became textually reinvented through colonial romanization efforts (van Ophuijsen's standardizations) as "book Malay," or *Melayu buku*. Courtly Malay eventually dominated the region through the colonial dissemination of government publications and textbooks in Latin orthography. Against this courtly standard adapted by the Dutch colonial state, Pramoedya opposed a baser, unstandardized Malay: the "people's Malay" (*Melayu rakyat*) or "working Malay" (*Melayu kerdja*), a variety favored by interinsular merchants and the archipelago's lower classes. *Melayu rakyat* was a variant in which the region's masses could speak "on an equal basis" regardless of background, class, and ethnicity but which eluded colonial circuits of textual standardization.[68]

Pramoedya characterized the fluidity and openness of *Melayu rakyat* as a sign of inclusivity across lines of ethnicity and class. As noted by literary critic Hilmar Farid Setiadi, Pramoedya emphasized across his "Lentera" commentaries: "There was no need for strict grammatical rules, nor even a standardized spelling system. The language was also open to changes and was able to absorb new words without difficulty."[69] As opposed to the variant privileged by the colonial state, Pramoedya identified this unstandardized *Melayu rakyat* as the true lingua franca of the archipelago (*Melayu lingua franca*) in which early literary experiments and foundational forms of print culture emerged beyond the direct control of the eminent Dutch colonial publishing house in the Indies, Balai Pustaka, established in 1908.[70] Pramoedya noted that late nineteenth- and early twentieth-century literary experiments, sidelined by colonial literary histories, had been written in this lower, more egalitarian variant of Malay. The variant had been largely dismissed by postindependence scholars and intellectuals within Indonesia as an unstandardized and unruly "wild writing" (*batjaan liar*), a bias inherited from Dutch colonial bureaucrats and publishers.

As Pramoedya would frequently explore in other publications on "proto-Indonesian literature" (*sastra pra-Indonesia*), the consequences of this colonially overdetermined exclusion were that a virtually lost corpus of protonational literature existed beyond public recognition, due to constrained understandings of what qualified as legitimate forms of writing.[71] Revisionist approaches to local literary history were, by Pramoedya's estimation, necessary to realign Indonesian collective memory with the nation's cultural precursors in nonofficial circuits of vernacular print. Reimagining the beginnings of a non-elite (and non-elitist) vernacular print language in "people's Malay," Pramoedya's fictional tetralogy, the *Buru Quartet*, follows the fortunes of Minke, a fictional protagonist based on the late nineteenth- and early twentieth-century print pioneer Tirto Adhi Surjo, tracing his establishment of the first natively owned publishing platforms for vernacular newsprint.[72] The *Buru Quartet* dramatizes the rationale behind Minke's more populist, egalitarian choice of language for print (*Melayu rakyat*), ultimately forgoing an elitist affiliation with Dutch (despite his training in Dutch schools for native Javanese aristocrats) and forgoing his filial attachment to a more aristocratic and courtly Javanese mother tongue (*kromo*).[73]

Minke's choice of "people's Malay" as a print language is revealed as an increasingly political tactic, with the protagonist orienting his envisioned reading public away from metropolitan centers of colonial influence in the Netherlands and away from exclusionary circles of native elites in the colonies (including Javanese bureaucrats, among them members of the aristocratic association Budi Utomo, portrayed in the novel as a relatively collaborationist association).[74] Minke's linguistic choices as traced within the tetralogy follow his developing sympathies across class lines, extending to a rural peasantry exploited by Dutch-dominated trade monopolies. He comes to realize that an ostensibly liberal Dutch "ethical policy" that promotes "Westernized" education for native elites relies on discriminatory double standards and functionally supplies native, white-collar labor to sustain the Dutch commercial exploitation of the Indies; and his political sensibilities extend to a shared community of the disenfranchised whose stories of disempowerment are exchanged through a publicly unstandardized, interethnic vernacular print in "people's Malay." His sympathies ultimately progress toward a broader interinsular consciousness and an emerging proto-nationalism, as he recognizes the need for forms of economic leverage and political solidarity to counter entrenched colonial networks of material exploitation. To this end, the quartet traces Minke's growing sense of urgency when promoting an independent native press, in the wake of editorial distortions by Dutch-owned publishing houses on politically sensitive or volatile topics of colonial corruption and economic disenfranchisement.

Within his tetralogy on the foundations of the vernacular press, Pramoedya presents a pastiche of the paraliterary, tracing what surfaces from oral anecdotes and underclass narratives into newsprint in "people's Malay" and presenting through narrative vignettes systemic forms of colonial exploitation that provoked the earliest stirrings of proto-national consciousness. Drawing inspiration from the corpus of newsprint left behind by the historical figure Tirto Adhi Surjo, with certain embellishments for dramatic effect, Pramoedya's tetralogy builds from what might be called paraliterary archives to narratively reconstruct a panorama of colonial-era wrongs in the turn-of-the-twentieth-century Dutch East Indies. These include vignettes of sexual exploitation, oral accounts on the brutalization of peasant labor that barely rise to the notice of conventional Dutch newsprint, and tales of broken familial ties among class-conscious Javanese who would sell their daughters as concubines to Dutch officials or excommunicate sons who rebel against Dutch superiors. The colonial-era wrongs depicted include stories of mass neglect and the inhumane sequestration and burning of peasant villages amid a pandemic—an inhumanity contrasted with the careful preservation of capital and labor required for Dutch sugar monopolies. And the wrongs include tales from a corrupt colonial judicial system reliant on double standards that segregate natives from their colonial rulers—a judicial system that assumes unequal rights between colonizers and colonized, Muslims and Christians (despite political talk of "ethical policies" and the liberal elevation of natives as a matter of political "Association").

Against a narrative array of colonial hypocrisies, the inevitable failures of Dutch policies of "Association" between a colonial metropole and its culturally assimilating, "modernizing" subjects in the Dutch East Indies appear through Minke's publications, unmasking the corrupt grounds of an exploitative policy masquerading as benevolent colonial reform. The need for a free, independent, native press to convey such wrongs in unvarnished form—in an interethnic, local language of broad popular appeal, capable of addressing the full array of these injustices among Holland's diverse colonial subjects—appears a growing urgency as the quartet progresses. Pramoedya's *Buru Quartet*, while elevating the virtues of a more representative print culture in "people's Malay," in this way presents a critique of Dutch policies of "Association" (with characters often explicitly referencing the term).[75]

If Pramoedya's earlier historical novel, *Arus Balik*, portrays the ushering of the Indonesian archipelago into a new age of commercial exploitation, the *Buru Quartet* anticipates the decline of the region's last European empire on material grounds. It equally asserts the nineteenth- and early twentieth-century Dutch Empire's unviability on the basis of its own internal policy contradictions, with ostensibly liberal Dutch policies of "Association" revealed for their failures through exposés daringly featured in the counterimperial print experiments of the fictional protagonist based on Tirto Adhi Surjo.[76] As Minke ultimately realizes in ways that complement his print activism, the tactical promotion of a free, economic basis of open exchange offers the material (and linguistic) basis for solidarity across the multiethnic, "multi-*bangsa*" archipelago—particularly given the general political inertia of the Dutch-educated class of Javanese *priyayi* (aristocrats) to which he belongs.[77]

The third novel in the *Buru Quartet*, *Jejak Langkah* (*Footsteps*), anticipates the grassroots corrosion of European commercial monopolies in the region, with the rise of counterimperial forms of interinsular trade and mercantile solidarity envisioned by the protagonist as a precursor to regional and national autonomy. Among Minke's culminating achievements is the formation of the region's first grassroots, trade-based political organization, the Sarekat Dagang Islam (SDI), an Islamic commercial association aspiring to serve as a counterweight to imperial Dutch monopolies. This association of Muslim merchant-traders has as its ideological basis a nonethnic membership, appearing in Pramoedya's text to be a non-nativist, nonfeudalistic association, inclusive across lines of class. Building in part from biographical details drawn from the life of Tirto Adhi Surjo, who, like the fictional Minke, founded the Indonesian region's first interethnic, Muslim trade association (in addition to promoting early newsprint in *Melayu rakyat*), the fictional SDI tragically fails, due to the persistence of internal antagonisms within the organization.

Jejak Langkah in this regard traces how the Muslim commercial association falters in part due to infighting and internal competition between diasporic Arab and non-Arab Muslims among its membership (a dynamic partially consistent with the historical Sarekat Dagang Islam founded by Adhi Surjo, which, as in the novel, became an increasingly "nativist" organization after the development of these disagreements).[78] This aspirationally egalitarian Muslim trade association, as the novel implies, was beset by an economic classism predicated on vestigial notions of preeminence (and, by extension, material entitlements) that privileged members of a diasporic Arab lineage within the Islamic commercial organization, alienating Arab members from their non-Arab counterparts. A critique of cultural and ethnic chauvinism within the interethnic archipelago therefore emerges within the quartet—a critique that implicates fracture points both within the global Muslim community and within regionally autonomous, local grassroots organizations that could have united against a common colonial European presence. Through such details, the subtle traces of *ʿajam* (non-Arab) and Arab ethnic tensions surface in the twentieth-century Indonesian novel as a matter of proto-national controversy.

We can observe a shared concern across *Arus Balik* and the *Buru Quartet*, despite their portrayal of distinct imperial thresholds in the Indonesian archipelago. Both serve as a cautionary tale on the failures of economic solidarity and interinsular alliance across ethnic differences in the context of a progressively Islamized Indonesia.[79] However, as portrayed across these fictions, historical missteps were in part due to forms of racial and religious chauvinism that endangered would-be alliances, leaving behind a region vulnerable to external co-optation and commercial exploitation across religious and ethnic or "racial" divisions.

Through the *Buru Quartet*, Pramoedya's intervention into the national historiography of the first Muslim commercial trade association (Sarekat Dagang Islam) appears through his emphasis on its interethnic aspirations, characterizing it as a fundamentally homegrown, grassroots organization rather than an ideologically derivative one, passively following or emulating foreign directives and models of political association in other "centers" of global Muslim influence in the Middle East. Directly countering such notions of regional autonomy and ideological independence, however, are surveillance reports developed by the *Quartet*'s concluding narrator (and ultimate antagonist), the figure of Pangemanann, a native informant and colonial state inspector who peruses and redacts Minke's personal documents upon the latter's imprisonment. Against the claims of Minke himself, this final narrator concludes that local movements in opposition to the colonial state were co-optable and fundamentally indebted to foreign influences in their challenge to Dutch colonial dominance, as Setiadi has argued.[80] This conclusion builds on emergent strains of ethnographic colonial writing toward the late nineteenth and early twentieth centuries, a discourse that classed natives of the Dutch East Indies as relatively passive and culturally malleable subjects; by this logic, Indies natives were marginal Muslims, characterized as figures of intellectual lassitude, impressionable to foreign, ideological influences—a trend noted in previous chapters.

Vignettes of Minke's self-consciousness as a colonially educated figure who is perceived by his Dutch social superiors as an example of native malleability illustrate this tendency to view colonial Indies subjects as passive ideological receptacles. The *Quartet*, however, critiques the history of ostensibly liberal Dutch "ethical" policies for the reform and "modernization" of a rising generation of Dutch-trained elites. By following a Dutch-educated nationalist who refused to meet the expectations of Dutch policies of "Association," Pramoedya suggests that Indonesian nationalism and national culture emerged beyond the reach of colonial Dutch policy experiments. The autonomous grounds of Indonesian nationalism are underscored by a protagonist who ultimately refuses to perform for his Dutch superiors and educational patrons in the Dutch language, dignifying an Indonesian Malay print vernacular instead. Here one might see a resonance between Pramoedya's dignification of print platforms beyond the direct reaches of colonial policies of "Association" and the anti-assimilationist beginnings of vernacular print in Senegal, with Sembene's counter-francophone experiments through *Kaddu.*

Print Vernaculars and the Value of "Disarray"

Pramoedya explored the uneven effects of print capitalism (and print colonialism) in Indonesia under the Dutch colonial state, laying bare through his historical fiction and paraliterary texts the publicly underrecognized and underinventoried lineages of Indonesian national literature and print culture of the twentieth century. The dedication that Pramoedya brought to recovering the subaltern foundations of vernacular print in Indonesia parallels the forms of vernacular print activism that Sembene and his fellow founders of *Kaddu* pursued in Senegal. *Kaddu*'s "unofficial" experiments in Senegal, however, left the journal open to condemnation by then-president Senghor, who alleged that *Kaddu*'s print initiatives in a nonstandardized orthography unsanctioned by the Senegalese state left the "language question" in Senegal *en pagaille*—"a mess."[81] Such accusations of disarray and disorder by official figures are telling in their commonality: The forms of vernacular proto-Indonesian print that Pramoedya sought to dignify beyond the standardized efforts of the Dutch colonial state were also historically dismissed as orthographically disarrayed, unruly, or "wild."[82] To take seriously Sembene's and Pramoedya's parallel legacies, however, is to understand that such foundational print experiments—like those of *Kaddu* and Tirto Adhi Surjo (or "Minke" as his fictional double)—nonetheless sought to bridge the segregated literacies that became the legacy of European empires in Senegal and Indonesia. Such segregated literacies left behind a "multitude of traces" without a colonial, state-sanctioned "inventory."[83]

Sembene's and Pramoedya's work on local language dynamics equally challenges linguistically constrained definitions of the literary, drawing attention to the public oversight of a historically forsaken, lost corpus of literary texts and narrative traditions within each region. In the wake of Indonesian independence, Pramoedya considered the premise behind local debates on the "backwardness" (*kemunduran*) of Indonesian literature and the need for Indonesian "literary development" fundamentally flawed. At fault was not Indonesia's offerings to a world literary corpus, he contended, but, rather, the limiting definition of what qualified as literature, overdetermined by colonial inheritances that homogenized and constrained what stood for "modern" and "universal" standards of the literary.[84] Sembene, for his part, famously rejected colonially inherited linguistic constraints on the literary by advancing a two-front struggle against Senegal's segregated literacies and the literary schisms they engendered. He both embraced filmmaking in vernacular languages as a way to extend the limits of the literary and founded an unprecedented print platform for writing in local vernaculars.

Although Pramoedya and Sembene are often separately associated with realist trends in leftist fiction in an emergent "Third World" literary canon, the foregoing observations suggest other commonalities across their work; their vernacular print activism at the convergence of Arabic and Latinate "script-worlds" and in the shadow of both Eurocentric and Arabocentric language hierarchies connects them beyond their more critically acknowledged innovations in realist prose.[85] Even after the widespread colonial introduction of romanized literacies in the regions of French West Africa and the Dutch East Indies, their parallel legacies reveal that egalitarian sensibilities relative to Arabic as a language of prestige persisted in late twentieth-century historical fiction and print. Pramoedya's and Sembene's literary work in Indonesia and Senegal can thus be seen as a by-product of the generative tensions between monolingual and plurilingual ideologies in the shadow of scriptural Arabic.

9

Pluralism Sanctified

And among His wonders is the creation of the heavens and the earth, and the diversity of your languages and your colors. In these are signs for mankind [or "for those who know"].

—QUR'AN 30:22

IS IT POSSIBLE to reconcile the story of Babel—on the confounding of human languages as a curse from God—with Qur'anic verses on linguistic diversity as a benediction and divine sign? The question has puzzled interpreters who have inherited both traditions, the Babelian narrative and Qur'anic teachings, yielding inventive reflections on the diversities of human speech as an otherworldly sign. Moroccan literary critic Abdelfattah Kilito, for example, arrays a series of historical responses to the question by Muslim theologians, probing a sequence of Qur'anically inflected readings of the Babelian myth in an essay collection entitled *The Tongue of Adam*. In his own interpretation of these readings, he draws connections between the Babel story and accounts of Edenic expulsion through an imaginative conclusion. Kilito surmises that all languages according to Qur'anic injunctions are equal, that plurilingualism might be construed as an Edenic human condition (and perhaps Adam himself spoke in many tongues), but that *rivalry* between languages among Adam's descendants amounts to God's Babelian curse—*not plurilingualism itself.*[1]

If we were to ask where such reconciliations between the Babel story and Qur'anic verses on language diversity resurface in contemporary Arabic writing, a clear answer emerges in the prose of Naguib Mahfouz, one of the twentieth century's most prominent Arabic language authors and an Egyptian

Nobel laureate. Mahfouz, the focus of this chapter, also grappled with the stories of Eden and Babel, adapting both in interconnected ways. His corpus, as we shall see, aligns with Kilito's idealization of parity between languages, drawing from Qurʾanic notions that language diversity is a sign of divine wonder—of sublimity and power—rather than only a sign of humanity's alienation from God.[2]

Mahfouz's novel *al-Ḥarāfīsh* (*The Rabble*) features a subtle re-creation of the Babelian story, probing the meanings of human linguistic diversity and inscrutability from the vantage point of diglossic Egypt (where colloquial speech differs from a more prestigious ritual and literary standard). Within the novel, a figure mourning his beloved raises to the heavens a towering "minaret without a mosque" in an emblematic quest to escape his own mortality. Believing himself liberated of his human constraints, he imagines himself alone in the tower's environs, privy to the songs of the stars and the secrets of life, which are conveyed through sacred chants—*anāshīd ʿajamiyya*—in a language inscrutable and foreign to all others in his Cairene alley.[3] The story of this pseudo-Babelian tower draws to a close with the figure's madness and death. Its legacy impresses on the man's last descendant an insight akin to Walter Benjamin's: Despite our collective yearning for absolute transparencies, an "instantaneous dissolution" of the foreignness between languages "remains out of human reach." The yearned-for dissolution can only be indirectly intuited through moments of awe in the face of this insuperable foreignness.[4]

Through this allusive rewriting of a pseudo-Babelian parable in the novel he considered his most accomplished, Mahfouz probed in narrative form the value of unbridgeable opacities between languages.[5] He embedded throughout *The Rabble* lines of "sacred" *ʿajamiyya* verse, which he intended to leave untranslated, so as not to be easily comprehended by the average reader of Arabic.[6] The novel tempers monoglossic attachments to Arabic as a sacralized language by upholding the value of heteroglossia—"the diversity of [our] languages"—as itself a human marvel and divine sign, a notion implied by this chapter's epigraph from the Qurʾan.

Rallied to defend differences of language and color (or "race") across a transregional *umma*, the term *ʿajamiyya* is a concept vital for understanding the egalitarian dimensions of this critically underexamined novel. As previously discussed, *ʿajamiyya* is conceptually protean and difficult to define even in Arabic; as an Arabocentric and at times pejorative term for non-Arabic speech, it also resists translation within European languages and assumed distortive associations when colonially translated (as "nationally" non-Arab or "racially" Indo-Aryan speech forms in opposition to Arab and Semitic languages). Meeting this translational challenge is nonetheless necessary to clarify Mahfouz's allegorical claims on translingual and interracial parity, especially as they align with certain Islamic teachings and traditions, including the verse cited in the chapter epigraph. As illustrated by interpretive traditions on the Prophet Muhammad's last sermon, which proclaimed the equality between *ʿarab* and *ʿajam*, black and white, the term *ʿajamiyya* has framed dynamics of ethnolinguistic stratification and parity within arabophone Muslim communities historically. It therefore frames a sanctified right to equality across difference in ways that illuminate Mahfouz's legacy within a transregional arabophone canon—a matter implicating readers well beyond his principal audience within the Middle East.

By setting his most renowned allegorical treatments of equality between *ʿarab* and *ʿajam*, black and white, in the prosaic spaces of urban Cairo, however, Mahfouz implicates local dynamics of linguism, colorism, and classism informed by Egypt's unique position as a site of African subcolonization. Historically subject to Ottoman and British imperial control but bearing its own imperial ambitions across its Sudanese borders, Egypt continues to reckon with its fraught racial history of domestic slavery and colorism, linguistic prejudice, and discrimination against its Sudanese neighbors and its southern populace in Upper Egypt.[7] Mahfouz's narrative therefore throws into relief the local stakes of Islamic ideals of parity in the quotidian spaces of contemporary Egypt, given Egypt's historical position as a site both colonized and colonizing. Where Mahfouz's writing challenges forms of linguistic chauvinism in experimental form, language appears as but one dimension through which he probed the contours of social parity and racial equality in Egypt as an interimperial space.

Two patterns stand out across Mahfouz's later experimental novels, of which *The Rabble* is a prime example: the critique of ethnocentric entitlements across dynastic forms of succession and the critique of religious certitudes and practices of interpretive closure. Through these critiques, Mahfouz characterizes the boundaries of both Egyptian Arab identity and Muslim belonging in fluid ways. Attuned to these fluid Egyptian Arab and Muslim boundaries, the literary parable *The Rabble* proclaims the value of epistemic humilities when confronted with the mysteries of linguistic diversity.

Mahfouz's elevation of heteroglossia—and of *ʿajamiyya* otherness—illuminates his position as an Egyptian author who repeatedly probed the pluralist dimensions of an Islamic legacy within Egypt and who explored Egypt's position as a site of territorial and cultural hybridity.[8] In Mahfouz's later experimental fiction, Arabic appears dissociated from cultural purism. These works instead reconcile Arabic with an openness to the foreign, with the strange or uncanny, and with the genealogically—and therefore linguistically—unknown or unknowable. Mahfouz's elevation of heteroglossia therefore seems to align his experimental fiction with idealist Islamic traditions that extol ethnic or racial parity and interpret linguistic pluralism as a matter of divine sanction.

Mahfouz's career extended from an early fixation with pharaonic Egypt in the 1930s through many of Egypt's postindependence political transitions, up until his death in 2006. His sympathies and personal affiliations fell to leftist and socialist circles throughout his career—sympathies that many critics believe translated into his fiction.[9] His novels stylistically evolved in the postindependence context, moving away from a realist early style to a more formally experimental one by the late 1950s. Several of his allegorical texts, as we shall see, continued to gesture to the familiar Cairene quarters of his youth. His rewritings of the Edenic story of expulsion, *The Children of the Alley*, and of Babelian elements in *The Rabble*, for example, are set in Cairo's historically medieval neighborhoods. Tragedy struck in connection to one of these texts, which changed the course of Mahfouz's life and writing. After a troubling bout of controversy, censorship, and death threats over *The Children of the Alley*, Mahfouz was the target of an assassination attempt by an extremist member of the Muslim Brotherhood who accused the author of blasphemy. Mahfouz's injuries from a knife attack (in 1994) resulted in his near-paralysis and gave rise to his more sporadic fits of writing until his passing.[10]

This chapter observes how Mahfouz's experimental fiction explores Egypt's layered inheritances while presenting egalitarian critiques of dynastic rule, ethnocentric entitlement, and inflated claims of moral and religious authority on the grounds of charismatic filiation. To illustrate these broader concerns within his fiction, I analyze a selection of Mahfouz's experimental novels in ways that foreground the stakes of *al-Ḥarāfish* (*The Rabble*), where he projects onto a metalingual register the egalitarian values that he probes elsewhere in his experimental texts.[11] I begin by highlighting the dynamics of hierarchy and parity across three of his other novels: his novel on political succession in Egypt, *Before the Throne*; his oneiric *Journey of Ibn Fattouma*, which probed the boundaries between "Muslim" authenticity and "pagan" strangeness; and his prophetic allegories in *Children of the Alley*. These novels collectively explore

Islamic ideals of ethnolinguistic parity—parity between *ʿarab* and *ʿajam* (Arab and non-Arab) and *sudān* and *bayḍān* (black and white)—against the shifting, relational thresholds of Egyptian Muslim identity and territorial belonging as Mahfouz imagines them. The chapter begins by giving relatively brief treatments of these three novels before more extensively foregrounding Mahfouz's portrayal of egalitarianism and translingual parity in *The Rabble*.

In probing the thresholds between a pre-Islamic past and an Arabized present in Egypt, Mahfouz's fiction is similar to that of the West African Sembene and the Indonesian Pramoedya. As noted in the previous chapter, Sembene and Pramoedya—fellow leftists, as well as two of Mahfouz's most accomplished literary counterparts—privileged positionally vernacular languages relative to Arabic. Mahfouz, however, chose to write in a "higher" register of literary Arabic (*fuṣḥā*) over a colloquial Egyptian alternative (*ʿāmmiyya*).[12] Despite this choice, Mahfouz nonetheless was able to convey a positionally subaltern, vernacular literary sensibility in his fiction.

Mahfouz professed throughout his career an attachment to *fuṣḥā* as a literary medium that unified an otherwise dialectally fractured Arabic reading public. However, he qualified this attachment by characterizing his role as an author to be one of refashioning *fuṣḥā* into a medium that could "come close to the minds of ordinary people," thereby giving it "something of life's forms" ("nawʿa min al-ḥayāt").[13] In *The Rabble*, he wrote in high literary Arabic to capture the interiority of ordinary arabophone listeners entranced and estranged by inscrutable *ʿajamiyya* chants—chants that symbolize a diversity of languages by the novel's end.[14] He thus implied that colloquial Egyptian Arabic (*ʿāmmiyya*) need not be the sole bearer of a positionally subaltern vantage point relative to sacred speech, nor *fuṣḥā* the sole medium of ritual transcendence.

Mahfouz's formal choices in his refashioning of *fuṣḥā* as a medium capable of reflecting the interiority of ordinary Egyptians have been a matter of critical debate, with some scholars observing a colloquial cadence to his *fuṣḥā* or a reliance on colloquial terms despite his stated avoidance of *ʿāmmiyyāt*.[15] My contribution instead draws attention to formal choices made by Mahfouz that gain meaning when understood through the dynamics traced in previous chapters, on the coexistence of Arabic and *ʿajamiyyāt*. He was able to deploy *fuṣḥā* as a malleable literary medium, bringing to life a creative mimesis of subordinate sensibilities in the face of sacralized speech represented by inscrutable verses of *ʿajamiyya*.[16] Although his attachment to *fuṣḥā* and stated avoidance of colloquialisms might seem to align Mahfouz with a relatively monoglossic or purist defense of high literary Arabic, formal experiments in his own writing qualify such impressions.

Although Mahfouz, Pramoedya, and Sembene are often separately associated with realist trends in leftist fiction in an emergent "Third World" or Asian-African literary canon, this chapter offers alternative grounds for comparing their legacies.[17] Across regions historically connected by ritual Arabic—from West Africa to the Middle East and Southeast Asia—generative tensions between monolingual and plurilingual ideas contributed to their pioneering literary innovations in the shadow of vernacular language debates, as each author reimagined the twinned historical processes of Islamization and Arabicization in local terms. With distinctive local inflections, idealist strains across their fiction allegorically defend the values of heteroglossia, cultural pluralism, and parity in the wake of an imperial past.

Judging an Egyptian Past

Late in his career, Mahfouz published *Before the Throne* (*Amām al-ʿArsh*), a novel that offered a panoramic survey of Egypt's successive rulers, with each of them theatrically resurrected, paraded, and judged before a divine tribunal. The novel presents each Egyptian ruler as a transient presence tested by questions of legitimate succession across a shifting historical frame, moving from an ancient pharaonic past to the postrevolutionary rule of Anwar Sadat. A posthumous challenge to each ruler's legitimacy is advanced through the inclusion of a prosecutorial character who represents an anonymous "everyman"—a forgotten rebel leader named Abnum. This forgotten leader, according to the novel's inventive fictions, reigned over ancient Egypt in a time of political chaos after its early pharaonic kingdoms, but his controversial position as an underclass regent meant his exclusion from later Egyptian chronicles. Rising from Egypt's "rabble," Abnum's presence amounts to an imaginative retrieval on behalf of the disenfranchised, demanding a reckoning with Egypt's past through the single metric of parity for the region's common masses. Although his persistence is tempered by his reactionary challengers, his protests run through the narrative as a constant refrain, as though reminding Mahfouz's readers of history's lost populist substrates.[18]

Although the novel falls short of a direct critique of Egypt's theocratic history, it challenges discriminatory Arabocentric practices after the Arab Muslim conquests of the seventh century in ways that mirror the pluralist ideals of the Southeast Asian and West African historical fictions examined in the previous chapter. The novel, however, equally challenges the grounds of a reverse racism that asserts the pre-Islamic superiority of purist Coptic bloodlines against an allegedly foreign Arab presence. Implicating the novel's own status as a genre emerging from an agonistic ethnic and religious history, the cultural genealogy of twentieth-century Egyptian Arabic writing surfaces within *Before the Throne* through the rivalry it portrays between two historical languages of public chronicle in Egypt: Coptic and Arabic. The narrative's insistence on equality and "justice" (in Abnum's terms) assumes a particular inflection when retracing Egypt's transformation as a region Islamized and Arabicized.[19]

Through the testimonials of progressively minoritized Coptic Egyptian characters, the Arab Muslim conquests of Egypt are at first presented favorably—not as a foreign invasion per se but as the consequence of a deal brokered by Coptic leaders to allow for a higher degree of Egyptian independence from a foreign Byzantine church. Increasingly marginalized members of Egypt's once Coptic Christian majority, however, attest to the gradual attenuation of Islamic ideals of pluralism and interethnic parity once promised by an early Muslim Arab leadership in Egypt. ("How quickly leaders forget their religion," as one fictional witness remarks.)[20] The autonomy of Egypt's Coptic community under Arab governance eventually falters, according to the novel, due to the growing decadence of Egypt's new Muslim leadership after the caliph ʿUthman. Coptic scribes and Coptic-Arabic translators remark on the increasingly forcible displacement of Coptic by Arabic for official use. They note that after an initial period in which subaltern Egyptians enjoyed freedom of worship under Arab rule, Egypt's populace converted to Islam under growing duress, leaving Islam's egalitarian beginnings a forgotten worldly ideal within the region.

Mahfouz's choice to retell this seismic transition through gradually minoritized Coptic figures is in line with his tendency to frame Egypt's history through its internal margins. In doing so, he challenges purist notions of Egyptian belonging. Notwithstanding claims by pharaonic dynasts and their twentieth-century emulators that Egypt's "throne" should fall to ethnically pure native bloodlines—a notion debated and popularized by a number of Coptic intellectuals who asserted that Copts were the direct descendants of pharaonic Egyptians—the boundaries between foreign and indigenous appear fluid across the novel.[21] Mahfouz therefore seems to parody two opposing claims that surfaced across Egyptian nationalist debates: claims that aligned Egyptian identity either with notions of Arabic-Islamic cultural superiority or, in contrast, with a pre-Islamic patrimony to which Coptic communities might be presumed the most authentic heirs.[22] The novel challenges both presumptions. As implied by the initially positive portrayal of the (foreign) Arab conquests, and by the "everyman" whose claims to Egyptian governance transcend entitlements by dynastic pedigree, moral legitimacy rather than nativism determines the right to rule Egypt.

Mahfouz's own disavowal of purist approaches to Egyptian belonging complements these allegorical dimensions of *Before the Throne*. In an interview later in his career, he dissociated himself from controversial claims popularized by intellectuals such as Salama Musa and Taha Hussein, who respectively aligned Egypt in more purist terms with pharaonic Coptic or Euro-Mediterranean origins, distancing Egypt from its associations with Arabness, Asianness, and Africanness.[23] Being Egyptian, Mahfouz countered, meant instead affiliating with a shared regional history while embracing a constitutional pluralism on behalf of Egypt as a common territorial "homeland":

> It is said that we are of pharaonic, not Arab, descent, that we are northerners and not Africans, or that we are Mediterranean peoples who have no roots in Asia. In my opinion our homeland is the source of our identity, something that has nothing to do with race. Egyptians represent an integral culture, formed by races of different civilizations—Arabs, Sudanese, Turks, and Moors, as well as ancient Egyptians. The common denominator has been our homeland, which has made one people of migrants of many races and civilizations, fusing their traits to form our national and cultural identity. Once we were pharaonic. We became Greco-pharaonic, then Greco-Roman-pharaonic. Then we were Copts—at least until the Arabo-Islamic conquest. So how can we separate and distinguish all these cultural elements that have been molded together over the centuries to form a single nationality? [. . .] We must not try to deconstruct this national character and reduce it to its original components, because that would cause it to lose all its cohesion. It would be like reducing water to oxygen and hydrogen—gases drifting away and disappearing in the air.[24]

Mahfouz's belief in the pluralism of an Egyptian past suggests an ethical valence to several of his texts, many of which extend a sense of pathos to the apparently foreign relative to the (implicitly) Egyptian Arab narrating self. Indeed, such statements by Mahfouz on the risks of ethnic chauvinism to Egyptian national integrity present a prism (or cipher) through which several of his experimental novels can be understood against enduring forms of colorism and linguism in Egypt. Through the dignification of *sudān* and *ʿajam* bearers of sanctified messages in his most accomplished allegorical novels, scenes of uncanny recognition or near-recognition connect the narrating self to the foreign and the obscure across lines of "language" and "skin color"—*alsinatikum wa-alwānikum.*[25] In the remaining texts considered in this chapter, one can see how Mahfouz inscribes episodes of uncanny resemblance in his narratives to unsettle the boundaries between *sudān* and *bayḍān*, *ʿajam* and *ʿarab*, Muslim selfhood and pagan strangeness, to expose the foreign in the familiar—or the stranger within the self.

Islamocentrism and the Uncanny

Conjuring an Islamocentric vision of the world, *The Journey of Ibn Fattouma* (*Riḥlat Ibn Faṭṭūma*) progresses through spaces segregated between the "realms of Islam" (*dār al-Islām*) and non-Muslim regions beyond (*dār al-ḥarb*).[26] Although the travelogue divides Muslim from non-Muslim realms, it raises questions about the thresholds of Islam's integrity across these divisions through a sequence of eerie and oneiric episodes. Moments of the uncanny unsettle the thresholds of "Muslim" selfhood and pagan "strangeness," as the narrative interrogates who authoritatively speaks for Islam against a pagan "other" in a hyperviolent world in search of its own deliverance. The narrative begins with a realist descriptive style in its account of the protagonist's disenchantment with his native land, described as overrun by materialism and moral corruption. The style of the novel then shifts to a more parodic and dreamlike register, as the narrative follows the protagonist's quest for redemption beyond his North African homeland, crossing the thresholds from his native *dār al-Islām* into non-Muslim regions encompassed by the oppositional term *dār al-ḥarb*.

The fictional travelogue relies on an imaginative cartography derived from both an Arab/Islamocentric and techno-Eurocentric (Cold War–era) vision of the world, even as it destabilizes the moral relevance and certitudes of both "centers." On these grounds, Mahfouz's narrative portrays peripheral regions through which the vague specter of Asiatic and sub-Saharan African subalternity—and paganism—appears relative to a North African regional "homeland." Civilizational "progress" in this fictional world seems indexed not only to an Islamic cultural custodianship represented by an implicitly North African homeland in *dār al-Islām* but also by global measures of technical and military domination fronted by regions of the veiledly Euro-American (and Russo-Soviet) global North.[27] *Ibn Fattouma* as such plays on global hierarchies both

Islamocentric and techno-Eurocentric, even as the narrative ultimately unsettles the moral relevance of both hierarchies in a bellicose world.

Many critics read the narrator's passage through "pagan" regions—from the crudely sub-Saharan *dār al-Mashriq* through the exoticized, Asiatic *dār al-Ghurūb*—as part of an allegorical journey through human history. In this reading, as the protagonist travels through the non-Muslim realms of *dār al-ḥarb*, he ventures from primitive to civilized realms.[28] The insufficiency of such an evolutionary interpretation, however, lies in its neglect of a crucial set of textual cues that caricature forms of black African and Asiatic difference from an implied Arab Egyptian narrator. (In some cases, the caricatured representations are comparable to depictions in the original travelogue of the fourteenth-century Moroccan jurist Ibn Battuta, from which Mahfouz has taken his title.) Scenes of "primitive" lands that begin the journey appear racially marked by a naked, darker-skinned populace. However, the penultimate destination of the novel is not the apex of "modern" civilization but a second site of seminakedness and technical weakness. Characterized by civilizational inertia, this region has been invaded (like its black African counterpart) by more advanced military powers. Such details challenge interpretations of the narrative voyage as an allegory of human progress from a primordial past to a globally violent present and instead suggest that it moves through marginalized spaces of the present that merely appear to exist in a state of civilizational lag.

As a fictional travelogue, Mahfouz's novel builds on historical precedents within the medieval Arabic travel genre of the *riḥla*, of which Ibn Battuta's text is a prime example.[29] It nonetheless assumes a marked difference from its near-namesake. For Mahfouz's narrative appears not as the account of a religious pilgrimage with a principal destination (as was the case for the itinerant Ibn Battuta) but, instead, proceeds as an aimless and unresolved quest through variant dystopias, marked by episodes of the uncanny. Across these dystopian realms, unsettling representations of extreme Asiatic and sub-Saharan African otherness appear in Mahfouz's text, throwing into relief the boundaries of Egyptian Arab Muslim selfhood as represented by the novel's principal narrator. The portrayal of regions peripheral to both an Islamocentric/Arabocentric and techno-Eurocentric worldview marks Mahfouz's novel as a postcolonial text, where the thresholds of "pagan" sub-Saharan Africa and East Asia appear doubly marginalized.[30]

The narrator first passes through a vaguely sub-Saharan, desertlike realm peopled by inhabitants "of bronze skin" and described through the grossest stereotypes of black otherness: by a proximity to the bestial, associated with ritual strangeness and a coarse rythmicality, singing chants "distinguished by a barbaric crudeness" ("mumayizzat al-waḥashiyya wa-l-khashūn").[31] Such stereotypes are amplified by descriptions of libidinous excess and forms of governance synonymous with slavery, as though the region's darker inhabitants are inclined to extremes of passive subordination or tyranny. To conclude that a Muslim (Arab Egyptian) narrator while visiting this nominally "pagan" realm simply re-encounters his own civilizational antecedents appears therefore a serious underreading. This is especially true given Mahfouz's position as an Egyptian author writing for an implicitly North African Arab readership—a public inheriting a troubled history of violent conflict with its "darker" southern neighbors. Building on a different style of "Far Eastern," Asiatic caricature, *dār al-Ghurūb* features a second region of exoticized, "pagan" strangeness: A land of "reactionless" figures, the realm is marked by "silent," "half-naked" sages, "dozing or in a trance," surrounded by passive followers who chant in eerie tones or who otherwise appear "deaf, dumb, and blind."[32]

The narrative at times cuts through these differences with episodes of uncanny recognition and rises to a critique of violence across these eventually invaded "African" and "Asian" realms. Nevertheless, an important qualification here deserves mention. There is a disconcerting contrast between Mahfouz's caricatural representations of the veiledly African and Asiatic non-Muslim "pagan" or "idolatrous" other and those characterized with greater pathos and multidimensionality by Sembene and Pramoedya.[33] Here, one might mention Ghenwa Hayek's vital observation that it is unsettling but necessary to draw attention to troubling patterns of racialized representation in (already subaltern) postcolonial Arabic fiction, which may appear tempered and therefore underrecognized in English translation.[34] Their salience is uncontestable in Mahfouz's novel—both in English translation and in the original Arabic—despite their critical oversight.

Episodic moments of the uncanny—of recognition and identification across lines of otherwise alienating difference—offer a possible redemptive horizon for the narrative against these troubling patterns of caricature. Within the vaguely sub-Saharan *dār al-Mashriq*, for example, where the protagonist contemplates the similarity between his pagan hosts and his pagan ancestors, he encounters a darker-skinned woman curiously identical to his (implicitly lighter-skinned) beloved left behind in his native *dār al-Islām*. His "pagan" bride is described as "bronze and naked, but [. . .] her face very closely resembled Halima, my lost love."[35] Tempering the differences between his Muslim compatriots and his "pagan" hosts, the narrator observes to himself, "[O]ur religion is wonderful, but our life is pagan [*jāhilī*]."[36] He also concludes that "our own erring, in the land of Revelation [*dār al-wāḥī*] is more shocking than the rest of mankind" and rhetorically asks, "[W]ho is worse [. . .] he who claims divinity through ignorance or he who exploits the Qur'an for his own ends?"[37] In the wake of these musings, his pagan lover's devastation upon the conquest of her homeland by a neighboring region and the enslavement and disappearance of the children they share amid this violent invasion build toward a critique of the global bellicosity that leaves both the narrator and his pagan lover in a state of alienation and constant displacement.[38]

Also troubling a teleological reading of the narrative as it moves from allegedly more primitive to more advanced regions is the novel's parodic thrust: Justifications of violence imposed on "primitive" sites by more "advanced" regions are parodied in the novel through scenes of endless bellicosity. Sequential scenes of invasion and conflict suggest that regions portrayed in the narrative exist in a synchronous pattern of contemporary global violence—one from which "the abode of Islam" (*dār al-Islām*) offers no clear sanctuary. Mahfouz's narrative as such gains poignancy when read against controversial ideas in circulation among some of his earliest associates on the nature of non-Muslim "paganness" and on the need to take up arms for the cause of Islam's global reform and expansion. One former associate of Mahfouz, the literary critic and eventual ideologue and propagandist of Egypt's Muslim Brotherhood Sayyid Qutb, influentially argued that pagan (*jāhiliyya*) states were not a temporal marker differentiating eras before and after Islam; for Qutb, paganness was instead a perennial state of contamination and risk to the global Muslim community across time and space. Qutb notoriously claimed that pagan (*jāhiliyya*) sensibilities were pervasive in the contemporary twentieth century, deserving a constant and, if necessary, violent corrective in the name of Islam.[39]

Mahfouz's novel parodies notions that paganness is a contemporary condition that infringes upon the boundaries of a true or authentic Islam. Within Mahfouz's text, what "Islam" stands for—and who is entitled to represent it—appears to be an open question: For Islam appears as deracinated in its "native" abode as the self-proclaimed Muslim appears alienated in *dār al-ḥarb*. Mahfouz's travelogue is a narrative of decentered authority, offering a panoramic view of a polycentric religious community internally undone and externally unredeemed, with its most ardent defenders endlessly engaged in a disappointed quest for deliverance.

The narrator's encounters with fellow Muslims across the realms of *dār al-ḥarb* occasion another relevant insight: that Muslims recurrently fail the test of mutual recognition, experiencing forms of uncanny estrangement both within and beyond the narrator's homeland. Traveling through *dār al-Ḥalba* (often interpreted as an allegorically North American or Western European space), he finds himself amid a diasporic Muslim community. There, he is locked into unresolved debates with other Muslims on the nature of Islam itself—its demands for social parity, its constraints on personal freedoms, and its openness to renovation and reform.[40] The travelogue, then, from within an internally contested Islamocentric worldview, unexpectedly raises a mirror to the homeland of the narrating self (*dār al-Islām*), provoking fundamental confusions about who ultimately speaks for Islam. The novel, in other words, begins with an "Islamocentric" notional division of the world only to destabilize this division, to probe the terms of its own deracination, and to question its thresholds of integrity.

Mahfouz's narrative seems to play on the possibility that *dār al-Islām* is not a worldly site at all but, rather, an elusive state of peaceable existence—that its relational other, *dār al-ḥarb*, is therefore not a territorially demarcated (or knowable) horizon beyond *dār al-Islām* but, in fact, a pervasive and perennial condition of violence—a condition from which the protagonist seems in constant flight as a global refugee, rather than a pilgrim with a known destination. Reflecting a global order in which the realms of war (*dār al-ḥarb*) are pervasive, and *dār al-Islām* as a sanctuary is everywhere denatured and unrecognizable to itself, the narrative leaves the reader with a vision of the world in constant suspension, a world of existential uncertainties and indeterminacies, if not of territorial ambiguities.

Social Credit and Divine Sanction: The Marginal Messenger in *Children of the Alley*

First released in 1959, *The Children of the Alley* (*Awlād Ḥāratinā*) was Mahfouz's most controversial novel, and in 1994 his attempted assassin was an extremist member of Egypt's Muslim Brotherhood who objected to its alleged secularism and to its portrayal of Islam, Christianity, and Judaism as three equal faiths. Against such views, Mahfouz asserted that the novel was a fundamentally "Islamic" text undeserving of its public controversy.[41] By suggesting how underexamined dimensions of the narrative animate Islamic teachings on egalitarianism and ethnolinguistic parity, my interpretation of the novel supports Mahfouz's defense.[42]

The novel centers on a family of charismatic visionaries legible as veiled representations of Moses, Jesus, and the Prophet Muhammad descending from a common patriarch, the enigmatic "Gabalawi." Catalyzing the plot is a primordial transgression: Gabalawi's first son, Adham, steals into his father's chambers to catch a glimpse of his father's will, hoping to discern the future as ordained by the mysterious patriarch. The transgression results in his expulsion from his father's idyllic house, leaving generations of Adham's descendants to quarrel over their imagined entitlements, with fratricidal results. The nostalgic desire for proximity to Gabalawi and his hearth and the shared yearning for a just inheritance emerge as constants within the narrative. Against this backdrop, three charismatic descendants of the patriarch episodically appear and respond to this collective yearning for reunion with Gabalawi. Inviting comparison with figures of Judaic, Christian, and Muslim tradition (as Moses, Jesus, and the Prophet Muhammad), each bears a message of equal inheritance to Gabalawi's descendants, renewing an egalitarian ideal among Gabalawi's warring descendants across different epochs.

The novel's narrative sequence presents a pattern of prophetic idealism and cyclical corruption characteristic of the classical Arabic literary genre of Islamic *qiṣaṣ al-anbiyāʾ* (stories of the prophets).[43] The sequence emphasizes a shared message of parity with different generational contours, conveyed to each visionary in dreams and uncanny sightings or near-sightings of Gabalawi. Gabal, a Moses-like figure, is portrayed as uplifting an exploited people laboring in bondage, an underclass among Gabalawi's descendants. His message of redemption and equality for the disenfranchised, however, remains circumscribed, becoming a pretext for claims to superiority among his later devotees. The novel then shifts in focus to Rifāʾa, a Jesus-like figure, who advances a radical message of parity through an eschewal of the material world but who fails by his gentleness to survive his detractors. With his death, he leaves his ideals without a defender, ultimately bequeathing his teachings to bellicose followers who betray its pacifist origins. The character of Qāssem then appears, a Muhammad-like figure portrayed as the final heir to an earlier prophetic line (also in keeping with the genre of prophetic stories). The message of Qāssem, again one of social parity like those of his forebearers, is beset after his death by disagreements about the nature of his message and his lived example, as his later defenders adopt sinister tactics of extortion and coercion for material gain.[44]

After Qāssem's demise, a final figure emerges as a potential successor (or usurper) in this prophetic line: ʿArafa, whose name means "knowledge" in Arabic and whose appearance in the novel is often read as an emblem of "secular knowledge."[45] In an act of transgressive curiosity, ʿArafa intrudes into Gabalawi's house, killing one of Gabalawi's menservants before escaping the scene. Upon hearing of the death of his manservant, Gabalawi himself is rumored to die of shock, but not before dictating a cryptic last message to his maidservant to convey to ʿArafa: that Gabalawi, against all expectations, was "pleased" with ʿArafa upon his deathbed.[46]

Critics have often interpreted this turn of events as symbolizing the overthrow of religious sensibilities by "science" or "secular knowledge," as ʿArafa's transgression indirectly leads to the seemingly omnipotent Gabalawi's demise (representing the "death of God," if Gabalawi is believed to allegorize the divine and ʿArafa is believed to represent "worldly" knowledge).[47] Yet, given the nature of Gabalawi's final message of his contentment with ʿArafa, such scenes represent perhaps not a pure displacement but an allegorical (if ambiguous) reconciliation between sources of worldly knowledge and divine gnosis. The secrets of this conciliation, however, remain obscure; Gabalawi's demise is never directly described or seen, its occurrence is announced through rumor, and Gabalawi's final will is never revealed. Nor is the nature of ʿArafa's "knowledge" ever fully exposed, as his "scientific notes" are buried by sinister gangsters who bludgeon him to death, leaving him "screaming in a language that no one knew."[48]

Despite this lack of transparency, the novel's climactic scene suggests that an embrace of parity—across lines of class, gender, and skin color—is a requisite for receiving messages of conciliation between worldly and divine forms of knowledge. Significant in this regard is Gabalawi's decision to entrust his vital last words, his deathbed message, to a subordinate figure, marginalized by her gender and by her darker complexion: Gabalawi's black, female servant. Though ʿArafa visibly struggles to believe her, she is the chosen messenger of Gabalawi's final message of satisfaction with him. In the moments of narrative pause and incredulity in the confrontation between Gabalawi's servant and ʿArafa, when her credibility is challenged and questioned, the drama of her social subordination is in the balance: Her status as a figure marginalized by virtue of her gender, her class, and her darker complexion is at play (as suggested by other passages in which blackness is mocked by an Iblis- or Lucifer-like figure, Idris).[49] But also at play is an invitation to read across these lines of difference and to recognize the familiar in the strange through subtle textual cues.

This climactic scene provokes a subtle moment of uncanny recognition, for Gabalawi's servant-messenger resembles, and bears a social status equal to, the matriarch from whom all of humanity descends in the world of the novel. The

"Eve" figure—the wife of Adham (and ʿArafa's own ancestress)—is introduced earlier in the text as a black slave of Gabalawi. Adham's mysterious mother is also introduced as a black slave woman (*jāriya*) of Gabalawi: She is a humble matriarch whose favor with Gabalawi according to the "devil's" mockery augurs a future dominated by "servants and slaves" (*khadam wa-ʿabīd*)—the latter term an Arabic epithet for "blacks" but related to the term for "worshipper" in devotional contexts (*ʿabd Allah* or *ʿibād Allah*).[50] One might therefore see in ʿArafa's final confrontation with a humble but subtly matriarchal figure elements of the uncanny, as ʿArafa struggles to recall whether he has seen this messenger before, challenging presumptions of difference across lines of color or race, class, and gender through this scene. The novel also allegorically equates piety (among *ʿibād*) with divine subordination through this scene, for it is Gabalawi's slaves (*ʿabīd*)—rather than his self-entitled and estranged descendants—who enjoy his constant proximity and shelter: Those closest to Gabalawi (or God), and thus poised to convey his ultimate message, are the most devoted of his slaves—or worshippers (*ʿabīd*/ *ʿibād*, both plural forms of *ʿabd*). The novel allegorically animates the conditions of closeness to God (Gabalawi) in line with the Islamic teaching that there is "no difference between black and white" and that the "highest among God's devotees [or "servants," *ʿibād*] is the most pious"—a teaching that subtly dignifies the novel's humble final messenger.[51]

Earlier passages in the novel reinforce the notion that characters of the maidservant's station deserve elevation. For example, Qāssem's slave woman (*jāriya*) is jubilant upon receiving Qāssem's message of universal parity.[52] That all of humanity descends from a doppelgänger of Gabalawi's final messenger reinforces this egalitarian subtext. Embedded in this climactic scene, then, is the implication that to believe Gabalawi's message means to elevate the marginalized as a matter of social trust. A belief in Gabalawi's last word, in other words, depends on the credit implicitly granted to those through whom it is conveyed—here in an invitation for the final protagonist, ʿArafa, to see elements of the self in the apparent stranger. Mahfouz's narrative therefore dramatizes what the application of egalitarian precepts in line with a certain tradition of Islamic idealism at their limit involves: an unsettling of extant social and racial hierarchies, reaching into the most mundane forms of domestic stratification.

The scene in which the prevailing conciliation between Gabalawi and ʿArafa is conveyed emphasizes the importance of social currency in the reception of charismatic messages. It implies, in other words, that a belief in parity across lines of class, gender, and skin color is a requisite for receiving this message of conciliation between (allegorically) worldly and divine forms of knowledge. Gabalawi's egalitarian injunctions, then, subtly impose themselves on the figure of ʿArafa through a drama of social trust. Enfolded within this allegorical story on faith's reconciliation with secular knowledge is a demand that the message of their conciliation be embraced through dignifying underclass figures as credible sources. To this end, the novel enjoins readers to confront the possibility that an embrace of social trust across lines of difference is itself a gesture of piety—parity not merely as an otherworldly ideal but as an imperative for the here and now.

By embedding this allegorical narrative in the mundane setting of a pseudo-Cairene *ḥāra* (or alley), with its implied dynamics of colorism, classism, and gender hierarchies, the novel advances an egalitarian subtext that speaks to two resonant horizons. It throws into relief the local stakes of such ideals of parity in the quotidian spaces of contemporary Egypt (a region with a troubled racial history of domestic slavery and of discrimination against its southern populace in Upper Egypt and against its Sudanese neighbors).[53] It equally draws upon the idealist, Islamic traditions of parity traced in previous chapters, which claim that there is no difference between black and white, *ʿajam* and *ʿarab*, but for the piety of each believer. As historian Louise Marlow has written of this tradition of egalitarian idealism, disparate practices of interpreting such ideals of equality have resulted in claims by more socially conservative exegetes that divine injunctions of equal status between believers pertain to the hereafter rather than the worldly present; by this logic, the demands of parity between *ʿarab* and *ʿajam*, black and white, need not unsettle existing social hierarchies.[54] Through a subtle, allegorical embedding of imperatives of equality in the prosaic spaces of a fictional Cairene alley, Mahfouz's novel is legible as a direct challenge to such deferrals. Parity—between black and white, *ʿarab* and *ʿajam*, associated with certain Islamic narrative traditions (and stories of the Prophet Muhammad's last sermon)—here coincides with a social imperative of contemporary urgency. It is indeed a worldly equality for the present, rather than for the hereafter.

The Sacred Unrevealed: Inscrutable Chanting in *The Rabble*

In his later experimental novel *al-Ḥarāfīsh* (*The Rabble*), often interpreted as a rewriting of *Children of the Alley*, Mahfouz reframes the injunction of parity with subtle but equally striking inferences of solidarity between *ʿarab* and

ʿ*ajam*, interweaving an egalitarian sensibility through translingual dimensions of his work.[55] As in *Children of the Alley*, a charismatic dynastic line is central to *The Rabble*. It, too, begins with an enigmatic founding patriarch and evolves through transgenerational conflicts among the patriarch's descendants across competitive lines of succession. Each line of descent assumes a local inflection in the all-too-human quest for social distinction and material entitlements among the genealogically ennobled. Although again set in the provincial space of a vaguely Cairene alley (*ḥāra*) and featuring semirecognizable common sites such as a local Sufi monastery (*takiyya*), *The Rabble* demands a double vision of its reader. Subtle referents direct readers' attention beyond the provincial, toward an allegorical subtext. Dramatizing the risks of infighting among descendants of a common patriarch (the character Ashur), whom some critics compare with the Prophet Muhammad, *The Rabble* seems to challenge the value of charismatic genealogies. The novel suggests that entitlements derived from a charismatic—or prophetic—bloodline offer no redemption to the common masses or "rabble" (the eponymous *ḥarāfīsh*).[56]

While *Children of the Alley* presents its allegorical account of charismatic descent through a sequence of "prophetic stories," *The Rabble* engages with these themes in formally more subtle but equally subversive terms. This is particularly true if literary critic Rasheed El-Enany's claim is correct that characters in *The Rabble*—particularly the first patriarch and his final descendant—are legible as fictional doubles of the Prophet Muhammad through certain biographical details. (These include, for example, veiled allusions to the status of the Prophet Muhammad as having been orphaned as a child, like the first patriarch in the novel.)[57] Such an interpretation arguably renders *The Rabble* not just an anti-genealogical text but an anti-sharifian one. The novel may, in other words, satirize the practice of social stratification and hierarchy that endures within many Muslim communities—hierarchies that exalt those who claim direct descent from the Prophet Muhammad. As several scholars have observed, such claims not only confer an aura of religious charisma and social distinction on these descendants but often translate into material and, in some cases, state-sanctioned entitlements—extending to enduring political dynasties whose legitimacy derives from claims of prophetic descent.[58]

Like *Children of the Alley*, *The Rabble* is an episodic novel largely peopled by characters whose presence in the narrative is short-lived. The impression left by this transience is that *The Rabble* represents a hyperviolent realm in which misfortune and death strike often and at random, and the collective search for deliverance from this state of constant risk remains endless and open. Exceptions, however, exist to this general pattern. The narrative at times slows to describe certain figures in higher detail, betraying their most profound moments of interiority. Through this deceleration, several figures cast a long narrative shadow across the text. Among them are the patriarch of the charismatic family line, whose unknown origins and status as an orphaned foundling stand in ironic contrast to his glorification as the founder of a prestigious bloodline. A second example is the patriarch's most arrogant descendant: a man notorious for his pyrrhic quest to overcome his mortality by building a mosqueless minaret towering toward the heavens. A final descendant, a second Ashur, concludes the novel. He destroys this pseudo-Babelian minaret, appearing as a redemptive figure with a final message of egalitarian deliverance to his mass of followers. This final character promotes a vision of parity that undercuts notions of inherited leadership based on claimed entitlements and genealogical descent, instead advocating a practice of self-governance anchored in the collective—in the eponymous "rabble."[59]

Along with the novel's succession struggles, an enigmatic motif recurs across the text: Lines of inscrutable, sacralized *ʿajamiyya* chants repeatedly rise from the local monastery of the novel's setting. As Mahfouz made clear to his English language translator, Catherine Cobham, although these lines are identifiable as Persian poetry by the fourteenth-century poet Hafez, they were intended to remain untranslated and obscure to the intended Arabic language reader.[60] Mahfouz considered their enduring inscrutability—their protean meaning and shifting interpretation by diverse characters across the text—to be a powerful emblematic force within the novel, as he claimed in later interviews.[61] As Mahfouz implied, these *ʿajamiyya* lines impose upon their fictional hearers (and symbolize to Mahfouz's arabophone readers) both the interpretive openness and the esotericism of sacral speech. Inscrutable (*ʿajamiyya*) chants emanating from the monastery within the world of the novel thus introduce new horizons of meaning throughout the text and ultimately mark the final protagonist's utopian visions.

This narrative soundscape of inscrutable *ʿajamiyya* lines of sacred poetry, sung by disembodied voices from within the mysterious confines of the alley's monastery, appears first as a way of establishing a somber and mysterious mood for the opening scenes. These lines of verse accompany the narrative's opening discovery of the foundling infant who would become the patriarch of the novel. But their presence later assumes an allegorical significance, as the obscurity of these sacred chants is compared with the obscurity of the child's origins. As the orphaned child relentlessly searches people's faces for signs of his unknown parentage, the hidden meaning of the lines of sacred verse is likened to the obscure identities of the child's parents, hidden behind the faces of strangers:

ومن شِدّة حُزنِهِ استمع إلى أناشيد التَكية بحب.
معانيها المُتَرَنِمة تُخَتفى وراء الفاظِها الأعجمية كما يُختَفى أبوأه وراء وجوهِ الغُرَباء.[62]

> And through the intensity of his sadness, he listened to the chants of the monastery with love. Their harmonious meanings seemed hidden behind their inscrutable expressions [*alfāẓihā al-āʿjamiyya*], just as his parents were hidden behind the faces of strangers.[63]

Here, then, the experience of *ʿajamiyya* otherness—of sacralized, linguistic inscrutabilities—is compared with a search for the familiar amid the strange or uncanny, with moments of near-recognition in the relentless quest for the self in the stranger. With the orphaned child confronting his possible kinship to the unknown, the novel seems to begin with a parable on the inscrutability of our common origins. This passage arguably revisits Sufi parables on the endless search for the beloved amid the strange and obscure (a theme probed in Mahfouz's other stories of spiritual quest).[64] The very notion of strangeness is presented as an open riddle, as every passing stranger offers a possible cipher to the child's origins and sense of self. The orphaned child's experience of an obscure or uncanny language also seems to allegorize the unknowable ties that bind self to stranger, mother tongue to foreign speech (*ʿajamiyya*). When read through the plotlines of the novel, the inaugural sense of self-estrangement experienced by the child gains an ironic meaning against his eventual position at the origins of a charismatic bloodline. This bloodline, of course, confers on his descendants an array of social presumptions and material entitlements.

Lines of *ʿajamiyya* verse continue to recur throughout the text like a refrain, surfacing in scenes of irresolution and transformation among the patriarch's descendants. Their appearance invites moments of transient interiority among those who hear the enigmatic chants, at times impressing upon them a sense of their embodied constraints. In passages where *ʿajamiyya* chants rise to prominence, they often appear to characters as a source of solace and constancy. At the same time, the chants throw into relief the feelings of alienation experienced by those who seek to decipher their meaning.

Ashur's most notorious descendant, Galal, a figure of exceptional hubris, dramatically illustrates the frustrations of a symbolic confrontation with the *ʿajamiyya* chants. He sees the inscrutable verses as taunting him, representing the opacity of death itself. In a quest to overcome his mortality, he brokers a Faustian bargain: He constructs his quasi-Babelian minaret without a mosque, a structure described as "a strange minaret" rising "toward infinity."[65] The Babelian tower ascends as a counterpoint to the humble monastery from which the *ʿajamiyya* chants rise. Imagining himself within its confines to be omniscient, omnipotent, and immortal, Galal believes himself alone able to capture the meaning of the inscrutable voices and the sounds of the stars in this towering space: "At the top [of the tower] the language of the stars was audible, the whisperings of space, the prayers for power and immortality."[66] Galal's, however, is an empty bargain: He and his pseudo-Babelian minaret eventually recede from narrative view after his tragic murder, leaving his tower to fall into ruin and his legacy to be overrun by rumors of his madness.

To passages in which inscrutability appears like a curse, a cruel and taunting presence, the novel's concluding scenes offer a redemptive possibility. These scenes invite readers—along with the protagonist—to intuit the nature of inscrutability as a sublime marvel and heteroglossia as a divine sign.

Heteroglossia as a Divine Sign

The novel's conclusion focuses on a final protagonist who emblematically destroys the pseudo-Babelian tower of his arrogant forefather and whose insights are intertwined with a distinctive interpretation of the *ʿajamiyya* chants. These sacred chants had throughout the text reflected an array of mental states through the reactions of their hearers, underscoring the interpretive ambiguities and elusive meanings associated with sacralized speech (symbolized through an experience of *ʿajamiyya* otherness). The novel's final protagonist, the second Ashur, therefore emerges as a direct challenger to his more arrogant predecessors, given his promotion of a final message for the common masses within the novel's setting: The "rabble" have no need, in his prophetic vision, for a single leader descending from an eminent bloodline for their redemption. The collective *ḥarāfīsh* embody their own salvation, he proclaims, as he enjoins them to assume the mantle of self-governance building from an equal distribution of wealth.[67] This final protagonist's vision of a more equitable social order, based on a form of self-governance anchored in the broadest collective sense of the people, in effect renders him (and his charismatic lineage) dispensable.

Through the novel's visionary final scenes, this last protagonist infers what the verses of *ʿajamiyya* inscrutability represent. He senses that the verses are an extension of his idealist insights on parity: Not merely corruptions or divergences from a purer Arabic, the *ʿajamiyya* inscrutabilities are a sublime sign of diversity. Of the protagonist's concluding visionary moments, the novel explains:

لحظة من لحظات الحياةِ النادرة التي تُسْفِر فيها عن نورٍ صافٍ.
لا شَكْوى من عضو أو خاطرة أو زمان أو مكان.
كأن الأناشيد الغامضة تُفْصِح عن أسرارِها بألف لسان.
وكأنما أدركَ لِمَ تَرَنَّموا طويلا بالأعجمية وأغلقوا الأبواب.

> It was a moment rare among life's moments, glowing with a pure light. No grievance in body or mind, time or space. As though the obscure chants had eloquently expressed their secrets in a thousand tongues [*tufṣiḥ ʿan asrārihā bi-alf lisān*]. And as though he understood why they [that recited them] sang in *ʿajamiyya* [*bi-l-āʿjamiyya*] and locked their doors.[68]

In this climactic passage, Ashur hears lines of verse that are both obscure in meaning and sublime. In hearing these inscrutable chants, he realizes that it is "as though" he were hearing the "secrets" of an irreducible heteroglossia, "eloquently expressed" in "a thousand tongues" (*alf lisān*).[69] In this final scene of transcendence and revelation, *ʿajamiyya* otherness symbolizes the irreducible differences of human speech—not a corruption of the clear but a divine marvel of "secret eloquence." Mahfouz's diction in Arabic emphasizes this mystical synthesis of two opposing experiences of obscurity and clarity of expression: Whereas qualities of inscrutability and eloquence (*ʿujma* and *faṣāḥa*) are conventionally opposed in classical texts on Arabic linguistics, in this passage, they appear as though mutually illumined ("al-anāshīd al-ghāmida [*al-āʿjamiyya*] tufṣiḥ ʿan asrārihā [. . .] ").[70]

What is potentially subversive about the novel, and this particular scene, is the linguistic inversion on which it operates. (This is particularly the case if, as Rasheed El-Enany suggests, the final protagonist invites comparison with the figure of the Prophet Muhammad.)[71] *ʿAjamiyya*, rather than a clear and eloquent Arabic, mediates an experience of sacred transcendence; and literary Arabic (*fuṣḥā*), by contrast, occupies a status relatively mundane, common, and prosaic. To underscore the stakes of this inversion, we might recall the self-referential characterization of the Qurʾan as a "clear Arabic revelation" as opposed to an *ʿajamiyya* one—in verses emphasizing the Qurʾan's clarity and eloquence over an *ʿajamiyya* counterfactual.[72] These verses have long been rallied to defend the cultural prestige of Arabic as a sacralized medium across language debates where such terms, *ʿajam* and *ʿarab*, are invoked. Against monoglossic defenses of Arabic as a singular language of sacred mediation, however, this final passage of Mahfouz's novel (allegorizing an experience of *ʿajamiyya* otherness) suggests that it is our intuition of heteroglossia as a worldly presence, our inference of the seemingly infinite diversity of language forms, that equally mediates an experience of sacral transcendence.

This may seem on first appearance a heterodoxy. But in defense of such claims stands Surat al-Rum's message in the Qurʾan (30:22) as cited in this chapter's epigraph, which posits that the difference between languages (or tongues) is also a divine sign, rendering heteroglossia itself a divine marvel and an illumination "for those who know."[73] The novel's final message on the sublimity of heteroglossia is subtle and indirect and straddles the boundaries of what qualifies as orthodoxy and heterodoxy in Islamic terms; in contrast to biblical myths of plurilingualism as a post-Babelian curse, symbolized by a quasi-Babelian minaret in the text, the novel presents visions (or aural intuitions) of heteroglossia as a benediction—even amid opacities of meaning to the ordinary hearer.

These lines of inscrutable verse by the novel's end, then, symbolically represent a linguistic multiplicity in lieu of a monoglossic, literary Arabic as a sanctified medium. Within Mahfouz's experimental fiction, opacity itself invites an experience of the sublime and demands an interpretive openness amid the unbridgeable differences between human speech forms. In my analysis of this literary work—in its symbolic portrayal of the differences between human languages in their imagined totality—the sanctified value of parity across language difference is inferred. This is a notion alluded to through the promise of an egalitarian idealism yearned for among the novel's characters. The novel's ultimate portrayal of heteroglossia and linguistic difference might be compared with Walter Benjamin's notion of "pure language": Amid the chasm between languages, one might nonetheless infer (as a kind of marvel) parallel drives for human expression and meaning, notwithstanding the impossibility of reconciling those differences, of "instantaneously dissolving the foreignness" between languages.[74]

The implications of allowing *ʿajamiyya* verse to stand in for the sacred (relative to Arabic *fuṣḥā* as a prosaic alternative) are several; not least among them is the implication that it is not merely monoglossic ideologies of language that advance the sensibilities of a ritual, Islamic high culture but, in fact, the exceptional diversity of human language—heteroglossia itself—that may serve this function. This dimension of Mahfouz's fiction aligns his literary experiments with the long tradition of debates on Arabic's coexistence with a diversity of non-Arabic languages and colloquials that has been discussed throughout this book.

In this connection, a final point on the politics of Arabic diglossia (or *ʿāmmiyya* and *fuṣḥā*) in Egypt deserves emphasis. As a defender of *fuṣḥā* as a literary medium as opposed to Egyptian colloquial Arabic (*ʿāmmiyya*), Mahfouz accomplishes an exceptional feat of mimesis by using *fuṣḥā* as a prosaic medium and *ʿajamiyya* as a language of sacralized prestige in *The Rabble*. His main characters across his text, a common "rabble" (or *ḥarāfīsh*)—were they truly meant to represent ordinary Egyptians in "real life"—could be presumed native speakers of *ʿāmmiyya* (or Egyptian colloquial Arabic).[75] Consider, then, that instead of the text directly representing the position of an estranged colloquial *ʿāmmiyya* speaker relative to high ritual Arabic, it is the chasm between a sacralized *ʿajamiyya* elevated above literary Arabic (*fuṣḥā*) that conveys this difference in analogous terms. In other words, Mahfouz seems to dramatize a subaltern experience of sacralized or esoteric language forms by portraying *heteroglossia* as a divine sign and *ʿajamiyya* inscrutability as sacred speech, leaving *fuṣḥā* a formidable medium of prosaic literary illusion.[76]

By the end of the novel, the term *ʿajamiyya*, then, takes on new meanings—mediating more than the uncanny, more than self-alienation in the face of the garbled or the strange; it also approaches a medium of transcendence, moving beyond its often pejorative associations in Arabic literary terms. In keeping with its broader challenge to social entitlements borne of charismatic genealogies, the novel's conclusion suggests through a final scene of gnosis and transcendence that we are all obscure of origin, constrained of body, and humbled by the irreducible diversity of human speech.

Mahfouz has been lauded for his exceptional literary hand in composing realist fiction, giving life to vivid characters rendered through an extraordinary psychological intimacy and pathos. He therefore mystified many of his critics by his choice of what he considered his most accomplished novel, his more formally experimental work *The Rabble*.[77] By the standards of high literary realism established through his earlier works such as *The Cairo Trilogy*, his preference was unexpected. For the characters in *The Rabble* are flatly drawn relative to the more vivid literary portraits in his realist texts; its plot moves at a rapid and disorienting pace, leaving critics puzzled by its repetitive patterns and transient protagonists. Some scholars have elevated *The Rabble* by aligning it with the traditional genre of the Arabic *malḥama*, the "epic" or "saga," though this was a term that Mahfouz was himself reluctant to attach to the title of his novel (often still published in Arabic as *Malḥamat al-Ḥarāfīsh*). By the logic of such generic alignments, however, the novel might be understood as a hybrid literary experiment, vested with folkloric elements and an oral narrative style, animating its episodic repetitions, narrative pace, and flat modes of characterization. Others have claimed that to appreciate *The Rabble* as an allegorical saga, the novel must be viewed as a reworking of Mahfouz's earlier and more controversial allegory of three coexistent faiths, *Awlād Ḥāratinā* (*The Children of the Alley*). Critics have also considered *The Rabble* to be one of Mahfouz's most "cinematic" works, connecting the novel's schematic narrative style to his experiences as a popular screenwriter in the 1950s and 1960s. Amid controversies over the novel's form, some have proposed that *The Rabble* parodies the mercenary currents of Egyptian politics at the time of its publication (in the late 1970s). Readers have speculated whether the novel's inscrutable chants, given their placement in a work legible as political satire, reflect the corruptions of political discourse in an increasingly authoritarian Egypt.[78]

To these suggestions, I offer the following claim. To appreciate Mahfouz's text as a literary accomplishment, an ideological statement, and a subversive literary gesture, one needs to grapple with the term that Mahfouz sutures within *The Rabble*: *ʿajamiyya*, the Arabic term for the foreign, the inscrutable, the opaque and accented. Building on the observations of this book's earlier chapters on language politics and literary form, we can more fully appreciate the weight of this term as it wends its way through Mahfouz's text, suturing its meaning to the vanishing horizons of Arabic speech, sacralized language, and ethnolinguistic otherness in Arabic contexts. In this way, the term presents a cipher, a key, for understanding the egalitarian contours of this critically underappreciated novel. One of the challenges involved, however, in critically elevating this text, and translating its importance to a world literary audience, lies in the fact that the term *ʿajamiyya* is itself conceptually obscure even in Arabic. Difficult to fix in meaning, the term stubbornly resists translation into the dominant European languages of world literary criticism.[79] In light of the way that the term has historically framed the complex dynamics of ethnolinguistic and racial stratification within arabophone communities, however, it is nonetheless worth the trouble of working against this translational difficulty to impress upon a broader audience the gravity of Mahfouz's allegorical gestures in *The Rabble*.

On these grounds, *The Rabble* is a radically egalitarian novel. I would even venture to call it a boldly anti-genealogical text that places the very notion and value of charismatic lineage (*ansāb*) under suspicion.[80] With exceptional formal subtlety, it equally uses literary Arabic (*fuṣḥā*) to dramatize a subaltern sensibility relative to a sacralized diversity of languages. Mahfouz's novel offers a subtle commentary on the politics of diglossia in arabophone Egypt and the politics of heteroglossia across a global Muslim community. As an intervention on long-standing language debates about literary and ritual Arabic's coexistence with its colloquial and "foreign" others, it presents an imaginative conciliation.

To clarify the stakes of Mahfouz's work, and in particular *The Rabble*, I refer again to the useful analogy offered by Tobias Warner, who proposes that one might compare polycentric linguistic influences on literary works with threads, with language debates emerging as the intractable "knots" that tie and bind them within a broader world literary fabric.[81] We might think of such influences converging in Mahfouz's work as the cross-threads of literary Arabic, Egyptian colloquial Arabic, and non-Arabic languages (*fuṣḥā*, *ʿāmmiyya*, and *ʿajamiyyāt*, respectively). This convergence or mutual interference has been perennially controversial, but purist efforts to disentangle the knotted influence of languages wrought across time are rarely successful. Such efforts, Warner claims, simply tend to reconfigure those entangled cross-threads, yielding new entanglements and configurations in literary form. Warner's analogy implies that the reconfigured knots of agonistic, linguistic influences are where we see literary innovation taking hold, at the convergence of linguistic controversies and the changing contours of the literary, as formal innovations invite critics to reassess how languages dynamically interact.[82] When Mahfouz, then, sutures the term *ʿajamiyya* into his *fuṣḥā* text, he derives his innovations from long-standing linguistic controversies, weaving together the cross-threads of *ʿāmmiyya*, *ʿajamiyya*, and *fuṣḥā* to develop an extraordinary reconfiguration of their influences. This reconfiguration yields a subtle egalitarian message of parity between languages, as evident in the final passage of his most accomplished work, *The Rabble*. This conceptual seam—this reference to *ʿajamiyya* otherness within his novel—stitches his narrative together with other texts that share an Arabic-Islamic inheritance, associated with an idealized parity between *ʿarab* and *ʿajam* across a world literary space. Mahfouz's narrative extends a sense of pathos not just to the arabophone "rabble"—an arabophone rabble or common public who implicitly express themselves through *ʿāmmiyya* speech—but to the subaltern, inscrutable, *ʿajami* other, whose very presence illuminates the originary mysteries and heteroglossic intuitions of the Arab (or arabophone) self.

CONCLUSION

Comparative Literature and Transregional Arabophone Studies

And an old priest said, Speak to us of Religion.
And he said:
Have I spoken this day of aught else?
Is not religion all deeds and all reflection,
And that which is neither deed nor reflection,
but a wonder and a surprise ever springing in the soul,
even while the hands hew the stone or tend the loom?

—KAHLIL GIBRAN [JUBRĀN KHALIL JUBRĀN], *THE PROPHET*

WHEN THE LEBANESE POET Kahlil Gibran's aphoristic verse collection *The Prophet* was translated into Indonesian in the 1970s, it was at first a resounding success within the world's most populous Muslim-majority republic. The translation's initial popularity, however, seemed to rely on mistaken assumptions about the poet's background. Local Muslim readers assumed that Gibran, an Arab Maronite Christian, was a fellow Muslim engaging in Qur'anically inspired forms of devotional writing. In the wake of greater public awareness of Gibran's background, booksellers in Indonesia reported a drop in the sales of Gibran's poetry after many readers learned of his Christian heritage. This drop occurred notwithstanding the enduring appreciation of Gibran's writing among more cosmopolitan Indonesian literary circles, in which critics reacted with dismay at the religious bias evident through such discriminatory and provincial patterns of reception. Despite the continued teaching of Gibran's poetry in several Indonesian Islamic schools (*pesantren*), a number of Muslim critics and public commentators dismissed his poetry as culturally derivative, implying that Gibran's poetic insights were merely a form of borrowed light from more authentic Qur'anic or Islamic sources.[1] By the distorted logic of these latter figures, and of readers who initially welcomed the Arab poet's translated verse as an exemplar of "Islamic literature," Arab writers seemed destined to cleave to imitative re-creations of Islamic source texts.

As this story of misprision implies, the association between Islam and ethnolinguistic Arabness appears to have been so heavily conflated in the Indonesian popular imagination by the late 1970s that it enabled an initial eclipse of Gibran's status as an Arab religious minority. Gibran, a bilingual anglophone and arabophone poet, emigrated at a tender age to the United States. He penned his most frequently translated and internationally popular work, *The Prophet*, in English (in 1923); it was translated into almost eighty languages, including Arabic (in 1926). His transnational visibility as a minority Arab Christian with a globally itinerant past, however, appears to have been obscured by a popular language bias that came to prevail in Indonesia at the time of Gibran's translation. Close identifications of Arabness with Islam meant that, for the average Indonesian reader, the very notion of an Arab Christian writer with cosmopolitan affiliations and plural language abilities seemed less plausible than the vague identitarian equation of ethnolinguistic Arabness and Islamic cultural purism. Such an equation, of course, neglected (and did a disservice to) the manifest values and historical salience of both Arab diversity and Islamic pluralism.

I mention this anecdote as it suggests the limited circulation by the late twentieth century of certain forms of cultural literacy between the Middle East and predominantly Muslim Indonesia in Southeast Asia, two regions once connected by Arabic as a language of precolonial commercial and cultural contact. The lesson of Arabic's history and evolving status as an interreligious or suprareligious literary medium in North Africa and West Asia had somehow failed to travel across these older circuits of exchange. Equally impeded, such anecdotes suggest, was the lesson that Arabic (and Arab diasporic) literature had diverse cosmopolitan informants during the Arabic *nahḍa* in the nineteenth and early twentieth centuries. This failure perhaps also underscores the success of some Indonesian Muslim religious leaders and Islamic ideologues who, as we have seen, had long invested in the symbolic conflation of Muslim piety with ethnolinguistic Arabness across multiple spheres of public discourse in postindependence Indonesia.

These observations imply the risks of misrecognition and impeded circulation across arabophone sites, against the spirit of Asian-African exchange celebrated at the Bandung Conference, risks to which this book has offered an intervention. By retracing connections across language debates in the Middle East, Southeast Asia, and sub-Saharan West Africa, I have explored the stakes of disaggregating Islam and ethnolinguistic Arabness across a diversity of sites, to reveal nuances in literary texts and episodes in literary history that unsettle their conflation. Across histories of Arabic contact with other languages, multilingual traditions of Islamic devotional writing challenge the practice of equating Arabness with Islam, both within and beyond custodial centers of Arabic culture in the Middle East. In addition, Arabic's evolving contact with "foreign" (non-Arabic) and "common" dialect influences gave rise to suprareligious attachments to *fuṣḥā* (high literary Arabic) and to literary innovations that questioned the very thresholds of ethnolinguistic Arabness itself. In weaving these observations together, the preceding chapters have revealed perennial tensions between monoglossic attachments to Arabic as a ritual medium and defenses of multilingualism arising through a diversity of historical texts. Such tensions between heteroglossic ideals and monoglossic defenses of Arabic had important effects across language debates engaged on both "secular" and "religious" terms.

Recognizing this tension gives greater visibility to historical claims of cultural and "racial" or ethnolinguistic parity across a transregional expanse. It equally makes visible the plight of minoritized cultural forms as they persisted within twentieth-century Asian and African writing and Arabic and Islamic contact zones. Bringing visibility to these dynamics of hierarchy and parity, this book has shown how tensions between linguistic diversity and orthodox Islamic attachments to Arabic were interpreted across a broad political and ideological spectrum in late colonial and decolonizing contexts. The identification of Arabic literacies with Islamic cultural assimilation, reinforced by the twinned historical processes of Islamization and Arabicization across the regions we have considered, contended with two centrifugal forces gaining momentum during the nineteenth century and across the twentieth. One such force was the genesis of new forms of (proto-)national self-consciousness emerging against a European colonial or Ottoman imperial presence, which lent urgency to the reappraisal of ethnic and linguistic differences within a transregional, Muslim community. The second was the evolving politicization of Arabic as an interreligious mark of identity within North Africa and West Asia.

Although Arabic's global role is often understood through its associations with Islamic ritual and precolonial merchant commerce within Asia and Africa, I hope to have shown that Arabic's global importance exceeds these associations when viewed against the rise and fall of European empires in the nineteenth and twentieth centuries. Through a large-scale historical reconstruction of connections across Asia and Africa—encompassing evidence from the 1820s through the end of the twentieth century—the book traced how Arabic transformed into an anticolonial medium and symbol, but one bearing an ambivalent relationship to anticolonial nationalisms and counterimperial writing; its transregional and interethnic reach complicated its position in emerging debates about indigeneity and national belonging across a diversity of sites.

Early chapters of this book observed how European colonial constructions of Arabic as a global force—a force that required colonial moderation or containment—conditioned the language's growing anticolonial associations. The book also uncovered the following pattern, whether in British-occupied Egypt, as a center of Arabic print, or in French West Africa and the Dutch East Indies, where Arabic was colonially displaced: Arabic's characterization by many Orientalist and colonial figures as a globally underclass language relative to Europeanized alternatives conditioned how subaltern authors rallied to its defense. Defensive attachments to Arabic, however, coexisted with disagreements among writers and intellectuals over its relevance to questions of indigeneity and emerging nationalisms and to ideals of religious pluralism with the formation of new nation-states (as shown in the book's final chapters).

One of the core conclusions of the book, therefore, is that the global history of Arabic bears an essential but complicated relationship to the rise of counterimperial writing across vast distances—as authors and intellectuals across several generations grappled with cultural asymmetries imposed by imperial Europe and debated how Arabic, as an interethnic language, might assume new roles and symbolic values with the fall of European empires. The story of this relationship between Arabic as a global force and counterimperial writing has nonetheless largely receded from scholarship within postcolonial studies, especially beyond the Middle East—just as Arabic's historical complexities have yet to be fully appreciated by many people on the ground in places such as Indonesia, where Arabic is often perceived in ways that flatten out its many dimensions. A renewed understanding of Arabic's global position is needed to compare and connect regional cultural histories separated by distance and by former imperial divisions, allowing for corrective approaches to the study of postcolonial literatures, anticolonial nationalisms, and the circulation of pluralist ideas in Arabic's cosmopolitan shadow.

By focusing on the comparative histories of national and decolonizing literatures that developed amid an Arabic scriptural and cosmopolitan standard, I hope to have offered an important contrast to literary histories that rely on European models, which tend to focus on the evolution of vernacular literatures from a Latin imperial, ecumenical, and scriptural tradition. The comparative studies presented here show the limits of two commonly held arguments (or biases) about the position of Arabic relative to other languages and "vernaculars." The first is that Arabic would be unilaterally displaced as a matter of secular progress in keeping with a Eurocentric or Latinate precedent; the second is that Arabic was a virtually untranslatable language due to its ritual vocation within Muslim communities. Contrary to both assumptions, an array of evidence in this book attests to more liminal or interstitial cultural dynamics.

The stakes of these conclusions are clear when we return to the questions that opened this book. European national cultures and vernacular-language literatures are often interpreted through their development against a Latin imperial or ecumenical tradition. How, then, might the study of national and vernacular literatures developing within an Arabic scriptural context compare? What implications might this have for how we assess cultural developments in decolonizing contexts—or national cultures defined and transforming through both European imperial pressures and the cultural impact of ritual or Qur'anic Arabic? As the evidence across this book demonstrates, a process of progressive "vernacularization" cannot be understood as paradigmatic across Arabic-Islamic contact zones, nor do we find a unilateral, defensive attachment to Arabic as a sacralized language against the supposed corruption of worldly alternatives in literary form. By comparing the fate of Arabic and its "vernacular" others across regional and imperial lines, we move beyond a single, unified paradigm to encompass the fate of Arabic relative to other languages and dialects. The coexistence (and tensions) of Arabic as a transregional medium of prestige relative to other languages endures as counterevidence. If anything can be understood as paradigmatic across these historically "Arabic-Islamic" contact zones, it is perhaps the perennial tension between heteroglossic and monoglossic ideologies of language in the specter of Arabic, rather than a definitive or unequivocal determination as to which language—"sacred" or "vernacular"—most endures in the competition for a literary and often politicized public standard.

These tensions are aesthetically and culturally generative. Instead of giving rise to a kind of cultural disorder, a corruption of the sacred, or an administrative disarray, the enduring and controversial coexistence of ritual Arabic and vernacular languages has inspired important literary and cultural innovations. Across a great cultural and linguistic variance, questions about ethnolinguistic and cultural parity have been addressed in aesthetically generative ways, rendering different visions for egalitarian futures in either national or regional terms or across an imagined transregional Muslim community.

The risks of overlooking this pattern of egalitarian idealism are considerable: Not least is the risk of missing the idealist attachments to cultural pluralism and parity that emerged within both arabophone communities and interethnic Muslim communities, in the specter of Arabocentrism and Islamocentrism. Regionally segregated and Eurocentric modes of reading and historical comparison fail to fully discern these dynamics as they extend to vital debates on language, religious differences, and ethnicity or race in decolonizing contexts across twentieth-century literary domains. This book has presented a methodological alternative, highlighting what can be gained by comparing the historical presence of Arabic across regional distances and diverse linguistic communities.

The evidence and conclusions presented within this book raise vital questions about the need to reconfigure disciplinary (and interdisciplinary) work across Arabic-Islamic contact zones. Arabic, however, is rarely studied through its transregional dimensions or across broad comparative contexts as a contact language. Often confined to Middle East studies in the United States, Arabic training is conventionally limited to Islamic studies in West African and Southeast Asian scholarly contexts. The position of Arabic as a transcontinental contact language with mixed ideological valences is, therefore, seriously underserved by prevailing disciplinary configurations. Studying the territorial and ideological ambiguity of Arabic as an interethnic, interreligious (or nonreligious), and transregional medium warrants a more capacious approach.

To address these shortcomings, I propose taking cues from the disciplinary shifts that gave rise to "Sinophone studies" beyond the regional limitations and ideological underpinnings of "Chinese studies," privileging, according to Shu-mei Shih, "the Sinophone's resistance to the hegemonic call of Chineseness."[2] In foundational scholarship on Sinophone studies, the emerging field was envisioned as a means to engage the "polyphonic" and "polyscriptic" character of Sinitic language communities beyond China, as well as minority cultures within China "where Mandarin is adopted or imposed."[3] Such an analogy can help us to envision reconfigured horizons for a global, more polycentric "arabophone studies" at the interstices of other disciplines and in ways encompassing the history and transregional afterlife of an Arabic "cosmopolis" or "scriptworld."[4]

The term "arabophone" is currently used in French-speaking North African contexts and within French scholarship to denote Arabic language writers and speakers, often against the "francophone." Given, however, the geographic breadth and diversity of Arabic speakers and Arabicized language literacies—transregionally, interimperially, and across an ideological spectrum—the term "arabophone" could designate a more globalized field that as yet does not formally exist, one that might support comparative literary and cultural studies with broader interdisciplinary valences. Emerging from the margins and interstices of Middle East studies, African studies, Asian studies, Islamic studies, and postcolonial studies, what could comparative "arabophone studies" become on a truly global scale? Perhaps it could build from emerging transregional and comparative scholarship within the field of Arabic studies itself—including, for example, on *the nahḍa*'s linguistic debates and histories of translation, *ʿāmmiyya* writing, digraphia across changing print technologies, diasporic *mahjar* publications, and Asian-African literary exchanges. And perhaps it could reinforce current Africanist efforts to develop an emerging and more global field of "*ʿajami* studies," an interdisciplinary field whose purpose, according to Fallou Ngom, is the scholarly elevation of *ʿajami* texts and the study of "centuries-old interplays between Islamic and local traditions."[5]

A more globalized and translingual field of "arabophone studies" might reassess the impact of Arabic as a charismatic language and script across a diversity of regional sites and in contact with an array of other languages and cultural creoles. While probing the relationship between Arabic and the many languages traditionally considered marginal to Islamic studies, it might also reassess the impact of religious influences on nominally nonreligious texts—and nominally "secular" pressures on the religious.[6] Building through a multiplicity of Arabic contact zones, it could take as its comparative common ground the historical presence of Arabic, as both language and script, while inviting a diversity of centripetal comparisons across cultural forms in non-Arabic languages as counterpoints; at the convergence of Arabic and

ʿajamiyyāt, arabophone studies would necessarily cede to comparative literary and cultural studies at these limits.

Taking its cue from Sinophone studies, a broadened arabophone studies could also claim greater comparative attention to Arabic as a transregional language and script connected to both an imperial past and a colonially subaltern history. Arabic's changing fortunes as an imperial acrolect and script that became in many contexts a postcolonial basilect with a globally controversial (and often colonially marginalized) writing system might be further explored. This dual framing of Arabic would offer an important basis for developing arabophone studies as a regionally polycentric field in which questions of cultural parity and ethnolinguistic hierarchy are central. In imagining the contours of comparative arabophone studies, encompassing a diversity of languages positioned within a shared Arabic "scriptworld," the position of Arabic's literary margins—speakers of dialects and of foreign tongues relative to literary or ritual Arabic and writers of other languages in Arabic script—could gain increased visibility. The horizons of a globalized arabophone studies might also allow for a more neutral stance toward purist ideas about ritual Arabic while retracing Arabic's shifting symbolic value in multilingual contexts.

The promise of a more polycentric arabophone studies designating "many decentered sites of contestation" (to borrow Françoise Lionnet's characterization of francophone studies) should not, however, blind us to the field's potential limitations.[7] Arabophone studies might, in this regard, draw insights from debates in analogous fields. As a disciplinary designation, could "arabophone" imply a more inclusive horizon than "Arabic" for a prospective field? Or might it in practice reinscribe dynamics of peripherality relative to an "Arabic" literary and regional center (as has been argued of francophone, anglophone, and Sinophone studies in the past)?[8] Does the term "arabophone," in other words, threaten to collapse into the nebulous specter of an Arab(ic) imperium in ways that reprivilege hierarchies of a bygone era in North Africa and West Asia? In addition to thinking about imperially informed hierarchies, it could also be fruitful to consider what relationship the term "arabophone" would (or could) have to what Ronit Ricci has more neutrally called in South and Southeast Asia an Arabic "cosmopolis"—that is, interconnected sites of Arabic literary diffusion and linguistic contact borne of commercial histories and regional proximities rather than imperial conquests.[9] The mercurial dynamics of borders and boundaries within and beyond native speech communities are here implicated.

Moving toward such a collective scholarly ideal would necessarily involve further conceptual work in connection with Arabocentric limit concepts: the terms *ʿajam* and *ʿajamiyya* (and, by extension, *ʿujma*), demarcating the vanishing horizons of the Arabophone against the *xenophone*.[10] Beyond their conceptual canonization within the Qurʾan, these terms carry meanings, implications, and values that have been re-created and reinvented across a diversity of contexts. As we have seen, across arabophone realms, the notion of *ʿajamiyya* otherness serves as an illuminating point of refraction on dynamics of stratification and parity, but one whose meaning is difficult to translationally fix. As a prismatic concept, its surface meanings—and arcs of illumination—change depending on its contextual surroundings. It can stand categorically for languages or vernaculars in Arabic orthography (as it does in many continental African regions); it can also name the accented, debased, and garbled, designating the ethnolinguistically or "racially" marked (in Arabocentric texts). At times, it names an allegedly corrupted distance from sanctified speech and charismatic eloquence (in Islamic contexts). And yet, it also names a threshold of ethnolinguistic inclusion for subaltern Muslims who claim the equality of non-Arab (*ʿajam*) speakers to Arabs. When surfacing within colonial-era Orientalist commentaries, *ʿajamiyya* gains additional meanings. It may name the historical and ideological thresholds of the "Muslim world," framing an Islamic precept of "racial" or "national" equality (between Arabs and their "racial others")—an egalitarian precept dismissed by some Orientalists as "Muslim propaganda." In late colonial and postcolonial contexts, the ideal of parity between *ʿarab* and *ʿajam* also informs subaltern debates about the legitimacy and genealogy of emerging nationalisms within a global *umma*. Overlooking the protean and accretive meanings of these concepts means missing an expansive and vastly interconnected history, with implications central to the literary and extended well beyond it.

The preceding observations suggest horizons for literary comparisons and methods that move beyond Eurocentric paradigms and disciplinary configurations. My own approach has sought to elevate connections across Asian and African regions through the politics of language, to render more visible egalitarian and pluralist ideas within Arabic-Islamic contact zones historically. But a final word of caution and nuance is warranted. If the book's larger lessons on the fluid boundaries of realms arabophone and arabographic are taken to their logical conclusion, the very notion of Asian-African writing as a closed literary corpus connected through Arabic but "writing back" to imperial Europe deserves to be questioned—particularly given the porous and shifting boundaries of Europe as itself a historically arabophone site. A global examination of Arabic-Islamic contact zones, in other words, challenges the fixity both of ethnolinguistic "Arabness" and of "Europe" as a region culturally distinct from the "Arabophone." Arabophone and arabographic influences, after all, spread liberally across the Mediterranean basin, vitally impacting the formation of "European" languages and literatures from Iberian to Ottoman contexts. Diasporic migrations and scholarly exchanges—including by *ʿajami* Orientalists—render these boundaries even more porous. The beginnings of the sixteenth-century European novel, it might also be remembered, built from the pretext of *ʿajami* (*aljamiado*) fragments surfacing in post-*reconquista* Spain, evincing a history of arabophone contact that unsettles the very idea of a culturally discrete Latinate Europe.[11] I emphasize again the strange appearance of a sixteenth-century Iberian Arab Muslim fleeing the Spanish reconquest as a refugee in a twentieth-century Indonesian novel (*Arus Balik*), an appearance that speaks to the spectral connection between two historically arabophone regions—Europe's Western extreme and insular Southeast Asia.[12] What Sukarno once called the artery of European imperialism that passed from the Strait of Gibraltar to the Strait of Malacca, in other words, presents an underexamined sequence of arabophone connections and a palimpsest of vital traces and agonistic histories for which literary texts offer a significant source of recuperation.[13]

NOTES

Notes to Preface

1. Niloofar Haeri, *Sacred Language, Ordinary People: Dilemmas of Culture and Politics in Egypt* (New York: Palgrave Macmillan, 2003), 2.

2. Haeri, *Sacred Language*, 9.

3. Haeri, *Sacred Language*, 11.

Notes to Introduction

1. Thomas Van Erpe, a foundational Dutch Orientalist of the seventeenth century and author of an early Arabic-Latin grammar (1613), for example, made this claim based on merchant traveler accounts. See John Robert Jones, *Learning Arabic in Renaissance Europe, 1505–1624* (Leiden: Brill, 2020), 15–25. For seventeenth- to eighteenth-century Dutch perceptions of Arabic as an unrivaled language of Asian-African commerce, see Jan Loop, *Johann Heinrich Hottinger: Arabic and Islamic Studies in the Seventeenth Century* (Oxford: Oxford University Press, 2013), 1–2.

2. Ahmed Sukarno, "Address by the President of Indonesia (Bandung, 18 April 1955)," in *Collected Documents of the Asian-African Conference* (Jakarta: Agency for Research and Development, Department of Foreign Affairs, Republic of Indonesia, 1983), 5.

3. Alfred Le Chatelier, *L'Islam dans l'Afrique occidentale* (Paris: G. Steinheil, 1899), 364–65. Unless otherwise noted, all translations are my own.

4. On these persistent tendencies and their challenges, see Aamir Mufti, *Forget English! Orientalism and World Literatures* (Cambridge: Harvard University Press, 2016), 32–35; Shaden Tageldin, "Beyond Latinity, Can the Vernacular Speak?" *Comparative Literature* 70, no. 2 (2018): 114–31; and Waïl Hassan, "Arabic and the Paradigms of Comparison," in *Futures of Comparative Literature: ACLA State of the Discipline Report*, ed. Ursula Heise (Abingdon, U.K.: Routledge, 2017), 191–92.

5. See Rebecca C. Johnson, *Stranger Fictions: A History of the Novel in Arabic Translation* (Ithaca: Cornell University Press, 2020), 6–8, on Arabic as a frequently invoked "limit" case for discussions of linguistic untranslatability in comparative literary studies. See also Shaden Tageldin, "Untranslatability," in *Futures of Comparative Literature: ACLA State of the Discipline Report*, ed. Ursula Heise (Abingdon, U.K.: Routledge, 2017), 234–35; Emily Apter, *The Translation Zone: A New Comparative Literature* (Princeton: Princeton University Press, 2006), 94–108, 278; and Emily Apter, *Against World Literature: On the Politics of Untranslatability* (New York: Verso, 2013), 254–55.

6. Tobias Warner, *The Tongue-Tied Imagination: Decolonizing Literary Modernity in Senegal* (New York: Fordham University Press, 2019), 255.

7. Warner, *Tongue-Tied Imagination*, 255.

8. James Joseph Errington, *Linguistics in a Colonial World: A Story of Language, Meaning, and Power* (Malden, Mass.: Blackwell, 2008), vii.

9. On the implications of such conceptual entrenchments, see Anne Laura Stoler, *Duress: Imperial Durabilities in Our Times* (Durham: Duke University Press, 2016), especially 5–10, 17–32.

10. Mary Louise Pratt, *Imperial Eyes: Travel Writing and Transculturation*, 2nd ed. (New York: Routledge, 2008), 7.

11. Pratt, *Imperial Eyes*, 8.

12. See Apter, *Translation Zone*, 5–6.

13. Benedict Anderson, *Imagined Communities: Reflections on the Origin and Spread of Nationalism* (New York: Verso, 2003), 36.

14. Ronit Ricci, *Islam Translated: Literature, Conversion, and the Arabic Cosmopolis of South and Southeast Asia* (Chicago: University of Chicago Press, 2011), 4, 24. On Arabic's cosmopolitan position among a multilingual populace, see also Muhsin al-Musawi, *The Medieval Islamic Republic of Letters: Arabic Knowledge Construction* (Notre Dame: University of Notre Dame Press, 2015), 44-48, 50-58, 68-72; and Karla Mallette, *Lives of the Great Languages: Arabic and Latin in the Medieval Mediterranean* (Chicago: University of Chicago Press, 2021), 71-85.

15. Ricci, *Islam Translated*, 245.

16. See Niloofar Haeri, "Form and Ideology: Arabic Sociolinguistics and Beyond," *Annual Review of Anthropology* 29 (2000): 61–87; and Niloofar Haeri and William M. Cotter, "Form and Ideology Revisited," in *The Routledge Handbook of Arabic Sociolinguistics*, ed. Enam Al-Wer and Uri Horesh (New York: Routledge, 2019), 243–58.

17. See Anwar Chejne, *The Arabic Language: Its Role in History* (Minneapolis: University of Minnesota Press, 1969); Jaroslav Stetkevych, *The Modern Arabic Literary Language: Lexical and Stylistic Developments* (Washington, D.C.: Georgetown University Press, 2006); and Haeri, "Form and Ideology."

18. Webb Keane, "Language and Religion," in *A Companion to Linguistic Anthropology*, ed. Alessandro Duranti (New York: Blackwell, 2004), 437.

19. Yasir Suleiman, *The Arabic Language and National Identity: A Study in Ideology* (Washington, D.C.: Georgetown University Press, 2003), 57.

20. These include verses 16:103, 26:198, and 41:44 (twice). Suleiman, *Arabic Language and National Identity*, 42–44; and Yasir Suleiman, *Arabic in the Fray: Language Ideology and Cultural Politics* (Edinburgh: Edinburgh University Press, 2013), 51–65.

21. Sunil Sharma, "Redrawing the Boundaries of *'Ajam* in Early Modern Persian Literary Histories," in *Iran Facing Others: Identity Boundaries in a Historical Perspective*, ed. Abbas Amanat and Farzin Vejdani (New York: Palgrave, 2012), 49–62. On these linguistic taxonomies as canonized by the ninth-century polymath al-Jahiz, see Suleiman, *Arabic in the Fray*, 66–82.

22. See Michael Cooperson, "'Arabs' and 'Iranians': The Uses of Ethnicity in the Early Abbasid Period," in *Islamic Cultures, Islamic Contexts: Essays in Honor of Professor Patricia Crone*, ed. Behnam Sadeghi and David Abulafia (Leiden: Brill, 2015), 364–87.

23. See Meikal Mumin, "The Arabic Script in Africa: Under-studied Literacy," in *The Arabic*

Script in Africa: Studies in the Use of a Writing System, ed. Meikal Mumin and Kees Versteegh (Leiden: Brill, 2014), 41–76; and Ousmane Kane, *Beyond Timbuktu: An Intellectual History of Muslim West Africa* (Cambridge: Harvard University Press, 2016), 54–56. Across continental Africa and Asia, however, other distinct regional taxonomies for naming these (*ʿajami*) practices of local writing and transcription also arose (e.g., *ki ajami* in Swahili, *Wolofal* in Wolof, and *jawi* in Malay).

24. See Cooperson, "'Arabs' and 'Iranians,'" 365–66.

25. As translated in Louise Marlow, *Hierarchy and Egalitarianism in Islamic Thought* (Cambridge: Cambridge University Press, 1997), 21 n. 43. On traditions of the Prophet Muhammad's farewell sermon, see also Marlow, *Hierarchy and Egalitarianism*, 21–25; and Ignaz Goldziher, *Muslim Studies*, vol. 1, trans. C. R. Barber (New Brunswick, N.J.: Aldine Press, 2006), 71–72.

26. On traditions of the Prophet Muhammad's last sermon in connection to colorism, see Goldziher, *Muslim Studies*, 71–75. See also Dawud Walid, *Blackness and Islam* (Wembley, U.K.: Algorithm/Islamic Human Rights Commission, 2021), 27–28; Chouki El Hamel, *Black Morocco: A History of Race, Slavery and Islam* (Cambridge: Cambridge University Press, 2013), 63.

27. See Marlow, *Hierarchy and Egalitarianism*, 18–19, 21, 174.

28. As translated in Roy Mottahedeh, "The Shuʿûbîyah Controversy and the Social History of Early Islamic Iran," *International Journal of Middle Eastern Studies* 7 (1976): 164.

29. Tarif Khalidi, trans., *The Qurʾan: A New Translation* (New York: Penguin Classics, 2008), 326.

30. See Abdelfattah Kilito, *The Tongue of Adam* [*La Langue d'Adam*], trans. Robyn Creswell (New York: New Directions, 2016), 22–30.

31. See Nadav Samin, *Of Sand or Soil: Genealogy and Tribal Belonging in Saudi Arabia* (Princeton: Princeton University Press, 2015), 1–3.

32. See Bruce Hall, *A History of Race in Muslim West Africa, 1600–1960* (New York: Cambridge University Press, 2011), 9–16; and Ghenwa Hayek, "Whitewashing Arabic for Global Consumption: Translating Race in *The Story of Zahra*," *Middle Eastern Literatures* 20, no. 1 (2017): 93–95, 100–101.

33. See Cemil Aydin, *The Idea of the Muslim World: A Global Intellectual History* (Cambridge: Harvard University Press, 2017), 3–13, 58-64.

34. On these legacies of the Bandung Conference, see Brian Russell Roberts and Keith Foulcher, *Indonesian Notebook: A Sourcebook on Richard Wright and the Bandung Conference* (Durham: Duke University Press, 2016), 2–8.

35. Warner, *Tongue-Tied Imagination*, 5–9, 17-23.

36. Djelal Kadir, "To World, to Globalize: World Literature's Crossroads," in *World Literature in Theory*, ed. David Damrosch (Chichester, U.K.: Wiley Blackwell, 2014), 264–70.

37. For an overview of these debates, see David Damrosch, ed., *World Literature in Theory* (Chichester, U.K.: Wiley Blackwell, 2014); and Theo D'haen, César Domínguez, and Mads Thomsen, eds., *World Literature: A Reader* (New York: Routledge, 2013).

38. See David Damrosch, *What Is World Literature?* (Princeton: Princeton University Press, 2004), 281–82, 288–303. See also Tobias Warner's reading of Damrosch in *Tongue-Tied Imagination*, 17–19.

39. Pheng Cheah, *What Is a World? Postcolonial Literature as World Literature* (Durham: Duke University Press, 2016), 3–5, 16–19.

40. Aamir Mufti, "Orientalism and the Institution of World Literatures," in *World Literature in Theory*, ed. David Damrosch (Chichester, U.K.: Wiley Blackwell, 2014), 339. See also Mufti's *Forget English!*, 19–34, 206–252.

Notes to Chapter 1

I am grateful to Liam Klein for his assistance with the epigraph's translation from Dutch.

1. Christiaan Snouck Hurgronje, "De Islam en het rassenprobleem," February 8, 1922, rector's lecture presented at the 347th anniversary of Der Leidsche Hoogeschool (Leiden: E. J. Brill, 1922), 5, available at https://play.google.com/books/reader?id=cKdBAQAAMAAJ&pg=GBS.PA2&hl=en.

2. See Marwa Elshakry, "Knowledge in Motion: The Cultural Politics of Modern Science Translations in Arabic," *Isis* 99, no. 4 (December 2008): 714; Marwa Elshakry, *Reading Darwin in Arabic* (Chicago: Chicago University Press, 2013), 87–89, 246–47, 260; Samah Selim, "Languages of Civilization: Nation, Translation and the Politics of Race in Colonial Egypt," *Translator* 15, no. 1 (2009): 151–54.

3. See Edmund Burke III, "The First Crisis of Orientalism 1890–1914," in *Connaissances du Maghreb*, ed. Jean Claude Vatin (Paris: Editions du Centre national de la recherche scientifique, 1984), 213–26.

4. See, for example, Edward Said, *Orientalism* (New York: Vintage, 2003), 134–50; and Maurice Olender, *Languages of Paradise: Race, Religion, and Philology in the Nineteenth Century* (Cambridge: Harvard University Press, 1992), 59–78.

5. Ernest Renan, *Histoire générale et système comparé des langues sémitiques* (Paris: Imprimérie Imperiale, 1863 [1855]), 347, 353–54.

6. See Olender, *Languages of Paradise*, 59–78, 115–35.

7. Renan, *Histoire générale*, xii–xiii.

8. Renan, *Histoire générale*, 346–47.

9. Renan, *Histoire générale*, 365.

10. Renan, *Histoire générale*, 10, emphasis in the original.

11. See Ibn Khaldun, *Kitāb al-ʿIbar wa-Dīwān al-Mubtadaʾ wa-l-Khabar fī Ayyām al-ʿArab wa-l-ʿAjam wa-l-Barbar* (Cairo: ʿAbd al-Maṭbaʿa al-Miṣrīyya bi-Būlāq, 1867), 358–509, esp. 477–79; and Ibn Khaldun, *The Muqaddimah*, trans. Franz Rosenthal (Princeton: Princeton University Press, 2005), 428–33.

12. Ernest Renan, "Islam and Science (*L'Islamisme et la science*, 1883)," in *What Is a Nation? and Other Political Writings*, trans. and ed. M.F.N. Giglioli (New York: Columbia University Press, 2018), 271–72.

13. Renan, "Islam and Science," 272.

14. See Olender, *Languages of Paradise*, 59–78, 115–35.

15. See Rifaʿa Rafiʿ al-Tahtawi, *An Imam in Paris: Account of a Stay in France by an Egyptian Cleric (1826–1831)* [*Takhlīṣ al-Ibrīz*], trans. Daniel L. Newman (London: Saqi, 2011), 335.

16. See Lawrence Conrad, "Ignaz Goldziher on Ernest Renan," in *The Jewish Discovery of Islam*, ed. Martin Kramer (Tel Aviv: Moshe Dayan Center for Middle Eastern and African Studies, Tel Aviv University, 1999), 137–80; David Moshfegh, *Ignaz Goldziher and the Rise of* Islamwissenschaft *as a "Science of Religion"* (Ph.D. dissertation, University of California, Berke-

ley, 2012), 194–97; Olender, *Languages of Paradise*, 115–35. Goldziher directly expressed his objections in a memorial lecture for Renan (delivered on the occasion of Renan's death in 1892 to the Hungarian Academy of Sciences), published as "Renan mint orientalista." As Moshfegh notes, Goldziher equally challenged Renan's association of Persian Islam with Aryan racialization in a 1900 lecture published as Ignaz Goldziher, "Islamisme et Parsisme," *Revue de l'histoire des religions* 43 (1901): 1–29.

17. Goldziher's letter was written to Hartmann on August, 24, 1896, here quoted in translation from Moshfegh, *Ignaz Goldziher*, 194–95.

18. Goldziher, cited in Moshfegh, *Ignaz Goldziher*, 194–95.

19. See Goldziher, *Muslim Studies*, especially 50–57, 74–75, 98–99. Goldziher's original term for "egalitarian" doctrine is *gleichheitslehre* in German (translated by Stern and Barber as "equalitarian teachings"); see, for example, Goldziher, *Muslim Studies*, 73. Conrad ("Ignaz Goldziher," 165) notes that Goldziher's scholarship was generally published in German after preliminary drafts in his native Hungarian.

20. See Goldziher, *Muslim Studies*, 27–100.

21. Goldziher, *Muslim Studies*, 71.

22. Goldziher, *Muslim Studies*, 55.

23. Goldziher, *Muslim Studies*, 111–12.

24. Goldziher, *Muslim Studies*, 112–15.

25. Goldziher, *Muslim Studies*, 99, 135, 141, and elsewhere.

26. Goldziher, *Muslim Studies*, 142, 144.

27. See H. T. Norris, "*Shuʿūbiyyah* in Arabic Literature," in *ʿAbbasid Belles Lettres*, ed. Julia Ashtiany, T. Johnstone, J. Latham, and R. Serjeant (Cambridge: Cambridge University Press, 1990), 31–47; and Suleiman, *Arabic in the Fray*, 55.

28. Snouck Hurgronje, "De Islam en het rassenprobleem," 11.

29. Snouck Hurgronje, "De Islam en het rassenprobleem," 10.

30. Snouck Hurgronje, "De Islam en het rassenprobleem," 13.

31. Snouck Hurgronje, "De Islam en het rassenprobleem," 14.

32. On this postwar context, see Léon Buskens, "Christiaan Snouck Hurgronje, 'Holy War,' and Colonial Concerns," in *Jihad and Islam in World War I*, ed. Erik-Jan Zürcher (Leiden: Leiden University Press, 2015), 29–52.

33. Snouck Hurgronje, "De Islam en het rassenprobleem," 5.

34. Snouck Hurgronje, "De Islam en het rassenprobleem," 23–26.

35. Christiaan Snouck Hurgronje, *Politique Musulmane de la Hollande: Quatres Conférences par C. Snouck Hurgronje Conseiller du Ministère des Colonies Néerlandaises pour les Affaires Indigènes et Arabes*, Collection de la Revue du Monde Musulman, vol. 14 (Paris: Ernest Leroux, 1911), 23–24.

36. Burke, "First Crisis of Orientalism."

37. Edward G. Browne, "L'Avenir de l'Islam [Enquête par Edmond Fazy]," *Questions Diplomatiques et Coloniales* 11, no. 102 (May 15, 1901): 593.

38. Snouck Hurgronje, *Politique Musulmane de la Hollande*, 21, 24.

39. Snouck Hurgronje, *Politique Musulmane de la Hollande*, 22–24.

40. Snouck Hurgronje, "De Islam en het rassenprobleem," 17–18, 20.

41. Snouck Hurgronje, *Politique Musulmane de la Hollande*, 23–24.

42. Snouck Hurgronje, *Politique Musulmane de la Hollande*, 22.

43. Snouck Hurgronje, *Politique Musulmane de la Hollande*, 29–32.

44. Snouck Hurgronje, *Politique Musulmane de la Hollande*, 24–26.

45. Browne, "L'Avenir de l'Islam," 593.

46. Browne, "L'Avenir de l'Islam," 593.

47. Snouck Hurgronje, *Politique Musulmane de la Hollande*, 22. See also Snouck Hurgronje, "De Islam en het rassenprobleem," 13–14 and 20, where he more directly states, "The racial doctrine of the Islamic system has greatly contributed to its initial, not insignificant, success, and it serves as an everlasting ornament to this international community."

48. Browne, "L'Avenir de l'Islam," 592.

49. See Falih Husayn, "The Participation of Non-Arab Elements in the Umayyad Army and Administration," in *The Articulation of Early Islamic State Structures*, ed. Fred M. Donner (New York: Routledge, 2012), 265–89.

50. French Arabist Edmond Doutté, for example, promoted a North African (Moroccan) sultanate led by an Arab Qurayshi "Sharif," to challenge "the Sultan of Istanbul," whom, he claimed, "is only a Turk." See Edmond Doutté, "L'Avenir de l'Islam [Enquête par Edmond Fazy]," *Questions Diplomatiques et Coloniales* 12, no. 112 (October 1, 1901): 397–99. See also Christiaan Snouck Hurgronje, "L'Avenir de l'Islam," *Questions Diplomatiques et Coloniales* 12, no. 106 (July 15, 1901): 78–80, on the theoretical legitimacy of Arab as opposed to non-Arab caliphal figureheads. See also Marwan Buheiry, "Colonial Scholarship and Muslim Revivalism in 1900," *Arab Studies Quarterly* 4, nos. 1–2 (1982): 1–9, 11–12; and Joseph Massad, *Islam in Liberalism* (Chicago: Chicago University Press, 2015), 63–73.

51. See Buheiry, "Colonial Scholarship"; Zachary Lockman, *Contending Visions of the Middle East* (Cambridge: Cambridge University Press, 2010), 91–93; Massad, *Islam in Liberalism*, 63–73. Responses to the inquiry were published through *Questions Diplomatiques et Coloniales* in several installments between May and October 1901 (see vols. 11–12, nos. 102, 106–7, 112–13).

52. See, for example, Edmond Fazy's introduction, "L'Avenir de l'Islam," *Questions Diplomatiques et Coloniales* 11, no. 102 (May 15, 1901): 579–80. On Ottoman Turkish claims to pan-Islamic unity in the late nineteenth century, see Jacob Landau, *Pan-Islam: History and Politics* (New York: Routledge Library Editions, 2016), 1–64.

53. Goldziher's own contribution to the inquiry offered a different emphasis, focusing on scholarly "historicism" and the threads of progressive reform latent within Islam itself, while emphasizing the need for Muslim scholars to emulate European rationalist models. In both Browne's and Goldziher's responses to the inquiry, the influence of Renan's earlier polemics on "Islam and science" seem evident. See Ignaz Goldziher, "L'Avenir de l'Islam," *Questions Diplomatiques et Coloniales* 11, no. 102 (May 15, 1901): 600–602. On Goldziher's colonial politics and contribution to the inquiry, see Massad, *Islam in Liberalism*, 69; and Katalin Rac, "Arabic Literature for the Colonizer and the Colonized: Ignaz Goldziher and Hungary's Eastern Politics 1878–1918," in *The Muslim Reception of European Orientalism: Reversing the Gaze*, ed. Susannah Heschel and Umar Ryad (New York: Routledge, 2019), 80–102.

54. Bernard Carra de Vaux, "L'Avenir de l'Islam [Enquête par Edmond Fazy]," *Questions Diplomatiques et Coloniales* 11, no. 102 (May 15, 1901): 580.

55. Carra de Vaux, "L'Avenir de l'Islam," 581.

56. Carra de Vaux, "L'Avenir de l'Islam," 581–85.

57. Carra de Vaux, "L'Avenir de l'Islam," 581.

58. Carra de Vaux, "L'Avenir de l'Islam," 585.

59. Carra de Vaux, "L'Avenir de l'Islam," 587.

60. Carra de Vaux, "L'Avenir de l'Islam," 588, emphasis in the original.

61. Buheiry, "Colonial Scholarship," 9.

62. See Burke, "First Crisis of Orientalism."

63. Snouck Hurgronje, "L'Avenir de l'Islam," 78–81.

64. Snouck Hurgronje, "L'Avenir de l'Islam," 78.

65. Snouck Hurgronje, "L'Avenir de l'Islam," 80–81.

66. Snouck Hurgronje, "L'Avenir de l'Islam," 82.

67. Snouck Hurgronje, "L'Avenir de l'Islam," 78.

68. Snouck Hurgronje's ambivalence to Arabic nonetheless deserves mention. He described Arabic in "De Islam en het rassenprobleem" (14–15) as a historical marvel—an impressive, fluid medium that coexisted with a diversity of other languages—but characterized it as a regressive literacy in his policy memoranda, including his 1901 *Questions Diplomatiques et Coloniales* submission and his 1911 *Politique Musulmane de la Hollande.* This latter position is implied by his promotion of romanization in the Dutch East Indies. As with his writing on Islamic practices of inclusivity and parity, his shift in emphasis seemed to depend on context, accommodating both his role as a colonial functionary and his later position as a university rector.

69. On this process, see John Hoffman, "A Foreign Investment: Indies Malay to 1901," *Indonesia* 27 (1979): 65–92; and Jeffrey Hadler, *Places Like Home: Islam, Matriliny, and the History of Family in Minangkabau* (Ph.D. dissertation, Cornell University, 2000), 317–25.

70. See Henry de Castries, "L'Avenir de l'Islam [Enquête par Edmond Fazy]," *Questions Diplomatiques et Coloniales* 12, no. 113 (November 1, 1901): 533. In English translation, see Buheiry, "Colonial Scholarship," 9–10. On Islam's "tolerance," "principles of equality," and "assimilative faculties," see also Henry de Castries, *L'Islam: Impressions et Études* (Paris: A. Collin, 1897), 64–60, 101–5, 181–90.

71. Alfred Le Chatelier, "Introduction," in Christiaan Snouck Hurgronje, *Politique Musulmane de la Hollande: Quatres Conférences par C. Snouck Hurgronje Conseiller du Ministère des Colonies Néerlandaises pour les Affaires Indigènes et Arabes,* Collection de la Revue du Monde Musulman, vol. 14 (Paris: Ernest Leroux, 1911), 1–3.

72. See Martin Kramer, "Surveying the Middle East," *Asian and African Studies* 24 (1990): 89–107; and Burke, "First Crisis of Orientalism."

73. See Kramer, "Surveying the Middle East."

74. Alfred Le Chatelier, *Politique Musulmane: Lettre au "Standard"* (Tours: E. Arrault, 1907). Le Chatelier lamented that the British paper *The Standard* published his letter in abridged form, prompting him to republish a complete version in French as a pamphlet. For the English publication, see Alfred Le Chatelier, "German Mussulman Policy, Its Widespread Character," *The Standard,* April 18, 1907, 5.

75. Le Chatelier, *Politique Musulmane,* 11.

76. Le Chatelier, *Politique Musulmane,* 58–59, 64–65.

77. Le Chatelier, *Politique Musulmane,* 13–14.

78. Le Chatelier, "Introduction." Le Chatelier's praise of Dutch Muslim policy anticipates

Snouck Hurgronje's later position as an advisor to France on Moroccan Islam and Berber customary law. See Mona Abaza, "Ada/Custom," in *Words in Motion*, ed. Carol Gluck, Anna Tsing, and Abraham Itty (Durham: Duke University Press, 2009), 67–82; and Mahmood Mamdani, *Define and Rule: Native as Political Identity* (Cambridge: Harvard University Press, 2012), 34–42.

79. Both Dutch and French officials during this period were engaging with a reorientation of colonial policy, with the Dutch establishment of an "Ethical Policy" (or policy of "Association") in the wake of a controversial and exploitative system of *cultuursteelsel* and with French shifts away from failed policies of "Assimilation" in North and West Africa. See H. L. Wessling, "The Dutch Colonial Model in French Colonial Theory, 1890–1914," *Proceedings of the Meeting of the French Colonial Historical Society* 2 (1977): 107–30; and Raymond Betts, *Assimilation and Association in French Colonial Theory 1890–1914* (Lincoln: University of Nebraska Press, 2005), 35–38. On the evolution of policies of "Association" in the French colonial context, see Betts, *Assimilation and Association in French Colonial Theory*, 120–32. For a more critical view, see G. H. Bousquet, *A French View of the Netherlands Indies*, trans. Philip Lilienthal (London: Oxford University Press, 1940), especially 8–21, 75–94.

80. See Harry Benda, "Christiaan Snouck Hurgronje and the Foundations of Dutch Islamic Policy in Indonesia," *Journal of Modern History* 30, no. 4 (December 1958): 338–47; and Harry Benda, *The Crescent and the Rising Sun: Indonesian Islam under the Japanese Occupation, 1942–1945* (The Hague: W. Van Hoeve, 1958), 21–23.

81. See Snouck Hurgronje, *Politique Musulmane de la Hollande*, 37–38, 97–102. For further context, see Benda, "Christiaan Snouck Hurgronje"; and Karel Steenbrink, *Dutch Colonialism and Indonesian Islam: Contacts and Conflicts 1596–1950* (Amsterdam: Rodopi, 2006), 87–145.

82. Snouck Hurgronje, *Politique Musulmane de la Hollande*, 82–86.

83. Benda, *Crescent and the Rising Sun*, 23.

84. Cited here is Benda's overview of Snouck Hurgronje's conclusions; see Benda, "Christiaan Snouck Hurgronje," 344. For Snouck Hurgronje's original comments, see *Politique Musulmane de la Hollande*, 109, 117. Snouck Hurgronje directly employs the term "association" at 108–33. For context, see Benda, "Christiaan Snouck Hurgronje," 344–47; and Willem Otterspeer, "The Ethical Imperative," in *Leiden Oriental Connections, 1850–1940*, ed. Willem Otterspeer (Leiden: E. J. Brill, 1989), 204–29.

85. Snouck Hurgronje, *Politique Musulmane de la Hollande*, 108–33.

86. On Snouck Hurgronje's promotion of romanization, see Hoffman, "Foreign Investment"; and Hadler, *Places Like Home*, 317–25.

87. Snouck Hurgronje, *Politique Musulmane de la Hollande*, 30–32.

88. Snouck Hurgronje, *Politique Musulmane de la Hollande*, 30.

89. Cited in Christopher Harrison, *France and Islam in West Africa, 1860–1960* (Cambridge: Cambridge University Press, 1988), 51–52.

90. Le Chatelier, *Politique Musulmane*, 92.

91. Le Chatelier, *Politique Musulmane*, 93.

92. Le Chatelier, *Politique Musulmane*, 94.

93. Le Chatelier, *Politique Musulmane*, 93–94.

94. Le Chatelier, *Politique Musulmane*, 95.

95. On this association of Arabic with underclass status in West Africa, see Ousmane Kane,

Non-Europhone Intellectuals (Dakar: Council for the Development of Social Science Research in Africa, 2012), especially 43–49.

Notes to Chapter 2

To foreground this chapter's framing of *ʿajami* as a relational category, a simplified transliteration (for *āʿjamī*) has been used in the epigraph.

1. Suleiman, *Arabic in the Fray*, 52–57; Noha Radwan, *Egyptian Colloquial Poetry in the Modern Arabic Canon* (New York: Palgrave Macmillan, 2012), 12–17; and Tageldin, "Beyond Latinity," 121–30.

2. On influential theorizations of this spectral connection, according to which "[Arabic] dialects differed according to the (more or less close) contact [of Arabs] with [non-Arabs]," see Ibn Khaldun, *Muqaddimah*, 457.

3. See Stephen Sheehi, *Foundations of Modern Arab Identity* (Gainesville: University Press of Forida, 2004), 4–14, 24–45; Ami Ayalon, *The Arabic Print Revolution: Cultural Production and Mass Readership* (Cambridge: Cambridge University Press, 2016), 18–32, 154–93; and Hoda Yousef, *Composing Egypt: Reading, Writing, and the Emergence of a Modern Nation* (Stanford: Stanford University Press, 2016), 77–87. On translation and the *nahḍa*, see Elshakry, "Knowledge in Motion"; Johnson, *Stranger Fictions*; and Shaden Tageldin, *Disarming Words: Empire and the Seductions of Translation in Egypt* (Berkeley: University of California Press, 2011).

4. Al-Tahtawi, *Imam in Paris*, 189.

5. See Suleiman, *Arabic Language and National Identity*, 43–45, 57. Jan Retsö suggests that the concept was in pre-Islamic circulation before its Qurʾanic instantiation; Jan Retsö, *The Arabs in Antiquity: Their History from the Assyrians to the Umayyads* (London: Routledge Curzon, 2003), 24–62.

6. Amidu Sanni, "The Discourse on *Laḥn* in Arabic Philological and Literary Traditions," *Middle Eastern Literatures* 13, no. 1 (2010): 9; and Nafusa Zakariyya Saʿid, *Tarīkh al-Daʿwa ilā al-ʿĀmmiyya wa-Athārihā fī Miṣr* (Alexandria, Egypt: Dār Nashr al-Thaqāfa, 1964), 4–7. On the implications of these historical exchanges for more recent language debates, see Walter Armbrust, *Mass Culture and Modernism in Egypt* (Cambridge: Cambridge University Press, 2001), 37–55.

7. See Tageldin, *Disarming Words*, especially 114–19, 126–27; and Elliott Colla, *Conflicted Antiquities: Egyptology, Egyptomania, Egyptian Modernity* (Durham: Duke University Press, 2007), 121–36.

8. Al-Tahtawi, *Imam in Paris*, 127, 129; Rifāʿah al-Ṭahṭāwī, *Takhlīṣ al-Ibrīz fī Talkhīṣ Bārīz* (Cairo: Mustafa al-Babi al-Halabi and Sons Press, 1958), 76, 78.

9. On the significance of this dynamic given the cartographic indeterminacy of Arabocentric boundaries dividing the *bilād al-sudān* from its northern counterparts, see Eve Troutt Powell, *A Different Shade of Colonialism: Egypt, Great Britain, and the Mastery of the Sudan* (Berkeley: University of California Press, 2003), 26–63; Heather Sharkey, *Living with Colonialism: Nationalism and Culture in the Anglo-Egyptian Sudan* (Berkeley: University of California Press, 2003), 16–24; Omnia El Shakry, *The Great Social Laboratory: Subjects of Knowledge in Colonial and Postcolonial Egypt* (Stanford: Stanford University Press, 2007); and El Hamel, *Black*

Morocco. On comparable, stratified portrayals of sub-Saharan Africans within major literary texts of the Arabic *nahḍa*, see also Johnson, *Stranger Fictions*, 154–58.

10. Al-Ṭahṭāwī, *Takhlīṣ al-Ibrīz*, 5, 80; al-Tahtawi, *Imam in Paris*, 106, 132. He also uses *ʿajam* to occasionally refer to a *Persian* populace; see al-Ṭahṭāwī, *Takhlīṣ al-Ibrīz*, 76.

11. Al-Tahtawi, *Imam in Paris*, 107–9, 125–26. On this opposition (*badāwa* and *ḥadāra*) and its linguistic implications, see Ibn Khaldun, *Kitāb al-ʿIbar*, 101–28, 317–18, 491–94; Ibn Khaldun, *Muqaddimah*, 98–99, 294–95, 438–41. Publishing after al-Ṭahṭāwī, Zaydān offers a compelling account of the ambiguity of the term *Arab* and of its ethnonymic development in nineteenth-century Arabic texts; see Jurji Zaidan, "Pre-Islamic Arabs," trans. Paul Starkey, in Thomas Philipp, *Jurji Zaidan and the Foundations of Arab Nationalism* (Syracuse: Syracuse University Press, 2014), 283–84.

12. See al-Tahtawi, *Imam in Paris*, 357. On Egyptian distinctiveness, al-Ṭahṭāwī characterizes ancient Egyptians' descendants as Copts but considers their language moribund (335–36). See also Colla, *Conflicted Antiquities*, 121–26.

13. Al-Tahtawi, *Imam in Paris*, 357.

14. Al-Tahtawi, *Imam in Paris*, 334–57 and 255–59.

15. Al-Tahtawi, *Imam in Paris*, 185–92.

16. Al-Ṭahṭāwī appears to draw on classical traditions of boast poetry (*mufakhara*), a corpus referenced in his epilogue among other passages. For context, see al-Musawi, Muhsin, *Medieval Islamic Republic of Letters*, 56-57; Norris, "*Shuʿūbiyyah* in Arabic Literature"; and H. N. Kennedy, "The ʿAbbasid Caliphate: A Historical Introduction," in *ʿAbbasid Belles Lettres*, ed. Julia Ashtiany, T. Johnstone, J. Latham, and R. Serjeant (Cambridge: Cambridge University Press, 1990), 1–15.

17. Al-Tahtawi, *Imam in Paris*, 176–83, 373–74.

18. Al-Tahtawi, *Imam in Paris*, 373–74.

19. See Tageldin, *Disarming Words*, 136–41.

20. Aḥmad Fāris al-Shidyāq, *Leg over Leg; or, The Turtle in the Tree: Concerning the Fariyaq, What Manner of Creature He Might Be* [*Al-Sāq ʿalā al-sāq fī mā huwa al-Firyāq*], Bilingual ed., trans. Humphrey Davies, vols. 1–4 (New York: New York University Press, 2013–14), vol. 2, 48–49. For a counterpoint on al-Shidyāq's "disarticulation" of Arabic from scripture, see also Rana Issa, "Scripture as Literature: The Bible, the Qurʾan and Aḥmad Fāris al-Shidyāq," *Journal of Arabic Literature* 50 (2019): 29–55.

21. On al-Shidyāq's conversions, see Kamran Rastegar, *Literary Modernity between the Middle East and Europe: Textual Transactions in Nineteenth-Century Arabic, English, and Persian Literatures* (New York: Routledge, 2007), 101–25.

22. Al-Shidyāq, *Leg over Leg*, vol. 2, 48–49.

23. On al-Shidyāq's Turkish fluency, see Rana Issa, "Al-Shidyāq-Lee Version (1857): An Example of a Non-synchronous Nineteenth-Century Arabic Bible," in *Senses of Scripture, Treasures of Tradition: The Bible in Arabic among Jews, Christians and Muslims*, ed. Miriam L. Hjalm (Leiden: Brill, 2017), 313.

24. Al-Shidyāq, *Leg over Leg*, vol. 2, 66–67. See also Anna Ziajka Stanton, *The Worlding of Arabic Literature: Language, Affect, and the Ethics of Translatability* (New York: Fordham University Press, 2023), 70–79.

25. See, for example, al-Shidyāq, *Leg over Leg*, vol. 3, 298–99, where a Persian figure (referred

to as an *ʿajami* or a *rajul min al-ʿajam*) is mocked for his status as an accented speaker of Arabic.

26. Al-Ṭahṭāwī, *Takhlīṣ al-Ibrīz*, 129; al-Tahtawi, *Imam in Paris*, 190, emphasis added.

27. Al-Tahtawi, *Imam in Paris*, 189; al-Ṭahṭāwī, *Takhlīṣ al-Ibrīz*, 129.

28. Al-Tahtawi, *Imam in Paris*, 189; al-Ṭahṭāwī, *Takhlīṣ al-Ibrīz*, 129.

29. See Tageldin, *Disarming Words*, 125–26. Al-Ṭahṭāwī's acknowledgment of parallel forms of eloquence across languages is not unique, notably appearing in Ibn Khaldun, *Kitāb al-ʿIbar*, 508–9 (Ibn Khaldun, *Muqaddimah*, 458–59)—a detail Renan, who borrows from Ibn Khaldun, overlooks.

30. On perceptions of these shifts among writers during the nahḍa, see Tageldin, *Disarming Words*; Abdelfattah Kilito, *Thou Shalt Not Speak My Language*, trans. Waïl Hassan (Syracuse: Syracuse University Press, 2008), 56–85; and Tarek El-Ariss, "On Cooks and Crooks: Aḥmad Fāris al-Shidyāq and the Orientalists in England and France (1840s–1850s)," in *The Muslim Reception of European Orientalism: Reversing the Gaze*, ed. Susannah Heschel and Umar Ryad (New York: Routledge, 2019), 14–38.

31. Al-Shidyāq, *Leg over Leg*, vol. 4, 354–55. On al-Shidyāq's broader characterizations of French Orientalists in Paris, see vol. 4, 282–87, 304–7. See also El-Ariss, "On Cooks and Crooks."

32. Al-Shidyāq, *Leg over Leg*, vol. 4, 429–83.

33. Al-Shidyāq, *Leg over Leg*, vol. 4, 436–37.

34. Al-Shidyāq, *Leg over Leg*, vol. 4, 428–29. Al-Shidyāq's original term for (what I refer to here in quotations as) "authorities" is *āsatīdh*, a term that El-Ariss ("On Cooks and Crooks," 24) contrasts with *āsatīdha* ("professors" in Arabic) and translates as "pseudo-professors."

35. Al-Shidyāq, *Leg over Leg*, vol. 4, 428–41.

36. On this perceived loss of authority, see El-Ariss, "On Cooks and Crooks"; and Jeffrey Sacks, *Iterations of Loss: Mutilation and Aesthetic Form, Al-Shidyaq to Darwish* (New York: Fordham University Press, 2015), 77–114.

37. The terms *ʿajam* and *ʿajami(yya)* for "foreignness" can be contrasted with an alternative phrase used in the text, *alsinat al-ajānib*, which more directly and less pejoratively refers to "foreigner's languages"; see, for example, al-Shidyāq, *Leg over Leg*, vol. 3, 41. Other terms designating "foreignness" in the text include *ajnabī*/*ajānib* and *gharīb* for "strangers" and specific ethnonyms such as *afrānj* for "Franks" or "Europeans" and *fārsī* and *hindī* for "Persian" and "Indian" characters.

38. See, for example, al-Shidyāq, *Leg over Leg*, vol. 1, 38–41 (1.1.4).

39. Al-Shidyāq, *Leg over Leg*, vol. 2, 386–87.

40. The text implies this difference between colloquial and literary registers rather than performing the difference, as the manservant's statement is conveyed in a more literary register.

41. See Rana Issa, "Rakākah and the Petit Quarrel of 1871: Christian Authors and the Competition over Arabic," in *Language, Politics and Society in the Middle East: Essays in Honour of Yasir Suleiman*, ed. Yonatan Mendel and Abeer Alnajjar (Edinburgh: Edinburgh University Press, 2018), 157–59. For further context on this rivalry, see Abdulrazzak Patel, *The Arab* Nahḍah*: The Making of the Intellectual and Humanist Movement* (Edinburgh: Edinburgh University Press, 2013), 102–26; and Adrian Gully, "Arabic Linguistic Issues and Controversies

of the Late Nineteenth and Early Twentieth Centuries," *Journal of Semitic Studies* 12, no. 1 (1997): 109–13.

42. See, for example, Yaʿqūb Ṣarrūf, "al-Kalimāt al-āʿjamiyya" ["Foreign Words"], *al-Muqtaṭaf* 15 (1891): 52–53; and ʿAbd al-Qādir al-Maghribī, *Kitāb al-Ishtiqāq wa-l-Taʿrīb* (Cairo: Maṭbaʿat al-Hilāl, 1908), 6–7, cited in Stetkevych, *Modern Arabic Literary Language*, 7. For an overview of these language debates, see Gully, "Arabic Linguistic Issues"; and Patel, *Arab* Nahḍah, 102–26. See also Elshakry, "Knowledge in Motion," 716–19.

43. See Elshakry, "Knowledge in Motion," 718–19; and Stetkevych, *Modern Arabic Literary Language*, 6–7. See also Shaadi Khoury, *Instituting Renaissance: The Early Work of the Arab Academy of Science in Damascus, 1919–1930* (ProQuest Dissertations Publishing, 2016), 109–59.

44. This is Jaroslav Stetkevych's summary overview; see Stetkevych, *Modern Arabic Literary Language*, 6. For relevant passages, see al-Maghribī, *Kitāb al-Ishtiqāq wa-l-Taʿrīb*, 6–7, 18–25, 47–49.

45. Aydin, *Idea of the Muslim World*, 36.

46. Al-Maghribī, likely drawing from Zaydān, cites the European term for "Semitic language" communities (*al-shuʿūb al-sāmī*) to frame *ʿarabiyya-ʿajamiyya* dynamics in evolutionary terms. Although he considered Arabic as a historically evolved "Semitic" language, he viewed its "evolution" (*irtiqāʾ*) as the consequence of Arabic's *ʿajamiyya* contacts after Islam's expansion—therefore privileging very different terms for "Semitic" language evolution than European philologists; see al-Maghribī, *Kitāb al-Ishtiqāq wa-l-Taʿrīb*, 6–7, 30–37, 47–49. See also Jurji Zaidan, "The Philosophy of Language and the Arabic Vocabulary" [*Al-Alfāẓ al-ʿArabiyya wa-l-Falsafa al-Lughawiyya*, 1886], trans. Hilary Kilpatrick, in Thomas Philipp, *Jurji Zaidan and the Foundations of Arab Nationalism* (Syracuse: Syracuse University Press, 2014), 192; Anne-Laure Dupont, "How Should the History of the Arabs Be Written? The Impact of European Orientalism on Jurji Zaidan's Work," in *Jurji Zaidan: Contributions to Modern Arab Thought and Literature*, ed. George C. Zaidan and Thomas Philipp (Bethesda, Md.: Zaidan Foundation, 2013), 85–121; and Marwa Elshakry, "Between Enlightenment and Evolution: Arabic and the Arab Golden Ages of Jurji Zaidan," in *Jurji Zaidan: Contributions to Modern Arab Thought and Literature*, ed. George C. Zaidan and Thomas Philipp (Bethesda, Md.: Zaidan Foundation, 2013), 123–44.

47. See Tageldin, "Beyond Latinity."

48. Controversies over Zaydān's efforts to frame the history of an Arab or Muslim *umma* through European social-scientific concepts (nationalism, race, evolution) throw these dynamics into relief; see Dupont, "How Should the History of the Arabs Be Written?" 108–21. For context, see Sheehi, *Foundations of Modern Arab Identity*, 159–62; and Ami Ayalon, *Language and Change in the Arab Middle East: The Evolution of Modern Political Discourse* (New York: Oxford University Press, 1987), 21–23, 27–28. The term al-Maghribī employs for the "naturalization" of non-Arab (*ʿajam*) converts—*tajannus*—into an *umma* is etymologically related to the Arabic term that has since evolved to mean "citizenship"—*jinsiyya*—in Arabic; in current legal contexts, the Arabic term *tajannus* has also come to refer to the "naturalization" of foreign citizens. The term "racialized" here refers back to Aydin, *Idea of the Muslim World*, 3–14.

49. On this "vernacularization" thesis, see Anderson, *Imagined Communities*.

50. See Jurji Zaidan, "The Arabic Language: A Living Being Subject to the Laws of Evolution" ["al-Lugha al-ʿArabiyya bi-ʿItibārihā Kāʾin Ḥayy"], trans. Hilary Kilpatrick, in Thomas

Philipp, *Jurji Zaidan and the Foundations of Arab Nationalism* (Syracuse: Syracuse University Press, 2014), 227–28. The genesis of Zaydān's ideas on Arabic's comparative evolution would be published under an early title—*Al-Alfāẓ al-ʿArabiyya wa-l-Falsafa al-Lughawiyya,* 1886—and refined in a later 1904 publication—*Al-Lugha al-ʿArabiyya bi-ʿItibārihā Kāʾin Ḥayy*. See Thomas Philipp, "Evolutionary and Historical Approaches to the Arabic Language," in *Jurji Zaidan and the Foundations of Arab Nationalism* (Syracuse: Syracuse University Press, 2014), 53–64.

51. Zaidan, "Arabic Language," 237.

52. Zaidan, "Arabic Language," 227–28.

53. Al-Tahtawi, *Imam in Paris,* 335–36, 338. Al-Ṭahṭāwī (*Takhlīṣ al-Ibrīz,* 278) translates "dead" and "living" into "used" and "abandoned" (*mustaʿmala* and *mahjūra*). His translation of "vernacular" (*dārija,* 280) positions it as a subcategory of "living" languages, describing it as "received" speech among languages still in use (*mustaʿmala*). Etymologically related to the term *daraja,* meaning "to spread," *dārija* is now often considered an equivalent term to *ʿāmmiyya*; see Ziad Fahmy, *Ordinary Egyptians: Creating the Modern Nation through Popular Culture* (Stanford: Stanford University Press, 2011), 5.

54. Al-Tahtawi, *Imam in Paris,* 335–36.

55. On the implications of these debates on *fuṣḥā,* or literary Arabic (*al-ʿarabiyya al-kitābiyya*), see Yousef, *Composing Egypt.*

56. Dufferin Report, The Earl of Dufferin to Lord Granville, Cairo, February 6, 1883, 65.

57. For further context, see Gully, "Arabic Linguistic Issues," 87–95; and Yousef, *Composing Egypt,* 144–45.

58. See William Willcocks, "Syria, Egypt, North Africa and Malta Speak Punic, Not Arabic: In Egypt during the Forty Years of the British Occupation," extract from *Bulletin de L'Institut d'Egypte* 8 (Cairo: Imprimerie de L'Institut Français D'Archéologie Orientale, 1926), 1–37. These arguments resume those presented by Willcocks during a speech at the Ezbekiyya Club in Cairo in 1892, published as William Willcocks, "Li-mā lam tūjad Quwwat al-Ikhtirāʿ ladā al-Miṣriyyīn al-Ān," *al-Azhar* 6, no. 1 (January 1893): 1–10. See Saʿid, *Tarīkh al-Daʿwa.*

59. Willcocks, "Syria, Egypt, North Africa and Malta Speak Punic, Not Arabic," 5–7.

60. Willcocks, "Syria, Egypt, North Africa and Malta Speak Punic, Not Arabic," 5.

61. Willcocks, "Syria, Egypt, North Africa and Malta Speak Punic, Not Arabic," 4.

62. Jurji Zaidan, "Literary and Colloquial Arabic," trans. Paul Starkey, in Thomas Philipp, *Jurji Zaidan and the Foundations of Arab Nationalism* (Syracuse: Syracuse University Press, 2014), 196–98.

63. These ideas were expressed across Zaydān's articles: Zaidan, "Literary and Colloquial Arabic," 196–98; and Jurji Zaidan, "The Writers and Readers of Arabic: (1) Writers; (2) Authors," trans. Hilary Kilpatrick, in Thomas Philipp, *Jurji Zaidan and the Foundations of Arab Nationalism* (Syracuse: Syracuse University Press, 2014), 200–201. For further context, see Anne-Laure Dupont, "What Is a *Kātib ʿāmm*? The Status of Men of Letters and the Conception of Language according to Jurjī Zaydān," *Middle Eastern Studies* 13, no. 2 (2010): 171–81.

64. Zaidan, "Literary and Colloquial Arabic," 196.

65. See Zaidan, "Literary and Colloquial Arabic."

66. Zaidan, "Arabic Language," 237. See also Zaidan, "Literary and Colloquial Arabic."

67. Tageldin, "Beyond Latinity," 127; and Dupont, "What Is a *Kātib ʿāmm*?"

68. Jurjī Zaydān, "Kuttāb al-ʿarabiyya wa-qurrāʾuhā," *al-Hilāl* 7, no. 13 (April 1899): 393–94.

69. Jurji Zaidan, "The Writers and Readers of Arabic" ["Kuttāb al-ʿarabiyya wa-qurrāʾuhā," 1899], trans. Hilary Kilpatrick, in Thomas Philipp, *Jurji Zaidan and the Foundations of Arab Nationalism* (Syracuse: Syracuse University Press, 2014), 220. For the original, see Zaydān, "Kuttāb al-ʿarabiyya wa-qurrāʾuhā," 396.

70. Zaidan, "Writers and Readers of Arabic," 220; Zaydān, "Kuttāb al-ʿarabiyya wa-qurrāʾuhā," 396–97.

71. Zaidan, "Writers and Readers of Arabic," 220; Zaydān, "Kuttāb al-ʿarabiyya wa-qurrāʾuhā," 397.

72. Zaidan, "Writers and Readers of Arabic," 224; Zaydān, "Kuttāb al-ʿarabiyya wa-qurrāʾuhā," 400.

73. See Ayalon, *Arabic Print Revolution*, 29–32.

74. Le Chatelier, *Politique Musulmane*, 11–12. Le Chatelier is indirectly referencing here a British publication on the nationalization of "realms in trust" as an imperial risk; see Rudyard Kipling and Charles Sydney Goldman, *The Empire and the Century: A Series of Essays on Imperial Problems and Possibilities by Various Writers* (London: John Murray, 1905).

75. Le Chatelier, *Politique Musulmane*, 13–14.

76. News of Zaydān's publications and their translation into other "Muslim world" languages appeared in Le Chatelier's *Revue du Monde Musulman*, which regularly surveyed emerging publications within the "Muslim world." See, for example, Lucien Bouvat, "La presse musulmane," *Revue du Monde Musulman* 1, no. 1 (November 1906): 122–29; Lucien Bouvat, "Histoire de la civilisation arabe," *Revue du Monde Musulman* 13, no. 3 (March 1911): 581–82; C. Desormeaux, "La Renaissance arabe," *Revue du Monde Musulman* 4, no. 4 (April 1908): 837; and C. Desormeaux, "L'Oeuvre de Georges Zaïdan," *Revue du Monde Musulman* 4, no. 4 (April 1908): 838–45. On Zaydān's appearance in the journal, see Dupont, "How Should the History of the Arabs Be Written?" 94–95. See also Kramer, "Surveying the Middle East."

77. Aydin, *Idea of the Muslim World*, 3–14.

78. Zaydān, "Kuttāb al-ʿarabiyya wa-qurrāʾuhā," 393–94.

79. Marwa Elshakry's account of this process is illuminating: "Race was an increasingly popular nineteenth century term with no universally agreed equivalent in Arabic. [. . .] Some translators played off older classical or religio-moral notions of human difference by using the phrase '*ṭabaqāt al-ʾumma*' (literally strata of people), utilizing the classical term '*ʾumma*' (as in the concept of a Muslim *ʾumma*), meaning 'community, peoples' or, later, 'nation.' Other renditions, such as '*al-ʾasnāf al-basharīyah*' or '*al-ʾanwāʿ al-basharīyah*' (meaning 'human types' or 'human kinds,' respectively), gave general terms for the 'type' or 'kind' of the specifically biological connotation of 'species': Darwin's *Origin of Species*, for instance, was similarly rendered into Arabic as *ʾAṣl al-ʾanwāʿ* [The origin of types]." Elshakry, "Knowledge in Motion," 714; and see Elshakry, *Reading Darwin in Arabic*, 87–89, 246–47, 260. Experimental translations for notions of race included terms such as *ʿunṣur* (e.g., *al-ʿunṣur al-sāmī*, the "Semitic element")—a term that eventually gave rise to the current Arabic term for "racism," *al-ʿunṣuriyya*. Zaydān appears to have been among the first to publish a systematic overview in Arabic of Semitic Aryan philological/racial categories current in European scholarship (categories that he also translates with some ambiguity as *ṭāʾifa*—"factions"), though Orit Bashkin traces Arab interest in these divisions to the 1830s. See Jurjī Zaydān, *Al-Alfāẓ al-ʿArabiyya wa-l-*

Falsafa al-Lughawiyya (Beirut: Maṭba'at al-Qidīs Jāwrjīyus, 1886), 5–7; Orit Bashkin, "On Noble and Inherited Virtues: Discussions of the Semitic Race in the Levant and Egypt, 1876–1918," *Humanities* 10, no. 88 (2021): 1–20. On other translations within social-scientific texts, see El Shakry, *Great Social Laboratory*, 55–61; and Selim, "Languages of Civilization." See also El Hamel, *Black Morocco*, 60–105.

80. On the nuances of Zaydān's use of both *lughat al-ʿāmma* and *ʿāmmiyyāt*, see Tageldin, "Beyond Latinity," 126–27.

81. See Jonathan M. Hall, *Hellenicity: Between Ethnicity and Culture* (Chicago: University of Chicago Press, 2002), 211–13; and Plato, *Statesman* (262c–63a), cited in Mary-Louise Gill, "Methods and Metaphysics in Plato's *Sophist and Statesman*," in *The Stanford Encyclopedia of Philosophy*, Spring 2020 ed., ed. Edward N. Zalta, https://plato.stanford.edu/archives/spr2020/entries/plato-sophstate.

Notes to Chapter 3

1. See Ousmane Kane and John Hunwick, "Senegambia III: Writers of the Murīd *Ṭarīqa*," in *Arabic Literature of Africa, vol. 4: The Writings of Western Sudanic Africa*, ed. John O. Hunwick (Leiden: Brill, 2003), 396.

2. The regional prestige of Arabic over *ʿajami* alternatives was prevalent but not uniformly accepted in West African Muslim communities; see Fallou Ngom, *Muslims beyond the Arab World: The Odyssey of* ʿAjami *and the Murīdiyya* (New York: Oxford University Press, 2016), 8–29, 59–67; and Fallou Ngom, "Aḥmadu Bamba's Pedagogy and the Development of ʿAjamī Literature," *African Studies Review* 52, no. 1 (April 2009): 99–123. The region of Senegal was considered by French colonial authorities as militarily "pacified" by the 1890s, when the French colony of L'Afrique Occidentale Française was formed.

3. On Bamba's teachings on ethnolinguistic parity as enshrined within Murid devotional communities and charismatic texts, see Ngom, *Muslims beyond the Arab World*, 41–69.

4. On Bamba's exiles as documented in French colonial texts, see Cheikh Anta Babou, *Fighting the Greater Jihad: Amadu Bamba and the Founding of the Muridiyya of Senegal, 1853–1913* (Athens: Ohio University Press, 2007), 115–61.

5. See Allen F. Roberts, Mary Nooter Roberts, Gassia Armenian, and Ousmane Gueye, *A Saint in the City: Sufi Arts of Urban Senegal* (Los Angeles: University of California, Los Angeles, Fowler Museum of Cultural History, 2003).

6. My use of these terms—"symbolic capital" and "accommodation"—is based on precedents in David Robinson's *Paths of Accommodation: Muslim Societies and French Colonial Authorities in Sénégal and Mauritania, 1880–1920* (Athens: Ohio University Press, 2000). See also Donal B. Cruise O'Brien, *The Mourides of Senegal: The Political and Economic Organization of an Islamic Brotherhood* (Oxford: Clarendon Press, 1971).

7. On the endurance of this segregation and its implications, see Kane, *Non-Europhone Intellectuals*.

8. Harrison, *France and Islam*, 9–56. Harrison nonetheless documents that such perceived antagonisms coincided with the French colonial administration's early reliance on Muslim intermediaries.

9. Governor Faidherbe (1860), cited in Didier Hamoneau, *Vie et Enseignement du Cheikh Ahmadou Bamba* (Beirut: Al-Bouraq, 1998), 51.

10. Governor de Lamothe, speech to Senegalese interpreters, 1893 (published in 1894), cited in Alice Conklin, *A Mission to Civilize: The Republican Idea of Empire in France and West Africa, 1895–1930* (Stanford: Stanford University Press, 1997), 84. Robert Arnaud, first head of the Bureau of Muslim Affairs established by Governor Roume in 1906, declared in a similar vein that "Islam should never be anything other than religious belief [and] must not evolve in the sense of Turko-Egyptian nationalism nor in the political traditions of Muslim states, but in the sense of French Ideas"; see Harrison, *France and Islam*, 97.

11. General de Trentinian, Governor of French Sudan, Annual Report of 1898, cited in Harrison, *France and Islam*, 34.

12. Trentinian, cited in Harrison, *France and Islam*, 34.

13. Governor Merleau Ponty (1908–14), paraphrased in Harrison, *France and Islam*, 51.

14. Harrison, *France and Islam*, 22–33.

15. This is Conklin's translation of the original French *mise en valeur* (see *Mission to Civilize*, 79–80).

16. A program of economic consolidation (*mise en valeur*) intensified under the Roume administration (1902–8), with infrastructural development serving a colonially consolidated regional market; see Conklin, *Mission to Civilize*, 79–80. The French continued to rule from the coasts and to implement a program of unequal development between urban coastal centers (St. Louis, Dakar) and a rural interior still governed by a brutal legal code known as the *indigénat*. The elimination of the *indigénat* and the electoral enfranchisement of rural areas in the 1940s inaugurated a trend of political alliances brokered between French-educated urban elites and Muslim clerics with a strong rural following. See Sheldon Gellar, *Senegal: An African Nation between Islam and the West*, 2nd ed. (Boulder: Westview Press, 1995), 9–11.

17. Conklin, *Mission to Civilize*, 84.

18. Ponty, Governor-General of L'Afrique Occidentale Française, circular, May 8, 1911, cited in Harrison, *France and Islam*, 51–52. Paul Marty reports on two circulars issued by the regional governor-general (May 8 and September 18, 1911) "suppressing" the administrative use of Arabic, amid broader reforms in customary law and Islamic tribunal courts; Paul Marty, *Études sur l'Islam au Sénégal*, vols. 1–2 (Paris: Ernest Leroux, 1917), vol. 2, 213–14. Marty (qtd. in Harrison, *France and Islam*, 128–29) suggests that Arabic's marginalization was already beginning upon Ponty's appointment in 1908 and was assiduously advanced by subsequent governors-general through at least 1918. Such changes also supported Ponty's aim to bypass the use of provincial chiefs and limit the influence of traditional marabouts in favor of a newly trained francophone elite, selected independently of traditional aristocratic lineages (an objective known as Ponty's *politique des races*, first articulated in 1909). See Conklin, *Mission to Civilize*, 115, 118.

19. One might, in this regard, discern the influence of Alfred Le Chatelier on his protégé Paul Marty, the French colonial official who changed the course of French Islamic policy in West Africa after 1912. Le Chatelier and his *Revue du Monde Musulman* would remain the exclusive publisher of Marty's ethnographic work; see Harrison, *France and Islam*, 115.

20. Phérivong, cited in Harrison, *France and Islam*, 86.

21. Harrison, *France and Islam*, 51, 64.

22. Harrison, *France and Islam*, 64.

23. Harrison, *France and Islam*, 108. Marty's own suggestion to romanize local vernaculars in addition to promoting French, as presented in *Études sur l'Islam au Sénégal*, vol. 2, 106–8, appears to have nonetheless gone unheeded.

24. This was the case after French colonial officials were forced to reassess their reliance on local interpreters in St. Louis, after the deaths of several of their most reliable translators in the closing decade of the nineteenth century. See Robinson, *Paths of Accommodation*, 80–85; and Harrison, *France and Islam*, 33–49.

25. Ponty, cited in Conklin, *Mission to Civilize*, 131.

26. Conklin, *Mission to Civilize*, 132.

27. Harrison, *France and Islam*, 11, 57.

28. Harrison, *France and Islam*, 62–65.

29. Marty, *Études sur l'Islam au Sénégal*, vol. 2, 26–28. On Marty's ethnographic overview of Mauritanian and Murid elites, see vol. 1, 1–65, 217–300. For an overview of scholarship on French colonial and Murid "accommodation," see Ngom, *Muslims beyond the Arab World*, 12–16.

30. Harrison, *France and Islam*, 91–117.

31. Marty, *Études sur l'Islam au Sénégal*, vol. 1, 281.

32. Marty, *Études sur l'Islam au Sénégal*, vol. 1, 281. See also vol. 2, 3–4, 295, for comparable restatements. Marty cites the *Questions Diplomatiques et Coloniales* inquiry on the "future of Islam" (May 15, 1901) to justify this characterization of Islamic "heterodoxy" among racially diverse Muslim communities and discerns within Senegal's *Islam noir* a "latent and confused patriotism" that threatens to further fracture along rival ethnic lines among black Muslims (vol. 1, 285–86).

33. Marty, *Études sur l'Islam au Sénégal*; and Harrison, *France and Islam*, 108–9.

34. Marty, cited in Harrison, *France and Islam*, 108.

35. Marty, cited in Harrison, *France and Islam*, 128–29. For a compelling deconstruction of these colonial impressions, see Rudolph Ware, *The Walking Qur'an: Islamic Education, Embodied Knowledge, and History in West Africa* (Chapel Hill: University of North Carolina Press, 2014), 163–202.

36. The term "black neophyte" is Marty's, glossing Moroccan and Mauritanian Arab perceptions; see Marty, *Études sur l'Islam au Sénégal*, vol. 1, 270–71. The ethnographic notion of *Islam noir* developed soon after Marty took office as head of AOF's Muslim Affairs Bureau in 1912; his surveillance findings and policy recommendations were first published in 1917 as *Études sur l'Islam au Sénégal* through the *Revue du Monde Musulman*. See Harrison, *France and Islam*, 94–97, 105–17.

37. Robinson, *Paths of Accommodation*, 94–96, 231–35, on Sidiyya Baba's influence on French ethnographic codifications of *bayḍān/sudān*; and Harrison, *France and Islam*, 33–40, 111–36.

38. See Babou, *Fighting the Greater Jihad*, 58–60.

39. See Babou, *Fighting the Greater Jihad*, 117–21, on conflicting accounts and controversies over Bamba's tribunal and exile.

40. Though "Yoonu géej gi" was written by Ka, Murid sources claim that it draws from Bamba's own epistolary account of these events in "Jawabu Abdulatif." See Babou, *Fighting the Greater Jihad*, 126; and Ngom, *Muslims beyond the Arab World*, 121–22.

41. Cited in Babou, *Fighting the Greater Jihad,* 126 n. 61.

42. Robinson, *Paths of Accommodation,* 236.

43. Ahmadu Bamba Mbakke, "Asīru" (Touba, Senegal: Darou Khoudoss Touba, [n.d.]), 6 and 16, ll. 1–2, 49. My translation is informed by Sana Camara's version: Ahmadu Bamba, *Sheikh Ahmadu Bamba: Selected Poems,* trans. Sana Camara (Leiden: Brill, 2017), 73–79.

44. Mbakke, "Asīru," 8, l. 10.

45. Ngom, *Muslims beyond the Arab World,* 149–50.

46. Ahmadu Bamba Mbakke, "Jāwartu" (Touba, Senegal: Darou Khoudoss Touba, [n.d.]), ll. 25–27. Bamba's original term in this final line, "ahl al-Kitāb," "people of the book," may more literally mean "Christians," though it is commonly interpreted in this poem to refer to French colonizers. See Bamba, *Selected Poems,* 85.

47. A *karāma* is the miracle of a saint, not to be confused with the notion of *ʿijaz/mʿujiza,* the miracle of the Prophet's eloquence; see Babou, *Fighting the Greater Jihad,* 136.

48. After his return from exile in Gabon, Bamba rewrote many of his earlier poems informed by his new mastery of Arabic, including, for example, "Jadhb al-Qulūb" and "Munawwir al-Sudūr." See Babou, *Fighting the Greater Jihad,* 135 n. 100.

49. Ahmadu Bamba Mbakke, "Jadhb al-Qulūb," in *Majmūʿa Mubāraka li-Sheikhunā Ahmad al-Khadīm* (Touba, Senegal: Darou Khoudoss Touba, [n.d.]), 10, ll. 28–29.

50. Ahmadu Bamba Mbakke, "The Keys to Paradise" ["Mafātīḥ al-Jinān wa Maghlāqa al-Nirāni"], emphasis added, translation based on an excerpt in Fernand Dumont, *La pensée religieuse d'Amadou Bamba* (Dakar: Les Nouvelles Éditions Africaines, 1975), 296–97.

51. Ahmadu Bamba Mbakke, "Light of Two Hearths" ["Nūru al-Dārayni"], translation based on excerpts in Dumont's *La pensée religieuse d'Amadou Bamba,* 287–89, 292–93.

52. On colonial French constraints over Bamba's movements, see Ngom, *Muslims beyond the Arab World,* 115–23, 155–59, 184–90.

53. Babou, *Fighting the Greater Jihad,* 61, 143–52.

54. See Babou, *Fighting the Greater Jihad,* 152; and Ngom, *Muslims beyond the Arab World,* 174–77, 196–97, 241–42.

55. Ngom, *Muslims beyond the Arab World,* 174–77; and Babou, *Fighting the Greater Jihad,* 148–52.

56. Ahmadu Bamba Mbakke, "Masālik al-Jinān" (Touba, Senegal: Darou Khoudoss Touba, [n.d.]), 5.

57. On these pejorative terms, see Ngom, *Muslims beyond the Arab World,* 25–29, 144; Hall, *History of Race in Muslim West Africa,* 9–16; Sharkey, *Living with Colonialism,* 16–24; Hayek, "Whitewashing Arabic for Global Consumption," 93, 97–99; and Eve Troutt Powell, *Tell This in My Memory: Stories of Enslavement from Egypt, Sudan and the Ottoman Empire* (Stanford: Stanford University Press, 2012), 1–6.

58. Babou, *Fighting the Greater Jihad,* 149–50.

59. Sidiyya Baba, cited in Babou, *Fighting the Greater Jihad,* 62. See Robinson, *Paths of Accommodation,* 184.

60. Sidiyya Baba, cited in Babou, *Fighting the Greater Jihad,* 62, originally transcribed in Paul Marty, "Cheikh Sidiya et sa voie," *Revue du Monde Musulman* 31 (1915–16): 29–133, at 39.

61. Marty, *Études sur l'Islam au Sénégal,* vol. 2, 31, 57.

62. Marty, *Études sur l'Islam au Sénégal,* vol. 2, 3–4, 15–16, 78–81.

63. Marty, *Études sur l'Islam au Sénégal*, vol. 2, 78–81.

64. Marty, *Études sur l'Islam au Sénégal*, vol. 1, 58.

65. Robinson, *Paths of Accommodation*.

66. Harrison, *France and Islam*, 157.

67. Local commemorations of the *hijra* in Senegal developed through the Murid practice of *maggal* (meaning "commemoration" in Wolof), an annual pilgrimage by Bamba's followers to Bamba's last location in Senegal (Touba) before his trial and exile to Gabon. See Ngom, *Muslims beyond the Arab World*, 190–92; and Cheikh Anta Babou, "Contesting Space, Shaping Places: Making Room for the Muridiyya in Colonial Senegal, 1912–45," *Journal of African History* 46, no. 3 (2005): 405–26.

68. On French impressions of the Murid's growing economic autonomy, see Ponty, cited in Harrison, *France and Islam*, 113. See also Cruise O'Brien, *Mourides of Senegal*, 52, 163–87.

69. Ngom, *Muslims beyond the Arab World*, 19–29.

70. See Fallou Ngom, "Linguistic Resistance in the Murid Speech Community in Senegal," *Journal of Multilingual and Multicultural Development* 23, no. 3 (2002): 214–26; and Ngom, "Aḥmadu Bamba's Pedagogy."

71. "Rapport confidentiel sur les mourides d'Amadou Bamba, Janvier 1914," cited in Babou, *Fighting the Greater Jihad*, 171–72.

72. Ahmadu Bamba Mbakke, "Nahju Qaḍāʿi al-Ḥāji," cited in Babou, *Fighting the Greater Jihad*, 85, translation modified.

73. Warner, *Tongue-Tied Imagination*, 118–51; and Arame Fal, "OSAD's Experience in the Publishing of Books in National Languages," in *Literacy and Linguistic Diversity in Global Perspective: An Intercultural Exchange with African Countries*, ed. Neville Alexander and Brigitta Busch (Strasbourg: Council of Europe Publishing, 2007), 31–38.

74. Ngom, *Muslims beyond the Arab World*, 57–69.

75. Quoted in Ngom, *Muslims beyond the Arab World*, 63. Bamba's statements within the anecdote invoke the Prophet Muhammad's final sermon.

76. Sëriñ Muusaa Ka, "Barsan," cited in Albert Gérard, *African Language Literatures: An Introduction to the Literary History of Sub-Saharan Africa* (Harlow, U.K.: Longman, 1981), 73. On Ka's defense of Wolof as a devotional language, see Ngom, *Muslims beyond the Arab World*, 59–67.

77. Sëriñ Muusaa Ka, "Taxmiis bub Wolof," quoted in Ngom, *Muslims beyond the Arab World*, 60.

78. Ngom, *Muslims beyond the Arab World*, 60.

79. Conklin, *Mission to Civilize*, 138.

80. The earliest Wolof vocabularies were transcribed into English and Dutch in the late seventeenth and early eighteenth centuries, but early missionary attempts to transcribe native languages in Latin script were largely unsystematic and limited in impact. See Desmond Cole, "The History of African Linguistics to 1945," in *Current Trends in Linguistics: Linguistics in Sub-Saharan Africa*, vol. 7, ed. Thomas E. Sebeok (The Hague: Mouton, 1971), 18; P.E.H. Hair, "The Contribution of Early Linguistic Material to the History of West Africa," in *Language and History in Africa*, ed. David Dalby (New York: Africana Publishing Corporation, 1970), 52; and Judith T. Irvine, "Minerva's Orthography: Early Colonial Projects for Print Literacy in African Languages," *Social Dynamics* 45, no. 1 (2019): 26–52.

81. On the history and broader impact of this marginalization of Arabic and Arabic script literacies in Senegal, see Kane, *Non-Europhone Intellectuals*; and Ngom, *Muslims beyond the Arab World*, 4–10, 245–51.

82. See Sana Camara, "*A'jami* Literature in Senegal: The Example of Sëriñ Muusaa Ka, Poet and Biographer," trans. R. H. Mitsch, *Research in African Literatures* 28, no. 3 (1997): 163–82; and Ngom, "Aḥmadu Bamba's Pedagogy."

83. Fallou Ngom, "West African Manuscripts in Arabic and African Languages and Digital Preservation," in *Oxford Research Encyclopedia of African History* (Oxford University Press, 2017), 1–28, accessed December 31, 2019, https://hdl.handle.net/2144/29017.

84. Fal, "OSAD's Experience," 35.

Notes to Chapter 4

1. On his pride of linguistic passing in Arabic, see Hamka, *Kenang-Kenangan Hidup II* [*Life Memoirs II*], 3rd ed. (Jakarta: Bulan Bintang, 1974), 120–21, 124–25. Hamka's memoirs present a relatively positive account of his pilgrimage, reserving more critical impressions for his journalistic writing (*Pelita Andalas*, August 2, 4, 6, and 13, 1927). See James R. Rush, *Hamka's Great Story: A Master Writer's Vision of Islam for Modern Indonesia* (Madison: University of Wisconsin Press, 2016), 63–65, on this contrast. *Jawi* is an Arabic ethnonym often used for Malay Southeast Asian pilgrims and communities, especially in the Arabian Peninsula. See Michael Francis Laffan, *Islamic Nationhood and Colonial Indonesia: The* Umma *below the Winds* (New York: Routledge, 2003). The term *jawi* is also an Arabic-derived designation for Malay written in Arabic or modified Arabic scripts. See Ricci, *Islam Translated*, 170–82. Following Laffan and Ricci, "Jawi" is capitalized as an ethnonym, not as a designation for Malay in Arabic script (*jawi*).

2. On this transformation within regional publishing, see Ahmat Adam, *The Vernacular Press and the Emergence of Modern Indonesian Consciousness, 1855–1913* (Ithaca: Cornell University Studies on Southeast Asia, 1995); Laffan, *Islamic Nationhood*, 142–80; and Kevin Fogg, "The Standardisation of the Indonesian Language and Its Consequences for Islamic Communities," *Journal of Southeast Asian Studies* 46, no. 1 (2015): 86–110. "Hamka" was an acronym the writer popularly employed in lieu of his full name, Hadji Abdul Malik Karim Amrullah.

3. Hamka's father was among the founders of the pan-Islamic Arabic-script periodical *al-Munir*. See Rush, *Hamka's Great Story*, 41–72.

4. Laffan, *Islamic Nationhood*, 180.

5. On the Muhammadiyah movement cofounded by Hamka's father, see Khairudin Aljunied, *Hamka and Islam: Cosmopolitan Reform in the Malay World* (Ithaca: Cornell University Press, 2018); and Rush, *Hamka's Great Story*, 53–67.

6. Farchad Poeradisastra, "Memang, Kebenaran Harus Tetap Disampaikan," in *Hamka di mata hati umat*, ed. Nasir Tamara, Buntaran Sanusi, and Vincent Djauhari (Jakarta: Sinar Harapan, 1983), 158.

7. See Rush, *Hamka's Great Story*, 136–40.

8. Hamka, "Pengaruh Huruf atas Bahasa dan Bangsa" ["The Influence of Script beyond Language and Nation"], *Hikmah* 107 (February 16, 1952): 18.

9. On this global process of "racialization," see Aydin, *Idea of the Muslim World*.

10. On *Islam dan Ideologi*, see Rush, *Hamka's Great Story*, 85–126.

11. See Fogg, "Standardisation."

12. See Hoffman, "Foreign Investment," 65.

13. Hoffman, "Foreign Investment," 65–71.

14. Hoffman, "Foreign Investment," 76–82, 87–89.

15. Hadler, *Places Like Home*, 319–30. The interregnum occurred after Napoleon's invasion of Holland.

16. Hadler, *Places Like Home*, 292–310. See also Olender, *Languages of Paradise*.

17. Hadler, *Places Like Home*, 303–13, 319–23.

18. Hadler, *Places Like Home*, 306.

19. Hoffman, "Foreign Investment," 74–77.

20. Hoffman, "Foreign Investment," 77.

21. Pijnappel (1860), summarized in Hoffman, "Foreign Investment," 77. This recommendation was also expressed in 1876 by J.R.P.F. Gonggrijp, a missionary society teacher and lecturer who trained officials for assignments to the Indies and also supported a transition to Latin orthography for Malay.

22. Holle (1860), cited in Steenbrink, *Dutch Colonialism and Indonesian Islam*, 79.

23. Steenbrink, *Dutch Colonialism and Indonesian Islam*, 78–79.

24. Holle, cited in Steenbrink, *Dutch Colonialism and Indonesian Islam*, 86.

25. This is Harry Benda's paraphrase of Snouck Hurgronje's ideas on "Association." See Benda, *Crescent and the Rising Sun*, 27.

26. See Benda, *Crescent and the Rising Sun*, 24–25; and Laffan, *Islamic Nationhood*, 90–95.

27. Snouck Hurgronje, cited in Laffan, *Islamic Nationhood*, 90. See also Jan Just Witkam, "Christiaan Snouck Hurgronje: Lives and Afterlives," in *Scholarship in Action: Essays on the Life and Work of Christiaan Snouck Hurgronje (1857–1936)*, ed. Léon Buskens, Jan Just Witkam, and Annemarie van Sandwijk (Leiden: Brill, 2021), 89–92; and Wim van den Doel, "Snouck Hurgronje and the Colonial Administration of the Dutch East Indies," in *Scholarship in Action: Essays on the Life and Work of Christiaan Snouck Hurgronje (1857–1936)*, ed. Léon Buskens, Jan Just Witkam, and Annemarie van Sandwijk (Leiden: Brill, 2021), 292–94.

28. On the Acehnese case, see Anthony Reid, *The Blood of the People: Revolution and the End of Traditional Rule in Northern Sumatra* (Kuala Lumpur: Oxford University Press, 1979), 21–24; and Bukhari Daud, *Writing and Reciting Acehnese: Perspectives on Language and Literature in Aceh* (Ph.D. dissertation, University of Melbourne, 1997), 115–39.

29. Laffan, *Islamic Nationhood*, 145, referencing *Circular* 468 (May 22, 1894). Snouck Hurgronje played a vital but controversial role in native administration and educational reform during this time. See van den Doel, "Snouck Hurgronje and the Colonial Administration of the Dutch East Indies"; and Kees Van Dijk, "The Scholar and the War Horse: The Aceh War, Snouck Hurgronje, and Van Heutz," in *Scholarship in Action: Essays on the Life and Work of Christiaan Snouck Hurgronje (1857–1936)*, ed. Léon Buskens, Jan Just Witkam, and Annemarie van Sandwijk (Leiden: Brill, 2021), 334–53.

30. See Hadler, *Places Like Home*, 324–28; and Hoffman, "Foreign Investment," 88–89. Snouck Hurgronje himself was nonetheless aware of the issue that dialectal differences could not be fully captured through romanization, textually distorting the realities of spoken Malay usage; see Rachel Leow, *Taming Babel: Language in the Making of Malaysia* (New York: Cambridge University Press, 2018), 85.

31. Although evidence points to French officials emulating Dutch policy precedents, it is possible that by 1910–11 Snouck Hurgronje borrowed the French term "Associationism" to describe policy ideals he had long promoted in the Dutch East Indies since the 1890s. See Léon Buskens and Annemarie van Sandwijk, "Introduction: Images of a Scholar in Action," in *Scholarship in Action: Essays on the Life and Work of Christiaan Snouck Hurgronje (1857–1936)*, ed. Léon Buskens, Jan Just Witkam, and Annemarie van Sandwijk (Leiden: Brill, 2021), 9–11; and Peter Hamburger, "Orientalist or Master Spy: The Career of Christiaan Snouck Hurgronje," in *Scholarship in Action: Essays on the Life and Work of Christiaan Snouck Hurgronje (1857–1936)*, ed. Léon Buskens, Jan Just Witkam, and Annemarie van Sandwijk (Leiden: Brill, 2021), 557–60. Whether the Dutch or the French were first to coin the term ("Association"), the correlative rise of a policy by this designation is indisputable. These parallel Dutch and French policy developments have yet to be extensively explored. On the early influence of late nineteenth-century Dutch policies (seen largely as a successful role model) in French colonies, see Betts, *Assimilation and Association in French Colonial Theory*, 35–38, 120–32. For additional scholarship on "Association" in the Dutch colonial context, see Elsbeth Locher-Scholten, "Association in Theory and Practice: The Composition of the Regency Council (ca. 1910–1920)," in *Between People and Statistics: Essays in Modern Indonesian History*, ed. Francien van Anroij and Dirk H. A. Kolff (The Hague: Martinus Nijhoff, 1979), 209–11. For a later comparison of both policies in French West Africa and the Dutch East Indies by one of Snouck Hurgronje's former French students, see Georges-Henri Bousquet, *La politique musulmane et coloniale des Pays-Bas* (Paris: P. Hartmann, 1939).

32. It may be safely assumed that Snouck Hurgronje's lectures enjoyed a French audience well before their June 1911 translation and formal publication through the *Revue du Monde Musulmane* (under Le Chatelier's direction). Snouck Hurgronje's policy recommendations were published in French at a time that closely coincided with the issuance of two circulars by French West Africa's Governor-General Ponty (in May 8, 1911, and September 18, 1911), "suppressing" the use of Arabic for administrative purposes and within the colonial court system. Both circulars also outlined official advisements on the reform of customary law and Islamic tribunal courts, a subject on which Snouck Hurgronje was a known expert and for which he later served as an advisor to French officials in Morocco. Reports of these circulars are found in Marty, *Études sur l'Islam au Sénégal*, vol. 2, 213–14, where Snouck Hurgronje's influence might be seen in passages advising against the outward appearance of "religious persecution" but recommending an "immediate, vigorous, repressive action" against "politico-religious agitators" (see vol. 1, 291–92). See also Marty's notes on Hajj surveillance (vol. 2, 24–25), a second subject on which Snouck Hurgronje was a known authority. Both Marty and Snouck Hurgronje were notably publishing their recommendations through the *Revue du Monde Musulman*.

33. Anderson, *Imagined Communities*, 45. See also Hendrik M. J. Maier, "From Heteroglossia to Polyglossia: The Creation of Malay and Dutch in the Indies," *Indonesia* 56 (October 1993): 57; and Adam, *Vernacular Press*, 59–78.

34. Although van Ophuijsen was instructed by Snouck Hurgronje to follow the voweling standards of the "cultivated Malays of insular Riau," he appears to have fallen back on the West Sumatranese Minang dialect in his postulation of a romanized standard; see Hoffman, "Foreign Investment," 87–90. See also Hadler, *Places Like Home*, 327–29. Van Ophuijsen's orthographic work was followed by an authoritative grammar in 1910; see Maier, "From Heteroglos-

sia to Polyglossia," 55. The widespread colonial adoption of this standard began in 1902, when J. H. Abendanon (colonial director of education) decreed that van Ophuijsen's spelling would be used in Dutch-mandated school systems. See also Doris Jedamski, "Balai Pustaka: A Colonial Wolf in Sheep's Clothing," *Archipel* 44, no. 1 (1992): 24.

35. Hadler, *Places Like Home*, 302. The Dutch colonial bureau and publisher for popular literature (Balai Pustaka) was nationalized in the postindependence context.

36. Hadler, *Places Like Home*, 294.

37. Hamka ("Pengaruh Huruf") highlights Arabic's lexical influences on Malay and its historic use as a political medium to justify Indonesia's return to the Arabic script.

38. See Laffan, *Islamic Nationhood*, 179–80.

39. See Hamka, "Tjatetan Editorial: Menjamboet Kongres Bahasa Indonesia," *Pedoman Masjarakat* 25 (June 22, 1938): 481.

40. Rush, *Hamka's Great Story*, 69.

41. *Pedoman Masjarakat* was published in Medan, North Sumatra, from 1936 to 1941. On these controversies, see, for example, Hamka's editorial "Fikiran Kita: Islam dan Nasional" ["Our Thoughts: Islam and the National"], *Pedoman Masjarakat* 42 (October 16, 1940): 825. Hamka's defense of Sukarno further progresses in an editorial series entitled "Faham Soekarno" ("Understanding Sukarno"), published in three parts, in *Pedoman Masjarakat* 18 (May 1, 1940): 344–45; 19 (May 8, 1940): 365–66; 20 (May 15, 1940): 385–86.

42. Rush, *Hamka's Great Story*, 86–87.

43. Hamka, "Islam dan kebangsaan," *Pedoman Masjarakat* 11 (March 16, 1938): 201.

44. For an overview, see Rush, *Hamka's Great Story*, 86–88. See also Hamka, *Negara Islam* (Padang Panjang, Indonesia: Penerbit Anwar Rasjid Padang Pandjang, 1946), 39–41, 82; and Hamka, *Islam dan Demokrasi* (Jakarta: Tjerdas, 1945).

45. Hamka, *Negara Islam*, 58–59; and Hamka, *Islam dan Demokrasi*, 47. See also Rush, *Hamka's Great Story*, 85–86.

46. Hamka, *Negara Islam*, 35, 92; and Hamka, *Islam dan Demokrasi*, 33, 35. See also Rush, *Hamka's Great Story*, 86–87.

47. Hamka, "Islam dan kebangsaan," *Pedoman Masjarakat* 11 (March 16, 1938): 201.

48. Hamka, "Islam dan kebangsaan" ["Islam and Nationalism"], *Pedoman Masjarakat*, January 4, 1939, 5.

49. Hamka, "Islam dan kebangsaan," *Pedoman Masjarakat*, January 4, 1939, 4.

50. Hamka, *Pedoman Masjarakat*, January 4, 1939, 26–27.

51. See Suleiman, *Arabic in the Fray*, 83–92. Some scholars have controversially considered this ideological alignment in nationalist writing to be the *shuʿūbiyya* currents of emergent nationalisms. See, for example, Sami Hanna and George Gardner, "*Al-Shuʿūbiyya* Up-Dated: A Study of the 20th Century Revival of an Eighth Century Concept," *Middle East Journal* 20, no. 3 (Summer 1966): 335–51; and Sami Hanna and George Gardner, *Arab Socialism: A Documentary Survey* (Leiden: Brill, 1969).

52. Between 1938 and 1940, Hamka tended to emphasize Indonesian cultural and linguistic autonomy while claiming the sustained ritual importance of Arabic. See, for example, Hamka, "Menjamboet Kongres Bahasa Indonesia"; and Hamka, "Tjatatan Editorial: Bahasa Indonesia di Volksraad," *Pedoman Masjarakat*, July 13, 1938, 541.

53. Hamka, "Bahasa didalam sembahjang," *Pedoman Masjarakat* 37 (September 11, 1940):

723–24. See also Hamka, "Soal2 Islam: Sembahjang dalam bahasa sendiri," *Pedoman Masjarakat*, August 14, 1940, 643.

54. Hamka claimed that conversationally speaking in Qur'anic Arabic was as odd as the speech of a Dutch Orientalist who, fresh off the boat upon arriving in Indonesia, addressed locals as though reading from a book in classical Malay. See Hamka, *Pedoman Masjarakat* 35 (August 28, 1940): 687–88.

55. Hamka, *Pedoman Masjarakat* 35 (August 28, 1940): 687–88.

56. See Hamka's postindependence work, *Islam dan Adat Minangkabau* (Jakarta: Pustaka Panjimas, 1984), as a counterpoint. The publication date and circumstances of prohibition are mentioned in Hamka, *Kenang-Kenangan Hidup II*, 1st ed. (Jakarta: Usaha Penerbitan Gapura, 1951), 23. His other earlier works before his shift to romanized publishing include a series of sermons written in Arabic, *Khatīb al-Umma* (*Address of the* Umma, 1925), and a story written in Minang dialect in Arabic script, *Si Sabariah* (1927–28).

57. Hamka, "Berita memperkenalkan," *Pedoman Masjarakat*, January 20, 1936, 1.

58. Hamka (*Kenang-Kenangan Hidup II*, 3rd ed., 31) explains that this original Arabic version was drawn from a literary textbook entitled *Bahrul Adab*; see also Hamka, *Kenang-Kenangan Hidup II*, 1st ed., 10–13.

59. Hamka, *Laila Madjnoen* (Jakarta: Balai Poestaka, 1932), 15–16, 18, 64.

60. Hamka, *Laila Madjnoen*, 3–4.

61. Hamka, *Laila Madjnoen*, 18.

62. Hamka, *Laila Madjnoen*, 50–52.

63. Hamka, *Laila Madjnoen*, 7–8, emphasis added; Arabic terms remain untranslated in keeping with the original.

64. Hamka, *Laila Madjnoen*, 9. The original reads *gadjil*; I presume that this is a typo of *gandjil* (strange).

65. Hamka, *Laila Madjnoen*, 5.

66. On this fictionalized utopianism and egalitarianism in the Hijaz, see Hamka, *Di Bawah Lindoengan Ka'bah* [*Beneath the Sanctuary of the Ka'bah*] (Jakarta: Balai Poestaka, 1938), 5–6, 23, 49–50, 52.

67. For examples of these appearances of Arabic in the Malay narrative, see Hamka, *Di Bawah Lindoengan Ka'bah*, 6–7, 35, 44, 47–49, where Arabic references appear religiously didactic.

68. Hamka, *Di Bawah Lindoengan Ka'bah*, 35, 47.

69. The Indonesian language was declared an emblem of national identity by the Indonesian nationalist youth movement in 1928 and became a topic of public scrutiny after the first natively organized conference on the Indonesian language in 1938. See Fogg, "Standardisation."

70. *Di Bawah Lindoengan Ka'bah* (*Beneath the Sanctuary of the Ka'bah*) idealizes the Hijaz as a utopian space and sanctuary for Indies pilgrims, whereas Hamka's most renowned novel, *Tenggelamnja Kapal "Van der Wijck"* (*The Sinking of the* Van der Wijck *Ship*), was inspired by the Egyptian author al-Manfalūṭī's text—itself an Arabic translation of a French novel (Alphonse Karr, *Sous les Tilleuls*); Hamka, *Tenggelamnja Kapal "Van der Wijck"* [*The Sinking of the* Van der Wijck *Ship*] (Jakarta: Balai Poestaka, 1939). *Di Bawah Lindoengan Ka'bah* and *Tenggelamnja Kapal "Van der Wijck"* were first published serially in *Pedoman Masjarakat*, before

their later publication by the colonial Dutch publishing house Balai Poestaka. See Alphonse Karr, *Sous les Tilleuls* (Paris: Michel Lévy Frères, 1857); and Muṣṭafā Luṭfī al-Manfalūṭī, *Mājdūlīn aw-Taḥta Ẓilāl al-Zayzafūn, Ta'līf Alfūns Kār* (Beirut: Dār al-Thaqāfa, 1969).

71. Anderson's precise term is "inner pilgrim" (*Imagined Communities*, 120).

72. The novel's self-referential aspect complements Hamka's journalistic writing in the 1930s and early 1940s, praising Sumatranese writers as the vanguards of Indonesian literary modernism; see among his *Pedoman Masjarakat* columns ("Kebudayaan" and "Dasar Kebudayaan"), published under a pen name, Aboe Zakij [Hamka], *Pedoman Masjarakat* 32 (September 24, 1936): 629–31; *Pedoman Masjarakat* 33 (September 30, 1936): 651–52; and *Pedoman Masjarakat* 40 (November 25, 1936): 791–92.

73. See Hans van Miert, "The 'Land of the Future': The Jong Sumatranen Bond (1917–1930) and Its Image of the Nation," *Modern Asian Studies* 30, no. 3 (July 1996): 591–616.

74. This innovation is equally clear when comparing Hamka's adaptation with the French original (Alphonse Karr's *Sous les Tilleuls*) on which *Majdūlīn* was based. On Hamka's *Merantau ke Deli* (1940), see also Jeffrey Hadler, "Home, Fatherhood, Succession: Three Generations of Amrullahs in Twentieth-Century Indonesia," *Indonesia* 65 (April 1998): 135; and Jeffrey Hadler, *Muslims and Matriarchs: Cultural Resilience in Indonesia through Jihad and Colonialism* (Ithaca: Cornell University Press, 2008), 152–55.

75. For Anderson's claims on the Indonesian novel as an effectively secular genre, see *Imagined Communities*. See also Jonathan Culler, "Anderson and the Novel," *Diacritics* 29, no. 4 (1999): 20–39.

76. Hamka himself continued to use Arabic and Arabic script for private correspondence through the 1970s until his death in 1981; see Roesydi Hamka's *Pribadi dan Martabat Buya Prof. Hamka* (Jakarta: Pustaka Panjimas, 1981), 207–10.

77. Hamka, *Pedoman Masjarakat* 35 (August 28, 1940): 687–88.

78. Hamka, "Pengaruh Huruf."

79. See Jedamski, "Balai Pustaka"; and Hadler, *Places Like Home*.

80. Hamka, "Pengaruh Huruf," 18.

81. Hamka, "Mengapa Hamka Dipenjara?" ["Why Was Hamka Imprisoned?"], interview, *Al-Islam* (Kuala Lumpur), May 15, 1974, 10–11.

82. Hamka, "Pengaruh Huruf," 18.

83. Hamka, *Kenang-Kenangan ku di Malaya* (Singapore: Setia Derma, 1957), 110. While this was originally printed in Arabic script, *jawi* and *rumi* versions are available at the National Library of Malaysia (Perpustakaan Negara Malaysia) in Kuala Lumpur. For Hamka's critique of "Javanisms" as undemocratic and of Arabic's marginalized status in Indonesia, see 103–9, 116.

84. On the publication's context in 1957, see Rush, *Hamka's Great Story*, 124; and Fogg, "Standardisation."

85. Hamka, *Tafsir al-Azhar*. Rush (*Hamka's Great Story*, 177, 190, 198) notes that the exegesis was virtually a work of translation. On Hamka's imprisonment, see Hamka's interview, "Mengapa Hamka Dipenjara?"

86. For satirical reactions to Hamka's defense of Arabic in the 1950s, see B.S., "Hamka bisa Bahasa asing" ["Hamka Can Talk Foreign"], *Harian Rakyat*, October 23, 1954.

87. Anthony H. Johns, "Qur'anic Exegesis in the Malay-Indonesian World: An Introduc-

tory Survey," in *Approaches to the Qur'an in Contemporary Indonesia*, ed. Abdullah Saeed (London: Oxford University Press, 2005), 17–18.

88. Hamka, "Sambutan Hamka Pada Cetakan Pertama" ["Hamka's Statement on the First Edition"], in H. B. Jassin, *Al Qu'ran Bacaan Mulia*, 4th ed. (Jakarta: Yaco Jaya, 2002), xvi. On earlier controversies over Qur'anic translation into *jawi*, see Nico Kaptein, "'My Dear Professor 'Abd al-Ghaffar.' The Letters of Sayyid 'Uthman to C. Snouck Hurgronje as a Reflection of Their Relationship," in *Scholarship in Action: Essays on the Life and Work of Christiaan Snouck Hurgronje (1857–1936)*, ed. Léon Buskens, Jan Just Witkam, and Annemarie van Sandwijk (Leiden: Brill, 2021), 395–98.

89. Laffan, *Islamic Nationhood*, 144.

90. See also Fogg, "Standardisation."

91. Laffan, *Islamic Nationhood*, 144.

92. Hamka, "Berita memperkenalkan."

Notes to Chapter 5

1. Léopold Sédar Senghor, "Les nationalismes d'outremer et l'avenir des peuples de couleur" ["Overseas Nationalisms and the Future of Peoples of Color"], in *L'encyclopédie française: Le monde en devenir (histoire, évolution, prospective)*, vol. 20, ed. Gaston Berger, Lucien Febvre, and Pierre Renouvin (Paris: Larousse/Société nouvelle de l'encyclopédie française, 1959), 6–11.

2. Sukarno, cited in Richard Wright, *The Color Curtain: A Report on the Bandung Conference* (Jackson: University Press of Mississippi, 1995), 136–37.

3. Sukarno, cited in Wright, *Color Curtain*, 137.

4. Sukarno, *Collected Documents*, 9.

5. Wright, *Color Curtain*, 199–201.

6. Wright, *Color Curtain*, 201.

7. Wright, *Color Curtain*, 200–201.

8. Wright, *Color Curtain*, 200.

9. Wright, *Color Curtain*, 136.

10. Wright, *Color Curtain*, 139.

11. Wright, *Color Curtain*, 139–40.

12. Wright, *Color Curtain*, 218.

13. Sukarno, quoted in Bob Hering, *Soekarno: Founding Father of Indonesia, 1901–1945* (Leiden: Koninklijk Institut voor Taal-, Land- en Volkenkunde Press, 2002), 264. Although he promoted this separation, Sukarno publicly characterized himself among Indonesians as a "Muslim reformist" rather than a "secularist."

14. See James R. Rush, "Sukarno: Anticipating an Asian Century," in *Makers of Modern Asia*, ed. Ramachandra Guha (Cambridge: Harvard University Press, 2014), 178–81.

15. For more on Chairil Anwar's involvement in the independence struggle, see Boen Oemarjati, *Chairil Anwar: The Poet and His Language* (Leiden: Brill, 1972), xiii–xxvi; and Hering, *Soekarno*, 364–83.

16. See Wright, *Color Curtain*, 119–23.

17. See Greg Fealy and Ronit Ricci, eds., *Contentious Belonging: The Place of Minorities in*

Indonesia (Singapore: Institute of Southeast Asian Studies Publishing, 2019); and Chiara Formichi, ed., *Religious Pluralism in Indonesia: Threats and Opportunities for Democracy* (Ithaca: Cornell University Press, 2021).

18. Wright, *Color Curtain*, 60, 107.

19. Wright, *Color Curtain*, 218.

20. Sukarno, *Collected Documents*, 11, original emphasis. *Pancha Sila* (*Panca Sila*) refers to five precepts that embody the pluralist foundations of the newly independent Indonesian state as envisioned by Sukarno in the 1940s. See Rush, "Sukarno," 184–89.

21. Sukarno, *Collected Documents*, 10–11.

22. Sukarno, *Collected Documents*, 11.

23. Sukarno, *Collected Documents*, 11.

24. This translation is based on Santoso's version: "[Truths] are indeed different, but they are of the same kind, as there are no divisions in Truth." See Mpu Tantular and Suwito Santoso, *Sutasoma: A Study in Javanese Wajrayana* (New Delhi: International Academy of Indian Culture, 1975), 578.

25. Tantular and Santoso, *Sutasoma*, 78–79.

26. Sukarno, *Collected Documents*, 11. On the significance and afterlife of this nationalist precept, see Formichi, *Religious Pluralism*, 1–13.

27. Sukarno, *Collected Documents*, 11.

28. Sukarno, *Collected Documents*, 10.

29. For a broader discussion of this connection, see chapter 4; and Fogg, "Standardisation."

30. Benedict Anderson, *Language and Power: Exploring Political Cultures in Indonesia* (Ithaca: Cornell University Press, 1990), 123–51.

31. Lucy Montolalu and Leo Suryadinata, "National Language and Nation-Building: The Case of Bahasa Indonesia," in *Language, Nation and Development in Southeast Asia*, ed. Hock Guan Lee and Leo Suryadinata (Singapore: Institute of Southeast Asian Studies Publishing, 2007), 39–50.

32. Benedict Anderson, "Languages of Indonesian Politics," in *Language and Power*, 140. Anderson directed his rejoinder (originally published in 1966) to colleagues such as Clifford Geertz and Herbert Luethy, who characterized these developments in more negative terms. Such claims about the nationalization of the Indonesian language as an ideologically generative medium rather than a hollow inauthenticity anticipate Anderson's later arguments about nationalism and vernacular print languages in *Imagined Communities*.

33. Fogg ("Standardisation") observes that this administrative privileging of romanized print over Arabic and other indigenous scripts rendered "rendered illiterate" and less publicly visible many historically arabophone political brokers after independence, especially those based in central Indonesian and outlying islands.

34. Anderson, *Language and Power*, 138.

35. Anderson claims that "Dutch remained the inner language of elite discourse" (*Language and Power*, 138). On practices of "internal" translation, see Webb Keane, "Public Speaking: On Indonesian as the Language of the Nation," *Public Culture* 15, no. 3 (2003): 515–16; and Keith Foulcher, *Pujangga Baru: Literature and Nationalism in Indonesia, 1933–1942* (Bedford Park, Australia: Flinders University Asian Studies Monograph Series, 1980), 58. See also H. B. Jassin, *Chairil Anwar: Pelopor Angkatan 45*, 3rd ed. (Jakarta: Gunung Agung, 1968), 9–10, 39.

36. "Double-minded" here builds on Anderson's notion of "two-mindedness" (*Language and Power*, 123–44).

37. Ahmed Soekarno [Dutch-era spelling of Sukarno], *Under the Banner of Revolution*, vol. 1, 1st ed. (Jakarta: Publication Committee, 1966), 359, 380–85 (henceforth cited as *UBR*); corresponding in Indonesian to Sukarno's collected speeches in Ahmed Sukarno, *Dibawah Bendera Revolusi*, rev. ed. (Jakarta: Yayasan Bung Karno dan Penerbit Media Pressindo, 2015), 420, 443–49 (henceforth cited as *DBR*).

38. *Marxisant* is Anderson's term (*Language and Power*, 137).

39. Sukarno admired and carefully studied Jaurès's speeches; see Sukarno's "The Power of the Throat" (1940), in *DBR* 401, 681/*UBR* 342, 585–88.

40. Jean Jaurès, "Pour la laïque, discours prononcé à la chambre en deux fois, les 14 et 24 Janvier 1910," in *L'Esprit du socialisme, six études et discours* (Paris: Éditions Gonthier, 1964), 134. On this borrowing from Jaurès (who had originally been speaking in promotion of secular socialism), see Sukarno's Endeh letters, in *DBR* 381–82/*UBR* 323–25; and his "Memudakan Pengartian Islam," in *DBR* 447/*UBR* 383. See also Bernhard Dahm, *Sukarno and the Struggle for Indonesian Independence* (Ithaca: Cornell University Press, 1969), 184–85, 206–7.

41. Sukarno, "Endeh Letter No. 9," in *DBR* 376–78/*UBR* 319–21. These ideas would be resumed and developed throughout later articles of the 1940s; see, for example, *DBR* 441–49/*UBR* 381–85.

42. *DBR* 381–82/*UBR* 324–25, original emphasis. Variations of this passage recurred across Sukarno's many controversial *Pandji Islam* and *Pemandangan* articles in the 1940s. See *DBR* 365, 369, 378, 547/*UBR* 309, 313, 321, 471.

43. *DBR* 381–82/*UBR* 324–25 (reprinted in *UBR* 434–36/*DBR* 505–7).

44. *DBR* 447/*UBR* 384. Sukarno often called this tendency toward interpretive scriptural closure the "casuistry of the *fiqh* people," the practice of an *Islam bila kaifa* (an "unquestioning Islam") (*UBR* 377/*DBR* 443) or an *Islam Sontoloyo* (an "addlepated Islam") (*DBR* 545/*UBR* 469). See also Sukarno's 1940 article "Saya Kurang Dinamis" ["I'm Insufficiently Dynamic"], in *UBR* 436/*DBR* 508.

45. *UBR* 364/original found in *DBR* 426. Sukarno used the term *panta rei* in comparable ways, to emphasize the importance of interpretive openness when reading scripture; see *DBR* 415/*UBR* 354.

46. Sukarno, "Why Has Turkey Separated Religion from the State?" ["Apa Sebab Turki Memisah Agama dari Negara?"], in *UBR* 391/*DBR* 456.

47. *UBR* 391 /*DBR* 456.

48. *UBR* 434–35 /*DBR* 505–6.

49. On Sukarno's critique of what he called a "theocratic dictatorship" and ideas about representative democracy, see *DBR* 503–5/*UBR* 433–34.

50. *UBR* 364/*DBR* 426.

51. Critics accused Sukarno of being an advocate of ethnocentric tribalism (*taʿsubiyya*) and a sectarian defector (*khariji*) intent on factionalizing the *umma*. See *DBR* 379–83, 413–14, 499–508/*UBR* 322–27, 353, 429–36.

52. Sukarno, "Endeh Letters Nos. 4, 11, 12," in *DBR* 368–69, 381–82/*UBR* 312, 323–25.

53. Mangunkusomo, quoted by Sukarno at *DBR* 567. Sukarno—brazen and unrepentant—

received this as high praise. See Sukarno, "Menjadi Pembantu *Pemandangan*" (originally published June 1941), in *DBR* 563–69/*UBR* 483–88.

54. *UBR* 371/*DBR* 433.

55. Mohammad Natsir, "Persatuan Agama Dengan Negara" ["The Unity of Religion and State"], in *Agama dan Negara dalam Perspektif Islam* (Jakarta: Media Da'wah, 2001), 112–13.

56. See Mohammad Natsir, "Syekh yang Maha Hebat," reprint, in *Agama dan Negara dalam Perspektif Islam* (Jakarta: Media Da'wah, 2001), 109–10; and *UBR* 390/*DBR* 455.

57. *DBR* 429–31/*UBR* 368–69.

58. Sukarno mentions the Latin script's association with *takfir* in his Endeh letters (*DBR* 380–81/*UBR* 323–24), republished in *Pandji Islam*, 1940 (*DBR* 542/*UBR* 467), and discusses "dis-Arabization" in "Re-juvenating the Concept of Islam" ["Me-mudahkan Pengartian Islam"], in *DBR* 429–23/*UBR* 368–69. In his *Pandji Islam* articles of the 1940s, Sukarno often deliberately cites non-Muslim, European Orientalists to provoke, criticize, and mock his ideological opponents. See, for example, his citations of Snouck Hurgronje and Tor Andrae in *DBR* 448, 548–49/*UBR* 383–84, 472.

59. Sukarno's most notorious entry into this fray was an incendiary article entitled "Rejuvenating the Concept of Islam," in *DBR* 413–49/*UBR* 353–85.

60. See Hendrik M. J. Maier, "Chairil Anwar's 'Heritage: The Fear of Stultification': Another Side of Modern Indonesian Literature," *Indonesia* 43 (1987): 1–29. On Chairil Anwar's literary canonization in Indonesia, see Jassin, *Chairil Anwar*.

61. Goenawan Muhammad aptly notes that the Indonesian term *aku* "has a connotation of arrogance," egocentrism, and "boastfulness"; see Goenawan Muhammad, "Aku," in *Sidelines: Thought Pieces from Tempo Magazine* [*Catatan Pinggir*], trans. Jennifer Lindsay (Jakarta: Lontar Foundation Lontar, 1994), 12.

62. Jassin, *Chairil Anwar*, 168. The poem was first published in November 1948, after a rival Islamist government (the Negara Islam Indonesia) and a communist rebellion (the "Madiun Affair") threatened Sukarno's republican nationalist leadership. See M. C. Ricklefs, *A History of Modern Indonesia since c. 1200*, 4th ed. (Stanford: Stanford University Press, 2008), 264–68; and Kevin Fogg, *Indonesia's Islamic Revolution* (Cambridge: Cambridge University Press, 2020), 105–22.

63. Rush, "Sukarno," 183.

64. Herbert Feith, *The Decline of Constitutional Democracy in Indonesia* (Ithaca: Cornell University Press, 1962), 24–25, 34.

65. Jassin (*Chairil Anwar*, 46–47) notes the likely influence on Chairil of Ezra Pound's "A pact with Walt Whitman" (particularly Pound's line: "we have one sap and one root"—"kau dan aku satu zat satu urat"). If Pound's poem was indeed an inspiration for Chairil's, it reinforces the affective transformation central to Chairil's poem, shifting from resentment and rivalry to a kind of truce (as was the case in Pound's short poem dedicated to Whitman as a rival). Chairil's choice of diction, *zat*, meaning "essence of the self," distinctly connects through Arabic and the Malay language to theologically oriented explanations of metaphysical unity. See Vladimir Braginsky, *Nada-Nada Islam dalam Sastera Melayu Klasik* [*Islamic Tones in Classical Malay Literature*] (Kuala Lumpur: Dewan Bahasa dan Pustaka Kementerian Pendidikan Malaysia, 1994), 17–18. *Zat*, in other words, is not a term or concept that borrows from an

English original, nor does it quite align with the solipsism/individualism (*ke-akuan*) for which Chairil is elsewhere known in Malay.

66. Chairil Anwar, "A Pact with Brother 'Karno," in *The Voice of the Night: Complete Poetry and Prose of Chairil Anwar*, rev. bilingual ed., trans. Burton Raffel, Southeast Asia Series no. 89 (Athens: Ohio University Center for International Studies, 1993), 127, translation modified.

67. See Masduki, *Public Service Broadcasting and Post-authoritarian Indonesia* (New York: Palgrave, 2020), 117–68.

68. See Braginsky, *Nada-Nada Islam*, 17–18.

69. See *UBR* 378 and 375, reappearing in *UBR* 354, 359, 368–71/*DBR* 415, 420, 433, 438. On the original controversial context of *panta rei*, see Dahm, *Sukarno and the Struggle*, 188.

70. *UBR* 371, 375.

71. *UBR* 391, 467–68. Goenawan Mohamad offers an overview of these rhetorical flourishes, concluding that Sukarno viewed Islam as a "liberating political energy" that resists "interpretive monopolization" by clerical circles. See Goenawan Mohamad, "Bung Karno dan Islam," in *Pembentuk Sejarah: Pilihan Tulisan Goenawan Mohamad*, ed. Zaim Rofiqi, Candra Gautama, Akhmad Sahal, and Rustam F. Mandayun (Jakarta: Kepustakaan Populer Gramedia, 2021), 10–34 [reprint of Goenawan Mohamad, "Bung Karno dan Islam," blogpost, September 8, 2010, accessed July 1, 2016, http://goenawanmohamad.com/2010/09/08/bung-karno-dan-islam/]; and Mohammad Ridwan Lubis, *Sukarno dan modernisme Islam* (Depok, Indonesia: Komunitas Bambu, 2010), 135–232.

72. Naziroeddin Rachmat, "'Api' Islam Apa Jang Dimaksudkan Oleh Bung Karno?" ["What 'Fire' of Islam Does Brother 'Karno Mean?"], *Hikmah*, May 26, 1956, 7. Sukarno continued to use the term *api Islam* after independence with such insistence that his collected speeches at religious events were republished under the title *Api Islam* in the 1960s. This article from the 1950s responds to Sukarno's continued attachment to the controversial turn of phrase.

73. Rachmat ("'Api' Islam Apa?" 7) also remarks that the *idhafatized* term is a grammatical absurdity in Arabic with no basis in Qur'anic scripture. On earlier exchanges from the 1940s, see Deliar Noer, *The Modernist Muslim Movement in Indonesia, 1900–1942* (London: Oxford University Press, 1973), 275–95, 318–24.

74. Rachmat, "'Api' Islam Apa?" 7.

75. Rachmat, "'Api' Islam Apa?" 7.

76. *UBR* 375.

77. This may be especially true given the poet's reputation for extreme deliberation and precision in his choice of diction. Chairil's poems were painstakingly reworked, as attested by his frequent editor and publisher H. B. Jassin. See Jassin, *Chairil Anwar*, 14; and Oemarjati, *Chairil Anwar*, xxiii.

78. Chairil Anwar, "Hoppla!" in *Voice of the Night*, 178. For the original Indonesian, see Jassin, *Chairil Anwar*, 139–40. This "manifesto" was first published in December 1945 as the transcript of one of Chairil Anwar's radio broadcasts. See Rudolf Mrázek, "Bridges of Hope: Senior Citizens' Memories," *Indonesia* 70 (2000): 39–40.

79. Anwar, "Hoppla!" 169.

80. See Maier, "Chairil Anwar's 'Heritage'"; and Keith Foulcher, "Politics and Literature in Independent Indonesia: The View from the Left," *Southeast Asian Journal of Social Science* 15, no. 1 (1987): 83–103.

81. Chairil Anwar, "Four Miscellaneous Aphorisms," in *Voice of the Night*, 178.

82. On public debates about the Indonesian language's ideological orientations and modes of lexical enrichment, see Fogg, "Standardisation."

83. See Jassin, *Chairil Anwar*; and Maier, "Chairil Anwar's 'Heritage.'"

84. Chairil Anwar, "At the Mosque," in *Voice of the Night*, 48–49.

85. See Jassin, *Chairil Anwar*; Maier, "Chairil Anwar's 'Heritage'"; and Sjuman Djaya's screenplay, *Aku: Berdasarkan Perjalanan Hidup dan Karya Penyair Chairil Anwar*, 2nd ed. (Jakarta: Metafor Publishing, 2003).

86. Chairil Anwar, "Prayer," in *Voice of the Night*, 69.

87. A collection of pastiches by students of a reformist (Muhammadiyah) Islamic school in 1990, for example, reinforces this perception of Chairil as a protean figure, with compositions ranging from emulations of Chairil's reverential poetry to staged rebukes of the poet as a "godless" atheist. See *Suara Jiwa: Antoloji Puisi Peringatan 41 Wafatnya Chairil Anwar* [*Voices of the Soul: An Anthology of Poetry Commemorating 41 Years since the Death of Chairil Anwar*], Institut Keguruan dan Ilmu Pendidikan Muhammadiyah Purworejo (Central Java), 1990.

88. Hamka's sermon reinterprets the final lines of Chairil's poem as a repentant deathbed prayer or a prayer spoken by a departed soul; Hamka, *Gema Islam* 10 (June 15, 1962): 30–33.

89. See Ricklefs, *History of Modern Indonesia*, 294–321; Benedict Anderson, "Bung Karno and the Fossilization of Soekarno's Thought," *Indonesia* 74 (2002): 1–19; and, on the reception history of Chairil's poetry between New and Old Order critics, Maier, "Chairil Anwar's 'Heritage,'" 25–28.

90. The satirical short story, "Langit Makin Mendung," was published under a pseudonym. Jassin's translation was first published as H. B. Jassin, *Al Qu'ran Bacaan Mulia*, 1st ed. (Jakarta: Djambatan, 1978).

91. See H. B. Jassin, *Kontroversi Al-Qur'anul Karim Bacaan Mulia* (Jakarta: Dinas Kebudayaan Propinsi DKI Jakarta bekerja sama dengan Dokumentasi Sastra H. B. Jassin Pusat, 2000); and Webb Keane, "Divine Text, National Language, and Their Publics: Arguing an Indonesian Qur'an," *Comparative Studies in Society and History* 60, no. 4 (2018): 758–85. Jassin fielded accusations that his Indonesian version had the "smell of Dutch and English translations" (*Kontroversi*, 374). See also Hamka, "Sambutan Hamka Pada Cetakan Pertama."

92. This observation builds from Warner's analogy in *Tongue-Tied Imagination*, 5–7.

93. On these orthographic changes and lexical enrichments, see Fogg, "Standardisation"; and Hoffman, "Foreign Investment."

94. Anderson, *Imagined Communities*, 134.

Notes to Chapter 6

1. See Saïd Aburish, *Nasser* (New York: St. Martin's Press/Thomas Dunne Books, 2004), 29–86; and Reem Abou-El-Fadl, "Building Egypt's Afro-Asian Hub: Infrastructures of Solidarity and the 1957 Cairo Conference," *Journal of World History* 30, nos. 1/2 (2019): 171–73.

2. See Radwan, *Egyptian Colloquial Poetry*, 1–7, 37–43.

3. Marilyn Booth, "Fu'ād Ḥaddād," in *The Routledge Encyclopedia of Arabic Literature*, ed. Julie Scott Meisami and Paul Starkey (New York: Routledge, 1998), 260.

4. This incisive characterization of Ḥaddād's poetry was coined by Ḥaddād's son Amin Ḥaddād (also an award-winning colloquial poet) in a commemorative documentary produced by the Egyptian television program *Ḥibr ʿalā al-Raṣīf*; see "Fuʾād Ḥaddād . . . Mutanabbī al-ʿĀmmiyya al-Maṣriyya" ["Fuʾād Ḥaddād . . . the Mutanabbī of Egyptian *ʿĀmmiyya*"], *Ḥibr ʿalā al-Raṣīf*, YouTube, uploaded by Alghad TV, August 15, 2020, https://youtu.be/_fdaBbwZQHo.

5. On this marginalization, see Radwan, *Egyptian Colloquial Poetry*, 1–4, 80–89; and Richard Jacquemond, *Conscience of the Nation* (Cairo: American University in Cairo Press, 2008), 84–85, 214–16. Haeri (*Sacred Language*, 127–41) documents the challenges faced by editors and publishers of the first journal dedicated to Egyptian colloquial Arabic poetry in the 1990s (*Ibn ʿArous*).

6. Radwan, *Egyptian Colloquial Poetry*; and Sayyid Dayfallah, *Ṣūrat al-Shaʿb bayna al-Shāʿir wa-l-Raʾīs* (Cairo: al-Kutub Khān li-l-Nashr wa-l-Tawzīʿ, 2015).

7. "Verbal play" is a translational approximation for the Arabic term *jinās*. On the original Arabic term's meaning and nuances, see Hany Rashwan, "Arabic Jinās Is Not Pun, Wortspiel, Calembour, or Paronomasia," *Rhetorica* 38, no. 4 (Autumn 2020): 335–70.

8. Joseph Massad offers a useful overview of the term's modern translation history in Arabic, in *Desiring Arabs* (Chicago: University of Chicago Press, 2008), 171–72; and in *Islam in Liberalism*, 159–60.

9. On "diglossia," a term drawn from Anglo-American linguistics, to describe the distinction between "high" (*fuṣḥā*) and "low" (*ʿāmmiyya*) varieties of Arabic in Egypt, see Radwan, *Egyptian Colloquial Poetry*, 11–17; Walter Armbrust, "The Split Vernacular," in *Mass Culture and Modernism in Egypt*, 40–55; Haeri, *Sacred Language*, xi, 1–21; Suleiman, *Arabic in the Fray*, 51–55; and Kristen Brustad, "Diglossia as Ideology," in *The Politics of Written Language in the Arab World*, ed. Jacob Hoigilt and Gunvor Mejdell (Leiden: Brill, 2017), 41–67. See also Kees Versteegh, *The Arabic Language* (Edinburgh: Edinburgh University Press, 2001), 173–97.

10. Gamal Abdel Nasser, *Egypt's Liberation: The Philosophy of the Revolution* (Washington, D.C.: Public Affairs Press, 1955).

11. See Haeri, *Sacred Language*, 52, 82–92, 94–111. Haeri notes that colloquial excisions in journalistic print varied based on a speaker's official status, class, or gender; such redactions ostensibly aligned with Nasser's higher social standing as head of state.

12. See Amin Ḥaddād's comments in "Fuʾād Ḥaddād . . . Mutanabbī al-ʿĀmmiyya al-Maṣriyya."

13. Radwan, *Egyptian Colloquial Poetry*, 37–43.

14. See Radwan, *Egyptian Colloquial Poetry*, 17–18. Radwan suggests that, through this historical process, canonical poetry (*shiʿr*) came to be associated with codified (Qurʾanically informed) standards of grammar and eloquence (*faṣāha*) (4, 19–23).

15. For further context, see Robert Tignor, *Modernization and British Colonial Rule in Egypt, 1882–1914* (Princeton: Princeton University Press, 2015), 94–110.

16. See Yousef, *Composing Egypt*, 144–47; Suleiman, *Arabic Language and National Identity*, 174–203; Fahmy, *Ordinary Egyptians*, 88–91; and Gully, "Arabic Linguistic Issues."

17. For an important account of this process, see Suleiman, *Arabic Language and National Identity*, 69–161.

18. Suleiman, *Arabic Language and National Identity*, 172–79, 193–94; Yousef, *Composing Egypt*, 33–39, 139–47; and Mike Holt, "Divided Loyalties: Language and Ethnic Identity in the

Arab World," in *Language and Identity in the Middle East and North Africa*, ed. Yasir Suleiman (Richmond, U.K.: Curzon Press, 1996), 11–24.

19. Yousef (*Composing Egypt*, 128, 136) and Tageldin ("Beyond Latinity," 121–24) suggest that this was a departure from earlier understandings of Arabic literacy as more fluid across "high" and "low" forms. See also Brustad, "Diglossia as Ideology."

20. Clive Holes, "The Use of Variation: A Study of the Political Speeches of Gamal Abd al-Nasir," in *Perspectives on Arabic Linguistics*, ed. Mushira Eid and Clive Holes (Ann Arbor: John Benjamins, 1993), 23, 29–33, 37. Nasser usually employed mixed registers in his public speeches and rarely spoke in pure *fuṣḥā*. When employing *fuṣḥā*, Nasser usually translated his intended meanings back into colloquial Egyptian Arabic (*ʿāmmiyya*), a tendency that Holes describes as an "exegetical" style of code-switching. See also Radwan, *Egyptian Colloquial Poetry*, 32.

21. See Ziad Fahmy on this "*ʿāmmiyya* paradox" in *Ordinary Egyptians*, 172–73.

22. On further connections between Nasser's rhetoric and Ḥaddād's diction, see Dayfallah, *Ṣūrat al-Shaʿb*, 105–204.

23. This analogy is borrowed from Warner, *Tongue-Tied Imagination*, 5.

24. On these biases, see Haeri, *Sacred Language*, 134–41. As incisively observed by Joel Beinin, "[T]he mere decision to write in colloquial Egyptian Arabic, even if not so intended, has often been perceived as a political act associated with a nationalist program of populism, anticlericalism (though not irreligion), and local Egyptian patriotism (*wataniyya*), as opposed to pan-Arabism (*qawmiyya*)." See Joel Beinin, "Writing Class: Workers and Modern Egyptian Colloquial Poetry (*Zajal*)," *Poetics Today* 15, no. 2 (1994): 192.

25. Dayfallah, *Ṣūrat al-Shaʿb*, 53, glossing al-Ḥillī's original manuscript on solecistic speech, *al-ʿĀṭil al-ḥālī wa-l-murakhkhaṣ al-ghālī*. See also Radwan, *Egyptian Colloquial Poetry*, 4, 19–23.

26. See Dayfallah's reading of al-Ḥillī: *Ṣūrat al-Shaʿb*, 53–55. Dayfallah describes this opposition as one between *jidd* (gravity) and *khalāʿa* (dissolution). Al-Ḥillī's original description of *barzakhī* verse was intended for *mawwāl*, a transcultural genre that he suggests emerged due to Arab contacts with non-Arab *mawālī* (clients of Arab tribes). See also Pierre Cachia, *Exploring Arab Folk Literature* (Edinburgh: Edinburgh University Press, 2011), 20–23.

27. Tageldin, "Beyond Latinity," 114.

28. Tageldin, "Beyond Latinity," 129–30.

29. This practice has been broadly adopted across historically Arabic-Islamic contact zones, with the *misaḥḥarātī* known as the *sahur* in Indonesia; West African traditions of Ramadan awakening to *sakara* drums extend this practice westward. Ḥaddād published *misaḥḥarātī* poems regularly beginning in 1964 during the month of Ramadan. As such, his corpus of *misaḥḥarātī* poems effectively chronicles major turning points in the late twentieth-century history of Egypt (from the Naksah, to the death of Nasser, until the poet's own passing in the mid-1980s).

30. See Radwan, *Egyptian Colloquial Poetry*, 23, on the connections between begging and the performance of *qūmā* by traditional *misaḥḥarātī*.

31. This uniform stanza begins all of Ḥaddād's poems and is drawn from the street cries of traditional awakeners.

32. Fuʾād Ḥaddād, *al-Aʿmāl al-Kāmila*, vols. 1–3 (Cairo: al-Hayʾa al-Miṣriyya al-ʿĀmma li-l-Kitāb, 2012), vol. 2, 15.

33. On the symbolic value of this term and concept, *fallāḥ*, see Suleiman, *Arabic Language and National Identity*, 34–35; and Samia Kholoussi, "Fallahin: The 'Mud Bearers' of Egypt's

'Liberal Age,'" in *Re-envisioning Egypt 1919–1952*, ed. Arthur Goldschmidt and Amy Johnson (Cairo: American University in Cairo Press, 2005), 277–311.

34. On the dual meaning of the term hajīn(a) to designate either a rapid steed (a racing camel) or a half-bred steed, see Martin Hinds and El-Said Badawi, eds., *A Dictionary of Egyptian Arabic* (Beirut: Librairie du Liban, 1986), 901; and Hans Wehr and J. Milton Cowan, eds., *A Dictionary of Modern Written Arabic*, 4th ed. (Urbana: Spoken Languages Services, 1994), 1200.

35. Ḥaddād left the verb *yehājīnā* ambiguous in the poem, opening up the meaning of "God's recompense"; its interpretation depends on the verb's presumed root, which could derive from *ha-ja-a'* (to mock) or *ha-ja-wa* (to rouse).

36. In Egyptian colloquial Arabic, the term would be pronounced *hagīn*/*hagīna* (as opposed to *hajīn*). Jack Forbes traces this connection between *hajīn*, *muwallad*, and *mulatto* through Iberian texts in *Africans and Native Americans: The Language of Race and the Evolution of Red-Black Peoples* (Urbana: University of Illinois Press, 1993), 140–47. For an overview of these interrelated terminologies (and of enduring hierarchies that subordinate "mongrelized" maternal bloodlines and cross-bred *hajīn*), see Josep Lluís Mateo Dieste, "Are There 'Mestizos' in the Arab World? A Comparative Survey of Classification Categories and Kinship Systems," *Middle Eastern Studies* 48, no. 1 (2012): 125–38. As Dieste notes, the term *hajīn* was frequently employed in early Muslim contexts for the child of an *ʿajamiyya* mother and an *ʿarab* father. For further context, see also Bernard Lewis, "The Crows of the Arabs," in *"Race," Writing, and Difference*, ed. Henry Louis Gates (Chicago: University of Chicago Press, 1986), 107–16.

37. Ḥaddād, *al-Aʿmāl al-Kāmila*, vol. 2, 16.

38. Dayfallah, *Ṣūrat al-Shaʿb*, 161–62.

39. Dayfallah, *Ṣūrat al-Shaʿb*, 161.

40. Ḥaddād, *al-Aʿmāl al-Kāmila*, vol. 2, 16–17.

41. As noted by Marilyn Booth, "Although the origins of what has come to be known as the classical ode may lie in the oral poetry of tribal Arabia, classical poetry is [now] at the center of the elite"—and written—"canon" in contemporary Egypt; see Marilyn Booth, "Colloquial Arabic Poetry, Politics, and the Press in Modern Egypt," *International Journal of Middle East Studies* 24, no. 3 (1992): 420. See also Yousef, *Composing Egypt*, 144–47.

42. On the lower literary status of Egyptian colloquial Arabic proverbs (*amthāl*), see Cachia, *Exploring Arab Folk Literature*, 51; and Wiebke Walther, "Proverbs," in *The Routledge Encyclopedia of Arabic Literature*, ed. Julie Scott Meisami and Paul Starkey (New York: Routledge, 1998), 622–24. Walther notes that, despite the genre's lower conventional standing, classical *fuṣḥā* references to *amthāl* suggest that such hierarchies were not always historically observed.

43. Ḥaddād, *al-Aʿmāl al-Kāmila*, vol. 2, 84–85. Across Ḥaddād's *misaḥḥarātī* poems, the speaker invokes the genre of the traditional *mawwāl* (colloquial poems performed as songs, traditionally associated with the popular music of an Egyptian underclass and distinguished by expressive emphases on vowel sounds). See Radwan, *Egyptian Colloquial Poetry*, 84, 99–100; and Cachia, *Exploring Arab Folk Literature*, 19–38. The mosques of al-Azhar and Sayyida Zaynab are among the most important religious sites in Egypt, respectively associated with one of the oldest universities in Cairo and with the burial site of the Prophet Muhammad's granddaughter (Sayyeda Zaynab) in Sunni Muslim traditions.

44. The publisher of Ḥaddād's collected works cites this line as "يمينُنا," though in keeping with the rhyme scheme in Egyptian colloquial, it should likely read "يمينا"; see Ḥaddād, *al-Aʿmāl al-Kāmila*, vol. 2, 86.

45. Ḥaddād, *al-Aʿmāl al-Kāmila*, vol. 2, 86. Expressions of this sentiment of the Prophet as guarantor are also traceable to folkloric epic traditions in rural Egypt, as noted in Cachia, *Exploring Arab Folk Literature*, 162.

46. Ḥaddād, *al-Aʿmāl al-Kāmila*, vol. 2, 102–3. A more literal, less rhythmic translation of the first two lines might read: "Awakener, Drummer."

47. Ḥaddād, *al-Aʿmāl al-Kāmila*, vol. 2, 103–4.

48. See Marlow, *Hierarchy and Egalitarianism*, 79–81.

49. Dayfallah, *Ṣūrat al-Shaʿb*, 200.

50. Dayfallah (*Ṣūrat al-Shaʿb*, 200) attributes this broader shift in Ḥaddād's corpus to the context of the Naksah after 1967.

51. Ḥaddād, *al-Aʿmāl al-Kāmila*, vol. 1, 23.

52. Ḥaddād, *al-Aʿmāl al-Kāmila*, vol. 1, 25–26.

53. Radwan (*Egyptian Colloquial Poetry*, 105) identifies the historical references within the poem more specifically with Salāḥ al-Din's 1187 battle of Ḥiṭṭin (Hattin).

54. Ḥaddād, *al-Aʿmāl al-Kāmila*, vol. 1, 27.

55. Dayfallah, *Ṣūrat al-Shaʿb*, 199–200.

56. Ḥaddād, *al-Aʿmāl al-Kāmila*, vol. 1, 27. The term *miʿrāj* alludes to the nocturnal ascent of the Prophet Muhammad to heaven. *Ṭāhā* refers to a group of letters opening the twentieth sura of the Qurʾan, also associated with one of the names of the Prophet Muhammad. The final line is drawn from the Qurʾan 61:13.

57. Attesting to its persisting centrality in an Egyptian national imaginary and soundscape, it was revived as a song of popular protest during the Arab Spring uprisings in 2011.

58. Ḥaddād, *al-Aʿmāl al-Kāmila*, vol. 3, 193. Noha Radwan (*Egyptian Colloquial Poetry*, 84) offers a more literal translation of the opening line ("I said to the bricks: Are you happy? They said Listen [. . .]").

59. Gamal Abdel Nasser, "Khiṭāb Taʾmīm Qanāt al-Suways" ["Speech on the Nationalization of the Suez Canal"], in *al-Majmuʿa al-Kāmila li-Khiṭāb wa-Taṣrīḥāt al-Raʾīs Gamāl ʿAbdel Nāṣir*, vol. 10, ed. Hoda Gamal Abdel Nasser (Cairo: al-Maktaba al-Akadimiyya, 2005), 755–806.

60. In a possible example of verbal play, the end of this line may also be legible as *al-kalima diyya* (meaning "the word restitution.")

61. Ḥaddād, *al-Aʿmāl al-Kāmila*, vol. 3, 193.

62. Classical conventions of praise poetry (*madīḥ*) and its neoclassical emulations in nineteenth-century Egypt revolved around the support of a court patron whose generosity court poets would laud in eulogistic form.

63. Ḥaddād, *al-Aʿmāl al-Kāmila*, vol. 3, 193–94.

64. Ḥaddād, *al-Aʿmāl al-Kāmila*, vol. 3, 196.

65. Salāḥ Jāhīn explains the genesis behind Fuʾād Ḥaddād's poetry collection *Ḥanibnī al-Sadd* in an article published in the journal *Ruz al-Yusuf*, October 22, 1956, cited in "Maqāl Nādir li-Ṣalāḥ Jāhīn ʿan Fuʾād Ḥaddād," *al-Tahrir*, October 22, 2014, accessed September 1, 2019, https://www.masress.com/tahrirnews/1344703.

66. On Ḥaddād's periods of imprisonment, reconciliation, and disenchantment with Nasser's regime, see Dayfallah, *Ṣūrat al-Shaʿb*, 182–203, and Hisham al-Salamuni, *Ḥikāyāt Wālid al-Shuʿarāʾ Fuʾād Ḥaddād* (al-Qāhira: al-Majlis al-aʿlā li-l-thaqāfa, 2017), 89-99.

67. Radwan, *Egyptian Colloquial Poetry*, 85.

68. Hala Halim, "*Lotus*, the Afro-Asian Nexus, and Global South Comparatism," *Comparative Studies of South Asia, Africa, and the Middle East* 32, no. 3 (2012): 571–77. Profiles of colloquial poets (such as Ḥaddād's close associate Salāḥ Jāhīn) and articles on Egyptian folk traditions were occasionally featured within the publication, but Arabic literary contributions were dominated by *fuṣḥā* writers. See also Edwar al-Kharrat and Nehad Salem, eds., *Afro-Asian Poetry: An Anthology* (Cairo: Permanent Bureau of Afro-Asian Writers, 1971), drawn from the journal's initial volumes.

69. Tageldin, "Beyond Latinity," 130.

70. Sukarno, *Collected Documents*, 11–12.

Notes to Chapter 7

1. Senghor, "Nationalismes d'Outremer," 6.

2. Senghor, "Nationalismes d'Outremer," 6.

3. Senghor, "Nationalismes d'Outremer," 9–10.

4. Senghor, "Nationalismes d'Outremer," 7.

5. Senghor, "Nationalismes d'Outremer," 7, original emphasis.

6. For an overview of these debates, see Warner, *Tongue-Tied Imagination*, 123–51; and Donal B. Cruise O'Brien, "The Shadow Politics of Wolofization," in *Symbolic Confrontations: Muslims Imagining the State in Africa* (New York: Palgrave Macmillan, 2003), 120–38.

7. On these diverse dynamics faced by Senghor, see Elizabeth Harney, *In Senghor's Shadow: Art, Politics, and the Avant-Garde in Senegal, 1960–1995* (Durham: Duke University Press, 2004), 34–35. Despite Senegal's "regional homogeneity" due to widespread Islamization and Wolof language use, "the greatest measure of social differentiation within Senegal historically and, to a certain extent, today, is the division by caste," according to Harney (3).

8. On these enduring segregations, see Warner, *Tongue-Tied Imagination*; Fal, "OSAD's Experience"; Fallou Ngom, "Ajami Scripts in the Senegalese Speech Community," *Journal of Arabic and Islamic Studies* 10 (2017): 1–23; and Kane, *Beyond Timbuktu*.

9. Senghor addressing the French National Assembly in 1946 characterized his religiously mixed family in the following terms: "Currently, all those who are not Muslims enjoy French status [citizenship]. Moreover, a single family can consist of Muslims and Catholics. In my own family, we are divided among Catholics, who have French status and favorable [political] representation, and Muslims, whose [civic] representation is sacrificed." See Léopold Sédar Senghor, "Transcription de l'Assemblée Nationale Constituante, 1ère séance du 18 septembre, 1946," September 18, 1946, Centre de Documentation des Archives Nationales de la République du Sénégal, Dakar.

10. On Senghor's mixed religious background, see Etienne Smith, "Religious and Cultural Pluralism in Senegal: Accommodation through 'Proportional Equidistance'?" in *Tolerance, Democracy, and Sufis in Senegal*, ed. Mamadou Diouf (New York: Columbia University Press, 2013), 157; and Lilyan Kesteloot, *Comprendre les poèmes de Léopold Sédar Senghor* (Issy-les-Moulineaux, France: Classiques Africains, 1986), 31, 92.

11. *Négritude* as a concept has been critiqued for promoting reductive notions of black racial unity. Anglophone critics such as Wole Soyinka and Ezekiel Mphahlele also insist that the term is an outgrowth of "assimilationist" French colonial policies and is therefore irrelevant in for-

mer British colonies; see Mphahlele, quoted in Irving Markovitz, *Léopold Sédar Senghor and the Politics of Negritude* (New York: Atheneum, 1969), 67. For an overview of these controversies, see Abiola Irele, *The African Experience in Literature and Ideology* (Bloomington: Indiana University Press, 1990), 67–116.

12. Aimé Césaire, "Conscience raciale et révolution sociale," *L'Étudiant noir* 1, no. 3 (May–June 1935): 1–2. On Césaire's inaugural article on *négritude*, see Christopher L. Miller, "The (Revised) Birth of Negritude: Communist Revolution and 'the Immanent Negro' in 1935," *PMLA* 125, no. 3 (2010): 743–49; and Raisa Rexer, "Black and White and Re(a)d All Over: *L'Étudiant noir*, Communism, and the Birth of Négritude," *Research in African Literatures* 44, no. 4 (2013): 1–14.

13. Harney, *In Senghor's Shadow*, 38.

14. On early records of the West African caste system, see Tal Tamari, "The Development of Caste Systems in West Africa," *Journal of African History* 32, no. 2 (1991): 221–50; and Thomas A. Hale, *Griots and Griottes: Masters of Words and Music* (Bloomington: Indiana University Press, 1998). The term *griot* is of uncertain (possibly Portuguese) origin for a bardic figure often designated in local languages by the terms *géwél/gewel* (Wolof), *kevel* (Serer), or *djeli* (in Mandinka).

15. On controversies over Senghor's code-switching, inclusion of African-language terms, and stylistic borrowings from *griotage* in his poetry, see, for example, Sylvia Washington Ba, *The Concept of Negritude in the Poetry of Leopold Sedar Senghor* (Princeton: Princeton University Press, 2015), 110–51; and Irele, *African Experience*, 67–116.

16. Judith T. Irvine, "When Talk Isn't Cheap: Language and Political Economy," in *The Matrix of Language: Contemporary Linguistic Anthropology*, ed. Donald Brenneis and Ronald K. S. Macaulay (New York: Routledge, 2018), 270.

17. Irvine, "When Talk Isn't Cheap," 274–75. The most common caste occupations include music-making and entertainment, in addition to metalworking, leatherworking, and woodworking. "Caste" communities are generically referred to as *nyeenyo/nyeenbe* in Wolof or *nyamakala* in Mandinka, among other regional variations. See Tamari, "Development of Caste Systems," 224, 241; and Hale, *Griots and Griottes*, 260.

18. See Tamari, "Development of Caste Systems," 221.

19. The Wolof terms for these distinctions are *géér* (noble) and *gewel* (underclass bard), corresponding in Senghor's native Serer to noble (*guelwar*) and bardic *kewel* or *kevel*; see Tamari, "Development of Caste Systems," 241–43. Wolof terms are predominantly used to designate casted communities in Senegal, likely reflecting the Wolofization of the region under the French Empire; see Cruise O'Brien, "Shadow Politics of Wolofization."

20. Irvine, "When Talk Isn't Cheap," 265. Although Irvine here describes Wolof communities, such differences in speech patterns (between bardic grandiloquence and higher-born restraint) are evident within other West African ethnic groups who sustain comparable communities of casted praise singers; see Tamari, "Development of Caste Systems."

21. Irvine, "When Talk Isn't Cheap," 275. On this patronage system, see 274–77.

22. Irvine, "When Talk Isn't Cheap," 275.

23. Léopold Sédar Senghor, *Léopold Sédar Senghor: Oeuvre Poétique*, 5th ed. (Paris: Seuil, 1990), 32.

24. Léopold Sédar Senghor, *Léopold Sédar Senghor: The Collected Poetry*, trans. Melvin

Dixon (Charlottesville: University Press of Virginia, 1991), 40; and Senghor, *Oeuvre Poétique*, 57. Eulogies to *guelwar* dominate Senghor's *Chants d'ombre* and *Ethiopiques* collections, but it is in *Hosties noires* where the motif is accompanied by statements of caste renunciation.

25. Senghor, *Collected Poetry*, 40.

26. Senghor, *Oeuvre Poétique*, 58.

27. Senghor, *Collected Poetry*, 40.

28. Senghor, *Oeuvre Poétique*, 83.

29. Senghor, *Collected Poetry*, 59–60.

30. *Guelwar* entitlements include having their lineage remembered, praised, and sung through a designated family of praise poets; see Tamari, "Development of Caste Systems," 225.

31. Senghor, *Collected Poetry*, 42; Senghor, *Oeuvre Poétique*, 63.

32. Senghor, *Oeuvre Poétique*, 63; Senghor, *Collected Poetry*, 44.

33. Senghor, *Oeuvre Poétique*, 63.

34. Senghor, *Collected Poetry*, 43.

35. Léopold Sédar Senghor, *Léopold Sédar Senghor: Poésie complète (édition critique)*, ed. Pierre Brunel (Paris: Centre National de la Recherche Scientifique Éditions, 2007), 286.

36. On this proverb, see R. P. Gravrand, "Le Gabou dans les Traditions Orales du Ngabou," *Ethiopiques: Numéro spécial revue socialiste de culture négro-africaine* 28 (October 1981): 50. My interpretation is informed by R. P. Gravrand's reading of the poem according to the *guelwar* oral traditions of Ngabou.

37. Senghor, *Collected Poetry*, 21, translation modified.

38. Senghor, *Oeuvre Poétique*, 32. See Pierre Brunel's commentary in Senghor, *Poésie complète*, 98; and Kesteloot, *Comprendre les poèmes*, 47.

39. Senghor, *Collected Poetry*, 18–19, translation modified.

40. Senghor, *Oeuvre Poétique*, 39.

41. See Souleymane Bachir Diagne, "La Négritude comme mouvement et comme devenir," *Rue Descartes* 83 (April 2014): 50–61.

42. See Léopold Sédar Senghor, *Les Fondements de l'Africanité ou Négritude et Arabité* (Paris: Présence Africaine, 1967); Shaden Tageldin, "The Place of Africa, in Theory: Pan-Africanism, Postcolonialism, Beyond," *Journal of Historical Sociology* 27, no. 3 (2014): 305–9; and Jane Hiddleston, *Decolonising the Intellectual: Politics, Culture, and Humanism at the End of the French Empire* (Liverpool: Liverpool University Press, 2014), 41–55.

43. Léopold Sédar Senghor, "La poésie négro-africaine de langue française," réception organisée par la Société des auteurs, compositeurs, et éditeurs de musique en l'honneur des poètes, Paris, January 30, 1979, Centre de Documentation des Archives Nationales de la République du Sénégal, Dakar, 7. On Arfang Sitokoto Dabo of Diao-Ba (1857–1971), often considered the greatest Mandinka *ʿajami* poet of his generation, see Fallou Ngom and Eleni Castro, "Beyond African Orality: Digital Preservation of Mandinka ʿAjamī Archives of Casamance," *History Compass* 17, no. 8 (2019): 1–16.

44. On Senghor's sponsorship of the Tuba Mosque project, see Cheikh Anta Babou, "The Senegalese 'Social Contract' Revisited: The Muridiyya Muslim Order and State Politics," in *Tolerance, Democracy, and Sufis in Senegal*, ed. Mamadou Diouf (New York: Columbia University Press, 2013), 131.

45. Léopold Sédar Senghor, "Laïcité," in *Liberté I: Négritude et Humanisme* (Paris: Seuil,

1964), 423. Ngom (*Muslims beyond the Arab World*, 64) notes that several Western-educated Murid intellectuals have welcomed such comparisons, embracing Bamba's status as a direct precursor to Senghor and the French *négritude* movement and considering themselves promoters of a parallel "Muriditude" movement.

46. Senghor, "Laïcité," 423.

47. Senghor, "Laïcité," 423.

48. Césaire, "Conscience raciale."

49. Bamba's efforts included the elevation of "casted" members of Wolof society to positions of clerical esteem and the promotion of intermarriage between casted and noncasted members of the Murid community; see Babou, *Fighting the Greater Jihad*, 99–100.

50. Babou, *Fighting the Greater Jihad*, 99–100. See also Cruise O'Brien, *Mourides of Senegal*, 56–57.

51. Ahmadu Bamba Mbakke, *Nahju Qaḍā'i al-Ḥāji: Fīmā min al-Adab ilayhi al-Murīd Yaḥtāj* (Rabat: Dā'irat Fatḥ al-Ghaffār, 2017), 45–46.

52. The term *ḥasab* designates inherited superiority (through the illustrious deeds of ancestral forebears) and is often paired with the term *nasab*, meaning "prestigious descent from an eminent bloodline." See Marlow, *Hierarchy and Egalitarianism*, 24–25, 99–100, 108–12.

53. Babou, *Fighting the Greater Jihad*, 99.

54. See Ngom, "Aḥmadu Bamba's Pedagogy." Within Murid devotional communities, poets are referred to as *taalifkat yi*, and singers are referred to as *jangkat yi* or *woykat yi*. In contrast to a traditional bardic underclass in which poetic eulogists and genealogists are considered socially subordinate, these poets (along with Wolofal scribes and copyists, referred to as *bindkat yi* or *moolkat yi*) are classed as scholars and figures of erudition (108–9). In this connection, however, one might nonetheless revisit the controversial claim by some historians that the extreme Murid subservience of followers or students (even erudite ones) to sheikhs may yet be an atavistic carryover of older systems of caste patronage; Babou, *Fighting the Greater Jihad*, 87–88. See also Ngom, *Muslims beyond the Arab World*, 15, 176, 235–37, on controversial assertions that traditional feudal hierarchies persist within the Murid order and on the attribution of sharifian (prophetic) genealogy to Bamba (which Bamba himself never claimed).

55. Senghor, "Laïcité," 422.

56. See Linda Beck, *Brokering Democracy in Africa: The Rise of Clientelist Democracy in Senegal* (New York: Palgrave Macmillan, 2008), 51–56.

57. Senghor, "Laïcité," 423. On the context of this speech, see Souleymane Bachir Diagne, "Religion and the Public Sphere in Senegal: The Evolution of a Project of Modernity," in *Crediting God: Sovereignty and Religion in the Age of Global Capitalism*, ed. Miguel E. Vatter (New York: Fordham University Press, 2011), 106–7.

58. See Mamadou Diouf, "The Public Role of the 'Good Islam': Sufi Islam and the Administration of Pluralism," in *Tolerance, Democracy, and Sufis in Senegal*, ed. Mamadou Diouf (New York: Columbia University Press, 2013), 6–7. On Senghor's inheritance of these colonial dynamics of "accommodation," see Diouf, "Public Role," 15–18; Beck, *Brokering Democracy*, 51–56; and Cruise O'Brien, *Symbolic Confrontations*, 194–95.

59. See Warner, *Tongue-Tied Imagination*, 123–51; and Cruise O'Brien, "Shadow Politics of Wolofization," on Senghor's arbitration over local language debates.

60. Léopold Sédar Senghor, "Le problème culturel en A.O.F. [1937]," in *Liberté I: Négritude et Humanisme* (Paris: Seuil, 1964), 19, final emphasis added.

61. See also Kane, *Beyond Timbuktu*, 160–77.

62. Léopold Sédar Senghor, "Vues sur l'Afrique noire ou assimiler, non être assimilés [1945]," in *Liberté I: Négritude et Humanisme* (Paris: Seuil, 1964), 39–69.

63. Senghor, "Vues sur l'Afrique noire," 67.

64. Senghor, "Vues sur l'Afrique noire," 68, emphasis added.

65. Senghor, "Vues sur l'Afrique noire," 55.

66. Senghor, "Vues sur l'Afrique noire," 55.

67. See Senghor, *Négritude et Arabité*, 9, 75–83.

68. Senghor, *Négritude et Arabité*, 60, 91; see also 50–68.

69. Senghor, *Négritude et Arabité*, 77, final emphasis added.

70. Senghor, *Négritude et Arabité*, 103.

71. See Tageldin, "Place of Africa, in Theory," 304–9; and Sophia Azeb, "Crossing the Saharan Boundary: *Lotus* and the Legibility of Africanness," *Research in African Literatures* 50, no. 3 (2019): 91–115.

72. On the limits of Senghor's commitment to dismantling these divisions across pan-African conferences from 1966 to 1977, see Andrew Apter, "Beyond Négritude: Black Cultural Citizenship and the Arab Question in FESTAC 77," *Journal of African Cultural Studies* 28, no. 3 (2016): 313–26.

73. The dearth of scholarship available to Senegalese francophone readers on West Africa's Arabic and *ʿajami* literature was not redressed until Amar Samb's groundbreaking 1972 dissertation, well after Senghor's Cairo speech. See Amar Samb, *Essai Sur La Contribution Du Sénégal à La Littérature D'expression Arabe*, Mémoires de l'Institut Fondamental d'Afrique Noire, no. 87 (Dakar: Institut Fondamental d'Afrique Noir, 1972).

74. See Harrison, *France and Islam*, 92–136, on *Islam noir* as a pejorative French colonial concept. The term's positive scholarly recasting appears in Vincent Monteil's *L'Islam Noir*, 3rd ed. (Paris: Seuil, 1980 [1964]), first published after Senghor's rehabilitation of the concept in 1963.

75. Césaire, "Conscience raciale." On the term "scriptworld," see David Damrosch, "Scriptworlds: Writing Systems and the Formation of World Literature," *Modern Language Quarterly* 68, no. 2 (2007): 195–219.

76. Harney, *In Senghor's Shadow*, 38, 42.

77. Quito Swan, "Blinded by Bandung? Illumining West Papua, Senegal, and the Black Pacific," *Radical History Review* 131 (May 2018): 58–81; Ulli Beier, "Léopold Sédar Senghor: A Personal Memoir," *Research in African Literatures* 33, no. 4 (2002): 8–10; Wole Soyinka, "Senghor: Lessons in Power," *Research in African Literatures* 33, no. 4 (2002): 1–2.

78. Frantz Fanon, *The Wretched of the Earth*, 1st ed. (New York: Grove Press, 1968), 235. On Senghor's diplomatic positions on Egypt and Algeria, see, respectively, Tageldin, "Place of Africa, in Theory"; and Apter, "Beyond Négritude."

79. Senghor, "Vues sur l'Afrique noire," 47–50.

80. See Harney, *In Senghor's Shadow*, 81–83.

81. Beier, "Léopold Sédar Senghor," 9.

82. Beier, "Léopold Sédar Senghor," 9. For further context, see Cornelia Panzacchi, "The

Livelihoods of Traditional Griots in Modern Senegal," *Africa: Journal of the International African Institute* 64, no. 2 (1994): 196–198.

83. Gary Wilder, *Freedom Time: Negritude, Decolonization, and the Future of the World* (Durham: Duke University Press, 2015), 8–13.

84. This conclusion builds on Wilder, *Freedom Time*, 241–59; and on Warner's critique of Benedict Anderson in *Tongue-Tied Imagination*, 21–22.

85. See Léopold Sédar Senghor, "Discours de L. S. Senghor, Président de l'Assemblée fédérale, Réception du General de Gaulle à l'Assemblée fédérale du Mali," December 13, 1959, Centre de Documentation des Archives Nationales de la République du Sénégal, Dakar, 6; and Léopold Sédar Senghor, "Interventions du Président Senghor Au Congrès du P.F.A., Dakar," August 1959, Centre de Documentation des Archives Nationales de la République du Sénégal, Dakar, 12.

86. See Wilder, *Freedom Time*, 241–59.

87. "Civilizational reciprocity" is Wilder's term (*Freedom Time*, 164).

88. See Amady Aly Dieng, *Mémoires d'un étudiant africain*, vol. 2 (Dakar: Council for the Development of Social Science Research in Africa, 2011), 48–49.

89. Association des étudiants Sénégalais en France [Senegalese section of FEANF], *Ijjib Volof: Syllabaire Volof.* (Grenoble: Imprimerie des Deux-Ponts, 1959). See also Fal, "OSAD's Experience," 36.

Notes to Chapter 8

1. Arabic writing in Wolof and Malay was locally known as (respectively) Wolofal or Wolof *ʿajami* and *jawi*.

2. See Cruise O'Brien, "Shadow Politics of Wolofization"; Johns, "Qurʾanic Exegesis in the Malay-Indonesian World"; and Hoffman, "Foreign Investment." On Islam's expansion, see Brian J. Peterson, *Islamization from Below: The Making of Muslim Communities in Colonial French Sudan, 1880–1960* (New Haven: Yale University Press, 2011); Ricklefs, *History of Modern Indonesia*, 36–49; and M. C. Ricklefs, *Mystic Synthesis in Java: A History of Islamization from the Fourteenth to the Early Nineteenth Centuries* (Norwalk, Conn.: Eastbridge, 2006).

3. On local controversies over Arabic in Senegal, see Ngom, *Muslims beyond the Arab World*, 8–29, 59–67; Ngom, "Linguistic Resistance"; and Kane, *Non-Europhone Intellectuals*. In Indonesia, see Fogg, "Standardisation"; and Noorhaidi Hassan, "The Making of Public Islam: Piety, Agency, and Commodification on the Landscape of the Indonesian Public Sphere," *Contemporary Islam* 3 (2009): 229–50. Controversies over Arabic use as a sign of piety, as noted by Hassan, reflect continued debates over religious pluralism and public blasphemy laws, as discussed in Formichi, *Religious Pluralism*.

4. On the term "from below" (*turun ke bawah*), see Pramoedya Ananta Toer, *Realisme Sosialis dan Sastra Indonesia* (Jakarta: Lentera Dipantara, 2003), 27–28; and Martina Heinschke, "Between Gelanggang and Lekra: Pramoedya's Developing Literary Concepts," *Indonesia* 61 (1996): 145–69.

5. See Hilmar Farid Setiadi and Razif, "*Batjaan Liar* in the Dutch East Indies: A Colonial Antipode," *Postcolonial Studies* 11, no. 3 (2008): 277–92. See also Hoffman, "Foreign Investment"; Adam, *Vernacular Press*; and Hilmar Farid Setiadi, *Rewriting the Nation: Pramoedya Ananta Toer and the Politics of Decolonization* (Ph.D. dissertation, National University of Singapore, 2014), 12.

6. Rossen Djagalov, *From Internationalism to Postcolonialism: Literature and Cinema between the Second and the Third Worlds* (Montreal: McGill-Queen's University Press, 2020), 62. Pramoedya led the Indonesian delegation, and Sembene was present as an associate of the Federation of Black African Students in France and the French Communist Party (as Senegal was still a French colony in 1958). See Hong Liu, "Pramoedya Ananta Toer and China: The Transformation of a Cultural Intellectual," *Indonesia* 61 (1996): 131–36; Rhoma Dwi Aria Yuliantri and Muhidin M. Dahlan, *Lekra Tak Membakar Buku: Suara Senyap Lembar Kebudayaan Harian Rakjat 1950–1965* (Yogyakarta, Indonesia: Merakesumba, 2008), 136–50; Françoise Blum, Gabrielle Chomentowski, and Constantin Katsakioris, "Au cœur des réseaux africano-soviétiques: Archives et trajectoire de l'écrivain-cinéaste sénégalais Ousmane Sembène," *Sources. Materials and Fieldwork in African Studies* 3 (2021): 99–135, accessed May 15, 2023, https://halshs.archives-ouvertes.fr/SOURCES/halshs-03418769; and Josephine Woll, "The Russian Connection: Soviet Cinema and the Cinema of Francophone Africa," in *Focus on African Films*, ed. Françoise Pfaff (Bloomington: Indiana University Press, 2004), 225–28. On connections between Afro-Asian literary exchanges in Tashkent and the first Asia-Africa conference in Bandung, see Duncan Yoon, "'Our Forces Have Redoubled': World Literature, Postcolonialism, and the Afro-Asian Writers' Bureau," *Cambridge Journal of Postcolonial Literary Inquiry* 2, no. 2 (2015): 233–52; and Elena Razlagova, "Cinema in the Spirit of Bandung: The Afro-Asian Film Festival Circuit, 1957–1964," in *The Cultural Cold War and the Global South: Sites of Contest and Communitas*, ed. Kerry Bystrom, Monica Popescu, and Katherine Zien (New York: Routledge, 2021), 118–28.

7. See Boroom Yoon ["The Explorer"], "Ubbi," *Kaddu* 1 (December 1971): 3–5; and Boroom Yoon ["The Explorer"], "Ubbi Editoryaal," *Kaddu* 2 (January 1972): 1–2. See also Taalibé yi ["Students"], "Ubbite Lekool yi ag Reforme bi," *Kaddu* 10 (November/December 1972): 1–6. Among the challenges to researchers working on the journal *Kaddu* is its inconsistent practice of authorial attribution. Although the journal lists contributors at the beginning of each volume, most articles were published under pen names (Sembene is believed to have contributed articles under the pen name "Ceddo"). Following Warner, *Tongue-Tied Imagination*, 119, I assume that Diagne and Sembene were responsible for editorials published under the pseudonym "Boroom Yoom" (or "B.Y."). I am indebted to Korka Sall for her assistance in preparing preliminary *Kaddu* translations from Wolof on which this translation and all others are based.

8. On this controversy, see W. Waalo bi, "Njangale Lakku Senegal Yi," *Kaddu* 3 (February 1972): 4; "Mbindinu lakki réew mi," editorial, *Kaddu* 15 (n.d. [likely between August 1973 and February 1974]): 2–5; "Kenu doginu baat yi," editorial, *Kaddu* 16 (n.d. [likely between January and March 1974]): 2–5; Sëriñ Sall, "Juróoméelu biyenaalu làkku Tubaab," *Kaddu* 17 (April 1974): 2; "Ubbiteefu *Kaddu*," editorial, *Kaddu* 23 (1978): 1–2; "Ceddo bi siggi ag ceddo ba Sëggulwoon," *Kaddu* 23 (1978): 2–4. See also Warner, *Tongue-Tied Imagination*, 118–51; and Moussa Daff, "L'aménagement linguistique et didactique de la coexistence du français et des langues nationales au Sénégal," *DiversCité Langues* 3 (1998), accessed August 29, 2011, http://www.uquebec.ca/diverscite.

9. Semiregular columns in Mandinka and Pulaar began in the journal's third volume: "Hello Pulaar," *Kaddu* 3 (February 1972): 15–16. *Kaddu*'s opening volume also mentioned plans to develop columns in Pulaar, Soninke (Sarakhole), Mandinka, and Jola for non-Wolof speakers. See Boroom Yoon, "Ubbi."

10. Seydou Nourou Ndiaye, "Un Pionnier de la presse dans les langues nationales," *Walfadjri/L'Aurore*, June 12, 2007, 8. See also Babacar Diop, Armand Faye, Yéro Sylla, and Amadou T. Gueye, eds., *L'impact des journaux en langues nationales sur les populations Sénégalais* (Dakar: Association des Chercheurs Sénégalais, 1990).

11. See "Ecriture: Mbind Mi," *Kaddu* 1 (December 1971): 2; and "Ecriture: Mbind Mi," *Kaddu* 2 (January 1972): 1, 16. The 1971 opening editorial of *Kaddu* clarified that the journal sought to "modernize" Wolof in the wake of foreign linguistic interference, by incorporating sounds (such as *j*, *z*) borrowed from the French language that did not "traditionally" exist in Wolof.

12. Pathé Diagne, in a personal interview with me in 2015, mentioned having developed the script and suggested that it was his own invention. The front matter in *Kaddu* 23 (February 1978) introduces this new script, which the journal called "Arafu Wolof" (as distinguished from Wolofal and "Arafu Tubaab," Arabic and Latin scripts).

13. "Bind ci sa lakk—Wolofal," *Kaddu* 23 (February 1978): 28. Although the poem remains unattributed in *Kaddu*, Pathé Diagne, in a personal interview with me in 2015, mentioned that it was one he had composed.

14. On these controversies, see Leonardo A. Villalón, "Negotiating Islam in the Era of Democracy: Senegal in Comparative Regional Perspective," in *Tolerance, Democracy, and Sufis in Senegal: Religion, Culture, and Public Life*, ed. Mamadou Diouf (New York: Columbia University Press, 2013), 235–55; and Alfred Stepan, "Stateness, Democracy, and Respect: Senegal in Comparative Perspective," in *Tolerance, Democracy, and Sufis in Senegal: Religion, Culture, and Public Life*, ed. Mamadou Diouf (New York: Columbia University Press, 2013), 224–25.

15. "Napoleon mbaa Araab bi? Deedeed! Du kenn ci noonu" ["Napoleon or Arabic? No Neither of Them!"], cited in D.S. and M.P.D., "Ubbi: Kodu Famiiy Bi," editorial, *Kaddu* 8 (September 1972): 1–4. For further background on the controversy, see Sëriñ Sall, "Xëtu diine ci kod bi," *Kaddu* 7 (August 1972): 9–10.

16. D.S. and M.P.D., "Ubbi," 2–3.

17. See Sëriñ Sall, "Xëtu diine ci kod bi".

18. D.S. and M.P.D., "Ubbi," 2–3.

19. Pathé Diagne, *Alxuraan ci Wolof* (Paris: Editions L'Harmattan, 1997 [1979]).

20. On national *defrancisation* and *desarabisation*, see Waa Senegal yi ["The Senegalese"], "Xewxewu jamano ji," *Kaddu* 8 (September 1972): 4. While attesting that national "*defrancisation, desarabisation, de-Christianisation*" were matters of public debate, this particular contributor, writing under a pseudonym, claims that the use of Arabic is harmless relative to the more exploitative use of French.

21. "Ubbi," *Kaddu* 19 ([December] 1974): 2–4. See also "Ndajem 'UNESCO' ci lakki Afrig yi," *Kaddu* 19 ([December] 1974): 3, 5. Both articles were published after a 1974 UNESCO meeting held in Bamako, Mali, on the promotion of African languages. UNESCO's final report on the conference indicates that Pathé Diagne (cofounder of *Kaddu*) was present; see UNESCO, "Meeting of Experts on the Use of Mother Tongues in Literacy Programmes in Africa, Bamako, 1974," 1975, accessed April 5, 2021, https://unesdoc.unesco.org/ark:/48223/pf0000015794. This issue of the journal in late 1974 also mentions an Asian-African conference in Beirut in December 1974, citing the importance of Asian- and African-language writing; see "Ndajem Liban," *Kaddu* 19 (1974 [likely December]): 3–4.

22. "Ubbi." *Kaddu* 19 ([December] 1974): 2–4.

23. Ceddo [Ousmane Sembene], "Moom sa reew," *Kaddu Espesiyal Sunu Indepandans*, March/April 1972, unpaginated first page. Within the same volume, see also features (without attributions) entitled "Sheyxu Umar ag Saamoori," *Kaddu Espesiyal Sunu Indepandans*, March/April 1972, 2, 8–9; "Ndaali Sheyxu Umar," *Kaddu Espesiyal Sunu Indepandans*, March/April 1972, 9–12; and "Ubbi Jëmmu Afrig konsiyans nasyonaal, xeexi tay yi ag seeni cosaan," *Kaddu Espesiyal Sunu Indepandans*, March/April 1972, 1–4. On the Malcolm X praise poem, see "Wàyu Malcom," *Kaddu* 3 (February 1972): 12–13.

24. B.Y., "NKrumaa," *Kaddu* 6 (July 1972): 1, 3–6, at 5. See also, on Nkrumah, "Njaal . . . Deewuk Kurumaa," *Kaddu* 4 (May 1972): 10; and "NKrumaa," *Kaddu* 5 (June 1972): 1–3, 6, 16.

25. *Kaddu*'s third volume was dedicated to contemporary African struggles (including against apartheid) and civil rights struggles in the United States. See Seetaankat bi, "Miryaam Makkeba ci Ndakaaru," *Kaddu* 3 (February 1972): 1–3; "Wàyu Miryaam," *Kaddu* 3 (February 1972): 10–11; "Wàyu Malcom" (an adaptation of Amiri Baraka/LeRoi Jones's poem written in tribute to Malcolm X, "A Poem for Black Hearts," published in *Negro Digest* 14, no. 11 [September 1965]: 58); and Xewcaakoon mi, "Amerigu nit ku ñuul," *Kaddu* 3 (February 1972): 7–9. See also a later article on Angela Davis: A. Salaam, "Angela Davis," *Kaddu* 4 (May 1972): 15–16.

26. See "Ubbi Jëmmu Afrig konsiyans nasyonaal, xeexi tay yi ag seeni cosaan." Although not directly cited, Cheikh Anta Diop's claim that ancient, pharaonic Egypt was a fundamentally "black" African civilization (to which later Hellenic cultures were indebted) is implied; see Cheikh Anta Diop, *Antériorité des civilisations nègres: Mythe ou vérité historique?* (Paris: Présence Africaine, 1967); and on Diop and Senghor's rivalry, see Warner, *Tongue-Tied Imagination*, 129–32.

27. See especially *Kaddu Espesiyal Sunu Indepandans*, March/April 1972.

28. "Sheyxu Umar ag Saamoori" (preceded by an opening contribution by Sembene under his pen name: Ceddo, "Moom sa reew").

29. For historical features on Lat Joor Joop, see Ibu Mbeng, "Lat Joor, ngoone Lattir: Ca mbañ ga," *Kaddu* 4 (May 1972): 1, 5–9; and B. Yoon, "Ubbi Editoryaal: Demokaraasi ag nguuru cosaan," *Kaddu* 4 (May 1972): 1–5. On al-Hadji Omar Tall, see "Sheyxu Umar ag Saamoori"; and "Ndaali Sheyxu Umar."

30. B. Yoon, "Ubbi Editoryaal: Demokaraasi ag nguuru cosaan," 3.

31. "Ndaali Sheyxu Umar," 12.

32. This gloss for the Wolof term *ceddo* is Sembene's; Annett Busch and Max Annas, eds., *Ousmane Sembène: Interviews* (Jackson: University of Mississippi Press, 2008), 113–14. Ngom (*Muslims beyond the Arab World*, 71) instead translates *ceddo* as traditional "crown soldiers." On the meanings of the term, see Philip Rosen, "Making a Nation in Sembene's *Ceddo*," *Quarterly Review of Film and Video* 13, nos. 1–3 (1991): 151.

33. The journal from its opening volumes had regular columns on cinema, with its first volumes in late 1971 and early 1972 introducing Sembene's film *Emitaï* and its final volume featuring the *Ceddo* controversy with Senghor. See "Ceddo bi siggi ag ceddo ba Sëggulwoon."

34. See Warner, *Tongue-Tied Imagination*, 148–49; and Mamadou Diouf, "History and Actuality in Ousmane Sembene's *Ceddo* and Djibril Diop Mambety's *Hyenas*," in *African Experiences of Cinema*, ed. Imrah Bakari and Mbye Cham (London: British Film Institute, 1996), 244.

For initial coverage of the censorship, see B. Biram Gassama, "'Ceddo' Baillonné!" *Andë Soppi*, June 1977.

35. Sembene, interview, *Framework* 7/8 (Spring 1978), cited in Warner, *Tongue-Tied Imagination*, 146.

36. See Beck, *Brokering Democracy*; and Mamadou Diouf, ed., *Tolerance, Democracy, and Sufis in Senegal* (New York: Columbia University Press, 2013).

37. Ousmane Sembene, dir., *Ceddo*, Filmi Doomireew, 1976.

38. On the film's indeterminate historical setting, see Warner, *Tongue-Tied Imagination*, 148–49; and Diouf, "History and Actuality," 244.

39. See Rosen, "Making a Nation," 155.

40. Sembene's novel *Le dernier de l'Empire* suggests that the Wolof term *guewel* comes from the word for "circle" (*geew*) and in its most literal sense designates "one who makes the rounds," a notion he plays on through his cinematography; Ousmane Sembene, *Le dernier de l'Empire*, 2nd ed. (Paris: L'Harmattan, 1985), 271. See also Manthia Diawara, "Popular Culture and Oral Traditions in African Film," in *African Experiences of Cinema*, ed. Imruh Bakari and Mbye B. Cham (London: British Film Institute, 1996), 214–15; and Rosen, "Making a Nation," 156–57.

41. Rosen explains that the *samp* is a "traditional challenge stick," "which gives [plaintiffs] the opportunity to articulate their grievances" ("Making a Nation," 151).

42. On this time line and on Pramoedya's early historical research into the Majapahit period, see Setiadi, *Rewriting the Nation*, 64–65.

43. See Setiadi, *Rewriting the Nation*, 90–95; and Sue Nichterlein, "Historicism and Historiography in Indonesia," *History and Theory* 13, no. 3 (1974): 261–72.

44. See Pramoedya Ananta Toer, "My Apologies in the Name of Experience," trans. Alex G. Bardsley, *Indonesia* 61 (April 1996): 6–7.

45. See Pramoedya, *Realisme Sosialis*; and Heinschke, "Between Gelanggang and Lekra."

46. See Savriti Scherer, "Globalisation in Java in the 16th Century: A Review of Pramoedya's *Arus Balik*," *Archipel* 55 (1998): 43–60; and Ricklefs, *History of Modern Indonesia*, 36–49.

47. Ananta Toer Pramoedya, *Arus Balik* (Jakarta: Hasta Mitra, 1995), 468.

48. On Galeng's ambiguous background, see Scherer, "Globalisation in Java."

49. One exemplary passage reads, "And now he understood: Tuban [his native kingdom] stood between Hinduism and Islam, without assuming a firm posture toward the Portuguese. [. . .] Tuban would have to challenge the Portuguese, without becoming [a Muslim theocracy], but also not for the sake of Hinduism." Pramoedya, *Arus Balik*, 243.

50. Pramoedya, *Arus Balik*, 740.

51. The term "positive hero" is drawn from Katerina Clark's reading of the "Socialist Realist" novel. See Katerina Clark, *The Soviet Novel: History as Ritual* (Bloomington: Indiana University Press, 2000); and, in Pramoedya's fiction, Annette Lienau, "The Ideal of Casteless Language in Pramoedya's *Arok Dedes*," *Comparative Studies of South Asia, Africa and the Middle East* 32, no. 3 (2012): 591–603.

52. The term "positionally vernacular" is Tony Day's, in "Locating Indonesian Literature in the World," *Modern Language Quarterly* 68, no. 2 (2007): 173–93.

53. The *syahbandar*, a Persian term meaning "lord of the port," or harbormaster, was

commonly deputized by local regents across precolonial Indian Ocean trade routes to welcome and allocate resources for incoming ships.

54. Christopher GoGwilt, *The Passage of Literature: Genealogies of Modernism in Conrad, Rhys, and Pramoedya* (Oxford: Oxford University Press, 2011), 205. GoGwilt also mentions Javanese in this connection, though the Iberian Arab *syahbandar* in fact prohibits its use among his subordinates; see Pramoedya, *Arus Balik*, 25–26.

55. GoGwilt, *Passage of Literature*, 205.

56. Scherer, "Globalisation in Java."

57. Pramoedya, *Arus Balik*, 125–26. On the dismissal of Javanese and its Sanskritized script by the *syahbandar* as a *tulisan kafir* (script of infidels), see 79.

58. Pramoedya, *Arus Balik*, 503–4.

59. On the semilegendary figure of Kalijage in Javanese popular narrative, see Ricklefs, *Mystic Synthesis*.

60. The term "truth-language" is Anderson's (*Imagined Communities*, 14, 36).

61. Pramoedya, *Arus Balik*, 147–48.

62. Pramoedya, *Arus Balik*, 144–46.

63. GoGwilt, *Passage of Literature*, 204–5. On relevant approaches to "interimperiality," see also Laura Doyle, *Inter-imperiality: Vying Empires, Gendered Labor, and the Literary Arts of Alliance* (Durham: Duke University Press, 2020), 15–27.

64. Day, "Locating Indonesian Literature in the World."

65. On Pramoedya's *Studi Percobaan tentang Sejarah Bahasa Indonesia* (*A Preliminary Study of the Indonesian Language*), see GoGwilt, *Passage of Literature*, 178.

66. On Pramoedya's articles and involvement in *Bintang Timur*, see Koesalah Soebagyo Toer, *Kamus Pramoedya Ananta Toer* (Sleman, Indonesia: Warning Books, 2018).

67. See Setiadi, *Rewriting the Nation*, 35–38.

68. The term "on an equal basis" is drawn from Setiadi's gloss of Pramoedya's "Lentera" columns (September 1963–April 1964) in *Bintang Timur*; see Setiadi, *Rewriting the Nation*, 37. Pramoedya also used the term *Melayu sekolah* (school Malay) to describe a colonially reinforced, formal Malay in opposition to *Melayu kerdja*. See Pramoedya, *Realisme Sosialis*, 126–27.

69. Setiadi, *Rewriting the Nation*, 36.

70. See Pramoedya Ananta Toer, *Tempoe Doeloe: Antologi Sastra Pra-Indonesia* (Jakarta: Hasta Mitra, 1982); and Setiadi, *Rewriting the Nation*, 36–38.

71. Pramoedya, *Tempoe Doeloe*; and Pramoedya, *Realisme Sosialis*.

72. On Tirto Adhi Surjo's pioneering status, see Adam, *Vernacular Press*, 108–24; and Pramoedya Ananta Toer, *Sang Pemula* (Jakarta: Hasta Mitra, 1985).

73. On the protagonist's shift to Malay across the quartet of novels, see, for example, Pramoedya Ananta Toer, *This Earth of Mankind* [*Bumi Manusia*], trans. Max Lane (New York: Penguin, 1996), 336–37; and Pramoedya Ananta Toer, *Child of All Nations* [*Anak Semua Bangsa*], trans. Max Lane (New York: Penguin, 1996), 57–63, 112–13, 186–89, which foreground the protagonist's culminating and foundational accomplishments in *Melayu rakyat* in the third novel of the series: Pramoedya Ananta Toer, *Footsteps* [*Jejak Langkah*], trans. Max Lane (New York: Penguin, 1996), 18–20, 189–93, 199–200, 277, 283–84.

74. On the portrayal of Budi Utomo in the novel, see Setiadi, *Rewriting the Nation*, 225–27.

75. Allusions to Dutch policies of "Association" (also referred to as Dutch "Ethical Policy") and to their backers, including Snouck Hurgronje, appear most prominently in the first two novels of the quartet: Pramoedya Ananta Toer, *Bumi Manusia* [*This Earth of Mankind*] (Jakarta: Hasta Mitra, 1980); and Pramoedya Ananta Toer, *Anak Semua Bangsa* [*Child of All Nations*] (Jakarta: Hasta Mitra, 1980). See Daniel Schultz and Maryanne Felter, "Education, History, and Nationalism in Pramoedya Toer's *Buru Quartet*," *Crossroads: An Interdisciplinary Journal of Southeast Asian Studies* 16, no. 2 (2002): 143–75.

76. On Adhi Surjo's press experiments, see Adam, *Vernacular Press*, 115–17; and Pramoedya, *Sang Pemula*. On Pramoedya's historical sources (including Tirto Adhi Surjo's diary) and research, see Setiadi, *Rewriting the Nation*, 65; and Takeshi Shiraishi, "Reading Pramoedya Ananta Toer's *Sang Pemula*," *Indonesia* 44 (October 1987): 129–39.

77. On "multi-*bangsa*" (*bangsa-ganda*) idealism, see Pramoedya Ananta Toer, *Jejak Langkah* [*Footsteps*] (Jakarta: Lentera Dipantara, 2006), 522–23, 540; and Pheng Cheah, *Spectral Nationality: Passages of Freedom from Kant to Postcolonial Literatures of Liberation* (New York: Columbia University Press, 2003), 249–341.

78. On the fictionalization of these interethnic tensions within SDI, see Pramoedya, *Jejak Langkah*, 518–24, 540–50, 626–29. As the narrative reveals (glossed by Setiadi, *Rewriting the Nation*, 190–91): "Although the Sarekat Dagang Islamijah was an effective tool of mobilization, it was also prone to internal division, particularly between the *saudagar* [merchants] of Arab descent and the natives." On the progressively nativist character of the historical SDI, see Adam, *Vernacular Press*, 115–17. On Pramoedya's historiographical interventions on the SDI, see Setiadi, *Rewriting the Nation*, 106–7.

79. My observation builds on Setiadi's suggestion (*Rewriting the Nation*, 190).

80. See, especially, Pramoedya Ananta Toer, *Rumah Kaca* (Jakarta: Lentera Dipantara, 2006), 1–15, 110–31, 195–229, 511–26, 596–646. See also Setiadi, *Rewriting the Nation*, 105–8, 195–206, 248–50.

81. Senghor, cited in Warner, *Tongue-Tied Imagination*, 134.

82. See Setiadi and Razif, "*Batjaan Liar*."

83. My phrasing here draws from Antonio Gramsci, cited in Said, *Orientalism*, 25.

84. Regarding the "backwardness" (*kemunduran*) of Indonesian literature relative to a global standard, see Pramoedya, *Realisme Sosialis*, especially 42–43, 57–82, 114–30; and Pramoedya, *Tempoe Doeloe*. For an overview of Pramoedya's arguments, see Setiadi, *Rewriting the Nation*, 53–59; and Christopher GoGwilt, "Postcolonial Philology and Nearly Reading the World-System in Print Form," *Modernism/modernity Print Plus* 2, no. 4 (2018), accessed May 15, 2023, https://doi.org/10.26597/mod.0038.

85. This may support Peter Kalliney's suggestion that "the Afro-Asian movement was more interested in the status of vernacular languages than in mimicking the literary techniques popular in the Soviet system." See Peter J. Kalliney, *The Aesthetic Cold War: Decolonization and Global Literature* (Princeton: Princeton University Press, 2022), 104. The *Buru Quartet* is often considered Pramoedya's highest achievement in the genre of "realist" fiction, a genre he promoted through his own critical text, *Realisme Sosialis*. Sembene's early fiction (*God's Bits of Wood*) is often upheld as an exemplar of his Socialist-Realist writing, following Carrie D. Moore's early treatment of the subject, *Evolution of an African Artist: Social Realism in the Works of Ousmane Sembene* (Ph.D. dissertation, Indiana University, 1973). See also Monica Popescu,

At Penpoint: African Literatures, Postcolonial Studies, and the Cold War (Durham: Duke University Press, 2020), 88–94, 113–20.

Notes to Chapter 9

1. Kilito, *Tongue of Adam*, 22–30.

2. Such claims of parity assume a poignancy in postcolonial Arabic contexts, given that quests to reconstruct "pre-Babelian" lineages of human speech gave rise to colonial-era hierarchies subordinating Arabic and Semitic languages to Indo-Aryan alternatives. See Maurice Olender, "From the Language of Adam to the Pluralism of Babel," *Mediterranean Historical Review* 12, no. 2 (1997): 51–59; and Olender, *Languages of Paradise*.

3. Naguib Mahfouz, *al-Ḥarāfīsh* (Cairo: Dār al-Shurūq, 2003), 451–61; Naguib Mahfouz, *The Harafish*, trans. Catherine Cobham (New York: Doubleday, 1994), 304–10.

4. Walter Benjamin, "The Translator's Task," trans. Steven Rendall, *TTR: Traduction, terminologie, rédaction* 10, no. 2 (1997): 157.

5. On Mahfouz's favoring of this novel, see Catherine Cobham, "Enchanted to a Stone: Heroes and Leaders in *The Harafish* by Najīb Mafūz," *Middle Eastern Literatures* 9, no. 2 (2006): 130–31; and Roger Allen, "*The Harafish* by Naguib Mahfouz, Catherine Cobham," *World Literature Today* 68, no. 4 (1994): 874.

6. As recalled by Catherine Cobham, Mahfouz's English translator, Mahfouz wished to retain the *ʿajamiyya* lines in transliteration rather than render them in English translation, to convey "how incomprehensible they sounded to the ordinary people" in the novel's setting and, by extension, to the implied Arabic language reader; see Catherine Cobham, "Five Questions with Catherine Cobham on the Translation of Mahfouz's 'Harafish,'" interview by Marcia Lynx Qualey, *ArabLit*, November 14, 2011, accessed November 1, 2018, https://arablit.org/2011/11/14/5-questions-with-catherine-cobham-on-translation-mahfouzs-harafish/. On these untranslated lines—inscrutable to the presumed Arabic reader—drawn from Persian poems by the Sufi poet Hafez, see Ziad Elmarsafy, *Sufism in the Contemporary Arabic Novel* (Edinburgh: Edinburgh University Press, 2012), 33–39.

7. Powell, *Different Shade of Colonialism*, especially "Black Servants and Saviors: The Domestic Empire of Egypt," 64–104; Powell, *Tell This in My Memory*; Fahmy, *Ordinary Egyptians*, 8–11, 27–29, 70–72; and El Shakry, *Great Social Laboratory*.

8. Mahfouz spoke frequently of Egyptian's hybrid position at the convergence of a pharaonic and Arab Islamic inheritance. See Michael Allan, *In the Shadow of World Literature: Sites of Reading in Colonial Egypt* (Princeton: Princeton University Press, 2016), 17–38, 94–114; Colla, *Conflicted Antiquities*, 234–72; Rasheed El-Enany, *Naguib Mahfouz: The Pursuit of Meaning* (New York: Routledge, 1993), 35–46, 119–211; Wen-chin Ouyang, *Politics of Nostalgia in the Arabic Novel: Nation-State, Modernity, and Tradition* (Edinburgh: Edinburgh University Press, 2013), 25–53, 165–99; Muhsin al-Musawi, *Islam on the Street: Religion in Modern Arabic Literature* (Lanham, Md.: Rowman and Littlefield, 2009), 71–208.

9. See El-Enany, *Pursuit of Meaning*, 22–28.

10. See Rasheed El-Enany, *Naguib Mahfouz: His Life and Times* (Cairo: American University in Cairo Press, 2007), 40–41; and Hosam Aboul-Ela, "The Writer Becomes Text: Naguib Mahfouz and State Nationalism in Egypt," *Biography* (Honolulu) 27, no. 2 (2004): 339–56.

11. On Mahfouz's formally experimental novels, which some critics have called "episodic" (El-Enany) or "polyphonic" (Mehrez), see El-Enany, *Pursuit of Meaning*, 128–74; El-Enany, *His Life and Times*, 108–35; and Samia Mehrez, *Egyptian Writers between History and Fiction: Essays on Naguib Mahfouz, Sonallah Ibrahim, and Gamal Al-Ghitani* (Cairo: American University in Cairo Press, 1994), 14, 92–93.

12. The term "positionally vernacular" is Day's ("Locating Indonesian Literature").

13. Naguib Mahfouz, *Najīb Maḥfūẓ: Ṣafaḥāt min Mudhakkirātihi wa-aḍwāʾ Jādīda ʿalā Adabihi wa-Ḥayātihi*, interview by Rajāʾ Naqqāsh (Cairo: Markaz al-Ahrām lil-Tarjamah wa-al-Nashr, 1998), 62–63. Mahfouz in this interview associates writing in *fuṣḥā* with "patriotic" and "religious" affiliations and presents it as a practical literary choice (both within and beyond Egypt). He credits his early education in Islamic schools and in classical literature for his attachment to *fuṣḥā* formed during the British occupation, when Arabic occupied a defensive and less prestigious position relative to English and French.

14. Mahfouz, *al-Ḥarāfīsh*, 598.

15. See Mahfouz, *Najīb Maḥfūẓ*, 61–62, on his avoidance of colloquialisms. See also Naguib Mahfouz, *Ataḥaddath Ilaykum* (Beirut: Dār al-ʿAwda, 1977), 60–61. In a statement frequently cited by critics to illustrate his hostility to *ʿāmmiyya*, Mahfouz compared the prevalence of *ʿāmmiyya* with a "disease" of ignorance and a by-product of Arab "educational failures" (in a 1965 interview); Mahfouz, quoted in Fuʾād Dawwārah, *ʿAshrat Udābāʾ Yataḥaddathūn* (Cairo: Dār al-Hilāl, 1965), 286–87. He nonetheless also claimed, in the same interview, to read literature in both *fuṣḥā* and *ʿāmmiyya* and believed that the rapprochement of *fuṣḥā* and *ʿāmmiyya* was the true "mission of the literary author" (*muhimat al-adīb*). On suggestions among critics that Mahfouz imbues his *fuṣḥā* with an *ʿāmmiyya* cadence or sensibility, approaching a literary middle ground between both registers, see Yusuf al-Shārūni, "Lughat al-Ḥiwar bayna al-ʿĀmmiyya wa-l-Fuṣḥā," *al-Majallah* (Cairo) 67 (August 1962): 40–54, especially 42–43; Sasson Somekh, *Genre and Language in Modern Arabic Literature* (Wiesbaden, Germany: Harassowitz, 1991); and Sasson Somekh, *The Changing Rhythm: A Study of Najīb Maḥfūẓ's Novels* (Leiden: Brill, 1973), 98–155. For more on Mahfouz and the issue of Arabic diglossia, see also El-Enany, *Pursuit of Meaning*, 41–42, 192–94; and Muhammad Siddiq, *Arab Culture and the Novel: Genre, Identity, and Agency in Egyptian Fiction* (New York: Routledge, 2007), 11, 137, 185.

16. In describing these verses as "inscrutable," I refer to their intended effect for a presumed Arabic language reader; see Cobham, "Five Questions."

17. In interviews, Mahfouz claimed that he occasionally adopted the term "realism" or "naturalism" to describe his earlier work, but it was a label first applied by literary critics rather than one he consciously emulated; see Mahfouz, *Ataḥaddath Ilaykum*, 48–61. On "realism" and "naturalism" in Mahfouz's fiction, see El-Enany, *Pursuit of Meaning*, xi–xii, 78–79, 196–97. On Mahfouz's engagement with the Afro-Asian Writers' Association, see Abou-El-Fadl, "Building Egypt's Afro-Asian Hub."

18. See Naguib Mahfouz, *Amām al-ʿArsh* (Cairo: Dār al-Shurūq, 2006), 17–12; Naguib Mahfouz, *Before the Throne*, trans. Raymond Stock (New York: Doubleday, 2012), 14–17.

19. Mahfouz, *Amām al-ʿArsh*, 84–90; Mahfouz, *Before the Throne*, 80–93.

20. Mahfouz, *Before the Throne*, 88; Mahfouz, *Amām al-ʿArsh*, 90.

21. On nativist entitlements to Egypt's "throne," see Mahfouz, *Before the Throne*, 33, 37, 102, 116, 132–37.

22. See Israel Gershoni and James Jankowski, *Egypt, Islam, and the Arabs: The Search for Egyptian Nationhood, 1900–1930* (New York: Oxford University Press, 1986); and Donald M. Reid, "Nationalizing the Pharaonic Past: Egyptology, Imperialism, and Egyptian Nationalism, 1922–1952," in *Rethinking Nationalism in the Arab Middle East*, ed. James Jankowski and Israel Gershoni (New York: Columbia University Press, 1997), 127–49.

23. Mahfouz, *Ataḥaddath Ilaykum*, 48–61. See also Tageldin, *Disarming Words*, 227–336; Gershoni and Jankowski, *Egypt, Islam, and the Arabs*, 164–274; Hussam Ahmed, *The Last Nahdawi: Taha Hussein and Institution Building in Egypt* (Stanford: Stanford University Press, 2021), 46–47, 136–37; Halim, "*Lotus*, the Afro-Asian Nexus, and Global South Comparatism," 575–76; and Mariam Aboelezz, "Language as Proxy in Egypt's Identity Politics: Examining the New Wave of Egyptian Nationalism," in *Language, Politics and Society in the Middle East*, ed. Yonatan Mendel and Abeer AlNajjar (Edinburgh: Edinburgh University Press, 2018), 129–32.

24. Naguib Mahfouz, *Naguib Mahfouz at Sidi Gaber: Reflections of a Nobel Laureate, 1994–2001. From Converstations with Mohamed Salmawy*, ed. Mohamed Salmawy (Cairo: American University in Cairo Press, 2001), 101.

25. Qur'an 30:22.

26. On these terms and on Ibn Battuta's *riḥla* as a precedent for Mahfouz's narrative, see Roxanne Euben, *Journeys to the Other Shore: Muslim and Western Travelers in Search of Knowledge* (Princeton: Princeton University Press, 2006), 86–88, 174–98.

27. The regions of *dār al-Ḥalba* and *dār al-Amān* are generally understood to represent Western Euro-American and Russo-Soviet blocs; see El-Enany, *Pursuit of Meaning*, 171–72.

28. While critics note the novel's disorienting temporal markers, El-Enany describes the narrative as "more of a journey in time than in space" (*Pursuit of Meaning*, 170–71). Ouyang's (*Politics of Nostalgia*, 25–50) reading of the novel from "past to present" (36) proposes that the novel ventures from "tribal paganism" to "aetheist(ic) communism" (28).

29. On comparisons to Ibn Battuta's travelogue, see El-Enany, *Pursuit of Meaning*, 168–70; and Ouyang, *Politics of Nostalgia*, 26–28, 46–47.

30. Ibn Battuta's travelogue, in other words, presumes the subordinate status of non-Muslim figures within sub-Saharan Africa and South/Southeast Asia in more unilateral terms relative to custodial Muslim Arab centers in West Asia and North Africa; see Ibn Battuta, *The Travels of Ibn Battutah*, trans. H.A.R. Gibb and C. F. Beckingham (London: Picador, 2002).

31. See Naguib Mahfouz, *Riḥlat Ibn Faṭṭūma* (Cairo: Dār al-shurūq, 2006), 25, 28–32; Naguib Mahfouz, *The Journey of Ibn Fattouma*, trans. Denys Johnson-Davies (New York: Doubleday, 1993), 23, 27–32. Johnson-Davies's English translation accurately renders some of the most offensive tropes from the original Arabic.

32. Mahfouz, *Riḥlat*, 114–35; Mahfouz, *Journey*, 133–44.

33. Mahfouz employs the term "idolatrous" (*awthanī*) to describe pagan inhabitants of *dār al-Mashriq* while comparing them with *jāhilī* (pagan, pre-Islamic) Arab ancestors and with dissolute contemporary Muslims (described as virtual "pagans" [*jāhilī*]); for example, the narrator states: "I criticize too harshly the outward signs of misery [poverty and neglect] in this pagan [idolatrous] country [*hadha al-balad al-awthanī*], which, being pagan, did perhaps have some excuse. But what excuse could I make for similar signs in my own Islamic country?" (Mahfouz, *Riḥlat*, 25; Mahfouz, *Journey*, 24). See also Mahfouz, *Journey*, 27, 41; Mahfouz, *Riḥlat*, 28, 41.

34. Hayek, "Whitewashing Arabic for Global Consumption," 101–2.

35. Mahfouz, *Riḥlat*, 26; Mahfouz, *Journey*, 24.

36. Mahfouz, *Riḥlat*, 25; Mahfouz, *Journey*, 24.

37. Mahfouz, *Riḥlat*, 28; Mahfouz, *Journey*, 27.

38. Their mixed children are described by the narrator as "uplifted by Islam," and the disappearance and enslavement of his "pagan" wife and children are due to a conflict masquerading as a war of "liberation." See Mahfouz, *Riḥlat*, 47–48, 59; and Mahfouz, *Journey*, 47, 59.

39. On Qutb's controversial ideas, see Roxanne Euben, *Enemy in the Mirror: Islamic Fundamentalism and the Limits of Modern Rationalism* (Princeton: Princeton University Press, 1999), 49–92. On Mahfouz's acquaintance with Sayyid Qutb, parodied in Mahfouz's novel *al-Mirāyā* (*Mirrors*), see El-Enany, *Pursuit of Meaning*, 23–24. See also Naguib Mahfouz, *Mirrors*, trans. Roger Allen (Cairo: American University in Cairo Press for Zeitouna, 1999).

40. For relevant passages on *dār al-Ḥalba*, including on controversies regarding homosexuality, the theatrical or artistic representation of religious figures, the consumption of alcohol, and the limits of religious freedom and pluralism, see Mahfouz, *Riḥlat*, 73–75, 80–81, 90, 93; Mahfouz, *Journey*, 84–86, 92, 103, 107. On the potential implications of such controversies and apparent contradictions—contradictions that Shahab Ahmed has argued might be understood as *constitutive* of "Islam" itself—see Shahab Ahmed, *What Is Islam? The Importance of Being Islamic* (Princeton: Princeton University Press, 2015), especially 72–73, 103–9, 246–97.

41. On this controversy and Mahfouz's response, see Mehrez, *Egyptian Writers*, 18–35; and Aboul-Ela, "Writer Becomes Text."

42. For an overview of these egalitarian teachings and precepts, see Kilito, *Tongue of Adam*, 23–24.

43. Ouyang, *Politics of Nostalgia*, 164–68.

44. On this sequence, see Naguib Mahfouz, *Children of the Alley* [*Awlād Ḥāratinā*], trans. Peter Theroux (New York: Random House, 1996), 144–45, 249, 359–60; see also Ouyang, *Politics of Nostalgia*, 165–68.

45. El-Enany, *Pursuit of Meaning*, 141–44; Ouyang, *Politics of Nostalgia*, 165–75.

46. Mahfouz, *Children of the Alley*, 437–38.

47. El-Enany, *Pursuit of Meaning*, 141–44; Ouyang, *Politics of Nostalgia*, 165–75; and Mehrez, *Egyptian Writers*, 19–24.

48. Mahfouz, *Children of the Alley*, 444.

49. Adham's wife, Umaima, the "Eve figure" of the text, and Adham's mother are both described as black *jāriya* or "slave women" and mocked by the devilish "Idris" (Iblis) for their social standing and complexion. See Naguib Mahfouz, *Awlād Ḥāratinā* (Cairo: Dār al-Shurūq, 2011), 13–15, 23–24; Mahfouz, *Children of the Alley*, 11–12, 19–20. Adham is equally derided as a "slave boy" due to his maternal lineage and darker complexion (*lawnihi al-ʾasmar*). Terms used in Mahfouz's Arabic original to describe these humbled figures—which include *ʿabd*/*ʿabīd*, meaning "slave" in Arabic but also a pejorative epithet for "black"—compound the narrative association of blackness with social subordination in the text. The connection between classism and colorism as conveyed by such pejorative Arabic terms fails to translate directly into the English version.

50. Mahfouz, *Awlād Ḥāratinā*, 13. The Arabic term *ʿabd* (slave/worshipper) yields two plural forms: *ʿibād*, more commonly used to describe worshippers, and *ʿabīd* (slaves); *ʿabd*/*ʿabīd*

are pejorative epithets for "blacks," associating dark skin with enslavement. The passage therefore seems to play on the Prophet Muhammad's last sermon proclaiming the equal status of blacks and whites, differentiated only by piety (or closeness to God). On these pejorative, prejudicial terms in Arabic, see Sharkey, *Living with Colonialism*, 16–24; and Hayek, "Whitewashing Arabic for Global Consumption," 93, 97–99.

51. This refers to the Prophet Muhammad's last sermon. Adham's mother recedes from view after being mocked by Idris/Iblis for her darkness and servitude, but her reappearance as Gabalawi's final messenger cannot be dismissed. The final messenger's intimate position as Gabalawi's black slave/wife is implied by her statement that Gabalawi "died in my arms" and by speculation that she "shared [her master's] room." See Mahfouz, *Children of the Alley*, 435–37; Mahfouz, *Awlād Ḥāratinā*, 563–69.

52. See Mahfouz, *Awlād Ḥāratinā*, 386; Mahfouz, *Children of the Alley*, 299–301.

53. Powell, *Different Shade of Colonialism*, especially "Black Servants and Saviors," 64–104; Powell, *Tell This in My Memory*; and Fahmy, *Ordinary Egyptians*, 8–11, 27–29, 70–72.

54. See Marlow, *Hierarchy and Egalitarianism*, 174–75.

55. See El-Enany, *Pursuit of Meaning*, 144–45; Ouyang, *Politics of Nostalgia*, 175–76; and M. M. Badawi, "Mamlakat Allah: Dirāsat fī Malḥamat al-Ḥarāfīsh," *Fuṣūl* 17, no. 1 (Summer 1998): 97–124, on *al-Ḥarāfīsh* as a rewriting of *Awlād Ḥāratinā*.

56. On historical meanings of *ḥarāfīsh*, see William Brinner, "The Significance of the *Ḥarāfīsh* and Their 'Sultan,'" *Journal of the Economic and Social History of the Orient* 6, no. 2 (1963): 190–215; and Cobham, "Enchanted to a Stone," 125–35.

57. On biographical similarities to the Prophet Muhammad, see El-Enany, *Pursuit of Meaning*, 157–59.

58. Singular terms for *ashrāf* and *assād* are *sharīf* and *sayyid*, respectively. On the historical and social dynamics associated with genealogical claims of proximity to the Prophet Mohammad and his tribe among the Quraysh, see Sarah Bowen Savant and Helena de Felipe, eds., *Genealogy and Knowledge in Muslim Societies: Understanding the Past* (Edinburgh: Edinburgh University Press, 2014), 1–10; and Kazuo Morimoto's contribution, "Keeping the Prophet's Family Alive: Profile of a Genealogical Discipline," in *Genealogy and Knowledge in Muslim Societies: Understanding the Past*, ed. Sarah Bowen Savant and Helena de Felipe (Edinburgh: Edinburgh University Press, 2014), 11–23. These dynamics within *al-Ḥarāfīsh* are subtle and indirect, as Mahfouz employs more neutral terms (*aʿyān* or *wujahāʾ*, or "notables") to refer to the eminent family at the center of the plot; see Ouyang, *Politics of Nostalgia*, 184–85.

59. Mahfouz, *al-Ḥarāfīsh*, 583–85, 593–96; Mahfouz, *Harafish*, 396, 402–4.

60. See Cobham, "Five Questions," on Mahfouz's intention to keep the *ʿajamiyya* chants inscrutable in English translation.

61. Naguib Mahfouz, "Najīb Maḥfūẓ: Youssef Wahbī fī dawr al-iqṭāʿī fī Mīrāmār," interview by Laila al-Atrash, al-Riwāʾīya wa-l-ʿIlāmiya Lailā al-Aṭrāsh, YouTube, October 25, 2020, https://youtu.be/j63XvfrS9R8.

62. Mahfouz, *al-Ḥarāfīsh*, 22.

63. My translation; see also Mahfouz, *Harafish*, 8–9.

64. See, for example, Naguib Mahfouz, "Zaabalawi," in *Modern Arabic Short Stories*, trans. Denys Johnson-Davies (London: Oxford University Press, 1966), 137–47.

65. Mahfouz, *Harafish*, 306. See also Mahfouz, *al-Ḥarāfīsh*, 451–61; Mahfouz, *Harafish*, 304–10.

66. Mahfouz, *al-Ḥarāfīsh*, 460–61; Mahfouz, *Harafish*, 310.

67. On the novel's utopianist ending, see El-Enany, *Pursuit of Meaning*, 158–90; Ouyang, *Politics of Nostalgia*, 184–90.

68. Mahfouz, *al-Ḥarāfīsh*, 598.

69. In the original Arabic, these final lines of *ʿajamiyya* verse remain untranslated and obscure. Cobham ("Five Questions") decided to translate these final lines into English, though Mahfouz was reluctant to agree and insisted that *ʿajamiyya* lines remain untranslated across the rest of the novel's English translation.

70. Mahfouz, *al-Ḥarāfīsh*, 598. This point is emphasized through Mahfouz's Arabic diction, as the verb *afṣaḥa* (*tufṣiḥ*) is etymologically related to the ideal of *faṣāḥa*; on this latter concept, see Suleiman, *Arabic in the Fray*, 70, 80–88.

71. On comparisons to the Prophet Muhammad, see El-Enany, *Pursuit of Meaning*, 157–59; and Cobham, "Enchanted to a Stone," 131–32.

72. Suleiman, *Arabic in the Fray*, 68–84; and Suleiman, *Arabic Language and National Identity*, 51–58.

73. See Qurʾan 30:22.

74. My paraphrase of Benjamin, "Translator's Task," 157, building on Lawrence Venuti's introduction to Lawrence Venuti, ed., *The Translation Studies Reader*, 3rd ed. (New York: Routledge, 2012), 71–77.

75. In interviews, Mahfouz claimed that the term *ḥarāfīsh* in this novel was meant to represent "the common masses" (*ʿāmmat al-shaʿb*); see Cobham, "Enchanted to a Stone," 124.

76. Mahfouz considered it an accomplishment that many of his readers seemed "not consciously aware of whether my characters are speaking *fuṣḥā* or *ʿāmmiyya*," believing that he had therefore surpassed older controversies over diglossia; see Mahfouz's interview with Mohamed Salmawy, *Naguib Mahfouz at Sidi Gaber*, 87.

77. See Cobham, "Enchanted to a Stone," 130–31; and Roger Allen's review, "*Harafish*," 874, claiming that the novel would likely "test the tolerance" of non-native readers of Arabic. One might observe, in contrast, the novel's largely favorable reception among Arabic language critics noted in Ouyang, *Politics of Nostalgia*, 184, 119–220.

78. On these interpretive trends, see Cobham, "Enchanted to a Stone," 125–26; El-Enany, *Pursuit of Meaning*, 144–45, 158–59; Ouyang, *Politics of Nostalgia*, 184–91; Nathaniel Greenberg, *The Aesthetic of Revolution in the Film and Literature of Naguib Mahfouz, 1952–1967* (Lanham, Md.: Lexington Books, 2014), xv–xvii, 28–30; and Badawi, "Mamlakat Allah."

79. Catherine Cobham's translation renders the term *ʿajamiyya* simply as "Persian" and in one case as "foreign." The choice unfortunately does not capture the original Arabic meaning of "inscrutability" or signal the Qurʾanic gravity of the term. Cobham ("Five Questions") notes the challenge to translators of these inscrutable lines in the novel, given that Mahfouz had intended for them to remain opaque to ordinary readers.

80. The notion of charismatic *ansāb* is here implicated. See "Ḥasab wa-Nasab," in *Encyclopaedia of Islam*, 2nd ed., ed. P. Bearman, Th. Bianquis, C. E. Bosworth, E. Van Donzel, and W. P. Heinrichs (Leiden: Brill, 2012), accessed August 23, 2019, http://dx.doi.org/10.1163/1573-3912_islam_SIM_2751; and F. Rosenthal, "Nasab," in *Encyclopaedia of Islam*, 2nd ed., ed.

P. Bearman, Th. Bianquis, C. E. Bosworth, E. Van Donzel, and W. P. Heinrichs (Leiden: Brill, 2012), accessed August 23, 2019, https://doi.org/10.1163/1573-3912_islam_SIM_5807. See also Savant and Felipe, *Genealogy and Knowledge in Muslim Societies*, 1–10.

81. Warner, *Tongue-Tied Imagination*, 5.

82. Warner, *Tongue-Tied Imagination*, 5–29.

Notes to Conclusion

1. See Khalil Gibran, *The Prophet* (New York: Alfred A. Knopf, 1923); and Eka Budianta, "Pengantar: Kahlil Gibran Kita," in *Kahlil Gibran di Indonesia, ed.* Eka Budianta (Depok, Indonesia: Badan Pelestarian Pusaka Indonesia, 2010), xv. On Gibran's Indonesian translation history in Indonesia, see Chairil Gibran Ramadhan, "Nabi, Dewa, dan Kahlil Gibran," in *Kahlil Gibran di Indonesia, ed.* Eka Budianta (Depok, Indonesia: Badan Pelestarian Pusaka Indonesia, 2010), 74–76; and Maman Lesmana, "Mengapa Mereka Enggan Menyebut Nama Gibran?" in *Kahlil Gibran di Indonesia, ed.* Eka Budianta (Depok, Indonesia: Badan Pelestarian Pusaka Indonesia, 2010), 151–62. The controversy concerned translations of *The Prophet* published in 1977 (after an earlier translation from 1949 had fallen into obscurity). On Gibran's Arabic and English reception, see Waïl Hassan, "The Gibran Phenomenon," in *Immigrant Narratives: Orientalism and Cultural Translation in Arab American and Arab British Literature* (New York: Oxford University Press, 2011), 60–76.

2. Shu-Mei Shih, "The Concept of the Sinophone," *PMLA* 126, no. 3 (2011): 711.

3. Shih, "Concept of the Sinophone," 711. See also Jing Tsu and David Der-wei Wang, eds., *Global Chinese Literature: Critical Essays* (Leiden: Brill, 2010); and Shu-mei Shih, Chien-hsin Tsai, and Brian Bernards, eds., *Sinophone Studies: A Critical Reader* (New York: Columbia University Press, 2013).

4. Ricci, *Islam Translated*, 13–20. See also generative questions on "post-monolingual" approaches to arabophone studies raised by Yasser Elhariry and Rebecca Walkowitz; Yasser Elhariry and Rebecca L. Walkowitz, "The Postlingual Turn," *SubStance* 50, no. 1 (2021): 8. Future scholarship might also consider as a precedent the liminal literary dynamics, forms of cultural nostalgia, and generative debates on orthographic change in the Turkish case observed by Nergis Ertürk in *Grammatology and Literary Modernity in Turkey* (New York: Oxford University Press, 2011). On "scriptworld" as a framing concept, see Damrosch, "Scriptworlds."

5. See Ngom, *Muslims beyond the Arab World*, 250–52; and Kane, *Non-Europhone Intellectuals*, 1–4, 57–60.

6. A convincing case for dissociating Arabic/Arabicized literacies from purely religious literacies and from globally "underclass" status (absent European language proficiencies) is also made in Kane, *Non-Europhone Intellectuals*, 44–45, 55–56. On problematic associations of religious literacies with noncosmopolitan status and a lack of critical erudition, see also Allan, *In the Shadow of World Literature*, 3, 7–9; and in former French colonial North African contexts, Hoda El Shakry, *The Literary Qur'an: Narrative Ethics in the Maghreb* (New York: Fordham University Press, 2019), 5–13.

7. Françoise Lionnet, "Universalisms and Francophonies," in *World Literature in Theory*, ed. David Damrosch (Chichester, U.K.: Wiley Blackwell, 2014), 307.

8. For an overview of relevant debates in francophone contexts, see Jacqueline Dutton,

"Francophonie and Universality: The Ideological Challenges of *Littérature Monde*," in *World Literature in Theory*, ed. David Damrosch (Chichester, U.K.: Wiley Blackwell, 2014), 279–92; Lionnet, "Universalisms and Francophonies." On anglophone counterpoints, see also Mufti, *Forget English!*, 12–20, 51–53; and Akshya Saxena, *Vernacular English: Reading the Anglophone in Postcolonial India* (Princeton: Princeton University Press, 2022), 6–28. See also Karen Thornber, "Rethinking the World in World Literature: East Asia and Literary Contact Nebulae," in *World Literature in Theory*, ed. David Damrosch (Chichester, U.K.: Wiley Blackwell, 2014), 460–79.

9. Ricci, *Islam Translated*, 1–21. See also al-Musawi, *Medieval Islamic Republic of Letters*, 50-58. Students of transregional arabophone studies might also take cues from recent work in South Asia in connection to language choice, code-switching, and caste, to consider how the use of Arabic in historically casted communities has reflected or transformed caste dynamics and caste marked literatures from West Africa to South and Southeast Asia. See Saxena, *Vernacular English*, 60–87, 98–100. See also Subramanian Shankar, *Flesh and Fish Blood: Postcolonialism, Translation, and the Vernacular* (Berkeley: University of California Press, 2012), 27–37, 94–102.

10. "Concept work" is Stoler's term (see *Duress*, 18–27). My use of the term "xenophone" is inspired by David Wang's insights on "xenophone" and "Sinophone" entanglements as a counterpoint. See David Der-wei Wang, "Introduction: Chinese Literature across the Borderlands," *Prism* 18, no. 2 (October 2021): 315–18. See also Haun Saussy, *The Making of Barbarians: Chinese Literature and Multilingual Asia* (Princeton: Princeton University Press, 2022), 1–10, 39–42, 85–139. Beyond sources previously cited on dynamics of alterity—or what might be understood as "xenophone" entanglements—across an Arabic/arabophone linguistic continuum, see relevant contributions to *Multilingual Literature as World Literature*, including, on the "inherently multilingual" qualities of Arabic, Wen-chin Ouyang, "Configurations of Multilingual Literature and World Literature," in *Multilingual Literature as World Literature*, ed. Jane Hiddleston and Wen-chin Ouyang (New York: Bloomsbury Academic, 2021), 282–85; and Claire Gallien, "The Heterolingual Zone: Arabic, English and the Practice of Worldliness," in *Multilingual Literature as World Literature*, ed. Jane Hiddleston and Wen-chin Ouyang (New York: Bloomsbury Academic, 2021), especially 71–73.

11. See Maria Rosa Menocal, *The Ornament of the World: How Muslims, Jews, and Christians Created a Culture of Tolerance in Medieval Spain* (Boston: Little, Brown, 2002), 256–60; and Suzanne Conklin Akbari and Karla Mallette, eds., *A Sea of Languages: Rethinking the Arabic Role in Medieval Literary History* (Toronto: University of Toronto Press, 2018).

12. Pramoedya, *Arus Balik*.

13. Sukarno, *Collected Documents*, 5.

SELECT BIBLIOGRAPHY

Abaza, Mona, "Ada/Custom," in *Words in Motion*, ed. Carol Gluck, Anna Tsing, and Abraham Itty (Durham: Duke University Press, 2009), 67–82.

Aboe Zakij [Hamka], *Pedoman Masjarakat* 32 (September 24, 1936): 629–31.

Aboe Zakij [Hamka], *Pedoman Masjarakat* 33 (September 30, 1936): 651–52.

Aboe Zakij [Hamka], *Pedoman Masjarakat* 40 (November 25, 1936): 791–92.

Aboelezz, Mariam, "Language as Proxy in Egypt's Identity Politics: Examining the New Wave of Egyptian Nationalism," in *Language, Politics and Society in the Middle East*, ed. Yonatan Mendel and Abeer AlNajjar (Edinburgh: Edinburgh University Press, 2018), 126–47.

Abou-El-Fadl, Reem, "Building Egypt's Afro-Asian Hub: Infrastructures of Solidarity and the 1957 Cairo Conference," *Journal of World History* 30, nos. 1/2 (2019): 157–92.

Aboul-Ela, Hosam, "The Writer Becomes Text: Naguib Mahfouz and State Nationalism in Egypt," *Biography* (Honolulu) 27, no. 2 (2004): 339–56.

Aburish, Saïd, *Nasser* (New York: St. Martin's Press/Thomas Dunne Books, 2004).

Adam, Ahmat, *The Vernacular Press and the Emergence of Modern Indonesian Consciousness, 1855–1913* (Ithaca: Cornell University Studies on Southeast Asia, 1995).

Ahmed, Hussam, *The Last Nahdawi: Taha Hussein and Institution Building in Egypt* (Stanford: Stanford University Press, 2021).

Ahmed, Shahab, *What Is Islam? The Importance of Being Islamic* (Princeton: Princeton University Press, 2015).

Akbari, Suzanne Conklin, and Karla Mallette, eds., *A Sea of Languages: Rethinking the Arabic Role in Medieval Literary History* (Toronto: University of Toronto Press, 2018).

Aljunied, Khairudin, *Hamka and Islam: Cosmopolitan Reform in the Malay World* (Ithaca: Cornell University Press, 2018).

Allan, Michael, *In the Shadow of World Literature: Sites of Reading in Colonial Egypt* (Princeton: Princeton University Press, 2016).

Allen, Roger, "*The Harafish* by Naguib Mahfouz, Catherine Cobham," *World Literature Today* 68, no. 4 (1994): 874.

Anderson, Benedict, "Bung Karno and the Fossilization of Soekarno's Thought," *Indonesia* 74 (2002): 1–19.

Anderson, Benedict, *Imagined Communities: Reflections on the Origin and Spread of Nationalism* (New York: Verso, 2003).

Anderson, Benedict, *Language and Power: Exploring Political Cultures in Indonesia* (Ithaca: Cornell University Press, 1990).

Anwar, Chairil, *The Voice of the Night: Complete Poetry and Prose of Chairil Anwar*, rev. bilingual ed., trans. Burton Raffel, Southeast Asia Series no. 89 (Athens: Ohio University Center for International Studies, 1993).

Apter, Andrew, "Beyond Négritude: Black Cultural Citizenship and the Arab Question in FESTAC 77," *Journal of African Cultural Studies* 28, no. 3 (2016): 313–26.

Apter, Emily, *Against World Literature: On the Politics of Untranslatability* (New York: Verso, 2013).

Apter, Emily, *The Translation Zone: A New Comparative Literature* (Princeton: Princeton University Press, 2006).

Armbrust, Walter, *Mass Culture and Modernism in Egypt* (Cambridge: Cambridge University Press, 2001).

Association des étudiants Sénégalais en France [Senegalese section of FEANF], *Ijjib Volof: Syllabaire Volof.* (Grenoble: Imprimerie des Deux-Ponts, 1959).

Ayalon, Ami, *The Arabic Print Revolution: Cultural Production and Mass Readership* (Cambridge: Cambridge University Press, 2016).

Ayalon, Ami, *Language and Change in the Arab Middle East: The Evolution of Modern Political Discourse* (New York: Oxford University Press, 1987).

Aydin, Cemil, *The Idea of the Muslim World: A Global Intellectual History* (Cambridge: Harvard University Press, 2017).

Azeb, Sophia, "Crossing the Saharan Boundary: *Lotus* and the Legibility of Africanness," *Research in African Literatures* 50, no. 3 (2019): 91–115.

B.S., "Hamka Bisa Bahasa Asing" ["Hamka Can Talk Foreign"], *Harian Rakyat*, October 23, 1954.

Ba, Sylvia Washington, *The Concept of Negritude in the Poetry of Leopold Sedar Senghor* (Princeton: Princeton University Press, 2015).

Babou, Cheikh Anta, "Contesting Space, Shaping Places: Making Room for the Muridiyya in Colonial Senegal, 1912–45," *Journal of African History* 46, no. 3 (2005): 405–26.

Babou, Cheikh Anta, *Fighting the Greater Jihad: Amadu Bamba and the Founding of the Muridiyya of Senegal, 1853–1913* (Athens: Ohio University Press, 2007).

Babou, Cheikh Anta, "The Senegalese 'Social Contract' Revisited: The Muridiyya Muslim Order and State Politics," in *Tolerance, Democracy, and Sufis in Senegal*, ed. Mamadou Diouf (New York: Columbia University Press, 2013), 125–46.

Badawi, M. M., "Mamlakat Allah: Dirāsat fī Malḥamat al-Ḥarāfīsh," *Fuṣūl* 17, no. 1 (Summer 1998): 97–124.

Baraka, Amiri, "A Poem for Black Hearts," *Negro Digest* 14, no. 11 (September 1965): 58.

Bashkin, Orit, "On Noble and Inherited Virtues: Discussions of the Semitic Race in the Levant and Egypt, 1876–1918," *Humanities* 10, no. 88 (2021): 1–20.

Beck, Linda, *Brokering Democracy in Africa: The Rise of Clientelist Democracy in Senegal* (New York: Palgrave Macmillan, 2008).

Beier, Ulli, "Léopold Sédar Senghor: A Personal Memoir," *Research in African Literatures* 33, no. 4 (2002): 3–11.

Beinin, Joel, "Writing Class: Workers and Modern Egyptian Colloquial Poetry (*Zajal*)," *Poetics Today* 15, no. 2 (1994): 191–215.

Benda, Harry, "Christiaan Snouck Hurgronje and the Foundations of Dutch Islamic Policy in Indonesia," *Journal of Modern History* 30, no. 4 (December 1958): 338–47.

Benda, Harry, *The Crescent and the Rising Sun: Indonesian Islam under the Japanese Occupation, 1942–1945* (The Hague: W. Van Hoeve, 1958).

Benjamin, Walter, "The Translator's Task," trans. Steven Rendall, *TTR: Traduction, terminologie, rédaction* 10, no. 2 (1997): 151–65.

Betts, Raymond, *Assimilation and Association in French Colonial Theory 1890–1914* (Lincoln: University of Nebraska Press, 2005).

Biram Gassama, B., "'Ceddo' Baillonné!" *Andë Soppi*, June 1977.

Blum, Françoise, Gabrielle Chomentowski, and Constantin Katsakioris, "Au cœur des réseaux africano-soviétiques: Archives et trajectoire de l'écrivain-cinéaste sénégalais Ousmane Sembène," *Sources. Materials and Fieldwork in African Studies* 3 (2021): 99–135, accessed May 15, 2023, https://halshs.archives-ouvertes.fr/SOURCES/halshs-03418769

Booth, Marilyn, "Colloquial Arabic Poetry, Politics, and the Press in Modern Egypt," *International Journal of Middle East Studies* 24, no. 3 (1992): 419–40.

Booth, Marilyn, "Fu'ād Ḥaddād," in *The Routledge Encyclopedia of Arabic Literature*, ed. Julie Scott Meisami and Paul Starkey (New York: Routledge, 1998), 259–60.

Bousquet, G. H., *A French View of the Netherlands Indies*, trans. Philip Lilienthal (London: Oxford University Press, 1940).

Bousquet, Georges-Henri, *La politique musulmane et coloniale des Pays-Bas* (Paris: P. Hartmann, 1939).

Bouvat, Lucien, "Histoire de la civilisation arabe," *Revue du Monde Musulman* 13, no. 3 (March 1911): 581–82.

Bouvat, Lucien, "La presse musulmane," *Revue du Monde Musulman* 1, no. 1 (November 1906): 122–29.

Bowen Savant, Sarah, and Helena de Felipe, eds., *Genealogy and Knowledge in Muslim Societies: Understanding the Past* (Edinburgh: Edinburgh University Press, 2014).

Braginsky, Vladimir, *Nada-Nada Islam dalam Sastera Melayu Klasik* [*Islamic Tones in Classical Malay Literature*] (Kuala Lumpur: Dewan Bahasa dan Pustaka Kementerian Pendidikan Malaysia, 1994).

Brinner, William, "The Significance of the *Ḥarāfīsh* and Their 'Sultan,'" *Journal of the Economic and Social History of the Orient* 6, no. 2 (1963): 190–215.

Browne, Edward G., "L'Avenir de l'Islam [Enquête par Edmond Fazy]," *Questions Diplomatiques et Coloniales* 11, no. 102 (May 15, 1901): 591–95.

Brustad, Kristen, "Diglossia as Ideology," in *The Politics of Written Language in the Arab World*, ed. Jacob Hoigilt and Gunvor Mejdell (Leiden: Brill, 2017), 41–67.

Budianta, Eka, "Pengantar: Kahlil Gibran Kita," in *Kahlil Gibran di Indonesia*, ed. Eka Budianta (Depok, Indonesia: Badan Pelestarian Pusaka Indonesia, 2010), xi–xv.

Buheiry, Marwan, "Colonial Scholarship and Muslim Revivalism in 1900," *Arab Studies Quarterly* 4, nos. 1–2 (1982): 1–16.

Burke, Edmund, III, "The First Crisis of Orientalism 1890–1914," in *Connaissances du Maghreb*, ed. Jean Claude Vatin (Paris: Editions du Centre national de la recherche scientifique, 1984), 213–26.

Busch, Annett, and Max Annas, eds., *Ousmane Sembène: Interviews* (Jackson: University of Mississippi Press, 2008).

Buskens, Léon, "Christiaan Snouck Hurgronje, 'Holy War,' and Colonial Concerns," in *Jihad and Islam in World War I*, ed. Erik-Jan Zürcher (Leiden: Leiden University Press, 2015), 29–52.

Buskens, Léon, and Annemarie van Sandwijk, "Introduction: Images of a Scholar in Action," in *Scholarship in Action: Essays on the Life and Work of Christiaan Snouck Hurgronje (1857–1936)*, ed. Léon Buskens, Jan Just Witkam, and Annemarie van Sandwijk (Leiden: Brill, 2021), 3–50.

Cachia, Pierre, *Exploring Arab Folk Literature* (Edinburgh: Edinburgh University Press, 2011).

Camara, Sana, "*A'jami* Literature in Senegal: The Example of Sëriñ Muusaa Ka, Poet and Biographer," trans. R. H. Mitsch, *Research in African Literatures* 28, no. 3 (1997): 163–82.

Carra de Vaux, Bernard, "L'Avenir de l'Islam [Enquête par Edmond Fazy]," *Questions Diplomatiques et Coloniales* 11, no. 102 (May 15, 1901): 580–88.

Césaire, Aimé, "Conscience raciale et révolution sociale," *L'Étudiant noir* 1, no. 3 (May–June 1935): 1–2.

Cheah, Pheng, *Spectral Nationality: Passages of Freedom from Kant to Postcolonial Literatures of Liberation* (New York: Columbia University Press, 2003).

Cheah, Pheng, *What Is a World? Postcolonial Literature as World Literature* (Durham: Duke University Press, 2016).

Chejne, Anwar, *The Arabic Language: Its Role in History* (Minneapolis: University of Minnesota Press, 1969).

Clark, Katerina, *The Soviet Novel: History as Ritual* (Bloomington: Indiana University Press, 2000).

Cobham, Catherine, "Enchanted to a Stone: Heroes and Leaders in *The Harafish* by Najīb Mafūz," *Middle Eastern Literatures* 9, no. 2 (2006): 123–35.

Cobham, Catherine, "Five Questions with Catherine Cobham on the Translation of Mahfouz's 'Harafish,'" interview by Marcia Lynx Qualey, *ArabLit*, November 14, 2011, accessed November 1, 2018, https://arablit.org/2011/11/14/5-questions-with-catherine-cobham-on-translation-mahfouzs-harafish/

Cole, Desmond, "The History of African Linguistics to 1945," in *Current Trends in Linguistics: Linguistics in Sub-Saharan Africa*, vol. 7, ed. Thomas E. Sebeok (The Hague: Mouton, 1971), 1–29.

Colla, Elliott, *Conflicted Antiquities: Egyptology, Egyptomania, Egyptian Modernity* (Durham: Duke University Press, 2007).

Conklin, Alice, *A Mission to Civilize: The Republican Idea of Empire in France and West Africa, 1895–1930* (Stanford: Stanford University Press, 1997).

Conrad, Lawrence, "Ignaz Goldziher on Ernest Renan," in *The Jewish Discovery of Islam*, ed. Martin Kramer (Tel Aviv: Moshe Dayan Center for Middle Eastern and African Studies, Tel Aviv University, 1999), 137–80.

Cooperson, Michael, "'Arabs' and 'Iranians': The Uses of Ethnicity in the Early Abbasid Period," in *Islamic Cultures, Islamic Contexts: Essays in Honor of Professor Patricia Crone*, ed. Behnam Sadeghi and David Abulafia (Leiden: Brill, 2015), 364–87.

Cruise O'Brien, Donal B., *The Mourides of Senegal: The Political and Economic Organization of an Islamic Brotherhood* (Oxford: Clarendon Press, 1971).

Cruise O'Brien, Donal B., "The Shadow Politics of Wolofization," in *Symbolic Confrontations: Muslims Imagining the State in Africa* (New York: Palgrave Macmillan, 2003), 120–38.

Culler, Jonathan, "Anderson and the Novel," *Diacritics* 29, no. 4 (1999): 20–39.

Daff, Moussa, "L'aménagement linguistique et didactique de la coexistence du français et des langues nationales au Sénégal," *DiversCité Langues* 3 (1998), accessed August 29, 2011, http://www.uquebec.ca/diverscite

Dahm, Bernhard, *Sukarno and the Struggle for Indonesian Independence* (Ithaca: Cornell University Press, 1969).

Damrosch, David, "Scriptworlds: Writing Systems and the Formation of World Literature," *Modern Language Quarterly* 68, no. 2 (2007): 195–219.

Damrosch, David, *What Is World Literature?* (Princeton: Princeton University Press, 2004).

Damrosch, David, ed., *World Literature in Theory* (Chichester, U.K.: Wiley Blackwell, 2014).

Daud, Bukhari, *Writing and Reciting Acehnese: Perspectives on Language and Literature in Aceh* (Ph.D. dissertation, University of Melbourne, 1997).

Dawwārah, Fuʾād, *ʿAshrat Udābāʾ Yataḥaddathūn* (Cairo: Dār al-Hilāl, 1965).

Day, Tony, "Locating Indonesian Literature in the World," *Modern Language Quarterly* 68, no. 2 (2007): 173–93.

Dayfallah, Sayyid, *Ṣūrat al-Shaʿb bayna al-Shāʿir wa-l-Raʾīs* (Cairo: al-Kutub Khān li-l-Nashr wa-l-Tawzīʿ, 2015).

de Castries, Henry, "L'Avenir de l'Islam [Enquête par Edmond Fazy]," *Questions Diplomatiques et Coloniales* 12, no. 113 (November 1, 1901): 532–35.

de Castries, Henry, *L'Islam: Impressions et Études* (Paris: A. Collin, 1897).

Desormeaux, C., "La Renaissance arabe," *Revue du Monde Musulman* 4, no. 4 (April 1908): 837.

Desormeaux, C., "L'Oeuvre de Georges Zaïdan," *Revue du Monde Musulman* 4, no. 4 (April 1908): 838–45.

D'haen, Theo, César Domínguez, and Mads Thomsen, eds., *World Literature: A Reader* (New York: Routledge, 2013).

Diagne, Pathé, *Alxuraan ci Wolof* (Paris: Editions L'Harmattan, 1997 [1979]).

Diagne, Souleymane Bachir, "La Négritude comme mouvement et comme devenir," *Rue Descartes* 83 (April 2014): 50–61.

Diagne, Souleymane Bachir, "Religion and the Public Sphere in Senegal: The Evolution of a Project of Modernity," in *Crediting God: Sovereignty and Religion in the Age of Global Capitalism*, ed. Miguel E. Vatter (New York: Fordham University Press, 2011), 102–16.

Diawara, Manthia, "Popular Culture and Oral Traditions in African Film," in *African Experiences of Cinema*, ed. Imruh Bakari and Mbye B. Cham (London: British Film Institute, 1996), 209–19.

Dieng, Amady Aly, *Mémoires d'un étudiant africain*, vol. 2 (Dakar: Council for the Development of Social Science Research in Africa, 2011).

Diop, Babacar, Armand Faye, Yéro Sylla, and Amadou T. Gueye, eds., *L'impact des journaux en langues nationales sur les populations Sénégalais* (Dakar: Association des Chercheurs Sénégalais, 1990).

Diop, Cheikh Anta, *Antériorité des civilisations nègres: Mythe ou vérité historique?* (Paris: Présence Africaine, 1967).

Diouf, Mamadou, "History and Actuality in Ousmane Sembene's *Ceddo* and Djibril Diop Mambety's *Hyenas*," in *African Experiences of Cinema*, ed. Imrah Bakari and Mbye Cham (London: British Film Institute, 1996), 239–51.

Diouf, Mamadou, "The Public Role of the 'Good Islam': Sufi Islam and the Administration of Pluralism," in *Tolerance, Democracy, and Sufis in Senegal*, ed. Mamadou Diouf (New York: Columbia University Press, 2013), 1–35.

Diouf, Mamadou, ed., *Tolerance, Democracy, and Sufis in Senegal* (New York: Columbia University Press, 2013).

Djagalov, Rossen, *From Internationalism to Postcolonialism: Literature and Cinema between the Second and the Third Worlds* (Montreal: McGill-Queen's University Press, 2020).

Djaya, Sjuman, *Aku: Berdasarkan Perjalanan Hidup dan Karya Penyair Chairil Anwar*, 2nd ed. (Jakarta: Metafor Publishing, 2003).

Doutté, Edmond, "L'Avenir de l'Islam [Enquête par Edmond Fazy]," *Questions Diplomatiques et Coloniales* 12, no. 112 (October 1, 1901): 390–99.

Doyle, Laura, *Inter-imperiality: Vying Empires, Gendered Labor, and the Literary Arts of Alliance* (Durham: Duke University Press, 2020).

Dufferin Report, The Earl of Dufferin to Lord Granville, Cairo, February 6, 1883.

Dumont, Fernand, *La pensée religieuse d'Amadou Bamba* (Dakar: Les Nouvelles Éditions Africaines, 1975).

Dupont, Anne-Laure, "How Should the History of the Arabs Be Written? The Impact of European Orientalism on Jurji Zaidan's Work," in *Jurji Zaidan: Contributions to Modern Arab Thought and Literature*, ed. George C. Zaidan and Thomas Philipp (Bethesda, Md.: Zaidan Foundation, 2013), 85–121.

Dupont, Anne-Laure, "What Is a *Kātib ʿāmm*? The Status of Men of Letters and the Conception of Language according to Jurjī Zaydān," *Middle Eastern Studies* 13, no. 2 (2010): 171–81.

Dutton, Jacqueline, "Francophonie and Universality: The Ideological Challenges of *Littérature Monde*," in *World Literature in Theory*, ed. David Damrosch (Chichester, U.K.: Wiley Blackwell, 2014), 279–92.

El Hamel, Chouki, *Black Morocco: A History of Race, Slavery and Islam* (Cambridge: Cambridge University Press, 2013).

El Shakry, Hoda, *The Literary Qur'an: Narrative Ethics in the Maghreb* (New York: Fordham University Press, 2019).

El Shakry, Omnia, *The Great Social Laboratory: Subjects of Knowledge in Colonial and Postcolonial Egypt* (Stanford: Stanford University Press, 2007).

El-Ariss, Tarek, "On Cooks and Crooks: Aḥmad Fāris al-Shidyāq and the Orientalists in England and France (1840s–1850s)," in *The Muslim Reception of European Orientalism: Reversing the Gaze*, ed. Susannah Heschel and Umar Ryad (New York: Routledge, 2019), 14–38.

El-Enany, Rasheed, *Naguib Mahfouz: His Life and Times* (Cairo: American University in Cairo Press, 2007).

El-Enany, Rasheed, *Naguib Mahfouz: The Pursuit of Meaning* (New York: Routledge, 1993).

Elhariry, Yasser, and Rebecca L. Walkowitz, "The Postlingual Turn," *SubStance* 50, no. 1 (2021): 3–9.

Elmarsafy, Ziad, *Sufism in the Contemporary Arabic Novel* (Edinburgh: Edinburgh University Press, 2012).

Elshakry, Marwa, "Between Enlightenment and Evolution: Arabic and the Arab Golden Ages of Jurji Zaidan," in *Jurji Zaidan: Contributions to Modern Arab Thought and Literature*, ed. George C. Zaidan and Thomas Philipp (Bethesda, Md.: Zaidan Foundation, 2013), 123–44.

Elshakry, Marwa, "Knowledge in Motion: The Cultural Politics of Modern Science Translations in Arabic," *Isis* 99, no. 4 (December 2008): 701–30.

Elshakry, Marwa, *Reading Darwin in Arabic* (Chicago: Chicago University Press, 2013).

Errington, James Joseph, *Linguistics in a Colonial World: A Story of Language, Meaning, and Power* (Malden, Mass.: Blackwell, 2008).

Ertürk, Nergis, *Grammatology and Literary Modernity in Turkey* (New York: Oxford University Press, 2011).

Euben, Roxanne, *Enemy in the Mirror: Islamic Fundamentalism and the Limits of Modern Rationalism* (Princeton: Princeton University Press, 1999).

Euben, Roxanne, *Journeys to the Other Shore: Muslim and Western Travelers in Search of Knowledge* (Princeton: Princeton University Press, 2006).

Fahmy, Ziad, *Ordinary Egyptians: Creating the Modern Nation through Popular Culture* (Stanford: Stanford University Press, 2011).

Fal, Arame, "OSAD's Experience in the Publishing of Books in National Languages," in *Literacy and Linguistic Diversity in Global Perspective: An Intercultural Exchange with African Countries*, ed. Neville Alexander and Brigitta Busch (Strasbourg: Council of Europe Publishing, 2007), 31–38.

Fanon, Frantz, *The Wretched of the Earth*, 1st ed. (New York: Grove Press, 1968).

Fazy, Edmond, "L'Avenir de l'Islam," *Questions Diplomatiques et Coloniales* 11, no. 102 (May 15, 1901): 579–80.

Fealy, Greg, and Ronit Ricci, eds., *Contentious Belonging: The Place of Minorities in Indonesia* (Singapore: Institute of Southeast Asian Studies Publishing, 2019).

Feith, Herbert, *The Decline of Constitutional Democracy in Indonesia* (Ithaca: Cornell University Press, 1962).

Fogg, Kevin, *Indonesia's Islamic Revolution* (Cambridge: Cambridge University Press, 2020).

Fogg, Kevin, "The Standardisation of the Indonesian Language and Its Consequences for Islamic Communities," *Journal of Southeast Asian Studies* 46, no. 1 (2015): 86–110.

Forbes, Jack, *Africans and Native Americans: The Language of Race and the Evolution of Red-Black Peoples* (Urbana: University of Illinois Press, 1993).

Formichi, Chiara, ed., *Religious Pluralism in Indonesia: Threats and Opportunities for Democracy* (Ithaca: Cornell University Press, 2021).

Foulcher, Keith, "Politics and Literature in Independent Indonesia: The View from the Left," *Southeast Asian Journal of Social Science* 15, no. 1 (1987): 83–103.

Foulcher, Keith, *Pujangga Baru: Literature and Nationalism in Indonesia, 1933–1942* (Bedford Park, Australia: Flinders University Asian Studies Monograph Series, 1980).

"Fuʾād Ḥaddād … Mutanabbī al-ʿĀmmiyya al-Maṣriyya" ["Fuʾād Ḥaddād … the Mutanabbī of Egyptian *ʿĀmmiyya*"], *Ḥibr ʿalā al-raṣīf*, YouTube, uploaded by Alghad TV, August 15, 2020, https://youtu.be/_fdaBbwZQHo

Gallien, Claire, "The Heterolingual Zone: Arabic, English and the Practice of Worldliness," in *Multilingual Literature as World Literature*, ed. Jane Hiddleston and Wen-chin Ouyang (New York: Bloomsbury Academic, 2021), 69–90.

Gellar, Sheldon, *Senegal: An African Nation between Islam and the West*, 2nd ed. (Boulder: Westview Press, 1995).

Gérard, Albert, *African Language Literatures: An Introduction to the Literary History of Sub-Saharan Africa* (Harlow, U.K.: Longman, 1981).

Gershoni, Israel, and James Jankowski, *Egypt, Islam, and the Arabs: The Search for Egyptian Nationhood, 1900–1930* (New York: Oxford University Press, 1986).

Gibran, Khalil, *The Prophet* (New York: Alfred A. Knopf, 1923).

Gill, Mary-Louise, "Methods and Metaphysics in Plato's *Sophist and Statesman*," in *The Stanford Encyclopedia of Philosophy*, Spring 2020 ed., ed. Edward N. Zalta, https://plato.stanford.edu/archives/spr2020/entries/plato-sophstate

GoGwilt, Christopher, *The Passage of Literature: Genealogies of Modernism in Conrad, Rhys, and Pramoedya* (Oxford: Oxford University Press, 2011).

GoGwilt, Christopher, "Postcolonial Philology and Nearly Reading the World-System in Print Form," *Modernism/modernity Print Plus* 2, no. 4 (2018), accessed May 15, 2023, https://doi.org/10.26597/mod.0038

Goldziher, Ignaz, "Islamisme et Parsisme," *Revue de l'histoire des religions* 43 (1901): 1–29.

Goldziher, Ignaz, "L'Avenir de l'Islam," *Questions Diplomatiques et Coloniales* 11, no. 102 (May 15, 1901): 600–602.

Goldziher, Ignaz, *Muslim Studies*, vol. 1, trans. C. R. Barber (New Brunswick, N.J.: Aldine Press, 2006).

Gravrand, R. P., "Le Gabou dans les Traditions Orales du Ngabou," *Ethiopiques: Numéro spécial revue socialiste de culture négro-africaine* 28 (October 1981): 50.

Greenberg, Nathaniel, *The Aesthetic of Revolution in the Film and Literature of Naguib Mahfouz, 1952–1967* (Lanham, Md.: Lexington Books, 2014).

Gully, Adrian, "Arabic Linguistic Issues and Controversies of the Late Nineteenth and Early Twentieth Centuries," *Journal of Semitic Studies* 12, no. 1 (1997): 75–120.

Ḥaddād, Fuʾād, *al-Aʿmāl al-Kāmila*, vols. 1–3 (Cairo: al-Hayʾa al-Miṣriyya al-ʿĀmma li-l-Kitāb, 2012).

Hadler, Jeffrey, "Home, Fatherhood, Succession: Three Generations of Amrullahs in Twentieth-Century Indonesia," *Indonesia* 65 (April 1998): 122–54.

Hadler, Jeffrey, *Muslims and Matriarchs: Cultural Resilience in Indonesia through Jihad and Colonialism* (Ithaca: Cornell University Press, 2008).

Hadler, Jeffrey, *Places Like Home: Islam, Matriliny, and the History of Family in Minangkabau* (Ph.D. dissertation, Cornell University, 2000).

Haeri, Niloofar, "Form and Ideology: Arabic Sociolinguistics and Beyond," *Annual Review of Anthropology* 29 (2000): 61–87.

Haeri, Niloofar, *Sacred Language, Ordinary People: Dilemmas of Culture and Politics in Egypt* (New York: Palgrave Macmillan, 2003).

Haeri, Niloofar, and William M. Cotter, "Form and Ideology Revisited," in *The Routledge Handbook of Arabic Sociolinguistics*, ed. Enam Al-Wer and Uri Horesh (New York: Routledge, 2019), 243–58.

Hair, P.E.H., "The Contribution of Early Linguistic Material to the History of West Africa," in *Language and History in Africa*, ed. David Dalby (New York: Africana Publishing Corporation, 1970), 50–63.

Hale, Thomas A., *Griots and Griottes: Masters of Words and Music* (Bloomington: Indiana University Press, 1998).

Halim, Hala, "*Lotus*, the Afro-Asian Nexus, and Global South Comparatism," *Comparative Studies of South Asia, Africa, and the Middle East* 32, no. 3 (2012): 571–77.

Hall, Bruce, *A History of Race in Muslim West Africa, 1600–1960* (New York: Cambridge University Press, 2011).

Hall, Jonathan M., *Hellenicity: Between Ethnicity and Culture* (Chicago: University of Chicago Press, 2002).

Hamburger, Peter, "Orientalist or Master Spy: The Career of Christiaan Snouck Hurgronje," in *Scholarship in Action: Essays on the Life and Work of Christiaan Snouck Hurgronje (1857–1936)*, ed. Léon Buskens, Jan Just Witkam, and Annemarie van Sandwijk (Leiden: Brill, 2021), 546–70.

Hamka, "Bahasa didalam sembahjang," *Pedoman Masjarakat* 37 (September 11, 1940): 723–24.

Hamka, "Berita memperkenalkan," *Pedoman Masjarakat*, January 20, 1936, 1.

Hamka, *Di Bawah Lindoengan Kaʿbah* [*Beneath the Sanctuary of the Kaʿbah*] (Jakarta: Balai Poestaka, 1938).

Hamka, "Faham Soekarno," 3 pts., *Pedoman Masjarakat* 18 (May 1, 1940): 344–45; 19 (May 8, 1940): 365–66; 20 (May 15, 1940): 385–86.

Hamka, "Fikiran Kita: Islam dan Nasional" ["Our Thoughts: Islam and the National"], *Pedoman Masjarakat* 42 (October 16, 1940): 825.

Hamka, *Gema Islam* 10 (June 15, 1962): 30–33.

Hamka, *Islam dan Adat Minangkabau* (Jakarta: Pustaka Panjimas, 1984).

Hamka, *Islam dan Demokrasi* (Jakarta: Tjerdas, 1945).

Hamka, "Islam dan kebangsaan" ["Islam and Nationalism"], *Pedoman Masjarakat*, January 4, 1939, 4–5.

Hamka, "Islam dan kebangsaan," *Pedoman Masjarakat* 11 (March 16, 1938): 201.

Hamka, *Kenang-Kenangan Hidup II*, 1st ed. (Jakarta: Usaha Penerbitan Gapura, 1951).

Hamka, *Kenang-Kenangan Hidup II* [*Life Memoirs II*], 3rd ed. (Jakarta: Bulan Bintang, 1974).

Hamka, *Kenang-Kenangan ku di Malaya* (Singapore: Setia Derma, 1957).

Hamka, *Laila Madjnoen* (Jakarta: Balai Poestaka, 1932).

Hamka, "Mengapa Hamka Dipenjara?" ["Why Was Hamka Imprisoned?"], interview, *Al-Islam* (Kuala Lumpur), May 15, 1974, 10–11.

Hamka, *Negara Islam* (Padang Panjang, Indonesia: Penerbit Anwar Rasjid Padang Pandjang, 1946).

Hamka, *Pedoman Masjarakat*, January 4, 1939, 26–27.

Hamka, *Pedoman Masjarakat* 35 (August 28, 1940): 687–88.

Hamka, *Pelita Andalas*, August 2, 4, 6, and 13, 1927.

Hamka, "Pengaruh Huruf atas Bahasa dan Bangsa" ["The Influence of Script beyond Language and Nation"], *Hikmah* 107 (February 16, 1952): 18.

Hamka, "Sambutan Hamka Pada Cetakan Pertama" ["Hamka's Statement on the First Edition"], in H. B. Jassin, *Al Qu'ran Bacaan Mulia*, 4th ed. (Jakarta: Yaco Jaya, 2002), xvi.

Hamka, "Soal2 Islam: Sembahjang dalam bahasa sendiri," *Pedoman Masjarakat*, August 14, 1940, 643.

Hamka, "Tjatatan Editorial: Bahasa Indonesia di Volksraad," *Pedoman Masjarakat*, July 13, 1938, 541.

Hamka, "Tjatetan Editorial: Menjamboet Kongres Bahasa Indonesia," *Pedoman Masjarakat* 25 (June 22, 1938): 481.

Hamka, Roesydi, *Pribadi dan Martabat Buya Prof. Hamka* (Jakarta: Pustaka Panjimas, 1981).

Hamoneau, Didier, *Vie et Enseignement du Cheikh Ahmadou Bamba* (Beirut: Al-Bouraq, 1998).

Hanna, Sami, and George Gardner, "*Al-Shuʿūbiyya* Up-Dated: A Study of the 20th Century Revival of an Eighth Century Concept," *Middle East Journal* 20, no. 3 (Summer 1966): 335–51.

Hanna, Sami, and George Gardner, *Arab Socialism: A Documentary Survey* (Leiden: Brill, 1969).

Harney, Elizabeth, *In Senghor's Shadow: Art, Politics, and the Avant-Garde in Senegal, 1960–1995* (Durham: Duke University Press, 2004).

Harrison, Christopher, *France and Islam in West Africa, 1860–1960* (Cambridge: Cambridge University Press, 1988).

"Ḥasab wa-Nasab," in *Encyclopaedia of Islam*, 2nd ed., ed. P. Bearman, Th. Bianquis, C. E. Bosworth, E. Van Donzel, and W. P. Heinrichs (Leiden: Brill, 2012), accessed August 23, 2019, http://dx.doi.org/10.1163/1573-3912_islam_SIM_2751

Hassan, Noorhaidi, "The Making of Public Islam: Piety, Agency, and Commodification on the Landscape of the Indonesian Public Sphere," *Contemporary Islam* 3 (2009): 229–50.

Hassan, Waïl, "Arabic and the Paradigms of Comparison," in *Futures of Comparative Literature: ACLA State of the Discipline Report*, ed. Ursula Heise (Abingdon, U.K.: Routledge, 2017), 191–92.

Hassan, Waïl, "The Gibran Phenomenon," in *Immigrant Narratives: Orientalism and Cultural Translation in Arab American and Arab British Literature* (New York: Oxford University Press, 2011), 60–76.

Hayek, Ghenwa, "Whitewashing Arabic for Global Consumption: Translating Race in *The Story of Zahra*," *Middle Eastern Literatures* 20, no. 1 (2017): 91–104.

Heinschke, Martina, "Between Gelanggang and Lekra: Pramoedya's Developing Literary Concepts," *Indonesia* 61 (1996): 145–69.

Hering, Bob, *Soekarno: Founding Father of Indonesia, 1901–1945* (Leiden: Koninklijk Institut voor Taal-, Land- en Volkenkunde Press, 2002).

Hiddleston, Jane, *Decolonising the Intellectual: Politics, Culture, and Humanism at the End of the French Empire* (Liverpool: Liverpool University Press, 2014).

Hoffman, John, "A Foreign Investment: Indies Malay to 1901," *Indonesia* 27 (1979): 65–92.

Holes, Clive, "The Use of Variation: A Study of the Political Speeches of Gamal Abd al-Nasir," in *Perspectives on Arabic Linguistics*, ed. Mushira Eid and Clive Holes (Ann Arbor: John Benjamins, 1993), 13–45.

Holt, Mike, "Divided Loyalties: Language and Ethnic Identity in the Arab World," in *Language and Identity in the Middle East and North Africa*, ed. Yasir Suleiman (Richmond, U.K.: Curzon Press, 1996), 11–24.

Husayn, Falih, "The Participation of Non-Arab Elements in the Umayyad Army and Administration," in *The Articulation of Early Islamic State Structures*, ed. Fred M. Donner (New York: Routledge, 2012), 265–89.

Ibn Battuta, *The Travels of Ibn Battutah*, trans. H.A.R. Gibb and C. F. Beckingham (London: Picador, 2002).

Ibn Khaldun, *Kitāb al-ʿIbar wa-Dīwān al-Mubtadaʾ wa-l-Khabar fī Ayyām al-ʿArab wa-l-ʿAjam wa-l-Barbar* (Cairo: ʿAbd al-Maṭbaʿa al-Miṣrīyya bi-Būlāq, 1867).

Ibn Khaldun, *The Muqaddimah*, trans. Franz Rosenthal (Princeton: Princeton University Press, 2005).

Irele, Abiola, *The African Experience in Literature and Ideology* (Bloomington: Indiana University Press, 1990).

Irvine, Judith T., "Minerva's Orthography: Early Colonial Projects for Print Literacy in African Languages," *Social Dynamics* 45, no. 1 (2019): 26–52.

Irvine, Judith T., "When Talk Isn't Cheap: Language and Political Economy," in *The Matrix of Language: Contemporary Linguistic Anthropology*, ed. Donald Brenneis and Ronald K. S. Macaulay (New York: Routledge, 2018), 258–83.

Issa, Rana, "Al-Shidyāq-Lee Version (1857): An Example of a Non-synchronous Nineteenth-Century Arabic Bible," in *Senses of Scripture, Treasures of Tradition: The Bible in Arabic among Jews, Christians and Muslims*, ed. Miriam L. Hjalm (Leiden: Brill, 2017), 305–23.

Issa, Rana, "Rakākah and the Petit Quarrel of 1871: Christian Authors and the Competition over Arabic," in *Language, Politics and Society in the Middle East: Essays in Honour of Yasir Suleiman*, ed. Yonatan Mendel and Abeer Alnajjar (Edinburgh: Edinburgh University Press, 2018), 148–64.

Issa, Rana, "Scripture as Literature: The Bible, the Qurʾan and Aḥmad Fāris al-Shidyāq," *Journal of Arabic Literature* 50 (2019): 29–55.

Jacquemond, Richard, *Conscience of the Nation* (Cairo: American University in Cairo Press, 2008).

Jassin, H. B., *Al Qu'ran Bacaan Mulia*, 1st ed. (Jakarta: Djambatan, 1978).

Jassin, H. B., *Al Qu'ran Bacaan Mulia*, 4th ed. (Jakarta: Yaco Jaya, 2002).

Jassin, H. B., *Chairil Anwar: Pelopor Angkatan 45*, 3rd ed. (Jakarta: Gunung Agung, 1968).

Jassin, H. B., *Kontroversi Al-Qurʾanul Karim Bacaan Mulia* (Jakarta: Dinas Kebudayaan Propinsi DKI Jakarta bekerja sama dengan Dokumentasi Sastra H. B. Jassin Pusat, 2000).

Jaurès, Jean, "Pour la laïque, discours prononcé à la chambre en deux fois, les 14 et 24 Janvier 1910," in *L'Esprit du socialisme, six études et discours* (Paris: Éditions Gonthier, 1964), 145–69.

Jedamski, Doris, "Balai Pustaka: A Colonial Wolf in Sheep's Clothing," *Archipel* 44, no. 1 (1992): 23–46.

Johns, Anthony H., "Qurʾanic Exegesis in the Malay-Indonesian World: An Introductory Survey," in *Approaches to the Qurʾan in Contemporary Indonesia*, ed. Abdullah Saeed (London: Oxford University Press, 2005), 17–40.

Johnson, Rebecca C., *Stranger Fictions: A History of the Novel in Arabic Translation* (Ithaca: Cornell University Press, 2020).

Jones, John Robert, *Learning Arabic in Renaissance Europe, 1505–1624* (Leiden: Brill, 2020).

Kaddu (Dakar: Éditions Papyrus, 1971–78):

Unattributed articles:

"Bind ci sa lakk—Wolofal," *Kaddu* 23 (February 1978): 28.

"Ceddo bi siggi ag ceddo ba Sëggulwoon," *Kaddu* 23 (1978): 2–4.
"Ecriture: Mbind Mi," *Kaddu* 1 (December 1971): 2.
"Ecriture: Mbind Mi," *Kaddu* 2 (January 1972): 1, 16.
"Hello Pulaar," *Kaddu* 3 (February 1972): 15–16.
"Kenu doginu baat yi," editorial, *Kaddu* 16 (n.d. [likely between January and March 1974]): 2–5.
"Mbindinu lakki réew mi," editorial, *Kaddu* 15 (n.d. [likely between August 1973 and February 1974]): 2–5.
"Ndaali Sheyxu Umar," *Kaddu Espesiyal Sunu Indepandans*, March/April 1972, 9–12.
"Ndajem Liban," *Kaddu* 19 (1974 [likely December]): 3–4.
"Ndajem 'UNESCO' ci lakki Afrig yi," *Kaddu* 19 ([December] 1974): 3, 5.
"Njaal . . . Deewuk Kurumaa," *Kaddu* 4 (May 1972): 10.
"NKrumaa," *Kaddu* 5 (June 1972): 1–3, 6, 16.
"Sheyxu Umar ag Saamoori," *Kaddu Espesiyal Sunu Indepandans*, March/April 1972, 2, 8–9.
"Ubbi," *Kaddu* 19 ([December] 1974): 2–4.
"Ubbi Jëmmu Afrig konsiyans nasyonaal, xeexi tay yi ag seeni cosaan," *Kaddu Espesiyal Sunu Indepandans*, March/April 1972, 1–4.
"Ubbiteefu *Kaddu*," editorial, *Kaddu* 23 (1978): 1–2.
"Wàyu Malcom," *Kaddu* 3 (February 1972): 12–13.
"Wàyu Miryaam," *Kaddu* 3 (February 1972): 10–11.
Articles published under pseudonyms:
A. Salaam, "Angela Davis," *Kaddu* 4 (May 1972): 15–16.
B.Y., "NKrumaa," *Kaddu* 6 (July 1972): 1, 3–6.
B. Yoon, "Ubbi Editoryaal: Demokaraasi ag nguuru cosaan," *Kaddu* 4 (May 1972): 1–5.
Boroom Yoon ["The Explorer"], "Ubbi," *Kaddu* 1 (December 1971): 3–5.
Boroom Yoon ["The Explorer"], "Ubbi Editoryaal," *Kaddu* 2 (January 1972): 1–2.
Ceddo [Ousmane Sembene], "Moom sa reew," *Kaddu Espesiyal Sunu Indepandans*, March/April 1972, unpaginated first page.
D.S. and M.P.D., "Ubbi: Kodu Famiiy Bi," editorial, *Kaddu* 8 (September 1972): 1–4.
Seetaankat bi, "Miryaam Makkeba ci Ndakaaru," *Kaddu* 3 (February 1972): 1–3.
Sëriñ Sall, "Juróoméelu biyenaalu làkku Tubaab," *Kaddu* 17 (April 1974): 2.
Sëriñ Sall, "Xëtu diine ci kod bi," *Kaddu* 7 (August 1972): 9–10.
Taalibé yi ["Students"], "Ubbite Lekool yi ag Reforme bi," *Kaddu* 10 (November/December 1972): 1–6.
W. Waalo bi, "Njangale Lakku Senegal Yi," *Kaddu* 3 (February 1972): 4.
Waa Senegal yi ["The Senegalese"], "Xewxewu jamano ji," *Kaddu* 8 (September 1972): 4.
Xewcaakoon mi, "Amerigu nit ku ñuul," *Kaddu* 3 (February 1972): 7–9.
Kadir, Djelal, "To World, to Globalize: World Literature's Crossroads," in *World Literature in Theory*, ed. David Damrosch (Chichester, U.K.: Wiley Blackwell, 2014), 264–70.
Kalliney, Peter J., *The Aesthetic Cold War: Decolonization and Global Literature* (Princeton: Princeton University Press, 2022).
Kane, Ousmane, *Beyond Timbuktu: An Intellectual History of Muslim West Africa* (Cambridge: Harvard University Press, 2016).
Kane, Ousmane, *Non-Europhone Intellectuals* (Dakar: Council for the Development of Social Science Research in Africa, 2012).

Kane, Ousmane, and John Hunwick, "Senegambia III: Writers of the Murīd Ṭarīqa," in *Arabic Literature of Africa, vol. 4: The Writings of Western Sudanic Africa*, ed. John O. Hunwick (Leiden: Brill, 2003), 396–462.

Kaptein, Nico, "'My Dear Professor 'Abd al-Ghaffar.' The Letters of Sayyid 'Uthman to C. Snouck Hurgronje as a Reflection of Their Relationship," in *Scholarship in Action: Essays on the Life and Work of Christiaan Snouck Hurgronje (1857–1936)*, ed. Léon Buskens, Jan Just Witkam, and Annemarie van Sandwijk (Leiden: Brill, 2021), 387–404.

Karr, Alphonse, *Sous les Tilleuls* (Paris: Michel Lévy Frères, 1857).

Keane, Webb, "Divine Text, National Language, and Their Publics: Arguing an Indonesian Qur'an," *Comparative Studies in Society and History* 60, no. 4 (2018): 758–85.

Keane, Webb, "Language and Religion," in *A Companion to Linguistic Anthropology*, ed. Alessandro Duranti (New York: Blackwell, 2004), 431–48.

Keane, Webb, "Public Speaking: On Indonesian as the Language of the Nation," *Public Culture* 15, no. 3 (2003): 503–30.

Kennedy, H. N., "The 'Abbasid Caliphate: A Historical Introduction," in *'Abbasid Belles Lettres*, ed. Julia Ashtiany, T. Johnstone, J. Latham, and R. Serjeant (Cambridge: Cambridge University Press, 1990), 1–15.

Kesteloot, Lilyan, *Comprendre les poèmes de Léopold Sédar Senghor* (Issy-les-Moulineaux, France: Classiques Africains, 1986).

Khalidi, Tarif, trans., *The Qur'an: A New Translation* (New York: Penguin Classics, 2008).

al-Kharrat, Edwar, and Nehad Salem, eds., *Afro-Asian Poetry: An Anthology* (Cairo: Permanent Bureau of Afro-Asian Writers, 1971).

Kholoussi, Samia, "Fallahin: The 'Mud Bearers' of Egypt's 'Liberal Age,'" in *Re-envisioning Egypt 1919–1952*, ed. Arthur Goldschmidt and Amy Johnson (Cairo: American University in Cairo Press, 2005), 277–311.

Khoury, Shaadi, *Instituting Renaissance: The Early Work of the Arab Academy of Science in Damascus, 1919–1930* (ProQuest Dissertations Publishing, 2016).

Kilito, Abdelfattah, *Thou Shalt Not Speak My Language*, trans. Waïl Hassan (Syracuse: Syracuse University Press, 2008).

Kilito, Abdelfattah, *The Tongue of Adam*, trans. Robyn Creswell (New York: New Directions, 2016).

Kipling, Rudyard, and Charles Sydney Goldman, *The Empire and the Century: A Series of Essays on Imperial Problems and Possibilities by Various Writers* (London: John Murray, 1905).

Kramer, Martin, "Surveying the Middle East," *Asian and African Studies* 24 (1990): 89–107.

Laffan, Michael Francis, *Islamic Nationhood and Colonial Indonesia: The* Umma *below the Winds* (New York: Routledge, 2003).

Landau, Jacob, *Pan-Islam: History and Politics* (New York: Routledge Library Editions, 2016).

Le Chatelier, Alfred, "German Mussulman Policy, Its Widespread Character," *The Standard*, April 18, 1907, 5.

Le Chatelier, Alfred, "Introduction," in Christiaan Snouck Hurgronje, *Politique Musulmane de la Hollande: Quatres Conférences par C. Snouck Hurgronje Conseiller du Ministère des Colonies Néerlandaises pour les Affaires Indigènes et Arabes*, Collection de la Revue du Monde Musulman, vol. 14 (Paris: Ernest Leroux, 1911), 1–3.

Le Chatelier, Alfred, *L'Islam dans l'Afrique occidentale* (Paris: G. Steinheil, 1899).

Le Chatelier, Alfred, *Politique Musulmane: Lettre au "Standard"* (Tours: E. Arrault, 1907).

Leow, Rachel, *Taming Babel: Language in the Making of Malaysia* (New York: Cambridge University Press, 2018).

Lesmana, Maman, "Mengapa Mereka Enggan Menyebut Nama Gibran?" in *Kahlil Gibran di Indonesia, ed.* Eka Budianta (Depok, Indonesia: Badan Pelestarian Pusaka Indonesia, 2010), 151–62.

Lewis, Bernard, "The Crows of the Arabs," in *"Race," Writing, and Difference*, ed. Henry Louis Gates (Chicago: University of Chicago Press, 1986), 107–16.

Lienau, Annette, "The Ideal of Casteless Language in Pramoedya's *Arok Dedes*," *Comparative Studies of South Asia, Africa and the Middle East* 32, no. 3 (2012): 591–603.

Lionnet, Françoise, "Universalisms and Francophonies," in *World Literature in Theory*, ed. David Damrosch (Chichester, U.K.: Wiley Blackwell, 2014), 293–312.

Liu, Hong, "Pramoedya Ananta Toer and China: The Transformation of a Cultural Intellectual," *Indonesia* 61 (1996): 119–43.

Locher-Scholten, Elsbeth, "Association in Theory and Practice: The Composition of the Regency Council (ca. 1910–1920)," in *Between People and Statistics: Essays in Modern Indonesian History*, ed. Francien van Anroij and Dirk H. A. Kolff (The Hague: Martinus Nijhoff, 1979), 209–11.

Lockman, Zachary, *Contending Visions of the Middle East* (Cambridge: Cambridge University Press, 2010).

Loop, Jan, *Johann Heinrich Hottinger: Arabic and Islamic Studies in the Seventeenth Century* (Oxford: Oxford University Press, 2013).

Lubis, Mohammad Ridwan, *Sukarno dan modernisme Islam* (Depok, Indonesia: Komunitas Bambu, 2010).

al-Maghribī, ʿAbd al-Qādir, *Kitāb al-Ishtiqāq wa-l-Taʿrīb* (Cairo: Maṭbaʿat al-Hilāl, 1908)

Mahfouz, Naguib, *al-Ḥarāfīsh* (Cairo: Dār al-Shurūq, 2003).

Mahfouz, Naguib, *Amām al-ʿArsh* (Cairo: Dār al-Shurūq, 2006).

Mahfouz, Naguib, *Ataḥaddath Ilaykum* (Beirut: Dār al-ʿAwda, 1977).

Mahfouz, Naguib, *Awlād Ḥāratinā* (Cairo: Dār al-Shurūq, 2011).

Mahfouz, Naguib, *Before the Throne*, trans. Raymond Stock (New York: Doubleday, 2012).

Mahfouz, Naguib, *Children of the Alley* [*Awlād Ḥāratinā*], trans. Peter Theroux (New York: Random House, 1996).

Mahfouz, Naguib, *The Harafish*, trans. Catherine Cobham (New York: Doubleday, 1994).

Mahfouz, Naguib, *The Journey of Ibn Fattouma*, trans. Denys Johnson-Davies (New York: Doubleday, 1993).

Mahfouz, Naguib, *Mirrors*, trans. Roger Allen (Cairo: American University in Cairo Press for Zeitouna, 1999).

Mahfouz, Naguib, *Naguib Mahfouz at Sidi Gaber: Reflections of a Nobel Laureate, 1994–2001. From Converstations with Mohamed Salmawy*, ed. Mohamed Salmawy (Cairo: American University in Cairo Press, 2001).

Mahfouz, Naguib, *Najīb Maḥfūẓ: Ṣafaḥāt min Mudhakkirātihi wa-Aḍwāʾ Jadīda ʿalā Adabihi wa-Ḥayātihi*, interview by Rajāʾ Naqqāsh (Cairo: Markaz al-Ahrām lil-Tarjamah wa-al-Nashr, 1998).

Mahfouz, Naguib, "Najīb Maḥfūẓ: Youssef Wahbī fi dawr al-iqṭāʿī fī Mīrāmār," interview by Laila

al-Atrash, al-Riwā'īya wa-l-ʿIlāmiya Lailā al-Aṭrāsh, YouTube, uploaded October 25, 2020, https://youtu.be/j63XvfrS9R8
Mahfouz, Naguib, *Riḥlat Ibn Faṭṭūma* (Cairo: Dār al-Shurūq, 2006).
Mahfouz, Naguib, "Zaabalawi," in *Modern Arabic Short Stories*, trans. Denys Johnson-Davies (London: Oxford University Press, 1966), 137–47.
Maier, Hendrik M. J., "Chairil Anwar's 'Heritage: The Fear of Stultification': Another Side of Modern Indonesian Literature," *Indonesia* 43 (1987): 1–29.
Maier, Hendrik M. J., "From Heteroglossia to Polyglossia: The Creation of Malay and Dutch in the Indies," *Indonesia* 56 (October 1993): 37–65.
Mallette, Karla, *Lives of the Great Languages: Arabic and Latin in the Medieval Mediterranean* (Chicago: University of Chicago Press, 2021).
Mamdani, Mahmood, *Define and Rule: Native as Political Identity* (Cambridge: Harvard University Press, 2012).
al-Manfalūṭī, Musṭafā Luṭfī, *Mājdūlīn aw-taḥta ẓilāl al-zayzafūn, ta'līf Alfūns Kār* (Beirut: Dār al-Thaqāfa, 1969).
"Maqāl Nādir li-Ṣalāḥ Jāhīn ʿan Fu'ād Ḥaddād," *al-Tahrir*, October 22, 2014, accessed September 1, 2019, https://www.masress.com/tahrirnews/1344703
Markovitz, Irving, *Léopold Sédar Senghor and the Politics of Negritude* (New York: Atheneum, 1969).
Marlow, Louise, *Hierarchy and Egalitarianism in Islamic Thought* (Cambridge: Cambridge University Press, 1997).
Marty, Paul, "Cheikh Sidiya et sa voie," *Revue du Monde Musulman* 31 (1915–16): 29–133.
Marty, Paul, *Études sur l'Islam au Sénégal*, vols. 1–2 (Paris: Ernest Leroux, 1917).
Masduki, *Public Service Broadcasting and Post-authoritarian Indonesia* (New York: Palgrave, 2020).
Massad, Joseph, *Desiring Arabs* (Chicago: University of Chicago Press, 2008).
Massad, Joseph, *Islam in Liberalism* (Chicago: Chicago University Press, 2015).
Mateo Dieste, Josep Lluís, "Are There 'Mestizos' in the Arab World? A Comparative Survey of Classification Categories and Kinship Systems," *Middle Eastern Studies* 48, no. 1 (2012): 125–38.
Mbakke, Ahmadu Bamba, "Asīru" (Touba, Senegal: Darou Khoudoss Touba, [n.d.]).
Mbakke, Ahmadu Bamba, "Jāwartu" (Touba, Senegal: Darou Khoudoss Touba, [n.d.]).
Mbakke, Ahmadu Bamba, "Jadhb al-Qulūb," in *Majmūʿa Mubāraka li-Sheikhunā Ahmad al-Khadīm* (Touba, Senegal: Darou Khoudoss Touba, [n.d.]).
Mbakke, Ahmadu Bamba, "Masālik al-Jinān" (Touba, Senegal: Darou Khoudoss Touba, [n.d.]).
Mbakke, Ahmadu Bamba, *Nahju Qaḍāʾi al-Ḥājī: fī mā min al-Adab ilayhi al-Murīd Yaḥtāj* (Rabat: Dā'irat Fath al-Ghaffār, 2017).
Mbakke, Ahmadu Bamba, *Sheikh Ahmadu Bamba: Selected Poems*, trans. Sana Camara (Leiden: Brill, 2017).
Mbeng, Ibu, "Lat Joor, ngoone Lattir: Ca mbañ ga," *Kaddu* 4 (May 1972): 1, 5–9.
Mehrez, Samia, *Egyptian Writers between History and Fiction: Essays on Naguib Mahfouz, Sonallah Ibrahim, and Gamal Al-Ghitani* (Cairo: American University in Cairo Press, 1994).
Menocal, Maria Rosa, *The Ornament of the World: How Muslims, Jews, and Christians Created a Culture of Tolerance in Medieval Spain* (Boston: Little, Brown, 2002).
Miller, Christopher L., "The (Revised) Birth of Negritude: Communist Revolution and 'the Immanent Negro' in 1935," *PMLA* 125, no. 3 (2010): 743–49.

Mohamad, Goenawan, "Bung Karno dan Islam," in *Pembentuk Sejarah: Pilihan Tulisan Goenawan Mohamad*, ed. Zaim Rofiqi, Candra Gautama, Akhmad Sahal, and Rustam F. Mandayun (Jakarta: Kepustakaan Populer Gramedia, 2021), 10–34. [Reprint of Mohamad, Goenawan, "Bung Karno dan Islam," blogpost, September 8, 2010, accessed July 1, 2016, http://goenawanmohamad.com/2010/09/08/bung-karno-dan-islam/.]

Monteil, Vincent, *L'Islam Noir*, 3rd ed. (Paris: Seuil, 1980 [1964]).

Montolalu, Lucy, and Leo Suryadinata, "National Language and Nation-Building: The Case of Bahasa Indonesia," in *Language, Nation and Development in Southeast Asia*, ed. Hock Guan Lee and Leo Suryadinata (Singapore: Institute of Southeast Asian Studies Publishing, 2007), 39–50.

Moore, Carrie D., *Evolution of an African Artist: Social Realism in the Works of Ousmane Sembene* (Ph.D. dissertation, Indiana University, 1973).

Morimoto, Kazuo, "Keeping the Prophet's Family Alive: Profile of a Genealogical Discipline," in *Genealogy and Knowledge in Muslim Societies: Understanding the Past*, ed. Sarah Bowen Savant and Helena de Felipe (Edinburgh: Edinburgh University Press, 2014), 11–23.

Moshfegh, David, *Ignaz Goldziher and the Rise of* Islamwissenschaft *as a "Science of Religion"* (Ph.D. dissertation, University of California, Berkeley, 2012).

Mottahedeh, Roy, "The Shuʿûbîyah Controversy and the Social History of Early Islamic Iran," *International Journal of Middle Eastern Studies* 7 (1976): 161–82.

Mrázek, Rudolf, "Bridges of Hope: Senior Citizens' Memories," *Indonesia* 70 (2000): 39–40.

Mufti, Aamir, *Forget English! Orientalism and World Literatures* (Cambridge: Harvard University Press, 2016).

Mufti, Aamir, "Orientalism and the Institution of World Literatures," in *World Literature in Theory*, ed. David Damrosch (Chichester, U.K.: Wiley Blackwell, 2014), 313–44.

Muhammad, Goenawan, "Aku," in *Sidelines: Thought Pieces from Tempo Magazine* [*Catatan Pinggir*], trans. Jennifer Lindsay (Jakarta: Lontar Foundation Lontar, 1994).

Mumin, Meikal, "The Arabic Script in Africa: Under-studied Literacy," in *The Arabic Script in Africa: Studies in the Use of a Writing System*, ed. Meikal Mumin and Kees Versteegh (Leiden: Brill, 2014), 41–76.

al-Musawi, Muhsin, *Islam on the Street: Religion in Modern Arabic Literature* (Lanham, Md.: Rowman and Littlefield, 2009).

al-Musawi, Muhsin, *The Medieval Islamic Republic of Letters: Arabic Knowledge Construction* (Notre Dame: University of Notre Dame Press, 2015).

Nasser, Gamal Abdel, *Egypt's Liberation: The Philosophy of the Revolution* (Washington, D.C.: Public Affairs Press, 1955).

Nasser, Gamal Abdel, "Khiṭāb Taʾmīm Qanāt al-Suways" ["Speech on the Nationalization of the Suez Canal"], in *al-Majmuʿa al-Kāmila li-Khiṭāb wa-Taṣrīḥāt al-Raʾīs Gamāl ʿAbdel Nāṣir*, vol. 10, ed. Hoda Gamal Abdel Nasser (Cairo: al-Maktaba al-Akadimiyya, 2005), 755–806.

Natsir, Moehammad, "Persatuan Agama Dengan Negara" ["The Unity of Religion and State"], in *Agama dan Negara dalam Perspektif Islam* (Jakarta: Media Da'wah, 2001), 112–13.

Natsir, Moehammad, "Syekh yang Maha Hebat," reprint, in *Agama dan Negara dalam Perspektif Islam* (Jakarta: Media Da'wah, 2001), 109–10.

Ndiaye, Seydou Nourou, "Un Pionnier de la presse dans les langues nationales," *Walfadjri/L'Aurore*, June 12, 2007, 8.

Ngom, Fallou, "Aḥmadu Bamba's Pedagogy and the Development of ʿAjamī Literature," *African Studies Review* 52, no. 1 (April 2009): 99–123.

Ngom, Fallou, "Ajami Scripts in the Senegalese Speech Community," *Journal of Arabic and Islamic Studies* 10 (2017): 1–23.

Ngom, Fallou, "Linguistic Resistance in the Murid Speech Community in Senegal," *Journal of Multilingual and Multicultural Development* 23, no. 3 (2002): 214–26.

Ngom, Fallou, *Muslims beyond the Arab World: The Odyssey of* ʿAjami *and the Murīdiyya* (New York: Oxford University Press, 2016).

Ngom, Fallou, "West African Manuscripts in Arabic and African Languages and Digital Preservation," in *Oxford Research Encyclopedia of African History* (Oxford University Press, 2017), 1–28, accessed December 31, 2019, https://hdl.handle.net/2144/29017

Ngom, Fallou, and Eleni Castro, "Beyond African Orality: Digital Preservation of Mandinka ʿAjamī Archives of Casamance," *History Compass* 17, no. 8 (2019): 1–16.

Nichterlein, Sue, "Historicism and Historiography in Indonesia," *History and Theory* 13, no. 3 (1974): 261–72.

Noer, Deliar, *The Modernist Muslim Movement in Indonesia, 1900–1942* (London: Oxford University Press, 1973).

Norris, H. T., "*Shuʿūbiyyah* in Arabic Literature," in *ʿAbbasid Belles Lettres*, ed. Julia Ashtiany, T. Johnstone, J. Latham, and R. Serjeant (Cambridge: Cambridge University Press, 1990), 31–47.

Oemarjati, Boen, *Chairil Anwar: The Poet and His Language* (Leiden: Brill, 1972).

Olender, Maurice, "From the Language of Adam to the Pluralism of Babel," *Mediterranean Historical Review* 12, no. 2 (1997): 51–59.

Olender, Maurice, *Languages of Paradise: Race, Religion, and Philology in the Nineteenth Century* (Cambridge: Harvard University Press, 1992).

Otterspeer, Willem, "The Ethical Imperative," in *Leiden Oriental Connections, 1850–1940*, ed. Willem Otterspeer (Leiden: E. J. Brill, 1989), 204–29.

Ouyang, Wen-chin, "Configurations of Multilingual Literature and World Literature," in *Multilingual Literature as World Literature*, ed. Jane Hiddleston and Wen-chin Ouyang (New York: Bloomsbury Academic, 2021), 282–303.

Ouyang, Wen-chin, *Politics of Nostalgia in the Arabic Novel: Nation-State, Modernity, and Tradition* (Edinburgh: Edinburgh University Press, 2013).

Panzacchi, Cornelia, "The Livelihoods of Traditional Griots in Modern Senegal," *Africa: Journal of the International African Institute* 64, no. 2 (1994): 190–210.

Patel, Abdulrazzak, *The Arab* Nahḍah*: The Making of the Intellectual and Humanist Movement* (Edinburgh: Edinburgh University Press, 2013).

Peterson, Brian J., *Islamization from Below: The Making of Muslim Communities in Colonial French Sudan, 1880–1960* (New Haven: Yale University Press, 2011).

Philipp, Thomas, "Evolutionary and Historical Approaches to the Arabic Language," in *Jurji Zaidan and the Foundations of Arab Nationalism* (Syracuse: Syracuse University Press, 2014), 53–64.

Poeradisastra, Farchad, "Memang, Kebenaran Harus Tetap Disampaikan," in *Hamka di mata hati umat*, ed. Nasir Tamara, Buntaran Sanusi, and Vincent Djauhari (Jakarta: Sinar Harapan, 1983), 155–64.

Popescu, Monica, *At Penpoint: African Literatures, Postcolonial Studies, and the Cold War* (Durham: Duke University Press, 2020).

Powell, Eve Troutt, *A Different Shade of Colonialism: Egypt, Great Britain, and the Mastery of the Sudan* (Berkeley: University of California Press, 2003).

Powell, Eve Troutt, *Tell This in My Memory: Stories of Enslavement from Egypt, Sudan and the Ottoman Empire* (Stanford: Stanford University Press, 2012).

Pratt, Mary Louise, *Imperial Eyes: Travel Writing and Transculturation*, 2nd ed. (New York: Routledge, 2008).

Rac, Katalin, "Arabic Literature for the Colonizer and the Colonized: Ignaz Goldziher and Hungary's Eastern Politics 1878–1918," in *The Muslim Reception of European Orientalism: Reversing the Gaze*, ed. Susannah Heschel and Umar Ryad (New York: Routledge, 2019), 80–102.

Rachmat, Naziroeddin, "'Api' Islam Apa Jang Dimaksudkan Oleh Bung Karno?" ["What 'Fire' of Islam Does Brother 'Karno Mean?"], *Hikmah*, May 26, 1956, 7.

Radwan, Noha, *Egyptian Colloquial Poetry in the Modern Arabic Canon* (New York: Palgrave Macmillan, 2012).

Ramadhan, Chairil Gibran, "Nabi, Dewa, dan Kahlil Gibran," in *Kahlil Gibran di Indonesia*, ed. Eka Budianta (Depok, Indonesia: Badan Pelestarian Pusaka Indonesia, 2010), 73–82.

Rastegar, Kamran, *Literary Modernity between the Middle East and Europe: Textual Transactions in Nineteenth-Century Arabic, English, and Persian Literatures* (New York: Routledge, 2007).

Razlagova, Elena, "Cinema in the Spirit of Bandung: The Afro-Asian Film Festival Circuit, 1957–1964," in *The Cultural Cold War and the Global South: Sites of Contest and Communitas*, ed. Kerry Bystrom, Monica Popescu, and Katherine Zien (New York: Routledge Taylor and Francis Group, 2021), 111–28.

Reid, Anthony, *The Blood of the People: Revolution and the End of Traditional Rule in Northern Sumatra* (Kuala Lumpur: Oxford University Press, 1979).

Reid, Donald M., "Nationalizing the Pharaonic Past: Egyptology, Imperialism, and Egyptian Nationalism, 1922–1952," in *Rethinking Nationalism in the Arab Middle East*, ed. James Jankowski and Israel Gershoni (New York: Columbia University Press, 1997), 127–49.

Renan, Ernest, *Histoire générale et système comparé des langues sémitiques* (Paris: Imprimérie Imperiale, 1863 [1855]).

Renan, Ernest, "Islam and Science (*L'Islamisme et la science*, 1883)," in *What Is a Nation? and Other Political Writings*, trans. and ed. M.F.N. Giglioli (New York: Columbia University Press, 2018), 264–80.

Retsö, Jan, *The Arabs in Antiquity: Their History from the Assyrians to the Umayyads* (London: Routledge Curzon, 2003).

Rexer, Raisa, "Black and White and Re(a)d All Over: *L'Étudiant noir*, Communism, and the Birth of Négritude," *Research in African Literatures* 44, no. 4 (2013): 1–14.

Ricci, Ronit, *Islam Translated: Literature, Conversion, and the Arabic Cosmopolis of South and Southeast Asia* (Chicago: University of Chicago Press, 2011).

Ricklefs, M. C., *A History of Modern Indonesia since c. 1200*, 4th ed. (Stanford: Stanford University Press, 2008).

Ricklefs, M. C., *Mystic Synthesis in Java: A History of Islamization from the Fourteenth to the Early Nineteenth Centuries* (Norwalk, Conn.: Eastbridge, 2006).

Roberts, Allen F., Mary Nooter Roberts, Gassia Armenian, and Ousmane Gueye, *A Saint in the*

City: Sufi Arts of Urban Senegal (Los Angeles: University of California, Los Angeles, Fowler Museum of Cultural History, 2003).

Roberts, Brian Russell, and Keith Foulcher, *Indonesian Notebook: A Sourcebook on Richard Wright and the Bandung Conference* (Durham: Duke University Press, 2016).

Robinson, David, *Paths of Accommodation: Muslim Societies and French Colonial Authorities in Sénégal and Mauritania, 1880–1920* (Athens: Ohio University Press, 2000).

Rosen, Philip, "Making a Nation in Sembene's *Ceddo*," *Quarterly Review of Film and Video* 13, nos. 1–3 (1991): 147–72.

Rosenthal, F., "Nasab," in *Encyclopaedia of Islam*, 2nd ed., ed. P. Bearman, Th. Bianquis, C. E. Bosworth, E. Van Donzel, and W. P. Heinrichs (Leiden: Brill, 2012), accessed August 23, 2019, https://doi.org/10.1163/1573-3912_islam_SIM_5807

Rush, James R., *Hamka's Great Story: A Master Writer's Vision of Islam for Modern Indonesia* (Madison: University of Wisconsin Press, 2016).

Rush, James R., "Sukarno: Anticipating an Asian Century," in *Makers of Modern Asia*, ed. Ramachandra Guha (Cambridge: Harvard University Press, 2014), 172–98.

Sacks, Jeffrey, *Iterations of Loss: Mutilation and Aesthetic Form, Al-Shidyaq to Darwish* (New York: Fordham University Press, 2015).

Said, Edward, *Orientalism* (New York: Vintage, 2003).

Saʿid, Nafusa Zakariyya, *Tarīkh al-Daʿwa ilā al-ʿĀmmiyya wa-Athārihā fī Miṣr* (Alexandria, Egypt: Dār Nashr al-Thaqāfa, 1964).

al-Salamuni, Hisham, *Ḥikāyāt Wālid al-Shuʿarāʾ Fuʾād Ḥaddād* (al-Qāhira: al-Majlis al-aʿlā li-l-thaqāfa, 2017).

Samb, Amar, *Essai Sur La Contribution Du Sénégal à La Littérature D'expression Arabe*, Mémoires de l'Institut Fondamental d'Afrique Noire, no. 87 (Dakar: Institut Fondamental d'Afrique Noir, 1972).

Samin, Nadav, *Of Sand or Soil: Genealogy and Tribal Belonging in Saudi Arabia* (Princeton: Princeton University Press, 2015).

Sanni, Amidu, "The Discourse on *Laḥn* in Arabic Philological and Literary Traditions," *Middle Eastern Literatures* 13, no. 1 (2010): 1–19.

Ṣarrūf, Yaʿqūb, "al-Kalimāt al-āʿjamiyah" ["Foreign Words"], *al-Muqtaṭaf* 15 (1891): 52–53.

Saussy, Haun, *The Making of Barbarians: Chinese Literature and Multilingual Asia* (Princeton: Princeton University Press, 2022).

Saxena, Akshya, *Vernacular English: Reading the Anglophone in Postcolonial India* (Princeton: Princeton University Press, 2022).

Scherer, Savriti, "Globalisation in Java in the 16th Century: A Review of Pramoedya's *Arus Balik*," *Archipel* 55 (1998): 43–60.

Schultz, Daniel, and Maryanne Felter, "Education, History, and Nationalism in Pramoedya Toer's *Buru Quartet*," *Crossroads: An Interdisciplinary Journal of Southeast Asian Studies* 16, no. 2 (2002): 143–75.

Selim, Samah, "Languages of Civilization: Nation, Translation and the Politics of Race in Colonial Egypt," *Translator* 15, no. 1 (2009): 151–54.

Sembene, Ousmane, dir., *Ceddo*, Filmi Doomireew, 1976.

Sembene, Ousmane, *Le dernier de l'Empire*, 2nd ed. (Paris: L'Harmattan, 1985).

Senghor, Léopold Sédar, "Discours de L. S. Senghor, Président de l'Assemblée fédérale, Réception du General de Gaulle à l'Assemblée fédérale du Mali," December 13, 1959, Centre de Documentation des Archives Nationales de la République du Sénégal, Dakar.

Senghor, Léopold Sédar, "Interventions du Président Senghor Au Congrès du P.F.A., Dakar," August 1959, Centre de Documentation des Archives Nationales de la République du Sénégal, Dakar.

Senghor, Léopold Sédar, "La poésie négro-africaine de langue française," réception organisée par la Société des auteurs, compositeurs, et éditeurs de musique en l'honneur des poètes, Paris, January 30, 1979, Centre de Documentation des Archives Nationales de la République du Sénégal, Dakar.

Senghor, Léopold Sédar, "Laïcité," in *Liberté I: Négritude et Humanisme* (Paris: Seuil, 1964), 422–24.

Senghor, Léopold Sédar, "Le problème culturel en A.O.F. [1937]," in *Liberté I: Négritude et Humanisme* (Paris: Seuil, 1964), 19.

Senghor, Léopold Sédar, *Léopold Sédar Senghor: Oeuvre Poétique*, 5th ed. (Paris: Seuil, 1990).

Senghor, Léopold Sédar, *Léopold Sédar Senghor: Poésie complète (édition critique)*, ed. Pierre Brunel (Paris: Centre National de la Recherche Scientifique Éditions, 2007).

Senghor, Léopold Sédar, Léopold Sédar Senghor: The Collected Poetry, trans. Melvin Dixon (Charlottesville: University Press of Virginia, 1991).

Senghor, Léopold Sédar, *Les Fondements de l'Africanité ou Négritude et Arabité* (Paris: Présence Africaine, 1967).

Senghor, Léopold Sédar, "Les nationalismes d'outremer et l'avenir des peuples de couleur" ["Overseas Nationalisms and the Future of Peoples of Color"], in *L'encyclopédie française: Le monde en devenir (histoire, évolution, prospective)*, vol. 20, ed. Gaston Berger, Lucien Febvre, and Pierre Renouvin (Paris: Larousse/Société nouvelle de l'encyclopédie française, 1959), 6–11.

Senghor, Léopold Sédar, "Transcription de l'Assemblée Nationale Constituante, 1ère séance du 18 septembre, 1946," September 18, 1946, Centre de Documentation des Archives Nationales de la République du Sénégal, Dakar.

Senghor, Léopold Sédar, "Vues sur l'Afrique noire ou assimiler, non être assimilés [1945]," in *Liberté I: Négritude et Humanisme* (Paris: Seuil, 1964), 39–69.

Setiadi, Hilmar Farid, *Rewriting the Nation: Pramoedya Ananta Toer and the Politics of Decolonization* (Ph.D. dissertation, National University of Singapore, 2014).

Setiadi, Hilmar Farid, and Razif, "*Batjaan Liar* in the Dutch East Indies: A Colonial Antipode," *Postcolonial Studies* 11, no. 3 (2008): 277–92.

Shankar, Subramanian, *Flesh and Fish Blood: Postcolonialism, Translation, and the Vernacular* (Berkeley: University of California Press, 2012).

Sharkey, Heather, *Living with Colonialism: Nationalism and Culture in the Anglo-Egyptian Sudan* (Berkeley: University of California Press, 2003).

Sharma, Sunil, "Redrawing the Boundaries of ʿAjam in Early Modern Persian Literary Histories," in *Iran Facing Others: Identity Boundaries in a Historical Perspective*, ed. Abbas Amanat and Farzin Vejdani (New York: Palgrave, 2012), 49–62.

al-Shārūni, Yusuf, "Lughat al-Ḥiwar bayna al-ʿĀmmiyya wa-l-Fuṣḥā," *al-Majallah* (Cairo) 67 (August 1962): 40–54.

Sheehi, Stephen, *Foundations of Modern Arab Identity* (Gainesville: University Press of Forida, 2004).

al-Shidyāq, Aḥmad Fāris, *Leg over Leg; or, The Turtle in the Tree: Concerning the Fariyaq, What Manner of Creature He Might Be* [*Al-Sāq ʿalā al-sāq fī mā huwa al-Firyāq*], Bilingual ed., trans. Humphrey Davies, vols. 1–4 (New York: New York University Press, 2013–14).

Shih, Shu-Mei, "The Concept of the Sinophone," *PMLA* 126, no. 3 (2011): 709–18.

Shih, Shu-mei, Chien-hsin Tsai, and Brian Bernards, eds., *Sinophone Studies: A Critical Reader* (New York: Columbia University Press, 2013).

Shiraishi, Takeshi, "Reading Pramoedya Ananta Toer's *Sang Pemula*," *Indonesia* 44 (October 1987): 129–39.

Siddiq, Muhammad, *Arab Culture and the Novel: Genre, Identity, and Agency in Egyptian Fiction* (New York: Routledge, 2007).

Smith, Etienne, "Religious and Cultural Pluralism in Senegal: Accomodation through 'Proportional Equidistance'?" in *Tolerance, Democracy, and Sufis in Senegal*, ed. Mamadou Diouf (New York: Columbia University Press, 2013), 147–79.

Snouck Hurgronje, Christiaan, "De Islam en het rassenprobleem," February 8, 1922, rector's lecture presented at the 347th anniversary of Der Leidsche Hoogeschool (Leiden: E. J. Brill, 1922), 5–26, available at https://play.google.com/books/reader?id=cKdBAQAAMAAJ&pg=GBS.PA2&hl=en

Snouck Hurgronje, Christiaan, "L'Avenir de l'Islam," *Questions Diplomatiques et Coloniales* 12, no. 106 (July 15, 1901): 73–82.

Snouck Hurgronje, Christiaan, *Politique Musulmane de la Hollande: Quatres Conférences par C. Snouck Hurgronje Conseiller du Ministère des Colonies Néerlandaises pour les Affaires Indigènes et Arabes*, Collection de la Revue du Monde Musulman, vol. 14 (Paris: Ernest Leroux, 1911).

Soekarno [Dutch-era spelling of Sukarno], Ahmed, *Under the Banner of Revolution*, vol. 1, 1st ed. (Jakarta: Publication Committee, 1966).

Somekh, Sasson, *The Changing Rhythm: A Study of Najīb Maḥfūẓ's Novels* (Leiden: Brill, 1973).

Somekh, Sasson, *Genre and Language in Modern Arabic Literature* (Wiesbaden, Germany: Harassowitz, 1991).

Soyinka, Wole, "Senghor: Lessons in Power," *Research in African Literatures* 33, no. 4 (2002): 1–2.

Stanton, Anna Ziajka, *The Worlding of Arabic Literature: Language, Affect, and the Ethics of Translatability* (New York: Fordham University Press, 2023).

Steenbrink, Karel, *Dutch Colonialism and Indonesian Islam: Contacts and Conflicts 1596–1950* (Amsterdam: Rodopi, 2006).

Stepan, Alfred, "Stateness, Democracy, and Respect: Senegal in Comparative Perspective," in *Tolerance, Democracy, and Sufis in Senegal: Religion, Culture, and Public Life*, ed. Mamadou Diouf (New York: Columbia University Press, 2013), 205–38.

Stetkevych, Jaroslav, *The Modern Arabic Literary Language: Lexical and Stylistic Developments* (Washington, D.C.: Georgetown University Press, 2006).

Stoler, Anne Laura, *Duress: Imperial Durabilities in Our Times* (Durham: Duke University Press, 2016).

Suara Jiwa: Antoloji Puisi Peringatan 41 Wafatnya Chairil Anwar [*Voices of the Soul: An Anthology*

of Poetry Commemorating 41 Years since the Death of Chairil Anwar], Institut Keguruan dan Ilmu Pendidikan Muhammadiyah Purworejo (Central Java), 1990.

Sukarno, Ahmed, *Collected Documents of the Asian-African Conference* (Jakarta: Agency for Research and Development, Department of Foreign Affairs, Republic of Indonesia, 1983).

Sukarno, Ahmed, *Dibawah Bendera Revolusi*, rev. ed. (Jakarta: Yayasan Bung Karno dan Penerbit Media Pressindo, 2015).

Suleiman, Yasir, *Arabic in the Fray: Language Ideology and Cultural Politics* (Edinburgh: Edinburgh University Press, 2013).

Suleiman, Yasir, *The Arabic Language and National Identity: A Study in Ideology* (Washington, D.C.: Georgetown University Press, 2003).

Swan, Quito, "Blinded by Bandung? Illumining West Papua, Senegal, and the Black Pacific," *Radical History Review* 131 (May 2018): 58–81.

Tageldin, Shaden, "Beyond Latinity, Can the Vernacular Speak?" *Comparative Literature* 70, no. 2 (2018): 114–31.

Tageldin, Shaden, *Disarming Words: Empire and the Seductions of Translation in Egypt* (Berkeley: University of California Press, 2011).

Tageldin, Shaden, "The Place of Africa, in Theory: Pan-Africanism, Postcolonialism, Beyond," *Journal of Historical Sociology* 27, no. 3 (2014): 302–23.

Tageldin, Shaden, "Untranslatability," in *Futures of Comparative Literature: ACLA State of the Discipline Report*, ed. Ursula Heise (Abingdon, U.K.: Routledge, 2017), 234–35.

al-Tahtawi, Rifaʿa Rafiʿ, *An Imam in Paris: Account of a Stay in France by an Egyptian Cleric (1826–1831)* [*Takhlīṣ al-Ibrīz*], trans. Daniel L. Newman (London: Saqi, 2011).

al-Ṭahṭāwī, Rifāʿah, *Takhlīṣ al-Ibrīz fī Talkhīṣ Bārīz* (Cairo: Mustafa al-Babi al-Halabi and Sons Press, 1958).

Tamari, Tal, "The Development of Caste Systems in West Africa," *Journal of African History* 32, no. 2 (1991): 221–50.

Tantular, Mpu, and Suwito Santoso, *Sutasoma: A Study in Javanese Wajrayana* (New Delhi: International Academy of Indian Culture, 1975).

Thornber, Karen, "Rethinking the World in World Literature: East Asia and Literary Contact Nebulae," in *World Literature in Theory*, ed. David Damrosch (Chichester, U.K.: Wiley Blackwell, 2014), 460–79.

Tignor, Robert, *Modernization and British Colonial Rule in Egypt, 1882–1914* (Princeton: Princeton University Press, 2015).

Toer, Koesalah Soebagyo, *Kamus Pramoedya Ananta Toer* (Sleman, Indonesia: Warning Books, 2018).

Toer, Pramoedya Ananta, *Anak Semua Bangsa* [*Child of All Nations*] (Jakarta: Hasta Mitra, 1980).

Toer, Pramoedya Ananta, *Arus Balik* (Jakarta: Hasta Mitra, 1995).

Toer, Pramoedya Ananta, *Bumi Manusia* [*This Earth of Mankind*] (Jakarta: Hasta Mitra, 1980).

Toer, Pramoedya Ananta, *Child of All Nations* [*Anak Semua Bangsa*], trans. Max Lane (New York: Penguin, 1996).

Toer, Pramoedya Ananta, *Footsteps* [*Jejak Langkah*], trans. Max Lane (New York: Penguin, 1996).

Toer, Pramoedya Ananta, *Jejak Langkah* [*Footsteps*] (Jakarta: Lentera Dipantara, 2006).

Toer, Pramoedya Ananta, "My Apologies in the Name of Experience," trans. Alex G. Bardsley, *Indonesia* 61 (April 1996): 1–14.

Toer, Pramoedya Ananta, *Realisme Sosialis dan Sastra Indonesia* (Jakarta: Lentera Dipantara, 2003).

Toer, Pramoedya Ananta, *Rumah Kaca* (Jakarta: Lentera Dipantara, 2006).

Toer, Pramoedya Ananta, *Sang Pemula* (Jakarta: Hasta Mitra, 1985).

Toer, Pramoedya Ananta, *Tempoe Doeloe: Antologi Sastra Pra-Indonesia* (Jakarta: Hasta Mitra, 1982).

Toer, Pramoedya Ananta, *This Earth of Mankind* [*Bumi Manusia*], trans. Max Lane (New York: Penguin, 1996).

Tsu, Jing, and David Der-wei Wang, eds., *Global Chinese Literature: Critical Essays* (Leiden: Brill, 2010).

UNESCO, "Meeting of Experts on the Use of Mother Tongues in Literacy Programmes in Africa, Bamako, 1974," 1975, accessed April 5, 2021, https://unesdoc.unesco.org/ark:/48223/pf0000015794

van den Doel, Wim, "Snouck Hurgronje and the Colonial Administration of the Dutch East Indies," in *Scholarship in Action: Essays on the Life and Work of Christiaan Snouck Hurgronje (1857–1936)*, ed. Léon Buskens, Jan Just Witkam, and Annemarie van Sandwijk (Leiden: Brill, 2021), 281–311.

van Dijk, Kees, "The Scholar and the War Horse: The Aceh War, Snouck Hurgronje, and Van Heutz," in *Scholarship in Action: Essays on the Life and Work of Christiaan Snouck Hurgronje (1857–1936)*, ed. Léon Buskens, Jan Just Witkam, and Annemarie van Sandwijk (Leiden: Brill, 2021), 327–73.

van Miert, Hans, "The 'Land of the Future': The Jong Sumatranen Bond (1917–1930) and Its Image of the Nation," *Modern Asian Studies* 30, no. 3 (July 1996): 591–616.

Venuti, Lawrence, ed., *The Translation Studies Reader*, 3rd ed. (New York: Routledge, 2012).

Versteegh, Kees, *The Arabic Language* (Edinburgh: Edinburgh University Press, 2001).

Villalón, Leonardo A., "Negotiating Islam in the Era of Democracy: Senegal in Comparative Regional Perspective," in *Tolerance, Democracy, and Sufis in Senegal: Religion, Culture, and Public Life*, ed. Mamadou Diouf (New York: Columbia University Press, 2013), 239–66.

Walid, Dawud, *Blackness and Islam* (Wembley, U.K.: Algorithm/Islamic Human Rights Commission, 2021).

Walther, Wiebke, "Proverbs," in *The Routledge Encyclopedia of Arabic Literature*, ed. Julie Scott Meisami and Paul Starkey (New York: Routledge, 1998), 622–24.

Wang, David Der-wei, "Introduction: Chinese Literature across the Borderlands," *Prism* 18, no. 2 (October 2021): 315–20.

Ware, Rudolph, *The Walking Qur'an: Islamic Education, Embodied Knowledge, and History in West Africa* (Chapel Hill: University of North Carolina Press, 2014).

Warner, Tobias, *The Tongue-Tied Imagination: Decolonizing Literary Modernity in Senegal* (New York: Fordham University Press, 2019).

Wessling, H. L., "The Dutch Colonial Model in French Colonial Theory, 1890–1914," *Proceedings of the Meeting of the French Colonial Historical Society* 2 (1977): 107–30.

Wilder, Gary, *Freedom Time: Negritude, Decolonization, and the Future of the World* (Durham: Duke University Press, 2015).

Willcocks, William, "Li-mā lam tūjad Quwwat al-Ikhtirāʿ ladā al-Miṣriyyīn al-Ān," *al-Azhar* 6, no. 1 (January 1893): 1–10.

Willcocks, William, "Syria, Egypt, North Africa and Malta Speak Punic, Not Arabic: In Egypt during the Forty Years of the British Occupation," extract from *Bulletin de L'Institut d'Egypte* 8 (Cairo: Imprimerie de L'Institut Français D'Archéologie Orientale, 1926), 1–37.

Witkam, Jan Just, "Christiaan Snouck Hurgronje: Lives and Afterlives," in *Scholarship in Action: Essays on the Life and Work of Christiaan Snouck Hurgronje (1857–1936)*, ed. Léon Buskens, Jan Just Witkam, and Annemarie van Sandwijk (Leiden: Brill, 2021), 73–113.

Woll, Josephine, "The Russian Connection: Soviet Cinema and the Cinema of Francophone Africa," in *Focus on African Films*, ed. Françoise Pfaff (Bloomington: Indiana University Press, 2004), 223–40.

Wright, Richard, *The Color Curtain: A Report on the Bandung Conference* (Jackson: University Press of Mississippi, 1995).

Yoon, Duncan, "'Our Forces Have Redoubled': World Literature, Postcolonialism, and the Afro-Asian Writers' Bureau," *Cambridge Journal of Postcolonial Literary Inquiry* 2, no. 2 (2015): 233–52.

Yousef, Hoda, *Composing Egypt: Reading, Writing, and the Emergence of a Modern Nation* (Stanford: Stanford University Press, 2016).

Yuliantri, Rhoma Dwi Aria, and Muhidin M. Dahlan, *Lekra Tak Membakar Buku: Suara Senyap Lembar Kebudayaan Harian Rakjat 1950–1965* (Yogyakarta, Indonesia: Merakesumba, 2008).

Zaidan, Jurji, "The Arabic Language: A Living Being Subject to the Laws of Evolution" ["al-Lugha al-ʿArabiyya bi-ʿItibārihā Kāʾin Ḥayy"], trans. Hilary Kilpatrick, in Thomas Philipp, *Jurji Zaidan and the Foundations of Arab Nationalism* (Syracuse: Syracuse University Press, 2014), 226–38.

Zaidan, Jurji, "Literary and Colloquial Arabic," trans. Paul Starkey, in Thomas Philipp, *Jurji Zaidan and the Foundations of Arab Nationalism* (Syracuse: Syracuse University Press, 2014), 194–98.

Zaidan, Jurji, "The Philosophy of Language and the Arabic Vocabulary" [*Al-Alfāẓ al-ʿArabiyya wa-l-Falsafa al-Lughawiyya*, 1886], trans. Hilary Kilpatrick, in Thomas Phillipp, *Jurji Zaidan and the Foundations of Arab Nationalism* (Syracuse: Syracuse University Press, 2014), 177–93.

Zaidan, Jurji, "Pre-Islamic Arabs," trans. Paul Starkey, in Thomas Phillipp, *Jurji Zaidan and the Foundations of Arab Nationalism* (Syracuse: Syracuse University Press, 2014), 275–90.

Zaidan, Jurji, "The Writers and Readers of Arabic" ["Kuttāb al-ʿArabiyya wa-Qurrāʾuhā," 1899], trans. Hilary Kilpatrick, in Thomas Philipp, *Jurji Zaidan and the Foundations of Arab Nationalism* (Syracuse: Syracuse University Press, 2014), 216–25.

Zaidan, Jurji, "The Writers and Readers of Arabic: (1) Writers; (2) Authors," trans. Hilary Kilpatrick, in Thomas Philipp, *Jurji Zaidan and the Foundations of Arab Nationalism* (Syracuse: Syracuse University Press, 2014), 199–215.

Zaydān, Jurjī, *Al-Alfāẓ al-ʿArabiyya wa-l-Falsafa al-Lughawiyya* (Beirut: Maṭbaʾat al-Qidīs Jāwrjīyus, 1886).

Zaydān, Jurjī, "Kuttāb al-ʿarabiyya wa-qurrāʾuhā," *al-Hilāl* 7, no. 13 (April 1899): 393–400.

INDEX

Abendanon, J. H., 305n34
Aceh: Snouck Hurgronje and, 26, 106; language of, 46; war in 106
adab (cultivation), 9, 56; in Bamba's didactic poetry, 89, 202
Adam: in Eden story, 247; hadith on, 37
accommodation, as colonial policy in French West Africa, 79–80, 84, 94, 95
acculturation: and Malay ethnicity in Indonesia, 121, 151; Muslim diversity and, 25, 36, 37–38,65, 78, 100, 211; *nahḍa* figures on, 51, 56–58, 73; Orientalist views on Islam and, 25–26, 33, 36–38; Senegal literary portrayals of, 231
Afro-Asian Writers' Movement: Afro-Asian Writers' Congress (Tashkent 1958), 220–21; connections to the Bandung Conference, 324n6; Mahfouz and, 331n17; Pramoedya and, 220–221, 324n6; Sembene and, 220–221 324n6. See also under *Lotus* (Journal of Afro-Asian Writing)
Ahmadou Cheikhou, 48
ʿajam(iyya) concept, 11–14, 24, 25, 50, 52, 53, 75–76; *ʿajami* studies, 279; al-Shidyāq's terms for, 293n37; Goldziher on, 31, 32–33; in Mahfouz, 248–49, 251, 265–72, 335n79; *patois* and, 27–28, 62; Renan's neglect of, 27–28; shifting meaning of, 54, 58, 64, 73, 248–49, 270, 281. *See also ʿarab* and *ʿajam* difference; "Arabness"
ʿajamiyyāt (non-Arabic languages), 12, 24, 28, 52, 53–54, 60–61, 63–66, 69, 78, 280. *See also under ʿāmmiyya; and* foreign languages and concepts
al-Azhar mosque (Cairo), 56, 316n43
al-Hilāl (journal), 70
al-Ḥillī, Ṣafī al-Dīn, 158–59, 315n26
al-Kindi, 29
al-Maghribī, ʿAbd al-Qādir, 53, 64–65, 75, 294n46
al-Manfalūṭī, Luṭfī, 113, 117–18, 306n70
al-Shidyāq, Aḥmad Fāris, 50, 53, 58–60, 61–66, 74
al-Ṭahṭāwī, Rifāʿah, 30, 52–53, 54–58, 60–61, 62, 67, 292n16, 295n53
al-Yaziji, Ibrahim, 63
Algerian independence movement, 212, 215
aljamiado, 282
Amadu Sheikhu, 86
ʿāmmiyya (Colloquial Arabic), as "common" language, 51, 54, 62, 66, 69; al-Shidyāq and, 63–64; bias against, 155–59; distinction between *ʿajamiyyāt* and, 63, 74–76; English translation of term, 159; Ḥaddād's use of, 153–57, 158, 159–60, 179, 185; Hamka on, 112; *Kaddu* on, 222–24; Nasser's use of, 158, 315n20; Mahfouz and, 251, 270, 272, 331n15; Zaydān on, 66–69
ʿAmr ibn al-ʿĀṣ, 57, 110, 173–74
Anderson, Benedict, 8, 17, 107, 118–19, 121–22, 136, 151, 309n32
ansāb (charismatic lineage), 272, 335n80
ʿAntar and ʿAbla (folk heroes), 183–84

A NOTE ON THE TYPE

This book has been composed in Arno, an Old-style serif typeface in the classic Venetian tradition, designed by Robert Slimbach at Adobe.